The Craft of Fiction

Essays in Medieval Poetics

Edited by
Leigh A. Arrathoon

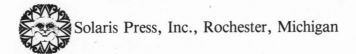

Solaris Press, Inc., Rochester, Michigan

©1984 by Solaris Press, Rochester, Michigan 48063
ALL RIGHTS RESERVED. Except for brief passages quoted in a
newspaper, magazine, radio or television review, no part of this book
may be reproduced in any form or by any means, electronic or
mechanical, including photocopying and recording, or by an information retrieval system, without permission in writing from the publisher.
Printed on permanent/durable acid-free paper
and bound in the United States of America

Designed by Leigh A. Arrathoon
Illustrations by Janet Anderson
Typeset by Vicky Harris
Cover photo by the Bibliothèque Nationale de Paris, taken from their
ms. fr. 112, XVe siècle, "Le Chevalier combattant un dragon."
Printed by McNaughton & Gunn, Ann Arbor, Michigan

Library of Congress Cataloging in Publication Data
Main entry under title:

The Craft of fiction.

Includes bibliographical references and index.
1. Literature, Medieval — History and criticism —
Addresses, essays, lectures.   I. Arrathoon, Leigh A.,
1942–
PN681.C7   1984   809'.02   84–20313

ISBN 0-933760-04-3

For Ray

Contents

12. "Playing Games with Fiction: *Les Quinze Joyes
     de Mariage, Il Corbaccio, El Arcipreste de Talavera*"   423
     Per Nykrog

13. "The Mediterranean's Three Spiritual Shores:
     Images of the Self between Christianity and
     Islam in the Later Middle Ages"   453
     Aldo Scaglione

List of Illustrations

Introduction

When Percy Lubbock wrote the *Craft of Fiction* in 1921, no one had yet "really contemplated" the form of a novel.[1] What he wanted to accomplish as a critic was to overtake the literary craftsman at his work; to *see* how the book was made.[2] But his efforts to capture and freeze the elusive magic of fiction met with frustration at every turn:

> To grasp the shadowy and fantasmal form of a book, to hold it fast, to turn it over and survey it at leisure—that is the effort of a critic of books, and it is perpetually defeated. Nothing, no power, will keep a book steady and motionless before us, so that we may have time to examine its shape and design. As quickly as we read, it melts and shifts in the memory; even at the moment when the last page is turned, a great part of the book, its fine detail, is already vague and doubtful.[3]

In spite of his sincere misgivings about his ability to accomplish the critical task before him, Percy Lubbock was a modest man. Although he never penetrated the mysteries of the book in the way he longed to do, his discussions of the devices of aesthetic distance and irony in *Madame Bovary*, of point of view, and of the differences between the pictorial and dramatic methods of representation in novels are still useful and illuminating to the modern reader.

It is also good for us to remember that every critical reading is a reconstruction of the author's work, a new novel, as Lubbock put it,[4] or a gloss in which the allegorical imagination of the reader reinvents the text, as Roger Dragonetti would have it (p. 369).

In training students to become literary critics we ought not to forget that Percy Lubbock taught us to be craftsmen: "the man of letters is a craftsman, and the critic cannot be less."[5] Not only is the critic an artisan whose art consists of reconstructing books so that other readers may appreciate the beauty of their craftsmanship, but the book itself is an artifact. The art of fiction . . . is no report, or mere narrative of events, but

ix

an image, liberated from the tangle of cross-purposes"[6] which obscure the meaning of events in real life. The artist chooses his materials carefully, and "with every touch that he lays on his subject, he must show what he thinks of it; his subject, indeed the book which he finds in his selected fragment of life, is purely the representation of his view, his judgement, his opinion of it. . . ."[7] As a result "the literary landscape that opens before the critic is whole and single; it has passed through the imagination, it has shed its irrelevancy and is compact with its own meaning. Such is the world in the book. . . ."[8]

Criticism has come a long way since 1921. We are more "scientific" now in the kinds of questions we know how to put to the text, and yet, we are still struggling to grapple with the slick and often treacherous surfaces of narrative fiction. The medieval book in particular eludes us on account of the alterity of the culture. Because objective documents from the period are rare, we find ourselves having to reconstruct the political, economic, and social text of the period, out of the lexical patterns of the literary text (Haidu's article).

What kind of world did the medieval author live in? What were medieval dwellings like? How was farming carried out? How were money and goods exchanged? What were the burning political and social issues of the day? The answers to these questions about a culture that flourished seven or eight hundred years ago are to be found in the text if we know how to discern them where they lie embedded in the fiction. And it is vital that we recover such information if we are ever to understand what the text means. How, for example, can the *Chastelaine de Vergi* (= *ChV*; Arrathoon's article) manage to greet her lover at home if she is married? Where is the husband? Scrutiny of the text reveals that she lives in a manor house while her husband is out protecting the castle of which he has charge.

A semiotic approach to another medieval narrative yields fruitful information about the medieval world of the twelfth century. By isolating the political isotopy in the text of Chrestien's *Yvain*, Peter Haidu is able to discover, among other things, that the essential political problem to which the text addresses itself is that of the necessity and destructiveness of the lower level knights as seen from the perspective of those who dominate society (p. 43). Such matters belong to the realm of the "extra-text," or those political, economic, and social materials that are reflected in the verbal schemes of the narrative and which can be reconstructed on the basis of the text.

But there are still other questions that are put to the medieval book in this collection of essays. For example, we need to know what kind of educational formation the medieval author had, what knowledge he shared with his listening audience, what books he read, and what books he could count upon his audience to have read and remembered. How did he and his public interpret the books in their culture? Eren Branch's article focuses upon the tale *in utramque partem*, which argues on both sides of the question in the manner of a Roman *controversia*. The *controversia* was a school exercise in declamation which Branch sees as underlying the construction of narratives like Boccaccio's *Teseida*. In order to make the argument she does, it was necessary for Branch to know that Seneca the Elder's collection of *controversiae* were part of the medieval school curriculum.

By the time *ChV* was written (ca. 1228–79), Aristotles' thinking on dialectical argumentation had been absorbed through the school system where it was practiced in the form of the disputation. Further, it is clear from the text of *ChV* that the anonymous author expected his public to be familiar with the *geu-parti*, a dialectically structured lyric debate about questions of love. Knowing this enables Arrathoon to investigate the confluence of the medieval university disputation, the *geu-parti*, and dialectically organized written narrative of the period.

But there are other kinds of books referred to in medieval narratives. Again the *ChV* poet counted upon his public to be familiar with the poems of the chastelain de Couci and the Tristan material. Our correct apprehension of his meaning depends upon our knowing what his audience knew. Similarly, Chrestien de Troyes expected his audience to be familiar with certain lyric poems (see Haidu and Hunt).

In short, it is perfectly possible to know at least some of the books a medieval author and his public had read or "heard" and how they understood those books by studying the functions of the intertextual relations in a given narrative. This is one of the ways in fact that the critic has of reconstructing the audience's reaction on the basis of the text. Another more obvious way to judge audience reception is by reading what scribes and contemporaries had to say about the work. In the case of *ChV*, for example, all of the medieval readers of the poem, whose opinions are extant, drew similar conclusions about the meaning of the poem. Their reactions show that they were responding to the poet's rhetoric which militates in favor of the male protagonist despite the narrator persona's insistence that this character has committed a tragic transgression against a law of love.

Another tool that helps us to reconstruct the audience is semiotic analysis. By isolating the various isotopies of the text and comparing these clusters of related terms with what is known from the historical documents of the period, the modern critic is able to reconstruct the experience of the medieval public and thus to receive the text in the way they must have done.

Related to the question of the kinds of books medieval people "read" and the way in which they understood those books, is the fact that we are dealing with a traditional literature. Medieval narratives were written in reference to previous narratives whose structures they frequently invert.[9] Thus D. D. R. Owen compares Guillaume Le Clerc's *Fergus*, with the works of Chrestien de Troyes, finding that *Fergus* bears an antiphrastic relationship to its sources. If the arms Perceval covets are red like the sun, the arms Fergus gets are red from rust! and so forth. By laying Chrestien's work alongside *Fergus*, as the text invites the reader to do, we catch the author's personal voice in the discrepancy between the model and its imitation (p. 66). Guillaume, Owen concludes, "may have been a second phase romancer, but he was a first-rate craftsman" (p. 79).

When an earlier narrative was not being inverted in the new narrative, the medieval listener was nevertheless often asked to lay other texts alongside the new one in order that these might serve as a kind of yardstick by which to measure the behavior of the narrator and other characters in the story at hand. Thus the chastelaine de Vergi's knight is supposed to be measured against the chastelain de Couci whose crusade song was probably sung when the reader reached verse 295 in the course of reciting the tale. Similarly, in Nykrog's article, the *Seven Joys of Mary*, a pious text exalting the sublimity of woman as she was symbolized in the Middle Ages by the acts of the Virgin Mary, is meant to be kept in mind during the reading of the cynical *Quinze Joyes de Mariage*, which presents the dark side of women and marriage.

To further illustrate the power of the intertext in medieval aesthetics — and by "intertext" I understand those elements such as lexical items, formulae, *topoi*, characters, and situations that are shared between texts — Tony Hunt uncovers a web of references in the *Yvain* to a lyric debate that took place in 1170-3 between Chrestien, Bernart de Ventadorn, and Raimbaut d'Aurenga. Chrestien's use of the device of allusion in this instance casts much light upon the way the reader is supposed to interpret Yvain's decision to leave his new bride in order to accompany Gauvain to the tournaments. There is irony in the invocation of Provençal lyrics emphasizing the lover's separation from his lady as advice for a safely-established husband. Chrestien's use of the device of allusion in this instance is thus an ironic foreshadowing of the unhappy consequences of Yvain's decision. Further, Yvain's behavior turns out to be an inversion of the behavior of the lover in Chrestien's "D'Amors qui m'a tolu a moi." In a word, the lyric debate is brought to bear upon the narrative where it is perpetuated rather than definitively resolved.

In all the articles that follow, the text is always at the center, always the final authority. But the question arises as to just what constitutes the text. Zumthor and Haidu believe that the correct way to edit a work written for oral delivery is to print all of the MS copies of it side by side because each MS version is seen as akin to a performance. With every performance, the work is created anew, just as, in a sense, with every reading, the reader recreates the book. While agreeing with this position for the edition of epic, drama, and lyric, Arrathoon views the text of a Chrestien de Troyes or a Chaucer as the production of an individual, a consummate artist, whose exquisitely crafted tales can only be debased by scribal intervention. Seen from this point of view, the establishment of the text of a romance is best carried out through the application of genre, as well as textual, theory to both the classification of the MSS and the emendation of the basic copy.[10]

Haidu and Zumthor are concerned with the orality of the extant texts. Haidu sees the *Yvain*, for example, as a written text transformed into an oral message which can be understood by an illiterate noble public. The book is the "symbolic representation of the political problems of the contemporary social text" and is received by "those who manipulate, create . . . and profit from the social, political, and economic organization of society" (p. 38).

Similarly, Paul Zumthor views Gautier d'Arras' *Eracle* as a text which can only be fully appreciated when it is read aloud, in performance. The edited text, he finds, is empty and very likely a far cry from what the author had in mind when he wrote his story. Twelfth-century romance, Zumthor argues, is a crossroads between the oral and the written word. Chrestien falls firmly into the Latin scriptural tradition, whereas authors like Gautier refused what they must have perceived as the "alienating exigencies of writing." The vernacular writer toward the end of the twelfth century vascillates between voice and writing, between what he senses as nature and what we would call culture—between an outside (the subject objectivized in performance) and an inside (the interiorization of the subject through writing).

The narrating voice in *Eracle* has an immediacy that narrators in written texts do not have. For example, the use of the adverb *or* 'now' suggests the presence of a speaker, while suspending the temporality of the narrative. This is a sign of an oral text because it helps to break down the barrier that the printed page erects between the narrating voice and the reader.

But in "L'Ecriture et la voix" Paul Zumthor does much more than make a case for orality in a written romance; he realizes the kind of craftsmanship Percy Lubbock hoped for in the literary critic by combining his own personal poetic discourse with a critical analysis that greatly enhances the modern reader's appreciation of a text long viewed as a disunified production. Zumthor describes *Eracle* as a "luminous" work of youth which, instead of going deeply into its subject like the romances of Chrestien de Troyes, "unfurls" in the manner of a picaresque novel. The unity of this "sonorous, disorganized, teeming text," is to be found in the "fascination" (cf. Nykrog's "narrative euphoria") which commands our attention throughout a narrative that "stretches out in an infinite succession of mottled events like life itself."

There are more signals of orality in the text of *Eracle* than in other texts of the period. But *Eracle* is not a *chanson de geste*. Rather the voice of *Eracle* is the fiction of voice, indiscernibly mixed together with all the other fictions of the romance. However, this particular fiction differs from the others in that it aspires to realize itself in sensorial experience, a transformation which takes place as soon as the romance is read to an audience. The performance is so profoundly "inviscerated in the text" that numerous passages are not easily understood upon silent reading. The text asks for a mimical or gestural gloss.

In contrast to Haidu and Zumthor's concern with the orality of some twelfth-century written narratives, Brynley Roberts is interested in the literariness of the Middle Welsh prose narratives which derive from the Welsh oral tradition. Although Roberts finds a limited use of formulaic expression in these stories, he concludes that the authors were as much indebted to contemporary literary theory for the presentation of their tales as they were to the oral tradition for the basis of their style and their narrative material. The use of the preposition *uchod* 'above' to refer to a previous incident is a sign of a written text because oral texts would use a temporal reference like "before." It is also a sign of literariness when a narrative is given significance beyond its progression to a satisfying conclusion. The originality of the Middle Welsh prose narratives, according to Roberts, lies in the authors' personal vision and their transformation of traditional and learned materials into unique narrative forms.

The structure of medieval literature is visibly conventional and repetitive (Haidu). Because modern literature is governed by an original aesthetic, modern readers easily become irritated with literary works whose most fundamental feature is repetition. From its gross structure to its microstructure, medieval narrative is characterized by parallels, echoes, and many other recurrent elements. Whereas modern aesthetics looks upon repetition as obvious and therefore artless, the medieval craftsman displayed his skill by reworking familiar patterns. If repetition was positively valued in the Middle Ages,[11] the explanation is possibly that the device reflected what medieval man perceived as the relationship between the created world and its creator. God was seen as the supreme, perfect, and immutable good; his creature, as a temporal good, subject to accident. Fashioned in the image of his creator, the creature was similar, but not identical to all the others of his kind as well as to his maker. Repetition in medieval art then mimics the created world as it appeared to medieval man, resemblance being a "middle term between absolute identity and absolute alterity."[12]

One manifestation of repetition in the structure of the first half of the *Yvain* is narrative supplementarity: the supplementation of one episode by another which completes it (Haidu's article). Another manifestation of the aesthetic of repetition is the dialectical structuring of narratives described by Tony Hunt in two important articles on the subject,[13] where one episode resembles the proposition in a disputation while another answers it, and so forth (see Arrathoon's article). The intertextual parallels discussed are another example of the same phenomenon, as are the reworking of the "good old days" *topos* in the *Yvain* (see Haidu, Hunt, and Arrathoon), or the antinomic verbal construction of *ChV* or the *Merchant's Tale*.[14]

In his prologue to *Erec et Enide*, Chrestien boasts of his "bele conjointure"[15] by which he means the artful putting together of his romance from "corrupt and disorganized" oral source materials. The end product of this "artful joining together" is a symmetrical narrative (i.e., one in which repetition occurs at every level).

Douglas Kelly remarks that the stories Chrestien used in the *Erec et Enide* are as seamlessly joined as the stones in the handle of the sword in Solomon's boat. By contrast, the prose romancers practiced a different art which Kelly calls "disjointure." In place of the pleasingly symmetric narrative design of a Chrestien de Troyes or the anonymous author of *ChV*, these writers developed an intricate system of interlace and dovetailing of narrative threads, each incident acquiring additional meaning by virtue of its relationship to the whole. The end product—the interlace—is still a regular design, but each part of the design is able to branch out into still other designs, filling and spilling out over the space allotted to it: in other words, quite distinct from the cleanly defined narrative blocks that result from *conjointure*. Kelly concludes that the strength of the *Lancelot-Graal* is precisely its ability to absorb *everything*. One of the devices that enables the romance to do this is an image like Solomon's boat which ingeniously unites biblical history from Adam to Christ and arthurian legend. Biblical typologies are now made to apply to the arthurian material. Like Solomon's boat, born of the *sen* 'wisdom' of Solomon and the *engin* 'craft' of Solomon's wife, the new romances only take on meaning when God adds his *senefiance* 'mark,' 'meaning.' In other words, as with Solomon's boat, correct apprehension of the prose romances occurs through faith. It seems to me that the only way such disparate elements as biblical history and arthurian legend can be united is through a belief in the similarities among creatures and between creatures and their creator. Thus *disjointure*, like *conjointure* is another facet of the aesthetic of repetition.

An article that illustrates the joy of the medieval aesthetic of repetition more clearly than any other in this volume is Eren Branch's "Rhetorical Structures and Strategies in Boccaccio's *Teseida*." The *Teseida*, Branch finds, is a two-sided tale (a tale *in utramque partem*)[16] which argues on both sides of the question in the manner of a Roman controversy. The central question in the *Teseida*, according to Branch, is the conflict between the ordering forces of the classical rhetorical tradition and the non-artistic rhetoric of brute force. The two-sided tale pattern is seen as the organizing principle of the work and as such informs many of its structures and themes. In the scene of the *boschetto*, for example, the rivals, Palemone and Archita, meet in a wood to discuss and eventually come to blows over the *partita* 'sharing' of Emilia's love. As Branch astutely remarks, "the word 'partita' (along with its cognates) occurs with conspicuous frequency throughout this scene," which is itself a *partita* 'debate' "over how a single woman might be *partita*" 'shared' (p. 146). The ruler Teseo arrives on the scene to mediate and to decide what punishment is to be meted out to the two men for breaking the law by fighting. Teseo analyzes the case, trying to reconcile the letter of the law (*ius*) with moral equity (*aequitas*), in the manner of a declaimer in a Roman *controversia*. Apparently Boccaccio's use of the two-sided tale pattern in the *Teseida* was both conscious and deliberate, as shown by the playful repetitions of it at various levels of his narrative. In fact Boccaccio's artful orchestration of this particular construct in his poem reveals the virtuoso at work, so confident of his craft that he has complete control over every device. This is medieval craftsmanship at its finest: the author engaging his listeners in a complex game, one facet of which was pattern recognition.

Closely allied to the structure of medieval narrative is the question of authorial intention. If the repetitive constructs of medieval literature reflect the relationship between the Creator and his creation, it stands to reason that, like God, in whose image he is created, the medieval author constructed his world in the book to be more or less like him, and to provide a set of *signa auctoris* for the reader. Like the world created by God, the world of the medieval book 'consists of traces of authorial intention, and intentionality is lodged throughout the created world.'[17]

Peter Haidu, whose article on "Repetition: . . ." I have been shamelessly paraphrasing, is uneasy about the whole question of intentionality in narrative, considering it a poor basis for literary analysis. If, of course, the critic were really "basing" his remarks about the work on an irresponsibly contrived hypothesis of intentionality, Professor Haidu would be quite right; however, what ought to happen in this kind of criticism, when it is competently done, is for the critic's perception of the author's purposes to be based upon the text. For example, Tony Hunt would appear to take intentionality for granted when he makes statements such as "he [Chrétien] wishes to alert his audience in this the most sophisticated and problematical of all his romances — to the complexities of reception" (p. 86) and "Chrétien's purpose is to strip away the hollow ideality of courtly romance" (p. 89). Because Tony Hunt's analysis of the *Yvain* as an "auto-reflective" romance is extremely perceptive we must ask ourselves how he knows what Chrestien's intentions were. The answer, of course, is that like any astute reader or listener, Dr. Hunt is responding to the *signa auctoris* strewn throughout the text and to the way in which these function together within the narrative as a whole. The question is, what are these signals, and how do we recognize them?

Arrathoon analyzes the devices of dialectical structure, rhetoric, repetition, frame (prologue/epilogue)-tale relationship, the degree of reliability of the narrator, the use of intertextual or outlandish language, outlandish ideas, allusiveness, intercalated lyric, irony, caring, distancing, verbal patterning, and tragedy in ethically-oriented narrative fiction, i.e., literary fiction that is chiefly concerned with human behavior rather than entertainment. As we see how these devices function and that they function together, a statement emerges from the text. The statement may take the form of a truth or "lesson," as in Jacques de Vitry's sermon exemplum where the male listeners are supposed to learn to avoid being "too fond lovers of their wives." By contrast, in narratives like "Calogrenant's Tale" and *ChV*, the function of the various devices in the narrative is to undermine the statement being made by an unreliable narrator, thus throwing the events of the story open for debate by the audience. These two kinds of ethically-oriented narrative fiction turn out to be mutually exclusive tale types. What emerges from this is analysis is that there are three possible purposes in medieval narrative fiction which serve as the organizing principles for all the structures of the work: *docere* 'to teach,' *movere*,' 'to move,' 'agitate,' or 'upset,' and *delectare*, 'to delight.' Because expository writing is often the reverse of the thinking process, Arrathoon begins with the discussion of narrative purpose that was really the conclusion to her research.

For Roy Pearcy the *fabliau* is a genre where opportunism is a virtue and where practical advice, rather than moral wisdom is frequently the point of the tale. The fabliau ethic is one of expediency, concerned with "strategies and tactics of survival in a space and time-bound world where resources are limited." What is expressed in these poems is the "need to maintain a delicate balance between freedom for the individual and the safeguarding of the social order from chaos." One form of chaos is the wife who obtains mastery over the husband because it is shameful for a husband to be subservient to a wife. Although the matter is dealt with in purely secular terms, we should perhaps keep in mind that it was Adam who ruled in the prelapsarian world (p. 262).

Although some fabliaux are merely entertainment, many have a *sentence* which while not moralistic, is far from arbitrary or capricious. *Fableors*, in fact, were no literary hacks, but competent craftsman whose statements as to the moral implications of their tales are usually bourne out by the moral concepts which can be extracted from their work (p. 274). Pearcy discerns seven different kinds of *sentence* in these poems which he thinks can be used as indicators in classifying the stories. What he finds is that there are two kinds of fabliaux: the *risée* whose chief purpose is entertainment, and the *essanple*, which is more concerned with moral content than entertainment. This conclusion correlates with Arrathoon's division of fabliaux into ethically-oriented and non-ethically-oriented fictions.

Nykrog, Dragonetti, and Arrathoon see literature as an elaborate game, organized by the author and played by the reader, who learns the rules of the game from the text. Per Nykrog focuses on two different kinds of games: (1) the writer who stacks the cards against himself by straining the reader's credulity so that the reader becomes suspicious of what he is being told by the narrator, as in *Les Quinze Joyes de Mariage*; (2) narrators who are so verisimilar that modern readers have taken them seriously, as with Boccaccio's *Corbaccio*. For Nykrog the storyteller proves his craftsmanship by maintaining an equilibrium between persuading the reader to believe everything he tells him and keeping the reader aware that what he is being asked to believe is not the truth. The narrator persona—or what Peter Haidu would term the "text enunciator"—in the game of fiction is a mask or fictional projection of the author which may or may not reflect the author's point of view.

If fiction is a game, then fiction is as St. Augustine found it to be, "enuntiatio falsa cum voluntate fallendi" (Nykrog). But let me cite Peter Haidu's thought-provoking definition of fiction from his classic article on "Repetition. . . ."

> In a specific, technical sense, *fiction*, considered an "etiolated use of language" by J. L. Austin, is more simply a *lie*: it is a turning away of language from its extralinguistic reference, and substitutes for that normative referential function a production of meaning which may take mimetic form, or which may turn into a simulacrum of the world, but which is essentially unbound and unpredictable. Fiction constitutes a turning away of language from what Austin considered its "serious" quality and what medieval theology considered its proper function as redeemed language: that of focusing on God's message as inscribed both in Scripture and in the created world. Fiction is man's disruption of language from its divinely ordained intentionality. . . .[18]

In a word, fiction can be an out and out lie, or it can be "straight," but even when it is straight, it is not referentially oriented. At its most mimetic, fiction is but an image of the world, having the form but not the substance of the represented object, even when its function is exemplary. Hence Boccaccio's defense of poetry in his *Genealogia Deorum* as hiding precious truth beneath the veil of fiction.

Aldo Scaglione treats us to a kind of medieval fiction most of us rarely study: islamic autobiography. Examining the autobiographies of Avicenna, al Ghazāli, Tamerlane, and Ibn Khaldūn, which he compares with western autobiography, Scaglione finds that Western writers tended to style themselves after the heroes of epic and hagiography, thus preventing the emergence of an individual from the text, whereas in Islam it was possible for an autocratic ruler to place himself upon a monumental pedestal since the collectivistic way of life that had produced him sanctioned his god-like superiority (p. 467).

The genre of autobiography is characterized by the imposition of an "*ex post facto* design upon a life" (p. 457), in other words, a fictionalization of that life. In portraying himself the way he wishes others to see him, the narrating voice in an autobiography is little different from a character like Chaucer's Merchant—i.e., a mask. This is especially true of a Tamerlane who is presented in his autobiography as a merciful and generous minister and ruler. By contrast, history depicts him as a butcher who massacred 100,000 Hindus among others.

Of the many "games" that can be played with fiction, a favorite is ambiguity. In his coruscating study of Jean Bodel's *Jeu de Saint Nicolas*, Roger Dragonetti captures the "shimmering ambiguity" of a difficult author, whose equivocal characters and chiaroscuro scenes are "like tides subject to celestial attraction." Both actions and characters bear a vertiginous resemblance to each other. For although the world of the *Jeu* is divided between Saracen and Christian, the two poles of the work reverse as the angle of vision varies. For example, the figure of St. Nicolas is extremely problematic. The saint is depicted as his image, which fails to carry out its duty to protect the king's treasure, and as a dream vision that swears like a tavern thief. He is called various names, among which "Honored Mohammed," "piece of wood," "wooden fetish," and "riffraff." More unsettling still, St. Nicolas has a pagan double, the image of Tervagan. If St. Nicolas' function is to protect and increase the king's gold (i.e., to serve as accomplice and protector of the king's greed), Tervagan gets more gold painted on his image each time the king desires propitious oracles. As Dragonetti puts it, the resemblances between Tervagan, to whom the king refers as "son of a whore" and St. Nicolas, who calls the thieves "sons of whores," are diabolical! In short, nothing is as it seems in this impishly elusive play where all the characters inhabit "the same country of dreams" and where even the language is polyvalent and ambiguous.

Barbara Sargent-Baur is concerned with a different kind of ambiguity: that of the signs of his wife's infidelity as interpreted by King Mark in Béroul's version of the *Tristan*. Since the evidence of the love affair is abundantly clear to the reader, one wonders at Mark's willful moral blindness. For example, it seems to me that his literal-minded interpretation of the sword placed between the sleeping lovers in the Morrois Forest might be seen as an image of and a warning to similarly imperceptive members of Béroul's listening audience. But Sargent-Baur's chief concern in her essay is with the interplay between truth and lies, and appearance and reality that creates the tension in the romance.

Characters are one of the two most fundamental elements in fictional narrative. The other, of course, is plot. Since it is almost impossible to write about narrative fiction without mentioning either the one or the other, or both, every writer in this book has something to say about characters and plot, at least in passing. In general, all the scholars writing here would probably agree that characters are not "real people," but the embodiments of ideas. They would also no doubt concur that while medieval characters may look psychologically verisimilar, their exemplary and emblematic functions keep them from being psychologically rounded like the actors in a modern novel. For example, Chaucer's Merchant, who is psychologically very believable, is nevertheless a patchwork of iconographical materials. In general, medieval narrators may be described as "masks" for the author, by which I mean 'false faces' which range from close mimeses of aspects of the author's mind to inversions of it.

Sarah Kay investigates the ways in which Greimas' categories of actor and plot interact in the *chansons de geste* of the twelfth and thirteenth century, with special emphasis on the *Raoul de Cambrai*, arguing both for the inseparability of character and plot and for the primacy of one over the other (p. 493).

Because medieval epic was a performed genre, epic characters are knowable in the same way as characters in a play, which is to say that in lieu of the privileged inside views we get about the actors in novels, we must judge epic characters by what we see them do. Moreover, the portraits in the epic are so traditional as to sap the characters' individuality. Nevertheless, Kay maintains that with a great deal of imagination on the part of the listener and a fine performance on the part of the *jongleur* it is possible to find psychological depth in epic characterization (p. 479).

The medieval aesthetic of repetition strongly affects the way we perceive character in epic because the hero is made to repeat the same actions over and over again, and the plot is so organized as to emphasize certain traits of the hero. Further, when the *chanson* was performed, individual scenes were dramatized at the expense of coherency of the whole with the result that consistency in characterization was frequently sacrificed to amplify the clash between the characters (p. 481). On the other hand, while the *laisses similaires* which present an act from different viewpoints, may seem to undermine characterization, they in fact enhance it because they complement more than they contradict each other (p. 482).

Finally, it is possible to see characterization in the epic as serving the moral or political thematic concerns of the work. "In such a case, character is subordinated to a plot conceived not just as a series of acts, but as the articulation of an ethical point of view" (p. 484).

In addition to the concerns she shares with the other writers in this volume, the aesthetic of repetition, intentionality and moral purpose, and the function of various devices, Kay is interested, as are Zumthor and Haidu, in the interaction of the performance text with the archetype or historical text with which it constantly comes into play. We are reminded, for example, that the narrative of a *chanson* is only one of several rival versions, all of which are to be measured against the *histoire* or ideal version. While the author and audience share a knowledge of the story behind the particular performance, the characters function in a present time, unaware that their story is history. However, at times, perhaps through a prophetic dream, the characters can "gain insight into the totality of the story in which they figure; and though they continue to enact the roles apportioned to them and to feel the emotions that are their lot, they do so with a curiously enhanced stature which can border on myth" (p. 488).

The Craft of Fiction: Essays in Medieval Poetics is a book about the art of medieval storytelling. Its chief concern is those aspects of medieval poetics that are knowable on the basis of the extant texts.

All of the scholars in this volume approach the Otherness of medieval culture with caution, realizing that whatever is to be understood by the modern reader about this ancient literature is to be gleaned from the text. When external materials, such as historical documentation and intertextual references, are brought to bear upon the analysis of a difficult passage, they are never forced upon the text which must always have the first and the last word in literary analysis. As I said earlier, this emphasis upon the importance of the text brings into sharp focus the problem of what properly constitutes the medieval text. Because reading aloud remained a deeply ingrained habit throughout the Middle Ages, the critic must always be able to envision the text as a performance, even though romance often displays the sophistication and interiority of the modern novel. Who then should have priority in determining the way the text is received today? The medieval performer who wantonly altered the words of the author or the author who earnestly wished his text to remain intact, safeguarded from the ignorant tampering of *jongleurs* and scribes? Should the text be presented to the modern reader as a series of "performances," each one layed beside the others in diplomatic transcriptions? Or should the archetype be reconstructed by the modern editor to appease the tortured shade of the author? One cannot help but think that Chrestien might have been grateful for the efforts of his modern editors, although it is possible that he would have been just as scornful of modern tampering with his text as he was with scribal intervention in his own day.

Although the essays in this book approach problems of interpretation with different methodologies, they are all asking similar questions of the text. The most important of these questions involve genre, structure and meaning, receptional aesthetics, the historical and social text into which the text is inserted, intentionality, the identification and function of the various narrative devices within the narrative as a whole, and the character not only of actors but especially of narrators who play such a key role in the meaning of the tales they tell.

The essays in this book are written for researchers, teachers, and students of medieval literature. Because these studies are fundamental, the major concepts are listed by key words below. Page numbers and definitions for the concepts have been withheld because it is hoped that the list may serve as a teaching tool when the book is used as a class text. Students should be encouraged to use the key words as a guide while they are reading the book.

Rochester, Michigan. June 21, 1984.

𝔑otes

1. Percy Lubbock, *The Craft of Fiction* (London: John Dickens and Co., 1921 and 1954, rpt. 1963), p. 3.
2. ibid., p. 274.
3. ibid., p. 1. Cf. pp. 5, 11.
4. Lubbock, pp. 16-17.
5. Lubbock, p. 20.
6. ibid., p. 19.
7. ibid., p. 67.
8. ibid., p. 19.
9. See Arrathoon, "La Châtelaine de Vergi: A Structural Study of an Old French Artistic Short Narrative," *Language and Style* 4 (1974), 151-80 and L. G. Donovan, *Recherches sur le Roman de Thèbes* (Paris: Société d'édition d'enseignement supérieur, 1975), rev. Arrathoon, *Romanic Review* 71 (1980), 88-89, and Eugene Vance, "Le combat érotique chez Chrétien de Troyes: De la figure à la forme," *Poétique* 12 (1972), 569. See also Owen, p. 49, and Hunt, pp. 85, 88 for example.
10. Arrathoon, *The Lady of Vergi* (Merrick, New York: Cross-Cultural Communications Press, 1984).
11. Peter Haidu, "Repetition: Modern Reflections on Medieval Aesthetics," *Modern Language Notes* 92 (1977), 880.
12. ibid., citing Robert Javelet, p. 878.
13. "The Dialectic of *Yvain,*" *Modern Language Review* 72 (1977), 285-99, and "Aristotle, Dialectic, and Courtly Literature," *Viator* 10 (1979), 95-129.
14. Arrathoon's article. Cf. *The Lady of Vergi* and "Antinomic Cluster Analysis and the Boethian Verbal Structure of Chaucer's *Merchant's Tale,*" *Language and Style* (1984), in press.
15. Douglas Kelly, "The Source and Meaning of *Conjointure* in Chrétien's *Erec* 14," *Viator* 1 (1970), 179-200, *Sens et Conjointure in the Chevalier de la Charrete* (The Hague: Mouton, 1966).
16. On the tale *in utramque partem,* see Wesley Trimpi, "The Quality of Fiction: The Rhetorical Transmission of Literary Theory," *Traditio* 30 (1974), and *Muses of One Mind: The Literary Analysis of Experience and Its Continuity* (Princeton: Princeton University

Press, 1983, pp. 301, 309, 334.

17. Peter Haidu, citing Marcia Colish, in "Repetition . . ." p. 879.
18. ibid., pp. 884–85.

List of Concepts

abelardian
acoustic image
acroistre . . . conte
actor
adjuvant
adventure / *avanture*
aenigmalogue
aenigmologist
aequitas
aesthetic distance /
   distance esthétique
alba
allegory
allusion
allusiveness
alterity
ambiguity / *ambiguïté*
Amors
analogical
anti-feminist
antancion
anti-novella
antinomic
antinomous
antiphrastic
antithetical / *antithétique*
antonyms
apocryphal
apologist
apologue
appearance and reality
archetypal
archetype
aristotelian
artifact
artisan
auctores
audience reception
augustinian
authorial commentary
authorial intention

authorial intervention /
   interventions d'auteur
auto-engendré
auto-reflective
autobiography
autorité

banal lordship
bardic
bestiary / *bestiaire*
binary opposition
boethian
boschetto / woodland
branch / *branche*
brevitas
burlesque

canso
captatio benevolentiae
caring
cavalcade
chanson de geste
chansons épiques
chanteurs de geste
chevauchée
chivalry
christology
chwedl / chwedleu
code
collocations
color / colores
comedy-comic
commentary /
   commentaire
commoratio
conflictuality
conjointure
conte d'avanture
contraception
contracts
controversia

convention of
   hospitality
conventional aesthetic
corronpre
courtly / *courtois*
courtly love
craft
craftsmanship
cyfarwyddyd /
   cyfarwyddiaid
cyfranc

debate poems
declamation
delectare
depecier
design
destinator / *destinataire*
device
dialectic
dialectical structure
dialogue
dianoia
diction sentencieuse
didactic
didacticism / *didactisme*
dilemma
disjointure
disputation / *disputatio*
disseminatory
distancing
docere
doubles
dynastic

ebostol
echoes / *échos*
eclogue
economic text
emblem
emblematic

XXV

péché originel
painne
parable
paradigm-paradigmatic
paradox-paradoxical
parallel structures
parallels / *parallélismes*
parody / *parodie*
parodic / *parodique*
partita
pattern-patterning
peasant / *vilain*
performance
peripeteia
phrases sentencieuses
picaresque
planh
platonic forms
plot
poetic discourse /
    discours poétique
poetics
point of view
political domination
political text
polysemous-polysemic
praexercitamenta
praexercitamina
problematic /
    problématique
program-programmatic /
    programme-program-
    matique
progymnasmata
prologue
propadeuctic
prosimetron
proverb / *proverbe*
purpose

quaestio
qualitas

quistioni d'amore
quizzical

reception
receptional aesthetics
recipient
recipient of the message
reflector
registre
remedium amoris
repetition
ressemblances
reversal technique
rhapsologue
rhetoric
rhetorical set piece /
    ensemble oratoire
risée
ritual
romance / *roman*
romans en prose
rounded character

san-sen
satire-satiric
scribe-scribal
scriptual
scripturaire
semantic / *sémantique*
seme
semiosis
semiotic / *sémiotique*
senefiance
sentence / *sententiae*
sermon
signal
signaling device
signifiant
signifié
signifier
social text
structure

supplementarity
surplus de sen
syllogism
symmetry / *symétrie*
symbol
synonyms
synonymy

taverne
tekmeria
tençon
text
text enunciator
topos-topoi
tradition orale
tragedy-tragic
transform
translatio studii
tropological
troubadours
two-sided tale / tale *in*
    utramque partem
type-typal
typologie
typology
typological-typologique
uncle
undercut
unity / *unité*
unreliable narrator
upside-down
utilitas

valorial
verbal schemes
verbal structure
virtuoso
vocalité
voice / *voix*

wish-fulfillment

ymddiddanion

1. Romance: Idealistic Genre or Historical Text?*

Romance is cursed by its name, at least for English speakers. In modern French and German, the same texts are designated as variants of the novel or of epic: *roman d'aventure, Abenteueroman, höfischer Roman, höfisches Epos* are terms in current use. The absence of a specific noun, the concomitant use of a compound, modified expression, suggests a broad range of narrativity of which *particular* cases represent variants. In English, however, since we have a *particular* noun, it has, presumably, reference to a *particular* group of texts: its use presupposes and indirectly asserts the existence of the group, as a group, by that very act of nomination. Language is inherently realistic, in the sense that word has in medieval philosophy: the concepts designated by words are posited as having a real existence independently of concrete reality. Thus, if the *verbum* exists, so then must the *res*. Existence follows nomination, no matter the evidence or the theoretical considerations that countermand that ideological mandate. In all modern European languages, there are concrete studies of particular texts that lead one to question the habitual generic definitions of romance and indeed the very pertinence of the concept of genres as applied to medieval texts, but old habits die hard.

Nor is it only medieval scholars who continue to invoke traditional and largely unexamined generic distinctions. The contemporary theologians of *la chose littéraire* continue to refer to "medieval romance" as the perfect incorporation of the genre's specific and differentiating traits, primarily in order to distinguish the more modern texts from the medieval. The medieval text then functions as a binary opposite to the modern, defining it oppositionally, arrogating to itself those traits that are negatively marked in the theoretician's literary vocabulary and, by implicational devolution, assigning to the modern texts those traits that are positively marked in his scale of literary value. In this manner, theory continues on its

1

ethnocentric and chronocentric journey without regard to the fact that it is thereby condemned to a purely circular circumnavigation of its own umbilicus, reaffirming the ignorance of both theoretician and reader in a perfect example of ideological reproduction. Not that "medieval" is the only path out of basing theory that merely reproduces already existing cultural assumptions: other non-modern, non-western bodies of literature are amply available, whether these are considered simply as "anthropological texts" or as examples of Oriental, African, Indian textuality, etc. But the extraordinary burgeoning of contemporary theory is largely based on modern European textuality, and therefore operates to reconfirm modern European cultural assumptions, just positing them as universally valid.

For students of the European tradition who have been formed by the same tradition, however, medieval literature does have a privileged place. It is simultaneously constitutive of European literarity, and yet represents a sufficiently great difference from the modern versions of literarity to render inacceptable the merely automatic repetitions of modern presuppositions in its domain. In truth, a small group of contemporary theoreticians has managed to avoid such chronocentric repetition in discussing medieval literature. Julia Kristeva tends to get her dates wrong but the theoretical issues she raises are most germane;[1] A. J. Greimas has not dealt extensively with medieval literature *per se*, but occasional references scattered throughout his works reveal a similar awareness.[2] A most interesting case is that of Umberto Eco. His early work argued for an opposition between modern works considered semantically "open," i.e., producing meaning in unlimited fashion, and medieval works, whose meaning was asserted as "closed," i.e., limited. In fact, this was a variant on an older, romantic opposition between "symbol" and "allegory" that went back at least to Goethe. But Eco's more recent theoretical work, incorporating a more sophisticated semiotics than was conceivable twenty years ago, acknowledges that earlier opposition is untenable,[3] and does so on the basis of a semiotics that is subtle and complex enough to account for both medieval and modern textuality (and perhaps non-European textuality as well, but that would require a different argument) while respecting their differentiating specificities.

In spite of such occasional recognitions—all three of the above, interestingly enough, represent different currents of semiotics—it remains a sad, unfortunate, but true fact that medievalism continues to inhabit, as Paul Zumthor recently noted, an intellectual ghetto,[4] allowing their mutual and complementary ignorances to protect the intellectual and professional investments of traditional medievalists and contemporary theoreticians. Thus it is that Fredric Jameson has recently resurrected Northrop Frye's theory of genres.[5] While medieval romance is relatively unimportant to Jameson's grandiose theory, it was an essential reference point for Frye's theory, providing him with an antecedent to English Renaissance romance—Spenser and Shakespeare primarily—in which the traits ascribed to "romance" were supposedly displayed in their purest state. Later versions of "romance," renaissance or modern, were seen as sophisticated, self-conscious "uses" of a genre that was inherently simple and naive—a usage that is still characteristic of Jameson. While it is not possible to deal with the details of Frye's and Jameson's theories here, the central attribute of the genre of "romance" as they see it ought to be recognized. That is the characteristic of "fantasy," as the textualization of an impulse of wish-fulfillment that is thought to preside at the conception of "romance." These terms are attractive in that they connect literary theory with psychoanalytic theory, albeit in a form of psychoanalytic theory that is earlier, perhaps more properly Freudian, than the Lacanian theory that becomes more important to Jameson in the rest of his book. Positing "romance" as characterized by "fantasy" that is the expression of (authorial and lectorial) "wish-fulfillment" does give rise to some questions, however. The concept of "fantasy" can have no independent existence: for it to have any meaning at all, it must be set in opposition to another term. It is a prime example of a theoretical term that derives its existence only from its location in a binary opposition. A domain of "fantasy" in literary theory can be asserted only in opposition to and within a framework of a referential theory of textuality, which sees the text as constituted by its relation to an extra-textual "reality" and which further sees that relation as being "serious" when the relation of text to its "real referent" is a correct relation. That is to say, "fantasy" functions within a theoretical frame of mimetism, as the exceptional opposite of the mimetic relation that is presumed to be the primordial and founding relation of text and "extra-text." In its simplest terms, that opposition is that between "realism" and "fantasy" on the semic category of representation:

/realism/   representation   /"fantasy"/

It is only against a presupposed norm of adequacy of representation, or "realism" of a type far broader than the nineteenth-century incarnation, and the judgment that a particular text or group of texts fails in the adequacy of its representation of an external reality, that the concept of "fantasy" can bear any sense as an element of literary theory.[6] As to the

notion of "wish-fulfillment," it is no more than a psychological rationali-
zation for the existence of "fantasy." It too presupposes an opposite, a
type of lectorial activity that is *not* wish-fulfillment, a type of reading
that is appropriate to texts whose function it is to communicate a serious,
responsible, and adequate representation of the referent. Insofar as text-
theory engages psychoanalysis, such a limited and limiting use of "wish-
fulfillment" is a travesty of the concept's import in Freudian theory. It is
not "romance" that is specified and constituted by the functioning of
wish-fulfillment, but any and all reading of a "literary" type (accepting
for the moment the notion of literature as we find it): all reading "for
pleasure," of poetry, of drama, of fiction, most obviously derive from
"wish-fulfillment." But are other types of the same activity — reading —
not infused with some kind of wish-fulfilling desire: the attorney's
perusal of the law, the doctor's incorporation of the information in the
latest issue of a medical journal, the engineer's analysis of another
engineer's blueprint, the philosopher's self-inscription in the body of western philosophy? These too must engage the individual at a sufficiently deep
level where a profound desire is fulfilled, either directly or indirectly in
the case of a process too easily decried by some contemporary writers on
psychoanalytic themes, that of sublimation. Wish-fulfillment *per se* does
not differentiate a putative genre of "romance" from other texts: on the
contrary, it indicates a mental functioning presupposed by the pleasur-
able reading of *all* forms of textuality. Its use as a criterion to differentiate a putative genre of "romance" is founded on sand.

As indicated, the problem is partly defined by the lack of direct
knowledge of some contemporary theoreticians of the texts signalled by
their reference to "medieval romance": it is interesting to note that all
three of the theoreticians I have named as exceptions to this misprision —
Eco, Greimas, and Kristeva — did some of their early work on medieval
texts, literary, philosophical, or linguistic. Another aspect of the problem, however, is defined by the very status of genre-theory within a
modern textual theory. By itself, the concept of genres can have two
aspects. One is that of a purely idealistic entity which transcends all historicity, much like Platonic Forms or Aristotelian types such as tragedy,
comedy, and epic; such was also Northrop Frye's theory of genres. In its
best modern examples, such an idealistic assertion of universal essences is
based on a broad knowledge of the European tradition, and the ignorance
or disregard of the textual production of other cultures, including that of
the Middle Ages. It thus represents an effort difficult to countenance

in the context of the contemporary anthropological consciousness of cultural relativity. The other version of genre theory is the historical, in which determinate definitions of genres are considered valid only within specified socio-historical limits. These definitions can base themselves on the material aspects of the text, such as its mode of production; the interpretation of the significance of that mode, in turn, depends on the interpretation of the cultural and historical context.[7] A more hazardous attempt is based, not on the material mode of textual production, but on its signifying mode of production.[8] Somewhere between these two extremes is the effort, well represented within traditional literary scholarship, to identify conventions agreed upon by authors and audiences at a given historical period, literary contracts "whose function is to specify the proper use of a particular cultural artifact."[9] That such contracts exist is certain: the question is, first, whether they are recuperable.

In the case of contemporary literature, a reader does not need to be an "ideal" reader, but requires only a reasonable incorporation of contemporary textual codes to enable him to consult the semiotic analogue to a Chomskyan linguistic competence, and perhaps compare it with that of other, equally endowed readers. While the interpretations generated by such contemporary competences will continue to vary (semiotic codes seem to bear less force of necessity than their linguistic counterparts), such a reasonably competent reader is unlikely to entirely misplace the focus of his attention in the reading of the text: such a reader is likely at least to head in the general direction of a pertinent problematic. In the case of somewhat earlier periods, the contracts that obtained at the time of the text's production can usually be reconstructed on the basis of prefaces, published criticism, manifestoes, and documents of a more private nature such as letters, diaries, and writer's notes. In the case of long distant periods, however, particularly where cultural continuity was interrupted at a given historical period, matters become more difficult. The status of such contracts becomes part of an epistemological difficulty of a different nature, one that approaches the epistemological difficulty of the anthropologist facing a social group belonging to a completely different culture than his own. In the case of classical literature, at least there exists a substantial body of written discussion of "literary" texts, from Plato and Aristotle to Cicero, Quintilian, and the grammarians, rhetoricians, and commentators of the late Empire. Even so, the received interpretation of a culture which is simultaneously constitutive of our own culture and yet profoundly foreign to it can be highly erroneous:

vide the critical tradition which, in spite of Nietszche, made of classical culture the epitome of Apollonian rationality in what can now seem only like a willful ignorance of its irrational characteristics.

The medieval case is yet more difficult. Such "documentation" as exists for the classical heritage — the various discussions of "literary" texts — is absent, particularly for the formative period of vernacular literature. With the exception of occasional asides incorporated within the texts themselves, generally brief, of a fragmentary and rhetorical nature, there is simply no recorded discussion of the vernacular texts of the eleventh and twelfth centuries. What discussions do exist, both of a technical nature (grammatical, rhetorical) and of a hermeneutic nature, are in Latin and address themselves to questions of the interpretation of religious texts. As a result, the contracts operative between vernacular authors and publics, between semiotic emitters and recipients in this period, remain of an implicit character: there is no textual basis to serve as evident historical documentation. On the one hand, that body of texts is characterized by a striking alterity from contemporary textual norms; on the other hand, their interpreter has far less historical guidance in their interpretation than in the case of closer bodies of textuality. The author-public contracts are, in fact, irrecuperable, at least for the French Middle Ages (phenomenological arguments can be made for a continuity of contact with medieval textuality in the English and German cases that may arguably differentiate them from the French). In such circumstances, the methodological decisions of the twentieth-century interpreter become all the more determinative of the type of reading he is to produce, and hence the type of meaning he is likely to find.

It must be stressed that no way out of that determining role can be found. There is no way to justify one's interpretative (or analytical) operations on a "historical" basis that elides the reader's critical responsibility. For the definition of what constitutes the historicity of a "historical" reading is itself open to extensive debate. With all their variety, modern notions of historicity differ profoundly from medieval notions of historicity. When it comes to the interpretation of ancient texts, the predominant medieval attitude was not at all "historical" but "modernist": it consisted of resolutely reading the classical texts such as Virgil and Ovid in terms of contemporary eleventh-or twelfth-century codes. Even the relative historicization of scriptural interpretation by the Victorines in the twelfth century focused on the first level of the biblical reading, its historical reading, not on the ultimate meaning to be attributed to its text.[10] Most important, however, is a decision prior to that of the interpretation of a particular text: it is that of the general character of the period in question, and implies an overall historiographical decision. Is it to be considered a unitary Hegelian whole, whose eventual semiotic content is such as was defined by those officially charged with the production and care of ideology by the social and institutional structures of the time, namely the men of the Church? Or are their productions as to the meanings of texts, society, and man, to be seen, precisely, as ideological constructs with a specific, historically defined role to play within the total social structure of their period? In the latter case, it is not the ideological production of the period that will determine a modern reading, but a modern view of the historical process and the functioning of that particular social structure that will provide the historical "meaning(s)" of the period and its textual production.

It is such a view of the historical process, and the essential role of social structures in determining social meaning, that is the founding and constitutive presupposition of my reading. The semiosis of any given historical period is to be read as an integral part of the social text of the period, not as defined by an ideology produced within that period and hence inevitably oriented toward the reproduction of that ideology as well as the protection and expansion of specific interests, but as participating in the conflictuality of the period which makes ideology necessary. Such a conflictuality is inherent in any period considered as historical and evolving: at least its traces are present at all social instances: the economic, the political, the legal, and the ideational which can be considered both cultural and ideological. That conflictuality is to be identified in the particular, concrete text by its encounter with a semiotics whose methodological structures are geared to the task of socio-historical analysis.[11] In the case of medieval texts, that encounter requires more concrete display of elementary interpretative moves than is customary in the analysis of modern texts. There, the familiarity of the reader with the text can more readily be taken for granted; more important, the logic that leads to particular semiotic identifications of syntactical and semantic kinds is more patent than in the medieval case. The encounter between the concrete medieval text and a socio-historically oriented semiotics will focus more on the actual construal of the semiotic object at a somehow "pre-analytic" level than is normally the case.

My choice of Chrétien de Troyes' *Yvain*, or rather, of its opening sequence, as the object of my discussion, will presumably not surprise any reader interested in medieval texts. It is not the "first" medieval romance in the chronological series, being preceded by the romances of antiquity and two of Chrétien's earlier texts, the *Erec* and the *Cligès*. Generally considered to be the finest of the author's completed works, the *Yvain* can be taken as a token of the putative type of "romance" and the inaugural text of the series. My reading, however, will resolutely address itself to the particular text in question, without regard to any possible role that reading might have in the elaboration of an eventual generic model: any such model ought to be worked out on the basis of a plurality of readings with similar presuppositions. An analysis of the entire narrative will be presented as part of a larger work currently in preparation:[12] the present reading will address itself only to the prologue and to Calogrenant's adventure. My goal is to draw out of the text a dimension which is in turn social, political, and economic, on the basis of close attention to its verbal and narrative complexity.

The Pro-logue

The Prologue of *Yvain* is, in fact, no pro-logue at all. It is not a metatextual segment ideationally related to the narrative but placed before the actual inception of the narrative. On the contrary, "prologue" and the inception of the narrative are entirely intertwined. Insofar as there is metatext, it begins after the inception of the narrative, and is thematically dependent thereon. The metatext comes into play only after an event, its agent, and its content are asserted: Arthur holds a feast at his court at Pentecost, at which a multitude of knights and ladies converse about various matters, including the abstract, ideational matter of the values to be associated with the court. This leads to a reflection as to the relative role of this ideology in earlier times and at the time of the enunciation: it is this content that can be specified as the material of the Prologue. The dependency of its ideological content on the framing narrative is clear.

So is its constitutive topos, that of the golden age. It is the same topos as appears at the beginning of the *Saint Alexis*. There too, an admirable past is compared to a regrettable present:

> Bons fu li secles al tens ancienur,
> Quer fet i ert e justice ed amor . . .
>
> [1-2]

> Bons fu li secles, ja mais n'ert si vailant.
> Velz est e frailes, tut s'en va declinant;
> Si'st ampairet, tut bien vait remanant.
>
> [8-10][13]

The basic semantic content of the topos is always:

past (+) *vs.* present(-),

and the two cases in question provide no exception. But this identity of fundamental semantic content from an intertextual structure only provides the basis for the analysis of the two cases' differential verbalizations. In the *Saint Alexis*, the Biblical references to Noah, Abraham, and David, "whom God loved so much," clearly establish the religious isotopy and the text's dependence on the institution of religion. The religious isotopy is not entirely absent from the *Yvain* prologue, but as we shall see, a reference to Pentecost is theologically trivial and polit ically ambiguous, and subordinated to a larger political isotopy. Exemplarity no longer devolves from the religious establishment and its ideological figures, but from the political institution of kingship:

Artus, li boens rois de Bretaigne
la cui proesce nos enseigne
que nos soiens preu et cortois . . .

[1-3][14]

If the political isotopy, centered around the thematic figure of kingship, continues to function throughout the narrative text—though not without extensive ambiguity—another intertextual reference indicates from the very beginning that its dominance presents inherent difficulties. The comparison of the present first line—

Artus, li boens rois de Bretainge—

with the first line of the *Roland*—

Carles li reis, nostre empereres magnes—

is hardly new. Both contain the following semantic contents: / nomination / + / king / + / positive qualification /. The ambiguity between "king" and "emperor" that obtains in the *Roland* has disappeared in *Yvain*, as has the possessive *nostre*, though that appears, semantically if not morphologically, in the second line: *la cui proesce nos enseigne*. In contrast to the *Saint Alexis*, enunciator and enunciatee are both represented within the enunciated text of both the *Roland* and the *Yvain*: the values in play within the enunciated text are thus pertinent to these two figures and the two ends of the semiotic process they represent, the production of the text and its reception. It is with what follows that the texts are differentiated. In the *Roland*, the first line leads immediately into a narrative whose valorial conflicts are embodied in the narrative action itself, without any mediating metatextuality: the implication of this

absence, of any overt specification of the values in conflict, is that such
conflict is absent. In the case of the *Yvain*, however, the nomination of
the immediate narrative agent, who will remain a major figure throughout the text, leads, not into the narrative directly, but into the function of
valorial exemplarity:

> . . . la cui proesce nos enseigne
> que nos soiens preu et cortois . . .

And by way of the ensuing narrative segment, the text leads to a discussion of ideological values.

The overtness of the ideological problematic in the *Yvain* suggests
the differentiation between narrative action and the values it bears. The
same narrative act can bear different values: in another register,
evenementiality or human action is ambiguous: inherently, and as a textual given from the very beginning of the text. Indeed, as we shall see, the
relationship between narrative event and its value is a central problematic
of this text. For the time being, it is ambiguity at the verbal level that is
explored. Arthur's first act is one that is simultaneously ritual, social,
and religious: he holds a special court for Pentecost. He does so via two
tropes. The first is a type of presuppositional play. The verbal structure
of the simile presupposes that the object in question will be compared to
another object: Achilles to the lion, for instance. It is thus an inversion
of normal linguistic presupposition to compare the object to itself, as
does this text: Arthur *tint cort si riche come rois*. The specific semantic
content of *riches* is uncertain: it can mean powerful, wealthy, or magnificent. Perhaps the most appropriate semantic attribution to be made
here, given the context, will be an ambiguous one combining the isotopies
of wealth and social effect as /expensive/ + /magnificent/. The syntactical construction that seems comparative and hence to lead to some
term other than that which constitutes the subject Arthur as King leads,
in fact, directly back to him:

> tint cort si riches *come rois*:

how else, indeed, should a king hold court, but as a king?

The second verbal game also has been noted before, though its implications in the context of our discussion have not. The time of the
court's assemblage is given as follows:

> a cele feste qui tant coste,
> qu'an doit clamer la Pantecoste,

in which the religious and financial isotopies are mixed by the repetition of the verbal element *-coste*. Its first occurrence, in the context of the term *riches* in the preceding line, is / financial /. It is only with the repetition of the verbal element *-coste* in "Pantecoste" that the possible Christological reference of *qui tant coste* is manifested: the introduction of the name of the religious festival retroactively bestows the religious and sacrificial dimension to the idea of "cost." The first pun sets into question the relationship between identity and difference, the second that between the financial and the religious, or perhaps better, between the material and the spiritual. A more appropriate ambiguity to the festival of Pentecost, the return of the Holy Spirit to the world of man, can hardly be imagined. Yet, as we have already seen, the relationship between narrative and value, also homologous to the distinction between matter and spirit, has already been put into question. The remainder of the "prologue" will continue the process of their differentiation. It is the opposition between the conjunction of values and their disjunction that is the ultimate metatheoretical problematic of this text, as of all texts of a post-lapsarian world.

The figures of Arthur and his court enter this textual world already defined by a close intertext. Already in Chrétien's earlier romances, *Erec et Enide* and *Cligès*, Arthur is named the best king in the world, the one who awards the prizes of honor and incorporation into an elite that is defined by his court. It is only there that a promising young noble can become a knight truly *preu* and *cortois*. In the earlier texts, the love associated with Arthur has been dynastic,[15] thus continuing the concerns of the earlier classical romances; in *Cligès*, an additional intertext of major import is that of *Tristan*, against which an elective love not subject to the social disarray brought on by the passion between *Tristan* and *Iseut* is posited and explored. It is in the *Yvain*, however, and presumably after the early lyric poems attributed to Chrétien, that the mode of love associated with the troubadours enters the world of romance, where it is socialized by its narrativization as part of a larger social scene, that of life at court. Arthur's court mingles in his palace at *Carduel en Gales*. It is introduced as a grouping organized along a sexual axis, with the ladies further sub-divided on marital lines:

> cil chevaler s'atropelerent
> la ou les dames les apelerent
> ou dameiseles ou puceles,
>
> [9-11]

with the further suggestion of a social dominance devolving on the ladies of the court. While some elements of structure thus obtain, these lines present a collection of individuals rather than a collectivity. It is only when the social intercourse of conversation begins, and an amorous ideology is displayed, that sufficient cohesion to found a collectivity occurs. The political subordination to the monarchical principle, the sexual and marital organization of society — so important to the feudal society's process of self-reproduction — are insufficient: it takes ideology to found a collectivity.

If an amorous ideology founds the collectivity of the court in *Yvain*, it also reveals, however, the discrepancies under all ideologies. Arthur's definition as exemplary, in the first couplet of the poem, locates him as the source of values, hence in the slot of the Destinator, not a surprising role for the figure of king with his intertextual relations. His thematic concretization as a good king, teaching his subjects to be *preu et cortois*, is followed, as noted, by the act, also positively marked, of holding the Pentecostal feast, at which his textual subjects wander about the palace halls and talk. At line 13, however, another figure appears, not concrete like the king, but abstract as an allegorical personification. While some of the court spoke of news (*noveles*),

> li autre parloient d'Amors,
> des angoisses et des dolors
> et des granz biens qu'orent sovant
> li deciple de son covant . . .
>
> [13-16]

Amors is another Destinator, allegorical and implicitly a value itself, with two stages of narrative evenementiality attributed to Love's subjects: an intermediary stage located on the isotopy of the passions (*angoisses, dolors*) and negatively marked, and an apparently final stage that is often reached by the subjects, that of the *granz biens*. This is not so much a matter of the distinction between instrumental and overall narrative programs, typical of a subject considered as individualistic, rational, and directed by will: it seems rather to imply a necessity of an overriding, perhaps metaphysical nature, the necessity of an exchange pattern in which a certain amount of dysphoria must be paid for the attainment of a possible euphoria.

In the social text of the 1170s, the decade of our text's probable composition, the actual relation between the King of France and his subjects was in a state of flux: we will return to this issue later. As the beginning of the *Yvain* has presented it so far, that relation is a purely ideological one. With the more abstract Destinator of *Amors*, however, the relationship is defined as that of a *covant*, a convention, an agreement, an accord:

a contract. In other words, the relationship of domination and subordination between this abstract Destinator and his subjects is the normal feudal one of a contractual accord. At the same time, the co-presence of *deciple* as the subjects of the *covant* establishes a religious isotopy that is also found in *Amors*: well-established as secular both in the troubadour tradition and in Chrétien's own early lyrics, love is also a "divinity." What is important here, for the moment, is the co-presence, in the text, of two Destinators whose relations to each other are, so far, unspecified: the abstract quality of love, treated, in the mode of allegory, as a narrative actor, but without the anthropomorphic concretization that is the usual status of narrative actors, and the concrete monarch, endowed with a particularizing name as well as the usual attributes of kingship (at least in texts where that actantial role is viewed positively). Whether these two figures are to be coordinated on a basis of equality, or one of domination/subordination, or on a conflictual basis, is so far uncertain. All we can be certain of at this point is the duality of the representation of the Destinator's role.

Right now, it is on the second Destinator that the text is focused. It is focused on the rule or discipline (*covant*) that the subjects of love's order are to follow, and does so in terms of power and veridictory categories. On the level of manifestation, these oppositions are figured in terms of a variant of the golden age topos. As in the prologue to the *Saint Alexis*, the past was good, the present is degenerate. It is degenerate because of the relation between ideology and power. An ideology, in order to be effective, must be felt and believed by those who pronounce it: it must be introjected. Here, it consists of the coordination of the traditional qualities from the warrior ethic—*preu et large et enorable*—with the new value, that of being *cortois* (ll. 22 f.). In other words, it requires the subsumption of the semantic traits of knighthood as a social class, already subordinate to the power of the *châtelains*, to the new power of centralized authority, simultaneously social, political, and economic, represented by court life. Its textual representation, at the moment, is the subordination of the warrior code to the newly narrativized love ethos. Yet even this historically new phenomenon is presented as already degenerating. The power of Love was formerly great, and her adherents were many, because the subjects' loyalty was true: they felt what they said, and as a result, the rule under which they were disciples or novices was sweet and good. Now, the power of Love is greatly decreased, and few are her adherents: by implication, its present rule is harsh. The transformation of

/ covant (+) + deciple (+) / $\rightarrow$ / covant (–) + deciple (–) /

is operated by the single veridictory change of /truth/ ⇒ /lie/. The specific transformation of these terms is the result of a change in the relation between words and feelings: those who claim to be lovers today turn love into fable and lie (*fable et mançonge an font*: l. 17), because they speak the words of love without feeling them:

> . . . cil qui rien n'en santent
> dïent qu'il aiment, mes il mantent.
>
> [26 f.]

Thus a true allegiance or loyalty is transformed into a false one by a transformation of feeling:

> (words + feeling) = (words − feeling).

Interestingly enough, it is as the result of this negatively valorized verbal behavior that the power of the Destinator is decreased:

> s'an est Amors molt abessiee;
>
> [20]
>
> or est Amors tornee a fable.
>
> [24]

The role and effectivity of ideology is briefly but clearly sketched out in this passage. As long as the subjects of the rule believe in the ideology, so that their words and feelings are positively conjoined, the ruler's hegemony and power remain intact, and the number of his or her subjects remains large. When ideological belief is sapped and the feelings and words disjoined, then ideology no longer performs its socially cohesive function: the adherence of the subjects to the ruler's hegemony is undermined, and their number—the source of the ruler's power—decreases. As a result, the rule turns harsher, though exactly what that means is not specified by the text. The continuity between this textual principle and the functioning of the political code of feudalism, in which respect of the hegemonic ideology and true adhesion of vassals to their contract with their overlord determines the latter's military, political, and eventually economic power, does not require rhetorical stress.

The conclusion to this non-prologue is simultaneously a transition back to the narrative:

> Mes or parlons de cez qui furent,
> si leissons cez qui ancor durent,
> car molt valt mialz, ce m'est a vis,
> uns cortois morz c'uns vilains vif.
>
> [29-32]

The text will now turn to its narration (*reconter*, l. 33), and the topic of the narrative will consist of the following semantic traits:

/ people / + / past / + / *cortois* / + / dead /,

rather than

/ people / + / present / + / *vilains* / + / live /.

Superficially, the Old French words retained opposed two social classes: the nobility and the peasantry. The literal meaning of the text is that "a dead noble is worth more than a live peasant." The terms historically opposed two locations: that of the court (though the etymology given by Greimas suggests a farm connection here too) *versus* that of the rural demense (*villanum*). From this topographical opposition the semantics of the terms moved synecdochically to the social classes that inhabit the two locations, the nobles attendant on the court as opposed to the peasants who remain on the demesne: topography defines social status. But the context shows that the meaning is not the correct meaning, and that a further transfer from the isotopy of social class to what appears to be a moral isotopy regarding the relation of / people / to their ideology takes place. For it is not really peasants that are in question. The *vilain vif* are those, noted earlier, who claim allegiance to *Amor* without feeling it and thereby *fable et mançonge an font*. These are hardly peasants: they are the noble participants of the court whose adherence to its ideology is merely verbal. The *vilains*, in other words, are those who have undermined the power of their Destinator, Love, by their lying: as love is courtly in the sense of being *of* the court, it is false nobles who are inculpated, not the peasants whose location is non-courtly. From topographical first, to social second, the term *vilains* is turned against those who originally defined themselves in opposition to it: the *cortois*, whose binary and definitional opposite are, precisely, the *vilain*. As a result, it is not only a moral judgment that is lodged against them, but their very social status that is put into question.

In the same passage, the triple deictics (*or, parlons, leissons*) signed the situation of enunciation. The first of these has occurred twice before (ll. 18, 24). It is now connected, not only with two verbs of present enunciation, but also with the function of judgment, noted above, and a concretized subject of enunciation: *molt valt mialz, ce m'est a vis* (l. 31). The subject of enunciation acknowledges both the subjectivity of his judgment, and affirms the function of judging itself. And yet it would be wrong to take the word "subjectivity" too seriously here. The subject of enunciation here speaks "subjectively" only in the technical, linguistic sense: he speaks *as* subject of enunciation. This does not imply, however, a unique, individual space removed from the gaze of others, a differentiated interiority, as with twentieth-century notions of the self and the subject. On the contrary, the enunciator has cautiously prepared the way by the repetition of the first person plural in the two preceding lines (*parlons, leissons*), identifying himself with his courtly audience: the immediate, surface meaning of the concluding antithetical phrase, apothegmatic in style, proposing a radical affirmation of noble value as against non-noble ignobility, can only continue that identification. One of the limits upon "twelfth-century individuality" is the continued identification of the subject with a social group, thus allowing a discourse that is simultaneously "subjective" and "objective."

Nevertheless, there is a difference between enunciator and the recipients of his message, a difference that is simultaneously technical and ontological. The contemporary analyst of this text reads it, and it is clear that its original composition was scriptorial. The original audience, however, was generally unlettered and illiterate: the text was written to be read aloud to an audience unable to decipher its graphemes. Thus, the verb *parlons* is not to be taken as a figurative usage meaning "let us take up" the topic in written language. The verb of (oral) speech was written, and is therefore duplicitous in a limited sense. While the written text does refer to the ensuing narrative in the register of orality, that orality was in fact the norm for the situation of enunciation that obtained. The text was simultaneously written and oral, a dual ontological status that has both cultural and socio-political ramifications.[16]

This last duality may stand for the several ambiguities located in this prologue that is not a prologue: indeed, it is hardly certain whether the next sentence should be considered as the final part of the "prologue" or the beginning of the narrative. It reverts back to the original Destinator, Arthur, and again deals with the issue of the verbal and its referent: the reputation of Arthur (*tesmoing, renons*), as incorporated in the tales told of him by Bretons, is approved by the enunciator, and its function as a reminder of

> il boen chevalier esleu
> qui a enor se traveillierent,
>
> [40 f.]

That is to say that the remembered tales of Arthur and his knights, undergoing *travail* for the sake of the traditional, early feudal value of *enor* (without mention of *cortoisie*), present a coherent, ideological whole worthy of being heard (*chose qui face a escoter*) and which in fact is spread far and wide (*an en parole et pres et loing*). Once again, the question of the relationship between the tale and its import, is raised by the text.

It must be clear that no simplicities are to be expected of a narrative that will incorporate these themes, and the play-out of these values. On the contrary, while narrative coherence is the mark of this text perhaps to a greater extent than of any other secular narrative of its time, that coherence is dependent precisely on the valorial complexity of the issues raised. It is perhaps not as an achieved unity of opposites, but as the process of their unification into a coherent narrative, that *Yvain* may best be considered. It is a narrative that raises fundamental issues of signification, ideology, and social organization. The fact that such issues are raised rather than answered by the prologue as well as by the narrative indicates that the metatext, while it does stand beside the narrative to reflect upon it, does not thereby obtain a position of privileged leverage. It has no purchase of an undoubted scheme of values that can be referred to as the ultimate "meaning" of the text. It is, instead, a segment of the text, couched in a somewhat different, more abstract linguistic register, but resolutely within the text as one element in its production of signification. That element is limited and even countered by other elements that are, first of all, comparable, and secondly, more telling in the total description of the text. The same applies to all metatexts: they do exist as a particular form of discourse, but as elements subsumed by particular textual structures. Above all, they do not absolve the contemporary reader from the responsibility of reading, nor the analyst-interpreter of the responsibility for his utterances regarding the text.

The Adventure of Shame

Before entering upon Calogrenant's discourse and adventure themselves, it is important to locate them within the overall narrative scheme of the *Yvain* as a whole. This scheme can be represented by the following formula:

$$A1 + N1 + X + A2 + N2,$$

where A = approach, N = nexus, and X = crisis. The nexus is the purpose of the preceding action, the subject's obtention of the object of his desire. The first approach and its nexus $(A1 + N1)$ represent a sequence with a somehow inadequate or unsatisfactory conclusion, as is revealed by the crisis which destroys that temporary conclusion. That crisis is in turn followed by a second approach which eventually leads to another resolution, presented as final by the text since it is the finality of the narrative. This structure is both repetitive and progressive, and derives from an analytic model applicable to a large number of texts.[17]

Within the (A1) section of the *Yvain*, two sequences are linearly juxtaposed in semantic opposition. After the Calogrenant-sequence which ends in failure, comes the Yvain-sequence through the same narrative events, with an additional *suppléance*, marked by all the signs of success. The (A1) section as a whole can be considered a preliminary test for the selection of the subject of the (B-2 + N-2) section, a kind of *triage* among the Arthurian knights for the role of narrative subject. The specific function of the Calogrenant-sequence, then, is to contrast Calogrenant with Yvain so as to differentiate the two, on some scale of values, in such a manner that the former is discarded as potential subject and the latter's potentiality as subject is actualized. Indeed, after the Calogrenant-sequence, his name will not be mentioned again during the rest of the text. (See the brief mention of him, avoiding his name, at l. 2184.) This general function of narrative linearity and paradigmatic contrast is clear. It should not lead to an expectation, however, that the Calogrenant-sequence is in itself a simple and unambiguous one. On the contrary, it is a highly complex narrative, incorporating major valorial ambiguities that will become constitutive of the text as a whole. It repays close analysis, as suggested by the text itself.

Calogrenant possesses one function of which there is no trace in his more successful cousin: in addition to being a knight, he is also a narrator. What is more, he is the narrator of his own adventure, and in a mode that sets him off from the narrator of the text as a whole. The latter produces a text that, as we have seen, is first of all a written script; within this script, Calogrenant is presented as an oral storyteller.[18] As such, he is entitled to a prologue of his own, a prologue which answers to the text-narrator's prologue in such a manner as to complete the latter and sketch out a figurative semiotic model of communication. *"Or escotez!,"* starts Calogrenant.

> Cuers et oroilles m'aportez,
> car parole est tote perdu
> s'ele n'est de cuer entandue.
> De cez i a qui la chose oent
> qu'il n'entandent, et si la loent;
> et cil n'en ont ne mes l'oïe,
> des que li cuers n'i entant mie;
> as oroilles vient la parole,
> ausi come li vanz qui vole,
> mes n'i areste ne demore,
> einz s'an part en molt petit d'ore,

se li cuers n'est esveilliez
qu'au prendre soit apareilliez;
car, s'il le poet an son oir
prendre, et anclorre, et retenir,
les oroilles sont voie et doiz
par ou s'an vient au cuer la voiz;
et li cuers prant dedanz le vantre
la voiz, qui par l'oroille i antre.
Et qui or me voldra entandre,
cuer et oroilles me doit randre,
car ne vuel pas parler de songe,
ne de fable, ne de mançonge.

[150-72]

There is a didactic tone about this passage that suggests the *grammaticus* of a cathedral school, about to exposit the rule of his art, or even the scriptural commentator addressing his brethren in the chapter. It is an extremely well-formed piece of rhetoric, and presents half of a theory of communication. Its connection to the earlier text-enunciator's (non-) prologue is partly at the level of the deep structure, but also appears at the level of manifestation. The two substantive lexemes of the last line are the same as those which occur toward the end of the (non-)prologue: those who lie by invoking Amor love falsely even though they feel nothing of it, *cil fable et mançonge an font* (l. 27). In both passages, the wrong kind of communication leads to fictive referentiality (*songe, fable, mançonge*), in opposition to the right kind of communication, which we will baptize "true speech," an expression not found in the text and which requires definition.

The (non-)prologue established a theory of the production of meaning, in which the alternatives were the conjunction of feeling and words, in the case of true speech, or their disjunction, in the case of false speech (the "dream, fable, or lie"). The same principle of the binary opposition between conjunction and disjunction operates in Calogrenant's prologue, but, in the figurative language of the text, applies to the relation between "heart" and "words" in the establishment of true and false reception. The verbs used indicate the essential identity between the two oppositions. The properly wakeful heart is ready to "take" or "capture" the words, to "enclose" them, to "retain" them (*prendre, et anclorre, et retenir*, l. 164): a military and feudal isotopy appears to operate through these lexemes, one according well with the status of the speaker. The text continues, however, with a topographic isotopy that is quite different: if the ears are path and channel (*voie et doiz*, l. 165) by which the voice comes to the heart, and the heart *takes* the voice *into* the chest cavity which *enters* there by the ear, the isotopy of interiorization is clear. The opposition of internality and externality is fundamental to Chrétien's theory of communication. Both on the side of production and on that of reception, the conjunction of the interior and the exterior is required for the true production and true reception of *parole*. The same binarism constitutes the emitter and the receiver of the message, who have equal roles to play in the process of communication. Calogrenant is about to tell a tale of his shame, not of his honor, and asks that it be taken with a conjunction of interiority and exteriority similar in his listeners to that which, by implication, characterizes his speech. Both Chrétien's and Calogrenant's prologue demand the unity of being and language. Interestingly enough, this is a point at which the introduction of the Abelardian concept of intentionality as a determinant of moral responsibility could be expected: no such intentionality is mentioned. While the figuration of the concepts appears to breathe new life into them, the basic conceptual structure outlined is not different from that which determines, say, the difference between a Roland or an Olivier on the one hand, and a Ganelon on the other, as speakers: one hides his being in his use of language, while the others reveal their being. What is perhaps different here is the new stress on the role of the reader: in this respect, Chrétien's theory bears a certain resemblance to contemporary semiotics.

Rhetorically, however, the two moments of this theory of communication produce different meanings. The first, figured in terms of the production of speech, is part of a structure instilling suspicion in the reader that ideological value and the value of narrative action may not, in fact, be conjoined. The second asks the recipients of a message, which is a narrative, to focus upon something other than only its words, for the entire process of interiorization described by the text has as its function the production of "understanding," as is repeated in the following lines.

> . . . parole est tote perdue
> s'ele n'est de cuer *entandue*.
> De cez i a qui la chose oënt
> qu'il *n'entandent*, et si la loënt . . .

> [151-4]

The local text-enunciator thus asks the listeners of his message to go beyond the mere words containing the narrative he is about to recount, and to not merely listen to the words on a superficial level, but to "take them in" so as to *understand* that which they bear, i.e. the value-content of their narrative. Meaning does not exist in the words alone, as they are borne in the air; nor is it produced in the moment of striking the ear. It is only as the words are transformed into what Saussure called an "acoustic image" that, within the being of the listener, they can acquire the "meaning" they have in the analogous interiority of the emitter. In both Chrétien de Troyes and Saussure, the inner / outer category, so finely deconstructed by Jacques Derrida in *La grammatologie*, is essential for the production and reception of meaning. For neither writer is the contemporary means of transcending that opposition available: the semiotic concept of the "code."[19]

The first lines of Calogrenant's sequence give both a definition of his overall program — though that has to be combined with semantic elements already touched on to be completed — and puzzling qualifications:

> Il m'avint plus de set anz
> que je, seus come païsanz,
> aloie querant aventures,
> armez de totes armeüres
> si come chevaliers doit estre . . .
>
> [173-7]

He seeks "adventures." The term will recur, when he explains his goal, in somewhat paradoxical terms, to the *vilain* he will meet on his way, but as a singular, modified so as to specify its valorial function. Asked what he wants to find, Calogrenant answers:

> —Avanture, por esprover
> ma proesce et mon hardement.
>
> [362 f.]

The essence of adventure is to remain undefined: *adventurus esse*, "that which is to happen," has no specific evenemential content. It is merely an empty projection upon the future. It is the name of a process, however, which does produce value, either of two: honor or shame. These are, in fact, no more than the positive and negative valorizations of the individual whose insertion is into the feudal system, the equivalent form of the thymic system in semiotics. As would be the case in the concretization of positive and negative values in any social system, the subject incorporating the value system of his society desires the positive value of the thymic category . . . a preference that "goes without saying." Thus, the overall narrative program of the subject of the present sequence can be defined as follows: to undergo *avanture* in such a manner as to demonstrate "honor." This can be represented formulaically:

$$S \longrightarrow 0 \ (0: S \longrightarrow 0 \ [0: \text{avanture}]) \longrightarrow S \cap O \ (\text{honor})$$

As we shall see, this narrative program is carried out with partial success: the subject will indeed find *avanture*, but its result will not be the desired one.

Along with the statement of the narrative goal, the passage cited contains a dual qualitative attribution to the subject. Such qualitative statements are important, since they imply characteristics of the narrative undertaken by the subject. On the one hand, the status of Calogrenant's encounters with the *vavasseur* and the *vilain* are marked by ambiguous valorizations. As pragmatic narrative programs of an instrumental level, they are successful. The subject obtains shelter from the first and information as to his goal from the second: both are thus adjuvants. At the purely narrative level, therefore, Calogrenant comes out of these encounters conjoined with positive valorizations. Insofar as the final goal of his adventure leads to an encounter that is the main test, these prior encounters may be considered qualifying tests that bestow positive markings on the subject. On the other hand, their manifestation on the textual level subtly suggests different valorizations. The encounter with the *vavasseur* is not only successful pragmatically, but also in the proper observance of the ritual of hospitality:[20] the ceremoniousness of that hospitality marks it as an ideological occasion. Nevertheless, minor narrative detail and language indicate that "something else" is going on. While the *vavasseur*'s entire household turns out to greet and cater to their guest, his daughter, *une pucele bele et gente* (l. 225), pays him special attention. She takes him to that location marked for special occasions, an idealized mixture of nature and culture, or perhaps the ideal culturization of nature, a *verger*:

> . . . ele me mena seoir
> el plus bel praelet del monde,
> clos de bas mur a la reonde,
>
> [236-8]

In this location, enclosed and conventionally containing beauties of sight and smell — the Garden of the Rose in Guillaume de Lorris' poem in the following century will only be the most striking development of the convention summarily indicated in our quotation — privileged narrative moments occur. And what privileged encounter might occur between the knight on his adventure and the young maiden, beautiful, noble, well spoken, well brought up and educated, full of "solace and of such a being" as to give the knight great pleasure and inspire him with the desire to never move out of the *verger* — ? The suggestion, made with delicacy, of a potential amorous encounter, is unmistakable: so is the abruptness of its interruption. Another occasion calls, a simultaneously pragmatic and social one, and its verbalization, certainly humorous, may also be taken with some seriousness:

mes *tant me fist*, la nuit, *de guerre*
li vavasors, qu'il me vint querre,
qant de soper fu tans et ore . . .

[245-7]

The pragmatic dimension, that segment of the narrative convention of hospitality that calls for the provision of food for the guest, interferes with another register composed of a dual isotopy: the erotic, and the erotic's function as the reward of the hero *after* his (successful) adventure. The text leaves unresolved the question of whether the *vavasseur* is merely protecting his daughter from the adventuresome knight, or whether the latter is not presuming to move a bit too rapidly from the qualifying test to the glorifying test, thus omitting the main test. The manifestation of this *solacium interruptus*, however, occurs in language that is perhaps ironic if taken literally, and yet the binary opposition of *guerre* vs. *pes* is such a fundamental one in both the social text of the period and in this particular text that one should not ignore its potential signification. In spite of the great courtesy and ceremoniousness with which the rear vassal treats his noble superior, there is a special sense in which they are "at war." At the least, a marking of success that is textually available is withheld from the subject. Nevertheless, the *vavasseur*, implicitly assuming the role of a sanctioning destinator for the moment, also communicates verbal markers of a positive nature to his guest: not for a long time had he sheltered a knight seeking adventure, and might he provide such shelter again upon his guest's return from his *aventure*?

The encounter with the *vilain* is even richer in semantic potential. The peasantry's appearances in "courtly romance" are rare, but it is not only because of its rarity that this episode is important: its significations are major. Having taken his leave of the hospitable family the following morning, Calogrenant goes on his way until he arrives at a nearby clearing in which wild bulls, bears and leopards are fighting. The conjunction of these beasts in a Breton forest has led referentially oriented scholars to shake heads and mutter that this must be a scribal error, since it is mimetically impossible. One text editor prefers to adopt the lesson of a secondary manuscript;[21] another scholar suggests a reading which, while not to be found as such in any manuscript, discards those animals that are geographically misplaced.[22] The editor of the text we are using, Mario Roques, shares their discomfort at the text of the primary manuscript in his note to this line, but has the wisdom to refrain from emendation. The problem is a false one. Medieval narrative does not proceed by reference to an extra-textual reality of an objective sort: it proceeds as a production of meaning, capable of invoking a wide variety of cultural codes, both secular and clerical, as well as inventing its own signifying relationships. In the present case, the meaning of the combat among the different types of wild animals is indicated quite clearly by the text: the animals,

> qui s'antreconbatoient tuit
> et demenoient si grant bruit
> *et tel fierté et tel orguel,*
> se voir conuistre vos an vuel,
> *c'une piece me treïs arriere . . .*

[279–83]

The knight attributes anthropomorphic qualities to the battle of the beasts: they are savage and proud, qualities, of course, that also lead men to combat, and particularly that class of men known as *chevaler*. It is worth noting that it is not the text enunciator that makes this attribution. At this point, as throughout Calogrenant-sequence, perception and the attribution of signification are relativized and attributed only to that particular enunciator: whether this is to be taken as an example of a far later narrative technique, that of "point of view" as defined by the practice and theory of Henry James and, after him, Norman Friedman and Wayne Booth, is another question altogether. The comment made above, as to the possible simultaneity of subjective and objective enunciation would lead one to avoid that kind of easy identification of rhetorical techniques and the ideological values they imply. Late nineteenth- and early twentieth-century "point of view" implies and depends upon contemporary views of the uniqueness of subjects, the relativization of "perspectives," and a potential solipsism that it would be difficult to sustain as operative in the twelfth century.

Not only is the semantic production of the text's mixed bag of animals specified in the text itself, but so is its pragmatic interpretation. The knight, in a displacement to be repeated, retreats: *une piece me treïs arriere*. Mere caution? Fear? The enunciator does not specify the *signified* of his own movement: the code is not provided, and the semantic limitation of the text remains undecidable in the reader's perception at this moment of the text. Perhaps the redundancy of later appearances of similar events will help us decide the specific isotopy in play. What is certain is that the event does not fit into the isotopy of the heroic. As noted earlier, it is the contrast with Yvain's later heroism that is the function of the Calogrenant-sequence. Along with the fighting animals, however, the narrative subject sees a peculiar creature, which has hitherto been studied best as an example of the convention of ugliness, the convention of inverted beauty in the portrait.[23] While there can be no question as to the ugliness of the *vilain's* portrait, it is worth understanding both the basis of the specific ugliness and its significance in context. The beginning of the description is general:

> Uns vilains, qui resanbloit Mor,
> leiz et hideus a desmesure,
> einsi tres leide criature . . .
>
> [286-8]

Certain traits are specifically and directly attributed to the *criature*: it has a big head, tangled hair, and a flat face, for instance. Most of the description, however, proceeds by similes which terms of comparisons are another mixed bag of animals: different aspects of the *vilain* are "like" a horse, an elephant, an owl, a cat, a wolf, and a boar. The point, that there is something animalistic about this *criature*, is reinforced by the paradox of his clothing, which is of leather coming *ou de teus tors ou de deus bués* (l. 311). Again, it is worth remarking that the perception of this animal isotopy is attributed to the enunciator of this text-segment, namely Calogrenant. This hierarchical dependency is implicit in the evenementiality that succeeds the description:

> An piez sailli li vilains, lués
> qu'il me vit vers lui aprochier;
> ne sai s'il me voloit tochier,
> ne ne sai qu'il voloit enprendre,
> mes me garni de desfandre . . .
>
> [312-6]

The peasant stands, and the knight prepares to defend himself against the possibility that this act implies the intent to "touch" him or to undertake some other action: whatever action, it might be aggressive, and requires, in the eyes of this knight, defensive preparation. Again, one may ask oneself what the appropriate signification is: fear or caution?

In any case, neither is called for. As the knight approaches, the *vilain* remains quiet, immobile and silent:

> si m'esgarda, ne mot ne dist,
> ne plus c'une beste feïst,
> et je cuidai qu'il ne seüst
> parler, ne reison point n'eüst.
>
> [321-4]

First, the knight infers from the peasant's standing up that danger might be present; secondly, he infers from the peasant's silence that it does not know language, any more than a beast does. Even more, he concludes that the peasant lacks *reison*, the distinguishing marker of humanity: later in the narrative, Yvain, crazed with grief, will in fact descend to the stage hypothesized by Calogrenant. As far as the *vilain* is concerned, however, Calogrenant is wrong on all counts, and remarkably wrong. For the moment, we may conclude that he is not a very good semiotician, at least when he addresses himself to the semiosis of what has been called the "natural world," that of gesture.[24] These discrepancies suggest a distantiation between the particular and temporary enunciator of the text within the text and his extratextual audience (no reactions from the textual audience are indicated at this point). It is not the difference between narrative and the point of view from which it is narrated that triangulates that distance, however, but the significances of the narrative proposed and denied by the narrative itself.

In spite of the grotesque and perhaps fearful appearance of the "creature," the knight screws up his courage (*tant m'anhardi*, l. 325) in order to speak to it. In a manner that is hardly flattering, he asks a question:

> . . . "Va, car me di
> se tu es boene chose ou non."
> [326f.]

"Are you a good thing or not?" translates the distance between himself and the *vilain* assumed by the knight. An animal, a possible source of danger, mute and yet threatening, Calogrenant sees "it" as a thing merely. The response and the ensuing dialogue not only reveal that the peasant is, indeed, some kind of man: it raises the question of commonality between the knight and the peasant, that is to say, the status of humanity itself. For the creature answers, simply, that it is a man:

> Et il me dist qu'il ert uns home.
> [328]

To creature, beast, and thing, the text opposes "man." If we may self-consciously fight off the associations with *King Lear* such a speech cannot but have for us, it is worth insisting that the issue of the relationship between both the animate and the inanimate worlds, and the relations between the differentiations of social class and another principle, located perhaps in "Nature," in "metaphysics," or in "religion," which asserts the principle of humanity in contradistinction to these social distinctions, is raised by the text. It only raises that question, however, and does not answer it here. As in the case of "point of view," however, it would be foolish to rush in with modern assumptions of equality, where all that is asserted is the presence of a common seme which, in itself, hardly denies the presence of the differentiating semes of appearance, class, and all the coded specifics the latter entails.

Under questioning, the *vilain* asserts his permanence and a function: he "guards" the beasts of the forest. Calogrenant expresses his amazement and disbelief. With reference to the fact that the *vilain* is at a mere clearing, the knight asserts that only by tying and enclosing a wild beast can it be "guarded." That is to say, only physical force can work, the principle, namely, that is at work in the knight's very existence, that of being a warrior. When the *vilain* denies this, the knight asks what else is possible. The answer is a complex one which implies a theory of political domination of some subtlety:

> "N'i a celi* qui s'ost movoir   */of the beasts/
> des que ele me voit venir,
> car quant j'an puis une tenir,
> si l'estraing si par les deus corz,
> as poinz que j'ai et durs et forz,
> que les autres de peor tranblent
> et tot en viron moi s'asanblant,
> ausi con por merci crier;
> ne nus ne s'i porroit fier,
> fors moi, s'antr'eles s'estoit mis,
> qu'il ne fust maintenant ocis."
>
> [342–54]

The fact of being able to wrestle one of the beasts and dominate it hand to horn strikes such terror into the others, that they all assemble around him as if to beg for mercy; as a result, the *vilain's* mere approach is sufficient to freeze the animals into place. Furthermore, his dominance over them is a personal one: no one else could trust himself to enter their territory, or he would be immediately killed. A dominance that is established by the selective and exemplary application of terror, with the result that the entire collectivity later submits without the application of such force, and submits not so much to a rule of law but to a particular individual who has personally established that dominance, that is the definintion of a pre-banal feudal lordship. Given the play of socio-political isotopies already identified, these principles are not foreign to the world Calogrenant inhabits. What is striking about the passage, therefore, is not its political and technical content, but the fact that it is being communicated to a noble by a peasant.

That it is a political isotopy of domination inherent within the *vilain's* narrative is confirmed by the redundancy of the level of manifestations, where his language specifies what is merely implicit in the narrative:

"Je gart si cestes et *justis*
que ja n'istront de cest porpris"

[339 f.];

. . .

"Einsi sui de mes bestes *sire* . . ."

[355]

The semantic field of *justicier* is both broad and crucial in the historical development of feudal society. The first three meanings given by Greimas are the following: 1) administer, govern; 2) dominate; 3) dispense justice. The primary semantic content, in this particular context, is the second: the *vilain* has just explained how he dominates the wild beast in the forest. One might leave it at that, and consider the use of the verb *justicier* to be "merely" metaphorical, except that the speaker repeats this complex of semic elements with the word *sire*. As with *justicier, sire* connotes semes of nobility, of political domination, of the goverance and administration of fiefs, both at the level of the local *châtelain* and at that of the ruler of the feudal principalities, and inserts the text at a specific moment in history. The original system of feudalism, as the political system of the medieval nobility, was based on a manorial exploitation of the land for local consumption. The major economic shift of the eleventh century had been the transformation of that closed, local economy into one geared toward the production of surplus value expropriated from the peasantry by the upper nobility under the forms of banal lordship, based on a greater quantity and circulation of silver coinage; the increased productivity that brought this coinage into the hands of the peasants; the development of trade at both regional and international levels; and the increased demand for luxury goods by a noble class newly enlarged, at the end of the eleventh century, thanks to the ennobling of the lower level knights, the *milites*. The essential political task of the twelfth century was the reintegration of the *châtellenies* of the preceding centuries of social and political fragmentation into the regional powers of the feudal principalities, the county of Champagne being one of the most successful and important of these. The essential textual connector of the isotopies of production, surplus value, and social class, comes later in the romance, towards the end of the Yvain section: it is the episode of the *château de pesme avanture*.[26]

In spite of a number of ideological efforts aimed at unifying the noble class—the adoption of the ritual of knighting by the entire nobility was one, the writing of a text like the *Yvain* another—the relations of its component elements to the sources of economic wealth and the exercise of power differentiated these elements profoundly. Banal lordship was not available to the entirety of the social class of the nobility: only the great, the powerful, the truly wealthy held the power of the ban. But the lower level knights performed an essential function within this political and economic system. Their duty of the *cavalcade*, the *chevauchée*, was a show of force destined to strike terror into the hearts of the peasantry by demonstrating the overlord's ever-present power and ensuring the continuation of the peasantry's productivity on the manor. In other words, while neither double function of terrorization and policing the territory nor its economic significance is mentioned by the text directly, the latter presents an inversion of it: from the victim of the nobility's police terror, the particular peasant produced by the text becomes its manipulator *vis-à-vis* the animal isotopy that is placed under his domination. While this textual manoeuver might be accounted for in terms of the descending ontological order implicit in the great chain of being, its specific verbalization calls into play a political structure which is reversed in the particular textual moment. Not only does the "literary" text construct itself out of the codes operative in the social text as a whole, it is also capable of taking the code's semantic elements and transforming them according to recognizable rules: here, the rule is something like the "inversion" of the peasant's role *vis-à-vis* the available elements of political power in his social structure.

This inversion receives a remarkable justification in the lines that follow. The isotopy of political power is subsumed by one of social ontology. As we saw, the knight cast doubt on the *vilain's* human status in asking what manner of thing he might be. The *vilain* now turns the tables on the knight, but far more courteously:

> " . . .
> et tu me redevroies dire
> quiex hom tu ies, et que tu quiers."

[356 f.]

The prefix *re-* signifies the reciprocity expected in a situation of communication: having responded to the knight's inquiry, the interlocutor now has the right to make the same inquiry of the knight. No formal education is required to understand the principle: it is inscribed in the linguistic practice that defines the speaker's competence. It is not that the *vilain* acts according to a principle that might be explicated by a John Austin or a John D. Searle in terms of speech-act theory, but rather that he implicitly asserts an equality of a linguistic type in the face of the obvious social and political inequality between himself and his interlocutor. The contradiction between the linguistic and the political isotopies here rejoins the earlier occurrences of the isotopy of (in)equality and the philosophical framework suggested by the seme of /humanity/.

The knight's response moves from the most obvious and platitudinous self-definition to self-pitying irony through a nice bit of intertextual transformation:

> "Je sui, fet il, uns chevaliers
> qui quier ce que trover ne puis;
> assez ai quis, et rien ne truis."
>
> [358–60]

That he is a knight, we have known from the beginning. This is not new information, but the reiteration of the category of social hierarchy, with its opposing terms of/nobility/ and /peasantry/. This redundancy provides the identity conjoining this utterance with the *vilain's*, enabling their difference to appear. The *vilain* defined himself as the ruler of a collectivity and specified the means by which his dominion is established and practiced. The knight, who in the social text is precisely the instrument of the establishment of such dominion by the noble who is the ruler, defines himself by an idealistic paradox that pales by comparison to the *vilain's* self-definition: he seeks what he cannot find. The assertion is actually more interesting and semantically richer when understood intertextually. In one of his "straight" love poems, William of Acquitaine has the lover exclaim:

> "Per tal n'ai meyns de bon saber
> Car *vuelh so que no puesc aver* . . ."
> ("Pus vezem de novelh florir")

The lover's inability to obtain what he wants is determined by the dominion exercised by the Lady, and her refusal to grant satisfaction to his desire: indeed, his non-success in the narrative of obtaining such satisfaction is the basis for the elaboration of that type of poem. The classeme is /necessity/, and thus the paradox is resolved narratively: its pragmatic affect is restrained to the sphere of the passions.[27] The statement that the lover has no less knowledge for being in that paradoxical state is thus justified. There is no such justification in the Old French transform. The seme of /necessity/ is quite absent: as we have seen, the isotopy of /love/ was excluded at the *vavasseur's* house, and the political isotopy invoked lends no justification for "avanture" either. Indeed, both his self-definition and his narrative take the subject quite outside the framework within which either love or dominion can operate, that of the court. While another social code will intersect with it in the second half of the narrative, the code of the subject's narrative is one that has been defined so far as an individualistic one. An argument has been made that the twelfth century witnesses the rise of the "individual."[28] There is a limited truth to the argument: the twelfth century sees the rise of a new definition of the "individual," but it must not be thought that the category or the phenomenon did not exist previously. Roland and Ganelon are both examples of the early knightly individualism that sets the particular against the interest of the social body in an explosion of pride, identifying the concrete individual with his lineage and threatening the continuity of the society as a whole. Nor is it only that individualism from an earlier feudalism that is troublesome. The specificity of Abelard's contribution to a theory of the human indivdual is in the moral domain, where the individual's intent in action becomes one of the determinants of the moral evaluation of his act. Such a contribution to moral philosophy, as important as it undoubtedly is historically, cannot lead to the presumption that the individual's proper name implies a Cartesian subject or a late twentieth-century American feeling (the term "concept" would be far too precise) of what is meant by a "self." The textual evidence is sparse. A comparison to the other major secular type, that of the *chanson de geste*, reveals a specific and limited form of narrative individualism: while the *chanson de geste* sets into action extensive groups of male subjects engaged in narrative programs of a military sort, twelfth-century romance typically sets into play an individual knight, sometimes accompanied, as are Erec and *Le bel inconnu*, by a specific Lady, engaged on an individual narrative program that proceeds by individual rather than group combat, and that ends in the (non-)acquisition of an erotic object. The "individualism" in question thus sets the narrative subject off from his collectivity and establishes a relation of an amorous nature as a narrative goal. The interiority which accompanies this intertextual transformation is limited to the themes associated with desire for the new feminine object, as when Yvain, towards the end of his narrative, finds he can no longer live without *amor* and hence returns to the magic fountain. In other words, the interiority that is textualized is most often that of the standard *topoi* of the love lyric . . . hardly tantamount to the introduction of a twentieth-century sense of the self! Not only is the twelfth-century sense of "individuality" thus limited, it is also not textualized with joyful connotations. On the contrary, it is the source of major narrative and social difficulty. It is precisely the conflicting claims of this "individualism" with the necessities of social organization that form the central problematic of romance since the earliest versions of the Tristan story and its mirror-image, Chrétien's *Cligès*.

At this particular point, the narrative subject is engaged on a narrative program which incorporates both evasion from social structure (the theme will be more marked in Yvain's version of the same adventure) and assertion of the earlier form of individualism, that associated with the epic. The valorial isotopy with which Calogrenant's tale is introduced by the narrator is the familiar one, to narrative subjects such as Roland, Ganelon, or the heroes of both the William cycle or that of the rebellious barons, of honor *vs.* shame. Among the knights sitting outside the royal chamber door was Calogrenant:

> une chevaliers molt avenanz
> qui lor a comancié un conte,
> non de s'annor, mes de sa honte.
>
> [58–60]

This seme is repeated a number of times during the narration and discussion of this sequence (ll. 527, 542, 560, 589; in the Yvain-sequence: 721, 748, 1535, 1537, 2242, 2282). Furthermore, asked by the *vilain* what he would like to find, the knight answers with values that are exactly those of the epic knights (*proesce* and *hardement*: l. 363), even though the means by which they are to be obtained—individual adventure—is quite different. While *avanture* sets into play the narrative program of an individual actor, its object, which is the subject's conjunction with the values of prowess and strength or courage, is the same as that which moves the heroes of the *chanson de geste*. Indeed, as in the *chanson de geste*, the honor or shame that result from the success or failure of this *avanture* are not individual values only, but those of the lineage to which the individual belongs: it is as a member of the same lineage that Yvain will set out to avenge his cousin Calogrenant. Thus, while the mode of narrative organization differs markedly from that of the epic, the values attributed to the subjects of the adventure of the magic fountain point to a continuity with the individualism of that past as social code and organization, rather than the birth of a new ethos. It must be stressed that the values of the warrior ethic are not the values affirmed by this text. On the contrary, they are set into play initially in order to be contrasted, first to the values of Yvain's adventure in repeating and continuing his cousin's sequence, and then, most important, to the values affabulated in the second half of the text, where it is the social organization of society that comes into question.

These, however, are not the immediate concerns of the text here. It focuses, rather, on the reversal of roles between the knight and the peasant. In the former's eagerness to prove his value as a knight—thus, to demonstrate his identity as a member of a given social class — he inverts the relation that obtains between that class and the class of the peasant before him. His request for information is made neither peremptorily nor on a basis of conversational equality. Instead, it is made with synonymies and a hypotactic structure that subordinates the speaker to his lowly interlocutor:

> "Or te pri et quier et demant,
> se tu sez, que tu me consoille
> ou d'aventure ou de mervoille."
>
> [364-6]

One who merely *asks* (*demant*) already defines himself by lack and pre-supposes possession of what would satisfy that lack on the part of the other. When that same subject supplies the synonymies of *pri et quier*, he clearly sets himself in an inferior position to that of the addressee. His own words thus continue and complete the paradox of the errant knight without a function and the lordly, justice-dispensing peasant. The latter disclaims all knowledge of such entities — "d'aventure ne sai je rien" — but proceeds to give the wandering knight the description of a quite extraordinary fountain and directions on how to reach it which precisely answer the knight's request. In fact, the peasant's description varies in certain details from the knight's, but is correct in all essentials. Invoking the traditional medieval distinction between words and things, one may conclude that, while the peasant hasn't got all the *verba* right, he certainly knows the *res*, whether this has to do with the adventure and the path that leads to it, or with the principles of feudal domination.

It is Calogrenant himself who, having described the fountain and its magic, will specify that, in its magical function as the determinant of a natural event, the fountain does fit one of the stated goals of his journey:

> "La *mervoille* a veoir me plot
> de la tanpeste et de l'orage . . .
>
> [432 f.]

Thus, the adventure of the fountain is a partial goal of the subject's narrative program as well as the final term of the trajectory which, starting at the center of Culture in Arthur's court, progressing through the mixed area of the sparsely populated forest represented by the two opposite social beings of the *vavasseur* and the *vilain*, finally leads to the encounter with a Nature that, as we will see, is far more complex than Calogrenant imagined. It is a Nature which is already culturalized; more than that, it is a Nature that is also humanized.

The beauty of the fountain itself is a mixture of the natural isotopy —
it is located next to a thickly grown pine that is the most beautiful ever to
grow on earth — and the cultural: on the tree hangs a basin of pure gold,
the finest ever to be sold in any market or fair. And what shall we say of
the emerald of which the fountain itself consists, or the four rubies with
which it is decorated, that they are of the domain of culture, or that of
nature? The question, clearly, is not readily answerable: we conclude
that, like all of the major encounters of the Calogrenant-sequence, it receives contradictory attributions: allowing of opposite, even contrary attributions. Throwing some of the fountain's water on the *perron* causes
the tempest Calogrenant is so eager to see: like modern science, medieval
magic is a human control over the natural elements. The resulting
tempest, however, described both by the peasant and the knight, represents Nature unchained: the sky breaks, the clouds cast rain, snow and
hail descend to earth in such violence that, along with the accompanying
thunder and the lightning, Calogrenant thought he would die a hundred
times. As the peasant noted, such a storm is not without effect in the
natural world: no beast remains in the forest, no stag nor any kind of
deer or boar or birds, said he. Other effects, on human social life, will be
specified later. The storm is clearly an extraordinarily vehement one.
Twice, the Subject who causes it expresses regret, perhaps guilt: he was
not wise (*sage*), and he would have been willing to repent immediately. Is
the technological explanation of the storm's vehemence to be taken literally or ironically: he threw too much water on the *perron*! If ironically,
is the enunciator conscious of the irony, or is it entirely at his expense?

The storm is followed by its opposite. Where violent disorder produced terror, now reigns the harmonious joy of birds covering the pine
tree and singing so that, while each sang a different tune, *molt, bien s'antr'
acordoient* (l. 466). The lexeme and isotopy of *joie* is repeated twice
before the description of the bird song and twice after, and leads quite expectedly to the conclusion that the enunciator and narrative Subject, now
in the role of recipient of a communication, thoroughly enjoys that song.
Yet the text, at the level of manifestation, makes a move to be repeated on
the narrative level: joy is to be followed by a paradoxical conclusion:

> . . . tant me plot et abeli
> que je m'an dui por fos tenir.
>
> [476 f.]

No more in the medieval codes than in the modern does natural beauty
per se, or the reaction of pleasure it occasions, normally lead to a judgment that one is mad to enjoy it.

If the natural marvel of the fountain seemed an adequate term and goal to Calogrenant's adventure, it unexpectedly leads to a further encounter, a *suppléance* that operates a radical transformation of value. If the storm constituted the end of the Calogrenant-sequence, its overall shape would be that of a narrative program successfully completed: the Subject could return to the court — the social, cultural, and narrative center of the Calogrenant-sequence — with a new integer of positive valorization. The unforeseen supplement of adventure, however, will transform this success into failure: we approach the explanation of the enunciator's and narrative subject's earlier judgment that his tale is *non de s'annor, mes de sa honte* (l. 60).

As Calogrenant is enjoying the harmony of the singing birds, another type of sound encroaches, its binary opposite. It is *tel noise et tel bruit* as to indicate, to Calogrenant at least, that a troupe of ten knights is riding towards him through the forest. In fact, a single knight appears, faster than a great eagle, fiercer than a lion — this is the same isotopy of animalistic description of a human as was used in connection with the *vilain*, but applied at a different social level and with nobler animals: the conclusion of a mixed ontological status is no less valid, however, — and immediately challenges Calogrenant at the top of his voice. This challenge is not merely an intersubjective phenomenon of two knights: it invokes socio-political and legal parameters, and establishes, quite literally, a state of war between the two actors. The knight of the fountain lodges a legal complaint (*je me plaing*) to the effect that Calogrenant had done him obvious damage, as a result of which he has incurred *honte*, as the result of an attack (*envaie*) which is equivalent to a state of war (*guerre*). The unleashing of the "natural" storm may have been brought about by magic means: it has had social, economic, and political effects, however, and leads to the further declaration by the knight of the fountain that his attacker will have neither truce nor peace from him (*n'avroiz de moi trives ne pes*): if Calogrenant acted against him by an act of war, the knight of the fountain will differentiate himself from his opponent by *declaring* war first, before actually engaging in combat. This is what Calogrenant did not do: his attack was *sanz defïance*, hence subject to prosecution as treason and, if death results from it, murder. Under the customary feudal code of law, it is the warning of the opponent that makes of individual combat a legal act: without such warning, one is a traitor and a murderer (ll. 491–516).[29]

To the earlier indication of fear and perhaps cowardice, Calogrenant now adds a new one. He explains his loss in combat as the result of size:

his opponent is taller by a head, and has a better horse. He despatches our decidedly unheroic subject, leaving him *honteus et mat* on the ground, taking away his horse. Calogrenant will return, to the *vavasseur*'s abode, *honteusemant* and *sans* horse, *sans* weapons, *sans* the accoutrements that, in his own earlier definition, identified his status as that of a knight and a member of the nobility (supra, p. 20). If he departed from the court and headed for adventure *seus come païsanz* but *armez de totes, armeüres/si come chevaliers doit estre*, he returns simply *seus come païsanz*. His shame, his de-gradation are obvious, and defined by his own terms. While the *vavasseur* to whom he returns receives him courteously, and while his household does the knight *grant enor*, that is a surface manifestation that does not change the knight's evaluation of his adventure:

> "Ensi alai, ensi reving:
> au revenir por fol me ting.
> Si vos ai conté come fos
> ce c'onques conter ne vos."
>
> [577-80]

His enunciation and the narration it comports concludes on the dual evaluation of both the content of his utterance (the *énoncé*), and on the enunciation itself. In both cases the judgment is not only a negative one: it is an extreme judgment, as will be demonstrated by the episode of Yvain's madness later in the romance. But that is another tale, to be considered at another time: now, let us draw a few conclusions from the present analysis.

Conclusion

The prologue that is not a prologue raises issues of an ontological sort. Both "What is the nature of textuality?" and "What are the limits of a text?" — separable but related issues — are implicit in a textual inauguration which, in the medieval context, acquires a material dimension absent from Derrida's brilliant philosophical discussions of the same issues.[30] The nature of this particular kind of text is a matter of general agreement among contemporary medievalists: written by an individual *scriptor* who used orally circulated materials, it was read aloud to a noble audience whose individual members remained largely illiterate. Both the enunciating subject of the text and the text itself are thus "split" along multiple axes determined by matters of social class, history, and the division of the dominant social class into secular and religious factions.

The question of the limits of the text is not that of its syntagmatic conclusion, though that is very much an issue in the discussion of medieval aesthetics: many texts are left "unfinished," or finished by another writer (as was Chrétien's *Lancelot*), and "continued" by writers other than the "original" one, sometimes at some temporal remove: thus, approximately half a century elapsed between Guillaume de Lorris' original *Romance of the Rose* and its "continuation," in what seems to most readers a very different vein, by Jean de Meung. In the same way, what seem to the modern reader fairly important changes wrought in the "original" manuscript are current, and not to be explained away as scribal errors, in the process of textual reproduction. The text is not the "property" of an individual: it is not only a matter of property rights as recognized by a copyright convention, but the fundamental attitude of the uniqueness, unity, and differentiated character of the text. It is the very materiality of the text that raises the question, in a twentieth-century frame of reference, of the ontological self-identity of the text. Obviously, this was most pronounced in the cultural domain of orality, in which the very concept of an "original" was not pertinent. The introduction of writing into the domain of secular textuality brought into that domain a limitation upon the endless oral play of the signifier, on the continually differentiated production of the same: the fact is that there now *was* an "original," and that modern scholars can judge that such and such a manuscript version is more or less close to that "original," even when the latter no longer exists. Material dissemination is not stopped, but limited. More important, its progress can be measured by the invention of Peter Abelard, the juxtaposition of different texts and the analysis of their differences. The contemporary attitude that, in the absence of an original, a printing of the integral text of the various redactions is undoubtedly correct; it implies that these various redactions are, in fact, different texts, not to be reduced to identity or sameness into a synthetic twentieth-century "reconstruction," as Joseph Bédier did with the Tristan legend. Other texts bearing some positive relation to a particular text—identity of agents, actions, conventions, ideology, etc.—define one aspect of the "extra-text," an aspect that is discussable in various ways, including that of intertextuality.

The *Yvain* is intertextual in its first line, in the topos that is constitutive of its non-prologial prologue, and in many other places as well. Indeed, it is the very nature of a conventional aesthetic to be intertextal, and only the beginnings of the study of medieval intertextuality have been accomplished: further studies of the conventional codes, their concrete embodiments, and their multiple intersections are needed. But the intertextual is only one aspect of the *Yvain's* "hors-livre." The text itself raises that question of the extra-text, and answers it most promptly, without unnecessary deferral. Beyond intertexuality, the extra-text is political. The prologial topos is developed in terms of a collectivity, a society, its governance, and its ideology. That these issues are raised in fictive terms, and presented in a remarkably smooth-flowing verse form — the rhymed octosyllabic couplet was not Chrétien's invention, but the systematization of the syntactical run-on over the limits of the rhyme was — has been allowed to obscure the nature of the issues raised by the text at its very beginning. The "extra-text" is not an unknown philosophical Other to a known metaphysical tradition, the repressed of millenia and their presuppositional unity. Nor does the alterity of the text — the Other it extrudes and posits — ground the social construction of reality in two radically different spheres, which might be organized on axes such as fantasy/reality, secular/religious, logocentric/disseminatory, etc. While alterity there is, it is not that of separate domains, to use the feudal vocabulary that has been ours in the discussion up to now. Since the issue is the governance and ideology of a collectivity, most of whose elements are set into play by the text we have discussed (peasantry, upper nobility including the king, lower nobility, and specifically the knight: the only major element of the contemporary secular order that is missing is that of the bourgeoisie, the inhabitants of the towns), it is one that is quite immediately present in the ontological reality of the text: that ontology is a social situation in which a scriptor (or another reader) transforms his written text into an oral message comprehensible to an illiterate noble audience located in its court: the center of power, the center of governance, the center of the administration of the economic and political realms. The realm is not the king's *royaume* (*regalem*), the monarchical kingdom, for the general development toward centralization has not yet solidified at the royal level, as is too readily forgotten:[31] that will occur only with the reign of Philip Augustus in the early years of the following century. At the time of Chrétien's career, the general tendency toward centralization has only reached the level of the region or, better, the return of the earlier feudal principalities under the great barons (counts or dukes) who surround the king's *demesne* and whose alliances threaten the king's *demesne*: Normandy, Blois, Anjou, and the two at which Chrétien worked in unknown capacities: Champagne and Flanders. The immediate audience for his symbolic representation of the political problems of the contemporary social text is quite precisely composed of those who manipulate, create (largely in reaction to the pressures of the productive peasantry), and profit from the social, political, and economic organization of society.

The production of the signifier is thus a concrete social situation in which the codes of signification constitute both entities that a traditional criticism hypostasizes as radical alterities: the author, and its audience. In fact, that concrete social situation shows them to be inextricably enmeshed: it is only our textual ideology—not without precise links to a political ideology—which allows for their separation as hypostasized others. The semiotic concept of the code in the sophisticated version developed by Umberto Eco allowing for code-switching and contradiction,[32] is an enabling means of reconstructing a rather complex signifying situation.

Given the complexity of this situation of signification, it would be a strategic error to foreclose its exploration by grounding it in the kind of dualistic typology of signifying procedures suggested by the Tartu group.[33] Its assumption of certain principles taken over from information theory valorizing the shock value of the anomalous cannot but transform the perception of a textual system whose constitutive principle is that of repetition used to represent differentiations of value. It is essential to conceive of that textual system in a manner that avoids the negativity implicit in the introduction of a notion such as "entropy" into its analysis. On the contrary, that repetitiousness—differentiated from the modern concept of repetition which has received great attention from contemporary theoreticians, first of all by its overtness—has to be assumed as a given without deleterious effects on the process of signification, though it does require an attitudinal change in the modern reader, whose value-systems (ideological, textual) are questioned by the encounter with texts that not only represent a different value-system but do so by means that are "offensive" to modern textual values.

This principle is a corrective not only to an older traditional scholarship grounded in the virtue of "originality" in the (post-) romantic sense,[34] but as well to the latter's contemporary opponent, the philosophical attack on the "originary" foundation of the "western metaphysical tradition." This critique—whose philosophical value we are not competent to judge—takes a number of forms, one of which is directly pertinent to our analysis of the text. A means of narrative structuration has been identified, which could have been called "the unexpected narrative extension," but which we have named "supplementarity," in recognition of Derrida's extensive discussions of textuality. In a way, our use of the term is different from his, and is in fact its contrary: in our use, the term has positive value. The possibility, perhaps the need, for *suppléance* for Derrida, implies the inevitable incompleteness of the text, hence its inherent deconstructive quality along with the deconstruction of the western metaphysics the discourse apparently implies.[35] In our discussion, the principle of supplementarity has quite a different character: it is a positive means of narrative construction. Moreover, it can be argued that supplementarity is an essential principle of narrative construction in this text, particularly in its first part. As we have seen, Calogrenant's successful search for a *mervoille* leads to the supplementary *aventure* of his combat with the knight who defends the fountain, a supplement that transforms the narrative, successful up to now, into an ignominious defeat. But that supplement will lead to another, Yvain's successful wooing of Laudine, who is the positive hero's reward that was witheld from Calogrenant in the miniepisode of the *vavasseur*. But Yvain's successful *aventure* is in turn completed by yet a further supplement, the crisis that intervenes between him and Laudine. And finally, the entire second part of the romance—longer than the first—can be thought a necessary supplement to the first part, in order to right that adventure (by a series of adventures, be it noted, that do not use the principle of narrative supplementarity). Supplementarity in multiple stages, either confirming or overthrowing the prior narrative, is thus an essential aspect of the narrative structure of this text. This poses a number of theoretical questions. Is the difference between deconstruction and textual construction merely one of a different critical "point of view"? That is doubtful, especially in view of the fact (which has to be taken as a fact for the moment, even though it is only an assertion of the present enunciator) that the second half of the narrative, serial in construction, is not supplementary.[36] Is the present enunciator mistaken in construing the presence of the supplement as constructive rather than deconstructive? That might be quite possible, but it is not only the positive and non-supplementary second half that argues against this view, but also the simple fact (which this time is not merely an assertion of the enunciator) that the text *is* actually constructed (in part) on the basis of supplementarity, and that it is thus supplementarity that enables the text to exist and to produce significations, whether polysemic or disseminatory. Whether the text is thought of as pure phenomenon, prior to meaning, as a vector of possible meanings before some more limited signification is imposed on it, or as a hierarchized system of semantic relations, it exists, before it deconstructs. A value of positivity attends supplementarity, both onto/logically and in narrative priority.

The logic of the supplement is only one of many repetitions that are more overt, right at the surface of the text or to the narrative, than in modern texts. I have already discussed the issues of the conventionality of medieval textuality elsewhere.[37] It is the existence of such conventions, as well as their overtness, that makes a theory of genres attractive for the discussion of medieval texts, since it is precisely the conventional that is both the indicator and the very material stuff out of which genres are made. Such conventions, subject to dilation or compression in the affabulation of any particular narrative discourse, can equally well be considered the properly textual codes on which both narrative and discourse depend. There is harm neither in their identification and analysis, nor in their use for the purpose of textual analysis, as long as one essential principle is retained. That principle can best be explained by referring to the twin Jakobsonian principles of selection and combination in linguistic practice. A battery of conventions does exist, and can perhaps be organized as a paradigm (though that is a real question) from which the particular writer can select his *Stoff* in the affabulation of his narrative. That affabulation, of course, will consist of the particular combination of the selected materials. But it is that particular combination — just like the construction of a new sentence, possibly producing a new meaning — that will produce the significations of the text. The fact that words are always repeated (except for the hapax, relatively rare) does not affect the potential for a sentence expressing a new meaning: its composition of old, repeated words nevertheless allows saying the unsaid. In the same way, the fact that a text is composed of established, conventional materials does not preclude its potential for producing significations that have not been produced before. Indeed, it is the extraordinary and specific achievement of medieval literature to have explored this possibility, ignored by modernity and an aesthetic of "originality" as well as by a philosophical stance determined by its opposition to an "originary" metaphysics, as fully as possible.

The conventionality, repetitiveness, and supplementarity of the text do not prevent its historicity: on the contrary, they are the preconditions thereof. It is not at all the case that the tight, intertextual imbrication of the particular text in the textual system of its period precludes or even impedes the production of significances that we consider social, political and economic, though it is true that these textual characteristics have grossly impeded the recognition by modern critics and scholars — the highly specialized forms of readers who professionally occupy themselves with texts — of the kind of signifying process that might be found in these texts. In *Yvain*, the first narrative event of the text is the exclusion from the field of political relevance of the figure of the King, who can't even stay awake for the social celebration of an important religious festival. The second event is the display of discord at his court, supposedly the center of courteous civilization in the fictional world, particularly as ruled by a figure who is a second Destinator — a second Destinator? an anti-Destinator? in any case, *another* Destinator — the figure of *Amors*. That discord, breaking the rules of the politeness required at court, is a representation of the same type of behavior, albeit less violent and hence less damaging, as the behavior of the *barons* of the epic: pridefully individualistic and going against both social norms and political interests. The form of social organization that is foregrounded in both epic and in the first part of the *Yvain* is that of the lineage, and its associated value-system and ideology, the opposition honor / shame. It is this value-system that leads Calogrenant to shameful defeat and Yvain to a victory that entails the killing of his opposite number — all we know about Esclados le Ros are positional qualities that Yvain will take on (Laudine's husband, hence lord of the fief and defender of the fountain) — and, by a supplementary twist of the narrative, to marriage with Lady and fief. The problem with the value-system incorporated in the narrative system is the same as that which was repeatedly faced by the epic series: the specific combination of actantial characteristics and lineage-ideology led to blood-feuds destructive of social cohesion and the political order. At the beginning of the last quarter of the twelfth century, when Chrétien is writing, this further implies a disruption of the stability and peace required by the new economic system, the transformation of manorialism into banal lordship, hence including components of local production of goods for exchange, the expropriation of surplus value by the political means of taxation and judicial fines, as well as regional and international trade (especially important to a Count of Champagne whose principality was host to what has been called "six annual" fairs, but which in fact amounted to a permanent center of international exchange).[38] In their actantial characteristics, then, the knights, recently ennobled but essentially still the retainers of an earlier epoch, posed a threat to the world that defined the upper nobility's well-being. Yet, another necessity weighed upon the latter, which was continued control over the enormous mass of the population constituted by the peasantry, both as a work force in agricultural production and as a source of that surplus value to be expropriated now, no longer in the form of farm goods such as grain, animals, or the services on the lord's fields, but in monetary form. The means by which this control functioned was the employment of the lower-level knights as a permanent police presence, representing the overlord who retained the power of taxation and the levying of fines, but who affirmed either actual or potential force through the knights who served him: their regular expeditions into the countryside, the *chevauchée* that was specified in the feudal contract that bound them to their overlord, had as its function first to strike terror into the hearts of the peasants, so as, second, to assure their continuation as productive agricultural workers on the *demesne*, and thirdly, their rendering unto the overlord his due: taxes and such fines as he levied upon them. Thus, the lower-level knights played an essential role in the political and economic system of the later twelfth century, which had nothing to do either with kingship or the original justification of the class of the *bellatores*, the defense of the realm against outside enemies.

Elements of this structure—social, political, and economic—are scattered throughout Chrétien's work, though never brought together in one place. One would not expect such an analytic sketch of the social text in a romance, or even a novel, after all: it is neither within the conventions of the text nor is it likely in the signifying situation we sketched out at the beginning of these concluding remarks. Nevertheless, it can be said that this is the essential political problem to which this particular text addresses itself: the problem created by the dual, even contradictory qualities of the Subject's Adjuvants in the social text: the lower-level knights, their necessity and their destructiveness, seen from the perspective of those who dominate society. Accepting the valorial framework of their traditional mode of organization, the first part of the text plays out the narrative possibilities that ideology allows for: failure and success, shame and honor. It is the second part of the *Yvain* which, invoking both a different mode of textual organization and a radically different organization of society, will give the positive response to the negative first part of his text.

Peter Haidu
University of Illinois
Urbana, Illinois

Notes

* © 1984 by Peter Haidu

1. See Julia Kristeva's *thèse de troisième cycle, Le Texte du roman* (Paris: Mouton, 1970), and "Le texte clos," in *Semiotiké: Recherches pour une sémanalyse* (Paris: Seuil, 1969), pp. 113–42.

2. In fact, an early publication was that of a desk dictionary of Old French: A J. Greimas, *Dictionnaire de l'ancien français* (Paris: Larousse, 1968).

3. Umberto Eco, *L'Oeuvre ouverte*, tr. C. Roux de Bézieux (Paris: Seuil, 1966); much the same attitude exists in "The Poetics of the Open Work" published in 1962, the same year as the Italian original, *Opera aperta*, in *The Role of the Reader* (Bloomington: Indiana University Press, 1979), pp. 47–66; and both the title essay in that book and the one on "Peirce and the Semiotic Foundations of Openness: Signs as Texts and Texts as Signs" (pp. 175–99).

4. Paul Zumthor, *Parler du moyen âge* (Paris: Ed. de Minuit, 1980).

5. Fredric Jameson, *The Political Unconscious* (Ithaca, NY: Cornell University Press, 1981).

6. See W. Ostrowski, "The Fantastic and the Realistic in Literature: Suggestions on How to Define and Analyze Fantastic Fiction," *Zagadnienia rodzajow literackich* 9 (1966), 54–71, cited by Tzvetan Todorov in *Introduction à la littérature fantastique* (Paris: Seuil, 1970).

7. Marie-Louise Ollier, "Demande sociale et constitution d'un 'genre': la situation dans la France du XIIe siècle, *Mosaic* 8, iv (1975) 207–16. The two classical discussions of medieval genre theory are those of Hans-Robert Jauss, "Littérature médiévale et théorie des genres," *Poétique* 1 (1970) 79–101, and Paul Zumthor's fourth chapter in the *Essai de poétique médiévale* (Paris: Seuil, 1972), "L'organisation hiérarchique," pp. 157–87.

8. Juri M. Lotman, B. A. Uspenskij, V. V. Ivanov, V. N. Toporov, and A. M. Pjatigorksij, "Theses on the Semiotic Study of Cultures (As Applied to Slavic Texts)," in *The Tell-Tale Sign*, ed. Thomas A. Sebeok (Lisse: De Ridder Press, 1975), pp. 57–84.

9. Jameson, *Political Unconscious*, p. 106. The view that genres represent contractual conventions between authors and their public is hardly new: see Pierre Kohler, "Contribution à une philosophie des genres," *Helicon* 2 (1939), 135–42 ("Congrès de Lyon: IIIᵉ Congrès International d'Histoire Littéraire, Lyon, mai-juin 1939: Les genres littéraires. . . ."). The psychological vocabulary of this article should not be allowed to cloud its essentially structuralist, even Jakobsonian principle: "Avant de combiner, il faut choisir." (p. 138.)

10. Beryl Smalley, *The Study of the Bible in the Middle Ages* (Oxford: Clarendon Press, 1941).

11. See my "Text and History: The Semiosis of Twelfth-Century Lyric as Socio-Historical Phenomenon (Chrétien de Troyes, 'D'Amors qui m'a tolu . . .')," *Semiotica* 33 (1981), 1–62; and "Semiotics and History," *Semiotica* 40 (1982), 187–228; note that I use the words "analysis" and "interpretation" interchangeably.

12. "The Semes of History: Structures of Contradiction in Medieval French Literature."

13. *La Vie de Saint Alexis*, ed. Christopher Storey, Textes Littéraires Français, vol. 148 (Geneva: Droz; Paris: Minard, 1968).

14. Chrétien de Troyes, *Le Chevalier au lion (Yvain)*, ed. Mario Roques, Classiques français du Moyen-Age, vol. 89 (Paris: Champion, 1960).

15. Donald Maddox, "Kinship Alliances in the *Cligès* of Chrétien de Troyes," *L'Esprit créateur* 12 (1972), 3–12; see also his *Structure and Sacring: The Systematic Kingdom in Chrétien's "Erec et Enide"* (Lexington, Ky.: French Forum, 1978), on the figure of Arthur in Chrétien's first romance.

16. Ollier, "Demande sociale," and Haidu, "Le Sens historique du phénomène stylistique: La sémiose dissociative chez Chrétien de Troyes," *Europe* no. 641 (Oct. 1982), 36–47.

17. Haidu, "Narrativity and Style in Some Twelfth-Century Romances," *Yale French Studies* 51 (1974), 133–46.

18. See Marie-Louise Ollier, "Le discours en 'abyme' ou la narration équivoque," *Medioevo Romanzo* 1 (1974), 351–64; "The Author in the Text," *Yale French Studies* 51 (1974), 26–41.

19. Saussure does use the term, but in a vague, metaphoric manner that equates it with *langue: Cours de linguistique générale*, ed. T. de Mauro (Paris: Payot, 1972), p. 31.

20. On the convention of hospitality, see Matilda Tomaryn Bruckner, *Narrative Invention in Twelfth-Century French Romance: The Convention of Hospitality (1160–1200)* (Lexington, Ky.: French Forum, 1980).

21. Chrétien de Troyes, *Yvain*, ed. Wendelin Foerster (Halle: Niemeyer, 1926); cf. Mario Roques' critical note to l. 278, in the edition cited above.

22. F. Bar, "Sur un passage de Chrétien de Troyes (*Yvain*, ll. 276–85)," *Studi in honore I. Siciliano* 1 (Florence: Olshki, 1966), 46–50.

23. On the descriptive convention of beauty and its inversion, see Alice Colby, *The Portrait in Twelfth-Century French Literature* (Geneva: Droz, 1965).

24. See A. J. Greimas, "Conditions d'une sémiotique du monde naturel," in *Du sens* (Paris: Seuil, 1970), pp. 49–91.

25. On this shift, see Georges Duby, *Guerriers et paysans*, (Paris: Gallimard, 1973), pp. 191–200.

26. See my article, "The Hermit's Pottage: Deconstruction and History in 'Yvain'," *Romanic Review* 74 (1983), 1–15; also in *The Sower and His Seed: Essays on Chrétien de Troyes*, ed. Rupert T. Pickens (Lexington, Ky.: French Forum, 1983), pp. 127–45.

27. See "Text and History . . . ," *supra*, fn. 11.

28. Colin Morris, *The Discovery of the Individual, 1050–1200*, (London: SPCK, 1972); Robert W. Hanning, *The Individual in Twelfth-Century Romance* (New Haven, Conn.: Yale University Press, 1977).

29. R. Howard Bloch, *Medieval French Literature and Law*, (Berkeley: University of California Press, 1977), pp. 35–7.

30. See especially the deconstruction of the inner / outer category, starting in Jacques Derrida, *De la grammatologie* (Paris: Ed. de Minuit, 1967): and "Hors-Livre," the non-preface to *La Dissémination* (Paris: Seuil, 1972).

31. As, for example, in the conclusion of R. Howard Bloch's often brilliant book, *Etymologies and Genealogies* (Chicago: University of Chicago Press, 1983).

32. Umberto Eco, *A Theory of Semiotics* (Bloomington: Indiana University Press, 1976); of particular interest for medieval studies is also his introductory essay bearing the same title as the book in which it is published, *The Role of the Reader* (Bloomington: Indiana University Press, 1979).

33. *Supra*, n. 8.

34. Though it seems to have roots: Roland Mortier, *L'Originalité: une nouvelle catégorie esthétique au Siècle des Lumières* (Geneva: Droz, 1982).

35. See especially "Le supplément de copule," in Jacques Derrida, *Marges* (Paris: Ed. de Minuit, 1972), pp. 209-46, and *passim*.

36. See "The Episode as Semiotic Module," to appear in *Poetics Today*.

37. Haidu, "Making it (New) in the Middle Ages: Toward a Problematics of Alterity," *Diacritics* (Summer 1974), 1-10, and "Repetition: Modern Reflections of Medieval Aesthetics," *Modern Language Notes* 92 (1977), 875-87.

38. Jacques Le Goff, "L'apogée de la France urbaine médiévale," in *La Ville médiévale: des Carolingiens à la Renaissance*, ed. Jacques Le Goff, in *Histoire de la France urbaine*, ed. Georges Duby, 2 (Paris: Seuil, 1980), 257.

2. The Craft of Guillaume Le Clerc's Fergus

To follow in the footsteps of Chrétien de Troyes could not have been easy for aspiring practitioners of Arthurian verse romance. By the beginning of the thirteenth century, his works were so widely admired that to venture into the same genre was to risk invidious comparisons. How could a poet hope to outshine him in his dexterous handling of the octo-syllabic couplet, his lively presentation of events, the vividness of his descriptions, his creation of character through dialogue? How could one recapture the learned wit of his asides, the warmth of his humour, the finesse of his irony? And how should one set about disclosing with so little insistence such broad vistas for debate and reflection? In short, how was it possible to compete with his intelligent sophistication? Yet Chrétien had popularised these stories of King Arthur and his knights, and there was a ready public for more of them. Here lay the opportunity, and the dilemma, faced by the "second-phase" romancers, among whom, some time in the early thirteenth century, we can number Guillaume le Clerc.[1]

Not to be confused with his moralistic namesake from Normandy, Guillaume seems to have composed in the Picard dialect; but his identity eludes us, and where and when he composed *Fergus* remains a matter for speculation.[2] It is nevertheless a question that has preoccupied scholars for a century or more, largely to the exclusion of a proper appreciation of his romance as one of the best in its genre. Beate Schmolke-Hasselmann has recently done something to redress the balance; but even she has devoted more attention to the poem's provenance and circumstances of composition than to its literary qualities.[3] This extra-textual concern is understandable; for both Fergus and his father appear to be based on historical prototypes, and the geographical precision of the action, set in southern Scotland, is quite exceptional in the whole of Arthurian romance. The temptation to seek an explanation in local patronage or even political ambitions is strong but perhaps, as we shall see, best resisted.

The story makes Fergus the son of the powerful, but base-born *vilain* Soumilloit, whose stronghold is located in the region we know as Galloway. Martin, in his edition, quite reasonably identified the hero with the historical Fergus of Galloway, who died in 1161, and his fictional father with Somerled, the so-called Lord of the Isles, who also lived in the middle of the twelfth century and was indeed related, though only distantly, to Fergus. It was the latter's great-grandson, the celebrated Alan of Galloway, whom Martin proposed, but without discussion, as the likely patron of Guillaume le Clerc. Other scholars followed his lead, and M. Dominica Legge suggested a possible occasion for the commissioning of the romance: the marriage of Alan in 1209 to Margaret, niece of the Scottish king.[4] In 1951 Joan Greenberg, while accepting that Guillaume had first-hand knowledge of at least parts of southern Scotland, spoke against the hypothesis of Alan's patronage; and in this she has been supported by Beate Schmolke-Hasselmann, who believes that *Fergus* was instead composed for Dervorguilla of Galloway and her husband John of Baliol, probably between 1234 and 1241. She views the story of Fergus' social ascent as propaganda in the context of the Baliols' designs on the Scottish throne for their sons.[5] We are asked, then, to see in Guillaume's work a unique example of an ancestral romance with an Arthurian setting, a poem honouring and perhaps furthering the political aspirations of historical figures prominent on the Scottish scene during the first half of the thirteenth century. One second-phase composer would have found an ideal outlet for his talents.

If this were the case, we might expect Guillaume to give some small sign of his indebtedness to a patron, or at least to present his story in a way flattering to the family in question and hinting at a serious purpose beneath any superficial extravagance or humour. This was certainly within his capacity, for as we get to know his work, we gain the impression of a very able craftsman with a shrewd intelligence, a good appreciation of the meaning and nuances of words, and a refined sense of structure, overall and in detail. But rather than approaching his poem with a preconceived notion of an underlying intention or attitude, let us initially let it speak for itself as to a contemporary public, of whatever rank, that was well versed in the literature of the day and not least, like Guillaume himself, in the romances of Chrétien de Troyes. The opening episodes will especially repay close attention, since by them the tone is set for the whole work, and expectations are aroused in the mind of the reader or hearer (it is to the latter, the "escoutans" that Guillaume wishes joy in his final line).

There is no formal prologue to give us an inkling of the poet's purpose or approach: instead, we are introduced at once to King Arthur's court at Cardigan on the feast of St John. There were present, says Guillaume, many courtly knights whom he could name if he wished to take the trouble. In fact he proceeds to specify Gauvain and his dear companion Yvain, Lancelot, Perceval "Qui tant pena por le graal" ("who strove so arduously for the Grail" l. 14), Erec, Saigremor and Kay, adding that numerous others were there whose names he cannot give, not having learnt them. Two points strike us. Firstly there are the seemingly casual and contradictory statements about the naming of the knights. These might be dismissed as being simply a naïve and clumsy use of cliché — and yet Guillaume will turn out to be a careful chooser of words, hardly likely to have perpetrated this lapse unwittingly and at the very beginning of his work. Secondly, the short list he does give includes the heroes of each of Chrétien's Arthurian romances. So from these opening lines we are entitled to draw at least the provisional conclusion that the poet is inviting us, while not taking him too seriously, to carry with us as we read *Fergus* our memories of Chrétien's own tales.

Justification of this view quickly follows, as our thoughts are directed to the beginning of *Yvain*. Consider the following parallels. *Yvain*[6]: Arthur holds court in Carlisle at Pentecost; after the meal, the knights follow the ladies to tell tales or speak of love; the King leaves their company to rest and tarry with the Queen; she suddenly intrudes upon a group of knights including Gauvain and Yvain ("Se fu leissiee antraus cheoir" l. 66), one of whom notices her and springs to his feet. *Fergus*: after the meal on the feast day at Cardigan, the knights stay in the halls to swap stories of their exploits; Gauvain leads Yvain aside, for their love is greater than that of Achilles or Patroclus; as they converse together, the King comes upon them suddenly ("se laisse entr'els caoir" l. 38); Gauvain notices him and springs to his feet.

This is no simple plagiarism. Guillaume has used Chrétien's series of incidents to reproduce the familiar scenario, within which the startling changes he has made stand in sharp relief. Not only has he dismissed the ladies from the court scene, but the only talk of love (a major topic in Chrétien's opening) is of that between Gauvain and his companion Yvain. When the irruption comes, it is not by the Queen, but by a King Arthur who, in contrast to Chrétien's lethargic monarch, cuts a figure both imperial and imperious as he proceeds to call for his knights' immediate departure to hunt a white stag sighted in the forest near Carlisle. All this leaves the impression that Guillaume's concern is first to turn our thoughts to Chrétien and then systematically to overturn what our memory supplies. In other words, he is carefully using what might be termed a "reversal technique." Whether the misogynistic undertones that result in this case are deeply felt by the poet or merely the casual by-product of his technique is a question wakened in our minds; and we shall be alert to any later developments that may point towards an answer.

Erec et Enide was Guillaume's source for the hunting of the stag. There Arthur's proposal of the hunt had been opposed by Gauvain: here his nephew promptly agrees, and the chase is engaged at a furious pace, with the King offering his golden cup to the one who takes the quarry. Guillaume affects an epic tone as he describes the pursuit by way of Jedburgh ("Gedeorde"), the Lammermuirs ("Landemore"), the forest of Glasgow ("Glascou") and Ayr ("Aroie"), with Perceval le Galois outstripping the rest to bring the stag finally to bay in Ingeval, usually identified with Galloway. There the inhabitants are quite uncivilised,

> Que ja n'enterront en mostier.
> Pas ne leur calt de Diu proier:
> Tant sont niches et bestiaus.
>
> [197-9]

> [for they will never go to church. They care nothing for praying to
> God, so uncouth and bestial are they.]

Irony lies here for those who know Chrétien's *Conte du Graal*, for the unflattering epithets are the very ones applied there by Arthur to the young Perceval, fresh from his native Welsh forest;[7] and even earlier in that romance one of the knights who had come upon the lad and failed to get any sense out of him had said much the same:

> ". . . Galois sont tuit par nature
> Plus fol que bestes an pasture:
> Cist est aussi come une beste."
>
> [243-5]

> ["The Welsh are all more naturally stupid than grazing beasts: this one
> is just like a beast."]

We think too of Perceval's own ignorance of church-going as we read the lines from *Fergus*. Oblique though they are, these parallels Guillaume draws between the Welsh and the Gallovidians will prove of some significance. The latter did in fact have at this time a reputation for rough and barbaric manners, reflected in four of the manucripts of the *Conte du Graal,* where Galloway is described as

> Une terre molt felenesse
> Et si i a gent molt perverse. (After l. 6602 in MSS *C P S U*)

> [a very evil land with very perverse people.]

Having brought the hunt to a glorious conclusion, Perceval receives the golden trophy from the King. Yet Guillaume has slyly undercut the whole affair and distanced us from it by inserting a few incongruous details. To elude its pursuers the stag had hurled itself into a raging torrent — but to no avail, since it was close by a broad bridge, which the royal party crossed with ease. Perceval spurred after it with raised lance (normal hunting practice?); but in the end it was his hound that caught it, forced it into a pond and dragged it under by the nose so that it drowned ("Now it can drink, if it is thirsty!" says Guillaume). Since Perceval has ridden up to find it already dead, the following evident reminiscences of Roland's last stand at Roncevaux have an almost derisive ring: he sets his horn to his mouth and, to announce the kill, sounds it "a longe alaine" ("with a long blast" l. 237: cf. *Chanson de Roland l.* 1789); Arthur hears the call as he rides with his men and bids them hasten to Perceval's aid; they arrive on the scene — only to find him on foot drying off his hound; as night is falling, they pitch camp on the spot. It seems in keeping with the bathetic elements in this account that Perceval on receipt of his prize should hand it straight over to Gauvain. That incident, however, was based on one in *Cligés*.

Guillaume has not yet introduced his hero. The unforewarned might well suppose that this early narrowing of the focus to Perceval means that he will fill the role. In that case (though he should by now be on guard against making the easy assumption), his expectation will shortly be overturned. Eventually he will recognise that the false trail has been laid not out of inadvertence or mere perversity on Guillaume's part, but with a specific artistic purpose. With hindsight it will become clear that the real hero has been presented as a "neo-Perceval" and that the early prominence given to the Welsh knight has served to establish him firmly in our minds as a point of reference. But for the moment, his stature in our eyes is being slightly reduced by gentle innuendo. This will work to the profit of his supplanter, whilst for us the newcomer's character will gain by the comparison an extra dimension on which our imagination can work.[8]

Heading back for Carlisle, the royal cavalcade passes, on the borders of Ingeval, the castle of a *vilain* of Pelande (another name, it seems, for Galloway). Perched on a great rock, it has hurdles all around and a tall crenellated tower built not of stone but of earth. The name of its low-born, but wealthy owner is Soumilloit. Governer of the whole country, he had taken a noble wife, who has given him three handsome sons, who daily herd his sheep or plough his land for him. King Arthur gazes with admiration at the stronghold of this "vilains rustes campestre" ("rude, low-born rustic" l. 334). We may be less impressed. For even if, as some have suggested, the description could fit one of the primitive fortresses common in Galloway in Guillaume's day, this is a romance, and he has put us in no mood to ponder possible flashes of documentary realism. We wonder rather what he is up to now with his bucolic potentate lording over an earthen castle.

As the scene unfolds, his game becomes clearer. Having put us in mind of the *Conte du Graal,* he takes Chrétien's account of Perceval's adventures in his native "gaste forest" and plays with its elements, accepting some in a more or less distorted form, reversing others. Although I shall speak now of Fergus and Perceval, Guillaume follows Chrétien in not disclosing his hero's name for some time: the one is initially referred to as "li fius au vilain" ("the *vilain's* son" l. 381), the other was "li filz a la veve dame" ("the son of the widowed lady," *Conte du Graal* l. 74). Fergus is the eldest of three brothers, Perceval the youngest of three. We meet Fergus labouring at the plough, Perceval as he went out to see the labourers in the fields; he was armed with javelins, Fergus carries a club. The *vilain's* son sees Arthur and his company, whom he recognises as knights, and is terrified: Perceval was fearless before the party of knights, whom he did not recognise as such. Fergus accosts one of the retinue and asks for information: one of the knights sought information from Perceval. Fergus learns that this is Arthur with his knights of the Round Table: Perceval learnt that these were Arthur's knights. The reaction of each is to rush home, fired with a desire to go to the royal court; and soon after, both leave with this purpose, Perceval in the face of his mother's distress and reluctance to see him go, Fergus after his mother has overcome his father's opposition.

This episode and the teasing technique Guillaume uses in adapting Chrétien's presentation of his young hero will prove, I believe, to hold the master key for the unlocking of his whole romance. But I will not anticipate my conclusion here: let us rather consider now certain other features that help to raise the work far above the level of servile imitation. Not least there is Guillaume's ability to bring a scene to life by the injection of vivid, original details. Thus he shows us Fergus rushing back to the castle in order to equip himself and set off after the royal party before they have too long a start. Nevertheless he stops to unharness and dismantle his plough, and arrives before his father, pouring with sweat and carrying on his shoulders the ploughshare, which he flings to the ground. The *vilain,* hearing his intention and request for arms, would have belaboured him with a great stick, had he not been physically restrained by the lad's mother.

There follows an exchange between Soumilloit and his wife where we glimpse another of Guillaume's gifts, namely his enlivening of the dialogue

with a vein of sharp repartee. It is deftly introduced. The *vilain,* asking
Fergus why he should want arms instead of being content like his brothers
with dressing in sheepskins and herding cattle, applies to him the common
term of abuse "Fius a putain" ("Son of a whore" 480). His wife bridles:
by St. Mungo (the patron saint of Glasgow), this is to label her a whore,
whereas there are many fine knights in the family—but on *her* side!

Soumilloit capitulates and has a suit of armour fetched from a chest
where it had lain for thirty-two years or more. It is as scarlet as the sun
rising over Ethiopia—not, though, from some rich pigment, but from
the rust it had collected. Here again is a nice twist of Chrétien's tale, for
we recall how Perceval too became a "red knight" when he appropriated
the armour of the Chevalier Vermeil. As we see Soumilloit fling the
equipment down onto a black cloth and Fergus hastily put it on, we remember too the contrasting scene in Chrétien's first romance where Erec
sat in dignity on a precious rug in order to don his silver, rust-proof
hauberk and other gleaming armour.[9] So Guillaume is skilfully developing
his technique of borrowing some features from Chrétien and reversing
others to achieve a fresh and delightfully amusing situation. At the same
time he adds touches of his own. Fergus, unspurred, leaps into the saddle
of one of the plump, powerful local horses that can run more easily over
a quaking bog than can any man on foot. As well as a short, broad
sword, a smoke-blackened lance and an antique shield, he carries a knotted
scourge; then ("You can tell he was foolish," says the poet) he demands
his javelins and axe, and fastens them to his saddle-bow. That is how, to
the great distress of his mother and the others, he rides forth with couched
lance to look for Arthur and his company.

With our hero in the saddle, we can pause to take stock of our reactions
to the romance so far. If the rather off-hand manner in which Guillaume
had introduced his story had not encouraged in us too close a commitment to characters and events, this distancing process has been reinforced by
his persistent deflection of our attention to Chrétien's works and
especially the *Conte du Graal.* There, Perceval had been a person in his
own right with whom we rapidly formed a bond of sympathy. In contrast, we find ourselves looking at Fergus as it were through the immature
Perceval and so at one remove. The Welsh knight as he actually appears in
Guillaume's work is the established member of Arthur's company, yet
not perhaps to be taken entirely seriously, since we have been aware of
some slight undercutting of the image of heroic chivalry he presents in
the hunt scene. Here and elsewhere a gentle irony seems to break the surface. The simple Fergus, for instance, is seized by the ambition not just

to go to Arthur's court, but to become one of his counsellors (this becomes a leitmotif: 1. 422, cf. ll. 664, 745, 750, 860-1) — in fact we shall never see him in this role. Does one even sense a mildly condescending attitude towards the subject-matter or, conceivably, the genre itself? In any case, we do not feel prompted to take the romance seriously as anything but a piece of pure entertainment; and on this level, we can only admire the author's talent for vivid narrative, description, and dialogue and, above all, his skill in selecting, shaping, and organising his material.

Fergus soon shows his mettle, and Guillaume his taste for grisly detail, in an encounter with four robber knights. The outcome is his arrival at the royal court in Carlisle with the heads of two of them strung by their beards to his saddle-bow, along with the axe and javelins he had just used with such lethal effect. There the foolish youth ("Li vallés qui ne fu pas sages" l. 726) goes straight up to the King and, on Arthur's enquiry, reveals his name for the first time. He has come far, he says, to be his counsellor. Kay has found the perfect butt for his barbed tongue. I abridge: "You truly look like a royal counsellor. We were at our wits' end ('tout . . . desconsillié' l. 752) and were much in need of the counsel we now have, if God gives you long life. He has sent us aid; for you seem a valiant, courtly knight, skilled in arms. Your helmet, shining with gold, suits you well, as does the shield hung at your neck; and better still that fine, white lance in your hands. You certainly know how to strike great blows with lance and sword, and with them have cut off many a head. The fool told the truth when he said a knight would come who would go to La Nouquetran to take the horn and the wimple (pennon?)[10] from the lion's neck, then sound the horn thrice and fight the pitch-black knight to avenge those he has beheaded." Kay's remarks (ll. 749-93) are neatly turned, moving from the play on *consilliers / desconsillié / consel* to the sarcastic antiphrasis in his picture of Fergus and the enigmatic account of the task he should (and eventually will) perform. They are a good example of the witty, carefully framed, and functional dialogue in which Guillaume shows both mastery and delight.

There are models in Chrétien (and especially in *Yvain*) for Kay's malicious outburst, as there are too for Gauvain's telling reproof. I am not, however, aware of any likely source for the strange mission urged on Fergus. La Nouquetran, where Merlin dwelt for many a year and which, we learn, is on the Noire Montagne, has not been identified. Perceval's adventures offer no real analogy. If the thought occurs to us that the horn and wimple might have been substituted for Chrétien's lance and Grail, it will be dismissed when a more obvious parallel appears in the latter part of the romance. A wimple (or pennon) seems a trivial object for a quest; though we may recollect that in the short and less than serious romance *La Mule sans frein* (where one also catches faint echoes from the *Conte du Graal*), Gauvain had been put to immense pains to retrieve a mislaid bridle, described at one point as a foolish trifle.[11] Irreverently, perhaps, one thinks of another text associating a lion and a wimple: Thisbe's in the Old French *Piramus et Tisbé.*[12] We are puzzled, but hardly concerned, so little incentive does Guillaume give us to take his story seriously.

Swearing by St. Mungo, Fergus warns this "knight with the braided hair" (l. 825) that he will pay for his insults (Guillaume, as Chrétien before him, will use this determination to get even with Kay as a leitmotif in the rest of the romance). Arthur pacifies him and diplomatically diverts his attention from the seneschal by asking how he came by the heads dangling behind him. Fergus explains, then asks if he may become the King's counsellor on condition that he first undertake the adventure at the Noire Montagne. Arthur tries to dissuade him from the enterprise; but when Fergus insists that he would not wish Kay to turn out a liar, he agrees. Fergus takes his leave to seek lodging in the town.

The young hero is being consistently and well protrayed. He shows his provincial origins as he swears: "Par saint Mangon qu'est a Glacou [Glasgow]" (l. 845), and Guillaume has described him more than once as a simpleton; but he is certainly not witless. When unprovoked, he has a certain native politeness. His main traits, though, are his impetuosity, stubbornness and sublime self-confidence, coupled with an attractive youthful exuberance. It is true that we have seen all this before in Perceval. But Fergus is more than a stereotype, if only because of the original and engaging way in which Guillaume reveals these qualities.

The scene that follows is full of delicacy and humour. Fergus finds no one in the town to give him lodging or directions. A fine drizzle falls that seeps through his hauberk as he rides to and fro. Eventually he thrusts his lance into the ground beneath the overhanging upper storey of a house and, leaning against it, dozes off. Spotting this handsome youth from a window, a comely maiden hurries down to ask what he is doing there at that hour. Politely he asks for lodging; and the girl offers him hospitality, subject to the approval of her father when he comes home from court. Two serving-lads who go to stable his horse are terrified by the sight of the heads hanging at the saddle. Fergus once more relates his encounter with the robbers; and the girl, much impressed, orders the heads to be put out of the way where they will cause no harm or fright ("U ne facent mal ne paor" MS *A* l. 984—the reading of MS *P* is more down to earth: "Que ne rengent mauvaise odour" ["So they do not give off a foul smell"]!). This is Fergus' first meeting in the romance with a member of the fair sex other than his mother; and bearing in mind that by about this point in Chrétien's works, his heroes have already had their first taste of love (though limited in Perceval's case to his perfunctory romp with the tent-maiden), we await developments with some anticipation.

Of Fergus, we are assured that

> Molt fust biaus, s'il n'eust le vis
> Camosé des armes porter.
> Et s'il se seüst atorner
> A la maniere d'Engleterre,
> On ne seüst en nule terre
> Nul plus bel chevalier, ce cuit.
>
> [992-7]

[He would have been very handsome had his face not been bruised from the armour he had been wearing. And had he known how to dress in the English fashion, I think one would not have known a fairer knight in any land.]

Indeed, the damsel is delighted with his whole appearance, apart from his rustic garb. They talk of this and that until the meal is served. Guillaume will not tell us of all the courses, for fear of drawing out his narrative and spoiling it, he says: he has something better to tell and will turn to a quite different matter. So in the best romance tradition, he has perfectly set the stage for Fergus' introduction to the delights (or distress) of *amour courtois*. It is as the maiden, her face aglow,[13] sits beside Fergus that her father, the King's chamberlain, suddenly returns from court. Those familiar with *Le Chevalier à l'épée*,[14] where the father uses his daughter as a snare for visiting knights, may think this bodes no good. Guillaume has ensured us a moment of some suspense.

Anticlimax follows. The chamberlain proves to be a willing and gracious host, whilst his daughter, in whom, to be frank, Fergus has shown small interest, fades into the background. The creation and abrupt dispersal of suspense is no novel technique in medieval literature, being found notably in texts with a burlesque flavour: Chrétien, for instance, uses it to good effect in *Lancelot;* and in *La Mule sans frein* the whole narrative is regularly punctured by moments of anticlimax amounting to bathos. So here, for the second time, we find Guillaume pointedly dodging the courtly love theme (having departed from his model by omitting it from his opening scene). Yet the surprise he has caused us is to some extent misplaced, since despite the fact that he is bearing arms, Fergus has not yet gone through the ritual of knighthood; and only a knight can be a true courtly lover.

It soon appears that the chamberlain is to play a role similar to that of Gornemant de Goort in the *Conte du Graal,* initiating the young man into his new status. A comparison of the two episodes conveniently illustrates a contrasting aspect of the poets' techniques, namely Chrétien's fondness of a provocative ambiguity as against Guillaume's greater directness and precision. The institution of knighthood was clearly of interest to them both, though how far their presentation of it reflects contemporary reality and how far it is conditioned by literary tradition is debatable.

In the *Conte du Graal* Perceval had learnt from the knights he met in the forest of the "king who makes knights" (l. 494); and his mother had told him how his own brothers had received knighthood from the hands of kings. He too, she said, must go to the royal court and would himself become a knight before long. But Perceval needed no urging. Away he went to find Arthur and, riding straight into his hall,

> "Feites moi chevalier," fet il,
> "Sire rois, car aler m'an vuel."
>
> [972-3]
>
> ["Make me a knight, sir King," he says, "for I want to be off."]

Despite his preoccupations, Arthur was polite and promised to do as Perceval wished. However, the lad coveted the arms of the King's aggressor, the Chevalier Vermeil; so without further ado he pursued and slew him, and with the aid of a squire, Yvonet, stripped him of his gear. Yvonet then helped him into the armour and girt the sword on him. Shortly afterwards, when the squire spoke to Arthur of "your knight who was here" (l. 1213), the King asked if he meant the young Welshman, the "vaslet galois" (l. 1219).

Perceval did not return to court but told Gornemant de Goort, whom he next encountered, that he had been there. And what was he doing at court? — "'Chevalier m'a fet / Li rois'" ("'The King made me a knight'" ll. 1369-70), said the lad, whereupon Gornemant commented that he thought Arthur had concerns other than the making of knights. Who had given him the arms he was bearing? Perceval told his whole story, to which the worthy man reacted by giving him some martial training and then, in the morning, insisted that he change his rough clothes for new.

> Et li prodon s'est abeissiez,
> Si li chauça l'esperon destre:
> La costume soloit teus estre
> Que cil qui feisoit chevalier
> Li devoit l'esperon chaucier.
>
> [1624-8]
>
> [And the worthy man bent down and fitted on his right spur: that was the custom that the man conferring knighthood should fit on the spur.]

Next, youths came forward to arm him;

> Et li prodon l'espee a prise,
> Si li çainst et si le beisa
> Et dit que donee li a
> La plus haute ordre avuec l'espee
> Que Deus et feite et comandee:
> C'est l'ordre de chevalerie,
> Qui doit estre sanz vilenie.
>
> [1632-8]

[And the worthy man took the sword, girt him with it, and kissed him, saying he has bestowed on him with the sword the highest order created and ordained by God, namely the order of chivalry that must be free from wickedness.]

With Chrétien's account of the knighting we may compare and contrast Guillaume's. In the course of their after-dinner conversation, the chamberlain asks Fergus:

> "Fustes vos onques chevaliers?"
> Et cil dist qu'il le cuidoit estre.
> "Chevaliers sui je, par ma teste!
> Car li bons vilains m'adoba
> Quant a cort servir m'envoia.
> Si me donna un bon cheval:
> N'a millor jusqu'en Ingeval.
> E s'ai hauberc et lance et hiaume:
> N'a millor en tot cest roiaume
> Vostre roi a mon ensient.
> Adoubés sui a mon talent."
>
> [1110-20]

["Have you ever been knighted?" And he said he believed he had. "I am a knight, by my head! For the good *vilain* dubbed me when he sent me to serve at court. And he gave me a fine horse: there's none better this side of Ingeval. And I have hauberk, lance and helmet: none better here, I think, in your king's whole realm. I'm dubbed as I would wish to be."]

Seeing the young man's ignorance, the chamberlain extracts from him a promise to do something for him on the morrow that will redound to his honour. Only then does he disclose what Fergus must do. He is to go to court and there, newly equipped, will receive from the King his sword and the accolade and become a novice knight, "chevaliers nouvials" (ll. 1151). The chamberlain himself will fit the spurs. Fergus is taken aback:

> "Serrai je chevaliers deus fois?
> Dont ne m'adouba Soumilloit
> Li vilains qui chier me tenoit?"
> "Bials frere, mentir ne t'en quier:

Nus ne puet faire chevalier,
S'il n'est chevaliers ensement."

[1174-9]

["Shall I be made knight twice? Was I not then dubbed by Soumilloit,
the *vilain* who loved me well?" — "Good brother, I have no wish to lie
to you: none can make a knight unless he is also a knight."]

The following morning sees Fergus inducted into the world of chivalry,
and with full honour. On the urging of Gauvain, who recalls how the
aspiring Perceval had once been driven from the court by Kay's malicious
tongue and who declares his wish to become Fergus' companion, Arthur
has arms and armour brought. Gauvain himself sets the helmet on the
lad's head; then Perceval brings the sword given him by his own host
(that is, Gornemant) and hands it to the King for him to gird it on. The
chamberlain fits the right spur, Yvain the left; and now Fergus is ready to
mount his own Galloway steed and take his shield and lance.

Guillaume, then, while parading his familiarity with the knighting
of Perceval, has seen fit to tidy up and clarify in his account some slight
ambiguity in his source. For anyone who had wondered why, in Chrétien's
story, Perceval had not been a knight from the moment Yvonet had
helped him into the Chevalier Vermeil's armour and strapped on his
sword, he is ready with the answer. It is supplied by the chamberlain,
who spells out in full the conditions Gornemant had tactfully left un-
spoken: only a knight can make a knight — and Yvonet had been a mere
squire. So Guillaume has not merely adapted and expanded his model: he
has added a personal explanatory footnote.

This technical clarification is not, however, the feature of his scene
that most claims our attention, nor, we suspect, was it Guillaume's chief
reason for so insistently evoking memories of Perceval at this point. For
by the end of the investiture scene it is clear that he has been reinforcing
in our minds the parallel between his hero and Chrétien's for a particular
purpose: to exhibit Fergus publicly as a "neo-Perceval." The picture he
has already given of Perceval is not over-flattering. By introducing him
as the one who strove so arduously for the Grail, he had left us to reflect
on his doubtful success in that enterprise. Then, despite his receiving the
prize for taking the white stag, we were not wholly impressed by the manner of his achievement. For Fergus the signs seem more propitious. He
spends the night before his dubbing in a room marvellously decorated
with sun, moon, and all the stars in the firmament: the symbolism promises well. Then, unlike Perceval, he receives knighthood at the hands of
Arthur himself, with other of Chrétien's heroes eager with their services

and the great Gauvain seeking his companionship. But it is Perceval's bestowal of the sword that has the greatest significance; for the passing on of this very symbol of knighthood can be interpreted as more than a courteous and generous act, in fact as the surrendering by the donor of his illustrious place in the Arthurian hierarchy to the young aspirant from Galloway. Were we in any doubt, we have Guillaume's repeated assurance of Fergus' future status:

> Si fu puis li miudres armés
> Qui onques fust de mere nés
> Fors que Gavain en vel oster.
> Cil ne trova onques son per
> Ne par honme ne fu matés.
> Por ço vel qu'il en soit ostés.
> Et nequedent nus fors cestui
> N'est de Gauvain miudres de lui.

> [1419-26]

[And thereafter he was the best warrior ever born of mother, though I would make an exception of Gauvain, who never found his equal or was overcome by any man. That is why I would except him. Nevertheless, apart from him, Gauvain, there is none better than he.]

Guillaume's words are unequivocal and provide the context for subsequent events. However we have viewed Fergus so far, we must now recognise him as destined to take over Perceval's role and transcend him as a knight. Thus, unlike those poets who sought to follow in Chrétien's footsteps by continuing and aspiring to complete his *Conte du Graal,* Guillaume, still with that work as his chief point of reference, has preferred to pension off its hero and substitute another, who shows a strong family likeness, but will eventually outstrip him in achievement. It was a bold step, tongue in cheek or not, to take up the challenge posed by Chrétien's preeminence in the romance field; and this is the moment Guillaume has chosen to bring his ambition into the open, with an independence of spirit that can only be admired.

Fergus proudly bestrides his horse, and with such vigour that the animal almost bursts. When a court fool predicts the success of his mission to the Noire Montagne, Kay is so incensed he would have hurled him into the fire but for his fear of what the others would think (another reversal here of Chrétien who, when Perceval came to court, had shown Kay actually kicking a fool into the fire). Important as a clue to Guillaume's artistic purpose is the fact that whereas in Chrétien the fool had foretold Perceval's revenge on Kay, a relatively minor incident, in *Fergus* the prediction concerns the main quest we know of: the knight from the

Noire Montagne will come to submit to Arthur and surrender the wimple and horn. Such anticipation of major events, more characteristic of epic than of romance, suggests that Guillaume is less concerned with offering his public the bait of narrative suspense than with entertaining them by the manner of the telling. We shall later find the success of a second quest, even more vital to Fergus' ultimate happiness, being prophesied by another mysterious figure; and the proviso that he must have the courage to attempt the task scarcely fills us with foreboding. The delights of the journey promise to be more significant for us than the eventual arrival.

Fergus rides forth, proud as a lion, but to his chagrin finds no adventures that day. Towards evening he comes to the stronghold of Lidel (Liddel Castle, now Newcastleton); and there on the bridge he sees a gentleman and a maiden taking their leisure. We are put in mind of Perceval's meeting with Gornemant de Goort outside his castle; and Gornemant had a niece, Blancheflor, though we never see them together. So when the *preudome* at Lidel turns out to be the uncle of the girl, Galiene, our equation is complete, and we look forward with some relish to a rehandling of the Perceval-Blancheflor affair.

With the assurance that Galiene was ripe for giving and receiving love, Guillaume devotes some fifty well-cast, if largely conventional lines to a description of her beauty and qualities. Is the hyperbole, we wonder, a trifle exaggerated? The girl holds the stirrup for Fergus to dismount. But this places him in a quandary; for though his nature bids him show her honour and reverence, he has no savoir-faire, says Guillaume, beyond what little the chamberlain had taught him. However, guided by *nature,* he takes Galiene's hand; and she reciprocates most willingly. With a display of Ovidian rhetoric, the poet describes how Love's skill at archery is exercised at the girl's expense, as Fergus' beauty promptly steals her heart. Seated beside him on a couch and trying to conceal her emotion from her uncle, she is still too timid to engage him in conversation (we note the contrast with the eloquent Blancheflor), whilst he remains dumb through ignorance. The delicate humour in the presentation of this scene yields little to Chrétien in its charm.

So for the second time in his romance Guillaume has set up a conventional courtly love situation, but again only to make sport of our expectations. In response to his host's enquiry, Fergus has told of his quest (not failing to mention Kay's gibes) and has been warned of the folly of seeking out a foe who has already taken the heads from over a thousand men. That night Galiene suffers all the emotional torments of a Soredamors as she tosses in her bed and delivers herself of a monologue that runs something like this: "Fergus, fair *ami*! —But how can I be so bold as to call him *ami*? I've never seen him before today, and tomorrow he'll be off and not remember me: he can't take an *amie* wherever he finds lodging. But he'll never know the depth of my love unless I tell him. Tell him? No: I'd rather die than make the first approach! I'll forget him. My father wants to marry me to a king who may be more handsome—but no, that is impossible, and if Fergus knew what I'd said he would never love me. Love me? But he doesn't, otherwise he would have said so—though perhaps he didn't know how to. And tomorrow he'll by away with all his beauty and valour, which I would increase if I could." Eventually, however, with her scruples overcome, she leaves her bed to go

> Au chevalier qui se dormoit
> Ne de rien a li ne pensoit
> Ne ne savoit que est amors.
> Onques n'en ot eü dolors.
>
> [1885-8]

[to the knight who was asleep with no thought of her and no knowledge of love. He had never suffered its pains.]

Galiene, then, has reverted to her Blancheflor role, and we wait for Fergus to bring her solace by drawing her into his bed. Not at all! Certainly, when she raises the sheets to place her hand on his breast and he wakes to look into her tear-stained face, his first reaction is to draw her a little towards him, but only to ask what she wants. To her elegant talk of her heart, now lost to him but which she would wish returned, he bluffly disclaims all knowledge of it and says that, were it in his possession, he would have no desire to keep it. Galiene, undeterred, makes her final avowal:

> "En vostre main (ne doutés mie!)
> Tenés et ma mort et ma vie."
> Fergus li respont en riant:
> "Pucele, je vois el querrant
> Que amors ne que druerie.
> J'ai une bataille aatie,
> Que jou vaurai avant parfaire.
> Mais quant je venrai el repaire,
> Se je en puis vis escaper,
> Par chi m'en vaurai retorner.
> Adonques, se vos bien volés,
> Ma druerie et m'amistés
> Sera vostre sans contredit."
>
> [1949-61]

["Have no doubt that in your hand you hold my death and my life." With a laugh, Fergus replies to her: "Maiden, my quest is for something other than love and wooing. First I wish to carry out a contest I am

intent on. But on my return, if I get out of it alive, I will come back this
way. Then, if you wish, you shall certainly have my love and affection."]

Galiene's first reaction to this barely mitigated rebuff is to swoon; her
second is to repair to her bed, swearing to have nothing more to do with
love. Yet this brings no consolation:

> Une eure dist que s'ocirra,
> Si serra sa dolors finie.
> Une autre dist, nel fera mie:
> Car ele feroit grant outrage.
> Onques feme de son lingnage
> Ne s'ocist onques por amor.

[1990–5]

[At one moment she said she would kill herself and put an end to her
grief. At another she said she would not, for that would be an outrageous act. Never had any women of her family killed herself for love.]

So in the end she decides go back to her father in Lothian and forget
about it all. In the morning, when Fergus takes his leave, she lowers her
head and finds it hard to speak to him. Courtly love, it seems, has come
off second best to family pride and plain common sense. Amusing in
itself, the episode shows more subtle undercurrents of humour when we
match it against its source.

With an assurance to his host that he will return that way "if no
other adventure detain him," Fergus makes his way to the Noire Montagne, at which point we seem to leave the real world for a landscape of
fantasy: the precipitous path to La Nouquetran, once Merlin's home,
had been constructed by a giant; the view from the summit encompasses
"la mer d'Illande . . . Engleterre et Cornuaille" (ll. 2110–11); faced with a
painful ascent on foot, Fergus tethers his horse to the world's finest olive
tree. Now Guillaume proceeds to tease both us and his hero, exciting our
apprehension then dispelling it (promptly for us, only after some embarrassment for Fergus), craftily undermining what we had looked forward
to as a supreme heroic exploit. Of the lion Fergus expects to find at La
Nouquetran he sees no trace: in fact it is in a marble chapel with doors of
gilded ivory guarded by a hideous giant armed with a mallet. But the
giant is motionless, being, we are told, of bronze, whilst the lion from
whose neck hang the horn and wimple is carved from ivory. Fergus, however, thinks the giant alive and asks him politely and repeatedly how he
may find the lion. On receiving no reply, he hurls a rock at the figure,
shattering both its arms, then launches an assault with his sword. Only
then does he realise it is inanimate, and in his shame hopes no word of his
mistake ever reaches Arthur's court. He seizes the horn and wimple without

opposition; but when he sets the whole countryside ringing with three great blasts on the former (another wry reminiscence of Roland?), the folk who hear say he would have done better just to filch it quietly. Thus the whole episode is a masterpiece of ironically deceived expectations, a further example of a technique plainly dear to Guillaume, and exploited before him by Chrétien (as, for instance, in Lancelot's use of his magic ring to dispel or reveal the absence of enchantment).

The horn-call has alerted the Black Knight, who has nothing white about him save his teeth; so when Fergus returns with his trophies to his steed, he has to face the fury of this, Arthur's most deadly enemy. Guillaume's description of the combat is conventionally epic and almost ritualistic in style, but given individuality by the invective the two level at each other. This is the type of salty, bloodthirsty dialogue in which Guillaume revels, eagerly displaying his gifts as an expert and witty manipulator of the spoken word: there is something almost Voltairian in his taste for the cutting ironic shaft. Having defeated his opponent, Fergus packs him off to surrender to Arthur, bearing with him the horn and wimple and a few caustic words for Kay.

That same day, having sought and failed to find further adventures, he decides to comply with his host's request and return to Lidel: we are not told here that any thought of Galiene was in his mind. Guillaume appears to be still treating the love relationship as a no doubt interesting, but inconsequential affair: the change when it comes is melodramatic. Fergus finds the castle's inhabitants plunged into deep gloom at the sudden disappearance of Galiene, who had vanished without a word to her uncle while he was setting the hero that morning on the road to the Noire Montagne. The grieving man does not know where to seek her — in Ireland, England, Scotland, or Lothian; but he puts on a brave face and asks Fergus how he has fared that day. His questions, however, are put in vain, for now Fergus in turn is sunk in despair as his lost *amie* alone occupies his thoughts. Rather than engaging our sympathy for the young knight, this sudden reversal of his attitude leaves us wondering what we are to make of the delayed *coup de foudre*. We have already come to know Fergus' impetuous nature and the spontaneity of his emotions, but is there not deliberate humour in the presentation here of his extravagant reaction to the loss of Galiene? Not for the first time, Guillaume has unsettled us; but it will soon become evident that this change of direction is closely associated with, perhaps even occasioned by, his turning now to *Yvain* as his leading source of inspiration: there as here the hero, having neglected love for chivalric prowess, is precipitated into a state of distress and mental confusion by the sudden assertion of love's claim. We may be tempted to read into Guillaume's account (as earlier with the knighting episode) some elements of personal commentary on Chrétien's text.

The circumstances of Yvain's crisis are well known: after his rejection by Laudine, he lost his wits in a severe bout of *folie amoureuse*; wandering like a wild man, he was found and restored to physical health, narrowly avoiding a relapse when chance led him back to his lady's fountain. This is the narrative scheme that Guillaume proceeds to adapt, not without some use of the "reversal technique" already noticed.

Fergus' affliction is as sudden as Yvain's. It is first indicated in his somewhat obtuse reaction to his host's account of Galiene's departure he knows not where:

> Fergus, qui pensoit a s'amie
> Tant que perdu ot son espoir,
> "Sire, por Diu, dites me voir
> Se la pucele o le cler vis
> Est issue de cest païs,
> Si ne savés u ne quel part?"
>
> [2599–2604]

[Fergus, whose thoughts were so set on his beloved that hope had left him, (said): "Sir, in God's name, tell me truly if the bright-faced maiden has left this land without your knowing where or in what direction."]

Fergus, however, does not lose his senses as entirely as had Yvain. True, he does not know whether it is day or night, whether it is fine or raining. Vanquished by love as he now is, his mind turns solely on Galiene, so that he talks only at cross-purposes with his host when questioned on the day's adventure. He launches into a 68-line lament nicely balancing Galiene's earlier 65-line soliloquy and matching it too in that both invoke family reasons in seeking to justify resistance to love. Fergus reflects that his father never indulged in the folly of such love: why then should he?

> "Dius, quel eschar, qui me vel metre
> El renc de cels qui nuit et jor
> Por saudees servent Amor!
> Et je por coi ne m'i metroie?
> Car je mius ore en vaudroie.
> Por choi? por ço qu'el mien espoir
> Doi je bien bele amie avoir."
>
> [2685–91]

["God, how ridiculous I am to want to join the ranks of those who night and day serve as Love's mercenaries! And why should I not join them? For in doing so I would increase my worth. Why? Because it seems to me I should indeed have a beautiful mistress."]

Like Galiene, he remains able to consider the situation rationally, though in his case he opts for love and, ignoring the example of his *vilain* father, consciously casts himself in the role of the *fin amant* of courtly tradition. His host, though, expresses disapproval:

> . . . "Sire, ne vos estuet
> Tel dol mener, se vos volés,
> Ne n'est drois que vos dementés.
> N'apartient pas a chevalier,
> Por pucele ne por moillier
> Doie ja faire itel sanblant
> Que on nel tiengne por enfant.
> Vos le devés laissier ester.
> A moi pertient li dementer,
> A moi pertient li dolors faire:
> Mais vos de ce n'avés que faire."
>
> [2747–57]

["Sir, if it please you, you should not show such grief: it is not right to vent your anguish. It is not proper for a knight to make such a fuss over a girl or a woman, lest he be thought childish. You should have done with this. The anguish is my affair, and it is my affair to grieve: but this is not for you."]

The host's attitude may be thought merely to reflect the generation gap, or else to illustrate one contemporary opinion of the falseness of courtly love. The fact that Fergus does not take the advice may not necessarily correspond to the poet's own feelings: we are left free once again to question the whole concept and acceptability of *fin amor*, and in particular of the lover's total self-surrender to the power of love. Was Fergus right deliberately to choose this course? Or, thinking back to Chrétien, had Yvain shown culpable weakness in his *folie amoureuse*?

That Guillaume, in advertising more than dissembling his debts, wished us to make such mental reference to Chrétien seems ever more likely. As with effective parody, we are given the opportunity to catch in the discrepancy between model and imitation something of the author's personal voice. So by this stage in the romance alert and informed readers or hearers might have their attention divided between the lively narrative and a presumed undercurrent of authorial comment that is not necessarily sequential, but may consist simply of casual reflections on Chrétien's stories or on the conventions and ideals they embody.

Fergus, then, leaves Lidel without delay; and for the rest of the work we follow him in his single-minded quest for Galiene. Riding pensively that night, he comes across a belligerent and hideous dwarf standing guard over a tent in which sleep a knight and his *amie*. Provoked by the dwarf, he drubs him soundly, and the fellow's cries waken the sleeping couple. The upshot is a combat enlivened as usual by sharp verbal exchanges and ending with knight, dwarf, and *amie* being despatched to Arthur's court; but it is engaged only after Fergus has offered to defend his case at law. This is not the only occasion on which Guillaume betrays legal interests that tend to lower the courtly tone to a more matter-of-fact level. Indeed, the very next incident involves a dispute over the payment of toll to a robber, who ends up with a shattered arm, lying flat in a bog, and promising in his turn to report to King Arthur. In both these combat descriptions Guillaume further indulges his taste for the grotesque, the dwarf's master having been half scalped by a sword-cut.

Between his bouts of activity, Fergus has been wandering as his horse took him, plunged into gloomy thoughts of his love. But, not having eaten for two days,

> Or li fait li fains oblier
> Le grant cuire de son penser
> Qu'il avoit vers s'amie chiere.
>
> [3240-2]

[now hunger makes him forget the deep care that filled his thoughts for his dear love.]

Chancing upon fifteen robber knights sitting at an alfresco meal in a forest bower, he partakes uninvited of their feast, then, when they cause trouble, kills one with a spit still charged with its capons, and puts all but two of the others to the sword. The survivors, of course, are sent to the court. That evening, wearied, we are told, by his travels and by bearing arms (not, it seems, by his combats), he falls asleep beneath a pine.

The scene switches to the court, where Arthur is holding a council to seek advice on what to do about his foe the Black Knight. Kay is ready with more sarcasm at Fergus' expense and is wittily rebuked by Gauvain, when suddenly the knight in question arrives with message, horn and wimple, to be closely followed by the others Fergus has defeated. Gauvain's recommendation of mercy for the captives is adopted by the King, whom we leave lamenting the loss of the young hero. The latter is now back in the saddle, engulfed once more in his grief for Galiene. In this state he remains a full year, his clothes falling into tatters, eating raw what game he could catch, thin as his horse, his hair long and untended.

This section of the romance, so evidently inspired by *Yvain,* is lively in the telling and contains more hints of irony, incongruity, and mild comedy that call into question Guillaume's serious intentions and commitment to the fate of a young man whose empty stomach makes him forget for a time his broken heart. The humour excuses (indeed partly springs from and may justify) Fergus' too mechanical behaviour: he is treated with a smiling indulgence not unlike that shown to his hero by the author of *Aucassin et Nicolette*—though the *chantefable,* of which certain features hereabouts strongly remind us, would have been unknown to, and so no source of distraction for, Guillaume's contemporaries. Nevertheless, the more reflective among them might by now have found their attention frequently wandering from the characters and plot to the enigmatic strategy of this quirkish poet.

Fergus' rovings bring him to a fine woodland in which is a beautiful fountain that provides health and happiness for those who drink. Fortune, we are assured, has led him there; for after his tribulations he is to be raised to the very heights. A draught of its water at once replaces his care with joy, whilst a dwarf, who appears from a nearby chapel and has prophetic gifts, greets him by name to tell him that with courage he will recover Galiene. First, though, he must go to Dunostre (Dunnottar) and win the shining shield from the hairy hag ("la vielle moussue" l. 3738) who guards it. Fergus declares he could wish for nothing more:

> "Se Dames Dius par son plaisir
> Me voloit aveuc li posser
> Et tos mes mesfais pardonner
> Que je onques vers lui mespris,
> Se Galiene o le cler vis
> Fust en infer en tenebror,
> S'iroie je: por soie amor
> Lairoie paradis la sus
> Por venir aveuc li ça jus
> Sofrir mal et painne et torment
> Dusques au grant forsjugement."

[3763-73]

> ["If the Lord God were pleased to take me to Himself and pardon all the misdeeds I ever committed against Him, and if bright-faced Galiene were in the darkness of Hell, there would I go: for love of her I would leave Paradise above to join her down below and suffer ill, hardship and torment until the great Judgment Day."]

We recognise from *Yvain* the marvellous fountain with its neighbouring chapel, but crossed here, it seems, with the fountain of life or rejuvenation; and for Fergus it brings not bitter memories and renewed grief, as in Chrétien, but forgetfulness of care and, through its attendant dwarf, the assurance of ultimate success in his quest (we have seen before Guillaume's use of *praemonitio,* more characteristic of epic than romance). The key to Fergus' success will lie in his obtaining a radiant talisman which, he learns, has protective powers. It is tempting to see in this shield Guillaume's substitution for Chrétien's Grail. He had characterised Perceval at the beginning of his romance as the knight "Qui tant pena por le graal" (l. 14); now Fergus is told of the great hardship he must undergo in his quest for the wondrous shield before he can be reunited with Galiene (Guillaume's Blancheflor surrogate). If we accept the analogy, it is the more amusing to find the object in the care not of a beautiful maiden but of an old hag wielding a scythe — an extreme example, perhaps, of Guillaume's "reversal technique." It may also be of significance that Fergus specifically questions the dwarf about the shield's nature, in contrast to Perceval's silence on the subject of the Grail. As for Fergus' irreverent reflections on Heaven and Hell, we find here another thought-provoking parallel to the *chantefable,* where Aucassin makes a similar declaration.

Fergus rides from the fountain:

> Tot son pensé et son corage
> A torné a chevalerie.
> Et nequedent pas n'i oblie
> S'amie la gente, la sage.
> Amors un poi le rasouage,
> Et saciés bien qu'il aimme asés.
> Or est ses travaus atenprés
> Por ce qu'il set qu'ele n'est morte.
> Bonne esperance le conforte
> Et li nains qui dit li avoit
> Que par l'escu recouverroit
> Cele que tant ot desiree.
>
> [3879-90]

[He has turned his whole thought and will to chivalry. And yet in that he does not forget his noble and wise beloved. Love brings him some consolation, and you may be sure his love is great. Now his anguish is tempered, since he knows she is not dead. He is comforted by firm hope and by the dwarf's assurance that through the shield he would recover her whom he had so desired.]

In *Yvain* and indeed *Erec et Enide* Chrétien had posed the problem of the conflicting claims of love and chivalry. Here, Guillaume takes the opportunity to tell us that his hero has now struck the proper balance, thus dispelling any doubts we may have had on this score. Fergus' *travaus,* moreover, is mitigated by the knowledge that he will recover Galiene: Yvain, in contrast, had affirmed that only when his lady restored her goodwill, "Lors finera mes travauz toz" (*Yvain* l. 4592).[15] So Guillaume is continuing to impress on us the fact that Fergus will achieve his goal, implying that our entertainment will derive more from authorial virtuosity than from suspense.

We are past the mid-point of the romance, and now it gathers pace, with fresh adventures and incidents following thick and fast, but with the poet's quizzical bent still much in evidence. There is irony in the fact that on his way to Dunnottar Fergus passes through Lothian without knowing that his *amie* is now lady of that land (her father, having died, as we learn later). By way of the Castiel as Puceles (Edinburgh) he proceeds to the Port la Roïne (Queensferry), where the sea (i.e. the Firth of Forth) divides Lothian from Scotland (the name "Escoche," l. 3918, designating the northern part of present-day Scotland). Taking ship to make the crossing, he falls foul of the rascally crew but gets the better of them in a lively affray, lands below the Saracen (!) castle of Dunfermline, and rides where Fortune leads until, after more than two months, he spies a tower and the marvellous radiance that comes from the shield. On the bridge to the castle the hag awaits him, hissing and scowling beneath her shaggy mane, her scythe at the ready. After a brisk and bloody encounter, which the old woman does not survive, Fergus discovers in a courtyard the shield hanging from a marble pillar and guarded by a dragon bigger than that slain by Tristan. This too he kills before leaving with the shield, which he fits to his arm again and again with endearingly childish delight. There is no dialogue with these combats, but a good deal of black humour in their grisly detail. For example, the hag having embedded her scythe in a pillar, Fergus severs her hands before dealing the death-blow; and when he goes to take the shield, he fails to notice the dragon until he steps on a beam where it is sleeping and which strikes it on the ear; in its turn the beast knocks Fergus against the pillar with its tail, but, surprised to see his own blood flowing, he summons his strength and beheads it. With grotesque details like these Guillaume spices, almost to the point of travesty, typical romance situations and conventions; and his hero is still, now and then, made the butt of a humour innocent of malice but informed by a slightly perverse imagination.

Fergus leaves Dunnottar and sails in a leather-merchant's ship to Queensferry, with realism in the telling replacing the grotesque fantasy of the previous episode. From a conventional meeting with three shepherds he learns that Galiene is besieged in Roxburgh by a powerful king and in a desperate plight (the parallel with Blancheflor under siege in Belrepeire is thus re-established and will be reinforced later, as when we are told that the king aspires to the lady as well as the land). Bent on her rescue, he takes a wrong road to the Mont Dolerous at Maros (Melrose) where, on the bridge before the castle, he finds the dead hag's gigantic husband wielding a massive club. With heavy irony, Guillaume has warned that "Au fel gaiant parler l'estuet" ("He must speak with the wicked giant" l. 4443). Words are indeed bandied in the poet's usual wittily sarcastic vein; and they herald epic blows, one of which kills Fergus' horse; but the *coup de grâce* is delivered by the hero's sword as the already maimed giant pins him under his arm, thinking to hurl him into a torrent. There follows a domestic interlude that adds to the variety. In the castle Fergus finds the giant's son being massaged by two newly captive maidens. He makes short work of this "son of the foul devil," then discovers and breaks in a mettlesome horse to replace his own before submitting to the tender care of the damsels, who heal his wounds and restore him to fitness in three days.

The stage is set for the final extended act, the events of which can be briefly told. At Melrose Fergus spies from a window Roxburgh under siege. He arms and rides to the rescue. Skirmishing incognito with the besiegers, he slays the royal seneschal, unhorses the king's nephew Artofilas and sends the steed to Galiene with the compliments of the Knight of the Shining Shield, before returning secretly to Melrose. A week of such forays persuades the aggressor king to seek advice from his council of barons. Artofilas proposes an ultimatum: the surrender of both Lothian and its lady as the price of peace. Artofilas himself delivers the terms to Galiene and offers to settle the issue by fighting a duel with her champion, whereupon she rashly declares that in eight days she will find a knight to challenge two of them. When none of her own men is willing to undertake the contest, she regrets her offer; but her attendant Arondele volunteers to seek out the anonymous knight, or else one of King Arthur's company. However, finding Arthur's court dispersed in search of Fergus, she heads back for Roxburgh by way of Melrose. There, without recognising him, she confides in Fergus, who asks if her mistress has no lover to champion her. — Only he with whom she fell in love at Lidel, says Arondele. After some obliquely reassuring words from Fergus, she returns to her despairing lady. Seeing Artofilas and his uncle arrive for the duel, Galiene is about to cast herself down from her highest tower, when a mysterious voice bids her look towards the woods. They seem to blaze with the brilliance of the approaching hero's shield. Soon Artofilas is slain; and Fergus, forcing the king to submit, directs him to make peace with Galiene and greet her in veiled terms on his behalf before giving himself up to Arthur. Galiene now realises the identity of her saviour.

The king is pardoned by Arthur who then, on Gauvain's advice, proclaims a tournament to be held at Gedeorde (Jedburgh), with the winner to take a wife of his choosing. This, they hope, will attract Fergus to court. Galiene hears the news and, with her men's approval, decides to travel to Jedburgh, where she may find "celui o le biel escu" (ll. 6341-2). Sure enough, Fergus comes to the tourney, but incognito. On the first day he utterly humiliates Kay and defeats Lancelot and various others. On the second, he overcomes Saigremor and, with some reluctance, Perceval (this is significant in that his superiority over his *alter ego* is demonstrated in physical terms by Guillaume). All week he triumphs. After the arrival of Galiene, who declares she will only wed the Knight with the Fair Shield, Gauvain undertakes to encounter the victor of the previous days and attempt to persuade him to present himself to Arthur. The plan works, and the lovers are reunited. Arthur makes over to Fergus Galiene, Lothian, and, for good measure, Tudiele (Tweeddale). Fergus sends to Melrose for the two damsels who had tended him there, and his marriage to Galiene is celebrated at Roxburgh, where they are crowned to rule as king and queen and enjoy their *fin amor*. No man knows more of their story, says Guillaume — and may it bring joy to those who hear it!

A bald summary gives little idea of the quality of the narrative. It is zestful and well articulated, full of nicely varied incident, exploiting cleverly the opportunities for irony provided by Fergus' incognito and his presence within sight of Roxburgh while he is being sought throughout the realm of Arthur, who can himself offer no succour to Galiene, since his knights are absent on the same quest. Certain motifs recur to stitch the tale together, most prominent being the continuing perversity of Kay and Fergus' determination to obtain a revenge, which, when it comes, is comically complete.

There is variety both in the alternation of contrasting scenes and in their detail. Personal touches reinvigorate the conventional: on the battlefield a friendly man-at-arms, from whom Fergus borrows a lance and by whom he sends the captured steed to Galiene; the aggressor king surprised by the hero in his attempt to carry his nephew's corpse from the field; Arthur sleepily whittling a stick and not eating with the others as he laments the loss of Fergus. Sometimes Guillaume adds a spice of mystery, as when Arondele says that, though born in the region, she had never known of the castle at Melrose, or when an unidentified voice calls Galiene back from the brink of suicide. (He often hints through authorial comment or the dialogue, particularly in the latter part of the romance, that divine providence is at work attending to the happy outcome of events.) Occasionally, too, he leavens the narrative with moments of quite delicate lyricism. There is the conventional *reverdie* element introduced when we return to Arthur's court: it was May-time, when woods and meadows grow green, and each true lover sings new songs and ditties for his beloved. Of a more individual cast is Galiene's lament for the long-lost Fergus: she does not know whether he is alive or dead — but were he dead, the sun would have lost a third of its brilliance; and he is so handsome that should he ever wear sackcloth and she fine silks, his beauty would seem a hundred times greater than hers, his face bright as a rose on May-morning.

One passage that associates the supernatural, lyricism, surreptitious humour, and a dash of that realism frequently injected by Guillaume is the account of Galiene's near-suicide. She has climbed to the top of her tower:

> D'ilueques esgardoit son salt.
> Entor li estraint durement
> Ses dras, qu'ele veut vraiement
> Que li vens ne s'i enbatist
> Ne que il le contretenist.
>
> [5718-22]

[From there she measured her leap. She gathers her clothes tightly about her, determined that they should not be caught by the wind and the jump impeded.]

Commending Fergus to God, she crosses herself and puts her head through the window.

> Mais Dius ne le vaut endurer
> Que illuec une ame perdist.
>
> [5740-1]

[But God will not suffer a soul to be lost there.]

When a mysterious voice tells her to look to the woods and she sees them afire with the exceptional brilliance of the shield, Guillaume explains: that morning a moderate dew moistened the shield, which had the property that when it was wet, its paintwork reflected the sun's rays with added intensity. So the reader is carried along, with the fantastic made to seem almost plausible through the precision of the detail Guillaume supplies — with a sly wink, perhaps.

Humour, though a major feature of the romance, is not so constantly obvious that we may not sometimes be left trying to read the poet's mind or catch the ironic curl of his lips. A favourite outlet for it is when a physical clash between opponents allows a mixture of situational comedy and verbal thrust and parry. The duel between Fergus and Kay gave Guillaume an opportunity he did not waste. At the tournament Kay, as in *Yvain,* demands the first joust. Fergus loses no time in sending him flying, head first like an acrobat, into a muddy brook, where his helmet sticks into the ground. Fergus jeers that he is ill-mannered to fish in his river without permission. Still, the King will have plenty of fish to eat—how lucky for him to have such a fine steward! But Kay must be keen on his sport to have made a net of his coat of mail so that no eels could get through. He must not clean the river out, though, or there will be nothing for anyone else to catch. The hero goes off, rocking with laughter, leaving others to extract the seneschal from the mire. On this occasion, Kay is speechless.

Guillaume shares out his gift for barbed repartee among several of his characters. Even the golden-tongued Gauvain had found sarcastic words to level against Kay, and been reproved by Arthur for it. Yet there is no real pettiness in the character of the King's nephew, who is presented throughout the romance as the ideal representative of chivalry: he is a wise counsellor to Arthur, *courtois,* frank, open-hearted, loyal, and courageous. We are told that Fergus became the best knight ever, but for Gauvain, who never had his peer; and by the end the two are staunch companions. There is no hint here of that rather irresponsible flirtatiousness we already glimpse in Chrétien. So if one is looking for an exemplary element in the work, one finds it most unambiguously in this consistently admirable portrait—a fact that must shed doubt on the notion that Guillaume was a democrat before his time,[16] unless even Gauvain is to be taken with a pinch of salt.

Less conventional is the picture we have of Galiene. In her declaration of love, then her sudden disappearance from Lidel, Guillaume has already shown her impulsive nature. She is no different when we see her under the stress of the siege at Roxburgh. Faced by Artofilas with his ultimatum, she puts on a bold face and, treating him as a drunkard, bandies sharp words with him before declaring her intention to find a champion. But once he has left, she repents her rashness and turns to her knights to see if any will act as her champion, for money or out of patriotism. There are no volunteers; and one of them even accuses her of acting without their counsel. Eventually, in despair, she says she will give her wealth and herself to any man who will defend her. Later, when she has been rescued and hears of the tournament at Jedburgh, she does call her council to advise her on marriage, though we are assured she would have gone to court anyway (reminding us of Laudine's intention to wed in *Yvain*). There is some depth to this portrayal of Galiene, whom we get to know rather better than her main prototype, Blancheflor. She is fiercely proud and headstrong, passionate, yet recognising in rational moments her own fallibility (she should have waited at Lidel for Fergus to return; her offer to Artofilas was misguided); and this fallibility is underlined by Guillaume to the point where our earlier suspicions of his mildly misogynistic attitude are reawakened.

Galiene's *folie* is used as a minor leitmotif in the Roxburgh episode. On her rejection of the ultimatum, Artofilas rails against her and her sex:

> "Pucele, ne m'en mervel mie:
> Feme estes, si dites folie.
> Et por ce pas ne m'en mervel,
> S'avés respondu sans consel.
> Feme estes et feme soiés."
>
> [5220-4]

["Maiden, I am not at all surprised: you are a woman and talk nonsense. And that is why I am not surprised that you have given an unadvised answer. You are a woman, and a woman you must be."]

To this, says Guillaume, she responded with boastful temerity and "grant folie" (l. 5235) in making her offer to find a champion. Indeed, Artofilas' departure leaves her dejected and pensive, regretting now that she had proposed the combat "Par son mal sens, par sa folie" (l. 5275). When she seeks help from her men, she is told by a spokesman that they are not responsible for her "faus dis" (l. 5288): she has made her bed and must lie in it, and "Sens vaut molt mius que estoutie" ("Good sense is worth far more than rash temerity" l. 5293 – a possible reminiscence of *Roland* ll. 1724-5). The idea of feminine inadequacy is expressed later by Galiene herself: firstly when she tells her council that she intends to marry, since she cannot govern her land any longer without a man's help, and secondly when she explains to King Arthur her need for protection since the death of her father, for

> "Mauvaissement est gouvernee
> Terre que a feme repaire.'"
>
> [6648-9]

["A land left to a woman is badly governed."]

Not only does Guillaume in this way directly question the good sense and competence of women, but towards the end of his romance he even takes a step towards "de-glamourising" them through the person of Galiene. Surprisingly, if with becoming modesty, she herself declares Fergus' beauty to outshine hers a hundredfold. Then, when Fergus sheds his incognito, he becomes the main centre of attention at her expense. He and Gauvain embrace and kiss for as long as one would take to walk four bowshots (and this in Galiene's presence); then hand in hand they go to the King, to whom Gauvain presents the young knight as "Mon cier conpaignon et mon dru" ("My dear companion and beloved friend" l. 6807) even before asking Fergus for his love and companionship. Arthur in turn welcomes Fergus with kisses, and only then draws him aside with Gauvain and Galiene to ask if he will accept the lady and her land. With more politeness than evident enthusiasm, he accepts her and she him if that be Arthur's wish. In commenting on the reunited couple, Guillaume observes that if Fergus loves Galiene, she loves him three times as much. After "les noces Fergus" ("Fergus' wedding" l. 6950), when Arthur is about to leave with his company, the hero and Gauvain are seen lavishing on each other more kisses and embraces. Thus, in the concluding scenes, the mutual affection of the two knights is given more prominence than that between Fergus and Galiene, being not merely stated, but openly demonstrated. Is Guillaume, we wonder, joining in the love versus chivalry debate initiated by Chrétien and hinting that, for him, the chivalric ties are the more important?

For the last time, he awakens specific memories of Chrétien's work, and with disturbing effect. As Gauvain bids Fergus that tender farewell,

> . . . li amoneste et prie
> Que il ne laist chevalerie
> Por sa femme, que n'est pas drois.
> "De pluissors gabés en serois."
> Fergus bien li afie et jure,
> Ja n'ora parler d'adventure
> Qu'il n'i aille, s'il a santé.
> A cest mot se sont desevŕe.
>
> [6961-8]

[he urges and begs him not to abandon chivalry for his wife, for that is not right. "For many you would be a laughing-stock." Fergus swears and fully pledges him that he will never hear of an adventure without seeking it out, given good health. With this, they parted.]

This is a direct reminiscence of Gauvain's ill-fated advice to Yvain, the cause of that knight's betrayal of Laudine and subsequent trials. In the context, it is so gratuitous that we are forced to see in it a teasing authorial comment, beyond which we can only peer enquiringly. The fact that a few lines later Guillaume signs off leaving Fergus and Galiene as rulers and lovers in Roxburgh takes us only to the immediate horizon. A doubt has been mischievously cast over their enduring happiness. Perhaps we are being asked to reassess Chrétien's story, with its too neatly happy ending, and see Yvain as a fool to be shackled in the end (if he was) to his wife and territory at the expense of his chivalry. Has Guillaume, then, finally taken a stand that Chrétien was too undecided — or tactful, or deliberately provocative — to adopt?

However we answer that question, it has become abundantly evident that Guillaume's relationship to Chrétien is not that of a dull plagiarist brazenly flaunting his sources before our eyes. It may be that his main purpose was entertainment rather than sidelong criticism of certain literary or real-life attitudes. The fact remains that his manner of using Chrétien throws mutual light on their romances: we are able to see parts of the master's work through the eyes of Guillaume, a near-contemporary; and in turn we can appreciate how a second-phase romancer could add "depth of field" and intriguing resonances to his own text as an added stimulus to his public's imagination. So we return to the problem of the identity of this public whose familiarity with Chrétien and other literature circulating at the time would give them the key to Guillaume's more subtle effects. In particular, was it insular or Continental?

There is in my view nothing in the romance that points to specific patronage. There is certainly nothing in the presentation of Galloway or its *vilain* ruler Soumilloit that could be found flattering by any person with connections in that direction; and a female benefactor would have been unlikely to appreciate the whiff of anti-feminism we have detected from time to time. Although Lothian is presented in favourable terms and Fergus attains its kingship, there is no obvious reason to read into this any personal commitment on Guillaume's part.

Fergus was composed and, I have suggested, was designed to be appreciated with close reference to Chrétien. Central to Guillaume's scheme was the establishment of his hero as a "neo-Perceval." He too was to aspire to the heights of chivalry from obscure beginnings, and these had to be established from the outset. Perceval le Galois had emerged from "la gaste forest soutainne" ("the wild remote forest," *Conte du Graal* l. 75): where in Britain beyond the margins of the courtly Arthurian world was he to locate his own hero's home? Perhaps he had already decided on his name, Fergus, which would have made the choice of Galloway logical. Alternatively, the idea of the region could have come first, again under the inspiration of Chrétien: we saw in the *Conte du Graal* the reference to Galloway as an evil land inhabited by perverse people, and this reflects its reputation at the time. A more tenuous link with the master is that Perceval's parents hailed from "les Isles de mer" (*Conte du Graal* ll. 419, 425), normallly identified with the Hebrides,[17] of which the historical Somerled claimed the lordship. In any case, on the model of Perceval of Wales, Guillaume chose to tell of a Fergus of Galloway. Such playing with names and identities was a not uncommon technique in his day; and it is interesting to find two other poets using pseudonyms, Paien de Maisières and Sarrasin, coined as antonyms of Chrétien's own name.[18] Guillaume's device probably sprang from a similar antiphrastic turn of thought.

If his inspiration did indeed begin with the identity of the protagonist, it would have followed naturally that his activities should take place in northern Britain. Then, given his taste for realism tempering the fantasy of the story, it is understandable that he should choose to introduce it in the form of real places, if he knew of them. It is unnecessary to assume that such knowledge could have come only from his living in the area. There were large numbers of settlers of French origin in southern Scotland at this period, including many from Flanders and Picardy;[19] and merchants and travellers kept the lines of communication open. Guillaume might himself have paid a visit in the past or, just as plausibly, have found an informant to give enough idea of the geography for his purposes, or even have worked from some written account. The country was far from being a *terra incognita* at the beginning of the thirteenth century, and events there were well chronicled.[20]

Linguistic evidence points to Guillaume's being a Picard; and the bantering, irreverent spirit that permeates his work is found in numerous texts produced during the thirteenth century in that general area. This is no argument against his having resided in Scotland; but the fact that his romance does not seem to have left any mark on insular literature or even, as far as we can tell, to have been known north of the Channel may be more significant. Against this we can set the certainty that it had some circulation on the Continent, since a Middle Dutch version, *Ferguut,* is extant from the fourteenth century. In addition, there is strong evidence that *Fergus* was known to and used by the authors of three French texts from the north-east. That it was one of the sources of *Huon de Bordeaux* is generally recognised.[21] With *Hunbaut*[22] it shares the episode of the hero's purloined meal; and though the direction of the relationship cannot be proved, *Fergus* is likely to be the earlier text. Most intriguing is the probability that it was used quite extensively by the author of *Aucassin et Nicolette,* with which it shares tonal as well as narrative elements, some of which we have noticed.[23] All this places *Fergus* firmly in the literary milieu of the area to the north-east of the Ile-de-France; and since this region saw its dissemination, it must have a strong claim to being its place of composition.

My conclusion, then, is that when Guillaume first presented his hero dressed in the costume, slightly askew, of Perceval le Gallois, he was giving us fair warning that what he offered for our pleasure was a kind of literary masquerade in which we would chance upon old friends in new guises and more or less familiar happenings in a fresh setting. To this end he turned his rather prankish skills, teasing us with his reversals, his false climaxes, even with his mock-serious moments. To realise this is to be on our guard against reading too weighty a purpose into his text: better (as has been my aim in these pages) to note and appreciate his tricks as he plays them than try to fit them all into some more grand design.

Guillaume le Clerc I see above all as a literary man with literary interests, a poet who freely followed his own talents without needing to harness them to the requirements of a patron or wishing to use them in the promotion of any social or political cause. He was no moraliser. As an artist, he built afresh from old materials, but using individual techniques within a broad tradition of irreverent and partly ironic humour. From his lines a quite distinct personality emerges. Paradoxically for a dealer in the fantastic, he was a realist with a legalistic streak that makes sporadic appearances; intelligent and sharp-witted; more conservative than reformist as regards the chivalric function and code of conduct; betraying a hint of what today might pass as "male chauvinism," more typical of the epic genre in which, one suspects, he may well have composed. First and foremost, though, he was a lover of literature and himself a formidable spinner of words with a sound sense of structure and form: a second-phase romancer but a first-rate craftsman. But because of his chosen technique he has lived too long in Chrétien's shadow. It is high time we recognised the significance of his work in the evolving history of the romance and saluted him as one of its most gifted and subtle exponents.

D. D. R. Owen
University of St. Andrews
Scotland

𝔑otes

1. On the whole subject of these post-Chrétien romances see Beate Schmolke-Hasselmann, *Der arthurische Versroman von Chrestien bis Froissart,* Beihefte zur *Zeitschrift für Romanische Philologie,* vol. 177 (Tübingen: Niemeyer; 1980).

2. Guillaume le Clerc, *Le Roman des aventures de Fregus,* ed. Francisque Michel (Edinburgh: Abbotsford Club, 1842); *Fergus,* ed. Ernst Martin (Halle: Buch. des Waisenhauses, 1872). I shall quote from Martin's edition, adding diacritical signs and modifying the punctuation as necessary. A new edition, *The Romance of Fergus,* ed. Wilson Frescoln (Philadelphia: William H. Allen, 1983), appeared when this study was in proof.

3. Schmolke-Hasselmann, *Der arthurische Versroman,* and "Le Roman de *Fergus*: technique narrative et intention politique," *An Arthurian Tapestry: Essays in Memory of Lewis Thorpe,* ed. Kenneth Varty (Glasgow: published on behalf of the International Branch of the Arthurian Society . . . at the French Department of the University of Glasgow, 1981), pp. 342–53.

4. M. Dominica Legge, "Some Notes on the *Roman de Fergus,*" *Transactions of the Dumfriesshire and Galloway Natural History & Antiquarian Society,* 3rd series, 27 (1950), 163–72. See also Margaret Schlauch, "The Historical Background of *Fergus and Galiene,*" *Publications of the Modern Language Society of America* 44 (1929), 360–76; and E. Brugger, "'Pellande,' 'Galvoie,' and 'Arragoce' in the Romance of *Fergus,*" *A Miscellany of Studies in Romance Languages & Literatures Presented to Leon E. Kastner,* ed. Mary Williams & James A. de Rothschild (Cambridge: W. Haffer, 1932), pp. 94–107.

5. Joan Greenberg, "Guillaume le Clerc and Alan of Galloway," *Publications of the Modern Language Society of America* 66 (1951), 524–33.

6. Quotations are from the edition by Wendelin Foerster, *Der Löwenritter (Yvain) von Christian von Troyes* (Halle: Niemeyer, 1887).

7. "Tant est nices et bestïaus" (l. 1299). I quote from the edition by Alfons Hilka, *Der Percevalroman (Li Contes del Graal) von Christian von Troyes* (Halle: Niemeyer, 1932).

8. Much of this has been clearly seen by Beate Schmolke-Hasselmann, *Der arthurische Versroman,* pp. 130 ff.

9. Wendelin Foerster, ed., *Erec und Enide* (Halle: Niemeyer, 1890), ll. 2627–63.

10. Old French *guimple* (as English "wimple") can also mean "pennon"; but there is no evidence to indicate which sense is intended here.

11. Ed. R. C. Johnston and D. D. R. Owen, *Two Old French Gauvain Romances* (Edinburgh: Scottish Academic Press, 1972). See l. 253.

12. *Piramus et Tisbe,* ed. C. de Boer (Paris: classiques français du moyen âge, 1920). See ll. 668 ff.

13. The reading "vis alumé," l. 1046, has been questioned by Leo Jordan, "Zum altfranz. Fergusroman," *Zeitschrift für Romanische Philologie* 43 (1923), 163–4; but if it is allowed, the sense is probably "glowing with love."

14. *Le Chevalier à l'épée,* ed. Johnston & Owen, *Two Old French Gauvain Romances.*

15. "Then my whole *travauz* will be at an end." There has been some debate as to the meaning here of *travauz:* Guillaume's use of the word in a context influenced by his knowledge of Chrétien's text supports the meaning "torment, anguish."

16. This was Leo Jordan's view in "Zum altfranz. Fergusroman," pp. 184–6. It is disputed by Beate Schmolke-Hasselmann, *Der arthurische Versroman,* pp. 136 ff.

17. Cf. G. D. West, *An Index of Proper Names in French Arthurian Verse Romances 1150–1300* (Toronto: University of Toronto Press, 1969), p. 92.

18. See D. D. R. Owen, "Two More Romances by Chrétien de Troyes?," *Romania,* 92 (1971), 246–60.

19. See, e.g., G. W. S. Barrow, *The Anglo-Norman Era in Scottish History* (Oxford: Clarendon Press, 1980).

20. For instance, the *Chronicle of Melrose* (which I am not proposing as a source) contains most of the places named in *Fergus*.

21. See E. Brugger, *"Huon de Bordeaux* and *Fergus," Modern Language Review* 20 (1925), 158–73; *Huon de Bordeaux,* ed. Pierre Ruelle (Bruxelles: Presses universitaires de Bruxelles, 1960), p. 75.

22. *Hunbaut, altfranz. Artusroman des XIII. Jahrhunderts,* ed. Jakob Stürzinger and Hermann Breuer (Dresden: Gedruckt für die Gesellschaft für romanische Literatur, 1914).

23. The case for the influence of *Fergus* on *Aucassin et Nicolette* cannot be argued here; but as evidence, I would adduce a run of parallels, including those mentioned above, as well as the apparent transposition into a prose section of the *chantefable* of a couplet from *Fergus.* See D. D. R. Owen, "Chrétien, *Fergus, Aucassin et Nicolette,* and the Comedy of Reversal," in *Chrétien de Troyes and the Troubadours: Essays in Memory of the Late Leslie Topsfield,* ed. Peter S. Noble and Linda M. Paterson (Cambridge: St. Catharine's College, 1984), pp. 186–94.

3. Beginnings, Middles, and Ends: Some Interpretative Problems in Chretien's Yvain and Its Medieval Adaptations

The purpose of the present chapter is to relate three aspects of medieval poetics to problems of literary interpretation. The three aspects chosen are the exploitation of rhetorical conventions, the use of intertextual reference, and the role of the didacticism inherent in narrative conclusions. Through a comparison of three writers who are treating the same material, the story of Yvain or The Knight of the Lion, I hope to show how they approach these three aspects of their poetic craft in a different spirit and, hence, draw from them different effects. Chrétien de Troyes's romance of *Yvain*[1] in its beginning (prologue and *mise en scène*), middle (the *peripeteia* occasioned by Gauvain's parenetic intervention), and end (the contrived reconciliation of hero and wife) exemplifies the chosen aspects of medieval poetics in a striking and challenging form which, it is hoped, will reveal the exhilarating complexity of medieval narrative art at its best.[2] Further, as the subject of a number of medieval adaptations, the *Yvain* lends itself to a comparative approach through which interpretative problems can be viewed in a medieval perspective. In addition, the study of Chrétien's romance alongside its medieval adaptations brings to the fore a fundamental problem of medieval poetics, namely the relationship between the creative faculty of the individual writer and the authority of his source.[3]

Some interesting ways of looking at the medieval prologue are suggested by the following two passages:

> *De principiis litterarum*: Item notandum quod *exordium* aliquando large sumitur, scilicet illud totum quod antecedit narrationem; aliquando stricte, scilicet proverbium (vel illud quod est in loco proverbii).

Est autem exordium rethoricum principium ad persuadendum. Pro-
emium est preordinacio libri ad instruendum. Prologus est inductivus
sermo subsequentis operis, sive contineat talia prohemialia sive non.
Epigrama est principium continens causam et similitudinem, et modum
agendi demonstrans. Thema est principium divine predicationis. Pre-
facio est principium in divinis cantibus et ministeriis, ut hic: "Exultat
iam angelica turba celorum, etc."[4]

Argumentum est res ficta que licet non fuerit tamen extitisse poterit.
Insinuatio est oratio quedam dissimulatione et circuitione obscura
animum auditoris subiens. Dispositio est rerum inventarum in ordine
distributio. Inventio est rerum verarum aut verisimilium excogitatio.
Exordium est oratio auditores idonee conparans ad aliquam dictionem.[5]

The first passage, from John of Garland's *Parisiana Poetria* (c. 1220?), is
clearly influenced by the school tradition of the *accessus* and indicates a
number of different functions of the prologue. The second passage is
taken from a collection of moral and theological definitions arranged in
the MS under the rubric *Libellus magistri Hugonis Sancti Victoris,*[6] and
demonstrates the overlap of rhetoric and ethics which marked the
reading habits of twelfth-century humanism. We can therefore expect to
find in writers of that period a variety of sophisticated strategies concerning the *entrée en matière*.

I have examined elsewhere the formal structure of the prologue to
Yvain[7] and concluded that Chrétien first (ll. 1–41) employs the technique of *insinuatio*, by which he avoids any direct announcement of the
traditional motives of composition: *auctor, materia, intentio (causa),
utilitas* and *titulus*. He then recoups the loss incurred by this use of *cir-
cuitio* by placing a conventional *captatio benevolentiae* in the mouth of
Calogrenant (ll. 149–74) in whom the exegetical pretensions of such an
exordial device contrast with the naive incomprehension which accompanied the experience he describes. The result is that Chrétien's audience
is apprised of the need to reflect conscientiously on the meaning of what
it hears whilst being deprived of any guiding indications of the work's
theme or *modus agendi*. From the interpretative point of view, therefore,
the rhetoric of the prologue is characterised first of all by obliqueness or
indirection, uniquely amongst Chrétien's prologues and precisely because
Yvain will prove to be a playful subversion of the whole romance genre.
Obliqueness governs access to all the work's major components: the hero
is introduced obliquely through his *cosin germain,* Calogrenant; Laudine
is similarly presented via an *entremetteuse*, Lunete; the chivalric theme
("parcere subiectis et debellare superbos") is mediated by a lion.[8] The
dramatis personae are never announced but, rather, revealed,[9] and it is

difficult to say at what precise point Yvain is first clearly recognised as the hero.

A second characteristic of Chrétien's exordial rhetoric is paradox and irony.[10] Whilst presenting the twin themes of the genre — chivalry (in its moral and military aspects, *preu et cortois*) and love — Chrétien carefully inverts expectations. He is writing in the age of love *par excellence*, yet he argues that in his time *amor* is "mout abeissiee" and "tornee a fable."[11] Concomitantly his claim that Arthur's reign was a Golden Age of love is never justified, for it is *amicitia*, not *amor*, that informs the successful relationships of his romance. The valour and courtesy of the Arthurian past are also promptly queried through the acrimonious dispute which surrounds Calogrenant's report of his ignominious defeat. Indeed, Arthur's authority in the story is never unambiguous. Finally, the *sententia* of ll. 31-2 is an unexpected inversion of the verse of Ecclesiastes "Melior est canis vivus leone mortuo" (9: 4).

A third feature of the romance's opening is its marking of reception by an audience as an integral narrative problem. The initial "expository" adventure is subject to different reactions from an inscribed audience: several knights have assembled to hear Calogrenant's tale (*conte*) "non de s'enor, mes de sa honte" (l. 60). Calogrenant is unwilling to continue with the queen as audience (ll. 119-23), but she is insistent that he narrate his story, even though she apparently takes Kay's enthusiasm for the performance (ll. 125-30) as sarcastic (ll. 131-41). Calogrenant both accedes with the utmost reluctance (ll. 142-8) and at the same time emphasises the importance of "right understanding."[12] This inscribed recitation so completely evokes the *métier* of the romancer that Calogrenant unmistakably adopts the role of courtly narrator: "Car ne vuel pas parler de songe, / Ne de fable ne de mançonge / Don *maint autre* vos ont servi" (ll. 171-3). Even if *maint autre* is intended to refer to knights, the formulation is irresistibly reminiscent of romance *exordia* (cf. *Yvain* ll. 24 & 27!). The effect of Calogrenant's narration is to stir Yvain to action and precipitate an uncourtly dispute, Kay judging Yvain's reaction to be inappropriate. It is certainly clear that Yvain has not received the tale with "right understanding" and later completely misunderstands the nature of Esclados's complaint. Chrétien here encourages in his audience a constructive independence in the midst of the interplay of recitations and reactions.[13] The whole tale is passed to another narrator: " . . . la reïne maintenant / Les noveles Calogrenant / Li [= Arthur] reconta tot mot a mot; / *Que bien et bel conter li sot.* / Li rois les oï volantiers" (ll. 657-61). Why does Chrétien thus begin his romance with a tale-within-a-tale which is begun no fewer than three times? The answer is that he wishes to alert his audience—in this the most sophisticated and problematical of all his romances—to the complexities of reception.[14] He has already exploited obliqueness and irony in his *exordium*, and the *mise en scène* which follows shows him at his most subversive, carefully establishing multiple contrasts with the *exordium*. An ironic hinge—the adversative *mes* of l. 42 (cf. ll. 49, 60)—links the two. The expectations aroused by the *insinuatio* are frustrated: Arthur's status is implicitly withdrawn (*il s'oblia*) with his extraordinary (note the emphatic repetition of *mout* in ll. 42, 44, 45) retiral from the court festivities; talk of love (l. 13) is replaced by Calogrenant's "conte . . . de sa honte" (l. 60); the "buen chevalier esleü" (l. 40) are involved in an unmannerly dispute which scarcely reveals them as *preu et cortois* (cf. Kay's sarcasms at ll. 72, 74, 79, and 80 where precisely these qualities are disputed). In other words, the *mise en scène* specifically effaces those elements which formed the substance of the *insinuatio*: Arthur (ll. 1-7), love (ll. 8-32), Arthur (ll. 33-41).

It is significant that after this dialectical introduction, with all its internal discrepancies, Chrétien should give such prominence, through Calogrenant's preamble and recitation, to the problems of reception and interpretation, problems which challenge the audience's discrimination throughout the romance.[15] It has not, for example, been pointed out that the origin of the *coutume* at Pesme Avanture bears a striking resemblance to the adventure of the knight-errant Calogrenant:

> . . . li rois de l'Isle as Puceles
> Aloit por aprandre noveles
> Par les corz et par les païs,
> S'ala tant come fos naïs . . .
>
>   [5257-60]

Like Calogrenant's quest, it issues in *honte* (cf. ll. 5117, 5133, 5173, 5220, 5264, 5267, 5292): it is not an amusing fiction, *fable* (l. 5272). Above all, it illustrates the complexities of reception (in both the social and literary senses) and interpretation. The hostile reception given to Yvain by the townspeople, which leaves him so indignant (see the closely linked passages ll. 5119-22, 5136-41), has to be *interpreted* for him by "une dame auques d'aage,/Qui mout estoit cortoise et sage" (ll. 5143-4) who explains "por mal ne te dïent/Nule chose, einçois te chastïent" (ll. 5145-6). As Calogrenant emphasised *de cuer antandre*, so now Yvain is guided by his heart to judge the ambiguity (ll. 5168-74) of the situation:

> Mes mes fos (Guiot: fins) *cuers* leanz me tire,
> Si ferai ce, que *mes cuers* viaut.
>
>   [5176-7]

The ambiguity of the *coutume* is brought home again by the sight of the three hundred silk weavers:

> Oevres font, qui *mout m'abelissent,*
> Mes ce me *desabelist mout,*
> Qu'eles sont de cors et de vout
> Megres et pales et dolantes.
>
> [5230-33]

Again, Yvain has need of an interpreter (ll. 5250 ff.) who shows that the *coutume* really enshrines a chivalric adventure—in two senses: it was the knight-errantry of the "rois de l'Isle as Puceles" which created it, and it is chivalric valour which alone will dispel it (ll. 5288 ff.) and secure the *delivrance* of the silk workers. Just as we sense that we have here a thematic strand of chivalric romance inscribed within a romance adventure, Chrétien introduces the vignette of the young girl in the garden reading to her parents "un romanz, ne sai de cui" (l. 5366),[16] an episode which is decisively associated with Chrétien's present romance and its prologue by the renewed complaint about audiences' lack of interest in love (ll. 5393-6). The spatial movements of the hero at Pesme Avanture, from his entry through the gateway (ll. 5178 ff.) to contemplation of the *prael clos* (l. 5191 —no *hortus conclusus* this!), his passage through the *grant sale haute et nueve* (ll. 5190, 5347), and his arrival in *un vergier,* during which he is both granted (ll. 5142 ff., 5250 ff.) and denied (ll. 5237-8) the help of an "interpreter," these movements may be read as metaphorical indications of the problems of reception and interpretation posed by Chrétien's whole romance.[17] It is noteworthy that the narrator himself declines to solve these problems, just as Chrétien does:

> *Je ne sai,* se il le deçoivent,
> Mes a grant joie le reçoivent
> Et font sanblant, que il lor pleise,
> Que herbergiez soit a grant eise.
>
> [5407-10]

As in the prologue, there is a play on *coster,* here in connection with the young girl's attendance on the hero:

> Si li vest et ses braz li cost,
> Or doint Des, que trop ne li cost
> Ceste losange et cist servise!
>
> [5423-5]

As a final touch to the complexity of this episode and its literary and linguistic analogies we discover that what seemed to be a purely military challenge involving the knight's willingness to fight has an amatory concomitant (ll. 5486 ff.): if victorious, the knight must accept the hand of the young daughter of the lord of the castle. This is a neat allusion to the chivalry topos,[18] which is at the heart of the chivalric romance, but which is, I believe, deliberately dismantled in *Yvain*—here, at any rate, the lord of the castle's "solution" is rejected. When we discuss the conclusion of the work we shall see that the true beneficiaries of the reconciliation are the people of Laudine's castle: so here, it is the silk workers who gain from Yvain's intervention. Chivalric activity is *not* placed in the service of love! The host's final reaction (ll. 5756-70) is as unsympathetic as Laudine's final submission—a graceless acceptance of what cannot be altered! Love and chivalry do not concur!

Chrétien's introduction to *Yvain* thus sets the tone for the whole romance: it is oblique, ironic, and, above all, auto-reflective.[19] Love, chivalry *and their mediation* in a sophisticated (because school-inspired) romance narrative mode form the subject of the work. The romance has become auto-reflective, examining its own methods and presuppositions and making interpretation an integral part of its thematic design.

That the introduction is intimately connected with the meaning of the romance as a whole is further illustrated by the consistently divergent path taken by Chrétien's adaptor, Hartmann von Aue, whose *Iwein* was produced within twenty-five years of its model.[20] Hartmann substitutes for Chrétien's obliqueness and irony the same directness and clarity which characterise his treatment of the main narrative. It is likely that he could not presuppose in his audience a knowledge of romance other than that gained from his own *Erek* (the prologue of which is unfortunately lost) and that the ironising, self-referential opening of the *Yvain* would have so perplexed his listeners as to be counterproductive. Hartmann therefore recasts the whole introduction, approaching his audience "perspicue et protinus" (Cicero, *De invent.* 1. 15. 20) in a *principium* the explicit articulation of which contrasts with the ambiguities of Chrétien's *insinuatio*. Whilst the purpose of the latter is to undermine the security of the audience and impose at once the necessity for an independent, interpretative stance, Hartmann's prologue establishes a safe relationship with his audience in which listener, author, and subject-matter are linked in a programme based on the *dulce et utile*. The consolidation of this relationship is effected in a clear tripartite structure: *sententia* (ll. 1-3), *exemplum* (ll. 4-20), *titulus* (ll. 21-30). The prologue has become essentially a *commendatio* of Arthur, who is held up to admiration for his pursuit of chivalric honour: "der mit rîters muote / nâch lobe kunde strîten" (ll. 6-7); he bore, and his name still bears, "der êren krône" (l. 10); "er hât den lop erworben" (l. 15), and whoever follows his example "ist lasterlîcher schame/iemer vil gar erwert" (ll. 18-19).[21] There is no appearance of irony, and the prologue acts as a clear advertisement of a genre, Arthurian romance, in a way that becomes characteristic of the thirteenth-century romances.[22] The poet defends his subject-matter as an appropriate vehicle for the investigation of chivalric honour and the qualities (*rehte güete*) which it calls forth. The age of Arthur provides a suitable framework for the exploration of knighthood. Hartmann sets off the praise of Arthur at the beginning of his work because he is *not* concerned to reproduce Chrétien's ironic juxtapositions and to subvert the apparent qualities of Arthur's court.[23] He at once attenuates Chrétien's contrasts. The ideality of the court is elaborated without the negative contrast with more recent times. The *wunschleben* (l. 44) is accepted without denigration of the present and the hyperbole is not designed so that it may then be undercut. Chrétien's complaint about love—the ironic core of his *insinuatio*—is completely dropped! The narrator's attitude to contemporary life is much more sympathetic and rests, above all, on the peculiar compensation that can be obtained from literary re-creation, a defence surely of Hartmann's role as both adaptor and individual creator:

> mich jâmert waerlîchen,
> und hulfez iht, ich woldez clagen,
> daz *nû bî unseren tagen*
> selch vreude niemer werden mac
> der man *ze den zîten* pflac.
> doch müezen wir ouch *nû* genesen.
> ichn wolde *dô* niht sîn gewesen,
> daz ich *nû* niht enwaere,
> dâ uns noch mit ir maere
> sô rehte wol wesen sol:
> *dâ* tâten in diu werc vil wol.

[48-58]

This represents a confident affirmation of Hartmann's control of his material.[24] Whilst Chrétien's purpose is to strip away the hollow ideality of courtly romance, Hartmann defends fiction as a source of *delectatio*,[25] of the restoration of the *vreude* enjoyed by Arthurian society, and as an instrument of moral survival. The literary creator can clarify and teach through his re-presentation of reality. Small wonder, then, that so many critical studies have been devoted to Hartmann's sensitive and complex narrative presentation.

Elements of Chrétien's *insinuatio* are now redistributed to the *mise en scène* with significant alterations. Talk of love is *not* prominent (see

ll. 62-72), the behaviour of Arthur and his Queen does *not* cause conster-
nation and is *not* recorded as exceptional: they retire "mê durch geselle-
schaft geleit/dan durch deheine trâkheit" (ll. 83-4);[26] Kâlogrenant is
unwilling to relate his story, *not* before the Queen, but before Keiî
(ll. 217-9), because the latter is an unsympathetic listener, always trying
to find fault (see ll. 137-58); even Keiî envisages the possibility that he
may be in the wrong (ll. 183-4, cf. 223-5, 228-9). The specifically literary
or exegetical allusions of Kâlogrenant's *captatio benevolentiae* are reduced by the fact that Hartmann introduces earlier a passage which emphasises the heart as the seat of morality rather than of understanding or
intellectual perception (see ll. 157-8, 193-203, independent of Chrétien,
and cf. ll. 838-44) and by the further fact that Kâlogrenant's preamble
contains nothing of Chrétien's repeated oppositions *cuer-oroille, antan-
dre-oïr* (H. ll. 243-58),[27] despite the existence of a similar topos in Middle High German,[28] and is really a simpler request for a polite, respectful
hearing.[29] Hartmann's treatment of the introduction has a moral character,
which is lacking in Chrétien, as well as a more penetrating psychological
analysis of the characters. From the beginning there are significant differences between the French and German romances: Chrétien is critical,
dialectical, and oblique, concerned to subvert the audience's sense of security
and its assumptions, whilst Hartmann reinforces his audience's sense of
security by announcing the genre with a warm commendation of Arthur, a
more explicit analysis of the characters and close attention to the exemplary
value of what he relates. Hartmann's legitimation of literature (*maere*) is no
doubt linked with his constant concern for clarification of his source and his
interest in moral qualities: through *Iwein* we may reach a better understanding of *rehte güete*.[30] Whereas Chrétien is already moving in the direction of
literary burlesque (the subversion of courtly romance conventions and ironic
manipulation of the poses of *fin amor*), Hartmann is less concerned with the
manipulation of literary fictions and more interested in the exigencies of
social reality and the problematics of lordship. *Yvain* and *Iwein* will prove to
be two very different productions.

The Middle English adaptation, *Ywain and Gawain*,[31] was probably
made for a baronial court in the North of England over one hundred and
fifty years after the appearance of Chrétien's poem. The consistency with
which the author proceeded saved it from becoming one of the farragi-
nous productions all too typical of the Middle English romances.[32] The
emphasis throughout is fairly and squarely on chivalry as demonstrated
by the possession of *trowthe*. The religious invocation with which the
work begins (ll. 1-6) brackets Ywain *and* Gawain as "knightes of þe tabyl

rownde" (1. 5) and as protagonists of the story. That the major theme of the romance is chivalry is then reinforced by the description of Arthur: "Of al knightes he bare þe pryse" (1. 11); "In werld was none so war ne wise" (1. 12, see *knyghtes war and wyse* at 1. 21 and cf. 1. 1241). There is a constellation of elements which may point to the figure of Arthur as a symbol for Edward I. "þe Kyng of Yngland, / þat wan al Wales with his hand / and al Scotland" (11. 7-9) may evoke Edward's conquest of Wales in 1274-86 and his attempted subjugation of Scotland with the Scottish campaign of 1296 or the taking of Stirling Castle in 1304.[33] Edward's epitaph *pactum serva* seems appropriate to the theme of *trowthe* in the romance. Of Arthur it is asserted that "Trew he was in alkyn thing" (1. 13). Of love there is no mention, but rather of "dedes of armes and (of) veneri" (1. 26), of "gude knightes" (1. 27)," þaire gude dede" (1. 29), of "þe lose þai wan with speres-horde" (1. 45) and of the honour which accrued to those who were "stif in ilka stowre" (1. 31). The *laudatio temporis acti* and complaint at the degeneracy of the present give a significant prominence to *trowthe:*

> þai tald of more *trewth* þam bitw[e]ne
> þan now omang men here es sene.
> For *trowth* and luf es al bylaft,
> Men uses now a noþer craft.
> With worde men makes it *trew* and stabil,
> Bot in þaire faith es noght bot fabil;
> With þe mowth men makes it hale,
> Bot *trew trowth* es nane in þe tale.
>
> [33-40]

The English poet identifies this quality of *trowthe* in "þe flowre of chevallry" represented by Arthur's court. His prologue is devoted not to generic indications (no reference to the Bretons' belief in Arthur's imperishable name) nor to an idealisation of Arthur, but to the exemplification of the primacy of *trowthe*.[34] He believed with Arveragus in *The Franklin's Tale* that "Trouthe is the hyeste thyng that man may kepe" (1. 771).[35] The directness of expression which characterises the poet's revelation of his interests continues throughout the work. The concern for chivalric honour is so great that there is no reference to Colgrevance's adventure being "de sa honte": it is merely "a chance" (1. 60), the report of "a stowre" (1. 61), a "selly case" (1. 107, cf. "þis ferly fare," 462). Colgrevance himself is upgraded to a warrior "of mekyl mane" (1. 58), "þat hende knight" (1. 112).[36] The importance of the heart in his *captatio benevolentiae* is linked with the central quality of *trowthe*: "And wordes wo so *trewly* tase, / By þe eres into þe hert it gase" (11. 145-6). *Ywain and Gawain*

is a poem which commends true chivalry and identifies it with the possession of *trowthe*: reliability in keeping one's word.[37] The crisis depicts the
hero as "traytur untrew and trowthles" (l. 1626): he must learn to become
a "trew knyght" (l. 2189). The English poet therefore remodels the introduction to the romance in order to present clearly the theme of his
tale. In this he differs from both Chrétien and Hartmann.

Technically, the *peripeteia* of the *Yvain* is located in the moment of
the hero's overstaying his leave from Laudine (see ll. 2694 ff), but inter-
pretatively it is clear that greater significance attaches to the motivation
of the hero's leave itself. Whereas the expiry of the limit of time is
reported almost perfunctorily (ll. 2672 ff), the parenesis which determines
Yvain's departure is described at length and is the occasion, in both Chrétien and Hartmann, of important intertextual references which illustrate
a less familiar aspect of medieval poetics.

Gauvain's speech to Yvain (ll. 2484–538) has traditionally been considered as a statement or *mise au point* of the main problem which the
romance is said to treat, namely the relationship between love and chivalry and the coordination of the two. The reference in Hartmann to
Erec's *verligen* (Iw. ll. 2787ff) has, furthermore, confirmed critics in their
view that this problem is the same coin as in the *Erec*, only viewed here
from the other side. The theory's most vulnerable point is that to be valid
it demands that we take Gauvain's words seriously as reasonably and
satisfyingly appropriate to Yvain's situation. Is such a view plausible?
Lines 2479–83 make it quite clear that Arthur's company wished to take
Yvain back to court with them and to this end had tirelessly campaigned
the whole week long. Their motives for doing so could scarcely have anything to do with a theory of love and were most likely connected with the
honour of the court, that is, with showing the court the successful aveng-
er of the humiliation inflicted on one of its members.[38] It therefore seems
mistaken to see in Gauvain's speech the expression of a generally held or
publicly endorsed theory about love and chivalry to which Yvain is failing to conform. After a whole succession of evidently futile attempts,
Gauvain's is a last desperate effort at persuading or putting pressure on
Yvain, in which he relies on the strength of his intimacy with the hero
(which in turn provides a motive for his wanting Yvain to accompany
him). The farrago of *raisonnements* and *non-sequiturs* which make up
his speech only confirms that it is neither expository nor exemplary (see

Gauvain's own tongue-in-cheek admission of its unreality in ll. 2527-38), but simply hortatory. It is, in fact, thoroughly literary, a burlesque of courtly romance conventions, particularly the chivalry topos.

Gauvain's first argument centres on the theme of degeneration and improvement, *anpirier* (ll. 2488, 2494, 2497) and *amander* (l. 2489). The warning seems ludicrously premature, for Yvain has only been married a week, and there is not the slightest indication that any deterioration in his chivalric status will take place. On the contrary, the necessity of defending the fountain supports the opposite inference, and Yvain's valour has already been proved superior to that of the paragon Esclados. Given the difficult circumstances of Laudine's remarriage, it is hard to see how Yvain's reputation would be diminished by some concession to marital life. Yet, Gauvain insists:

> Amander doit de bele dame,
> Qui l'a a amie ou a fame.
> Ne n'est puis droiz, que ele l'aint,
> Que ses pris et ses los remaint.
>
> [2489-92][39]

Why this process should be precluded by Yvain's present situation, in which there has been no lack of stress on the service which he must render Laudine, is not at all clear. Gauvain is simply trying to alarm his friend.

The second argument is concerned with advocating the acquisition of chivalric reputation: "Or primes doit vostre pris croistre!" (l. 2499). As defender of the fountain, however, Yvain has already increased his stock by defeating Kay and, indeed, by having defeated Esclados in the first place. The argument seems malapropos because it is in the very nature of Yvain's new union that he must defend his wife's fountain and lands against all challengers (ll. 2033-35). This duty is far more important as a social reality than romance ideals of chivalric renown. Gauvain's conception of

> "Celui, qui de neant anpire
> Quant il est del reaume sire."
>
> [2497-8]

seems to contain a contradiction when applied to Yvain's situation. The old saw, "assez songe, qui ne se muet" (l. 2507) has no relevance to a knight henceforth committed to the defence of the fountain, but, of course, Gauvain's view of the nature of chivalric activity is different from that which the hero will later embrace, and his own constant mobility presents more than one problem for those who seek his aid. Gauvain's own chivalry is the stuff of which literature is made, but, in its lack of discrimination, it reveals an inner vulnerability. The selfish demand for the company of his friend at the tournaments (themselves already under considerable criticism as a temptation for knights[40]) contains a clear irony:

> "Or ne devez vos pas songier,
> Mes les tornoiemenz ongier,
> Anprandre estorz et fort joster,
> *Que que il vos doie coster!*"
>
> [2503-6]

This appeal to a romanticised myth of chivalric activity is again purely persuasive and of no practical relevance to Yvain's circumstances. It takes its place, however, in the web of contrasted conceptions of chivalry which is at the heart of *Yvain*: Calogrenant's fruitless searching for futile, arbitrary *avanture*; Kay's blustering but ineffectual adoption of the role of champion of the court; Gauvain's interventions as something of a chivalric butterfly; the juvenile wanderings of the lord of L'Isle as Puceles; Yvain's overzealous and ill-considered assault on the fountain and its defender; that combination of strength and humility first indicated by the lion and harnessed by the hero to the service of *publica utilitas*.

Finally, Gauvain resorts to an argument concerning love:

> *"Biens adoucist par delaiier.*
> Et plus est buens a essaiier
> Uns petiz biens, quant il delaie,
> Qu'uns granz, que l'an adés essaie."
>
> [2515-8]

This Ovidian sentiment (cf. ll. 2519-23 and *Ars amat.* (3. 573) of epicurean flavour, originally relating to the physical enjoyment of love, easily coalesced with the more abstract theory of Courtly Love, in which delay might increase the value of love in its ennobling effect as well as the pleasure of obtaining it.[41] Most important, line 2515 represents an intertextual reference of some complexity. It occurs in the fifth strophe of Chrétien's own lyric "D'Amors, qui m'a tolu a moi":

> Cuers, se ma dame ne t'a chier,
> Ja mar por çou t'en partiras:
> Tous jours soies en son dangier,
> Puis qu'empris et comencié l'as.
> Ja, mon los, plenté n'ameras,
> Ne pour chier tans ne t'esmaier.
> *Biens adoucist par delaier.*
> Et quant plus desiré l'auras,
> Plus t'en ert douls a l'essaier.
>
> [5:37-45][42]

The lyric has several links with *Yvain*: the complaint at the deceivers in love who yet obtain their *joie* (1: 7-9; cf. *Yvain* prologue); the gift of the lover's heart to his lady (2: 16; *Yvain* ll. 2639 ff.); the rejection of Tristan's love (4: 28 ff). The real interest of the lyric, however, lies in its connection with two troubadours, Bernart de Ventadorn and Raimbaut d'Aurenga, who themselves entertained a poetic correspondence. In *Can vei la lauzeta mover* Bernart used Tristan as a *senhal* for Raimbaut who had compared himself to Tristan in *No chan per auzel ni per flor*. In the latter poem we find the following lines:

> Carestia, esgauzimen
> M'aporta d'aicel repaire,
> On es midonz, qe.m ten gauzen
> Plus q'ieu eis non sai retraire.
>
> [49-52]

Aurelio Roncaglia has suggested that Carestia is a *senhal* for Chrétien[43] and that in *D'Amors, qui m'a tolu a moi* Chrétien imitates Bernart's poem *Can vei la lauzeta mover*, whilst at the same time replying to Raimbaut, the lines "Onques du buvrage ne bui / Dont Tristan fu enpoisonnez" (ll. 28-29) being a response to Raimbaut's "Car ieu begui de la amor . . . celada." Chrétien's poem therefore reflects a polemic between three poets in the period ca. 1170-73 in which the Champenois takes issue with both his southern rivals, opposing the lover's despairing renunciation in Bernart's poem and the Tristan-like fatality which is celebrated in Raimbaut's verses.[44] He does this by rejecting *plenté* and commending *chier tans*:

> Ja, mon los, plenté n'ameras,
> Ne pour chier tans ne t'esmaier.
>
> [41-42]

Line 42 of *D'Amors, qui m'a tolu a moi* recalls Ovid's "Copia tollat amorem" (*Rem. Am.* 541) and "Pinguis amor nimiumque patens in taedia nobis / vertitur et, stomacho dulcis ut esca, nocet" (*Amores* 2. 19. 25-26). The *chier tans* is an Ovidian idea, which passed to the troubadours and became an indispensable element of *fin amor*. As Roncaglia shows, the troubadours adopted Chrétien's term as *carestia / cartat* and opposed it to *viltat*.[45]

The importance of this web of intertextual references is threefold: (1) It suggests that Gauvain's advice to Yvain, like so much else in the romance, is based on a consciously literary convention or ideal. (2) It reveals the irony of the scene, for Gauvain's words evoke before the now safely established Yvain Provençal lyrics which emphasise the lover's despair and separation from his lady![46] It is thus an ironic anticipation of Yvain's fate with which we are confronted in the intertextual references. (3) The closest parallel to the speech in *Yvain*, Chrétien's own lyric, is a neat inversion of this fate: the lover is resolute, sustained by his "fins cuers et bone volentez" (l. 31), his heart will never abandon the lady, though she ignores him — he cannot separate from her ("Et je, qui ne m'en puis partir / De celi vers qui me souploi, / Mon cuer, qui siens est, li envoi," ll. 14-16). The lover of Chrétien's lyric behaves "Conme cil qui ne set a gas / Amors servir ne losengier" (ll. 53-54), but Yvain will be later denounced as "Le desleal, le traïtor, / le mançongier, le jeingleor" (*Yvain*, ll. 2719-20)!

The intertextual references thus brilliantly establish a tension or ambiguity concerning two different attitudes: the despair and separation of the Provençal lyrics, and the resolute rejection of separation in Chrétien's lyric. On which side will Yvain fall? There will emerge an ironic discrepancy between the advice of Gauvain and the condition to which it leads Yvain, the bookish recommendations of the *fin amant*[47] adumbrated by Gauvain resulting in the contented lover's loss of *joie*.

Whereas Chrétien's Gauvain exploits a burlesque of Ovidian and Courtly Love doctrines for purely selfish purposes, the German Gâwein behaves quite differently. Hartmann drops the motif of the court's desire for Iwein's return and makes Gâwein take the hero on one side and deliver his much more substantial admonition privately:

> her Gâwein der getriuwe man
> vuorte hern Iweinen dan
> von den liuten sunder.
>
> [2767-9]

In Hartmann Gâwein's advice is to be taken much more seriously, for it is predicated on Ciceronian moral values, not on literary fictions. Whilst Gauvain is little concerned to depict his friend's situation with any real finesse and credibility (his opening remark [ll. 2484-6] is quite peremptory), Gâwein applies himself to a careful diagnosis of Iwein's predicament, beginning with a general moral analysis (ll. 2771-80) completely absent from Chrétien and which takes up the motifs of *saelde* and *êre* with which the *Iwein* opens and closes. This takes us into the world, not of Ovidian love casuistry or Provençal love poetry, but of the Boethian philosophy of history, in which *saelde* finds its correspondence in *fortuna* (and is also used in the romances in the sense of *beatitudo* or *felicitas*).[48] Iwein has taken his chances and been rewarded by fortune: he has matched his opportunities with his initiative (ll. 2770-4) — many a man toils but "enhât der saelden niht" (l. 2778). Iwein's *arbeit* is *saeleclîchen an geleit* (l. 2780) — harnessed to fortune. The tenor of Gâwein's speech is thus entirely serious, philosophical even. He wishes Iwein to continue to take advantage of every opportunity to advance in honour and to build on his good fortune. The intertextual reference, which now occurs, to the romance of *Erek* shows how serious Hartmann is about the hero's pursuit of *güete*, the *benignitas* which Cicero praises and which is appropriate to the prince or ruler. The enemy of Arthurian civilisation is complacency. Only now does Hartmann take up Chrétien's text (ll. 2787 ff.; *Yvain*, ll. 2484 ff.), but he soon innovates. The immediate danger to Iwein is illustrated by Erek's *verligen:*

> "kêrt ez niht allez an gemach;
> als dem hern Êrecke geschach,
> der sich ouch alsô manegen tac
> durch vrouwen Ênîten verlac.
> *wan daz er sichs erholte*
> *sît als ein rîter solte,*
> *sô waere vervarn sîn êre.*
> der minnete ze sêre."
>
> [2791–8]

What needs to be emphasised here is that, as well as indicating Erek's mistake, Gâwein also draws attention to his recovery and thereby reminds his audience of the glorious ending of the earlier romance. The reference to Erek is not a purely negative *exemplum* as many critics have thought. In fact, it is not really uxoriousness that worries Gâwein.[49] What he is most concerned with is the prestige of knighthood, *rîterschaft* (see ll. 2806, 2857, 2910). The prologue presented "künec Artûs *der guote,* / der mit *rîters muote,* / nach *lobe* kunde strîten" (ll. 5–7) and showed that the pursuit of *rehte güete* issues in *saelde und êre* (ll. 1/3). This chivalric *Tugendlehre* has a firm Ciceronian basis. In the greatly influential *De officiis* Cicero declares:

> Sed expositis adulescentium officiis, quae valeant ad *gloriam* adipiscendam, deinceps de *beneficentia* ac de liberalitate dicendum est; cuius est ratio duplex; nam aut opera *benigne* fit indigentibus aut pecunia. (*De Officiis.* 2. 15:52)

This passage on kindness and largesse was of considerable importance for the chivalric ethos and was transmitted by William of Conches in the *Moralium dogma philosophorum.*[50] I have argued elsewhere[51] that Cicero's discussion of liberality with its reference to Alexander was known to Chrétien when he wrote the prologue to the *Conte du Graal.* Cicero is clear, however, that *beneficentia* (later *benignitas*) is superior to *liberalitas,* as *opera* are superior to *pecunia:*[52]

> Facilior est haec posterior, locupleti praesertim, sed illa lautior ac splendidior et viro forti claroque dignior. (*De officiis.* 2. 15. 52)

> Quam ob rem id quidem non dubium est, quin illa benignitas, quae
> constet ex opera et industria, et honestior sit et latius pateat et possit
> prodesse pluribus. (*De officiis*. 2. 15. 54)

A chivalric age can hardly fail to have been impressed by Cicero's suggestion, also in Book 2 of the *De officiis*,

> Prima igitur est adulescenti commendatio ad gloriam, si qua ex bellicis
> rebus comparari potest, in qua multi apud maiores nostros ex-
> stiterunt. (*De officiis*. 2. 13. 45)

He further recommends strength of character and association with the great (for a medieval knight, Arthur!) as steps to the attainment of honour (*gloria*). The point of our discussion is thus that Gâwein provides an entirely serious analysis, along moral lines, of Iwein's situation. Erek redeemed his fault by acts of chivalric service, *opera* inspired by *benignitas*, the *rehte güete* associated with Arthur. The Ciceronian basis of the chivalric ethos, complemented by an awareness of God's grace, is fundamental to Hartmann's view of *rîterschaft*.[53] Iwein is summoned away to maintain that *rîterschaft*, to pursue the *güete* or *benignitas* "quae constet ex opera et industria."

However, the celebrated depiction of the *Krautjunker* which Hartmann now introduces (ll. 2807–59) adds to the ethical dimension of Iwein's position a sociological one. Gâwein is also concerned with *rîterschaft* as the prestigious apanage of a social class. The portrait of the *Krautjunker* reminds us of the self-conscious upward push exercised by the ministerials, of whom Hartmann was one, in the eleventh and twelfth centuries.[54] Gâwein accepts the economic prudence displayed by the *Krautjunker*, with a reservation: "der wirt hât wâr, und doch niht gar" (l. 2850). In the face of the rising bourgeoisie the knights comprising the lesser nobility and ministerials could not hope to survive without sound economic husbandry, yet the latter had also to be made to serve the maintenance of a distinctive life-style which preserved their identity. Gâwein thus tells Iwein: "nu müget ir *mit dem guote*/volziehen dem muote" (ll. 2907–8), the reference being to *rîters muote* (l. 5). The *krautjunker* displays anxiety about two things: the upkeep of *daz hûs*, which "muoz kosten harte vil" (l. 2850 cf. 2825, 2834) and the situation of his wife: "ich sorge um mîn wîp:/diene weiz ich war ich tuo" (ll. 2836–7). It is precisely the same concerns which remain potential problems for Iwein, dangers within the generally accepted framework of good house-keeping:

> "iu hât erworben iuwer hant
> ein schoene wîp unde ein lant."
>
> [2781–2]

> "iu hât verdienet iuwer hant
> eine künegîn unde ein lant."
>
> [2879-80]

Preoccupation with his wife and the maintenance of his territory could lead Iwein to forego the characteristic activities of knighthood, just as the *Krautjunker* claims "daz er danne vür die zît / sül weder *rîten* noch *geben*" (ll. 2810-11). Without the exercise of knighthood, including the ceremonial show and ostentatious power of the tournament, Iwein might regress to the stage where, like the *Krautjunker*,

> "er geloubet sich der beider,
> vreuden unde cleider
> die nach rîterlichen siten
> sint gestalt und gesniten."
>
> [2813-6]

The portrait of the *Krautjunker* thus points to the maintenance of a distinctive chivalric life-style which alone safeguards the knightly class in the face of increasing obsolescence. So insistent is Gâwein on the preservation of *rîterschaft* that any reference to love would have seemed out of place.

Hartmann cannot, of course, completely ignore the love element: Iwein is, after all, being summoned away from his newly won wife! At the end of his speech, therefore, Gâwein adverts to the problem of amatory responsibilities (not amatory pleasures!) and argues that true *rîters muot* which manifests itself in knightly deeds is alone pleasing to a woman and that no devotion which eschews them can be welcome: "ich rede als ichz erkennen kan" (l. 2859). This may be true, of course, of his own amatory relationships, since they do not involve marriage. His advice is somewhat simplistic: Iwein should have complete confidence in his wife:

> "ein wîp die man hât erkant
> in alsô staetem muote,
> diun bedarf niht mêre huote
> niuwan ir selben êren."
>
> [2890-3]

He tells Iwein: "bevelhet ir liut unde lant" (l. 2889). His advice is clearly one-sided: he sees the situation only from the male point of view and, overestimating Iwein's maturity,[56] fails to see that his friend's new responsibilities make him one who "muoz deste dicker heime sîn" (l. 2853). Rather, he turns the argument on its head and suggests that Iwein's newly found resources permit for the first time an appropriate display of chivalry which will consolidate his status:

"irte iuch etewenne daz guot
michels harter dan der muot,
nû muget ir mit dem guote
volziehen dem muote."

[2905-8]

Unlike Gauvain, he clearly envisages a fixed period of leave:

". . . gewinnet mit minnen
der küneginne ein urloup abe
zeinem tage der vuoge habe."

[2886-8]

The significance of Gâwein's intervention in Hartmann is that it invokes, not the fictional ideas of poetry in an obvious temptation of the hero, but the problems of a social class, the ministerials, in an attempt to secure an appropriate advertisement of the knightly class by a man who has just inherited the resources to do so. For Hartmann, Iwein is guilty of no fault in complying with Gâwein's advice: the culpable error lies purely in the *Terminversäumnis*. The defence of the chivalric ethos in a rapidly changing society is an entirely serious theme. That Iwein currently lacks the qualifications for the task is no criticism of Gâwein, and Hartmann is later at pains to defend the premier representative of Arthurian knighthood.[57] The function of the intertextual references in Chrétien and Hartmann could scarcely be more contrasting. In *Yvain* the intertextual reference is purely amatory; it points to a dilemma circumscribed by the literary poses of a number of lyric poets polemically engaged with each other, and it is ironically fashioned in order to *undermine* our confidence in the wisdom of the hero's decision, as he submits to temptation in what is an obvious testing of his powers of discrimination and his tenacity of purpose. In Hartmann, on the other hand, the intertextual reference *supports* rather than undermines the hero's decision, since the allusion to Erek, far from being completely negative, gives a clear indication that he retrieved the situation by the exercise of his chivalry (ll. 2795-7) — *als ein rîter solte*. This reference to chivalric success, reinforced by the memory of the *Erek's* triumphant conclusion, thus encourages belief in a happy outcome of Iwein's decision. The different effects which Chrétien and Hartmann draw from these two instances of intertextuality merely point up the fundamental difference between their two romances. Hartmann's work remains solidly based on the importance of social relations and cohesion as guaranteed by the central notion of *triuwe*, whereas Chrétien is content to burlesque his hero's adventures in love through the skillful interplay of literary roles which constitute an ironic reflection of some of the conventions of courtly romance. It is the lion which leads us out of the world of literary fiction into the world of political ethics, a world which in *Iwein* we never leave.

As might be expected, *Ywain and Gawain* shows no resort to the technique of intertextuality. The author understandably excises Gawain's exaggerated references to courtly doctrines, the topicality of which would be completely lost to a fourteenth-century English audience. The emphasis throughout is on chivalry:

> " . . . Sir, if þou ly at hame,
> Wonderly men will þe blame.
> þat knyght es no thing to set by,
> þat leves al his chevalry . . ."
>
> [1455-8, cf. 1. 1475]

The different social ethos of the poem is clearly illustrated by the following radical modification of Chrétien's reference to *jalos* (l. 2502):

> "For when a knyght es chevalrouse,
> His lady es þe more jelows,
> Also sho lufes him wele þe bet."
>
> [1463-5][58]

It is also noteworthy that, as in Hartmann, appeal is made to the argument that the knight may now fittingly match his life-style to his new resources:

> "þou has inogh to þi despens,
> Now may þow wele hante turnamentes."
>
> [1469-70]

The stress throughout the much abbreviated episode is on Ywain's public reputation as a knight, and accommodation of renewed chivalric adventures to the fact of his recent marriage and to his wife's love is not regarded as problematic. For the English poet the central action of the hero is not his compliance with Gawain's requests, which seem designed to enhance his chivalry, but his negligence in forgetting the term set by Alundyne which is an offence against the poet's ideal of knightly *trowthe*. There is no note of burlesque humour in Gawain's speech and no intertextual reference, since the argument is regarded as self-justifying.

The conclusion of a medieval romance is worth individual study for at least three reasons: (1) it involves the audience's expectations of the genre; (2) it illuminates the thematic development of the preceding narrative, for its customary function is to bring together or unify the various strands of the plot; (3) its propensity to didacticism sheds light on problems of interpretation in the work as a whole. In each of these three aspects the *Yvain* marks an ironic manipulation of conventions, for the colophon (ll. 6814-8) betrays how little audience expectations have been satisfied, the perjury trick unites the work's themes (love and chivalry) on only the most superficial, technical level, and the final characterisation of Laudine completely inhibits the desired moral inference that Yvain has atoned for his fault and reconquered his lady's love. The ending of *Yvain* is every bit as subversive of romance conventions as the beginning was.

The conclusion presents an obvious paradox. The Knight of the Lion has established his chivalry in a very *different* way from the old Yvain, but he rewins his wife in precisely the *same* manner as he first conquered her.[59] It is quite misguided to embrace the comfortable view that the hero has now made himself worthy of being reunited with Laudine: such a thought occurs to neither partner. Yvain determines to force himself on her out of sheer desperation (ll. 6511-26) and this depiction of his decision deprives his desire for Laudine of any teleological role in the sequence of his chivalric adventures. Laudine herself demonstrates no recognition that Yvain has any moral claim on her. The strategy by which she is won for him involves the same procedures as before. The same tactics, however, do not secure the same response. In contrast to the former "Sachiez donc, bien acordé somes" (l. 2036) comes "Bien m'avez au hoquerel prise! / Celui, qui ne m'aimme ne prise, / Me feras amer maugré mien" (ll. 6761-3). Everything that the audience desires to hear is withheld or contradicted. Has Laudine forgiven Yvain in her heart and reawakened her love for him?

> "Miauz vossisse tote ma vie
> Vanz et orages andurer!
> Et se ne fust de parjurer
> Trop leide chose et trop vilainne,
> Ja mes a moi por nule painne
> Pes ne acorde ne trovast.
> Toz jorz mes el cors me covast
> Si con li feus cove an la çandre,
> Ce, don je ne vuel or reprandre,
> Ne ne me chaut del recorder,
> Puis qu'a lui m'estuet acorder."
>
> [6766-76]

One cannot overlook the Ovidian metaphor (ll. 6772f)[60] now functioning as an antitype of amatory desire (contrast ll. 1777-80 and 2519-23). Yvain, for his part, makes no suggestion of possessing any right to his

wife such as might have been engendered by a sense of new moral worth.
He begins with a cliché:[61]

> ". . . Dame! misericorde
> Doit an de pecheor avoir.
> Conparé ai mon fol savoir,
> Et je le dui bien conparer.
> Folie me fist demorer,
> Si m'an rant coupable et forfet.
> Et mout grant hardemant ai fet,
> Quant devant vos osai venir."
>
> [6780-87]

In declaring that he has "paid for" his folly Yvain does not refer to his chivalric adventures, and it is likely that he is alluding here to the episode of his
madness and the grief which he has experienced in his separation from
Laudine (cf. l. 6802)—this, as we shall see, is how Hartmann seems to have
understood it. The proverbial nature of the *pecheor* theme suggests that it
indicates no more than that Yvain has misbehaved. *Folie* and *fol savoir*
seem simply to indicate lack of judgement and understanding. Nothing in
this speech, therefore, convincingly establishes a link between Yvain's request for reconciliation and the substance of his chivalric adventures with
the lion. Moreover, of sincere forgiveness and true love there is not a trace.
What do we have here if not the systematic dismantling of the chivalry topos,
the subject of Gauvain's notorious advice? The ideology of knightly love service according to which the man's chivalric acts are inspired by love of a lady
and in turn intensify her devotion to him is completely belied here and the
bottom knocked out of courtly romance. At no point is it ever suggested that
Yvain's adventures are pursued in respect of his love for Laudine, and, cor-
respondingly, there is no indication that she is impressed by them. Laudine
acts entirely under duress and makes no secret of her bitter resentment. To
underscore this frustration of expectations Chrétien proceeds to assure his
listeners of the idyll of which they have just been cheated:

> Ore a mes sire Yvains sa pes,
> *Si poez croire*, qu'onques mes
> Ne fu de rien nule si liez,
> Comant qu'il ait esté iriez.
> Mout an est a buen chief venuz;
> Qu'il est amez et chier tenuz
> De sa dame, et ele de lui.
> Ne li sovient de nul enui,
> Que par la joie les oblie,
> Qu'il a de sa tres chiere amie.
>
> [6799-808]

The irony is evident. That Chrétien was well aware of how little conviction his ending carried is clearly demonstrated by the colophon with its anticipation of scribal interference and its ironic expression of Chrétien's unwillingness to see it changed:

Del *Chevalier au Lion* fine
Crestiiens son romanz einsi;
Qu'onques plus conter n'an oï,
Ne ja plus n'an orroiz conter,
S'an n'i viaut mançonge ajoster.

[6814-8]

The conclusion of *Yvain* conspicuously fails to satisfy the expectations predicated of the genre. Love and chivalry are not depicted, in the final analysis, as mutually enriching. Perhaps the knighthood of the *Chevalier au Lion* is indeed superior to that of Yvain—but not in Laudine's eyes. Perhaps the penitent lover does develop greater insight into love's ways—but this has no influence on his chivalry, and apparently none on his decision to revisit the fountain and seek reconciliation ("Que par force et par estovoir/Li covandroit feire a lui pes/Ou il ne fineroit ja mes/De la fontainne tormanter/Et de plovoir et de vanter" [ll. 6522-26]). The two themes are simply not bound together. Absolutely no amatory motivation is provided for the hero's chivalric exertions. His inner life is hidden from us. Psychology is subordinated to exemplariness. The hero's later chivalric career is a public demonstration, not a personal odyssey. How love and chivalry are to be reconciled remains an open question.

It is clear at once that neither Chrétien's image of the Belle Dame sans Merci (Laudine)[62] nor his presentation of a wily *entremetteuse* (Lunete) appealed to Hartmann. The problem was how to integrate Chrétien's female characters into a world of dependable human relationships in which the central quality of *triuwe* was safeguarded. That the problem did indeed centre on women is delightfully underscored by Lûnete's tongue-in-cheek allusion to the ambiguity of their role:

"ich bin ein wîp: naem ich mich an
ze râtenne als ein wîser man,
sô waer ich tumber danne ein kint."

[7851-3]

"Welch guot wîp waere von der siten,
die ir ze vlîze woldet biten,
diu iht versagen kunde
einem alsô süezen munde?"

[7897-900][63]

The ironic self-deprecation actually points up the responsibility which Lûnete and her mistress have already exercised in the action of the romance and which they must now implement in a definitive fashion. In a further addition to Chrétien Lûnete presses home the need for absolute reliability and commitment regarding *Iwein* (who himself, of course, is a forceful reminder of a broken promise):

> "er ist ein harte staeter man
> nach dem ich da rîten sol,
> und bedarf dâ staeter rede wol.
> welt ir nâch im senden,
> diu wort mit werken enden
> der ich zem eide niht enbir,
> sô sprechet, vrouwe, nâch mir."
>
> [7916–22][64]

For a moment the roles of Iwein and Laudîne seem paradoxically reversed: it is Laudîne who must give evidence of *staete* to the man who broke his word. In fact, this is only the first of a number of additions which raise the crucial question of whether Hartmann has refashioned Chrétien's conclusion in such a way as to suggest that Laudîne shares a measure of guilt with the hero. When Lûnete greets Iwein she offers the following observations on his experiences:

> "dâ habt ir iuch genietet,
> *ein teil von iuwern schulden,*
> *und von ir unhulden*
> von der iu dienete diz lant
> und diu mich ûz hât gesant,
> einer langen arbeit."
>
> [7960–65]

Does this statement contain implicit criticism of Laudîne? It must be remembered that in Hartmann it is Lûnete herself who berates the hero after the *Terminversäumnis* and who defends her lady who is unable to avenge herself (ll. 3111–96). Whereas Chrétien's Lunete tells her lady "Dame! pardonez li vostre ire!" (l. 6756), the phrasing in Hartman leads us away from, rather than towards, Laudîne's own disposition: "Vergebent im sine missetât" (l. 8071). It is not so much a trace of guilt as a degree of softening of attitudes which is in evidence at this point. Whilst in Chrétien the coercion exercised by the oath is not compensated for by any emotional concession on the part of Laudine (see, for example, ll. 6772–76), who accedes to the inevitable with bad grace, Hartmann's Laudîne already hints at a retreat from inflexibility:

"der zorn ist mînhalp dâ hin.
gedienen müez ich noch umb in
daz er mich lieber welle hân
danner mich noch habe getân."
[8093–6]

This suggestion of reciprocity prepares the way for a much more striking innovation. Iwein's ecstatic recognition of "mîner vreuden ôster-tac" (l. 8120) secures from Laudîne an emotional expression of sympathy and a plea for forgiveness which culminate in her falling at the hero's feet in an unexpected gesture of submission (ll. 8121–36):

"her Îwein, lieber herre mîn,
tuot genaedeclîchen an mir.
grôzen kumber habet ir
von mînen schulden erliten:
des wil ich iuch durch got biten
daz ir ruochet mir vergeben,
wand er mich, unz ich hân daz leben,
von herzen iemer riuwen muoz."
[8122–9]

This passage does not fit into its context as comfortably as some would wish. Hartmann has, it should be noted, stuck remarkably closely to Chrétien's earlier indications of constraint and smouldering resentment (ll. 8077 ff., 8083 ff., 8089–91), and at the end of the romance he shares his source's ironic distancing (*waenlich* ll. 8148, 8159; *waen ich* l. 8157; *ichn weiz* l. 8160).[65] In Chrétien the scepticism is being directed at what has all too obviously been contrived, but in Hartmann there is the danger of its weakening the credibility of Laudîne's "confession." But what is this "confession"? Is it a hyperbolic expression of sympathy for the hero's suffering or is it a frank acknowledgement of guilt? Does *von mînen schulden* mean simply "on my account"? The problem of interpreting the meaning and appropriateness of the "confession" is compounded by difficulties concerning the textual transmission of ll. 8121–36 which are contained in only three MSS![66] All of these MSS have certain weaknesses as witnesses. Wolff was confident enough to retain them in his critical text, but it is usually assumed that the lines belong to a later revision by Hartmann himself. The question remains: do they indicate guilt or compassion?

The case for the latter seems to me to be the stronger. Hartmann must have felt that the complete absence in Chrétien of any link between Yvain's "travauz"[67] and his reacceptance by Laudine left his suffering, and consequently his "reformed" identity, unrecognised. Indeed, my thesis is that this is precisely what Chrétien intended — to dismantle the chivalry topos by severing the links between the hero's chivalry and his lady's love. Hartmann thus sought to introduce a link between Iwein's suffering and his lady's attitude to him, and, indeed, to do so in order to effect a humanly credible basis for the reconciliation. The opportunity was there in a way that it was not present in Chrétien, for Hartmann has reorientated the problematics of the romance along the lines of political and social responsibility (*triuwe*), and this allows him to distinguish the political relationship of Iwein and Laudîne from their purely personal one. This point is best illustrated by the completely different orientation of the complaint against the hero in the two romances. In Chrétien "une dameisele" delivers the charge which is based *entirely* on Yvain as a lover. He claimed to be "verais amerre" (l. 2723), but had no understanding of "come li amant font" (l. 2760). There is a link with the complaint about love in the prologue, a link which is probably intended ironically, for Yvain has gone through the courtly ritual in wooing Laudine,[68] adopting the postures of feudal homage, and yet is revealed as false to his lady. Is it Yvain or the courtly stance which is being ridiculed? Whatever the answer, Yvain is criticised as a lover, rather than as a knight.[69] The verbal motifs of the speech of accusation, *cuer* and *anbler* (both occur five times), relate to the courtly casuistry concerning the exchange of hearts, and there is no reference whatsoever to the defence of Laudine's fountain.[70] It is from this disappointment in love that Laudine never really recovers. In Hartmann the scenario is conspicuously different. It is Lûnete who berates the hero (ll. 3111–96), regretting her own commitment to a man who has shown such neglect of his duties. In contrast to Chrétien the verbal motif which runs throughout the speech is *triuwe* (together with its compounds it occurs eleven times) the juridical connotations of which are uppermost in the context:[71]

> "nû ist iu triuwe unmaere.
> doch sulent ir in allen
> deste wirs gevallen
> die triuwe und êre minnent
> und sich des versinnent
> daz nimmer ein wol vrumer man
> âne triuwe werden kan."
>
> [3174–80]

Since Iwein lacks "rîters triuwe" (l. 3173), it would be shameful to King Arthur "hât er iuch mêre in rîters namen" (l. 3188). Laudine has ample cause to behave as she does in casting Iwein off, and her conduct is endorsed by Lûnete who feels equally dishonoured (ll. 3184–6, cf. 3150 ff.).

Iwein has grossly neglected his political responsibilities ("ir lîp unde ir lant, / daz ir daz soldet bewarn," [ll. 3158–9]). There is therefore no reason why Laudîne should be criticised for her conduct and led to "repent" in the reconciliation scene.[72] On the other hand, there is a personal as well as political dimension to the situation. Laudîne has been personally dishonoured by Iwein's individual treatment of her ("si ist iu ze edel und ze rîch / daz ir sî kebsen soldet," ll. 3170–1), and it is of this that she is mindful at the end of the romance where she complains, not of political *untriuwe*, but of him "der ûf mich dehein ahte enhât" (l. 8081), "der nie dehein ahte ûf mich gewan" (l. 8088). Understandably, in view of the promise she has just made, it is Iwein's attitude to her which causes her most anxiety, and she anticipates that she will have to expend some effort in changing the knight's attitude: "gedienen müez ich noch umb in / daz er mich lieber welle hân / danner mich noch habe getân" (ll. 8094–6). When, however, she hears Iwein's ecstatic reference to "mîner vreuden ôstertac" (l. 8120), her relief is such that she seizes the opportunity to restore their personal relationship by recognising the suffering he has endured on her account. This humanising touch by Hartmann, if not perfectly motivated and situated, is understandable.[73] In Chrétien the personal relationship of Yvain and Laudine is depicted in terms of a stylised literary fiction — courtly love. There is little human reality in their relationship: they speak to each other in literary metaphors.[74] This caused Hartmann real difficulty, since his elaboration of the Iwein-Lûnete relationship alone demonstrates his desire to accommodate the personal relationships in the romance to the ideals of *güete* and *triuwe*. Laudine's appearances are of such short duration and are so strongly "handlungsbedingt" that there were few opportunities to remodel her character and to humanise her.[75] The authenticity of lines 8121–36 might thus be defended on the grounds that it was one of the few ways in which Hartmann could provide a human basis, as distinct from mere fear of perjury, for the reconciliation of the hero and his lady. We have seen that Hartmann distinguishes a political and a personal dimension to Iwein's neglect of Laudîne. Lûnete has already provided full assurances concerning the political matter of the defence of the fountain by the Knight of the Lion. Laudîne's "confession" is less an expression of guilt than an emotional restoration of that reciprocity on the personal level which alone can give credibility to the contrived reconciliation which Hartmann found in his French source.

It has been strenuously argued,[76] however, that lines 8121–36 are authentic for a completely different reason, namely that Laudîne *is* guilty in a quite objective sense, since her conduct towards the hero, particularly as regards the fixing of the period of leave and the consequent sanctions, flouts all the known legal procedures of the time. This argument, however meticulously documented, really comes down to a complaint that the fundamental scenario and details of the *matière*, which Hartmann was scarcely free to modify, do not accord with medieval German law. It is no doubt true that Iwein has been convicted by the critics of too many offences in order to justify the apparent discrepancy between his guilt and the long and strenuous "Bewährungsabenteuer" which are normally regarded as a sort of "Sühnefahrt," but this should not lead us to accept that "das Missverhältnis zwischen der Schuld Iweins und dem Ausmass seiner Bestrafung während der Aventiurefahrt von Hartmann bewusst als eine Diskrepanz dargestellt wird, die von Laudine verursacht ist und Iweins Schuld relativiert." The paradoxes inherent in Laudîne's compact with Iwein, which is severely criticised by Hennig, are not only "stoffbedingt," but in the source are part of narrative requirements: the hero must be cast off, in order to pursue independently valuable adventures. Hennig's denial of the legal validity of this compact, her thoroughgoing "Überprüfung durch rechtliche Kriterien" surely imports standards which were not in Hartmann's mind (and could not possibly have been in Chrétien's!). The absolute conditions set by Laudîne, whether legally valid or not, are the symbolic expression of a moral duty, and without them Iwein's subsequent adventures could not take place. The "Willkür einer Minneherrin" displayed by Laudîne is poetically justified by the fact that she is being abandoned within a week of an extremely delicate remarriage. It is the hero's conduct at this point which would astonish the audience. Yet, Hennig argues that Lûnete's condemnation of the hero, which seems clear enough, is not endorsed by the narrator and is quite false. She concludes that the casting off of the hero is "eine unrechtmässige und unangemessene Bestrafung." It would thus follow that Laudîne is in need of forgiveness in the final scene. This view is unlikely to gain wide acceptance.

Nothing could be less problematic than the conclusion of the English *Ywain and Gawain* where the paradoxes and ironies are smoothed away. The lady Alundyne shows no vehement indignation at the discovery of Lunet's ruse, there are no histrionic objections and refusals, but a ready acquiescence: " . . . wheþer it torn to wele or ill, / þat I have said, I sal fulfill" (ll. 3991-2). Ywain acknowledges his fault quite specifically, "when þat I past my terme day" (l. 3998), and there is a general religious colouring absent from Chrétien. The reconciliation becomes much more convincing in the light of a passage like the following:

> þan sho asented saghteling to mak;
> And sone in arms he gan hir tak
> And kissed hir ful oft sith:
> Was he never are so blith.
>
> [4005-8]

Even the lion is not forgotten (l. 4025)! Chrétien's playful colophon is adapted to a conventional religious prayer. The problem of *trouthe* has been solved by the intervention of "trew Lunet, þe maiden hende" (l. 4014).

    This comparison of three critical moments in Chrétien's romance of *Yvain* and two of its medieval adaptations reveals that the orientation of all three works is individually distinctive. In Chrétien love and chivalry are kept apart and accorded quite different treatment. The chivalric theme is undeniably serious, supported by the image of the lion and illustrated in accordance with John of Salisbury's conception of knighthood and *publica utilitas*. The love theme is burlesqued as a topical literary fiction which does not command the ethical adherence of the author. What the new literary genre of the romance had joined, Chrétien ironically puts asunder. In Hartmann, however, love and chivalry are united in the political responsibilities of the hero, who is shown to depart from and subsequently return to the value of *triuwe*, moral commitment. Before the *Terminversäumnis* his chivalry is not, as in Chrétien, impugned and after it the criticism of him is directed at the knight, not, as in *Yvain*, at the courtly lover. In *Ywain and Gawain* the love element is entirely subordinated to the theme of chivalric *trowthe*, in which the keeping of one's word is all-important. The coordination of love and chivalry is not made to appear problematic. Ywain's mistake in the amatory sphere is merely a symptom of his chivalric immaturity. Thus the three versions of the Yvain story are so strongly individualised that they deserve the status of autonomous works in which the source has acted as a stimulus rather than as a constraint.

Tony Hunt
University of St. Andrews
Scotland

Notes

1. The edition used throughout is Chrestien de Troyes, *Yvain (Le Chevalier au Lion)*: The Critical Text of Wendelin Foerster with Introduction, Notes, and Glossary by T. B. W. Reid (Manchester: Manchester University Press, 1942; repr. 1952, etc.).

2. I thus seek to go beyond the disappointing superficiality of Ojars Kratins, *The Dream of Chivalry: A Study of Chrétien de Troyes's Yvain and Hartmann von Aue's Iwein* (Washington, D.C.: University Press of America, 1982).

3. See Carl Lofmark, *The Authority of the Source in Middle High German Narrative Poetry*, University of London, Institute of Germanic Studies, Bithell Series of Dissertations, 5 (London: Institute of Germanic Studies, 1981).

4. *The* Parisiana Poetria *of John of Garland*, ed. with introduction, translation, and notes by Traugott Lawler (New Haven: Yale University Press, 1974), p. 62.

5. MS Oxford, Bodleian Library, Laud Misc. 205 f. 3v.

6. The text occupies fols. 1r–3v.

7. Tony Hunt, "The Rhetorical Background to the Arthurian Prologue," *Forum for Modern Language Studies* 6 (1970), 1–23, especially 10–15; rpt. in *Arthurian Romance. Seven Essays,* ed. D. D. R. Owen (Edinburgh: Scottish Academic Press, 1973). See also Tony Hunt, "Tradition and Originality in the Prologues of Chrestien de Troyes," *Forum for Modern Language Studies* 8 (1972), 320–44, esp. 328–32.

8. See my article "The Lion and Yvain" in *The Legend of Arthur in the Middle Ages: Studies Presented to A. H. Diverres by Colleagues, Pupils and Friends*, ed. P. B. Grout et al. (Cambridge, 1983), pp. 86–98, 237–40 (notes). In an unpublished paper read to the Annual Colloquium of the London Medieval Society on Nov. 6, 1982, I was able to add to the references contained in the article the following: Pliny, *Nat. Hist.* 8. 19. 48; Rabanus Maurus, *De universo*, bk. 8, chap. 1, *Patrologia Latina* 3, 217; Nequam, *De laud. div. sap.* in Th. Wright, ed., *De nat. rer.* Rolls Series 34 (1863), 486; to Mr. Peter Dronke I owe the reference to the Confession of the Archpoet ("Parcit enim subditis leo rex ferarum / et est erga subditos immemor irarum, / et vos idem facite, principes terrarum: / quod caret dulcedine, nimis est amarum") in H. Watenphul and H. Krefeld, *Die Gedichte des Archipoeta* (Heidelberg: Winter, 1958), p. 76 (n. 10: str. 25). Further refs. to *Aen.* 6: 853 are Aug., *De civ. Dei,* pref. bk. 1 and Alcuin, *Monumenta Germaniae Historica* Ep. 4, p. 294. There is nothing new in I. Malaxecheverria, "El leon de Yvain y la degradación del símbolo," *Romance Notes* 22 (1981), 102–6, but the whole range of symbolic and human associations of the lion which might have been familiar to Chrétien and his audience are interestingly illustrated by the study of M. Igarashi-Takeshita, "Les lions dans la sculpture romane en Poitou," *Cahiers de Civilisation Médiévale* 23 (1980), 37–54.

9. See W. Bruce Finnie, "The Structural Function of Names in the Works of Chrétien de Troyes," *Names* 20 (1972), 91–4.

10. For Chrétien's use of irony see D. H. Green, *Irony in the Medieval Romance* (Cambridge: Cambridge University Press, 1979) and the review article by Tony Hunt in *German Life and Letters* 35 (1981), 98–104.

11. This is, of course, a theme of Bernart de Ventadorn's poem *Ges de chantar no.m pren talans* the first stanza of which runs: "Ges de chantar no.m pren talans, / tan me peza de so que vei, / que metre.s soli' om en grans / com agues pretz, onor e lau, / mas era no vei ni non au / c'om parle de drudaria, / per que pretz e cortezia / e solatz torn' en no-chaler," M. Lazar, ed., Bernard de Ventadour, *Chansons d'amour* (Paris: Klincksieck, 1966), p. 100, ll. 1–8. Chrétien may have had this in mind. On the other hand it is possible that his complaint in the prologue and at ll. 5392 ff. is directed against the *fin amor* of the troubadours as a topical literary fiction rather than a sincere emotion. He certainly seems to burlesque troubadour conceits in his romances, especially in Yvain's meeting with Laudine, and he may have abandoned the *Charrete* because its theme was ultimately inimical to him. See the important articles of F. Bogdanow, "The Love Theme in Chrétien de Troyes' *Chevalier de la Charrette*," *Modern Language Review* 67 (1972), 50–61; "The Tradition of

the Troubadour Lyrics and the Treatment of the Love Theme in Chrétien de Troyes' *Erec et Enide,*" in *Court and Poet*, ed. G. S. Burgess (Liverpool: Francis Cairns, 1981), pp. 79–92; "The Tradition of the Troubadours and the Treatment of the Love Theme in Chrétien de Troyes' *Chevalier au Lion*," *Arthurian Literature* 2 (1982), 76–91.

12. Chrétien may have got some of this from Gellius, see *Noctes Atticae*, ed. P. K. Marshall, (Oxford: Clarendon Press, 1968), 1. 65. 1–3: "Qui sunt leues et futtiles et inportuni locutores quique nullo rerum pondere innixi uerbis uuidis et lapsantibus diffluunt, eorum orationem bene existimatum est in ore nasci, non in pectore; linguam autem debere aiunt non esse liberam nec uagam, sed uinclis de pectore imo ac de corde aptis moueri et quasi gubernari . . . Ulixen contra Homerus, uirum sapienti facundia praeditum, uocem mittere ait non ex ore, sed ex pectore, quod scilicet non ad sonum magis habitumque uocis quam ad sententiarum penitus conceptarum altitudinem pertineret . . . "

13. On the complexities of presentation in Chrétien see P. F. Dembowski, "Monologue, Author's Monologue, and Related Problems in the Romances of Chrétien de Troyes," *Yale French Studies* 51 (1975) 102–14 and John L. Grigsby, "Narrative Voices in Chrétien de Troyes: A Prolegomenon to Dissection," *Romance Philology* 32 (1978–9), 261–73.

14. We must not confine this to aural reception, as is made clear by M. G. Scholz, *Hören und Lesen. Studien zur primären Rezeption der Literatur im 12. und 13. Jahrhundert* (Wiesbaden: Steiner, 1980), who shows that private reading is indicated by a far larger number of texts than has previously been allowed. Cf. the comments of F. Lebsanft in *Zeitschrift für Französische Sprache und Literatur* 92 (1982), 52–64. On the repetition of narrative performances in *Yvain* cf. R. Warning, "Formen narrativer Identitätskonstitution im höfischen Roman," *Grundriss der romanischen Literaturen des Mittelalters*, 4. 1: "Le Roman jusqu'à la fin du XIIIe siècle" (Heidelberg: Winter, 1978) [25–59] esp. 54 f.

15. I have drawn attention to some of these problems in my essay "Chrétien de Troyes' Arthurian Romance, *Yvain*" in *The New Pelican Guide to English Literature*, 1, *Medieval Literature*, pt. 2 The European Inheritance (Harmondsworth, 1983), 126–141. On the enforced critical activity of the audience see R. W. Hanning, "The Audience as Co-Creator of the First Chivalric Romances," *The Yearbook of English Studies* 11 (1981) [1–28] esp. 12–16.

16. The notion of inscribed audiences in *Yvain* and the *Charrete* and the links between the two are treated by Roberta L. Krueger, "Reading the *Yvain / Charrete*: Chrétien's inscribed audiences at Noauz and Pesme Aventure," *Forum for Modern Language Studies* 19 (1983), 172–87. I mention here the possibility that the reference to "un romanz, ne sai de cui" may be an ironic allusion to the *Charrete* which Chrétien abandoned to Godefroi de Leigni. The complaint about the current lack of interest in love (ll. 5394–6) might suggest that the *Charrete* had failed to find favour and that Chrétien here sardonically disowns it.

17. Cf. M. T. Bruckner, *Narrative Invention in Twelfth-Century French Romance. The Convention of Hospitality (1160–1200)* (Lexington: French Forum, 1980). I would not go so far as R. T. Pickens, *The Welsh Knight. Paradoxicality in Chrétien's Conte del Graal* (Lexington, Ky.: French Forum, 1977) who sees Chrétien's last work as an "exploded romance" which has as its central theme the inadequacies of linguistic signs.

18. See R. W. Hanning, "The Social Significance of Twelfth-Century Chivalric Romance," *Medievalia et Humanistica* n.s. 3 (1972), 3–29 and *id., The Individual in Twelfth-Century Romance* (New Haven: Yale University Press, 1977) especially pp. 54–60.

19. It is strange that this aspect of Chrétien has scarcely been treated by French specialists, though the idea has been familiar to Germanists for some time, see P. Kern, "Der Roman und seine Rezeption als Gegenstand des Romans. Beobachtungen zum Eingangsteil von Hartmanns *Iwein*," *Wirkendes Wort* 23 (1973), 246–52.

Notes

Notes   113

20. The edition used throughout is *Iwein: Eine Erzählung von Hartmann von Aue.* Herausgegeben von G. F. Benecke und K. Lachmann, neu bearbeitet von Ludwig Wolff, siebente Ausgabe, vol. 2 (Berlin: De Gruyter, 1968). For bibliographical details see Tony Hunt, "The Medieval Adaptations of Chrétien's *Yvain*: A Bibliographical Essay," in *An Arthurian Tapestry: Essays in Memory of Lewis Thorpe*, ed. Kenneth Varty (Glasgow: University of Glasgow, 1981), pp. 203–13.

21. See the important article of B. Nagel, "Hartmann 'zitiert' Reinmar. *Iwein* 1–30 und *MF* 150/10–18," *Euphorion* 63 (1969), 6–39, who sees in the prologue the expression of a specifically chivalric ideal and the reply by R. Endres, "Die Bedeutung von *güete* und die Diesseitigkeit der Artusromane Hartmanns," *Deutsche Vierteljahrsschrift* 44 (1970), 595–612.

22. See B. Schmolke-Hasselmann, "Untersuchung zur Typik des arthurischen Romananfangs," *Germanisch-Romanische Monatsschrift* 31 (1981), 1–13, and P. Kobbe, "Funktion und Gestalt des Prologs in der mittelhochdeutschen nachklassischen Epik des 13. Jahrhunderts," *Deutsche Vierteljahrsschrift* 43 (1969) [405–57] especially p. 421.

23. This should put us on our guard against too easily accepting what has become received wisdom, namely that Hartmann is concerned with a critique of Arthur and his values, a claim which has been exaggerated, see H. P. Pütz, "Artus-Kritik in Hartmanns Iwein," *Germanisch-Romanische Monatsschrift* 53 (1972), 193–7.

24. On the new degree of authorial self-consciousness which emerged in the 12th Century see Martin Stevens, "The Performing Self in Twelfth-Century Culture," *Viator* 9 (1978), 193–212.

25. See J. Suchomski, *Delectatio und Utilitas. Ein Beitrag zum Verständnis mittelalterlicher komischer Literatur*, Bibliotheca Germanica 18 (Bern: Francke, 1975), especially pp. 67 ff.; W. C. McDonald, "Die Deutung von Hartmanns Wendung 'swaere stunde senfter machen': Befreiung von 'Betrübnis' oder 'Langweile'?" *Studia Neophilologica* 46 (1974), 281–94; G. Olson, "The Medieval Theory of Literature for Refreshment and its Use in the Fabliau Tradition," *Studies in Philology* 71 (1974), 291–313.

26. Kurt Ruh, *Höfische Epik des deutschen Mittelalters*, Teil 1: *Von den Anfängen bis zu Hartmann von Aue* (Berlin: Erich Schmidt, 1967) p. 143, is surely right to describe this as "eine für Hartmann bezeichnende Korrektur Chrétiens." Cf. ll. 885–8, an elaboration of Chrétien l. 655.

27. In Chrétien *cuer* occurs 7 times, *oreilles* 5 times, *antandre* 5 times, and *oïr* 3 times. In Hartmann *ôren: herzen* occurs once, *merken* and *dagen* twice each.

28. See I. von Zingerle, "Herze und Ôren," *Germania* 8 (1863), 111–13.

29. Keiî, for example, is an unsympathetic listener, always trying to find fault, see the elaboration of Chrétien in ll. 137–58.

30. See V. Mertens, "Imitatio Arthuri: Zum Prolog von Hartmanns *Iwein*," *Zeitschrift für deutsches Altestum* 106 (1977), 350–8.

31. For bibliographical details see Hunt, "The Medieval Adaptations of Chrétien's *Yvain* . . . ," pp. 206 f., 211 f. (n. 21–25).

32. For recent surveys of the cultural background of the romances, see Janet Coleman, *English Literature in History. 1350–1400: Medieval Readers and Writers* (London: Hutchinson, 1981), pp. 41 ff.; P. Boitani, *English Medieval Narrative in the Thirteenth and Fourteenth Centuries* (Cambridge: Cambridge University Press, 1982), pp. 36–70.

33. See L. F. Salzman, *Edward I* (London: Constable, 1968); M. Prestwich, *The Three Edwards: War and State in England 1272–1377* (London: Weidenfeld and Nicolson, 1980).

34. On this quality see J. A. Burrow, *A Reading of Sir Gawain and the Green Knight*, (London: Routledge and Kegan Paul, 1965), pp. 42–50; S. S. Hussey, "*Sir Gawain* and

Romance Writing," *Studia Neophilologica* 40 (1968) [161–74] 172; K. Lippmann, *Das ritterliche Persönlichkeitsideal in der mittelenglischen Literatur des* 13. *und* 14. *Jahrhunderts*, diss. Leipzig (Meerane, 1933), pp. 11 ff., who discusses *trowthe* as "unerschütterlich festes Eintreten für das gegebene Wort, unbedingte Zuverlässigkeit im Einhalten von Versprechen und Gelübden" (p. 12). Lippmann draws attention to Middle English writers' emphasis on ethical character ideals and declares, "Neben der Betonung der *mesure* und der *meekness* zeigt der Vergleich mit den französischen Quellen die Vorliebe der Engländer für das Ideal der *trouthe*" (p. 54).

35. Cf. M. R. Golding, "The Importance of keeping 'trouthe' in *The Franklin's Tale*," *Medium Aevum* 39 (1970), 306–12.

36. Note, too, how at the end of his account Chrétien's "Einsi alai, einsi reving, / au revenir por fol me ting" (ll. 577–8) becomes "I fand þe folies þat I soght" (l. 456).

37. The importance of this theme (*triuwe*) in Hartmann's version of the Yvain story is brought out by Harald Scholler, "*Wâ sint diu werc? die rede hoere ich wol*: Ein Beitrag zur Interpretation von Hartmanns *Iwein*," in *Husbanding the Golden Grain: Studies in Honour of Henry W. Nordmeyer*, ed. L. T. Frank and E. E. George (Ann Arbor: University of Michigan Press, 1973), pp. 295–320, and Herta Zutt, *König Artus - Iwein - Der Löwe: Die Bedeutung des gesprochenen Wortes in Hartmanns Iwein* (Tübingen: Niemeyer, 1979). The theme is much more complex in Hartmann where legal questions are legion, see Edith Hagenguth, *Hartmanns Iwein. Rechtsargumentation und Bildsprache*, diss. Berlin, 1969.

38. This certainly seems to be the motive in *Iarlles y Ffynnawn* where Arthur negociates Owein's leave, and in the Swedish *Herr Ivan*, too, Arthur himself seeks to persuade Ivan to leave.

39. See L. Pollmann, *Die Liebe in der hochmittelalterlichen Literatur Frankreichs (Frankfurt M.: Klostermann,* 1966) p. 284 who observes, "Das 'amander doit' zeigt eindeutig, dass Chrétien hier höfische Liebe meint." Cf. Marcabru (ed. Dejeanne) 13, 25–7 and Arnaut Daniel (ed. Troja) 10, 8–10. In a treatise edited by A. Klein, Die altfranzösischen Minnefragen, diss. Marburg, 1910, on p. 48 we read "l'en ayme pour honneur et pour mieulx valoir."

40. See Ruth Harvey, *Moriz von Craûn and the Chivalric World* (Oxford: Clarendon Press, 1961), pp. 112 f. and R. Barber, *The Knight and Chivalry* (London: Longman, 1970), pp. 153 ff. See also J. J. Francis Firth, ed., *Robert of Flamborough . . . Liber Poenitentialis* (Toronto: Pontifical Institute of Medieval Studies, 1971), p. 134 § 128, and N. Denholm Young, "The Tournament in the Thirteenth Century," [1962] reprinted in *Collected Papers of N. Denholm Young* (Cardiff: University of Wales Press, 1969), pp. 95–120.

41. Cf. Klein, Die altfranzösischen Minnefragen, p. 42.

42. *Les Chansons courtoises de Chrétien de Troyes*, ed. M.-C. Zai (Berne: Lang, 1974), p. 79.

43. A. Roncaglia, "Carestia," *Cultura Neolatina* 18 (1958), 121–37. See now C. Di Girolamo, "Tristano, Carestia e Chrétien de Troyes," *Medioevo Romanzo* 9 (1984), 17–26 who tentatively proposes the identification of Carestia with Bernart.

44. On the Tristan theme in Chrétien see Zai, *Chansons courtoises*, pp. 97–100; H. Weber, *Chrestien und die Tristandichtung* (Berne: Lang, 1976); K. D. Uitti, "Intertextuality in *Le Chevalier au Lion*," *Dalhousie French Studies* 2 (1980), 3–13, who calls *Yvain* "Chrétien's most authentic 'anti-Tristan'" (p. 9). On the intertextuality of Chrétien's lyric see pp. 34–41 of Peter Haidu's study "Text and History: the Semiosis of Twelfth-Century Lyric as Sociohistorical Phenomenon (Chrétien de Troyes: *D'Amors qui m'a tolu*),"

Semiotica 33 (1981), 1-63. Haidu attaches great importance to monetary metaphors (pp. 27-34) and declares "If the dialectical argument of the poem — *biens adoucist par delaier* — is not really convincing in the amorous isotopy, it is entirely convincing in the economic isotopy." (p. 57.)

45. On the background of intertextual reference in the Troubadours see F. Pirot, *Recherches sur les connaissances littéraires des troubadours occitans et catalans des XIIe et XIIIe siècles*, Memorias de la Real Academia de Buenas Letras de Barcelona 14 (Barcelona: Real Academia de Buenas Letras, 1972), pp. 515-25.

46. Bernart's poem offers the closest possible link with *Yvain* in its evocation of the fickleness of the *domna*: "D'aisso's fa be femna parer / Ma domna, per qu'e.lh o retrai, / Car no vol so c'om deu voler, / e so c'om li deveda, fai." In Lazar ed., p. 182, ll. 33-6, cf. *Yvain* ll. 1640-4 and *Ars am.* 1: 755 f.

47. Besides the Ovidian references already noted in connection with the lyric, compare *Yvain* ll. 2519-23 with the depiction of the "vetus miles" in *Ars am.* 3: 573 ff. (cf. also *Heroides* 4: 19).

48. See F. P. Pickering, *Essays on Medieval German Literature and Iconography* (Cambridge: Cambridge University Press, 1980), pp. 95-109 ("Notes on Fate and Fortune") and 110-29 ("The 'Fortune' of Hartmann's Erec").

49. Though a ruler's relationship with his wife is the subject of extensive commentary in the *miroirs de princes*: see, for example, S. P. Molenaer, ed., *Li Livres du gouvernement des rois: A XIIIth Century French Version of Egidio Colonna's Treatise* De Regimine principum (Columbia: 1899; repr. London: Frank Cass, 1966), bk. 2, chap. 1-21, especially chap. 16-7 on restraint in sexual relations and chap. 19 on the dangers of jealousy. Cf. the *Secretum Secretorum* in *Opera hactenus inedita Rogeri Baconi*, Fasc. 5, ed. R. Steele (Oxford: Clarendon Press, 1920), Pt. 1, chap. 13, pp. 50-1.

50. See the edition by J. Holmberg (Uppsala: Almquist & Wiksells Boktryckeri 1929), pp. 20-1.

51. Tony Hunt, "The Prologue to Chrestien's *Li Contes del Graal*," *Romania* 92 (1971), 359-79. Cf. *Li Livres du gouvernement . . .* bk. 1, pt. 2, chap. 17-21.

52. The picture of the *Krautjunker's* domestic preoccupations may have been suggested by the discussion of property and its owner in *De officiis*. 1. 39. 138: "Ornanda enim est dignitas domo, non ex domo tota quaerenda nec domo dominus, sed domino domus honestanda."

53. See *Erek,* ll. 10085-100 and H. Naumann, "Hartmann von Aue und Cicero," *Deutsche Vierteljahrsschrift* 23 (1949), 285-7. For the importance of Cicero's *De officiis* see N. E. Nelson, "Cicero's *De officiis* in Christian Thought: *300-1300*," *University of Michigan Publications in Language and Literature* 10 (Ann Arbor: 1933), 59-160.

54. See K. Bosl, "'Noble Unfreedom': The Rise of the ministeriales in Germany," in T. Reuter, ed., *The Medieval Nobility. Studies on the Ruling Classes of France and Germany from the Sixth to the Twelfth Century*, Europe in the Middle Ages, Selected Studies 14 (Amsterdam: North-Holland Publ. Co., 1979), pp. 291-311; J. B. Freed, "The Origins of the European Nobility: The Problem of the Ministerials," *Viator* 7 (1976), 211-41 and *id.*, "The Formation of the Salzburg Ministerialage in the Tenth and Eleventh Centuries: An Example of Upward Social Mobility in the Early Middle Ages," *Viator* 9 (1978), 67-102. The reflection of these movements in the courtly romance has been argued by G. Kaiser, *Textauslegung und gesellschaftliche Selbstdeutung: Aspekte einer sozialgeschichtlichen Interpretation von Hartmanns Artusepen* (Frankfurt M.: Athenäum, 1973) (and, further, in *Euphorion* 69 [1975], 410-43) and criticised by Ursula Peters in *Euphorion* 69 (1975),

175-96, who argues that the romances were relevant to the ministerials precisely insofar as the latter had achieved parity with the nobility. That the latter remained the principal patrons of courtly literature is maintained by J. Bumke, *Ministerialität und Ritterdichtung. Umrisse der Forschung* (Munich: C. H. Beck, 1976). Chrétien seems to have been writing for the nobility of blood, see Tony Hunt, "The Emergence of the Knight in France and England *1000-1200*," *Forum for Modern Language Studies* 17 (1981) [93-114], 99.

55. In the *De officiis* Cicero stresses the need for advice (cf. Gâwein!) precisely at the moment of prosperity: "Atque etiam in secundissimis rebus maxime est utendum consilio amicorum iisque maior etiam quam ante tribuenda auctoritas . . . " (1. 26. 91). F. Martini, *Das Bauerntum im deutschen Schrifttum von den Anfängen bis zum 16. Jahrhundert* (Halle: Niemeyer, 1944), p. 35, compares Hartmann's description of the *Krautjunker* with a later complaint, concerning the Austrian ministerials, in the so-called *Seifried Helbling*. The domestic preoccupations of more than one *dienstman* at the Viennese court are unfavourably contrasted to the chivalric activities of literary heroes from the past (see ed. Seemüller, 15: 87 ff). Several of the poems in the collection display a critical attitude ca. 1291 to infringements of the social norms, including peasants aping the nobility and the nobility neglecting their own responsibilities.

56. See ll. 2899-901.

57. Note the distancing from criticism in ll. 3052-5: "*Man saget* daz mîn her Gâwein in/mit guoter handelunge/behabte unde betwunge/daz er der jârzal vergaz," and see also ll. 3029 ff.

58. It is unfortunate that the short speech contains a hapax which is difficult to construe: "For when þat he [= knight] has grete *endose*,/þan war tyme to win his lose" (ll. 1461-2). This may derive from a mistaken conflation of Chrétien 2498-9: "Quant il est del reaume sire,/Or primes doit *son* [MSS = vostre] pris croistre," so that the sense of *endose* would be "responsibilities" (cf. Stevick's "things to be done"). Or should the problematic lines be compared with the later lines 1469-70, *endose* being understood in the normal sense of OF *ados/endos* as "support, backing"?

59. Cf. *conseillier* in ll. 6556, 6580, 6582/1597, 1623, 1639, defence of the fountain in 6569/1624, the cowardice of the knights in 6564 ff, 6586 ff/1628 ff, and the lady's honour in 6571/1672.

60. Cf. *Cligés* ll. 603 ff. and *Met.* 4: 63 f.

61. See Reid ed., p. 216, note to l. 6780.

62. The parallel is pursued by A. R. Press, "Chrétien de Troyes' Laudine: A *Belle Dame sans Mercy?*", *Forum for Modern Language Studies* 19 (1983), 158-71, though I do not agree with his conclusions.

63. For similar instances of irony concerning women see ll. 3254-6, 7674-84, 8004-5.

64. See Ch. Huber, *Wort sint der dinge zeichen. Untersuchungen zum Sprachdenken der mittelhochdeutschen Spruchdichtung bis Frauenlob* (Munich: Artemis, 1977), p. 109 and Zutt, *König Artus-Iwein-Der Löwe* (see note 37).

65. All four occurrences of *waenlich* in Hartmann are found in the *Iwein*, cf. l. 2433.

66. The Dresden MS (Sächsischer Landesbibliothek M. 175(a) of ca. 1410-15, largely the work of a wilful Jewish scribe, is of little significance. The Giessen MS (Universitätsbibliothek 97) of ca. 1200-20 is the closest of all to Hartmann's time, but this factor does not make it automatically superior, and it is just as likely that alterations to Hartmann's ending were made by the spontaneous confusion or disapproval of a near contemporary, before a traditional interpretation or reception had become established. The Giessen MS becomes much less reliable towards the end and, on the strength of ll. 8149 ff. and 8121 ff., adds 32

lines after l. 8158. The "Ambraser Heldenbuch" (s.xvi in.) was based on a good model, but also becomes less reliable towards the end and lacks ll. 8133-6. For further details, see P. J. Becker, *Handschriften und Frühdrücke mittelhochdeutscher Epen* (Munich: Reichert, 1977), pp. 52 ff. For the texts of the endings see the *Studienausgabe* of Wolff's *Iwein* text by Thomas Cramer (Berlin: De Gruyter, 1968), pp. 225ff and Ch. Gerhardt, "*Iwein*-Schlüsse," *Literaturwissenschaftliches Jahrbuch* N. F. 13 (1972), 13-39. For a facsimile of the Giessen MS see *Hartmann von Aue: Iwein. Handschrift B*. Deutsche Texte in Handschriften 2 (Cologne: Böhlau, 1964). The present ending of *Iwein* was seen as an authorial revision by K. Zwierzina in *Zeitschrift für deutsches Altestum* 40 (1896), 235 ff.

67. See *Yvain* l. 4592 which is a crux. Incognito before Laudine, Yvain declares that when he regains his lady's pardon "finera mes travauz toz." Interpreting *travauz* here as "labours, chivalric exertions" would be the only way to provide a specific and explicit link between the hero's adventures and his love. It is more likely that *travauz* here means "travail, suffering, distress" and that Hartmann wishes to reinforce the link by depicting Laudîne's recognition of Iwein's "grôzen kumber" (l. 8124).

68. See F. Bogdanow, "The Tradition of the Troubadours . . . *Chevalier au Lion*," 82-84.

69. Note that it is not love which overcomes Yvain and recalls to his mind the promise to return (ll. 2694-703), as it is in Hartmann (ll. 3088-9).

70. See Hartmann ll. 3157-9.

71. See Zutt, *König Artus-Iwein-Der Löwe* (see note 37), p. 21.

72. When Iwein, incognito before Laudîne, says of "mîner vrouwen hulde" "der mangel ich ân schulde" (l. 5470) we must accept this, I think, as a rhetorical self-justification designed to elicit his lady's sympathy. When he assures her at the end "irn habt deheine schulde: / wan ich het iuwer hulde / niuwan durch mînen muot verlorn" (ll. 8133-5) we may see this, as the audience surely did, as setting the seal on the hero's new identity, which would have been compromised by any attempt to shift some of the burden of blame onto another. Cf. the explanation offered by Scholler, "*Wâ sint din werc?*", 318, n. 30.

73. Negative, unsympathetic judgements are offered by E.-M. Carne, *Die Frauengestalten bei Hartmann von Aue. Ihre Bedeutung im Aufbau und Gestalt der Epen* (Marburg: N. G. Elwert, 1970), pp. 133 f; A. K. Blumstein, *Misogyny and Idealization in the Courtly Romance* (Bonn: Bouvier, 1977) pp. 53 f. M.-N. Lefay-Toury, "Roman breton et mythe courtois: l'évolution du personnage féminin dans les romans de Chrétien de Troyes," *Cahiers de Civilisation Médiévale* 15 (1972) [193-204 & 283-93] argues that women make no contribution to the *sen* of *Yvain* and that the lion is "un substitut de Laudine" (p. 199), paints a negative portrait of Laudine (p. 204), and describes the ending as "escamoté . . . banal et abrupt, comme volontairement," all of which is seen in the context of a progressive "dégradation du rôle et du caractère de ses [= Chrétien's] figures féminines."

74. Helaine Newstead, "Narrative Techniques in Chrétien's *Yvain*," *Romance Philology* 30 (1976-7) [431-41], warns against overestimating the role of love in this romance, arguing that "the love scenes are bravura displays of the rhetorical language of amorous poetry" which overlay deception and guile and that the two themes of love and chivalry are "undeniably linked in the narrative but clearly differentiated in treatment." (p. 441).

75. For some other instances of 'humanising' details added by Hartmann, see M. Huby, "L'Interprétation des romans courtois de Hartmann von Aue," *Cahiers de Civilisation Médiévale* 22 (1979) [23-38], 36-7.

76. Beate Hennig, *"Maere" und "werc": Zur Funktion von erzählerischem Handeln im "Iwein" Hartmanns von Aue*, Göppinger Arbeiten zur Germanistik 321 (Göppingen: Kümmerle, 1981), 234 ff.

4. L'Invention dans les romans en prose*

Au moment où Alexandre Micha et Elspeth Kennedy[1] terminent leurs éditions du *Lancelot*, ce qui suscite déjà un regain d'intérêt pour les romans en prose, il serait bien téméraire d'entreprendre une vue d'ensemble, une synthèse à propos de ces romans. Une telle synthèse me paraît d'autant plus inopportune que nous n'avons pas encore d'éditions critiques pour tout le corpus des romans en prose. Les éditions Micha et Kennedy nous rappellent celles qui sont toujours en train de ressortir à la lumière — les *Tristan* en prose, le *Roman du Graal* post-Vulgate, *Perceforest* et d'autres,[2] — ainsi que le problème très complexe des versions variantes que l'on trouve dans de nombreux manuscrits des cycles romanesques. C'est un nouveau monde que nous commençons à explorer, à pouvoir explorer systématiquement, mais un nouveau monde dont la carte contient encore bien des terres inconnues, ou connues de nom seulement. Dans cent ans d'ici, notre carte du pays d'Arthur ressemblera-t-elle davantage aux cartes du XVIe et du XVIIe siècle qu'à celles de la cartographie moderne? La prudence s'impose.

Je me propose donc d'examiner non les romans en prose, mais l'invention de ces romans, et en particulier l'art de l'invention que l'on trouve illustré dans les images et exposé dans les interventions d'auteur les plus importantes des textes disponibles, notamment ceux du *Lancelot-Graal*.[3] Peut-être pourra-t-on ainsi du moins côtoyer ces vastes continents romanesques, identifier les formes et les qualités signalées par ceux-là mêmes qui les écrivirent et nous les transmirent. En faisant ces premières découvertes dans le nouveau monde des romans en prose, vaste et divers, il ne faudra pas pour autant oublier le vieux monde d'où ils sont sortis — le roman en vers du XIIe siècle. En effet, le roman en prose surgit du roman en vers, puis s'en détache et finit par s'y opposer.

On sait que l'appréciation des romans en vers peut être rehaussée par une juste connaissance de l'art des romanciers tel qu'ils l'expriment dans leurs

119

interventions – dans les prologues, les épilogues, les gloses et digressions qui interrompent parfois les récits.[4] Non que ces interventions parviennent à résoudre tous les problèmes – parfois même elles les aggravent. Cependant on continue de progresser dans l'éclaircissement de *matiere* et *sans* dans les romans en vers, de *conjointure*, des rapports entre les Anciens obscurs et les Modernes, et ces progrès facilitent la critique historique des textes en l'orientant dans le sens indiqué par la terminologie des romanciers eux-mêmes. Mais on n'a pas toujours étudié avec autant d'assiduité les déclarations des romanciers en prose sur la création littéraire, ou bien sur l'invention – terme qui convient mieux à une époque pour laquelle Dieu seul était capable de créer.[5] Cette hésitation vient en partie du fait que les interventions des prosateurs sont moins nettes, parfois plus allégoriques que celles des romanciers en vers. Choisissons comme exemple, et comme point de départ, la construction de la Nef de Salomon dans le *Lancelot-Graal*. C'est une image de l'invention romanesque.

Dans cet épisode, Salomon est remarquable par son *sens*, par sa capacité de penser et de proposer. Mais il n'a pas l'*engin*, c'est-à-dire la capacité de réaliser son propos. Selon la *Queste del saint graal* et l'*Estoire del saint graal en prose*,[6] Salomon voulait communiquer. Il voulait faire savoir à Galaad qu'il avait été informé du destin de celui qui devait achever la haute quête du graal. Mais il ne parvint pas à trouver, à inventer le moyen de faire aboutir ce projet. Salomon se tourna donc vers sa femme, "car il l'avoit trovee de si grant engin qu'il ne cuidast mie qu'il eust ame de si grant engin ou siecle."[7] C'est sa femme, dont l'*engin* subtil trompait toujours le *sens* vigilant de son seigneur,[8] qui invente la Nef qui portera le message de Salomon à travers les époques et les espaces jusqu'à Galaad. L'*engin* (< *ingenium*), c'est l'imagination dans une de ses acceptions médiévales : la capacité de rendre concrète une idée, et donc de réaliser une intention dans la matière.[9] Le *sens* de Salomon et l'*engin* de sa femme, précédemment opposés, coopèrent désormais et ne peuvent rencontrer d'échec. "Car il n'a ou monde chose de quoi je ne cuidasse venir a chief," proclame la femme, "au grant sens qui en vos est et a la grant subtilité qui est en moi."[10] Dans ce passage, *sens* ne renferme donc pas "subtilité," sans laquelle pourtant tout effort de la part de Salomon pour réaliser son *sens* restera vain. Il a beau chercher, il ne trouve, n'invente rien (Q 221.19–21, 222.3).

Salomon savait qu'il existe des inventions incomprises par les inventeurs eux-mêmes.[11] Quand sa femme eut parachevé la construction de la Nef, "Tu as, fist il, merveilles fetes" (Q 224.32–33). Mais, poursuit-il, il faudra que "Nostre Sires" y ajoute sa *senefiance*, son *conseil*, afin de réaliser la communication avec Galaad (Q 224.32–225.5). N'a-t-on pas le droit de dire – et sans doute les romanciers en prose se le dirent – que le

Chevalier de la charrette de Marie et Chrétien exigea, lui aussi, le *conseil* d'en haut afin d'être mené à bien? L'union du *sens* et de l'*engin* rappelle en effet celle de la *matiere* et du *san* de Marie de Champagne avec la *painne* et l'*antancion* de Chrétien.[12] Avec cette différence qu'ici, c'est la femme qui a le *san* et la *matiere*, et c'est l'homme qui invente et construit l'œuvre. Mais il y a une différence plus importante entre l'invention de Chrétien et celle de Salomon. C'est la présence du graal. Or le sens du graal échappe à l'énoncé direct dans toutes les versions de romans en prose.[13] Et cependant l'amour de Lancelot et Guenièvre dut attendre le graal avant d'être reconnu "ouvertement" pour le péché qu'il avait toujours été. Cette vérité s'insinue de plus en plus instamment dans le *Lancelot propre*,[14] avant de parvenir dans la *Queste* au jugement formel et absolu qui s'abat sur Lancelot avec toute la finalité et tout le tragique de l'irréparable (Q 126.18–33). L'intervention d'en haut est tout aussi nécessaire pour la Nef de Salomon. Des ministres descendent du ciel, l'arrosent d'eau bénite et ajoutent le *surplus* qui la transforme en *foi et creance* (Q 225.21–22; E 2: 483[136.24]), comme on lit sur le bord de la Nef au moment où, chargée de toute sa *senefiance*, elle s'éloigne dans sa navigation à l'aventure vers Galaad. La foi et la Nef, l'œuvre de Dieu et de l'*engin* de la femme, porte le *sens* de Salomon vers le dernier rejeton de sa famille. Cette Nef a désormais sa propre volonté, qui est celle de Dieu. C'est cette même volonté qui fit de la *Charrette*, du *Roman de la charrette*, une *Charrette* d'infamie où sont exposés les coupables de l'amour terrestre.

On sait que les romans en prose semblent avoir, eux aussi, leur propre volonté. Dans un article remarqué, Tzvetan Todorov conclut que "si l'auteur [à l'instar de la femme de Salomon] pouvait ne pas comprendre très bien ce qu'il était en train d'écrire, le conte, lui, le savait."[15] C'est en effet le conte qui, à travers tout le grand cycle, entrelace et délace les diverses aventures, détermine leurs rapports mutuels et, dans la lumière brillante du graal, manifeste la grâce ou la vengeance de Dieu. Le conte se raconte, comme la Nef se conduit. Cette technique qui utilise librement l'entrelacement est bien connue et n'a plus besoin d'être démontrée.[16]

Mais qui est l'auteur du *Lancelot-Graal*? En un sens, il y en a autant que de manuscrits du roman. L'auteur, c'est le scribe. Selon le Prologue à l'*Estoire du saint graal*, un premier scribe reçut l'original directement de la main du Christ (E 2: 9 [5.1–7]). Pieux mensonge? Sans doute, mais dans le sens où la *Divine Comédie* l'est aussi: ne retrouve-t-on pas chez notre scribe anonyme les doutes de Dante qui précèdent des révélations associées à des visions d'animaux mystérieux dans les forêts obscures? De part et d'autre, ce sont des allégories de l'inspiration divine.[17] Dans l'*Estoire*, Dieu donne son livre au moment même où il propose de mettre

un terme aux doutes de son scribe sur la Trinité (E 2: 9 [5.4–7]). C'est
Dieu qui inspire la mise à l'écrit du roman, après en avoir rédigé la première copie.[18]

Ce livre dieudonné, "ki n'estoit pas, en nule maniere, plus lons ne plus
les com est la paume d'un home" (E 2: 9 [5.2]), est un livre sur le saint graal
(E 2: 13 [5.37]), mais qui s'exprime "de langhe de cuer si que ja icele de la
bouce ne paraut" (E 2: 9 [5.8]). Seul le regard dans ce livre profitera à l'âme
et au corps, pourvu qu'on y regarde "issi com on i doit esgarder."[19] A cette
calme vision silencieuse, intime, on puisera une joie indicible, inimaginable.
C'est le *conseil* qui résout tous les doutes et conduit les âmes vers la foi.
"Tout chou avenra par la forche des paroles qui, en chest livret, sunt
escrites" (E 2: 10 [5.11]), nous assure le Prologue de l'*Estoire*.

Copier ce livre spirituel, c'est donc un acte de foi, par lequel le scribe
traduit le livre de "langhe de cuer" en "langhe de bouche." Mais comment
faire parler la "langhe de cuer" dans la *Charrette* de Marie et Chrétien?

On peut combiner diverses matières, comme le fait la femme de
Salomon avec les bois blanc, vert et rouge de l'Arbre de vie. Nous con-
statons en effet dans la *Charrette en prose* certaines additions à la
matière du roman de Chrétien. On y trouve notamment le corps de
Galaad, fils de Joseph d'Arimathie, dans la tombe destinée au sauveur
des prisonniers de Logres, c'est-à-dire Lancelot. A côté gît Syméon dans
une deuxième tombe. Celle-ci est destinée, comme la Nef de Salomon, au
Galaad fils de Lancelot. C'est lui qui portera au royaume arthurien le
conseil de Dieu, conseil qui aurait pu sauver la Table Ronde des plaines
de Salesbierres.[20] Ce conseil sera la grâce qui est le graal.

Mais d'où vient cette nouvelle conjointure dans le roman de Chrétien?
Pour répondre à cette question, essayons de retrouver l'assiette ferme de
l'histoire littéraire. La question se pose à propos de la constitution des
romans en prose avec les débris des romans en vers, l'héritage de Wace et
de Chrétien de Troyes. La popularité rapidement acquise des romans en
prose marque le début de la lente disparition des romans en vers au cours
du XIIIe siècle.[21] On n'a pas encore expliqué de manière entièrement
satisfaisante ce passage du roman français médiéval du vers à la prose.
Dire qu'on tourna en prose le roman en vers afin d'échapper aux men-
songes qu'impose l'usage de la rime n'est guère convaincant, si le point de
départ est un roman en vers, comme dans le cas de la *Charrette*.[22] Mais
un *Lancelot-Graal* en vers n'eût pas été une tâche insurmontable, vu les
Continuations de *Perceval* et l'*Ovide moralisé*, ainsi que les adaptations
en vers néerlandaises, vu aussi le fait que les romans en prose, dans leur
conception même, et dans leur élaboration au XIIIe siècle et plus tard,

sont l'œuvre de plus d'un auteur.[23] Donc, ce qui distingue les romans arthuriens en prose de ceux en vers, n'est pas tant, me semble-t-il, le fait qu'ils soient en prose, qu'une nouvelle conception de l'invention romanesque. Comme l'a fait remarquer récemment Daniel Poirion, la prose, elle aussi, "est un art fait de contraintes," qui a "sa discipline formelle et spirituelle."[24]

Chrétien et la plupart des autres romanciers en vers usent de deux facultés pour leurs inventions: ce sont celles que la *Queste* nomme *sens* et *engin*. Nous avons constaté que le *sens* de Salomon, son intention, c'est la communication. Ce qui correspond, dans la *Charrette* et le *Perceval*, à la remise de *matiere* et *san* à Chrétien par Marie de Champagne et par Philippe de Flandre. La réalisation de cette intention, c'est l'œuvre de Chrétien, comme la Nef de Salomon est le fait de sa femme. Dans les Prologues à ses deux romans, Chrétien insiste sur sa *painne* et son *antancion* — il *antant* et *peinne*, dans le *Conte du graal*, à *rimoier* son conte.[25] Ainsi passe-t-il de l'intention de communiquer à la communication, qui, elle, réalise cette intention assez générale de ses mécènes dans la conjointure du roman.

Ici s'impose une petite digression sur la terminologie littéraire de nos romanciers.

Hélas! cette terminologie n'a pas toujours l'exactitude qu'on pourrait souhaiter, surtout pour des termes d'application aussi large que *matiere* et *san*. Ainsi Chrétien parle-t-il du *san* de Marie de Champagne et de son propre *sans*, qu'il distingue de celui de Marie tout en l'associant à sa propre *antancion*. *Antancion* et *antandre* eux-mêmes, dans les Prologues de la *Charrette* et du *Conte du graal*, ne signifient pas "intention" comme la volonté de communiquer d'un Salomon, ou bien d'une Marie et d'un Philippe. *Antancion/antandre* y ont plutôt l'acception de pratiquer un art afin justement de réaliser l'intention des mécènes dans une conjointure.[26] Ainsi donc, *antancion* suppose pour Chrétien application, et, en particulier, l'application de son *sans* en tant qu'*engin* à l'invention et à l'élaboration de l'œuvre souhaitée par les mécènes.

L'auteur imagine son œuvre dans le sens médiéval d'inventer la matière qui, "jointe" ensemble, permet la communication. De Marie de Champagne à Chrétien de Troyes, on passe du *conte d'avanture* à la *bele conjointure*.[27] Ce passage réunit une matière *depeciee* et *corronpue* dans un beau roman. C'est le travail que Thomas d'Angleterre appelle *unir* et *en uni dire*[28] — travail ingénieux par lequel on agence les éléments divers de la matière dans un ensemble qui exclut toute retouche postérieure. "Tant en a fet, n'i vialt plus metre/Ne moins, por le conte mal metre,"[29] déclare Godefroi de Leigni à la conclusion de la *Charrette*. Quelqu'en soit le succès,[30] le principe du *noli me tangere* est absolu. Chrétien lui-même l'évoque à la fin du *Chevalier au lion* pour écarter la mouvance à laquelle le roman est exposé en quittant ses mains.

> Onques plus conter n'en oï
> Ne ja plus n'en orroiz conter
> S'an n'i vialt mançonge ajoster.[31]

Au XIIIe siècle on retrouve le même empressement à délimiter le roman dans la division en trois parties égales du *Roman du graal* post-Vulgate.[32]

Vains espoirs! Voici justement le scribe d'un manuscrit d'*Yvain* qui s'élève contre le droit d'auteur en ajoutant son propre Epilogue à celui de Chrétien: "Li sages hons si nous raconte / Que on puet bien acroistre .i. conte."[33] On sait le sort souvent réservé aux romans en vers et en prose dès que s'en emparent les scribes.[34]

Mais il y a une différence capitale entre Chrétien de Troyes et l'auteur du roman post-Vulgate tripartite. Celui-ci n'interdit pas les additions. Son propos, quoique personnel, est plus modeste. Il désire que ses lecteurs puissent reconnaître sa contribution et, en même temps, être sûrs de la recevoir intacte. Il s'attend à ce qu'un autre écrive le mystérieux conte du *Brait*.[35] Et il rattache ce qu'il fait au *Lancelot propre*, qu'il exclut de son livre "ne mie pour chou qu'il . . . n'i apartiegne et que elle" — l'histoire de Lancelot — "n'en soit traite,"[36] mais pour réaliser sa division tripartite. Cette partie de la totalité a, bien entendu, sa propre cohérence, comme l'a démontré Fanni Bogdanow.[37] L'addition sert non seulement à compléter le *Lancelot*, elle l'approfondit aussi en pratiquant la même espèce d'invention que celle pratiquée par le romancier Vulgate sur Chrétien et Robert de Boron. Comme le scribe du manuscrit d'*Yvain*, le rédacteur anonyme du roman post-Vulgate est persuadé que "on peut bien acroistre .i. conte": lui-même le fait dans le *Lancelot*.

Le roman en vers, dans sa forme classique, réduit une matière hétérogène et diverse à une œuvre achevée, parfaite — à la *bele conjointure*. Ainsi, pour celle d'*Erec et Enide*, Chrétien joint ensemble deux contes, celui du Blanc Cerf — le premier *vers* qui se termine par le baiser accordé à Enide[38] — et celui de l'Epervier qui prend fin avec le mariage d'Erec et d'Enide. Ce mariage glisse vers la crise conjugale, passe par les aventures de la quête, et enfin se résout dans la réconciliation, la Joie de la Cour et le couronnement à Nantes. Les matières diverses dans cette conjointure sont comparables aux pierres du pommeau de l'épée dans la Nef de Salomon, telles que la femme de Salomon les souhaitait: "si soutilment jointes"[39] qu'aucun regard humain ne pourrait les distinguer les unes des autres.

On pourrait croire la conjointure d'*Erec* faite, elle aussi, d'une seule pièce — ou plutôt on pourrait le croire, n'était la référence au premier *vers*. Or de telles références abondent dans le *Lancelot-Graal*, où même une conjointure comme celle de la *Charrette* — n'en déplaise à Godefroi de Leigni — s'entrelace avec d'autres contes et s'y relie par de complexes liens formels et narratifs. L'ensemble, comme la Nef de Salomon où se trouve l'épée aux étranges renges, est de bien *diverse façon*.[40]

Je n'apporte ici rien de neuf. Je ne fais que retrouver dans les interventions d'auteur des romans en vers et en prose la conception de la conjointure chez les premiers, de la diversité chez les derniers, conjointure et diversité telles qu'Eugène Vinaver les a définies. La conjointure, écrit-il, c'est "ce qui réunit, rassemble ou organise des éléments divers et même dissemblables" — c'est le *en uni dire* de Thomas d'Angleterre — puis "les transforme en un tout organisé,"[41] c'est-à-dire en conjointure. Mais une autre génération, qui prend son point de départ dans ces mêmes romans en vers, ouvrira la conjointure à l'expansion, une expansion susceptible de comprendre dans ses branchages des matières de plus en plus nombreuses, de plus en plus diverses, où — je cite toujours Eugène Vinaver — "chaque événement acquiert un surcroît de signification grâce aux rapports qu'il soutient avec ses antécédents et ses suites possibles."[42]

La conjointure fait donc place à la "disjointure," à l'insertion dans une matière donnée d'une nouvelle matière. Un scribe pratique à bon escient cette opération, en insérant le *Roman de Troie* dans sa versification de la Bible.

> Ja ne me poëz de rien poindre,
> Fors que de tant qu'ai fait desjoindre
> Ma matiere que conmençai:
> A lei tantost revertirai.[43]

Cette disjointure élevée en principe de composition permettra les multiples interventions pratiquées par les auteurs aussi bien que les scribes dans les manuscrits de nos romans en prose. La possibilité d'antécédents et de suites évoquée par Vinaver, et la disjointure qui intercale le *Troie* dans la Bible, font voir à quel point on s'éloigne de la conjointure intégrale d'un Chrétien de Troyes, pour qui toute addition est mensonge. L'exemple de la Nef de Salomon en est la preuve. On introduit dans la fiction arthurienne la matière biblique et rejoint ainsi la légende arthurienne et l'histoire biblique depuis Adam jusqu'au Christ et la christianisation de la Grande Bretagne.

Dans ce genre d'analyse, les exemples représentent un groupe d'œuvres assez diverses, qu'elles soient en vers ou en prose. Parmi les romans des XIIe et XIIIe siècles, il en existe maints dont la conjointure est moins *bele* que celles du maître champenois. Mais l'échec ne met pas nécessairement en question le principe, en l'occurrence le principe de la conjointure. Cependant, à partir du moment où ce principe, et donc la technique qu'il présuppose, se transforment, les nouveaux critères exigent un ajustement de notre perspective critique. Or on constate dans les romans des XIIe et XIIIe siècles la transformation par laquelle le roman passe de l'art de Chrétien de Troyes, celui de la conjointure, à l'art du cycle *Lancelot-Graal*, celui de la disjointure. Ce nouvel art ni ne s'impose d'un seul coup, ni ne s'en tient au seul roman en prose du XIIIe siécle. Il se décèle même dans les premiers romans en vers. Déjà Benoît de Sainte-Maure avait exprimé le désir d'écrire une mappemonde, qui serait en même temps une chronique universelle, et il présente le *Roman de Troie* et le *Chronique des ducs de Normandie* comme des ébauches dans ce projet pour lui irréalisable.[44] La *Charrette* elle-même est épisodique, et l'*Yvain*, en dépit de son Epilogue, n'hésite pas à faire allusion à la quête pour Guenièvre en Gorre afin d'expliquer l'absence de Gauvain en Logres[45] —allusion qui fait penser aux renvois de la post-Vulgate au *Lancelot* en prose. Les continuateurs s'emparent du *Conte du graal*, inachevé et énigmatique, pour l'amplifier bien au-delà d'une *bele conjointure* où l'auteur en principe "n'i vialt plus metre/ne moins, por le conte mal metre." Et en même temps que Chrétien lègue bien malgré lui le *Perceval* à ceux qui pensent bien "acroistre .i. conte" de matières diverses, Robert de Boron trouve une nouvelle source de signification dans les rapports que le graal et la Table Ronde peuvent entretenir avec leurs antécédents, et notamment avec Joseph d'Arimathie et, en s'inspirant sans doute de Geoffroi de Monmouth ou de Wace, avec Merlin et ses prophéties.

Le glissement depuis la conjointure vers la disjointure est évident dans le regret de ne pas pouvoir tout dire, qui se fait entendre après Benoît de Sainte-Maure: Robert de Boron explique l'absence de certains développements dans son cycle par sa faiblesse, peut-être sa maladie.[46] Lui aussi, comme Chrétien dans *Perceval*, ne pourra mener à bien son entreprise. En même temps, Robert insiste sur sa conclusion, la dernière partie du roman prévu, comme essentielle à la compréhension du reste.[47] Ce début d'une hiérarchie de contes s'achèvera par l'évocation dans la *Queste* des trois tables de la Cène, du graal et de la Table Ronde—tables qui sont comme les images des trois contes du *Lancelot-Graal*: celui d'Adam et du Christ, celui de Joseph d'Arimathie et celui d'Arthur. Le système de l'entrelacement et de l'enchevêtrement des fils narratifs de ces contes, l'accumulation et l'organisation des niveaux de cohérence—l'expression est de Jean Fourquet[48] — représentés par les trois tables, voilà ce qui détermine l'économie nouvelle du *Lancelot-Graal* et de ses suites réelles ou possibles. L'intégralité fait place à la divergence, la conjointure à la disjointure.

Cette évolution vers le roman cyclique, qui permet de *disjoindre* une matière par l'introduction d'une autre, se poursuit rapidement au cours de la période de transition qui nous intéresse. On la connaît par les manuscrits cycliques des chansons de geste étudiés notamment par Maurice Delbouille et Madeleine Tyssens.[49] Le cycle plus romanesque de *Huon de Bordeaux* en usera aussi.[50] Le roman en vers des *Sept Sages de Rome* se dérime,[51] puis se rallonge durant le XIIIe siècle.[52] Et il n'hésitera pas à puiser dans la matière de Bretagne pour les branches dites *Laurin* et *Kanor*,[53] pas plus que le *Lancelot-Graal* n'hésite à rattacher son histoire à l'histoire sainte, et notamment aux vies de Salomon et de sa femme.

Devant une telle exubérance, n'a-t-on pas le droit de s'écrier, comme Salomon à sa femme, "Tu as . . . merveilles fetes. Car se tuit cil dou monde estoient ci, si ne savroient il deviser la senefiance" (Q 224.32–225.1) de ces romans? Mais il ajoute: "se Nostre Sires ne lor enseignoit."[54] Et c'est justement ce qui arrive au scribe du Prologue de l'*Estoire*, quand le Seigneur lui donne son livre à copier. Ce qui lui permet de retourner de façon implicite les paroles de Salomon contre Chrétien de Troyes: "tu meesmes, qui l'as fete, ne ses que ele senefie" (Q 225.2–3). L'amour qui rend Lancelot supérieur dans la *Charrette* de Chrétien marquera désormais sa dégénération. La prose corrige, notamment dans l'aventure du cimetière dans la *Charrette en prose*, dans les réprimandes des ermites dans la *Queste*, ailleurs aussi.[55] Aveugle à la vérité parce qu'ébloui par son amour,[56] Lancelot erre entre la joie et la folie jusqu'aux échecs rencontrés dans la haute quête du graal. La correction de Lancelot, c'est la correction du roman en vers par le roman en prose. C'est la révélation de la foi dans la *matiere* et le *san* de Marie et Chrétien, comme c'est la foi qui rend compréhensible l'amalgame de l'histoire de Salomon et de la nef celtique de la navigation à l'aventure.

Il existait pour le roman en vers un art qui permettait aux auteurs de tisser une intrigue cohérente sans y sacrifier l'insolite, l'inattendu, le mystère de l'aventure merveilleuse. Ces deux niveaux de cohérence, Jean Fourquet les a trouvés dans les romans de Chrétien. Le plan mythique — le *conte d'avanture*, la source de l'aventure merveilleuse *depeciee* et *corronpue* par les jongleurs — y acquiert non seulement une nouvelle structure, mais aussi un *san* quand le romancier lui invente un contexte — ce que Jean Fourquet appelle le plan de cohérence courtoise. L'étrange y épouse le coutumier et la coutume devient merveilleuse. Le conte d'aventure capte le reflet de ce contexte dans les miroirs divers et diversement illuminés de ses épisodes. Le roman ainsi inventé réalise un équilibre très délicat entre le merveilleux et la signification que lui trouve Chrétien. On comprend que Chrétien n'admette aucune addition à ses romans. Même si toutes les aventures n'y sont pas essentielles à la cohérence de l'intrigue, on ne saurait rien supprimer, altérer, ajouter, sans entamer la conjointure, où il ne faut ni plus ni moins "por le conte mal metre." Chrétien entend puiser lui-même au conte d'aventure tout ce qu'il offre de merveilleux et de significatif.

Peu après que Jean Fourquet eut attiré notre attention sur les deux niveaux de cohérence chez Chrétien, Pierre Le Gentil nous faisait remarquer l'art de la mutation brusque — cette mouvance du texte médiéval consciemment et délibérément altéré par le copiste, le remanieur ou le nouvel auteur.[57] On sait que de telles mutations, qu'elles soient petites ou grandes, ne manquent pas dans la tradition manuscrite de Chrétien.[58] C'est justement ce que Chrétien craint dans l'Epilogue d'*Yvain*. Le roman le plus vulnérable, le *Conte du graal*, passe par là. On pourrait même dire que les continuateurs de celui-ci perdirent de vue tout niveau de cohérence — et leurs productions, de plus en plus longues, de plus en plus divergentes, semblent perdre le *Perceval* de Chrétien dans les eaux de ses tributaires. Le roman rejoint le conte d'aventure, *depecié* et *corronpu*! Voilà "l'inflation romanesque"[59] qui résulte de la domination de l'auteur par le scribe!

Pourtant, le graal restait toujours là, au bout du chemin, ce qui prouve que le récit — cette voie labyrinthine — menait toujours quelque part, même si le scribe, plus ou moins habile ou ingénieux, n'entrevoyait qu'obscurément ce but. Car il savait toujours que d'autres reprendraient la tâche, qui sauraient évoquer de leur propre perspective ce qui en dernière analyse échappe à l'expression totale: "ce que langue ne porroit descrire ne cuer penser . . . [la] començaille des granz hardemenz et l'achoison des proeces . . . les merveilles de totes autres merveilles."[60] Le graal, qui semble miroiter devant nos yeux — les mutations brusques nous en offrent des images variées, hétéroclites, contradictoires — finit par s'orienter vers une signification chrétienne et une origine dans l'histoire sainte. Le graal et la Cène, le graal et la Table Ronde: deux niveaux de cohérence, chrétienne et courtoise, doivent désormais s'intégrer, s'expliquer, finalement se juger à travers les ramifications des aventures merveilleuses.

Cette révision du roman arthurien ne manquera pas de rendre suspect, puis de condamner l'équilibre si précaire de la chevalerie et la clergie chez Chrétien depuis *Erec* et *Cligés*. En effet, quelle mutation plus brusque, plus radicale que celle du début de la *Queste*? "Ha, Lancelot, tant est vostre afere changiez puis ier matin! . . . car meillor i a de vos"

(Q12.28–13.2). Le graal finit par révéler comme caducs l'amour et la prou-esse traditionnels dans le roman arthurien. L'échec de la haute quête du graal et l'autodestruction de la chevalerie de la Table Ronde sur les plaines de Salesbierres en sont la preuve définitive. Et ce choc produit par le graal dépasse le *Lancelot propre* pour ne mourir, après avoir inspiré le *Merlin* et l'*Estoire en prose*, qu'au pied de la croix, juste avant le moment où, dans le saint sépulcre, Joseph d'Arimathie recueille les gouttes de sang qui transfor-ment l'*escuele* de la Cène en graal.[61] Encore une mutation brusque! D'autres fissures plus profondes se révèlent dans le paysage arthurien, des abîmes où se dessinent "les lignes fuyantes de l'arrière-plan"[62] — les mystères de la foi et de la volonté divine. Galaad dans la *Queste* figure le Christ, "de semblance ne mie de hautece,"[63] le Christ préfiguré lui-même par Adam et le péché originel. L'histoire arthurienne a rejoint les grandes typologies de l'histoire sainte.[64] Cette jointure changera tout.

La typologie établit des rapports entre certains événements. Adam, qui introduit par le péché originel le changement et donc l'histoire dans la vie humaine, préfigure le second Adam, le Christ qui rachètera le péché originel et donnera accès au salut. L'histoire dans la Vulgate commence immédiatement après ces événements, quand on descend le Christ de la croix, puis quand Adam et Eve quittent le jardin d'Eden.[65] L'histoire ar-thurienne s'y greffe avec le personnage de Galaad, qui est à la fois type du Christ et descendant de Salomon, lui-même dans la descendance d'Adam. La signification de tels liens et des événements qui les établissent échappe totalement à la rationalité humaine: ils ne sont l'effet ni de prophéties ni de volonté humaine. Comme la Nef de Salomon, ils manifestent dans l'histoire les "lignes de force" qui relient les moments, lignes de force qui ne fonctionnent dans l'histoire qu'aux moments voulus par Dieu (E 2: 19–20 [7.16–17], une force qui intervient dans le temps et y opère une dis-jointure. Dieu en tant que Trinité est la fusion et la fission dans l'unité mystique,[66] fusion et fission dont le cycle Vulgate offre l'image visible.[67] C'est la parole de Dieu que copie le scribe et qu'il transfère de la langue de cœur en celle de bouche. Dans ses ramifications et ses circuits divers, cette force qui est Dieu et qui, dit-on, a créé notre texte, se manifeste dans ses images — les personnages comme Galaad et Salomon, Adam et le Christ — pour changer la signification de toutes les aventures et toutes les merveilles dont se composait auparavant l'histoire arthurienne, et notam-ment celle du graal qui révèle, à ceux qui savent voir et lire avec les yeux du cœur, les merveilles de toutes autres merveilles.

Du roman en prose on peut bien dire, avec le scribe d'*Yvain*, "on peut bien acroistre .i. conte"! "Le récit" des romans en prose — je cite Emmanuèle

Baumgartner — "peut, au gré de l'écrivain, se développer d'une manière linéaire et rapide ou, au contraire, rayonner presque sans limites dans l'espace."[68] Même les détails en apparence inutiles, futiles, les épisodes répétitifs ou incomplets,[69] les aventures et merveilles qui foisonnent dans le *Lancelot-Graal* et ses suites se placent dans une conception plus haute, toujours implicite: celle où dominent les idées de la foi, de la grâce et de la Trinité, c'est-à-dire que les détails romanesques s'inventent sous l'inspiration divine. Sans doute préférerait-on retrouver plus souvent dans le *Lancelot* l'économie qu'on trouve dans la *Queste*, où sont supprimées les aventures de Lancelot et de Galaad dans les îles de mer "por ce que trop i covenist a demorer qui tout voldroit aconter qan qu'il lor avint."[70] Mais — on doit se le rappeler constamment — quelque saugrenues, quelque puériles que paraissent les aventures et les merveilles inventées par les prosateurs et leurs scribes,[71] quelque durs d'oreille que ceux-ci puissent se montrer à la langue de cœur, les aventures multiples sont toutes là à cause du graal, et s'entendent finalement toutes dans la perspective de la quête du graal, après laquelle, selon la *Mort Artu*, "les aventures del roiaume de Logres estoient si menees a fin qu'il n'en avenoit mes nule se petit non."[72] Le génie de cet art — le Prologue à l'*Estoire* le dit — c'est celui du scribe, humble ou prétentieux, qui cherche à faire comprendre la parole du cœur qu'il transcrit. La technique qui permet de telles interventions est celle de la disjointure telle que la pratique le scribe qui insère le *Roman de Troie* dans la Bible. C'est la technique contre laquelle s'insurge Chrétien de Troyes à la fin de l'*Yvain* au nom de la conjointure, principe qui interdit les retouches et les interventions d'autrui.

Donc, afin d'*acroistre*, on dut réviser l'art de Chrétien. Marie de Champagne et Chrétien avaient mis *sens* et *engin* au service de l'invention romanesque. Voilà ce dont l'invention humaine était capable! *Sens* et *engin* restent primordiaux même pour ceux qui, comme Jean Bodel, s'opposaient, non à la chevalerie et à l'amour exaltés dans la matière de Bretagne, mais à la matière de Bretagne elle-même, dont le romanesque plaisant semblait si vain parce qu'elle ne glorifiait pas les rois de France.[73] Afin de perdre irrévocablement tous les romans de vanité, même ceux traitant des matières de France et de Rome,[74] on dut faire appel à des instances plus hautes que la noblesse petite et grande du temps de Chrétien et de Jean Bodel. Il fallut faire appel à Dieu.

Comment faire parler Dieu? Cette question fondamentale recouvre une angoisse profonde, une angoisse qui se manifeste dans les doutes sur la Trinité qui sapent la foi du scribe anonyme dans le Prologue de l'*Estoire*. Et pourtant la réponse à la question est très simple et vient de la bouche de Jésus lui-même. *Quaerite et invenies* — cherche et tu inventeras. Cela est vrai aussi pour les scribes. Malgré son doute, le scribe du Prologue fait son devoir quand les portes du ciel s'ouvrent à lui, et il reçoit le livre du graal, qui s'exprime par la parole du cœur. Ainsi pourra-t-il ouvrir et éclaircir cette vérité à tous ceux qui écouteront son livre.

Afin de transcrire cette parole en langage humain, on greffa la branche arthurienne sur l'histoire sainte. Désormais l'histoire arthurienne se comprenait comme l'histoire se comprend dans l'Ancien et le Nouveau Testaments: en tant que typologie. Si aujourd'hui les érudits ne s'accordent pas sur toutes les allusions et les *incidences* bibliques et hagiographiques que l'on trouve dans le *Lancelot-Graal*,[75] on ne peut guère nier la fonction explicite et déterminante de l'Ecriture sainte en tant que livre d'histoire dans l'intrigue[76] — et non seulement dans la *Queste. Acroistre* l'histoire sainte de l'histoire arthurienne — comme le scribe le fit avec l'histoire troyenne — c'est imposer un jugement obscur, mais toujours possible, sur les tournois d'*Erec* et d'*Yvain,* sur l'adultère de Lancelot et Guenièvre, sur les folies de la chevalerie et de l'amour qui éclatent enfin au grand jour dans la *Queste* et la *Mort Artu*. Quel procédé plus efficace pour solliciter et donc pour gloser la matière et le sens des romans en vers! Et quel scribe du moyen âge échappait à la tentation de la glose?[77] L'opération se fait d'ailleurs d'elle-même, comme pour la Nef de Salomon, où le bateau de la navigation à l'aventure reçoit la matière nouvelle des bois blanc, vert et rouge qui permettent la consécration par la foi et le lien avec Galaad.

Cette Nef, c'est donc une idée qui se réalise grâce à l'inspiration divine, cette "force" dans les paroles du livre. Le *sens* conçoit l'idée de communiquer. L'*engin* trouve le véhicule: la *Charrette* de Marie et Chrétien. L'appel à Dieu donne à cette invention en apparence hétéroclite, merveilleuse aussi, une nouvelle signification biblique et historique. La Nef de Salomon, dans la chronologie arthurienne, établit le premier lien entre histoire biblique et histoire arthurienne.

Quand Marie de Champagne et Chrétien de Troyes, à l'instar de Salomon et sa femme, collaboraient à la composition du *Chevalier de la charrette*, ils ne prévoyaient point ce que la parole de Dieu en ferait. Mais le conte, lui, le savait, ce conte qui, au dire de son Prologue, est la parole de Dieu,[78] comme tout dans ce bas monde est sa création, quoi qu'en fasse la perversité humaine.

Le Prologue à l'*Estoire* prétend en outre que le livre reçu de la main du Seigneur contient le commencement du lignage du scribe (E 2: 12 [5.26–27]). C'est donc un livre généalogique. Galaad, notamment, descend de Salomon. L'arbre généalogique se reflète dans l'image des branches du *Lancelot-Graal*. Par exemple, les scribes qui, à la cour d'Arthur, enregistrent les aventures des chevaliers, commencent une fois par celles de Gauvain parce qu'elles sont le commencement d'une quête pour Lancelot, puis ajoutent celles d'Hector parce qu'il achève la quête de Gauvain, dont la sienne est par conséquent une branche. Ensuite viennent les aventures des dix-huit autres compagnons de la quête pour Lancelot. Et le conte de Lancelot, lui, "fu branche del Graal, si com il y fu ajoustés,"[79] ainsi que le conte du graal se greffe sur le grand tronc de l'histoire depuis la Création jusqu'à la fin du monde. Cet immense arbre généalogique qu'est le *Lancelot-Graal*, c'est la souche, le tronc et les ramifications d'aventures et de merveilles, qui, pénétrées de la force du Créateur, se tournent vers le graal comme vers leur soleil. Les lignes de force, pour employer toujours l'expression de Vinaver, qui relient les différentes branches du corpus, comme la Nef qui relie Salomon à Galaad, ou bien le graal qui rattache la carrière de Josephes à celle du Christ aussi bien qu'à celle de Galaad, ces lignes de force sont dans le livre de Dieu, en langue de cœur. L'arbre des scribes, leurs ramifications en langue de bouche en sont l'image. Image assez diverse, c'est le moins qu'on puisse dire—mais aussi image cohérente en dernière analyse. Jean Frappier nous rappelle que "ces divergences ne sont pas telles qu'elles disloquent le plan d'ensemble. L'élan mystique de la *Queste* et sa rigueur doctrinale ont failli rompre la perspective, mais ont failli seulement. Chaque auteur est resté assez complice de l'architecture générale pour rejoindre par quelque biais l'inspiration plus ou moins opposée à la sienne."[80] Ce jugement reste valable pour les additions postérieures au grand cycle Vulgate. La vérité qui les embrasse n'est pas une vérité d'ordre rationnel. Il ne s'agit pas, comme dans le *Conte du graal* de Chrétien, d'une série de questions dont les réponses résoudraient les doutes et satisferaient les exigences de la raison, terminant ainsi le conte dans une *bele conjointure*. La vérité du *Lancelot-Graal* se trouve ailleurs: dans la foi.

Seule la foi est susceptible de rendre compréhensible la multiplicité des inventions divergentes dans l'architecture des romans en prose. Pour les prosateurs, le reflet de la foi est le roman en expansion vers l'infini. Les aventures de Logres sont l'effet du graal qui transforme par les rayons de sa force quelque matière, quelque aventure qu'ils pénètrent. Même l'ancien niveau de cohérence mythique s'y retrouve: la force de Gauvain retrouvée à midi, les enchantements de la Douloureuse Garde, la navigation à l'aventure—débris tout cela de l'Autre Monde celtique. Les deux fins du roi Arthur, emporté par Morgain la fée et enterré à la Noire Chapelle se juxtaposent dans une belle énigme.[81] A la main qui reprend le graal dans la *Queste* répond celle qui sort des eaux pour saisir l'épée Escalibor à la fin de la *Mort*—*san* et *matiere* désormais disjoints pour toujours, absorbés dans leurs anciens domaines et séparés par la *mescheance* qui s'abattit sur le royaume de Logres après le départ de Galaad.

La puissance du *Lancelot-Graal* tient justement à sa capacité de tout absorber, même les contradictions et les épisodes incomplets, les adaptations étranges de scribes différents, sans perdre la *senefiance* inépuisable qui semble émaner du graal. Il existait une expression pour désigner de telles combinaisons: *concors discordia,* l'amalgame de la métaphore.[82] Or c'est la métaphore qui rend possible l'allégorie dans les romans en prose.

Ces unions "diverses" du mystique et du mythique sont analogues à celles tout aussi diverses du *sens* et de l'*engin*, de l'homme et de la femme. La signification de telles unions dans le *Lancelot-Graal* vient d'en haut. Ainsi l'union de Bohort et de la fille du roi Brangore est-elle un péché. Mais le péché est racheté quand Dieu donne fruit à leur union. Car Bohort et la fille du roi Brangore ne peuvent donner que ce que le *Lancelot* appelle la *façon*: Dieu donne le surplus—le fruit et l'esprit, c'est-à-dire, l'enfant Helain le Blanc,[83] comme il le fit dans la construction de la Nef de Salomon, qui n'était avant son intervention qu'une *façon*. Ce surplus ne s'exprime ni ne se glose à la manière de Marie de France ou Chrétien. Il descend sur l'œuvre comme son esprit—la parole du cœur qu'écoute le scribe de l'*Estoire* inspiré par ses visions ineffables.

A l'époque de Chrétien et des romans en prose, le travail de l'artiste est comparable à celui de Dieu et de ses agents.[84] La conception précède la réalisation: le *status archetypus* est antérieur au *status sensilis* dans l'invention, selon Geoffroi de Vinsauf, qui ne fait que reprendre après tant d'autres un lieu commun.[85] Mais la pleine connaissance de l'archétype est réservée à Dieu. Car lui seul est capable de l'inventer, ou bien de le créer. *Opus Dei est quod non erat creare*, nous rappelle Hugues de Saint-Victor.[86] La contemplation de l'œuvre de Dieu, évoquée dans le Prologue de l'*Estoire,* est visionnaire. La lecture du livre de Dieu, où la parole est celle du cœur, l'est aussi. Entre Dieu et les inventions du *sens* et de l'*engin*, passent les agents, comme les ministres qui consacrent la Nef de Salomon, comme la bête *diverse* qui mène le scribe du Prologue du livre visionnaire reçu au ciel vers le même livre retrouvé dans la chapelle d'un ermite et que le scribe transcrira. Ces agents réalisent la pensée divine dans la matière—*quod latuit ad actum producere*[87] est leur fonction, dit Hugues de Saint-Victor. Cette analogie force, peut-être excessivement, sa pensée, étant donné sa méfiance pour les inventions littéraires, ces appendices des arts.[88] Toujours est-il que, sous l'impulsion d'en haut, et ouvert à ce que la parole de Dieu peut dire sur l'histoire arthurienne, le scribe de l'*Estoire* se met à transcrire. Son travail, c'est de traduire la langue de cœur en langue de bouche — d'adapter la parole divine à la matière arthurienne, comme la femme de Salomon introduit le bois du paradis terrestre dans la nef celtique de la navigation à l'aventure.

Cette transcription exige bien des périphrases, bien des ambages dans les ramifications diverses des matières et des sens du roman si petit que Jésus-Christ lui présenta. Et c'est toujours Hugues de Saint-Victor qui décrit le mieux ce travail: *opus artificis est disgregata coniungere vel coniuncta segregare.*[89] La femme de Salomon elle-même fit couper le bois blanc, vert et rouge qu'ensuite elle chevilla au lit dans la Nef, ce bois qui représente dans ses trois couleurs, des extraits des vies d'Adam et Eve, de Caïn et Abel, rejoints dans la *Queste* et l'*Estoire*. Mais ce travail de la conjointure et de la disjointure[90] est vain sans l'apport de Dieu, nous apprend Alain de Lille, qui condamne les conjointures fabuleuses des poètes, ces monstruosités de l'invention humaine auxquelles manque la *senefiance* de Dieu.[91] Sans celle-ci, l'œuvre humaine reste incomplète, aussi *depeciee* et *corronpue* que la Nef de Salomon avant la consécration par la foi, comme la *Charrette* avant la mise en prose.

Coniungere, segregare: voilà le travail du scribe de l'*Estoire* que vont imiter ses émules. Chez Chrétien, le fruit de ce travail n'admet de tiers, pas même Dieu, cette Trinité que l'auteur de l'*Estoire* cherche dans son Prologue et qu'il invente dans son livre. C'est cette même Trinité connue par la foi qui bénit l'union de Bohort et la fille du roi Brangore, ainsi que celle de Lancelot et la fille du roi Pelles.[92] Du péché de Lancelot surgit Galaad, de la *Charrette* de Chrétien surgit le *Lancelot en prose*, quand descend la *senefiance* d'en haut sur le *sens* et l'*engin* humains. La conjointure ainsi conçue suppose en dépit d'elle-même — voir l'Epilogue d'*Yvain* — la disjointure, l'intervention préméditée qui complète ce qui semble *depecié* et *corronpu*. Accepter cette intervention, c'est accepter une nouvelle esthétique et un nouvel art, celui du scribe.

Je ne nie pas qu'en effet on puisse appeler les romans en prose ainsi que les romans en vers des conjointures. La critique le fait librement et ouvertement. Cependant il me paraît utile d'essayer de distinguer là où les faits imposent la distinction. La tendance d'un Chrétien de Troyes est de réunir sa matière de façon à cacher les jointures et les soudures et de faire de son œuvre une totalité intouchable. Celle des romanciers en prose prévoit plutôt l'intervention d'autres qui compléteront la conception originale. Cette distinction correspond évidemment aux faits. Il est donc opportun de trouver une terminologie susceptible de la rendre clairement.

Les termes conjointure et disjointure, correctement définis dans leur contexte historique, rendent la distinction de manière adéquate.

La préférence ne se fonde pas seulement sur la technique. Comme dans toutes choses au moyen âge, l'éthique y joue un rôle déterminant. La correction des romans de Chrétien dans les romans en prose porte sur des systèmes, des hiérarchies opposés. Le choix entre Dieu et la femme décide de leur importance relative dans la vie du chevalier. Le monde courtois où s'unissent le chevalier et la femme est un monde fermé, celui de la chevalerie *celestielle* s'ouvre à Dieu. Ce passage se manifeste dans la construction divergente des romans en vers et des romans en prose.

Pour le *Lancelot-Graal*, faire dominer l'homme par la femme — comme dans le cas de Lancelot — c'est mettre le subtil *engin* au-dessus du *sens*. Cette inversion reproduit le péché originel. L'*engin* dans le roman en prose, c'est le diable, celui même qui dupa Lancelot quand il s'éprit de Guenièvre (Q 125.7–126.11). La prose restaure la hiérarchie établie par Dieu, non seulement dans l'intrigue romanesque, mais jusque dans l'acte d'écrire, de transcrire la parole. Le scribe écoute désormais Jésus, non une Marie de Champagne.

Le graal et ses feux divergents rayonnent sur le travail de plus en plus étendu des scribes. Il semblait en effet au roi Henri que ce que Gautier Map avait fait dans la *Queste* ne suffisait pas.[93] D'autres estimaient nécessaire l'addition des débuts d'Arthur et des origines du graal. D'autres encore y adjoignaient le roman post-Vulgate, les autres cycles centrés sur Tristan, sur Guiron le courtois, sur maint autre chevalier, tous illuminés plus ou moins clairement par le graal. Cela est vrai aussi pour les petits changements de détails, pour les variantes préméditées. Le graal, l'origine et la source romanesque des aventures de Logres, est comme la graine de l'arbre et ses branchages. Le graal, c'est aussi la grâce, nous dit la *Queste*.[94] Inépuisable comme la foi, la grâce rend le graal inépuisable en aventures, irréductible, finalement inexprimable en langue de bouche. Avec le *conseil* de Dieu rendu possible par la foi, et donné au *sens* et à l'*engin*, ainsi qu'aux bons chevaliers de la *Queste*, les scribes peuvent copier, et ce faisant, inventer et amplifier le roman en prose qui est essentiellement le roman du graal. Plus humbles que Chrétien, ces scribes regardent pourtant plus loin que lui. Le graal leur dessilla les yeux et ouvrit leur *sens* et leur *engin* à cette simple vérité de l'invention romanesque: "on peut bien acroistre .i. conte." Mais cette vérité-là est autre que celle de Chrétien de Troyes.

Douglas Kelly
Université de Wisconsin (Madison)

Notes

*Version légèrement amplifiée de discours plénier présenté au XIIIe Congrès de la Société Internationale Arthurienne, tenu à Glasgow en août 1981.

1. *Lancelot: roman en prose du XIIIe siècle* [= Lm], éd. Alexandre Micha, 9 tomes, TLF [= Textes littéraires français] (Genève: Droz, 1978-82); *Lancelot do Lac: The Non-Cyclic Old French Prose Romance* [= Lk], éd. Elspeth Kennedy, 2 tomes (Oxford: Clarendon Press, 1980).

2. *Le Roman de Tristan en prose*, éd. Renée L. Curtis, t. 1 (Munich: Hueber, 1963), t. 2 (Leyde: Brill, 1976); voir aussi *Le Roman de Tristan en prose: les deux captivités de Tristan*, éd. Joël Blanchard, Bibliothèque française et romane, 15 (Paris: Klincksieck, 1976), et les éditions partielles suivantes: *Die Abenteuer Gawains, Ywains und Le Morholts mit den drei Jungfrauen aus der Trilogie (Demanda) des Pseudo-Robert de Borron: die Fortsetzung des Huth-Merlin nach der allein bekannten Hs. Nr. 112 der Pariser National Bibliothek*, éd. H. Oskar Sommer, Beihefte zur Zeitschrift für romanische Philologie, 47 (Halle: Niemeyer, 1913); *Les Enchantemenz de Bretaigne: An Extract from A Thirteenth Century Prose Romance "La Suite du Merlin,"* éd. Patrick Coogan Smith, University of North Carolina Studies in Romance Languages and Literatures, 146 (Chapel Hill: University of North Carolina Department of Romance Languages, 1977); *La Folie Lancelot: A Hitherto Unidentified Portion of the Suite du Merlin Contained in MSS B. N. fr. 112 and 12599*, éd. Fanni Bogdanow, Beihefte zur Zeitschrift für romanische Philologie, 109 (Tübingen: Niemeyer, 1965); *Le Roman de Perceforest (première partie)*, éd. Jane H. M. Taylor, TLF (Genève: Droz, 1979).

3. Il faudra évidemment être aussi prudent que possible, étant donné le manque d'éditions critiques qui permettraient de vérifier la terminologie et les commentaires des narrateurs sur l'art romanesque. Il faudra aussi tenir compte des différences entre les auteurs et, comme on le verra, les scribes: dans le roman en vers tous n'écrivent pas comme Chrétien de Troyes non plus.

4. Voir pour les romans en vers l'anthologie préparée par Ulrich Mölk, *Französische Literarästhetik des 12. und 13. Jahrhunderts*, Sammlung romanischer Übungstexte 54 (Tübingen: Niemeyer, 1969). A la bibliographie qui s'y trouve on peut ajouter Pierre Gallais, "Recherches sur la mentalité des romanciers français du moyen âge: les formules et le vocabulaire des prologues," *Cahiers de civilisation médiévale* 7 (1964), 479-93, 13 (1970), 333-47; D. Kelly, "Theory of Composition in Medieval Narrative Poetry and Geoffrey of Vinsauf's *Poetria Nova*," *Mediaeval Studies* 31 (1969), 117-48; Tony Hunt, "The Rhetorical Background to the Arthurian Prologue: Tradition and the Old French Vernacular Prologues," *Forum for Modern Language Studies* 6 (1970), 1-23; Tony Hunt, "Tradition and Originality in the Prologues of Chrestien de Troyes," *Forum for Modern Language Studies* 8 (1972), 320-44; Marie-Louise Ollier, "The Author in the Text: The Prologues of Chrétien de Troyes," *Yale French Studies* 51 (1974), 26-41; Pierre-Yves Badel, "Rhétorique et polémique dans les prologues de romans au moyen âge," *Littératur*

20 (1975), 81-94; Michel Zink, "Une Mutation de la conscience littéraire: le langage romanesque à travers des exemples français du XIIe siècle," *Cahiers de civilisation médiévale* 24 (1981), 3-27.

5. Alexandre Leupin, "Qui parle? Narrateurs et scripteurs dans la 'Vulgate arthurienne,' " *Digraphe* 20 (1979), 83.

6. *La Queste del saint graal* [= *Q*], éd. Albert Pauphilet, CFMA [= Classiques français du moyen âge] (Paris: Champion, 1980), pp. 220.7-226.7. *L'Estoire* [= *E*] est citée d'après la version longue d'Eugène Hucher, *Le Saint-Graal ou le Joseph d'Arimathie,* 3 tomes (Le Mans, 1875; réim. Genève: Slatkine, 1967) [avec renvois entre crochets à l'édition de H. Oskar Sommer, *Lestoire del Saint Graal,* t. 1 de *The Vulgate Version of Arthurian Romances* (Washington, D.C.: The Carnegie Institution, 1908)], 2: 469-84 [131.2-136.34]). La version longue du ms. British Library Royal 14.E.iii a été publiée par Frederick J. Furnivall, éd., *Seynt Graal, or The Sank Ryal: The History of the Holy Grail,* 2 tomes (London: Nichols, 1861-63). Voir à propos des deux versions F. Bogdanow, "The Relationship of the Portuguese *Josep Abarimatia* to the Extant French MSS of the *Estoire del Saint Graal,*" *Zeitschrift für romanische Philologie* 76 (1960), 343-46; et *The Romance of the Grail: a Study of the Structure and Genesis of a Thirteenth-Century Arthurian Prose Romance* (Manchester: Manchester University Press; New York: Barnes and Noble, 1966), p. 157.

7. *Q* 222.6-9; *E* 2: 473 [132.27-30].

8. *Q* 220.13-19, *E* 2: 469-70 [131.13-15]. Cf. le "sens" de Merlin (Lm via. 8, Lk 23.17) que Niniene "engigna" (Lm via.10, Lk 24.1).

9. Cf. Winthrop Wetherbee, "The Theme of Imagination in Medieval Poetry and the Allegorical Figure of 'Genius,' " *Medievalia et Humanistica* 7 (1976), 45-64; Kelly, *Medieval Imagination: Rhetoric and the Poetry of Courtly Love* (Madison: University of Wisconsin Press, 1978).

10. *Q* 222.1-3; cf. *E* 2: 473 [132.17-21]. Aminte usera de son *engin* pour tromper Lancelot et concevoir Galaad, enfant dieudonné s'il en fut! (Lm xcviii.25).

11. Au contraire de Marie de France, qui croyait que les Anciens savaient très bien ce que les gloses des Modernes devaient tirer de leurs écrits obscurs comme *surplus de sens*; voir Alfred Foulet et Karl D. Uitti, "The Prologue to the *Lais* of Marie de France: A Reconsideration," *Romance Philology* 35 (1981-82), 242-49.

12. Chrétien de Troyes, *Le Chevalier de la charrete,* éd. Mario Roques, CFMA (Paris: Champion, 1970), v. 21-29.

13. Sandra Ness Ihle, *Malory's Grail Quest: Invention and Adaptation in Medieval Prose Romance* (Madison: University of Wisconsin Press, 1983).

14. Jean Frappier, *Etude sur la Mort le Roi Artu,* 2e éd. (Genève: Droz, 1968), pp. 62-146, 440-55; Emmanuèle Baumgartner, *L'Arbre et le pain: essai sur La Queste del Saint Graal* (Paris: *Société d'édition de l'enseignement supérieur,* 1981), pp. 88-91.

15. "La Quête du récit," *Critique,* 262 (1969), 214. Cf. E. Baumgartner, "Du *Tristan* de Béroul au *Roman en prose de Tristan,* étude comparée de l'idéologie et de l'écriture romanesques à partir de l'épisode de la forêt de Morois," in Ernstpeter Ruhe et Richard Schwaderer, éds, *Der altfranzösische Prosaroman: Funktion, Funktionswandel und Ideologie am Beispiel des "Roman de Tristan en prose,"* Kolloquium Würzburg 1977, Beiträge zur romanischen Philologie des Mittelalters 12 (Munich: Fink, 1979), 22-24; cf. la discussion, pp. 43-45.

16. Depuis les travaux fondamentaux de Ferdinand Lot, Eugène Vinaver, Jean Frappier et Fanni Bogdanow. Pour *Perceforest*, voir L.-F. Flutre, "Etudes sur le roman de *Perceforêt,*" *Romania* 70 (1948-49), 475.

138 DOUGLAS KELLY

17. Benoît de Sainte-Maure joindra au sien *l'engin* du Saint-Esprit afin de mener à bien sa *Chronique des ducs de Normandie,* v. 2127-29, 28723-26, dans l'édition de Carin Fahlin, Bibliotheca Ekmaniana Universitatis Regiae Upsaliensis, 56, 60, 64, 3 tomes (Uppsala: Almqvist et Wiksells, 1951-67). Voir Badel, "Rhétorique," pp. 89-90.

18. Voir Valerie M. Lagorio, "The Apocalyptic Mode in the Vulgate Cycle of Arthurian Romances," *Philological Quarterly* 57 (1978), 2-3. Le Prologue à l'*Estoire* insiste longuement sur la présentation mystique du livre du Seigneur sur le Saint Graal. La *Vulgate* en effet se construit sur le travail de plusieurs "équipes" de scribes qui, tous, écoutent la vérité prononcée par la bouche de témoins d'autorité: au scribe de l'*Estoire* qui lit le livre du Christ correspondent Blaise qui enregistre les paroles de Merlin et les scribes à la cour d'Arthur qui font de même en écoutant les exploits des chevaliers de la Table Ronde, que ceuxci racontent lors de leur retour d'aventures merveilleuses. Voir sur ce sujet Leupin, "Qui parle?"

19. *E* 2: 10; le ms. de Sommer précise: "en parfonde creance" [5.12].

20. Lm xxxvii.28-42. Sur les changements apportés au texte de Chrétien dans la prose, voir Gweneth Hutchings, éd., *Le Roman en prose de Lancelot du Lac: Le Conte de la charrette* (Paris: Droz, 1938), pp. lii-lviii.

21. Voir Erich Köhler, "Zur Entstehung des altfranzösischen Prosaromans," dans son *Trobadorlyrik und höfischer Roman: Aufsätze zur französischen und provenzalischen Literatur des Mittelalters,* Neue Beiträge zur Literaturwissenschaft, 15 (Berlin: Rütten und Loening, 1962), pp. 213-23; Daniel Poirion, "Romans en vers et romans en prose," in t. 4.1: *Le Roman jusqu'à la fin du XIIIe siècle* dans *Grundriss der romanischen Literaturen des Mittelalters* [= *GRLMA*] (Heidelberg: Winter, 1978), 74-81. Pour les romans arthuriens en vers après Chrétien, voir Beate Schmolke-Hasselmann, *Der arthurische Versroman von Chrestien bis Froissart: zur Geschichte einer Gattung,* Beihefte zur Zeitschrift für romanische Philologie 177 (Tübingen: Niemeyer, 1980); et son chapitre "Der französische höfische Roman," dans *Europäisches Hochmittelalter,* éd. Henning Krauss, Neues Handbuch der Literaturwissenschaft 7 (Wiesbaden: Athenaion, 1981), 283-322.

22. Paul Meyer, "Prologue en vers français d'une histoire perdue de Philippe-Auguste," *Romania* 6 (1877), 494-98.

23. A ce propos, voir l'hypothèse de l'architecte romanesque proposée par J. Frappier, *Etude,* pp. 142-46, et *GRLMA,* 4. 1: 584-89. Que de nombreux "auteurs" aient participé à l'élaboration des différentes versions des romans en prose semble un fait acquis aujourd'hui. Mais on est très loin d'avoir défini les rapports éventuels entre ces auteurs, leurs contributions particulières et les modalités de leurs contacts dans la transmission du corpus *Lancelot-Graal.*

24. *GRLMA* 4. 1: 81

25. *Le Conte du graal (Perceval),* éd. Félix Lecoy, CFMA, 2 tomes (Paris: Champion, 1973-75), v. 62-63. Cette leçon est la même dans les éditions de Hilka et de Roach.

26. Faith Lyons, "*Entencion* in Chrétien's *Lancelot,*" *Studies in Philology* 51 (1954), 425-30; Kelly, *Sens and Conjointure in the Chevalier de la charrette* (Paris: Mouton, 1966), pp. 36-39.

27. Cf. *Erec et Enide,* éd. Mario Roques, CFMA (Paris: Champion, 1966), v. 9-22.

28. *Les Fragments du Roman de Tristan,* éd. Bartina H. Wind, TLF (Genève: Droz; Paris: Minard, 1960), Douce 836 et 839. Cf. Kelly, "*En uni dire (Tristan* Douce 839) and the Composition of Thomas's *Tristan,*" *Modern Philology* 66 (1969), 9-17.

29. *Charrette,* v. 7111-12.

30. A. Adams, "Godefroi de Leigni's Continuation of *Lancelot,*" *Forum for Modern Language Studies* 10 (1974), 295-99; David J. Shirt, "Godefroi de Lagny et la composition

de la *Charrette,"* *Romania* 96 (1975), 27-52. Une méprise de la part de Godefroi de Leigni — si méprise il y eut — sur un détail géographique peut-elle disqualifier un continuateur? Que dire alors de celle de Chrétien lui-même qui confond la chronologie de l'*Yvain?* Voir T. B. W. Reid, éd., *Yvain (Le Chevalier au lion)* (Manchester: Manchester University Press, 1942), v. 5061 f., note (p. 211).

31. *Le Chevalier au lion (Yvain),* éd. M. Roques, CFMA (Paris: Champion, 1971), v. 6806-08. Sur "cette volonté de conclusion et de complétude" dans le roman en vers, voir Albert Henry dans l'Introduction à son édition de *Cleomades,* dans le t. 5. 2, des *Œuvres* d'Adenet le Roi (Bruxelles: Editions de l'Université de Bruxelles, 1971), 643.

32. F. Bogdanow, *Romance,* surtout pp. 60-62, 220-21.

33. Dans le ms. B. N. fr. 12603, cité d'après Wendelin Foerster, éd., *Der Löwenritter (Yvain)* (Halle: Niemeyer, 1887), v. 6818 var. (p. 271). A. Micha date ce ms. du début du XIVe siècle; voir *La Tradition manuscrite des romans de Chrétien de Troyes* (Paris: Droz, 1939), p. 50. Cf. p. 231: "Un défaut remarquable chez ce ms. est celui qui consiste à développer de manière superflue une idée suffisamment claire."

34. Voir, par exemple, E. Kennedy, "The Scribe as Editor," in *Mélanges de langue et de littérature du moyen âge et de la Renaissance offerts à Jean Frappier,* 2 tomes (Genève: Droz, 1970), 1: 523-31. Pour le roman en vers, le cas du *Roman de Thèbes* est bien connu; voir Jean-Charles Payen, "La Mise en roman de la matière antique: le cas du *Roman de Thèbes,"* dans *Etudes de philologie romane et d'histoire littéraire offertes à Jules Horrent* (Tournai: Gedit, 1980), pp. 325-32; Guy Raynaud de Lage, éd., *Le Roman de Thèbes,* 2 tomes CFMA (Paris: Champion, 1968-71), 1: 5-9. Pour le *Tristan en prose,* cf. Renée L. Curtis, "The Manuscript Tradition of the *Prose Tristan* (Part I)," dans ses *Tristan Studies* (Munich: Fink, 1969), pp. 66-91.

35. Bogdanow, *Romance,* pp. 51-53. Sur le *Brait,* voir R. Curtis, "The Problems of the Authorship of the *Prose Tristan," Romania* 79 (1958), 328-35; A. Micha, *GRLMA,* 4. 1: 598.

36. Bogdanow, *Romance,* p. 62, n. 1.

37. *Romance.*

38. Kelly, "The Source and Meaning of *conjointure* in Chrétien's *Erec* 14," *Viator* 1 (1970), 195-98.

39. *Q.* 223.9; *E* 2: 476 [133.25-26].

40. *Q* 202.20; *E* 2: 446 [121.34: "de mout riche fachon"].

41. Engène Vinaver, *A la recherche d'une poétique médiévale* (Paris: Nizet, 1970), p. 107.

42. *A la recherche,* p. 138. Cf. aussi Vinaver, *Form and Meaning in Medieval Romance* (Leeds: Maney, 1960), pp. 11-13.

43. *Le Roman de Troie,* éd. Léopold Constans, Société des Anciens Textes Français [= SATF] (Paris: Firmin-Didot, 1908), 4: 435 (v. 13-16).

44. *Troie,* v. 23191-214; cf. *Chronique,* v. 177-84, et les descriptions qui accompagnent ces passages. Pour le roman en prose, on peut consulter avec profit E. Ruhe, "Repetition und Integration: Strukturprobleme des *Roman de Tristan en prose,"* in Ruhe et Schwaderer, *Der altfranzösische Prosaroman,* pp. 138-40.

45. *Yvain,* v. 3700-09. 3912-21. 4734-39.

46. *Le Roman de l'Estoire dou graal,* ed. William A. Nitze, CFMA (Paris: Champion, 1927), v. 34:95-514.

47. V. 3480-88.

48. Jean Fourquet, "Le Rapport entre l'œuvre et la source chez Chrétien de Troyes et le problème des sources bretonnes," *Romance Philology* 9 (1955-56), 298-312.

49. Maurice Delbouille, "Les Chansons de geste et le livre," in *La Tradition littéraire des chansons de geste,* Actes du Colloque de Liège (Septembre 1957) (Paris: Belles Lettres, 1959), pp. 295-407; Madeleine Tyssens, "Le Style oral et les ateliers de copistes," in *Mélanges de linguistique romane et de philologie médiévale offerts à M. Maurice Delbouille,* 2 tomes (Gembloux: Duculot, 1964), 2: 659-75; M. Tyssens, *La Geste de Guillaume d'Orange dans les manuscrits cycliques* (Paris: Belles Lettres, 1967). Voir aussi François Suard, *Guillaume d'Orange: étude du roman en prose,* Bibliothèque du XVe siècle 44 (Paris: Champion, 1979).

50. Voir Françoise Meunier, éd., *La Chanson de Godin,* Université de Louvain: Recueil de travaux d'histoire et de philologie, 4e série, fasc. 14 (Louvain: Publications universitaires de Louvain, 1958), pp. xi-xvi.

51. Sur ce terme, voir Mary B. Speer et Alfred Foulet, "Is *Marques de Rome* A Derhymed Romance?" *Romania* 101 (1980), 336-65.

52. Voir Henri Niedzielski, "La Formation d'un cycle littéraire au moyen âge: exemple des *Sept Sages de Rome,*" in *Studies on the Seven Sages of Rome and Other Essays in Medieval Literature Dedicated to the Memory of Jean Misrahi,* éd. H. Niedzielski, H. R. Runte et W. L. Hendrickson (Honolulu: Educational Research Associates, 1978), pp. 119-32.

53. Lewis Thorpe, *Le Roman de Laurin fils de Marques le sénéchal: A First Contribution to the Study of the Linguistics of an Unpublished Thirteenth-Century Prose-Romance,* University of Nottingham Research Publications 1 (Cambridge: Bowes and Bowes, 1950), vii; Kelly, "Motif and Structure as Amplification of Topoi in the *Sept Sages de Rome* Prose Cycle," in *Studies Misrahi,* pp. 137, 140-43.

54. *Q* 225.1-2. Cet émerveillement de Salomon manque dans l'*Estoire* (2: 479 [135.8-11)].

55. Par exemple, Lm lxv.25, lxxxv.2, xcviii.42; voir J-C. Payen, *Le Motif du repentir dans la littérature française médiévale (des origines à 1230)* (Genève: Droz, 1968), pp. 439-46.

56. *Q* 125.18-126.11; cf. *Q* 123.5-8.

57. Pierre Le Gentil, "Réflexions sur la création littéraire au moyen âge," in *Chanson de geste und höfischer Roman: Heidelberger Kolloquium 30. Januar 1961,* Studia Romanica 4 (Heidelberg: Winter, 1963), 9-20.

58. Voir A. Micha, *Tradition,* pp. 213-53.

59. Baumgartner, "Du *Tristan,*" p. 20. Voir à ce propos l'important article d'A. Leupin, "La Faille et l'écriture dans les continuations du *Perceval,*" *Moyen Age* 88 (1982), 237-69.

60. *Q* 278.4-7; voir Kelly, "*Translatio studii:* Translation, Adaptation, and Allegory in Medieval French Literature," *Philological Quarterly* 57 (1978), 297-306. Le scribe de l'*Estoire* évoque une expérience semblable en décrivant les merveilles qui le ravissent alors qu'il lit et réfléchit sur la version mystique du livre que Dieu lui présenta: "tuit li oel m'estincelerent en la teste et me fu avis que je eusse la cervele espandue" (2: 14, manque dans Sommer).

61. *E* 2: 65-66 [14.4-7 plus explicite].

62. Cf. Frappier, *Etude,* pp. 444-45.

63. *Q* 38.21; cf. 217.31-32.

64. Voir Baumgartner, *Arbre,* p. 93; Lagorio, "Apocalyptic Mode," pp. 1-22.

65. *Q* 134.14, *E* 2: 39-72 [12.30-15.13]; *Q* 210.29-213.13, *E* 2: 453-57 [124.26-125.30].

66. Cf. le rêve d'Evalac, *E* 2: 156-60 [27.29-28.11, 28.19-31].

67. Frappier, *Etude,* p. 448.

68. *Le "Tristan en prose": essai d'interprétation d'un roman médiéval* (Genève: Droz, 1975), p. 93. On trouve ici en quelque sorte la validation du récit *ab ovo.* Pour le *Tristan en prose* dans ses rapports avec la Vulgate, voir l'importante mise au point de E. Ruhe, "Repetition," surtout les pp. 151-55 et la Discussion, pp. 160-72; et la thèse récente de Colette-Anne

Storms-van Coolput, dont elle m'a très aimablement fait parvenir un exemplaire après la soutenance: *"Aventures querant et le sens du monde*: aspects de la réception productive des premiers romans du graal cycliques dans le *Tristan en prose,"* Louvain, 1982.

69. Voir Lm, notes aux pars iv.41, xxii.7, xlviii.24, xlix.38, l.4, l.30, liv.24, etc.; et Ruhe, "Repetition," pp. 147-54.

70. *Q* 251.29-30. Il s'y trouve pourtant quelques exemples: Lm lxxxvii.7 et 9, cvi.9.

71. Voir Roger Lathuillère, "Le Texte de *Guiron le courtois* donné par le manuscrit de Paris, B. N. n. acq. fr. 5243," *Etudes Horrent,* pp. 233-38.

72. *La Mort le Roi Artu,* éd. J. Frappier, 3ᵉ éd., TLF (Genève: Droz; Paris: Minard, 1964), par. 3.39-41.

73. Kelly, "Rhetoric in French Literature: Topical Invention in Medieval French Literature," in James J. Murphy, éd., *Medieval Eloquence: Studies in the Theory and Practice of Medieval Rhetoric* (Berkeley: University of California Press, 1978), pp. 237-39.

74. Voir, par exemple, Mölk, *Literarästhetik*, pars 64-65, 74-76.

75. V. Lagorio, "Pan-Brittonic Hagiography and the Arthurian Grail Cycle," *Traditio* 26 (1970), 29-61; Pauline Matarasso, *The Redemption of Chivalry: A Study of the "Queste del Saint Graal"* (Genève: Droz, 1979); Frederick W. Locke, *The Quest for the Holy Grail: A Literary Study of A Thirteenth-Century French Romance,* Stanford Studies in Language and Literature 21 (Stanford: Stanford University Press; London: Oxford University Press, 1960).

76. E. Baumgartner, *Arbre,* p. 82; J. Frappier, *GRLMA* 4. 1: 75-76.

77. Cf. E. Kennedy, "Scribe"; Micha, Lm I, p. xiii; E. Baumgartner, "Du *Tristan,"* p. 20. Ce qui ne les empêche pas de s'opposer aux additions après les avoir pratiquées eux-mêmes; voir la conclusion à la *Queste* dans le ms. Oxford Bodl. Rawlinson Q.b.6, fol. 360ʳ: "Si se test ore li contes atant des auentures du .s'. graal qui sont si menees a fin que apres ceste conte nem porroit nus riens dire qui nen mentist." Ceux qui avaient imaginé les romans en prose avaient l'esprit bien plus large que les scribes postérieurs comme celui-ci, car ils semblent avoir souhaité vivement le travail des continuateurs. Voir Vinaver, *Form.*

78. *E* 2: 439-42 [5.7, 119.10-120.8].

79. Lm lxxia.48; Lk 571.25-31. Cf. Lagorio, "Pan-Brittonic," pp. 40-42. Je ne prendrai pas parti ici dans le débat sur le *Lancelot* non-cyclique qui oppose A. Micha et E. Kennedy, le livre qui doit traiter en détail la thèse de celle-ci étant toujours sous presse au moment où je termine cet article. Il serait téméraire de ma part de me lancer dans un débat pour lequel la connaissance profonde et longuement acquise des manuscrits est essentielle. Une chose pourtant est claire: où qu'on situe la version courte par rapport à la version longue dans la chronologie de la Vulgate, la tradition manuscrite de l'une et de l'autre représente une mutation radicale dans la conception et donc la composition du *Lancelot en prose,* ce qui n'infirme en rien l'interprétation plus générale que j'avance ici sur la fonction du scribe et le principe de la disjointure dans l'élaboration des romans en prose. Même si le *Lancelot* version courte dut se terminer à la mort de Galehaut, comme le pense E. Kennedy, cette version particulière n'exclut pas les développements postérieurs dans les allusions à ce qui, dans la version longue, représente les suites de la mort de Galehaut, y compris la *Queste* (de Perceval seulement?) et, peut-être, de la *Mort.* Mais voir à ce propos Lk 2: 377-78 (n. 571.31).

80. Frappier, *Etude,* p. 455.

81. Payen, *Motif,* pp. 450-51.

82. Geoffroi de Vinsauf, *Poetria Nova,* in Edmond Faral, *Les Arts poétiques du XIIᵉ et du XIIIᵉ siècle: recherches et documents sur la technique littéraire au moyen âge* (Paris: Champion, 1958), v. 843 (p. 223).

83. Lm xlviii.25. Cf. Mathieu de Vendôme, *Ars versificatoria* 3. 50: "Et, si liceat res materiatas vocibus comparare, sicut in rebus animatis, ut in homine, tria possumus contemplari, scilicet vitalem spiritum, corporeae venustatem materiae et legitimam vivendi qualitatem, nec tamen alterum alterius est exclusivum, immo conjuncta melius comparantur et gratiorem habent efficatiam, similiter in metro venustas interioris sententiae et superficialis verborum ornatus et qualitas dicendi sese invicem hospitaliter recipiunt," in E. Faral, *Arts,* p. 179.

84. Par exemple, les anges, ou bien des personnifications comme celles de Genius, Nature, etc.

85. Kelly, "Theory," pp. 11–30.

86. *Didascalicon: de studio legendi,* éd. Charles Henry Buttimer, Catholic University of America Studies in Medieval and Renaissance Latin 10 (Washington, D.C.: Catholic University of America Press, 1939), 16.

87. *Didascalicon,* p. 16.

88. *Didascalicon,* pp. 54–55. Cf. "illorum . . . scripta . . . qui et brevem materiam longis verborum ambagibus extendere consueverunt, et facilem sensum perplexis sermonibus obscurare. Vel etiam diversa simul compilantes, quasi de multis coloribus et formis, unam picturam facere" (p. 54.) Sur *ambages,* voir maintenant Michelangelo Picone, "Dante e la tradizione arturiana," *Romanische Forschungen* 94 (1982), 2–6.

89. *Didascalicon,* p. 16.

90. Cf. E. Baumgartner, *Arbre,* pp. 111–41; Albert Pauphilet, *Etudes sur la Queste del Saint Graal* (Paris: Champion, 1968), pp. 157–90; noter surtout l'analyse des adaptations de textes bibliques, pp. 179–86.

91. *De planctu Naturae,* in Thomas Wright, éd., *The Anglo-Latin Satirical Poets and Epigrammatists of the Twelfth Century* (London, 1872; réim. Wiesbaden: Kraus, 1964), 2: 465–66.

92. Lm lxxviii.57–58.

93. *Mort* par. 1.

94. *Q* 15.33, 16.11, 271.9–10, 276.29.

5. Rhetorical Structures and Strategies in Boccaccio's Teseida

In his recent history of the tradition of classical rhetoric, George A. Kennedy concludes his discussion of the medieval period by distinguishing the "variety of rhetorics" that existed in the Middle Ages: he lists "classical rhetoric," "Christian rhetoric," the "non-artistic rhetoric of brute force, intimidation, and authority," and the "native forms of expression . . . in the vernacular languages." He adds that "the conflicts and interworkings of these rhetorics deserve more study than they have been given."[1]

Although Kennedy's necessarily cursory history does not mention the *Teseida*, Giovanni Boccaccio's ambitious vernacular epic set in ancient Greece, that poem provides an excellent example of the "conflicts and interworkings" of precisely the varieties of rhetoric that Kennedy lists, and it is on that poem that the present essay will focus. Combining conventions of classical epic with aspects of Italian *cantare*, the *Teseida* offers itself as a particularly appropriate fabric from which to unravel the several strands which Kennedy sees as making up medieval rhetoric.[2] To borrow his terms, the poem explicitly presents a conflict between the ordering forces of the classical rhetorical tradition and the "non-artistic rhetoric of brute force, intimidation, and authority"; by its location in the world of ancient Greece, the poem implicitly presents a conflict between the classical tradition and the "Christian rhetoric" of Boccaccio's contemporary world. At the same time, by its classical form and by its being written "nel volgar lazio" (12. 84. 8), the poem is an excellent example of the "interworkings" of the classical tradition, the vernacular language, and Christian rhetoric, as well as of the enrichment of both the vernacular language and Christian rhetoric by the "interworkings" of all three.

Although Boccaccio's familiarity with the classical and medieval rhetorical traditions has been well established,[3] the function of those traditions within the *Teseida* has not been discussed. In that poem, Boccaccio makes obvious use of many rhetorical conventions — structures and forms which had long before been borrowed from oratory and absorbed by literature in the general process of the "letteraturizzazione" of rhetoric.[4] Even a brief summary of the poem's plot can uncover a large number of rhetorical forms.

When approaching the *Teseida*, the reader is struck first perhaps by the presence of the letter form, a major focus of medieval rhetorical training and theory.[5] At the outset of the poem, the author dedicates his work to his lady, Fiammetta, with a letter that was to become during the sixteenth century an example of epistolary style.[6] The letter form reappears late in Book One (1. 99-111), when Teseo, the Athenian ruler who has set out to conquer the Amazons, exchanges bellicose letters with Ipolita, the Amazon chief.[7] During the battles between the Athenians and the Amazons, Teseo and Ipolita encourage their troops with persuasive, exhortative speeches (1. 23-35, 61-65), a form of oratory practiced by other characters on occasions later in the poem as well. In Book Two, as Teseo returns from the land of the Amazons having won the battle and gained Ipolita as his bride, he is accosted by a group of Argive widows who entreat him to leave his victory celebration and to march against Creon, the Theban tyrant who has forbidden proper burial to the women's dead husbands. The leader of the widows succeeds in persuading Teseo, using in her speech appeals by *ethos* (she and the other women are all of royal rank) and by *pathos* (contrasting their present wretched appearance and condition with their former station) as well as by logical argument (insisting that fame will come to Teseo from such a righteous exploit [2: 27-34]). Teseo defeats Creon, and, in the aftermath of the battle, Palemone and Arcita, two young Theban noblemen, are found by Teseo's soldiers. He brings them back to Athens and there imprisons them. Looking out from their prison window, Palemone and Arcita see Emilia, Teseo's young sister-in-law, and both men fall in love with her. In Book Three when, through the intercession of a friend, Arcita is released from prison and banished from Teseo's lands while Palemone is left in prison, each man laments his particular fate with a highly rhetorical *planctus* (3. 74-76, 77-79).[8] Arcita later returns to Athens in disguise (Book Four) and Palemone, learning of this, escapes from prison (Book Five). Finding themselves in very precarious situations, both men ask the gods for help (4. 43-48, 52-53, 75-77, 5. 30-32), with prayers that conform to classical formulas for such petitions.[9] In Book Seven, just before the tournament arranged by Teseo as a means of settling Palemone and Arcita's love rivalry over Emilia, the latter three characters all make prayers that also follow classical formulas. At several points during the poem characters are introduced according to the prescribed format for a *descriptio*.

The formulary quality of such *descriptio* is particularly conspicuous when, in Book Twelve, Emilia, whose appearance has already been recounted to us several times, is described yet again (12. 53–65): at this point the tournament is over — won by Arcita at the cost of his life — and Emilia has been persuaded by Teseo to accept Palemone in marriage. By its placement this highly conventional *descriptio*, unnecessary to the narrative, functions instead as part of the ritual of marriage and renewal that marks the end of the poem.

The general rhetorical tradition on which I would like to concentrate in the present essay, however, is that of the two-sided argument, the argument *in utramque partem*. The influence of the conventions of two-sided argumentation from the *controversia*, one of the classical legal rhetorical exercises practiced in the schools of declamation of the early Empire, through the *iudicia amoris* in Andreas Capellanus' *De Amore*, to the *quistioni d'amore* which figure so prominently in Boccaccio's own *Filocolo*, has been clearly and amply explicated.[10] Readers have also demonstrated Boccaccio's particular familiarity with both the work of Capellanus and the collections of Roman declamations which gained special popularity during the fourteenth century.[11] The argument *in utramque partem* — and especially in its permutations as pseudo-legal *controversia*, as the poetic debate, and, most specifically of all, as *quistione d'amore* — functions at several levels in the *Teseida*: it provides a pattern for specific scenes; it provides the central motif propelling the action of the poem; it has the further and double function of itself being one of the poem's thematic concerns as well as of providing an over-arching pattern for the presentation of those thematic concerns. The balance of this essay will take up the different uses in the *Teseida* of the rhetorical argument *in utramque partem*, finally considering the place of rhetoric *per se* — and particularly of the categories of rhetoric which Kennedy distinguishes — within the overall meaning of the poem.

The best example of the way in which the argument *in utramque partem* furnishes a pattern for a particular scene in the *Teseida* occurs in Book Five.[12] Arcita has managed to return in disguise to Athens where he enters the service of Teseo. Palemone, learning of this, escapes from prison and finds Arcita in a wood near Athens, hoping there to settle for good the question of which man has the greater claim on Emilia's love. After greeting each other in a friendly manner and exchanging stories of their experiences since they were last together (5. 39), the two men begin their dispute. Each argues his case for being more deserving of Emilia's love: Arcita insists that the risks he has taken in returning to Athens give

him the stronger claim to Emilia (41–42), and Palemone insists that the
bonds of friendship should move Arcita to relinquish Emilia to him (43).
As the scene progresses, the men's arguments, rather than resolving the
quistione, escalate the disagreement, until the exchange assumes the intensity of a debate. In fact, when Palemone directly challenges Arcita,

> "Però t'acconcia come me' ti piace
> dell'arme omai, e tua ragion difendi,"
>
> [5. 44. 1–2]

the interchange takes on the added character of a debate between *Verba*
and *Vis*: Palemone challenges Arcita to defend his words with his sword,
while Arcita urges that, since neither man has the slightest chance of
gaining Emilia, "piano amiamo intrambendui" (46. 7). Palemone, who
"più di ciò non volle udire" (48. 1–2), insists that even if it means his own
death, "tra noi convien che [Emilia] sia partita" (48. 4). The word
"partita" (along with its cognates) occurs with conspicuous frequency
throughout this scene,[13] and its use here points up with particular clarity
the central contradiction of the situation: two men are having a "partita"
over how a single woman might be "partita." Thus Palemone's use of the
word here neatly conflates the verbal structure of rhetorical disputation
and the physical reality of the disputed object. But, as Arcita points out,
there is not the slightest chance that he or Palemone could possibly win
Emilia, and so, confronting the essential inappropriateness of the "partita"—be it verbal or physical—he asks,

> "Dunque che vuoi pur far? Combatteremo,
> e con le spade in man farén le parti
> di quella cosa che noi non avemo?"
>
> [5. 52. 1–3]

The whole debate, as Arcita perceives, is based on an impossibility and
thus is a fictitious question. Furthermore, Arcita recognizes the difference between this rhetorical *quistione d'amore* and the worrisomely
real question of his own and Palemone's safety:

> ". . . Omè, ch'io temo
> lo 'mpedimento tuo, se non ti parti
> prima che 'l giorno sia, né sicur sono,
> s'io son riconosciuto, di perdono."
>
> [5. 52. 5–8]

Because this *quistione d'amore* will, by all the laws of probability,
remain only a fiction, Arcita would prefer to keep it at the level of rhetoric
rather than take it to the level of physical violence. Palemone persists,
however, and Arcita gives vent to an extended *planctus* (5. 55–60) in which

he recounts the long Theban history of violence and strife. He wonders how he could have been so foolish as to suppose that he and Palemone might be exempt from that history:

> "Or resta sopra noi, che ultimi siamo,
> del teban sangue, insieme n'uccidiamo."
>
> [5. 59. 7-8]

Arcita too is now convinced that he and Palemone must fight each other. He has been persuaded, however, not by Palemone's arguments, but by his own, now profoundly pessimistic view of the case. Seen as the concluding episode in Thebes' relentlessly accursed history, the conflict with Palemone (fictitious or not) now seems resolvable only through violence.

> "E e' mi piace, poi che t'è in piacere,
> che pure infra noi due battaglia sia;
> io sarò presto a fare il tuo volere."
>
> [5. 60. 1-3]

Arcita arms himself, asking the gods to witness his own innocence. He is not "cagion di battaglia" with Palemone, but rather, he says to Palemone,

> "Tu mossa l'hai e tu pur la vuoi fare,
> e pace schifi di voler con meco."
>
> [5. 63. 3-5]

By now neither man has many words: *Vis* has won over *Verba*.

Yet, despite both men's agreement to fight in order "che terminata fosse lor quistione" (66. 6), even that recourse does not resolve the impasse. For, after several skirmishes, the improbable does indeed come to pass:

> Ma come noi veggiam venire in ora
> cosa che in mille anni non avvene,
> così avvenne veramente allora
> che Teseo con Emilia d'Attene
> . . . .
> . . . nel boschetto entraro,
>
> [5. 77. 1-7]

and Teseo stops the fight.

After the identities of the two men have been revealed to him, Teseo, as the ruler whose decrees have been disobeyed, must decide the proper way to deal with the offenders. Now the argument has shifted from the rhetorical *quistione d'amore* of which man better deserves Emilia — a fictitious question far removed from the reality of Emilia's being unattainable, even unapproachable, by either one of them — to the legal and very real question of how the men shall be punished for their transgressions. Palemone has broken out of prison and Arcita has violated his decree of banishment, and therefore Teseo must arrive at a judgment, in each case deciding whether to treat the culprit severely or leniently.

The dispute, therefore, now moves from the earlier fictitious *quistione d'amore* and the debate between the forces of reasonable words and brute force to another form of argument *in utramque partem*: the *controversia*.[14] That particular classical rhetorical exercise involved a law or set of laws, frequently fictitious, in the light of which a fictitious legal case, set out in elaborate and usually sensational detail, was to be decided.[15] The declaimer of the *controversia* would argue, as if to a real judge, one side, or the other, or even both sides of the case, urging punishment or leniency by presenting the case in a particular light (or, to use the term from declamatory rhetoric, with the particular *color*) that would make his recommendation seem equitable. In fact, the laws by which the case was to be judged being frequently contradictory and even irreconcilable given the particular circumstances of the case, the declaimer strove to make a distinction between what was demanded by law and what by moral equity: the judgment fulfilling the law would not necessarily be the equitable judgment, given the *color* put upon the case by the declaimer.

Similarly, Teseo, now having to take into account both the laws of his country and the particular case of the two men before him, proceeds like a declaimer to analyze the case in terms of *ius* and *aequitas*, of what is legal and what is equitable. Also like the declaimer of a *controversia*, Teseo argues first one side. Putting both men to death would be easily justified by law:

> "Sì ch'io non ne saria mai biasimato
> se i' 'l facessi, né faria fallanza,
> ma serverei l'antica buona usanza."
>
> [5. 91. 6–8]

Teseo then argues for leniency, choosing to view the case in the light of his own past amorous experiences and to recall the forgiveness "ch'io . . . più fiate acquistai" (92. 4), and the *pietà* which was shown him in similar situations. Seeing the case under the *color* of his own experiences, Teseo decides that the morally right course is to spare the men: *aequitas* has prevailed over *ius*.

That question settled, there still remains the men's love question, the central issue after all in this woodland conflict. But what had earlier been a merely fictitious *quistione d'amore* — inasmuch as possessing Emilia, the object of debate, was in no way attendant upon winning the debate — has become a real legal question, for Teseo has the power of bestowing Emilia upon whichever man he chooses. Like the given circumstances of a *controversia*, the two men's claims to her must be adjudicated under the terms of a law and, having equal merit, those claims form an argument *in utramque partem*. Even now, after realizing that either young man would make a suitable and convenient husband for the nubile Emilia, Teseo still must deal with one inescapable fact:

> ". . . Non la può di voi aver ciascuno
> però convien ch'ella rimanga a l'uno."
>
> [5. 95. 7–8]

That fact carries the force of a law, and now Teseo must speak to the same law (only one man may marry one woman) and the same set of circumstances (both Palemone and Arcita wish to marry Emilia) that first prompted Palemone, in a jealous fury, to break out of jail ("Signoria / né amore stan ben con compagnia" [5. 13. 7–8]), and that later prompted him to do battle with Arcita ("ma più che d'uno [Emilia] esser non poria" [5. 40. 2]). Just as in a *controversia*, the given law, when applied to the given circumstances, results in an impasse.

We have come full circle, and the plan that Teseo proposes for ending "ogni quistione" (97. 1) is finally not a resolution but merely a postponement of the dispute.[16] The conflict is to be both delayed in time — for one year — and removed in place — from the *boschetto*, the pleasant woodland where the encounters have taken place, to Teseo's own *teatro*, a grandiose and elaborate arena in Athens. The significance of the regal setting for the second confrontation between the two men has been noted by many readers of Boccaccio's poem.[17] The significance of the woodland setting for their first confrontation, however, has not been recognized; nor has the function of that setting in placing the scene more firmly in rhetorical tradition been noted.[18]

The character of the men's meeting and the character of the woodland setting in which that meeting takes place stand in marked contrast to one another: the arguments of the two men, returning again and again to the devastating forces of violence and lust which inform their Theban doom, as well as the men's own attempt finally to settle matters through violence, are set against the most peaceful and pleasant of backgrounds. Indeed, the wood is always referred to as a "boschetto," whose diminutive form would seem to exclude all possibility of violence. As Palemone enters this wood and finds Arcita, the ambience is described:

> E poi che fu di sopra la rivera
> sotto il bel pino infra le fresche erbette
> che lì avea produtte primavera,
> vide dormire Arcita.
>
> [5. 34. 1–4]

As the scene progresses and the two men's dispute grows increasingly violent, we are reminded frequently of the details of this beautiful and serene
setting: there are trees (33. 2), singing birds (37. 2), green grass (67. 2),
flowers (69. 3), and even fresh water flowing in a nearby stream (69. 5–6).
These are of course the conventional features of a *locus amoenus*, which
is a pleasant place and also a literary *topos* with innumerable classical and
medieval antecedents.[19] Perhaps to emphasize the conventional nature of
this setting, its traditional features are repeated at a later point during
Palemone and Arcita's debate and then again when the scene is interrupted by the arrival of Teseo and Emilia (5. 76–78).

The equation of the *boschetto* with the traditional *locus amoenus* is
important for several reasons. First of all, the temperate and pleasant
woodland scene, a frequent setting for medieval debate poems, provides
one more link between this scene in Boccaccio's work and the conventions
of that particular genre.[20] Secondly, the image of the *locus amoenus* had
long been used in association with the classical exercises of declamation.
Twice in the Elder Seneca's collection of *controversiae*, for example, the
schools of declamation are characterized in similar terms: once as places
of "delicata umbra" and later as "umbrosi loci."[21] Each time, the image is
used as a way of contrasting the shaded protection of the declamation
halls with the dazzling sunshine of the "real" world outside. Although the
comparison is used as a criticism of declamation and of the unreality of
its debates, yet the point has been granted that the declamation hall in
fact provides a *locus amoenus*—a place removed from the real world and
therefore amenable precisely to discussions of hypothetical or fictitious
questions.[22] Thus Boccaccio's scene in which Palemone and Arcita confront each other in the pleasant *boschetto* outside of Athens is tied in yet
another way to the tradition of declamatory *controversia*: both by the
fact of its setting and by the function of that setting as a means of
isolating, and thereby permitting consideration of, a question that, to
Arcita at least, appears to be fictitious. In this regard the setting also
looks back to that of the *quistioni d'amore* in the *Filocolo* and forward to
that of the *novelle* in the *Decameron*: in both cases, questions of a
hypothetical and fictitious nature are brought under consideration within
a *locus amoenus* that is removed from and, for a time, not responsible to
the outside world.[23]

The woodland encounter among the protagonists of Boccaccio's
poem ends when, as must always happen, the contingencies of the real
world call the participants back from the *locus amoenus*: suddenly it is
noon, even the *boschetto* grows too warm, and Teseo realizes that

Arcita's wounds must be attended to by a doctor in the city (5. 103). Teseo leads the group back to Athens, although the central question dividing the two young Thebans has not yet been settled — neither by verbal debate, nor by physical violence, nor by royal intercession. All the same, this interlude in the wood has provided a time and a place where the question could be examined and clarified.

Seeming to recognize this, characters refer back to the scene on several occasions later in the poem, recalling words spoken and agreements made in the *boschetto*, as if they had gained from that place a special power or truth (e.g., 9. 60, 10. 29, 10. 80). During the tournament, Emilia, unable to decide between the equal claims of the two men fighting for her, wishes that Teseo could merely have left them "quando noi li trovammo nel boschetto" (8. 108. 2), for there, it seems to her, the dispute could have been resolved much more easily.[24]

The debate of the *Teseida* is finally resolved, however, and that resolution, to return to the categories introduced at the opening of this essay, is by means of the "non-artistic rhetoric of brute force . . . and authority." For the tournament which Teseo devises and in which he demands that Palemone and Arcita participate is in fact a contest, albeit well disguised in the elaborate trappings of civilization, of brute force. The result of the tournament and of the events which follow upon it, is that the debate between Palemone and Arcita over the love of Emilia is settled — at the price of Arcita's life. That debate, which began in the *boschetto*, has come full circle, as Arcita's corpse, the sacrifice necessary to a resolution, is now to be burned in the very same spot:

> . . . nel bosco, ov'e' rancura
> aver sovente soleva d'amore.
>
> [11. 13. 5–6]

After Arcita's funeral, Palemone supervises the building of a monument to his memory. This monument, like the pyre, is to be placed in the *boschetto*; it will contain Arcita's ashes, and on its walls are to be depicted "tutti i casi d'Arcita" (11. 69 and rubric). The purpose of these murals is to celebrate the events of Arcita's life, and the poem's narrator describes in detail each scene of the series (11. 70–87). As he does this, however, we learn that the murals actually tell the story of the poem, beginning with Teseo's return from the land of the Amazons, an event in which Arcita had no part. Although Palemone, under whose direction the temple is being built, would have known the facts of Arcita's life before both men were introduced into the poem after Teseo's defeat of Creon, still the murals correspond to the events of the poem, rather than to the events of Arcita's life. The effect of this incongruity is to suggest in yet another way that Arcita's death not only marks the end of his individual life but also provides a resolution to the whole story: the debate that began as a rhetorical *quistione d'amore* in the *boschetto* could only have been settled by the sacrifice of Arcita, whose ashes are now contained in an urn enshrined in the center of this temple built in that same *boschetto* (11. 90).

Taken overall, the narrative murals of the temple make a positive statement about the value of rhetoric—if we concede that these murals constitute a kind of visual rhetoric. At the same time the murals provide an example of rhetoric's limited potential for controlling human experience or even for controlling our memory of experience. In planning the murals, Palemone chooses to omit one event—Arcita's fatal fall from his horse, "acciò che mai non fosse ricordata" (11. 88). But this attempt to revise and reconstruct experience is futile, for

> . . . non poté la gente amenticallo,
> sì nel cor era di ciascuno entrata
> con greve doglia.
> [11. 88. 5–7]

Here the power of rhetoric is undercut, just as it was in the *boschetto* when reasoned argument proved powerless against the forces impelling Palemone and Arcita to violence.

Taking rhetoric as itself one of the themes of Boccaccio's poem, it becomes clear that the poem is offering us two different views of that theme: rhetoric is an important value and it is also ineffectual. On several occasions characters use rhetorical discourse in attempts to console other characters, but, then too, with only qualified success. In Book Nine, for example, Teseo tries to console Palemone's men for their defeat in the tournament by using intricate arguments assigning blame for their defeat to the gods. The speech over,

> piacque a costoro il parlar di Teseo,
> ben ch 'n parte non ver tenesser quello.
> [9. 61. 1–2]

Palemone's men accept Teseo's speech as rhetorical display, pleasing but fictitious. After Arcita's death, Teseo's father tries to console Palemone,

> ricordando le cose antiche e vere:
> le morti e' mutamenti e 'l duolo e 'l canto
> l'un dopo l'altro spesso ogn'uom vedere;

ma mentre che parlava, ognun piangeva,
poco intendendo a ciò che el diceva.

[11. 11. 4-8]

This speech, too, has only limited effect.

When rhetoric is used as a means of persuasion and exhortation it also brings mixed results: the various speeches urging greater effort in battle (1. 32-35, 61-65, 116-121; 2. 44-47; 7. 133-143) succeed in firing the men (or women) on to increased bravery and fortitude. When, however, in Book Twelve, Teseo sets out to persuade Palemone and Emilia to follow Arcita's dying wishes by marrying each other, suasive rhetoric and argument are not enough. Teseo begins by engaging Palemone in debate on the matter. Finding Palemone resistant to his argument, however, Teseo resorts to using his authority, commanding that "né parola di ciò incontro si faccia" (12. 32. 8). Turning then to Emilia, Teseo immediately issues a command: "Quel che io vo' farai che sia fornito" (12. 38. 8), and, when she, too, tries to argue the other side, Teseo brusquely dismisses her argument: "Questo dire è niente" (12. 43. 1). Finding that rhetorical argument does not immediately produce the result he desires, Teseo resorts to the authority of his office to move people to act in accordance with his will—a strategy that turns all preceding discussion of alternatives into mere rhetorical exercise and that is one more version of the "non-artistic rhetoric of brute force . . . and authority" that Kennedy distinguishes.

Rhetoric is double-edged, and, as final confirmation of that, there remains the unavoidable fact that, of the two lovers, Arcita is the one who believes in rhetoric and who is by far the greater talker, and yet it is Palemone who finally wins the object of their eloquence.[25] Like so many of the other values and attitudes that Boccaccio's poem would have us associate with classical pre-Christian times, rhetoric is seen from more than one angle and is presented as having more than one valence.[26] The poem thus finally becomes a thematic, as well as a narrative argument *in utramque partem:* the two-sided argument functions as the organizing narrative principle for the whole poem as well as for several individual scenes, and also as a central aspect of the poem's significance as well.

Early on in the *Teseida,* Boccaccio furnishes us with a particularly clear example—almost a paradigm, in fact—of this two-sided presentation of the theme of rhetoric. In Book One, Ipolita exhorts her Amazon troops with a long "diceria" urging them to put aside their hesitations and fears and to take arms against Teseo's invading army (1. 23-35). In the very clearly established ethical scheme of the poem, Ipolita is using rhetoric to persuade her Amazon subjects to fight an improper battle: the women, who have already disrupted the proper order by killing their husbands and fathers and setting up a kingdom of women, are in effect being urged to perpetuate that error by opposing Teseo and his Athenian troops who have come to reimpose the natural sovereignty of men over women. In Book Two, Teseo, also with a "diceria," exhorts his troops to take arms against the Theban tyrant, Creon (2. 44-47). Unlike Ipolita's earlier "diceria," this one is used to exhort an audience to fight a proper battle: in this case it is Creon who has disrupted the proper order by refusing customary burial rites to the Argive women's dead husbands, and Teseo is urging his men to join him in reestablishing this proper order.

Both these speeches are successful, and in this regard they offer a clear example of the ambiguous value of rhetoric: it can as easily persuade an audience to pursue an unjust cause as a just one. What invites more than a superficial comparison of the two speeches, however, is that they both contain numerous thematic and verbal echoes of that "orazion picciola" with which, Ulisse tells Virgil and Dante, he was once able to render his own "compagni . . . sì aguti / . . . al cammino, / che a pena poscia li avrei ritenuti" (*Inferno* 26. 121-23).[27] Ulisse, in his *orazione*, had given eloquent yet false counsel and ultimately led his followers to their doom. The two *dicerie* in Boccaccio's poem allude to, and thereby combine with, Ulisse's speech in Dante's work, to form a triangle fraught with moral contradictions.[28] The contrast between the ends urged in the two *Teseida* speeches as well as the contrast between the end urged by Ulisse and that urged by Teseo force the reader to go beyond the orations themselves and the immediate plots of the two poems, to a consideration of the overall context and purpose of the *Inferno* and the *Teseida*.

Appropriate terms for such a consideration, I would like to suggest, can be found in yet a third text, the Fourth Book of Boccaccio's *Filocolo*. There, in the Twelfth *quistione d'amore*, a young man must decide whether to enjoy a great pleasure before enduring a great trial, or vice-versa. Parmenione, the narrator of the *quistione*, argues that the man should first endure the trial, then, free of dreadful anticipation, enjoy the pleasure.

> Rispose a costui la reina: — Voi ne rispondete in parte come se degli eterni beni ragionassimo, per li quali acquistare non è dubbio che ogni affanno se ne dee prendere, e ogni mondano bene e diletto lasciare: ma noi al presente non parliamo di quelli, ma de' mondani diletti e delle mondane noie quistioniamo; a che noi rispondiamo, come prima

dicemmo, che ogni mondano diletto si dee più tosto prendere che
mondana noia ne segua, anzi che mondana noia per mondano diletto
aspettare, però che chi tempo ha e tempo aspetta, tempo perde.[29]

Fiammetta is reminding Parmenione that, as they sit in the garden posing
quistioni d'amore, they are discussing earthly rather than heavenly matters. His argument is one appropriate to heavenly goods, for which any
earthly trial should be endured—and compared to which all earthly
goods are as nothing. But, when the discussion is limited to earthly matters, as the group had agreed it would be, distinctions among earthly
goods must be made in earthly terms, and, considering the transitoriness of
earthly things, the pleasure in this case should be chosen over the trial.

Bringing this text to bear upon the triangle of speeches in the *Inferno* and the *Teseida*, it is clear that Dante's poem is to be aligned with
questions of "etterni beni." In the *Inferno* rhetoric and the power of
language itself are put into a divine, eschatological perspective and the
ultimate merit of that worldly and very classical value is thrown into
doubt.[30] The *Teseida*, however, is a poem aligning itself with questions
of "beni mondani" and therefore asking that we judge earthly matters,
such as the value of language and rhetoric, from an earthly perspective.
The allusions within Ipolita's and Teseo's speeches to the words of Ulisse
force us to acknowledge the radical difference between the eschatological
perspective of Dante's poem and the resolutely worldly perspective of
Boccaccio's.[31] Granting that worldly perspective, we are asked both to
acknowledge that rhetoric and other worldly values can be used towards
both improper and proper ends and also to take the further step of
distinguishing between those ends. Like the group in the garden of the
Filocolo, the reader of the *Teseida* must agree to accept the poem's specifically limited perspective and to judge the relative value of earthly
matters from that earthly point of view. We are asked to acknowledge
that, although earthly distinctions may become irrelevant from a divine
perspective, there is value in the creation of a perspective which is temporarily limited to the matters of this world and which therefore allows
such distinctions to be made.

To return to the rhetorical terms which have been the focus of this
essay, the *Teseida* presents itself as a debate on the values of the pagan
world. In this debate, or argument *in utramque partem*, Boccaccio does
not oppose pre-Christian values to Christian ones; rather he delineates,
within his particular classical framework, a double perspective on the
values of that world. Both *partes* of the argument have been generated by
the contradictions and conflicts inherent in the classical values themselves.

This is possible because, by setting his poem in pagan times, Boccaccio has granted himself a literary space in which to present certain qualities and values of the pre-Christian world without having to assess them from a Christian point of view. The poem itself becomes a *locus amoenus* where, removed from the absolute judgments of the Christian perspective, the qualities of a time long past can be considered in themselves. Of course reader and writer can only enter that *locus amoenus* from, and must always return to, the real world—a real world whose Christian perspective must ultimately transcend any questions of the feasibility of a pre-Christian ethical or philosophical code. Yet, Boccaccio's poem has provided a place amenable to the consideration of these questions.[32]

Although that Christian perspective must prevail outside of Boccaccio's poem, and the classical values of glory, fame, eloquence, and courage must ultimately be found insufficient, yet within the poem—the ultimate Christian perspective for a time suspended—we can consider the possibility that those classical values might indeed suffice. Viewed from the outside, that possibility is a fiction. Yet the poem, like a *locus amoenus*, affords a place where just such fictitious questions can for a time be entertained. The form of the argument *in utramque partem* has given to the poem a paradigm for the presentation of opposing views, and Boccaccio's appropriation of this form has enabled him to take under consideration for a brief space the ambiguous attractions of the classical world.

Eren Hostetter Branch
Cincinnati, Ohio

Notes

1. George A. Kennedy, *Classical Rhetoric and Its Christian and Secular Tradition from Ancient to Modern Times* (Chapel Hill, 1980), p. 194.

2. For the relationship of the *Teseida* to the classical epic tradition, see the "Introduzione" by Alberto Limentani in his edition of the poem, *Teseida delle nozze d'Emilia*, in *Tutte le opere di Giovanni Boccaccio*, 2 (Milan: Mondadori, 1964), 231–44. (All citations from the *Teseida* in this essay are taken from this edition and refer to book, stanza, and, when appropriate, line number.) See further Alberto Limentani, "Boccaccio 'traduttore' di Stazio," *La Rassegna della letteratura italiana* 64 (1960), 231–42; Piero Boitani, *Chaucer and Boccaccio*, Medium Aevum Monographs, n.s. 8 (Oxford: Society for the Study of Mediaeval Languages and Literatures, 1977), especially 1–71; David Anderson, "The Legendary History of Thebes in Boccaccio's *Teseida*, and Chaucer's *Knight's Tale*," Diss. Princeton University 1980, especially pp. 116–95. For the relationship of the *Teseida* to the Italian *cantare*, see Vittore Branca, *Il cantare trecentesco e il Boccaccio del Filostrato e del Teseida* (Florence: Sansoni, 1938).

3. The two books that demonstrate this with particular clarity are Vittore Branca, *Boccaccio medievale* (Florence: Sansoni,1970), and Giuseppe Billanovich, *Restauri boccacceschi* (Rome: Edizioni di Storia e Letteratura, 1945). For a list of books which may be presumed to have formed Boccaccio's library, see Antonia Mazza, "L'inventario della 'parva libraria' di Santo Spirito e la biblioteca del Boccaccio," *Italia medioevale e umanistica* 9 (1966), 1–74.

For the pervasive popularity during the fourteenth century of many of the rhetorical forms which will be discussed in this essay, see James J. Murphy, *Rhetoric in the Middle Ages: A History of Rhetorical Theory from Saint Augustine to the Renaissance* (Berkeley: University of California Press, 1974). For an examination of the far-reaching influence of declamatory forms in particular upon late-medieval literature, see Wesley Trimpi, "The Quality of Fiction: The Rhetorical Transmission of Literary Theory," *Traditio*, 30 (1974), 1–118. The present essay is deeply indebted to this illuminating discussion.

4. Kennedy, *Classical Rhetoric*, p. 109.

5. For an overview, see Murphy, *"Ars dictaminis*: The Art of Letter-Writing," in *Rhetoric in the Middle Ages*, pp. 194–268. For a more recent and more specific treatment, see Ronald Witt, "Medieval 'Ars Dictaminis' and the Beginnings of Humanism: a New Construction of the Problem," *Renaissance Quarterly*, 35 (1982), 1–35.

6. See Ernesto Travi, "L'introduzione al 'Teseida' e l'epistolografia del '500," in *Boccaccio Venezia e il Veneto*, ed. V. Branca and G. Padoan (Florence: L. S. Olschki, 1979), pp. 153–60, for a discussion of this letter.

7. Pertinent to this exchange of *dictamina* is Witt's distinction between the "rhetoric of harmony and that of conflict"; in the latter, he says, "one acknowledges conflict where it exists, and persuasion takes the form of debate" ("Medieval 'Ars Dictaminis,'" p. 15 and n. 34).

8. For an even more *conventional* planctus than this one employing the *ubi sunt* formula, see Arcita's dying lament in Book Ten (101–10).

9. For a discussion of the classical prayer formulae, see K. Buchholz, *De Horatio Hymnographo*, Diss. Konigsberg 1912, pp. 4–22 and E. Norden, *Agnostos Theos* (Leipzig and Berlin: Teubner, 1913), pp. 143–62.

10. See Trimpi, "The Quality of Fiction," esp. pp. 75–97.

11. See Branca, *Boccaccio medievale*, esp. pp. 227–35; Billanovich, ". . . *cum meum dictare non sit*," in *Restauri*, pp. 47–78; and Murphy, *Rhetoric in the Middle Ages*, pp. 39 and 131.

12. Other scenes and exchanges also showing the influence of the argument *in utramque partem* are the following: the letter of Ipolita to Teseo in its juxtaposition to the response by Teseo (1. 99–107, 109–11); Ipolita's speech to her Amazons, arguing the case first for continuing to resist Teseo's forces and then for surrendering to him (1. 116–21); the exchange between Teseo and Creon (2. 61–66); the two exactly balanced *planctus*, in which Palemone and Arcita each argues that his own situation is the more miserable (an implicit *quistione d'amore* that is made explicit in *The Knight's Tale*, Chaucer's version of the same story [lines 1347–52]) (3. 74–76, 77–79); Emilia's lament to Love in which she despairingly tries to decide between the claims of the two Thebans (8. 96–109); the debates between Arcita and Palemone and then between Arcita and Emilia, by which he tries to persuade the two of them to marry after his death (10. 38–51, 55–82); the debates between Teseo and Palemone and then Teseo and Emilia, by which he also tries to persuade them to marry (12. 6–37, 38–43).

13. See Bk. 5. 43. 7, 43. 8, 47. 3, 48. 4, 52. 2, 52. 6, 53. 3, 83. 3, 83. 5, 98. 1.

14. As introductions to the subject of declamation see S. F. Bonner, *Roman Declamation in the Late Republic and Early Empire* (Liverpool: University Press of Liverpool, 1949); M. L. Clarke, "Declamation," in *Rhetoric at Rome: a Historical Survey* (London: Cohen & West, 1953), pp. 85–99. For further treatment, see Henri Bornecque, *Les Déclamations et les déclamateurs d'après Sénèque le Père* (Lille, 1902); and Frederick H. Turner, "The Theory and Practice of Rhetorical Declamation from Homeric Greece through the Renaissance," *DA*, 32 (1972), 7119A (Temple University).

15. The *locus classicus*, perhaps, among *controversiae* is the case of "The Man who Raped Two Girls." The law there states that "A girl who has been raped may choose either marriage to her ravisher without a dowry or his death." The situation to be adjudicated is that "on a single night a man raped two girls. One demands his death, the other marriage." The case occurs, among other places, in bk. 1 (*Contr.* 5) of the collection of *controversiae* made by the Elder Seneca. (The translation is that by Michael Winterbottom for the Loeb Classical Library, *The Elder Seneca Declamations*, 2 vols. [Cambridge, Mass.: Harvard University Press, 1974], 1: 121.) Another example of the typically implausible and sensational character of so many of the *controversiae* occurs in *Contr.* 7.4:

> The Blind Mother who would not let her Son go.
> Children must support their parents, or be imprisoned.

> A man with a wife and a son by her set out abroad. Captured by pirates, he wrote to his wife and son about a ransom. The wife's weeping blinded her. She asks support from her son as he goes off to ransom his father; she demands that he should be imprisoned because he will not stay. (Winterbottom, 2: 85, 87.)

16. Boccaccio's main narrative source and poetic model for his own epic was the *Thebaid* of Statius. Considering that, the similarities between this scene in the *Teseida* and that in the *Thebaid* when Adrastus stops the fight between Polynices and Tydeus outside the gate of Argos (1. 382–525) deserve more notice than they have received. In both cases there is a fight between two young men (one of whom finds the other asleep) who are both in some way outlaws or exiles; that fight is interrupted and settled in each case by an older and wiser ruler, who induces the young men to become friends; in each case the ruler then recognizes the young men as potential husbands—in Adrastus' case for his two daughters, in Teseo's for his sister-in-law.

17. See Limentani's introduction to his edition of the *Teseida*; Boitani, pp. 12–18; Anderson, pp. 156–61; Janet Levarie Smarr, "Boccaccio and the Stars: Astrology in the 'Teseida,'" *Traditio* 35 (1979), 303–32. In particular, see Robert Hollander, "The Validity of Boccaccio's Self-Exegesis in His *Teseida*," *Medievalia et Humanistica*, n.s. 8 (1977), 163–83, as well as his discussion of the *Teseida* in *Boccaccio's Two Venuses* (New York: Columbia University Press, 1977), pp. 53–65.

18. Anderson (p. 186, n. 27) associates this *boschetto* with the "selva oscura" of Dante's *Inferno*. As I hope the following discussion will make clear, Dante's *selva* would serve as a far more useful gloss on the "selva vecchia" (*Tes.* 11. 18. 3) and "miserabil loco" (*Tes.* 11. 21. 1) that Teseo later orders cut down to build Arcita's pyre, than on this *boschetto* with its "erbetta fresca," "fiori," and "freschi liquori" (*Tes.* 5. 69 passim).

19. See Ernst Robert Curtius' discussion of "The Pleasaunce," in *European Literature and the Latin Middle Ages*, trans. Willard Trask, (New York: Harper & Row, 1963[2]), pp. 195–200.

20. For a discussion of the spring setting for medieval *débats*, see Rosamund Tuve, *Seasons and Months: Studies in a Tradition of Middle English Poetry* (Paris: Librairie Universitaire, 1933), pp. 36–38.

21. Quoted from *L. Annaei Senecae Oratorum et Rhetorum: Sententiae Divisiones Colores*, ed. H. J. Muller (Vienna, 1887), pp. 210, 372.

22. See Trimpi, pp. 81-85, for a discussion of the literary implications of this aspect of declamation.

23. There are three distinct "luoghi ameni" in the *Teseida*: the wood where Palemone and Arcita meet, the "tempio e la magione" where Palemone's prayer finds Venus, and the "luogo amen" where Arcita hopes his spirit might be taken after his death (10. 90. 3-5). The morally ambiguous values of the venereal *locus amoenus* (discussed at length by Hollander, "The Validity," pp. 170-73) combine with the attractions of the other two *loci amoeni*, to create the kind of thematic argument *in utramque partem* that is discussed below.

24. The *bosco* has the further and related appeal for Emilia of being the dwelling place of Diana and her followers. Emilia wishes again and again to be allowed to retire to the *boschi* and be a part of Diana's band (*Tes* 7. 79 ff.; 10. 80) — a far simpler existence than her present lot as subject of a *quistione d'amore*.

25. Not only is Arcita given the greater number of lines during the scene in the *boschetto* (as well as his lengthy speeches of bk. 10), but twice, after he has delivered an extended oration, it is merely remarked that Palemone did likewise (7. 128 and 7. 145).

26. Examples of other classical ethical motifs that are developed in the poem as thematic arguments *in utramque partem*: the love that unites first Teseo with Ipolita and later Palemone with Emilia (thereby also uniting Athens with its neighbors) is closely related both to the "folle ardire" that brings individual torment to Palemone and Arcita and to the illicit lusts that have brought public disruption for generations of Thebans; similarly the righteous anger that prompts Teseo to fight Creon and impels Juno to punish Thebes, is sometimes hard to distinguish from the belligerence that has led to unjust wars and to Arcita and Palemone's decision to fight each other so violently in the woods; the "arte," the "grazia," and the "cortesia" that smooth the workings of human and divine society in the *Teseida* are put into question when they appear as members of Venus' ambiguous retinue.

27. Quoted from *La Divina Commedia*, ed. Giuseppe Vandelli (Milan: U. Hoepli, 1958).

28. Cf. the first octave of Teseo's speech (2. 44, quoted above) and his *captatio* (". . . cari e buon commilitoni / che meco in tante perigliose cose . . ." [2. 45. 1-2]), and, in Ipolita's speech, 1. 24. 1, 1. 29. 5, and 1. 32. 4, with Ulisse's speech (*Inf.* 26, 112-20).

29. Quoted from the edition of the *Filocolo* by Antonio Enzo Quaglio in *Tutte le opere di Giovanni Boccaccio*, 1 (Milan: Mondadori, 1967), 447.

30. For one of the more recent discussions of the Ulisse episode, see Giuseppe Mazzotta, "Rhetoric and History," chap. 2 of *Dante, Poet of the Desert* (Princeton: Princeton University Press, 1979), pp. 66-106.

31. The *Teseida* maintains a worldly perspective, I would suggest, in spite of our brief view of the earth from afar, as Arcita's spirit looks back immediately after his death (11. 1-3). This brief removal from the affairs on earth functions in fact only to return us almost immediately to those affairs and does not affect either the characters' or the narrator's point of view or the focus of the poem.

32. By his device of adding a commentary to the poem, Boccaccio has made explicit and thereby further emphasized the distance between his poetic *locus* and his own contemporary real world. With his *chiose*, or notes (described by Hollander, "The Validity," pp. 164-68), Boccaccio provides a fourteenth-century gloss on what he has chosen to represent as the pagan world of his poem and by inferring the need to explain his purportedly classical epic, Boccaccio has in effect further classicized it. The *chiose* remind the reader again and again of the gulf between "then" and "now." At the same time, by establishing a sense of historical distance between pre-Christian and Christian times, the commentary

helps to create a place where the pre-Christian world can be considered apart from the absolute judgments imperative in the Christian perspective.

6. L'Écriture et la voix
Le Roman d'Éracle

On n'a de chance de parler bien que de ce qu'on aime: la condition, insuffisante certes, n'en est pas moins nécessaire. Si j'ai choisi de parler d'*Eracle*, c'est que j'aime ce roman qu'on a dit mal ficelé, dépourvu d'unité, parasité de digressions adventices.[1] Mais aussi — comme je le vois et l'entends — d'une ardeur où fusionnent en un chatoyant alliage cent éléments hétérogènes; d'une verdeur tour à tour caustique, galante, héroïque, attendrie; œuvre d'une lumineuse jeunesse (et quelle jeunesse n'a ses instants d'ennui, de retombée?), où le verbe tantôt colle à la nudité du vécu, tantôt claque au vent des paroles comme une bannière: joyeux, courant son train sans trop de souci des horaires, — à l'opposé de la science synthétisante, de la mesure intériorisée, du travail en pleine épaisseur sémantique, des récits, contemporains, d'un Chrétien de Troyes, lequel fut sans doute à la cour de Champagne, en quelque occasion entre 1170 et 1180, *compain* de Gautier d'Arras, l'auteur. L'un et l'autre clercs, vraisemblablement ecclésiastiques, — et rivaux, si l'on admet que le Prologue du *Chevalier de la Charette* réfère à la dédicace d'*Eracle*. Où Chrétien creuse et concentre en profondeur, Gautier déploie une histoire à la manière des futurs conteurs picaresques. *Eracle* étire, comme notre propre existence, comme celle de son héros, de la naissance à la mort, une infinie suite bigarrée d'événements tour à tour menus ou majeurs: la fin en paraît, jusqu' à deux pages de l'*explicit*, si lointaine en perspective que l'on a depuis longtemps cessé de l'attendre. Pourtant, ce roman compte cent vers de moins que *Cligès,* le plus bref de ceux de Chrétien.

Eracle ainsi condense en un temps de lecture — d'audition — plutôt court un temps narratif très long. D'où un surprenant effet, à la fois de retenue et d'expansion, de mouvement centripète et d'éclatement centrifuge. L'extrême diversité de la narration se ramasse, sans rien perdre de sa fraîcheur, dans le sens, non point même d'une intention évidente, mais de l'unicité d'une action: celle de Gautier, par laquelle il s'adresse à nous. La forte mais confuse unité de l'œuvre est l'unité d'une performance, avec tout ce qu'implique, dans l'usage que j'en fais, ce terme.

Les matériaux que manipula Gautier ont fait jadis, de la part d'A. Fourrier, l'objet d'un inventaire que l'on aime à croire exhaustif. Je n'en retiendrai qu'une conclusion: la pluralité des registres alternant dans le récit, et qui en font, en ce dernier tiers du XIIe siècle, au lieu géométrique de l'intertexte, un réceptacle et un miroir de tous les discours poétiques alors en formation dans la langue vulgaire du royaume de France.

Le Prologue, en sa littéralité, n'a rien d'équivoque: les vers 87–113 annoncent une biographie de l'empereur d'Orient Héraclius, successeur de Phocas au trône de Byzance, au VIIe siècle, et vainqueur du roi de Perse Chosroès auquel il reprit la relique de la Vraie Croix. Matière d'histoire antique, mais à laquelle l'épisode terminal—inspirant d'emblée l'affabulation—exige que soient conférées des connotations hagiographiques. D'où un montage d'éléments narratifs très approximativement extraits de lectures historiques et liturgiques; de souvenirs de quelques contes d'origine orientale; de discours peut-être alors communément tenus, en milieu chevaleresque, à propos de la Croisade; le tout lié de subtiles allusions aux événements du jour ou de la veille. L'ensemble tient encore du grand mouvement de divulgation jubilante des trésors de la narration antique, auquel nous devons, avec la fameuse "triade" (*Thèbes, Enéas, Troie*), les *Alexandre*, le fragment d'*Apollonius*, l'*Hector et Hercule* franco-italien.[2] La cohérence d'*Eracle* provient de là: elle s'identifie au regard que jette Gautier sur un passé ressenti comme exemplaire et fondateur, à la fois dans le temps et hors de lui, selon le mode de référence que, d'épisode en épisode, on y fait. Rien ne distingue en cela histoire, hagiographie, roman: même "type de fascination," selon l'expression qu'utilisent aujourd'hui plusieurs critiques allemands pour définir ce qui crée l'unité d'un genre.[3]

De son accession à l'empire jusqu'à sa victoire sur Chosroès, le règne d'Héraclius ne posait, à qui la qualité de l'information importait peu, aucun problème documentaire. La liturgie des fêtes de l'Invention et de l'Exaltation de la Sainte Croix suggérait, dans le sens désiré, une alternative à la fin de l'Héraclius "réel," devenu hérétique et vaincu par les Arabes! Le discours de la guerre sainte, dans cette partie de l'œuvre, parasite celui que Gautier emprunte aux chanteurs de geste, au point d'en évacuer toute mention "nationale." Restent les clichés:

> et maint hauberc menu maillé,
> maint hiaume a or bien entaillé;
>
> [5407-8]

(et maint haubert à mailles serrées,
maint heaume d'or bien gravé)

sainte a l'espee al puig d'or fin
qui ot esté roi Coustentin;
[5607-8]
(il a ceint l'épée à la poignée d'or fin
qui avait appartenu au roi Constantin)

des esperuns les cevaus brocent;
[5627]
(des éperons ils piquent les chevaux)

hurtent cevaus des esperons
et s'entrefierent es blasons;
[5705-6];
(ils piquent de leurs éperons les chevaux
et entrechoquent leurs écus)

et dessor l'aume a or le fiert;
[5718]
(et sur le heaume d'or il le frappe)

et bien d'autres référant directement à la pratique des chansons épiques: on pourrait en dresser la liste. Les vers 5704 à 5820 en sont tissus. Motifs typiques, plus nombreux encore: ordre du ciel engageant à la guerre, conseil des barons ("chez nous," puis "chez eux"), messagers, scène d'armement du chef, éloge du cheval, discours alternés avant l'assaut, "folie" des païens, combat singulier, carnage et baptême de masse des survivants . . .

Voilà qui fixait, comme on dit, l'isotopie. Cependant, l'enfance et la jeunesse d'Eracle restaient en blanc: l'"histoire" n'en disait mot. L'habileté de Gautier fut d'emboucher, d'entrée de jeu, la trompette hagiographique, selon une partition bien connue: parents Romains, pieux chrétiens, déjà mûrs mais stériles, engendrant enfin, grâce à la bienveillance divine, l'enfant souhaité. Ainsi, providentiellement marqué dès sa conception, Eracle (d'abord nommé Dieudonné . . . comme l'avait été le roi Philippe-Auguste!) le sera de façon manifeste à sa naissance: sa mère recevra d'un ange une charte par laquelle (dans les termes d'un conte féérique aux versions multiples, attestées de l'Iraq à l'Espagne et à la Scandinavie) Dieu accorde au nouveau-né le triple don de connaître infailliblement la valeur cachée des gemmes, des chevaux et des femmes. Dès lors, il suffit de broder, sur un arrière-fond de fourmillante et babillarde vie urbaine, une série d'anecdotes témoignant de l'héroïcité des vertus d'Eracle et de sa mère (Gautier s'est vite débarrassé du père, et n'insiste pas trop sur sa veuve), puis narrant, avec l'insistance qui se doit, la progressive découverte, par l'empereur alors régnant, des qualités du jeune *devin*—comme le désigne à plusieurs reprises le texte. Eracle devient conseiller et confident de son maître. Il lui a fait découvrir, dans la foule de ses jeunes sujettes, la perle rare, toute pudeur et beauté, aussitôt faite impératrice. Cependant, les jeunes nobles de la cour du comte de Blois Thibaut V, premier dédicataire du roman, attendent autre chose encore d'un récit de cette espèce. Chrétien de Troyes, au moment où Gautier entreprend *Eracle*, a déjà fait connaître, dans les mêmes milieux, son *Erec*, très probablement son *Cligès* (avec lequel *Eracle* n'est pas sans présenter certaines ressemblances apparentes), peut-être même *Le chevalier au lion*. Désormais, il faut, à l'aventure, son versant de galanterie courtoise: telle est la demande, donc la loi du marché. Rien de plus simple à combiner: d'un empereur, on glisse aisément à l'autre, et l'on identifie l'épouse du patron d'Eracle avec celle de Théodose (mais la traduction française de ce nom grec n'est-elle pas justement Dieudonné!), héroïne d'un roman populaire byzantin, fortement folklorisé, peut-être véhiculé jusqu'en Occident par la tradition orale. Gautier en adapte les grands traits, à commencer par le nom de la dame: Athénaïs. Partant en guerre, le mari méfiant place sa femme sous étroite surveillance, déjouée au bout d'un temps; adultère heureux, puis retour du mari et vengeance. Cela devient l'épisode central du roman, qu'une esthétique classicisante jugerait démesurément amplifié, à la manière des amours d'Enée et Lavinie dans l'*Enéas*, une dizaine d'années plus tôt: témoin du goût nouveau qui se répand alors dans les cours. De cette partie, Eracle demeure matériellement absent, mais il s'y trouve implicitement engagé: en refusant à Atanaïs la confiance qu'elle mérite, l'empereur a, pour une fois, désobéi aux conseils de son "devin," et celui-ci, au retour, prouve éloquemment l'innocence des amants. Convaincu d'être seul coupable, l'époux trompé se montre magnanime, rend sa liberté à l'infidèle et laisse triompher l' amour. Que la morale ecclésiastique s'en arrange comme elle pourra: ce qu'on nous raconte, c'est un cas de sainteté courtoise. D'où l'exultation de ces quelque quinze cents vers, leur liberté sereine, leur tendresse, leur humour espiègle ou coquin. Rencontre lors d'une fête publique, coup de foudre, longues hésitations des cœurs, intervention de l'entremetteuse, revendication répétée de la *fine amour*, rendant égaux ceux, et ceux-là seuls, qui la partagent dans la joie des corps. Univers transparent et sans problèmes, où la population entière de la ville proclame sa sympathie pour ceux qui aiment (v. 4877-81).

Tout cela est "littérature," dans le sens plein du latin médiéval *litteratura*: la tradition de ce qui fut écrit. Mais, plus encore, cela relève d'une pratique, proche en langue vulgaire de sa source toute fraîche, vibrante de l'affirmation d'une conscience: de la perception confuse mais heureuse, — obscure mais gaie science — d'une distance instaurée entre le texte et ce qu'il raconte, espace neuf d'une vérité sans référence qu'à soi; d'une autorité incontestable, gommant la barre qui, de la fiction, distingue à d'autres yeux la réalité, ou de quelque nom qu'on la désigne. D'où le merveilleux: j'entends surtout l'incessante merveille d'un récit naissant et renaissant de lui-même, auto-engendré dès que le premier vers en fut prononcé. Certes, sur le plan narratif, le "devin" Eracle pénètre avec aisance les secrets de la nature et du temps: ses ennemis l'accusent de sorcellerie. Il s'en explique, aux vers 1077-89: il n'est qu'un instrument de Dieu et son pouvoir réside dans la seule connaissance du *vrai*. Gautier, comme pour sceller ce message, répartit au fil de son roman sept fois (nombre aléatoire?) le couplet de rimes *miracle: Eracle*, dans cet ordre ou l'inverse. Miracle de la parole véridique, le héros, dans un monde de faux-fuyants, d'hypocrisie, d'ignorance, est porte-voix de l'Ordre providentiel: curieuse ressemblance entre Eracle et le prophète Merlin tel que l'ont figuré (dans une perspective d'abord toute laïque) à partir de 1135 Geoffroy de Monmouth puis Wace, avant que dans les années 90 du siècle Robert de Boron n'en fasse l'Elu de Dieu, l'anti-Antéchrist.[4]

A l'instant dramatique où, au vers 2584, après une longue recherche vaine, l'oeil d'Eracle discerne, dans une fillette de la rue, celle qu'il va choisir pour l'empereur, le texte le nomme *li Voirdisans*: appellation unique, nulle part ailleurs reprise, d'autant plus fortement en relief. Un thème récurrent traverse la narration: l'affirmation d'une véridicité, le rejet des discours mensongers ou vains. Exposé dès les vers 524-42, puis encore 1085-88, ce thème fonctionnalise le long épisode de la manifestation des trois dons d'Eracle. Ensuite, il figure, par rapport au texte, comme un plan de référence auquel renvoient périodiquement, en contexte négatif, des termes comme *mensonge* et *mentir, barat* et *bareter* (qui en sont synonymes), voire les équivalents *menteur, trichiere, losengier, gengleor*: ensemble, une quarantaine d'occurrences.

Dans l'espace de "vérité" miraculeuse ainsi engendré par le récit, résonne ce que les lecteurs universitaires modernes d'*Eracle* ont longtemps à l'envi décrié comme son "didactisme," sinon sa pédanterie moralisante. Je dirais plutôt que l'une des dimensions du discours de Gautier n'est autre que sa propre glose: glose qui, apparemment destinée à expliciter un message tenu pour vrai mais en quelque manière voilé, en constitue plutôt l'authentification interne, en ouvre la signifiance sur le champ illimité des possibles jusqu'à l'ironie, sinon, qui sait? au pastiche. C'est par ce moyen que, relativement à l'intertexte, le texte opère sa *translatio*.[5] Ce dernier terme, à la mode depuis quelques années chez les médiévistes français et américains, appartint au vocabulaire fondamental de la rhétorique. Le *Manuel* de Lausberg lui consacre une cinquantaine de paragraphes.[6] Liée à la *qualitas* de ce que l'on rapporte, la *translatio* tient à la fois de la métonymie et de la métaphore: ce qui la constitue, c'est le déplacement du fait déclaré dans l'espace sémantique, en principe sans bornes, qu'engendre le discours poétique. Tel est aussi bien, à un niveau plus général, le sens de l'expression de *translatio studii*, référant à une culture savante, fondée sur les Auteurs et intégrant à la compréhension de ceux-ci un "surplus de sens."[7]

La glose, dans *Eracle*, toute indissociable qu'elle est d'une narration dans la trame même de laquelle on l'a filée, prend çà et là figure explicite de commentaire. C'est cela, sans nul doute, qui gêna certains lecteurs, asservis au préjugé littéraire moderne. Le procédé en effet renvoie à des pratiques orales plus que d'écriture: enseignement, prédication, jugement. En tant que tel, il contribue à définir le registre poétique du roman.

Ce n'est point un hasard si le plus autonome de ces commentaires, expressément marqué dans le texte par une référence à l'Ecriture (v. 6089), est aussi le dernier de la série, relatif à l'Exaltation de la Croix, glorieux épisode final, terme d'une gradation engagée dès la conception du héros. La structure du passage est celle même d'une *lectio* allégorique explicite:

— action décrite:

> . . . si s'est tant esploitiés
> o le Vraie Crois qu'il en porte
> qu'il est venus pres de le porte . . .
>
>   [6084-6]
>
> (il s'est tant efforcé
> avec la Vraie Croix qu'il emporte
> qu'il est venu près de la porte)

— rappel du type scriptural qu'elle reproduit:

> Cil qui fu nés en Belleem
> vint par la . . .
>   [6091-2]
> (Celui qui naquit à Bethléem
>   passa par là . . .)
> suit une traduction résumée de Matthieu 21, 1–9
>   [6093-6113]

— interprétation allégorique:

> senefiance i a molt biele
>   [6114]
> (il y a là une riche signification)

que développent les sept vers suivants;

—définition de l'*utilitas* de cette leçon; (6121-23)

—jugement, par rapport au modèle typologique, de l'action en cours (v. 6124-31), ce qui entraînera, par delà une suite de la description (v. 6132-40), un rebondissement narratif annoncé aux vers 6141-48.

Le discours ici tient de l'homélie—narrativisée et dramatisée du seul fait de son resserrement en soixante-cinq vers. Ailleurs, le commentaire devient historique, introduisant ou expliquant un épisode par référence à telle coutume institutionnelle ou mentale:

> coustume estoit en icel tens . . . ;
>
> [374]
> (il y avait en ce temps-là une coutume)
>
> c'est pres coustume a tote gent
>   qu'il sont . . . ;
>
> [1994-95],
> (presque tout le monde a coutume
>   d'être . . .)

et l'exposé de la "coustume" emplit huit vers. La grande fête (autre point culminant du récit) où se rencontrent l'impératrice et son futur amant eut lieu, explique Gautier, en vertu d'un ancien usage romain—qu'il décrit en dix-neuf vers (3372-90), non sans avoir pris la précaution (3367-70) d'avouer que, certes, de nos jours cette fête est tombée en désuétude quoique

> encore le sevent bien maint home
>
> [3371].
> (bien des gens le savent encore)

Digression signalisatrice: l'accent narratif qui marque ainsi l'épisode résulte de ces remarques aimables, un peu décousues, au ton de causerie familière. Plus souvent, la glose se réduit à une très brève notation de l'auteur intervenant anonymement dans son récit pour en souligner quelque détail. Lorsque, durant la première épreuve imposée par l'empereur, Eracle est près de se noyer dans le Tibre, Gautier prévient notre inquiétude:

> N'a encor talent de morir,
> Dius le velt a son oeus norir.
>
> [977-78]
> (il n'a pas encore envie de mourir,
> Dieu veut l'élever pour son service)

Après qu'ait été prouvé le pouvoir divinatoire du jeune inconnu, le texte ajoute:

> Or est Eracles de grant pris,
> nus ne puet mais trover son maistre.

> Bien ait li sire quil fist naistre
> qu'en tout le monde n'en a tel!
>
> [998-1001]
> (voici Eracle objet d'une telle estime
> que nul ne peut lui trouver de maître.
> Béni soit le Seigneur qui le fit naître,
> car dans le monde entier il n'a pas son
> semblable!)

Quand est criée, à la demande d'Eracle, la grande foire aux chevaux, Gautier nous assure que

> encor l'ont maint home en memoire
> [1281]
> (bien des gens l'ont encore en mémoire)

On reconnaît au passage la formule.

La plupart du temps la glose revêt l'aspect d'une sentence, dont le propre est de fonder, selon le mode argumentatif, un discours d'autorité: énoncé autonome, mais ne fonctionnant, écrit M. L. Ollier, qu' "en rupture de cette autonomie, dans son lien nécessaire à un discours qui l'intègre," la sentence "se présente comme la majeure d'un syllogisme. Majeure et mineure le plus souvent suivent la conclusion: le syllogisme intervient comme justification."[8] La ligne de démarcation pourtant reste floue, qui distingue en principe la sentence du proverbe, préexistant, intertextuel, et sémantiquement révélateur d'analogie. En l'absence d'éléments de comparaison (qu'est-ce donc qui préexiste?), l'identification des proverbes proprement dits est malaisée: on n'hésite pas au vers 2244:

> car n'est pas ors tout canqu'il luist,
> (car tout ce qui luit n'est pas or)

ni aux vers 3560-61, déclarés tels par une formule connue:

> li vilains dist, s'est vérités,
> que bien s'abaisse qui s'aaise.
> (le paysan dit — et c'est très vrai —
> que bien s'abaisse qui se met à l'aise)

La répertoire de Morawski en fournit une variante, sous le numéro 2118. Les vers 1901-2 ont toute l'apparence stylistique d'un proverbe (je les cite selon la version *BT*, mieux intelligible que *A*, adoptée par l'éditeur):

> car puis que sire a cier son cien,
> tout li autre le sivent bien . . .
> (car quand le maître aime son chien
> tous les autres le suivent bien)

On pourrait se livrer longtemps à ce jeu de repérage. La vanité ne tarde pas à en apparaître, faute de critères sûrs. J'ai tenté du moins de relever dans le texte tous les traits de diction sentencieuse; un premier examen m'a conduit à fixer empiriquement les limites quantitatives de la "sentence": une phrase unique, d'une longueur inférieure à cinq vers. J'en ai compté 52, dont plusieurs énoncées par des personnages. Mais le niveau de discours qu'elles constituent est si fortement intériorisé dans la narration que ce nombre demeure à la fois approximatif et d'interprétation douteuse. Comment tracer, d'autre part, une frontière entre la sentence amplifiée, glosant moralement l'action, et ce que le texte lui-même nomme *sermon*? Le terme apparaît aux vers 5658 et 5697, pour désigner l'un des prêches par lesquels, au cours de sa grande guerre, Eracle tente de convertir à la foi chrétienne son adversaire. Ces prêches ne diffèrent toutefois, ni par leur étendue ni par leur fonction dramatique, de ceux qui émaillent les parties précédentes du roman. Sur ce point encore, mon approche est empirique. Je constate en effet l'existence d'agrégats de phrases sentencieuses, étalés sur plus de quatre vers, généralement une dizaine. Parfois, des figures, des exemples ou des références à quelque autorité extra-textuelle les amplifient; voire un souvenir, comme dans ces vers que prononce la vieille, si semblables à ceux d'une autre vieille, plus tard, chez Villon:

> A feme n'est pas de grant pris
> hom puis que trop en est soupris,
> mais celui aime, celui prise
> qui l'a sous pies, qui l'a souprise.
> Jel di por moi qui feme sui:
> ja ai je fait maint home anui;
> quant je estoie jovene touse
> je n'amaisse home por Toulouse
> por qu'il m'amast, ains l'amusoie
> ne mais du sien tos jors prendoie:
> a ceus le donoie a droiture
> qui de m'amor n'avoient cure.
>   [4149-60].
> (aux yeux d'une femme ne vaut pas grand'chose
> l'homme qui est trop épris d'elle,
> mais elle aime et estime
> celui qui la domine et dont elle s'est éprise.
> Je parle pour moi, qui suis femme:
> j'ai fait souffrir bien des hommes.
> quand j'étais toute jeune fille
> je n'aurais pas aimé pour un empire
> homme qui m'eût aimé: je m'en amusais,
> je lui soutirais au jour le jour son argent:

          et le donnais de tout cœur
          à qui n'avait cure de mon amour.)

Sémantiquement, de tels "sermons" intègrent à l'action un jugement porté sur elle. J'en ai relevé 33. Aucun d'entre eux ne compte plus de 30 vers consécutifs: les plus longs se rapportent aux vices des femmes et aux douleurs de l'amour (v. 2221-50 et 4688-4708); plusieurs, qui se succèdent au cours d'un même épisode, y introduisent une "moralisation" discontinue mais homogène: ainsi, cette trentaine de vers, en trois segments, 3040-46, 3065-75 et 3094-3104, plaidoyer pour la générosité et la confiance envers la femme aimée; ainsi encore, discours dans le discours, les six sermons, totalisant 46 vers, qui jalonnent le grand dialogue intérieur d'Atanaïs, dont ils constituent ensemble l'une des voix, déroulant, en contre-point des autres, une éloquente *reprobatio amoris*: v. 3571-86, 3659-63, 3669-72, 3676-81, 3685-93, 3701-6.

    Si je m'en rapporte à mes relevés, et compte tenu de leur approximation, la fréquence moyenne — donc la probabilité — des gloses (sous l'une ou l'autre de leurs formes: commentaire, proverbe, sentence, sermon) dans le texte d'*Eracle* est d'une pour 65 à 70 vers, densité, me semble-t-il, particulièrement forte. Pourtant, aucune de ces gloses ne pèse lourd; la grande majorité d'entre elles ne dure pas plus de trois, quatre, six vers, soit de six à quinze secondes de parole, un peu plus si le récitant introduit une pause. C'est là une forme de *brevitas* étrangère aux conceptions codifiées de la rhétorique, mais évidemment imposée par le souci de maintenir la vivacité et la mobilité de la parole, l'aspect cursif du discours, sans rien sacrifier de ce qui suggère la multiplicité de son sens.

    Un grand *art* (dans l'acception médiévale technique de ce terme) met en œuvre des éléments si divers. Gautier maîtrise à la perfection les ressources de la rhétorique. En témoigne une série d'ensembles oratoires dont une passion, vécue ou fictive, soutient la pathétique élégance verbale: ainsi, la plainte d'Atanaïs emprisonnée, v. 3227-60; la plaidoirie d'Eracle, v. 4961-5044; le discours de l'ange ordonnant la Croisade, v. 5327-78; la lyrique invocation de la Sainte Croix, v. 5897-5943, résonnant d'échos sonores, de refrains, scandée par l'apostrophe cinq fois répétée. Ces fragments, et quelques autres, passeraient sans peine pour modèles de la poétique lettrée de ce temps, jusqu'à l'affectation.[9] La première description d'Atanaïs, encore pauvre et inconnue, v. 2589-2606, respecte avec subtilité les règles de la *descriptio a cognatione* et *a natura*: trois vers de *narratio* introduisent les trois séries d'*attributa*, que suit une *descriptio superficialis* ornée de figures de *frequentatio*! Neuf cents vers plus loin, 3478-3513, y répond, plus longuement mais travaillée de la même manière, la description du beau Paridès, l'amant à venir. L'habileté de l'auteur comporte en cela néanmoins une double retenue: la brièveté de ces morceaux de bravoure et, plus encore, la discrétion de l'*ornatus*. Excellent artisan, Gautier ne fétichise pas son instrument. La personnification allégorique et la métaphore sont les seuls procédés d'*ornatus difficilis* auxquels il recourt assez souvent. Mais l'usage de l'allégorie relève, dans son discours, de la glose: ainsi, les tirades sur Envie, v. 1059-72, après le premier triomphe public d'Eracle; v. 4120-27, sur Désespérance, dans les exhortations de l'entremetteuse, à quoi répond, v. 4369-73, l'allusion à Espérance . . . Quant aux métaphores, L. Renzi observe avec justesse la luminosité du registre imaginaire auquel elles font en général appel: astres, gemmes, eau, feu, matières cosmiques concrétisant la relation figurale et qui la rendent comme tactile:

> se li plons art, que l'argens fonde,
> n'est mie drois qu'on le confonde.
> Nus ne doit por ce blasmer l'or
> que l'archaus solle le trésor;
> que puet li rose de l'ortie
> s'ele est vius erbe et amortie?
> Que puet la lune s'ele luist
> sor mainte cose qui molt nuist?
>
> [4827-34]
>
> (si le plomb brûle, que l'argent fonde,
> il est injuste de les confondre.
> Personne ne doit blâmer l'or
> de ce que du laiton souille le trésor.
> Que peut la rose de ce que l'ortie
> est herbe vile et comme morte?
> Qu' en peut la lune si elle luit
> sur mainte chose nuisible?)

Rien ne suspend l'élan de la parole, qui traverse sans obstacle ce champ d'images translucides; aucune obscurité n'arrête l'attention, invitant la pensée à en fouiller les profondeurs: c'est en extension que l'on saisit les choses, jusqu'aux cercles célestes où s'enchâssent nos destins.

C'est pourquoi l'*ornatus facilis* convient mieux au dessein de Gautier: les figures de mots surtout, du type accumulatif. A tout instant, elles surgissent dans le récit, entassant en une élégante jonglerie noms ou verbes, conjonctions ou formules syntaxiques équivalentes:

> . . . ses peres li vaillans,
> Mirïados li gens, le biaus;

si tint se mere les castiaus,
les viles et les fremetés,
les manoirs et les yretés;

[280-4]

(Son père, le vaillant,
le noble, le beau Mériados.
Sa mère géra les châteaux,
les villages et les forteresses,
les manoirs et tous les biens-fonds)

mar fu si biele creature!
Il ne fu lere ne triciere
ne baretere ne boisiere . . . ;

[949-50]

(c'est pour son malheur que vécut si belle créature!
Il ne fut larron ni tricheur
ni menteur ni trompeur)

de lui amer et conjoïr,
de lui servir, de lui joïr;

[1899-1900]

(de l'aimer, de lui donner de la joie,
de le servir, de jouir de lui)

. . . m'est vis que c'est raisons
que ma dame aut par ses maisons,
par ses viles, par ses castiaus,
par ses manoirs qu'ele a molt biaus;
verra les terres et le gent,
verra son or et son argent.

[3079-84].

(il me semble raisonnable
que ma Dame aille dans ses maisons,
dans ses villages, dans ses châteaux,
dans ses manoirs très beaux;
elle verra ses terres et ses gens,
elle verra son or et son argent)

Au niveau de l'organisation des ensembles, la gradation provoque un effet analogue, qu'elle consiste en un déplacement lexical, en un démembrement du message ou en distribution significative des masses. Du vers 4263 au vers 4341, Atanaïs, interpellant l'entremetteuse, passe de sœur à amie puis à mère! La scène hagio-comique où la mère d'Eracle décide de vendre son fils afin d'en distribuer le prix aux pauvres, v. 380-421, révèle progressivement l'énormité du marché envisagé, jusqu'à ce que l'enfant fixe lui-même les enchères: mille besants, une fortune. . . , Le pittoresque et charmant épisode du "concours de beauté" comporte huit volets de construction homologue: Eracle remarque et examine l'une des concurrentes, dont sont dépeintes les réactions, espoir et crainte; la perspicacité du devin saisit le vice caché; Eracle se détourne, passe sans s'arrêter devant soixante autres jeunes filles, puis le scénario se reproduit . . . à cela près que son étendue s'accroît considérablement. De la troisième à la septième candidate examinée, il s'abrège en revanche au point que les cinq scènes semblent n'en plus former qu'une seule, à rebondissements. Eracle interrompt cette quête vaine; et c'est alors que, fortuitement, il rencontre la petite Atanaïs. Or, les durées respectives des quatre séquences ainsi découpées ne paraisssent pas aléatoires: 74, 114, 168 et enfin 203 vers, nombres comparables en proportion à 3, 5, 7 et 9!

Amusement de virtuose? Je ne le pense pas, et reviendrai plus loin sur cette question. Du moins, toutes les figures que je signale ici n'empêchent-elles pas que, globalement, le langage d'*Eracle* ne soit, dans le sens canonique du terme, assez peu orné, et que de vastes sections du récit, dépourvues de *colores*, ne puissent être considérées (si l'on tient à ces classifications!) comme de *stylus humilis*. Le discours adhère alors directement à ce qu'il représente et, par un jeu de balance ou de compensation, le lexique s'enrichit et se nuance.[10] D'où l'ampleur, rare dans les romans du XIIe siècle (me semble-t-il; mais il nous manque un nombre suffisant de relevés complets), du vocabulaire concret d'*Eracle*.

Gautier d'Arras apparaît ainsi comme un admirable *conteur* — de ceux peut-être que Chrétien de Troyes accuse, au Prologue d'*Erec*, de "dépecer et corrompre" leur matière. Gautier n'a que faire des complaisances esthétiques par lesquelles certaine écriture savante sémantise, en le fixant, un discours. Sa démarche zigzagante le fait passer, d'un vers à l'autre (comme dans la scène de l'équarissage du poulain, v. 1860-90), de l'abstraction raffinée de l'univers courtois à l'apparente banalité et à la truculence de l'ordinaire. Mais ce contraste, en lui-même, ne fait pas *sens*: il fait *plaisir*. C'est là sa fin. D'où l'aspect centrifuge que, sous le regard, parfois prend l'oeuvre, son côté moins incohérent qu'irrémédiablement fragmentaire. Mais c'est là comme l'envers ou le complément de sa prestesse, de la vivacité de ses rythmes, aussi bien dans le mouvement grammatical que dans l'enchaînement des unités narratives: adverbes parsemant le texte, *tost, isnelement, sempres, delivrement, maintenant,* tous dénotant la vitesse, sinon la hâte; verbes comme *sauter sus*; dénégations répétées *sans demourement, sans longe atendue, ne detrïer*; phrases condensées en un *faire*:

> "Facent le feu!" Et cil le font.
>
> [1037]
>
> ("Qu'ils fassent le feu!" Et ils le font)
>
> Quanque le sire velt, si fist.
>
> [3175]
>
> (Tout ce que veut le seigneur, il le fit)

La partie qui pourrait être la plus statique du récit, les amours d'Atanaïs et Paridès (vers 3223 à 4722) est animée de trois manières, concourant à lui imposer un tel galop que l'on évite à peine la grivoiserie: la fête populaire, où s'échangent les premiers regards, continue, emmêlée à l'épisode amoureux, jusqu'à la fin de celui-ci; l'intervention bienveillante de l'entremetteuse entraîne une série d'actions burlesques, dans le récit desquelles on sent la présence intertextuelle du genre alors nouveau des fabliaux: le message dans le pâté, le creusement du tunnel, la fausse chute dans la gadoue et les gardiens dupés au nom de la pudeur féminine; enfin, où la convention romanesque exigeait un monologue de l'héroïne, Gautier place un étourdissant dialogue intérieur! La longue histoire de la manifestation des dons d'Eracle, étendue sur plus de deux mille vers éclate en trois épisodes dont chacun fourmille d'actions subordonnées, de personnages, de courts fragments descriptifs, de dialogues, de brefs discours, de notations ironiques. Rapidité unique, associée à tant de variété, dans la poésie de ce temps: les contes au sein du conte se succèdent, décalant la tonalité sans cesse: pittoresques (Eracle en vente au marché, v. 435-67), coquins (l'aspirante-impératrice songeant à son amant secret, v. 2259-2302), touchants (le manège pudique et l'effroi de la jeune Atanaïs chez sa tante, v. 2596-2664), héroïque enfin, la bataille sur le Danube (v. 5409-5837) où les motifs épiques, hâchés par l'octosyllabe, se précipitent (en dépit des discours insérés) sur un rythme haletant vers le carnage terminal.

Gautier est partout présent dans son récit et, manifestement, tient à le faire sentir. J'ai relevé, assez régulièrement réparties, 99 interventions d'auteur: une en moyenne tous les 65 vers, une toutes les deux ou trois minutes à l'audition! Leur fonction les diversifie: remarque en passant, à propos d'un personnage ou de l'épisode en cours (donc, assimilable à une glose); affirmation de savoir; citation ou référence; annonce d'événements à venir. Cinq seulement de ces interventions ont la forme d'une phrase à la troisième personne et constituent de brefs apartés (ainsi, v. 3840-42, 4388-90), dont le plus frappant, aux vers 3259-61, interrompt un monologue de l'héroïne. En revanche, 85 interventions se font à la première personne du singulier; 9, à la première personne du pluriel, qui tantôt peut s'interpréter comme un substitut de *je* (*si vos dirons d'Eracle humais*, v. 5092) (nous vous parlerons désormais d'Eracle) , tantôt comme englobant la communauté de l'auteur et des destinataires du roman

(*molt nos a en grant paine traite*, [elle nous a causé par là bien du malheur]
dit le vers 2090, par allusion à Eve). Aux vers 2907 et 5326, l'intervention
se réduit à un *nostre*, appliqué à *l'empereur*:

> Vint li angles Nostre Signor
> a nostre bon empereour.
> [5325-6]
> (L'ange de Notre-Seigneur vint
> à notre bon empereur)

On serait porté à entendre là un tour du langage parlé le plus familier.
Par ailleurs, 49 de ces interventions impliquent expressément le public,
par recours au pronom *vous*, çà et là, selon l'usage des jongleurs, appuyé
d'un *seigneurs*, ou parfois, comme aux vers 2083, 5119 et 6161, remplacé
par lui. Ainsi, v. 287,

> Avant savrés com ele fist;
> [979-80]
> (d'abord vous saurez comment elle s'y prit)
>
> S'oïr volés l'ovre et cerchier,
> oïr poés com Dius l'ot cier;
> [3513-4]
> (si vous voulez bien écouter ce récit et en comprendre le sens,
> vous pourrez entendre à quel point Dieu l'aima)
>
> Que ainques de mot n'i menti,
> ce saciés vos trestot de fi.
> [3513-4]
> (car jamais il ne dit un mot mensonger:
> sachez-le tous de façon sûre)

Quand alors un verbe à la première personne régit le *vous* (ou l'inverse),
un dialogue virtuel s'établit, qui s'actualise dans et par la communauté de
la performance:

> si com m'orrés el romans dire;
> [102]
> (comme vous m'entendrez dire dans ce roman)
>
> que jou Mirïados vous nom;
> [198]
> (que je vous nomme Mériados)

ainsi, vingt-et-une fois, d'un bout à l'autre du roman.

Plus d'une fois sur trois, l'auteur use d'une formule juxtaposant au
vous un *je* explicite (dans l'usage du XIIe siècle, fortement insistant): *je
vos di* (v. 939, 2020, 5502), ou les variantes *car je vos di* (v. 2989 et 3411),
mais je vos di (v. 2977), *mais je vos dirai* (v. 4412), *je vos di bien* (v.
2817), *jel vos di* (v. 2365) ou même *je vous cuic assés dire mius* (v. 3220).

Cet énoncé récurrent, on le constate, fonctionne à la manière des formules dites épiques; narrativement, il sert à introduire ou relancer un
épisode; et, sur le plan de la glose, il reprend en compte le motif de la
véridicité. La vigueur de l'affirmation est d'autant plus significative que
je vos di pourrait bien avoir appartenu au discours stéréotypé des
charlatans et thériaqueurs de place publique (ou à sa parodie traditionnelle): on ne le relève pas moins de 34 fois, en 165 lignes, dans le boniment jadis publié par Jubinal en appendice des *Oeuvres* de Rutebeuf, et
repris par E. Faral et J. Bastin dans leur édition, tome 2, p. 268-71.
Rutebeuf lui-même, dont le *Dit de l'herberie* pastiche très littérairement ce
texte ou un autre semblable, emploie (comme un trait typique?) quatre fois
la formule. Celle-ci, dans *Eracle*, met contextuellement en relief le fait
que plus du tiers de toutes les interventions d'auteur contiennent le verbe
dire (31 fois), un autre verbe de parole (tels *vanter* ou *faire devise*), ou inversement *oïr* (7 fois).

    C'est l'autorité du récit—la vérité d'*Eracle* non moins que celle
d'Eracle—que Gautier entend fonder sur cette parole dont la présence se
réaffirme sans cesse. En témoigne une tournure çà et là substituée à celle-
ci et renvoyant, non directement au discours de l'auteur, mais à la connaissance qu'il détient: *je cuit, al mien cuidier, ce m'est vis, mien esciënt*
et autres (ainsi, v. 966, 1290, 1642, 2017, 2453, 2459, 2592). C'est pourquoi

> ce vous voel por voir plevir;
>   [2932]
> (je vous en garantis la vérité)
>
> Signor, ce nen est mie fable,
> ançois est cose veritable . . .
>   [6173-4]
> (Seigneurs, ce n'est pas là une fable,
> mais bien une chose véritable)

Telle est, si je puis dire, l'intention première du texte: son *origine*. Contrairement à bien des auteurs ses contemporains, tel Chrétien de Troyes
aux Prologues de *Cligès* et du *Graal*, Gautier n'éprouve aucun besoin de
citer quelque modèle livresque, réel ou fictif, censé lui avoir fourni la
matière de son roman. Ou plutôt, il y renvoie exclusivement (et cela fait
grandement sens), à sept reprises (ce chiffre . . .), entre les vers 5119 et
6435, c'est-à-dire dans le récit de la reconquête de la Croix, terme du
roman et pour laquelle, nous le savons, l'auteur puisa l'essentiel de son information dans un *Passionnaire* jadis retrouvé par Faral. Or, les
références qu'il y fait suggèrent qu'il prend à son égard quelque distance:

un *livre* existe, évoqué au vers 6180; il est écrit en latin (v. 5119) et contient une ou des *estoire(s)* (v. 5126, 6089); cette histoire *dit* quelque chose (v. 5126) à ceux qui la *lisent* (v. 5119, 6089), spécialistes formant un groupe social déterminé (*cil qui . . .* v. 6089; *clers*, v. 6177), dont le *témoignage* nous garantit la *vérité* (v. 6178-6180). Mais Gautier ne semble pas se ranger d'emblée parmi ces privilégiés du savoir. Certes, il a accès à ce livre, il l'a *lu* (v. 6435); mais ce qu'il nous conte a séjourné dans sa mémoire: il nous en livre la *remembrance* (v. 6435). N'est-ce pas revendiquer, dans la véridicité même, une part à soi, la spécificité du verbe que l'on tient — liée à ce dire? Les vers 6100-6101, introduisant une citation littérale du texte évangélique (en français et en vers), confirment, me semble-t-il, cette interprétation:

> . . . je le vi
> en un livre dont me souvient.
> (. . . je le vis
> en un livre dont il me souvient)

La désinvolture de ce *vi* (rappelé, sinon corrigé, par l'*escrit* du vers 6306) accuse l'autonomie et la plénitude du *souvient*.

Les parties précédentes du roman ne comportent aucun effet de ce genre: lorsqu'au baptême le héros reçoit le nom d'Eracle, l'auteur précise *ensi l'oï dire* (je l'entendis ainsi dire); avant la course de chevaux, *ce m'a on dit certainement* (on m'a dit cela de façon certaine). C'est peu, et ces renvois, sans aucun doute fictifs, à la tradition orale, sont-ils mieux qu'une allusion amusée à la pratique des conteurs populaires? Seul élément hétérogène, le *ce truis lisant* (je trouve cela en lisant) du vers 1769, au début d'une tirade contre la médisance, relève d'un banal *ars praedicandi*. C'est à travers ces affirmations ambiguës, ces dénégations à demi-mot, ces allusions latentes, que le texte parle de lui-même, raconte sa propre poétique, en opération au sein de l'autre récit. En opération, non sur des sources qu'il filtrerait de telle ou telle manière, mais parmi un fourmillement de discours, ses multiples archétypes.[11] Hors de ceux-ci, *Eracle* est, comme oeuvre, littéralement impensable: lieu de leur convergence et de leur transformation, à travers ces signes que trace la main, dans une *remembrance* obsédée du miracle de la voix vive.

A plusieurs reprises, *Eracle* mentionne une activité d'écriture: mais elle constitue, soit un objet de description, élément de pittoresque, soit l'instrument, indifférent comme tel, de communication d'êtres hors du commun. C'est une lettre du ciel qui révèle les dons d'Eracle nouveau-né; Eracle devenu empereur écrit à ses vassaux pour les convoquer à l'ost, comme le fait de son côté le roi païen. Quant à la lettre d'amour d'Atanaïs, sa confection nous est exactement décrite (v. 4378-83): mais la scène vise à louer l'impératrice d'un talent donné pour rare:

> nul autre escrivain n'i apiele
> ne mais son cors . . .
> (elle ne fait appel à aucun autre scribe
> qu'elle-même . . .)

Ces vers 4380-1 achèvent l'éloge implicitement engagé au vers 4244:

> un livre tient et si i list.
> (elle tient un livre où elle lit)

Ecriture comme lecture sont ainsi considérées du dehors, au même titre que les autres actions humaines. La "vérité" n'est pas l'écrit; n'est peut-être pas même *dans* l'écrit — sinon, au sens tout extrinsèque de cette préposition, au sein des limites matérielles de la page inscrite: elle ne procède pas du texte comme tel; l'espace poétique où elle s'engendre est celui même où se déploie, en y résonnant, la parole. Dans son Prologue-dédicace, dans son Epilogue, et dans deux interventions d'auteur, Gautier parle de son propre ouvrage. Or, il n'emploie pas moins de quatre termes différents, en douze occurrences, et les connotations qui y sont liées dans le texte trahissent un attachement foncier à la vocalité, sinon (indirectement) à la gestualité même, du message. Au vers 2746, Gautier nomme son *conte*, mot dont il use ailleurs, ainsi que de *conter*, dans d'autres contextes (v. 15, 24, 38, etc.) renvoyant à diverses situations d'oralité: au vers 3809, *conter* est donné expressément comme synonyme de *dire*. Les vers 95, puis 102, emploient *roman*, en deux tournures syntaxiques non identiques: *assés vous dirai en romans*, c'est la locution bien connue, signifiant "en langue vulgaire" par opposition au latin; mais *si com m'orés el romans dire* semble prendre *romans* pour un nom, référant au récit qui va commencer. Reste que *roman* est lié à *dire* et qu'il véhicule quelque idée de translation de parole.

A six reprises apparaît *œuvre*, toujours déterminé (par *ceste, m', l'*) et dépourvu de toute ambiguïté dans son entourage immédiat. Mais le terme figure cinq autres fois dans le texte en un sens différent quoiqu'aussi clair: désignant l'action faite ou entreprise par quelqu'un (v. 2004, 5397), un objet travaillé (v. 5874, 5886), enfin de façon plus générale, une opération (*l'uevre de malisse*, v. 5360). Les connotations ici réfèrent à un agir concret, au produit résultant d'une dépense d'énergie physique: au jeu corporel d'une performance, autant ou plus qu'à l'investissement du langage dans une écriture.

Le mot de *traitié*, enfin, surgit deux fois, à des lieux éminemment stratégiques: au début, comme nom, et à la fin comme verbe, dans les deux phrases de signature que comporte le texte:

> Se Gautiers d'Arras fist ainc rien
> c'on atorner li doive a bien,
> or li estuet tel traitié faire . . .
>
> [1-3]
>
> (si Gautier d'Arras fit jamais rien
> dont on doive le feliciter,
> il lui faut maintenant faire un traité)

> Nous soit li Sainte Crois aidable
> dont Vautiers d'Arras a traitié!
>
> [6516-7]
>
> (que la sainte Croix nous soit secourable,
> dont Gautier d'Arras a traité!)

Ces passages évoquent l'usage latin de *tractatus*, désignant l'exposé magistral de quelque point de doctrine; ils renvoient explicitement, plutôt qu'à une technique scripturale comme telle, à la glose intégrée au récit. Le long éloge du comte Thibaut, qui suit immédiatement (v. 5-86) la première de ces mentions, en précise indirectement la portée: l'argument développé d'abord en faveur de ce prince n'est autre que son amour de la parole, son éloquence, la joie dont il témoigne ouvertement à l'audition de chanteurs, de musiciens ou de conteurs (v. 29-46).

Je n'entends pas, en formulant ces observations, faire dire aux mots plus qu'ils ne peuvent. Loin de moi l'idée de présenter Gautier comme un héraut de la poésie orale; ni son roman, comme une sorte de chanson de geste. Gautier m'apparaît plutôt, dans le texte d'*Eracle*, comme non encore asservi, en ce troisième quart du XIIe siècle, aux mentalités scripturales, alors en rapide expansion parmi les clercs de milieu courtois. Il serait utile d'instaurer sur ce point une comparaison avec *Ille et Galeron*, l'autre roman de Gautier et que celui-ci déclare (v. 5805-6 de l'édition Cowper) postérieur à *Eracle*. Certains critiques admettent que les deux ouvrages se trouvèrent quelque temps simultanément en chantier. Cela semble improbable.[12] Mais peu importe. On peut, non sans motif, se demander si Gautier – durant les dix ou quinze années (entre 1170 et 85) où l'on tient la preuve qu'il fut actif – ne fut pas déchiré entre deux conceptions esthétiques mal compatibles: celle qui privilégie la voix vive, et celle qui se fonde sur les propriétés et les implications de l'écriture. Gautier ne fut

pas le seul sans doute dans cette situation. L'enseignement même de la
rhétorique semble avoir maintenu ici une équivocité: vers 1210 encore, la
Poetria nova de Geoffroy de Vinsauf se termine par trente-cinq vers sur
l'*actio* (qu'en ont précédés soixante-deux sur la *memoria*):[13] sur un total
de 2 115 hexamètres, c'est peu de chose, et l'on comprend que les commentateurs aient négligé ce passage. Il n'en est pas moins lourd de sens,
assimilant poète et *recitator* (v. 2040, 2048), parole, visage, geste et
langage (v. 2031-2), prônant l'adéquation, à la chose désignée, des
tonalités vocales et gestuelles

> . . . sic ergo feratur ad aures,
> ut cibet auditum, vox castigata modeste,
> vultus et gestus gemino condita sapore.
>
> [2056-8]
>
> (qu'ainsi soit portée aux oreilles
> pour nourrir l'ouïe, modestement une voix maîtrisée,
> assaisonnée des saveurs jumelles de la mimique et du geste)

Il ne fait pas de doute à mes yeux que, pour l'écrivain Gautier d'Arras,
cette *actio* concernait bien davantage que le comportement d'un interprète; elle définissait la visée ultime d'un art, par delà la pragmatique de
l'écriture. Intériorisée, elle animait le discours entier, dès sa première
émergence, puis dans sa fixation sur le parchemin, et jusqu'à son
épanouissement dans le geste et la voix.

Ce geste, *Eracle* à tout instant le suggère, et souvent l'impose: je
reviendrai sur ce point. La voix vive, sans cesse il nous la fait entendre.
Les mots qui dans le langage courant la désignent, les verbes surtout,
parsèment le texte avec une telle densité qu'ils y tissent un réseau sémique
nuançant tous les autres effets de signification. Le récit se constitue sur
fond de paroles, au moyen de paroles, assumées dans le discours pro-
clamé véridique du narrateur et de *nostre empereour*. Les diverses interventions d'auteur comportent 44 fois le verbe *dire*, deux fois des sub-
stituts constitués en locutions factitives (*faire conte, faire devise*).
Quatre-vingt quinze monologues et dialogues sont attachés au récit par le
moyen d'un *dit-il* ou *il dit*, parfois remplacé par *fait-il*, très rarement par
répondre, une fois, inversement, par *ouïr (oïr porrés)*.[14] Rien là de bien
surprenant. Mais la narration proprement dite ne présente pas moins de
145 occurrences de *verba dicendi*, dont 138 de *dire*. On atteint, dans les 6
570 vers du texte, le nombre total d'environ 300 verbes de cette classe
sémantique, auxquels s'ajoutent quelques substantifs tels *canson* (v. 35),
cri (v. 6270) ou *diction* (v. 6260) . . . Y répondent des dizaines d'*oïr* ou

expressions équivalentes. Dieu, nous l'avons vu, communique par l'Ecriture son message: ici, la lettre déposée dans le berceau d'Eracle et dont, au reste, on nous résume le contenu sans en reproduire le texte (v. 234-44, puis 264-8). Les autres êtres surnaturels, eux, discourent: un ange, à trois reprises, v. 145-78, 5327-78, et 6185-6232; un diable, aux vers 5170-91.

Dans cet ouvrage, en dépit de sa première apparence superbement maîtrisé, et où rien ne s'abandonne au hasard, de tels dosages ne peuvent guère ne pas signifier: ne serait-ce qu'une nostalgie peut-être, ou bien un appel, un élan de l'être vers toutes ces voix, émanation de vie, preuve de la vérité de nos corps, truchement du Miracle, gage de jouissance, *hic et nunc*. Une volonté de les faire se dire dans cela même qu'on écrit; une sommation. C'est pourquoi *Eracle* exige d'être perçu comme un discours plus que comme un texte: comme un message-en-situation. Si l'on veut avoir prise à la fin sur son existence textuelle, on ne le pourra qu'en s'attachant à percevoir et à analyser son existence discursive. De là, à notre première lecture, l'impression d'*entendre* un conteur. Puis, l'impression se confirme; elle requiert l'interprétation. Des traits, des signaux que l'on repérerait aussi bien, plus dilués, dans d'autres textes de la même époque, ici présentent une insistance qui nous contraint à les sémantiser fortement.

A ceux que j'ai signalés jusqu'ici s'en ajoutent bien d'autres, dans l'ordre de la communication du savoir, du montage grammatical ou des modalités diégétiques. Ainsi, près de la moitié des interventions d'auteur constituent des déclarations variées sur le thème "je le sais." Cette revendication, réitérée en moyenne tous les cent cinquante vers, établit, d'un bout à l'autre du roman, une perspective axiale, celle d'une vérité dans le présent, d'une vérité-en-présence, c'est-à dire en performance—ce qui spécifie le thème général de la véridicité: cela est vrai *parce que* je suis là et prononce mes paroles. Affirmation si convaincue qu'elle rayonne au-delà de ce présent même, confirmant la coutume ou s'épanouissant en prophétie.

> Car je vos di bien sans doutance
> que grant cose est de coustumance,
> (car je vous dis bien avec certitude
> que c'est une grande chose que la coutume)

déclarent les vers 3409-10. Le couplet dont ils sont extraits valorise triplement cette vérité de *droit*:

—en en faisant un ressort narratif indispensable: cette *coustume*, celle de la grande fête, est la cause à la fois matérielle et formelle de l'adultère (cf. v. 3367-90), et par là de toute la seconde partie du roman;

—en l'introduisant doublement par la formule *je vos di*, dont j'ai noté la valeur, à la fois de haute véridicité et de socialité: dans la description de la coutume, v. 3588, et dans sa glose morale, v. 3409;

—en assumant ouvertement ainsi le discours de tous les conteurs, récitants, chanteurs traditionnels, dont la voix—fût-elle dédaignée par certains clercs—a pour fonction de maintenir dans le temps la cohésion du groupe.[15] Ailleurs, c'est l'avenir qu'engage d'ores et déjà la parole dite: un verbe au futur, surgissant dans la phrase, annonce quelque événement destiné à se produire plus tard dans le récit: ainsi, v. 5583-4 et 5586-7; parfois, cette forme verbale, en monologue intérieur, projette le personnage dans ses propres lendemains: ainsi, v. 1261-4, 4503-4. L'un de ces passages met en haut relief la fonction prophétique de la parole présente: au milieu de la longue plaidoirie d'Eracle en faveur d'Atanaïs, le *Voirdisant* écarte sur le long terme le voile de l'avenir:

> on dira cent ans ci après . . .
>
>   [5019]
> (on dira dans cent ans . . .)

évoquant la honte qui entachera le souvenir de l'empereur dans la mémoire de générations pas encore nées s'il ne pardonne pas une faute dont il est responsable; v. 5020-28 et 5043-4, Eracle prononce par anticipation les discours qui seront tenus dans ce lointain avenir. Et, pour marquer davantage la gravité de ses paroles, il rappelle sa qualité divinatoire (v. 5021) et à son tour (après l'auteur) recourt à la formule *je vos di*, ici du reste au passé car, de l'avenir où sa vision l'engage, il se retourne vers le présent, bouleversant l'apparente succession du temps.

Autre effet, cumulatif, d'oralité, à la surface lexico-syntaxique du texte: une sorte de familiarité savoureuse du ton—choix des mots et train de phrase—, difficile, certes, à apprécier et que l'on ne saurait ériger en critère, néanmoins contribuant à l'impression générale. Manière de réduire à deux mots la scène de la conception d'Eracle, au point de susciter négativement toute espèce d'allusion gaillarde:

> . . . et si l'apiele a lui
> si engenra en li celui . . . ;
>
>   [205-6]
> (. . . et il l'appelle alors à lui
> et engendra en elle celui)

de désigner l'enfant Eracle par *li petis* (v. 253); d'évoquer en quatre exclamations assez drues le bon sens et la faconde des chalands marchandeurs (v. 455-59) . . . La vieille entremetteuse, pour convaincre Paridès de sa puissance auprès des jeunes filles:

il n'i a nule, se je voel,
que je ne face en mon diu croire:
je parol bien el que d'estoire,
de patre notre et d'evangile!

[4175-78]

(il n'y en a pas une, si je le veux,
que je ne fasse croire en mon dieu:
je te parle de bien autre chose que d'histoire,
de patenôtre ou d'évangile!)

Des passages de ce genre truffent les deux premières parties; l'intention épique de la troisième s'y prêtait moins bien. Plusieurs interventions d'auteur sont de la même farine:

mais je demain trop longe lime,
je vois trop alongant me rime
car on n'i puet nul bien pinchier;
or vuel me bouce recinchier.

[47-50]

(mais je m'attarde trop,
j'allonge trop mon poème
sans qu'on puisse en tirer aucun profit.
Je veux maintenant rincer ma bouche)

N'est d'ui ne d'ier que il commencent,
(ça ne date ni d'hier ni d'aujourd'hui)

nous dit encore l'auteur, v. 1507, des Romains depuis longtemps déjà connus pour *gaingleor*!

Aussi bien, *Eracle*, comme texte, exhibe sa parenté avec diverses formes poétiques orales. C'est ainsi qu'à onze reprises, Gautier emprunte, au registre très formalisé des chanteurs d'amour les images printanières dont il jalonne le récit:

Biaus est li tans et clers li jors.

[1639]

(Beau est le temps, et clair le jour)

Ce fu par un bel jor d'esté

[1973]

(c'était par un beau jour d'été)

que s'en vint gaiment à la ville la foule des pucelles que guidaient de beaux et gents chevaliers *par grant douçor* (v. 1979). Le miracle de saint Curiace a lieu *un jor d'esté* (v. 5162), et ce même mot enjolive l'expression d'une très longue durée:

En tout le plus lonc jor d'esté
ne poroit on conter ne dire

de ces deus amans le martire.

[3840-2]

(Le plus long jour d'été entier
ne suffirait à raconter
de ces deux amants le martyre

Dans un contexte rappelant les chansons de *Bele Aélis*, Atanaïs (dont le
nom vient d'être prononcé pour la première fois — et n'est pas sans évoquer, par son initiale et sa finale, celui de la tendre héroïne de ce cycle
lyrique) est dite *li flors d'esté* (v. 2789); au vers 3123, elle est *la rose:*
Paridès amoureux la nomme *flors de rose* (v. 4267). Emprisonnée,
pleurant la solitude à laquelle on la condamne, la jeune impératrice la
compare longuement au sort heureux des oisillons pépiant ensemble dans
le bocage (v. 3882-91). Eracle, dans sa prière à la Croix, compare la
bonté du Christ au *rius de le fontaine* (ruisseau de la source) . . . expression qui, dans sa littéralité, est un cliché de "romances" et de
pastourelles. Les astres, le jour, les nuages même mouvants dans le ciel:
le texte boucle sa ronde au sein d'un cosmos luminescent, très discrète-
ment désigné par ces allusions éparses. Dès les vers 9-13, l'éloge du comte
Thibaut s'ouvre par une évocation d'aurore. Atanaïs, ignorant de quoi
peut-être on la punit, se demande avec une pathétique ironie si c'est de
l'errance des nuages ou du fait que la lune luit moins que le soleil et croît
et décroît dans sa course (v. 3244-7): simple figure, mais élégament
évocatrice — et à laquelle répond, aux vers 5659-71, un vigoureux passage
du sermon d'Eracle, qui, pour prouver au Persan la générosité du Dieu
chrétien, lui décrit les merveilles du firmament, les étoiles et leurs signes,
la clarté ocrée de la lune, la marche inlassable du soleil dans cette sphère
pourtant immuable. . . .

A l'opposé, les commentateurs ont noté les passages tenant, par le
langage et le thème, de la tradition des fabliaux et du conte "populaire."[16]
Ainsi, l'épisode du concours de beauté, farci de clichés "anti-féministes,"
enchâsse, selon l'analyse de Renzi, un fabliau complet, v. 2259-2367, con-
forme à toutes les règles du genre et à juger en tant que tel. Même jeu au
cœur de l'aventure adultère d'Atanaïs, pourtant entière sous le signe de
la *fine amour* (l'expression y revient constamment et le style en calque
celui des chansons de trouvères): la rencontre des amoureux chez l'entremetteuse suit un schème de conte apparemment très répandu. On en
rencontre des équivalents, selon Fourrier, aussi bien dans un *exemplum*
de Jacques de Vitry qu'aux vers 6194-6391 du *Roman du Châtelain de
Couci*, plus tard encore dans les *Cent nouvelles nouvelles* (n. 37), chez
Bonaventure des Périers, Noël du Fail et d'autres. . . .

Il convient d'élever le plan de comparaison jusqu'au niveau des comportements sémiotiques; et plutôt que d'invoquer l' interférence textuelle d'un genre particulier et relativement bien défini comme le fabliau, référer à l'usage — nécessairement intentionnel — de procédés de représentation spécialement accordés à de multiples effets de récitation publique plutôt que de lecture, modulant la voix et le geste, soulignant les contrastes et l'ironie, jouant des rythmes verbaux, variant significativement les débits, — et visant peut-être un auditoire plus large et mêlé que les *happy few* de l'entourage princier. Ainsi, telles figures superlatives, dénuées de sens littéral, mais efficaces, et que l'on ne comprend guère qu'accompagnées d'une mimique ou d'un geste: *por toute France*, v. 2210, pour signifier "partout au monde," dans la bouche de jeunes Romaines! Ou, dans la semonce adressée à son fils par Chosroès, quelque part en pays *sarazinois*, l'ordre d'aller conquérir l'empire entier d'Eracle.

> et Normandie, et France, et Flandre.
>
> [5310]

Une somme considérable d'argent, c'est (*l'or de*) *Toulouse* (v. 797 et 4156) ou *tout l'or . . . au roi englés qui molt en a* (v. 5881). Ainsi, de ces nombreux passages, parfois très brefs, où l'on reconnaît tel segment structurellement ou linguistiquement typique, provenu moins d'un conte identifiable que du vaste discours narratif, réglé par une longue tradition d'oralité, dont les contes constituent les manifestations concrètes, successives ou simultanées mais toujours instables. Duperies de conduite ou de langage, ironies amusantes ou tendres, traits touchants, expressions édifiantes: ainsi, les railleries hautes en couleur (et qui bientôt apparaîtront dérisoires) adressées par les Romains au jeune Eracle, v. 794-834, 886-924; ainsi, la scène tour à tour risible et attendrissante de l'achat du poulain, avec la plaisante pirouette finale (v. 1329-1498). Mêmes types de scènes, v. 2085-2129, 2381-92, 2542-68; comique trempé d'une sensiblerie qui en occulte la verdeur, dans les vers où la mère d'Eracle l'emmène, par le licou, au marché pour le vendre (v. 421-52); faux tragique de l'apparente noyade du héros (v. 936-76); tendresse tant soit peu ironique du sénéchal, couvrant Eracle de baisers (v. 1785-1824); jolie évocation, par Atanaïs, de la manière dont les petits enfants se comprennent entre eux, dans leur langage impénétrable aux adultes (v. 3620-27) . . .

Se retrouve ainsi, disséminé dans l'ouvrage, tout l'éventail des formes de dire qu'illustrent par ailleurs des textes aussi différents que le fabliau de la *Bourgeoise d'Orléans* ou le conte pieux de la *Housse partie* . . . textes dont il est difficile de ne pas penser que leurs auteurs les destinaient à la place publique. D'où certains trucs techniques, dont Gautier fait un large emploi. Ainsi, le suspense, toujours habilement ménagé, comme dans l'épisode de la foire aux gemmes, v. 779-833 et, surtout, durant la course de chevaux, v. 1621-1784, chef-d'œuvre du genre, qui peut faire haleter encore le lecteur moderne. Même effet dans la description des jeux (v. 3415-78) où l'on pressent, puis déjà l'on sait, puis impatiemment l'on attend, que surgisse l'amour . . . Ou, dans le combat où Eracle, v. 5720 puis encore v. 5760, reçoit un coup qui devrait être mortel. Suspense, d'une autre manière, de la dénomination des personnages: Atanaïs entre en scène au vers 2577; elle n'est désignée par son nom qu'au vers 2788; l'empereur de Rome, en scène dès le vers 672, ne l'est qu'au vers 2787! Quant au héros lui-même, il change de nom en trois vers: Dieudonné v. 225, Eracle v. 228. Autre truc: la multiplicité des exclamations et interrogations. Certes, ces tournures sont pour nous malaisément repérables, car c'est l'intonation plus que la syntaxe qui les marque en ancien français. Le nombre de points d'exclamation et d'interrogation dont l'éditeur a semé le texte imprimé ne donne sans doute qu'une image trop modeste de la densité de ces figures pour l'auditeur du XIIe siècle. J'en ai fait néanmoins le compte: 263 exclamations et 98 interrogations, affectant ensemble près de 500 vers, soit plus de 7% du texte. Une lecture à haute voix, tant soit peu expressive, accroîtrait probablement cette proportion.

Le vers contribue à cette instauration, dans le texte, d'un rapport privilégié à la voix. On en a fait la remarque à propos de Chrétien de Troyes.[17] La brisure, il est vrai, du couplet, où Frappier voyait une subtile recherche vocale, paraît beaucoup moins nette dans *Eracle* que dans *Erec*. Sur ce point, encore, après tous les autres, se marque l'irréductibilité de l'art de Gautier à celui de son émule. La norme qu'apparemment il s'est imposée comporte un double principe: une proposition s'étend sur un vers ou sur deux vers entiers; la phrase, quelle qu'en soit la longueur, sur un nombre entier de couplets. Les écarts restent nombreux; mais la variété rythmique provient plutôt des différences de longueur entre phrases, souvent fortement contrastives, et constituant, me semble-t-il, l'équivalent (ou le fondement) textuel d'un jeu d'acteur très animé. De même reste rare l'enjambement proprement dit, répartissant sur deux vers successifs les éléments d'un même syntagme: j'en ai relevé au plus une quarantaine sans grande netteté, et une dizaine seulement procédant, à l'évidence, de quelque intention dramatisante: ainsi,

puis fut nonmés el baptestire
Eracles
　　　　[227-8]
(puis il fut nommé au baptême
Eracle)

et mainte huissure bien ferree
a en le tor,
　　　　[3172-3]
(et mainte porte à ferrures
il y a dans la tour)

li crois qui tant est covoitie
pren,
　　　　[5374-5]
(la Croix si désirée
il prend,)

. . . ressoient arriere trait
li mur.
　　　　[6313-4]
(que soient reculés
les murs.)

De telles ruptures rythmiques ne se produisent, dans la chaîne narrative, qu'aux moments les plus intenses, comme un geste amplificateur.

Dans ce système dont la rigueur relative renforce l'efficacité des effets de déviance, les limites du vers sont bien marquées, lexicalement à l'initiale, phoniquement à la fin. De façon très largement prédominante, c'est un mot-outil non accentué qui commence le vers: déterminatif quelconque, préposition, conjonction ou adverbe de phrase. A eux seuls, conjonctions diverses et adverbes *ne, or, si* figurent en tête de 3007 vers, soit 45,8% du total:

1) *et:* 689 occurrences
2) *que* (conjonction et relatif): 484
    mais: 260
    car: 219
    qui et *cui:* 196
    quant, se, ains et les adverbes *ou* et *dont:* ensemble 489
3) *ne:* 309
4) *si:* 154

Ces adverbes, surtout *or*, méritent une attention particulière, par suite de leur fonction dans l'énoncé et de leur rapport à la discursivité orale ou oralisante.[18] *Or*, spécialement, au-delà de sa valeur temporelle, a pour fonction première de dénoter la présence du locuteur dans ce qu'il dit: il provoque une brève stase, suspendant la temporalité du récit. On peut s'attendre à ce que la fréquence de cet adverbe s'accroisse en situation de performance ou dans un texte structuré en vue de celle-ci. Dans *Eracle, or* commence 1,4% des vers; chez Chrétien de Troyes, selon la concordance établie par M. L. Ollier,[19] la moyenne générale (si l'on exclut la partie du *Lancelot* due à Geoffroy de Lagni) n'est que de 0,77%. Dans la *Mort Arthur*,[20] dont les 9 300 lignes de prose équivalent à peu près, en nombre de syllabes, à 14 000 vers, la proportion des *or(e)* initiaux de phrases ne dépasse pas 0,8%. Un écart aussi considérable porte nécessairement sens.

Quant aux rimes, je les ai examinées de près, à titre de sondage, dans les deux cents premiers vers de chaque millier (v. 1–200, 1001–1200, etc.), soit 1 400 vers en 700 couplets. Phoniquement banales (à part le récurrent *Eracle / miracle*), elles témoignent pourtant d'une recherche particulière: je relève en effet 146 rimes riches et 188 rimes bissyllabiques — dont plusieurs, en fait, trissyllabiques, ainsi *soit amendee / pieça mandee* v. 4047-8, voire exceptionnellement quadrissyllabiques ou davantage, comme v. 6049-50, *a fait departir / c'a fait dessartir*. Ces jeux sonores touchent, dans mon échantillon, 334 couplets, donc 668 vers, soit une proportion de 48%; pour les seules rimes bi- et trissyllabiques, 27%. Cette dernière proportion est, dans l'*Yvain* de Chrétien de Troyes, de 32[21]: différence, elle aussi, non négligeable et confirmant dans *Eracle* une tendance générale à une certaine négligence grammaticale en dépit d'une recherche de tous les raffinements aptes à accroître la tension discursive. Cette tendance n'est pas étrangère à celle que l'on constate universellement dans la poésie à destination orale.[22] Elle rendrait aussi bien compte de quelques "erreurs" de versification — dont, il est, au reste, tentant de laisser la responsabilité au copiste! Vers hypométriques: 3 588, dans une série de cinq couplets donnés par un seul des trois manuscrits:

> si que le verront la gent;
> (de telle sorte que les gens le verront)

5 991, en revanche, confirmé:

> di, feras tu autre cose?
> (dis, feras-tu autre chose?)

Vers hypermétriques:

> et celle fu jovenete et tendre,
>   [2595]
> (et celle-ci était jeunette et tendre)
> con jovene dame a son signor.
>   [2807].
> (comme jeune dame à son mari)

L'étrangeté, dans les deux derniers exemples, est due apparemment à la seule graphie: sans doute faut-il prononcer *jue(v)ne* et *juenete*. Reste qu'une oscillation par rapport à la norme rythmique peut être considérée, elle aussi, comme un trait fréquent de la poésie oralisée.[23]

La distribution de certains éléments constitutifs de la narration manifeste la même tendance générale. C'est ainsi que le nombre, la répartition et la structure des discours directs concourent à une valorisation, non seulement de la voix mais plus encore des procédés mêmes que peut exalter l'oralité du discours. Le récit contient 41 dialogues et 51 monologues, de toutes longueurs. Ils parsèment assez régulièrement le texte: le plus long passage qui n'en comporte aucun compte moins de trois cents vers (2787-3009) et remplit une fonction particulière, opérant la transition entre la découverte de l'adultère et le départ pour la Croisade. Je projette en tableau les données recueillies:

Nombre de vers dans les monologues: total 872
soit: pourcentage du texte 13,3%
Nombre de vers dans les dialogues: 2 123
pourcentage du texte 32,3%

Nombre de vers par	monologue		dialogue
un demi-vers	1		–
de 1 à 5 vers	13		–
de 6 à 12 vers	17	(de 9 à 12 vers)	3
de 13 à 25 vers	11		10
de 26 à 45 vers	3		12
de 46 à 70 vers	5		7
de 71 à 100 vers	–		5
de 101 à 120 vers	–		3
134 vers	1		
138 vers	–		1
180 vers	–		1

Longueur moyenne par monologue 17 vers
– dialogue 51 vers.

Tous ces chiffres sont éloquents. Non seulement près de la moitié du texte (45,6%) est "parlé," mais il est surtout dialogué—donc théâtralisé: 32,3% de sa longueur textuelle représente sensiblement plus en durée, ne serait-ce que par suite de la multiplication des pauses, même brèves, résultant du changement de locuteur. Les 41 dialogues comportent au total 240 répliques: les plus complexes en comptent respectivement 31, 18, 12, 11 et 10; les autres, de 2 à 9. D'où un mouvement constant, qui parfois se précipite, à mesure que les répliques se contractent en se répondant du tac au tac, à intervalles de un, deux, trois vers: ainsi, v. 451-62, 2338-61 ou, dans le cours du long dialogue intérieur d'Atanaïs, les vers 3587-99, 3631-84; ailleurs encore, soit au début soit à la fin d'un dialogue formé, en sa partie principale, d'un échange de plus amples discours: v. 291-334, 385-421, 850-76, etc. L'ensemble dialogué se trouve ainsi raccordé au rythme rapide du récit. L'effet est accusé par le mode d'attache narrative: à quelques exceptions près, (v. 607, 1167, 1521, 1614, 5640, 5944, 5992), un *dit-il, fait-il*, introduit les paroles du premier interlocuteur; celles des autres suivent sans autre marque que les tirets apposés par l'éditeur! D'où, à la lecture sur manuscrit, une fréquente obscurité que l'écriture ne suffit pas à dissiper. Parfois, l'auteur signale rhétoriquement par une apostrophe le début de répliques longues ou au contraire très serrées: ainsi, aux vers 3011-3162, ou dans la série des dialogues qui se succèdent aux vers 451 à 707. Mais, contrairement à ce que Frappier constatait chez Chrétien de Troyes,[24] les répliques entre elles, dans le dialogue, ne sont que de loin en loin liées par la rime. Gautier n'a pas sur ce point de système: la distribution des rimes dites mnémoniques, dans de longs dialogues comme ceux des vers 1520-1620 et 5944-6030, semble aléatoire. La versification renforce la relative autonomie des discours: en règle générale, monologues et dialogues commencent et finissent par un couplet entier. Une fois sur cinq, il est vrai, ce relâchement du lien sonore est compensé par un effet de rythme, le discours direct commençant ou finissant au milieu d'un vers.

L'auteur s'efforce, apparemment, d'atténuer l'opposition oratoire et dramatique existant entre discours dialogués et monologués. Il lui arrive de conjoindre, par le moyen d'une brève transition narrative, deux monologues en un dialogue de fait, comme aux vers 571-632 ou 4961-5065; ou un monologue avec le dialogue qui suit: ainsi, v. 4187-4202; voire, de donner à un long monologue de fait une courte réplique terminale qui le transforme rétrospectivement en dialogue: lorsque, aux soixante-seize vers du discours d'Eracle à ses barons (v. 5440-5515) répond en trois vers d'une seule voix l'armée, Gautier ne fait, il est vrai, qu'appliquer une recette de chanteur de geste . . . Cumulant ces procédés, il tempère ce que le pur monologue peut avoir de statique; il introduit dans le discours un élément quasi-polyphonique et virtuellement gestuel; à la voix du monologueur répond une contre-voix, révélant la présence d'un autre corps. De même, à plusieurs reprises, ce n'est pas entre deux interlocuteurs que s'échangent les paroles, mais entre un individu et une foule, dont l'intervention nous est rapportée comme unanime et, pour ainsi dire, chorale!:

Illuec l'arainnent plusor hom
et dient li: "Ma douce suer,
di nous de cest enfant le fuer."

[451-3]

(là plusieurs hommes l'interpellent
et lui disent: "Ma douce sœur,
dis-nous le prix de cet enfant")

Cet étrange dialogue continue sur douze vers. Ainsi encore, v. 1710-8. Plus souvent, ce sont des monologues collectifs, fonctionnant à la fois comme ressort narratif et comme bruitage: v. 789-93, 2198-2208, 2271-4, 6398-6407, 6411-5.

Une douzaine de discours grammaticalement directs sont pensés et non dits, par divers personnages. Ces "discours intérieurs" constituent (sur le plan de la figuration) des monologues, mais plusieurs, dans le récit des amours de l'impératrice, prennent forme dialoguée: longues interruptions dramatiques, où le héros, l'héroïne, déchirés, engagent une *disputatio* avec les parties dissociées d'eux-mêmes. Ainsi, les 134 vers de la plainte d'Atanaïs, v. 3227-3360; les 180 vers de ses hésitations amoureuses, 3543-3722; les étonnements de Paridès, v. 3736-98; la douce crainte de ce péché 3867-3919. O. Jodogne jadis suggérait, à propos de l'*Enéas*, que la technique littéraire du monologue, spécialement intérieur, consacre, en ce XIIe siècle, le passage d'une esthétique de conteur traditionnel à celle de romancier. A ce compte, l'usage — du reste raffiné — que fait Gautier de ce procédé nouveau en langue vulgaire impliquerait une volonté de l'intégrer au procédé plus ancien, de le subordonner à une conception de l'art qui fut celle des chanteurs de geste et restait celle des récitants de fabliaux. On pourrait ici renvoyer aux pertinentes remarques de M. L. Ollier sur la dramatisation par la parole chez Chrétien de Troyes, sur la valeur vocale du vers comme tel, exaltée dans le discours direct.[26] Certes. Reste que, des mêmes instruments linguistiques et rhétoriques, Gautier tire des effets plus fortement contrastants, en une plus urgente instance. J'ai opéré dans *Cligès* (choisi parmi les romans de Chrétien pour sa ressemblance approximative avec *Eracle*) un relevé des discours directs, selon les critères employés dans mon étude de Gautier. Le nombre total de ces discours est sensiblement le même: 98. Mais le nombre de vers qu'ils occupent diffère d'un tiers environ: pour 2 995 vers de discours (sur 6 570) dans *Eracle, Cligès* n'en présente que 2 028 (sur 6 664 vers), soit:

en monologues: 1 098 vers (16,5% du roman)
dialogues: 930 (14%)

Par ailleurs, *Cligès* compte 72 monologues pour 26 dialogues, soit en moyenne 2,75 monologues pour un dialogue; dans *Eracle*, cette proportion n'est que de 1,25. Encore les dialogues de *Cligès* comportent-ils moins de répliques: 2 (quinze fois), 3 (quatre fois), 5, 6 ou 10 (chacun, une fois), soit 85 au total, à peine plus du tiers de ce que l'on observe dans *Eracle*. Quant aux durées respectives des deux types de discours en question, elles témoignent dans *Eracle* d'une nette tendance—absente de *Cligès*—à l'expansion des dialogues et à la concentration des monologues. En chiffres absolus, ces durées sont dans *Cligès*:

de un demi à 12 vers:	49 monologues: 5 dialogues
de 13 à 20 vers:	13 monologues: 8 dialogues
de 21 à 100 vers:	9 monologues: 9 dialogues
plus de 100 vers:	3 monologues (de 150, 151 et 161 vers);
	2 dialogues (103 et 105 vers).

D'où les proportions suivantes:

nombre de dialogues de 13 à 100 vers: *Eracle* 34 (85% des dialogues), *Cligès* 17 (65%);

nombre de monologues de un demi à 12 vers: *Eracle* 31 (60%); *Cligès* 49 (68%).

J'interprète dans la même perspective l'absence presque totale en *Eracle* de discours indirects, fréquents au contraire chez Chrétien. J'en dénombre 18 dans le récit proprement dit (discours directs non comptés), chiffre dérisoire . . . et encore les vers 672-74 commencent-ils la phrase au style indirect pour passer chemin faisant à la première personne en enchaînant sur une réponse directe:

> . . . et l'empereres li demande
> si çou est voirs que on m'a dit.
> —Sire, ne sai . . .
> (. . . et l'empereur lui demande
> si c'est vrai ce qu'on me dit.
> —Sire, je ne sais)

Gautier semble se refuser, en narration, à ce type de discours, comme s'il étouffait la voix. En revanche, je compte dix discours indirects dans les interventions d'auteur et une vingtaine à l'intérieur des discours directs — situations de parole vive, neutralisant cet effet d'étouffement.

La composition d'*Eracle*—l'organisation des masses narratives—ne présente pas moins d'apparentes ambiguïtés que la structure lexico-syntaxique. A premier examen, le lecteur sans préjugé la trouve limpide dans sa linéarité et la successivité presque sans faille des épisodes. Seule la dernière partie comporte deux digressions narratives, de 120 vers environ chacune: l'histoire de la Vraie Croix, de Constantin à Chosroès (v. 5092-5215), retour en arrière indispensable à l'intelligence de ce qui suit; et le récit de l'entrée triomphale du Christ à Jérusalem (v. 6091-6120), expressément donné (v. 6121-4) comme une glose. En gros, le roman, dans sa lettre, semble constituer un triptyque: *enfances* d'Eracle, amours d'Atanaïs, reconquête de la Croix. La plupart des commentateurs se sont interrogés sur le sens de cette conjoncture, et l'intention que peut-être dissimule sa bizarrerie. Le second volet semble en effet interposé comme une immense digression dans l'histoire du triomphe progressif d'Eracle, cause de son accession à l'empire et par là de ses exploits futurs. L'auteur lui-même ne le déclare-t-il pas, ouvrant aux vers 2905-7 une parenthèse qu'il ferme aux v. 5088-9? On peut en douter: l'idée de digression provient, soit de la rhétorique traditionnelle (qui fait de la *digressio* une forme d'*amplificatio*) soit d'une conception moderne de l'"unité" de l'œuvre d'art, dont on sait combien elle fut étrangère à la plupart des poètes médiévaux.[27] Aussi bien, à y regarder de plus près, le récit n'est pas exempt d'incohérences, ni de ce qui, pour un goût formé aux traditions classiques, serait négligence: ainsi, entre les motivations de la mise en vente de l'enfant Eracle et les regrets ultérieurs qu'elle provoque (v. 374-644), on dénoncerait aisément la contradiction; aux vers 6072-8, dans la mention d'un fils cadet de Chosroès, une inutilité mal venue. . . .

Peu importe. La narration sans cesse se fuit elle-même, s'éparpille en détails, en jeux gracieux puis soudain en envolées savamment soutenues. Fondamentalement, le récit est fragmentaire. Gautier ne manque pas de nous le faire savoir au moyen d'une formule quatre fois répétée:

> v. 114: Huis mais voel m'oevre commenchier;
> (Désormais je vais commencer mon œuvre)

> v. 2746: Huimais commencera li contes;
> (Désormais commencera le conte)

> v. 5092: Si vos dirons d'Eracle humais;
> (nous parlerons d'Eracle désormais)

> v. 5110-11: Bon me seroit huimais a dire
> coment fu puis et rois et sire.
> (il serait bon désormais que je dise
> comment il devint roi et maître)

La dernière est une simple réitération de la troisième, ou celle-ci une annonce de celle-là. L'interprétation n'en fait pas moins difficulté. Le vers 2746 impliquerait que ce qui le précède constitue une introduction, une vaste *digressio* préliminaire occupant 42 percent de la durée totale du récit; à partir de là, restent 3 824 vers pour aller à la fin du roman; encore les vers 5092 puis 5110 les coupent-ils en deux tronçons. Si l'on tient à prendre ces formules pour révélatrices d'un plan d'ensemble, on en tire le découpage suivant:

1. v. 114 à 2745: 2 632 vers
2. v. 2746 à 5091: 2 346 vers
   ou v. 2746 à 5109: 2 364 vers
3. v. 5092 à 6514: 1 423 vers
   ou v. 5110 à 6514: 1 405 vers.

Les vers 1-113 et 6515-fin restent hors récit. Les formules 2 et 3 encadrent très approximativement l'épisode des amours d'Atanaïs: aux vers 2743-5 s'achèvent les préparatifs du mariage impérial; celui-ci se déroule aux vers 2800-10, et est conclu par l'éloge d'Eracle et un double éloge de la nouvelle souveraine, jusqu'au vers 2968—éloge interrompu, v. 2903-14, par une intervention d'auteur annonçant un changement de sujet et la prochaine conquête de la Croix, changement qui, en fait, se produit au v. 2969.

Ce n'est que là l'apparence d'un désordre. Les termes même par lesquels Gautier périodiquement revient sur son propos donnent plutôt à penser à un *patchwork* très attentivement conçu mais pièce à pièce, à mesure que l'ensemble se construit et s'étend. D'où, de la part des critiques diversité des lectures. Ou bien, faute d'articulations évidentes, on admet, comme le faisait A. Fourrier, que l'hétérogénéité des "sources" (ou prétendues telles) constitue une indication suffisante et justifie un certain découpage du texte; ou bien l'on part, comme L. Renzi, d'une conception rhétorique globale pour accuser les distinctions entre quelques parties du récit clairement opposables. D'où les divisions proposées—en deux, en trois, en quatre—et que l'on présente comme l'émanation d'un dessein inscrit dans l'œuvre. Reste une troisième option: lire dans *Eracle* une série de séquences enchaînées mais sans organisation hiérarchique: composition analogue à celle de la plupart des récits assez longs de tradition orale, projetés (quelles qu'en soient l'origine et la fonction) en performance.[28] Plurilogisme, expansion plutôt que concentricité: cela est vrai, en quelque mesure, de tout le genre romanesque en formation au XIIe siècle. Mais, là encore, Gautier reste en-deçà de la pratique nouvelle ou—peut-être, d'une autre façon—va plus loin qu'elle. A propos de Chrétien de Troyes, on a pu parler de polyphonie.[29] *Eracle*, plus composite que complexe, combine moins les voix qu'il ne les suscite, chacune à son tour, dans une temporalité rectiligne. Pas trace chez Gautier d'"entrelacement" . . . en dépit du vers 2903,

> ne voel pas ci entrelacier,
> l'ahan qu'il ot au porcacier
> qu'ensi ne vait pas le matire,
> (je ne veux pas développer ici
> la peine qu'il eut dans cette entreprise,
> car cela ne convient pas à mon sujet)

où *entrelacier* signifie, évidemment me semble-t-il, "introduire à contre-temps."

De l'une à l'autre des techniques romanesques qui, entour 1170-80, contrastaient ainsi, la différence toutefois n'est pas, comme telle, d'un plus ou moins de modernité; elle ne s'inscrit pas au barême d'un progrès historique. Elle manifeste l'affrontement—au-delà peut-être de la conscience qu'en eurent les contemporains—de deux poétiques coexistantes. *Eracle* possède un double trait commun avec la poésie de transmission orale telle qu'on peut l'observer encore, en quelques lieux de notre monde: à la fois—et, pour beaucoup de doctes universitaires, contradictoirement—une extrême et minutieuse complication du tissu textuel, et une souveraine, presque licencieuse, liberté de combinaison des ensembles. La forme ici est d'ordre désidéral: finalisante et idéale, et telle que l'œuvre entière ne peut, comme œuvre, constituer une totalité. Mais des fils se tissent dans la trame du discours qui, multipliés, entrecroisés, y dessinent un hiéroglyphe toujours incomplet . . . et dont seuls le ton de la voix, le geste, le décor achèvent le dessin dans la performance.

Le facteur déterminant, dans cette perspective, est la durée du récit: durée de parole et durée d'audition, l'une et l'autre aux limites plus ou moins nettement fixées par les conditions physiques, l'énergie des corps et les habitudes collectives. J'ai fait, par sondage sur deux fragments de cinq cents vers, un essai de lecture à haute voix d'*Eracle*, en y mettant un minimum d'expressivité, avec les pauses indispensables et en l'accompagnant de quelques gestes: par extrapolation j'en conclus qu'une lecture publique du roman entier exigerait un peu plus de quatre heures—beaucoup plus si le lecteur mimait certains passages, comme çà et là (en particulier dans les dialogues) le texte y invite instamment. Il ne paraît donc pas impossible que la composition du texte tienne en quelque façon compte de ce fait: une performance de quatre ou cinq heures est en effet mal concevable sans entractes. Ainsi, je constate que les trois "parties" du roman séparées par les *huimais* des vers 2746 et 5092, soit v. 1-2745, 2746-5091 et 5092-6570, durent respectivement, selon mon débit, une heure trois quarts, une heure et demie, et une heure.

Je me garderais bien de conclure. Du moins me semble-t-il de ce point de vue justifié d'examiner les longueurs en nombre de vers, des diverses unités narratives, ainsi que les proportions existant entre elles. Les résultats d'un tel examen seront d'autant plus vraisemblables que les nombres en cause comporteront quelque approximation. Il n'est en effet aucunement question ici d'un symbolisme numéral ni de construction crypto-arithmétique; mais bien d'une harmonie que l'art vocal d'un récitant ou d'un lecteur épanouit dans l'espace de la performance, où l'oreille, même exercée, ne peut percevoir les rapports de temps avec une rigoureuse exactitude. Tandis que l'écriture tend à une intériorisation des structures, la voix les objective, les gestualise. L'écriture d'*Eracle* se souvient, en cela aussi, de la voix, intègre à sa conscience d'elle-même sa certitude des performances à venir.

Plutôt que comme des figures de rhétorique, je supposerais que les proportions numérales fonctionnèrent en performance comme des figures d'*ars memoriae*, articulant à ce titre les parties de la narration, permettant par là divers effets de dramatisation rythmique, sinon — le cas échéant — de correspondances entre deux séances successives de récitation. L'*ars* crée un espace orienté où placer les jalons d'un discours: en chacun des lieux qu'on y détermine, se loge un élément auquel la parole, à tour de rôle, réfèrera. Il semble qu'*Eracle* transpose le système en durée: des moments remplacent les lieux, et des proportions simples suffisent à les définir. Il me paraît ainsi remarquable que l'exact milieu du roman, les vers 3283-85, coïncide avec le centre de la plainte d'Atanaïs emprisonnée où, en vertu d'une dramatique gradation, la malheureuse en vient à accuser les félons courtisans, les menteurs, bien plus, le *Maufés* lui même, qui n'est, dans l'œuvre, cité qu'ici (v. 3284), point nodal d'une ligne thématique qui, je l'ai signalé, traverse le roman entier et renvoie immédiatement à Eracle le *Voirdisant*. Au reste, cet instant marque, en durée, la fin du premier tiers de l'épisode des amours d'Atanaïs; aussitôt après, surgit le premier doute (v. 3300) et commence le dérapage vers l'inévitable adultère: effet soutenu de *climax*.

L'ensemble de l'épisode, des vers 2925-7 (intervention de l'auteur qui déclare laisser pour quelque temps de côté Eracle et entame, d'Atanaïs, un éloge destiné à dramatiser la suite) aux vers 5088-92 (*il n'afiert pas a ma matiere/que je plus die de Laïs,/de Pariden, d'Atanaïs*) (il ne convient pas au sujet/que j'en dise plus de Laïs,/de Paridès, d'Atanaïs) compte 2 170 vers. Les *enfances* d'Eracle l'ont précédé, coupées, après le vers 372, de manière à former deux sections nettement distinctes: les premières années, cachées, — puis la vie publique, comme il en va de Jésus dans les Evangiles de Matthieu et de Luc: v. 115-372 (soit 258 vers) d'une part; v. 373-2924 (soit 2 552 vers) de l'autre. Quant à la conquête de la Croix, aboutissant à l'institution de la Fête de l'Exaltation, elle commence au vers 5093 par un solennel prologue de vingt-six vers, le récit s'engageant au v. 5119 pour prendre fin au v. 6443. Le reste de la vie d'Eracle est expédié du v. 6444 au v. 6514. Suivent une invocation de trois vers et la signature, v. 6515-22. Le tout est encadré de deux dédicaces, v. 1-86 et 6523-70 (selon les manuscrits *A* et *B*; le dernier vers est numéroté 6568 dans l'édition). Entre les vers 86 et 115 enfin, est inséré un résumé de l'action.

Ainsi déchiffré, *Eracle* apparaît construit en masses assez simplement proportionnées:

hors narration:	114 vers
a. enfance cachée	258 —
b. vie publique (manifestation)	2 552 —
c. amours d'Atanaïs	2 170 —
d. conquête de la Croix	1 351 —
e. fin d'Eracle	71 —
hors narration	53 —

La relation narrative entre *b* et *a* est symétrique de celle qui unit *d* à *e*. Si l'on joint ces couples d'éléments, on constate que le récit se décompose en trois unités de respectivement 2 811, 2 170 et 1 422 vers, soit 43 percent, 33 percent et 22 percent de la durée totale du texte: nombres rapportés approximativement entre eux comme 4 à 3 et à 2. Aussi bien, la partie hors discours initiale a une durée double de la partie finale. Les mêmes rapports simples se retrouvent dans la distribution des sous-éléments, assez longs et complexes. Ainsi, les durées respectives des épreuves relatives aux dons d'Eracle (v. 673 à 2745) sont approximativement dans la relation de 4 à 5 et à 7, gradation qui met en relief la découverte finale d'Atanaïs; et chacune des épreuves présente la même structure: exposition, triple événement, conclusion, les proportions de ces cinq sous-unités demeurant identiques malgré l'allongement des durées: 4 à 7 et à ½. L'histoire des amours d'Atanaïs se décompose en deux séquences (naissance de l'amour — l'adultère), chacune divisée en quatre scènes de longueur sensiblement égale, 200 à 300 vers — soit, selon mon compte, dix à douze minutes par scène, une heure et demie pour l'épisode entier. La partie centrale de la conquête de la Croix — la guerre contre Chosroès — est précédée d'un prologue de durée égale, contant l'accession d'Eracle à l'empire, par suite même de la menace constituée par le Persan; suivent l'entrée à Jérusalem et l'Exaltation. La longueur de ces trois sections est, en gros, proportionnelle à 4, 4 et 3.

Ces divisions numériques ne correspondent pas exactement à celles qu'engendrent les *huimais* de l'auteur: elles ne sont pourtant pas incompatibles, mais s'appliquent l'une à l'autre comme, à un dessin, une copie légèrement décalée. Cela même me paraît significatif, comme le serait une mise en scène jouant l'improvisation.

Gautier accuse cet effet en parsemant son texte d'annonces, à la manière d'un conteur soucieux de maintenir l'attention tout en faisant valoir la continuité de sa matière. Trois interventions de ce genre, de longueur régulièrement décroissante (27, 15 puis 9 vers: proportion de 9 à 5 et à 3!), piquettent le récit à intervalles de dimensions comparables (entre 2 800 et 2 200 vers):

> v. 87-113, aussitôt après la dédicace, Gautier fournit un résumé des parties du roman concernant Eracle, mais ne dit pas un mot d'Atanaïs (sinon, par prétérition, v. 101: *par lui se maria li sire*) (grâce à lui le seigneur se maria); il entend donc préciser—et fixer dans l'esprit des auditeurs—la nature de son thème général, par rapport auquel tout ce qui surviendra d'autre sera amplification, ornement, détour;
> v. 2856-2914, après le mariage impérial, Gautier résume les épisodes précédents depuis le début du roman, en les présentant comme ce que le peuple romain connaît désormais de son devin, conseiller de l'empereur (v. 2856-82). Suit, après un éloge d'Eracle (v. 2883-99), l'annonce de ce qui va suivre: *l'uevre tote entiere / de nostre empereor Laïs / et de se feme Atanaïs (l'aventure toute entière / de notre empereur Laïs / et de sa femme Atanaïs)* (en fait, l'adultère et la séparation), puis l'ascension sociale d'Eracle et la conquête de la Croix; les vers 2909-14 répètent, en les abrégeant, les vers 105-113. Tout le passage constitue une stase dans la narration, à peu de distance (environ trois cents vers, soit douze à treize minutes de parole) de son milieu; enfin, v. 5110-18, est annoncée pour la troisième fois, immédiatement avant que n'en commence le récit, la conquête de la Croix.

Plusieurs autres annonces ponctuelles maintiennent çà et là l'auditeur en haleine: d'un type auctorial (*après dirai*) ou "pédagogique" (*orrés, savrés*). Ainsi, v. 287-90, 979-80, 3221-26, 4384; parfois il s'agit simplement de souligner l'importance de l'événement qui va survenir: v. 1049-50, 4388-90, 5895-6, 6141-8; à deux reprises, dans l'épisode d'Atanaïs, pour en hâter le suspense, v. 3424-5 et 3475-8. Divers procédés, cumulés avec ceux-ci, concourent à tendre le fil du récit, à y ramener une attention qu'à tout instant risquent de dissiper les bruits de la performance sinon le bruit même du texte qui se dit. Effets de raccourci, faisant passer du récit à sa glose au sein d'une même phrase, ainsi v. 3408-9; répliques dont la seule fin est de relancer, en le modulant, un monologue, comme v. 4101-4; transition écrasée, réduite au simple jeu des temps verbaux, ainsi v. 6454-5. Enfin, Gautier périodiquement mesure le temps du récit — qu'il importe, pour la compréhension auditive, de distinguer de la durée performancielle: il utilise tour à tour dans ce but plusieurs espèces de jalons. L'éditeur du texte l'a si bien perçu, qu'il a introduit çà et là une ligne en blanc, signalant l'un de ces jalons. Par malheur, son procédé est hâtif et manque de rigueur. Il suffit néanmoins à rendre probable l'existence, dans le texte, d'un système. Il pratique ainsi 59 coupures, précédant une phrase qui commence

> 24 fois par le nom du héros ou quelque autre agent humain,
> 17 fois, par une indication modale, de temps ou de lieu,
> 3 fois, par une combinaison des deux.

Des quinze coupures restantes, cinq précèdent un discours direct; trois, une intervention de l'auteur interpellant les auditeurs; deux, l'expression *molt par* + verbe; les autres semblent aléatoires, fondées sur le seul jugement porté par l'éditeur sur le contenu. Certaines d'entre elles pourraient aisément être déplacées: ainsi, pourquoi celle qui suit le vers 5840 ne suivrait-elle pas plutôt le vers 5850? Les deux coupures de la page 152 interviennent dans le cours d'un dialogue (après les vers 4918 et 4932).

Là me semble-t-il, n'est pourtant pas la question. Il apparaît que l'auteur a jalonné son texte de marques destinées à en manifester, en performance, par une pause ou un mouvement vocal, les articulations. Or, ces marques ne sont pas toutes de même nature. Trois espèces s'en détachent avec assez de netteté dans le fil du texte:

— les unes sont de nature stylistique: notation du type *biaus est li tens (v.* 1639, 1973, 2065, 3799); phrase isolée en discours direct, fonctionnant à la manière de fins de laisses épiques (v. 294) ou exclamation intervenant à la fin d'un discours (v. 2563, 2567); changement de temps verbal (v. 373, 652);

— d'autres relèvent de la syntaxe narrative: changement de lieu (v. 2542, 2799, 2969, etc.), changement de personnage (v. 2815, 5211, 5320), nomination d'un personnage (v. 2787, 4961, etc.);

— les plus nombreuses sont temporelles: ou bien, elles mesurent expressément la durée événementielle, par des phrases comme *au cief de set ans, au tierc jor* ou autres semblables, distribuées en particulier au cours des *enfances* d'Eracle (v. 141, 229, 252, 279, 345, 736) mais non absentes de la suite du récit (v. 2819, 2935, 2966, 3899, 5285); — ou bien, elles modalisent le temps narratif à l'aide de divers adverbes de discours (*lors puis, ains* temporel, *atant, ja*), surtout *or* dans la formule *or* + verbe + sujet (ainsi, v. 1059, 1499, 1766, 1919, 4919), dont la réalisation la plus remarquable, *or est Eracles*, réapparaît neuf fois.

Il arrive que deux ou trois de ces marques surgissent successivement à peu de vers de distance, se neutralisant en apparence: ainsi, aux vers 1245 et 1256, 1513 et 1517, 2065 et 2068, 3799, et 3805, 5192 et 5204, etc. On peut se demander si ce n'est pas là un moyen de laisser au récitant une marge de liberté dans l'interprétation "rythmique" du texte — analogue à ce que serait pour un chanteur une notation musicale incomplète (comme l'étaient les neumes), simple support d'exécution permettant des réalisations variées. Les effets, à ce niveau, purent (on l'imagine) être d'autant plus dramatiques en performance que le texte comporte une forte prédominance de verbes au présent: la plupart de ceux qui figurent dans les nombreux discours directs puis, en règle générale et comme par rayonnement de ces derniers, dans les phrases qui les suivent immédiatement; enfin, de façon plus aléatoire, très fréquemment ailleurs. Ainsi se trouve presque constamment — dans ce récit dont le vers, par sa répétitivité même, tend à estomper la profondeur temporelle — maintenue l'instance d'énonciation, le présent charnel et la continuité de la voix, dans le refus de cette "distance esthétique" où l'on a vu le secret de l'art de Chrétien de Troyes.[30]

Au sein de ce présent — de cette présence — substitué à l'histoire, les mouvements se dessinent en espace plutôt qu'en durée: des récurrences nombreuses, à plusieurs niveaux d'organisation, les mesurent en en inscrivant la trace. Certes, répétitions, parallélismes, échos périodiques ne sont le propre d'aucune espèce particulière de poésie. Jakobson voyait en eux le fondement de tout langage poétique; P. Haidu, dans leur usage médiéval, l'affirmation d'une Ressemblance dont l'idée constitue l'un des traits majeurs de cette civilisation: rien n'est absolument identique ni absolument autre; la Ressemblance opère la médiation entre Créateur et créature, référant, non à la chaîne de l'histoire mais à celle des valeurs de l'être. La pertinence de telles remarques n'empêche que, par ailleurs, un lien étroit, et sans doute fonctionnel, attache tout effet de récurrence à l'exercice de la voix.[31] Le texte à destin vocal est en effet par nature moins appropriable que le texte proposé à la lecture. Plus que lui, il répugne à s'identifier avec la parole de son auteur; plus que lui, il tend à s'instituer en bien commun du groupe au sein duquel il fonctionne. De là découlent deux caractères étroitement corrélés: d'une part, le "modèle" des textes oraux est plus fortement concret que celui des textes écrits: les fragments discursifs préfabriqués qu'il véhicule sont plus nombreux, mieux organisés et sémantiquement plus stables; d'autre part, à l'intérieur d'un même texte au cours de sa transmission, et de texte à texte (en synchronie et en diachronie) on observe des interférences, des reprises, des répétitions probablement allusives: échanges qui donnent l'impression d'une circulation d'éléments voyageurs, à tout instant se combinant avec d'autres en compositions provisoires. C'est pourquoi la multiplicité des récurrences dans un texte écrit contribue à rapprocher celui-ci, en tant que fonctionnement verbal — et fût-ce par fiction — des conditions habituelles de l'oralité.

L'auteur d'*Eracle* use d'un procédé formulaire remarquable en ce qu'il lui permet de constituer — à ras de texte mais simultanément aux niveaux rythmique, lexical et syntaxique — un système mouvant d'échos et de parallélismes. En effet, on l'a vu, près de la moitié des vers du roman commencent par une conjonction ou un adverbe de phrase; or, un nombre non négligeable de ces termes figure en tête de plusieurs vers successifs, constituant des séries itératives étirées et entrecroisées au long du texte; ainsi

et figure 59 fois en tête de deux vers consécutifs; 3 fois en tête de trois vers; 2 fois, en tête de quatre;

que, qui, ou, dont, ne et les conjonctions simples *quant, se, ains, car, mais* constituent 90 séries de deux vers, et 9 de trois;

or, onze séries de deux, et une de trois.

L'ensemble de ces récurrences, assez régulièrement distribuées, affecte 376 vers, soit 5,75 percent du total. Autre procédé, de même ordre: 86 vers commencent par le nom *Eracle* (parfois précédé d'un *d'* ou *qu'* non syllabiques), le plus souvent en fonction de sujet du verbe. C'est là comme une variante simplifiée du *Or est Eracles* déjà signalé. Sous ces deux aspects, la formule marque ainsi 1,45 percent des vers.

Souvent, l'auteur ponctue l'unité narrative (scène, épisode, action) de vers ou expressions à valeur de refrain, introduisant dans l'exposé, grâce à de menues variations, un rythme interne qui le dramatise et y figure comme l'ébauche d'un geste. J'en ai relevé par sondage plus de cinquante exemples; le nombre total doit être beaucoup plus grand. Ainsi:

> car cascuns ert en esperance
> [1951]
> (car chacun espérait)
> car cascune iert en bon espoir;
> [1955]
> (car chacune avait bon espoir)

con cele ki iert assenee
[2144]
(comme femme de bon espoir)
con cele qui ert couronee;
[2147]
(comme femme portant couronne)
et cerque molt, ce li convient
[1312]
(et il fouille partout — il le faut bien —)
cerque les mons, cerque les vaus.
[1316]
(fouille les monts, fouille les vallées)

Généralement, la répétition porte sur deux ou même trois vers consécutifs, suspendant le récit d'une manière qui accentue la dramatisation et fortifie la suggestion gestuelle. Ainsi:

n'a mais mestier c'on plus le maint
[1702]
(n'a plus besoin qu'on le mène davantage)
n'a mais mestier, autant se vaut,
n'a mais mestier qu'on le travaut!
[1707-8]
(n'a plus besoin, c'est la même chose,
n'a plus besoin qu'on le tourmente)

mar vi onques si grant riquece,
mar vi onques si grant honor;
[3782-3]
(pour mon malheur j'eus telle richesse,
pour mon malheur, si grand honneur!)

ou, évoquant les fêtes passées où l'on dansait,

tant mainte fois i ai alé,
tant mainte fois i ai balé
et mainte fois i ai sailli!
[3929-31]
(si souvent j'y suis allé,
si souvent j'y ai dansé
et souvent y ai bondi)

Ça et là un vers réapparaît, identique, après un assez long intervalle, se transformant ainsi en refrain proprement dit. Dans l'épisode de la vente d'Eracle, le même vers,

Fius, bien ait tele engenreüre!
(Fils, bénie soit telle descendance!)

est prononcé par la mère au moment, v. 421, où, la décision prise, elle part pour le marché, puis (v. 571) aussitôt après que l'affaire a été conclue.

Le refrain encadre ainsi une scène virtuellement théâtrale par le nombre des dialogues (110 vers sur 150), leur rythme, la brièveté des répliques et la présence, dans celles-ci, de vocatifs récurrents formant gradation et qui personnalisent fortement les interlocuteurs: *varlet, amis, sire* . . . Dans les séquences de la scène du concours de beauté chaque fois qu'Eracle ayant examiné une candidate et percé ses tares morales, se détourne, un refrain conclusif opère de légères variations sur le thème "Eracle en passe alors un grand nombre sans s'arrêter": il dédaigne ainsi, successivement, *soixante* candidates (v. 2256-8), puis *cent* autres (v. 2393-2406; 2451-2; 2478), de nouveau *soixante* (v. 2504), le septième refrain, atypique, renvoie aux précédents en les récapitulant:

> Eracle cerke tos les rens,
> ne trueve pucele en tos sens
> qui ait trestotes les bontés
>
> [2539-41]
> (Eracle parcourt tous les rangs,
> il ne trouve en tous sens de jeune fille
> qui ait toutes les vertus)

De même, les trois discours de l'ange qui, respectivement, inaugurent, confirment à son apogée, et concluent l'existence d'Eracle, s'attachent au récit au moyen d'une double formule, l'une introductive, l'autre terminale:

> uns angles vint en son devant
> et se li dist . . .
>
> [144-5]
> (un ange vint devant elle
> et lui dit . . .)
>
> vint li angles Nostre Signor
> . . . dist li . . .
>
> [5325-7]
> (vint un ange du Notre-Seigneur . . .
> lui dit . . .)
>
> vint un angles del ciel . . .
> et dist . . .
>
> [6183-4]
> (vint un ange du ciel . . .
> et dit;)

et, aussitôt après qu'il s'est tu:

> li angles Diu s'esvanuïst,
>
> [179]
> (l'ange de Dieu s'évanouit,)
> apres cest mot s'esvanuïst,
>
> [4379]
> (après ces mots s'évanouit,)

et voiant tos s'esvanuïst.

[6234]

(et sous leurs yeux s'évanouit)

Même si, comme il est probable, ce sont là ornements rhétoriques, Gautier les manie à la façon dont les chanteurs épiques manipulaient leurs formules,[32] et sans doute dans la même intention d'extériorisation du récit, tendant à manifester sensoriellement son artifice—ce qu'en d'autres temps on eût appelé sa poésie. Souvent, au cours des vers, il suffit d'un mot, réitéré à quelques lieux stratégiques, pour rapprocher ainsi de l'auditeur une partie de la narration, engager cet auditeur lui-même dans cette re-présentation, *mimesis* d'une présence: les *molt* accumulés de v. 1325-29, les *brocher, poindre, férir* de la course de chevaux, v. 1631, 1691, 1745, 1751, 1753, 1756; le *nièce* des vers 2755, 2760, 2765; le *grant duel* de v. 6479-81, et bien d'autres.

En dépit des incertitudes qui embrument encore le détail de cette histoire, on peut tenir pour établi que l'invention, au XIIe siècle, du discours narratif désigné par le terme de *roman* marque dans l'itinéraire poétique de l'Occident un commencement, peu s'en faut, absolu.[33] Globalement, le phénomène présente un aspect homogène: le même faisceau de causes produisit localement des effets tellement semblables que la tentation est forte pour le critique de les réduire à l'identité. Peut-être conviendrait-il d'insister, au contraire, sur la diversité. Ainsi, l'on ne saurait nier que le "roman," au carrefour de l'oralité poétique traditionnelle et de la pratique scripturaire latine, ne surgisse comme le résultat d'une réflexion active sur cette dualité du dire—comme une réaction au conflit d'autorité qu'elle engendre. Embouchés sur une matière jusqu'alors livrée aux seules transmissions orales, les romans dits "bretons" (tels, ceux de Chrétien de Troyes) en opèrent une transmutation en écriture, aussi radicale que celle dont pouvaient, dans leur atanor, rêver les alchimistes. Mais c'est l'opération inverse qui se perpètre dans les romans dits "antiques": une tradition écrite et latine s'y voit adaptée, grâce à une série de transformations, à certaines au moins des conditions de l'oralité—ne serait-ce que l'usage de la langue vulgaire et de ce que, sur tous les plans, il implique. D'où—pour prendre d'éminents exemples—dans l'*Enéas* non moins que dans *Erec* les éléments d'un dialogisme fondamental, la prise en charge simultanée de discours qui tendent, sans y parvenir, à se neutraliser l'un l'autre. Mais la tendance, ici ou là, est différemment polarisée, et l'on ne saurait sans abus la décrire dans les

même termes . . . pas plus que, s'agissant de chansons de geste, il ne
serait légitime d'alléguer d'un même souffle et pour le même argument le
Roland d'Oxford et la *Chanson de Guillaume!* Et encore, par rapport à
Enéas, à Erec, quid du *Tristan* de Béroul, de *Floire et Blancheflor* de
Waldef, tous plus ou moins contemporains? *Quid, d'Eracle?*

Entour 1200, dans un public déjà coutumier de telles lectures, semble çà et là se manifester la conscience de différences de nature. Ainsi,
l'auteur anonyme d'un *Miracle de Nostre-Dame*, évoquant les "bons
ménestrels" du passé, cite en exemple une liste, à cet égard significative:
Gautiers d'Arras, qui fist d'Eracle, Benoît de Sainte-More, "La Chèvre,"
Chrétien de Troyes et "Guiot"; éventail d'ouvrages aussi représentatifs
que dissemblables: *Eracle, Troie, Tristan*, les romans arthuriens, et (s'il
s'agit de Guiot de Provins) la *Bible* des "estats du monde." Le même
genre de considération pourrait avoir dicté le choix que firent les poètes
allemands du début du XIIIe siècle parmi les romans français qu'ils
jugèrent bon de récrire en leur langue: *Eracle* (adapté par Meister Otte),
Floire et Blancheflor, Troie, Tristan et les arthuriens *Erec* et *Yvain* de
Hartmann, le *Graal* de Wolfram. . . .

Ce que nous font entendre, collectivement, ces textes, c'est une
pluralité, non seulement de thèmes et de tons (peu importe), mais de
types de discours. Et ce qui, je le pense, distingue fondamentalement entre ceux-ci, c'est la position qu'ils occupent au carrefour que j'évoquais;
c'est la double relation qui les unit ou les oppose à l'écriture et aux
coutumes vocales, et s'inscrit dans la généalogie de leur forme. D'où la
question qu'ils soulèvent — moins du reste au niveau superficiel des
méthodes que dans l'ordre des principes épistémologiques: est-il
possible — voire, souhaitable — d'opérer, de tous ces ouvrages, la même
lecture *textuelle*, d'y pratiquer la même prise en compte de la totalité du
signifiant? Il faut, me semble-t-il, éviter de répondre par l'affirmative . . .
à moins que l'on ne suppose ici, gratuitement, une aporie critique.

Certes, comme on l'a dit, certaines œuvres de ce grand XIIe siècle
raisonnable en figurent le côté chaotique, archaïque peut-être ou
baroque.[35] *Eracle* est de celles-ci. Mais c'est moins ce caractère comme tel
que je mettrais en cause, que le trait initial dont il provient et qu'indirectement il manifeste: la prépondérance, parmi les valeurs mises en
jeu par l'écriture, de celles qui s'attachent au modèle performanciel, c'est-
à-dire vocal et — au sens complet du terme — *dramatique*. P. Dronke
naguère soulignait avec force l'aspect programmatiquement "a-gramma-
tical" d'une longue série de textes dès la fin du XIe siècle, tels (disait-il) le
Ruodlieb: par un refus de ce qui sans doute paraissait à certains auteurs
comme un asservissement aux exigences d'une écriture aliénante. Aussi

bien, Wolfram dans *Parzivâl* se vante d'être illettré, par quoi j'entendrais qu'il feint de repousser une conception totalisante de la lettre: ce que l'auteur glose aussitôt, (115.21 à 116.4) en déniant à son poème le statut de livre. L'écrivain de langue vulgaire, en cette fin du XIIe siècle, transite (dirais-je en paraphrasant G. L. Bruns)[36] entre la voix et l'écriture, entre ce qu'il ressent comme nature et ce que nous désignerions comme culture, entre un dehors et un dedans: il y pénètre, s'y installe mais conserve le souvenir mythifié d'une parole originelle, originale, issue d'une poitrine vivante, dans le souffle d'une gorge singulière, et non d'un assujettissement à l'autorité de l'écrit. Une contradiction loge au cœur du discours romanesque, par là même qu'il confère, à la langue *maternelle*, cette autorité-là: or, la langue maternelle est d'abord voix, et demande d'écoute. En reste la nostalgie qui souvent s'étouffe ou s'intègre à un projet autre; mais parfois, en revanche, s'exalte et travaille en profondeur l'écriture au point d'en abolir la *suffisance*. Dès lors, le signifiant tend à déborder ce qui s'est inscrit sur la page, à se répandre dans la matière théâtrale, non comme telle enregistrée, présente pourtant au sein du texte, sous l'aspect d'une volonté de performance, d'une "diction" au sens où ce terme réfèrerait à une rhétorique de la voix et à une grammaire des mouvements du corps. Ainsi, dans *Eracle*.

Tout se passe comme si, paradoxalement, le texte n'était plus que l'un des enjeux de l'action qui se noue et se dénoue en lui. Dans le récit qu'inscrit sa plume, l'auteur proclame l'immanence de valeurs qui sont celles de la voix aimée—innommée. Il procède en cela simultanément à plusieurs niveaux ou selon plusieurs axes:

—au niveau stylistique (trivial et le moins décisif), en adoptant tels procédés ou techniques assez fréquents dans la poésie orale pour constituer, par cumul, une allusion globale, voire une imitation efficace;

—au niveau thématique, en tissant dans le réseau narratif un motif récurrent qui réfère à la parole, au son ou à l'effet de la voix, à la puissance du verbe prononcé;

—dans l'axe des finalités, en situant le texte entier dans la perspective concrète d'une performance: en y intégrant les qualités spécifiques exigibles dans la réalité corporelle de celle-ci.

Ce sont là, je crois l'avoir montré, les trois aspects de cette épiphanie de la voix vive que constitue, en contradiction apparente avec son être d'écriture, le texte fourmillant, sonore, désordonné, heureux d'*Eracle*. C'est ainsi que Gautier d'Arras *incorpore* à son récit la poétique ambiguë qui l'engendre: la Voix d'*Eracle* est fiction de voix, indiscernablement emmêlée aux fictions constitutives du roman. Mais, différente de ces dernières, elle aspire à perdre ce statut, à se réaliser dans la vérité d'une expérience sensorielle: et cette mutation se produit en effet, dès qu'en performance un interprète "prend la parole" et, durant les quelques heures que dure une lecture ou une récitation, suspend l'effet d'écriture à l'oreille d'un auditoire réuni à seule fin d'entendre.

La finalité performancielle est si profondément inviscérée au texte que de nombreux passages ne sont facilement compréhensibles à la lecture muette que grâce aux artifices des éditeurs. Ainsi, de courts monologues rapportés par un locuteur au cours de son propre monologue comme paroles d'un tiers: seul un jeu de guillemets permet au lecteur de s'y retrouver (v. 5019-22, 5043-4, 5447-8, etc); de même, aux vers 3259-61, les parenthèses seules distinguent du discours d'Atanaïs la glose d'auteur qui s'y emmêle sans couper le fil de la phrase. Dans les dialogues, le passage d'un interlocuteur à l'autre, marqué souvent par une apostrophe, en général ne l'est que visuellement, par un tiret, dans l'édition. Les dialogues intérieurs, en particulier celui d'Atanaïs, seraient complètement incohérents sans ces truquages typographiques. Qu'est-ce à dire, sinon que, dans l'intention même de Gautier, le texte exige une glose vocale-tonale, mimique ou gestuelle? Lors même que le dialogue est jalonné d'apostrophes, celles-ci ne font que confirmer ce caractère en le théâtralisant de manière explicite. En ce sens, le texte que nous lisons grâce à G. Raynaud de Lage après E. Löseth—ne nous livre qu'une forme vide et sans doute profondément *altérée*—devenue autre—de ce qu'il devait être dans le dessein de son auteur: la figure d'une parole vive.

Paul Zumthor
Emeritus, University of Montréal

Notes

1. Il existe peu d'études d'ensemble sur ce roman. Voir: A. Fourrier, *Le Courant réaliste dans le roman courtois en France* (Paris: Nizet, 1960), p. 179-313, spécialt. 207-74 et, mieux, L. Renzi, *Tradizione cortese e realismo in Gautier d'Arras* (Padoue: CEDAM 1964). Je suis l'édition G. Raynaud de Lage (Paris: Champion, 1976), précédée d'une brève mais bonne introduction.

2. M. Zink, "Une Mutation de la conscience littéraire: le langage romanesque à travers les exemples français du XIIe siècle," *Cahiers de civilisation médiévale* 24 (1981), 3-27 (spécialt. 8-9).

3. Proposée par H. Kuhn, *Entwürfe zu einer Literatursystematik des Spätmittelalters* (Tübingen: Niemeyer, 1979).

4. P. Zumthor, *Merlin le prophète*, réédition (Paris: Slatkine-Champion, 1973), p. 30-36, 50-54, 126-46.

5. G. L. Bruns, "The Originality of Texts in a Manuscript Culture," *Comparative Literature* 32 (1980), 113-29 (spécialt. 118-122); cf. L. Dolezel, "Truth and authenticity in narrative," *Poetics Today*, 1 (1980), 7-25 (spécialt. 12-40).

6. *Handbuch der literarischen Rhetorik*, 3, Index, s.v. *translatio*.

7. Expression de Marie de France, v. 16 du Prologue des *Lais*, édition J. Rychner, (Paris: Champion 1966).

8. M. L. Ollier, "Proverbe et sentence: le discours d'autorité chez Chrétien de Troyes," *Revue des sciences humaines* 163 (1976), 329-57 (spécialt. 331 et 345).

9. Sur ces questions, voir Renzi, *Tradizione Cortese* p. 108-9, 121-4, 128, 133-7.

10. *Renzi*, p. 138-43.

11. Cf. L. Jenny, "Les stratégies de la forme," *Poétique* 27 (1976), 257-81 (spécialt. 257-62).

12. Introduction de l'édition d'*Eracle*, p. ix-xi et références.

13. E. Faral, *Les Arts poétiques* (Paris: Champion, 1923), p. 257-60.

14. Onze fois, l'attache de discours est *il pense*, introducteur d'un monologue intérieur. Je n'en tiens pas compte ici.

15. P. Zumthor, *Introduction à la poésie orale* (Paris: Seuil, 1983) p. 250-54.

16. Fourrier, *Le Courant réaliste*, p. 230-1, 257-60; Renzi, *Tradizione Cortese* p. 168-70, 188.

17. J. Frappier, "Brisure du couplet dans *Erec*," *Etudes d'histoire et de critique littéraire* (Paris, Champion, 1976), p. 101; M. L. Ollier, "Le présent du récit," *Langue française* 40 (1978), 100.

18. Sur *si*, v. Ch. Marchello-Nizia, *Recherches sur la structuration de l'énoncé en ancien et moyen français*, thèse de l'université de Paris-7, (1982), inédite, chapitres 3, 4 et 5; — sur *or*, j'ai eu connaissance des recherches communes, en cours, de M. L. Ollier et Ch. Marchello-Nizia.

19. A paraître.

20. Selon la concordance établie par P. Kunstmann, éditions de l'université d'Ottawa (1982).

21. Selon un sondage opéré sur 2000 vers d'*Yvain*: renseignement fourni par Ch. Doutrelepont, auteur d'une thèse, en cours de préparation, sur le rimaire de Chrétien de Troyes.

22. Zumthor, *Introduction*, p. 129-30.

23. *Ibid.*, p. 172.

24. Frappier, "Brisure du couplet . . .," p. 105-9.

25. O. Jodogne, "Le caractère des oeuvres antiques aux XIIe et XIIIe siècles," *L'humanisme médiéval du XIIe au XIVe siècle* (Paris: Klincksieck, 1964), p. 79; cf. E. Vinaver, *The Rise of Romance* (Oxford: Clarendon Press, 1971), p. 23-25.

26. Ollier, "Le présent du récit," p. 105-7.

27. W. Ryding, *Structure in Medieval Narrative*, (La Haye: Mouton, 1971), p. 115-61; cf. Lausberg, *Handbuch . . .*, paragraphes 340-42.

28. Zumthor, *Introduction*, p. 114-15, 132.

29. Vinaver, *The Rise of Romance*, p. 72-75; Ryding, *Structure in Medieval Narrative*, p. 61.

30. Ollier, p. 102-5; R. Pickens, "Historial Consciousness in Old French Narrative," *French Forum* (1980), p. 169; cf. P. Haidu, "Le sens historique du phénomène stylistique," *Europe* 642 (1982), 37-47 (spécialement 38-9).

31. P. Haidu, "Repetition: Modern Reflections on Medieval Esthetics," *Modern Language Notes* 92 (1977), 875-87; Zumthor, *Introduction*, p. 141-3.

32. Zumthor, *Introduction*, p. 116-19.

33. *Grundriss der romanischen Literaturen des Mittelalters*, (Heidelberg: Carl Winter, 4, 1, 1978), 1 partie, chap. 2 (p. 60-81) et 5 (p. 104-22).

34. Cité dans l'Introduction éd. F. Cowper d'*Ille et Galeron*, (Paris: Picard, 1956), p.x.

35. Renzi, *"Tradizione Cortese,"* p. 9.

36. Sur ces points, voir Bruns, "The Originality," p. 123-25 et références.

7. From Traditional Tale to Literary Story Middle Welsh Prose Narratives

The Welsh storytelling tradition has, from its earliest extant forms, been a prose tradition. Most of the verse remaining from the Old Welsh and medieval period is eulogistic and aristocratic in tone, and in its style is declamatory and allusive, often structured in lines or couplets forming phrases or sentences. There may be lines of impressionistic description, there are sometimes statements about external events, but there is no extended narrative. *Cywyddwyr* of the fourteenth and fifteenth centuries occasionally relate an anecdote or a fabliau-type escapade in the *cywydd* metre and there are a few dialogues, types of poetry which may derive from popular verse narrative forms; but such narratives, if indeed they existed, would probably have been anecdotal and brief, far removed in ethos and content from epic poetry. Tales were recited in prose in the Welsh tradition by professional storytellers who may, nevertheless, have been poets by training. The reference in the *Four Branches of the Mabinogi* to Gwydion and his friends visiting Pryderi's court in the guise of poets suggests as much:

> "Yes," said Pryderi, "we would like *cyfarwyddyd* [lore] from some of those young men." "Our custom, lord," said Gwydion, "is that the *pencerdd* [chief poet] should recite the first night one comes to a nobleman. I'll gladly recite *cyfarwyddyd*." Gwydion was the best *cyfarwydd* [storyteller] in the world. And that night he entertained the court with pleasant *ymddiddanion* [dialogues] and *cyfarwyddyd*, so that everyone in the court grew fond of him and Pryderi enjoyed speaking with him.

And later:

> "Porter," he said, "go in and say there are poets here from Morgannwg." The porter went. "God's welcome to them. Let them in," she said. They were greeted gladly. The hall was prepared and they went to eat. After eating she and Gwydion talked of *chwedlau* [stories] and *cyfarwyddyd* [lore]. Gwydion was a good storyteller.

211

Extant court poetry has many allusions to legendary characters, and less frequently it is possible to recognise references to episodes, but nevertheless it is difficult to relate precisely the role of poet as storyteller to what is known of bardic practice in the Middle Ages. Though the references quoted above may represent what the author believed to be past usage and as such may not be historically accurate, Irish evidence reveals the corresponding *filid* reciting tales to kings and lords. We must think of a complex situation, which our fragmentary evidence cannot adequately portray, and in which we need to distinguish between types of narrative varying in both material and status, the differing circumstances of recitation, and to relate these variable elements to grades of poets.[1]

Poetry was used as an integral element in one type of narrative. There exist in Middle Welsh series of *englynion* (three or four line stanzas) ranging from groups of three or four verses to more extended chains of twenty or more, which have been explained as the verse portions of narratives which have lost their prose setting. According to this theory, argued most cogently by Sir Ifor Williams,[2] some tales were told in prosimetron form wherein prose was used for narrative and verse for passages of heightened emotion, soliloquy, and dialogue. *Englynion* found in the Black Book of Carmarthen (ca. 1250) seem to be scraps of dialogue and greetings which need a context if they are to be comprehended. They appear to have been used to introduce a character or episode or to provide a framework for catalogues, though the precise narrative context may have been variable. The longer series of *englynion* associated with Llywarch Hen and Heledd are dialogues or long soliloquies of intense emotion, often elegiac in tone. Like other "character" poems of similar ethos in Irish and Old English these frequently have their own validity as lyric poems, so that it may not always be necessary to postulate a narrative setting in a strict sense, but rather the context of an established character or role within the story tradition.

These verse elements in narratives point to bardic involvement in storytelling for which, however, prose was the normal medium. The tales themselves were traditional, and no doubt many fulfilled more than simply an entertainment function in society. As in any preliterate society traditional lore about origins, tribal history, geography, toponymics, the Otherworld and the gods, the cosmos and human relationships, would have been expressed in narrative forms transmitted orally from one generation to another, but formulated and controlled by a learned class. In early and medieval Wales this would have been the poets who together with lawyers and mediciners formed the learned orders in society. Crucial as was the concept of praise of rulers in Indo-European society and its historical descendants, the poets were more than guardians of *regnum*. They were historians, genealogists, custodians of *cyfarwyddyd*, which we may define as that broad body of traditional learning which society regarded as important to its identity and functioning.[3]

Cyfarwyddyd, 'lore' being transmitted orally in narrative forms, became simply 'tale,' and the *cyfarwydd* (pl. *cyfarwyddiaid*) a storyteller. In the second reference above from the *Four Branches, cyfarwyddyd* retains something of its original meaning though in the first it already reveals its restricted use.

There were a number of other words for tale. Gwydion entertained the court with *ymddiddanion*, which in Modern Welsh is 'conversation,' but which the medieval context suggests was a type of narration.[4] Other words are *ebostol* (Latin *epistola*, or *apostolus* in its derived meaning of 'book of epistles'), homily, religious narrative, story; *dadl*, legal discussion, then an account; *cyfranc*, encounter, then a description of the encounter. *Ystoria* (Latin *historia*) seems to refer to texts emanating from a written rather than an oral background. It is used for a variety of texts, including religious and instructional manuals translated from Latin, but the crux passage occurs at the end of the *Dream of Rhonabwy*:

> And this *ystoria* is called the Dream of Rhonabwy And this is why no one, neither poet nor *cyfarwydd*, knows the Dream without a book, because of the many colours of the horses, the many rare hues both of their armour and accoutrements, and of the valuable cloaks and precious stones.

Such colourful descriptive passages would not have taxed the trained memory of an oral storyteller, indeed they are of the essence of his art, and the gloss is an attempt to explain why the tale was commonly read, not recited. It is the most consciously literary composition of all the extant tales and its place outside the traditional repertoire may be what is reflected in the use of *ystoria* to describe it. If so, the occurence of the word to describe *Peredur* and sections of *Geraint and Enid* becomes more significant.[5]

The more common word used for tale is *chwedl* (pl. *chwedlau*) which is related to the Welsh verb *heb*, 'says, speaks.' The word conveys the sense of spoken material and is the generic term for an oral traditional story. Most of the extant Middle Welsh tales use the word to describe themselves in a stereotyped closing sentence, "And this *chwedl* is called. . . ." The majority of the tragically few examples of Welsh medieval storytelling which have survived are versions of tales told by the *cyfarwyddiaid* and they are now known collectively in popular modern usage as the Mabinogion. This word, in fact, occurs only once in Middle

Welsh and is a scribal error found in a single manuscript. It gained currency after its use by Lady Charlotte Guest to denote the collection of Welsh stories which she translated into English in the years 1838–1849 and which she published in 1849 and 1877. This charming translation (not wholly accurate and occasionally bowdlerized) became known to generations of readers when it was issued in the popular Everyman's Library series, with the result that "The Mabinogion" has become a convenient, though historically unfounded, way of referring to the eleven Middle Welsh prose narratives which remain. In its correct form in Middle Welsh it refers only to the sequence of stories properly called *The Four Branches of the Mabinogi*. In this essay I shall avoid the term *mabinogion* and use *mabinogi* strictly to denote *The Four Branches*. This conforms more closely to Middle Welsh usage, but more important it will prevent our viewing the extant tales as a unified group, for one of my aims in this discussion is to examine the different ways in which and the varying degrees to which they have, as individual compositions, developed from being traditional tales to crafted stories.

Copies of the eleven stories are found in the Red Book of Hergest (ca. 1400), ten whole or in part in the closely related White Book of Rhydderch (1325–50), and a few fragments in earlier manuscripts. The texts are difficult to date, but the earliest seems to be "How Culhwch won Olwen" (*Culhwch and Olwen*), ca. 1050, followed by the *Four Branches*, ca. 1060–1120, *Cyfranc Lludd a Llefelys*, ca. 1200 (but also in a later expanded version), and perhaps a little later but of similar date to one another, the *Dream of Maxen, Owain, (The Lady of the Fountain), Geraint and Enid, Peredur; The Dream of Rhonabwy* may be later.[6] Allusions in these stories and in cognate sources testify to an extensive repertoire of oral tales the nature of which ranged from the mythical to the heroic and legendary and which also contained less significant material. Much was lost as the oral tradition weakened and died and the few stories which achieved written form in the medieval period are all that survive complete. They are examples of traditional Welsh narrative and as such they have been analysed and examined to see what they can reveal of Welsh legendary and mythical tradition, and how they can enrich our understanding of the art of the oral storyteller. They have deepened our appreciation of traditional medieval Welsh culture, but an overemphasis on the sources and the traditional contexts of these stories which stresses purely native elements and which sees them simply as written versions of oral narratives, tends to divorce them from their contemporary literary associations, and to cloud our appreciation of them as the conscious compositions of anonymous but individual authors. They are not to be viewed as written versions of oral stories as recalled by interested amateurs, but more positively as the work of *literati* using and shaping traditional material for their own purposes, whatever those may have been. Their sources are lost, so that it is impossible to specify what changes may have occurred in the passage from oral to written text. It is necessary to distinguish between traditional material and traditional tale, since we cannot even be sure that the tales which we have represent corresponding entities in the oral tradition, or whether our authors have re-arranged, conflated, and combined material, in short, have composed (in the sense of *compositio*) new stories. As we shall see, the structures of most of the Mabinogion stories appear to follow common medieval literary modes, while a long, architecturally designed narrative comprising four individual tales, like the *Four Branches*, must raise doubts as to whether the composition ever existed orally in this complete and sequential form, though each part may have existed within a conceptual entity. It has frequently been observed that the oral narrator's relationship to his text is different from that of the author. In the one case we see a performer, a variable text, a knowledgeable audience; stylistically we have a composition based on formulae, or at least conventional phrases, and familiar situations; structurally the text will be linear, chronological, and sequential. The written text, however, is fixed and it will be read rather than performed; its narration may be less direct but will lend itself to experimentation and its style will be less bound by convention, but it will be open to audience participation of a different kind, as listeners ponder the meaning of the narrative or enjoy literary skills more subtle than the purely aural.[7]

Nevertheless, in the early stages of the development of the literary tale the already established conventions of the oral storyteller would have been the overriding influence on an author's style, and though experience in other types of Welsh writing (e.g. legal) and in Latin and French literature would have provided patterns for structuring and presenting material, the basis of the style of these tales would have been the *cyfarwydd* or oral tradition. The written tales develop their own conventions and the extant stories share common features, so that we may describe these texts as being "*cyfarwydd* style writing," a consciously literary style which never became wholly divorced from the oral tradition which continued to flourish throughout the Middle Ages. It is an essentially narrative style in that sentences are made to flow one into another in a logical and harmonious progression. They are frequently linked by conjunctions, or joining phrases, *a* 'and,' *sef a wnaeth* 'this is what he did,' so that the reader is conscious of being moved along by the story. Though coordinate clauses or an elementary pattern of adverbial clause and main clause are the most usual, the syntactical pattern of clauses varies so that though the usual verbal tense is preterite or past continuous, writers avoid monotony by using, in addition to the simple verbal form, circumlocutions—verb-noun, e.g. *myned, + a wnaeth/a orug* 'go he did,' *sef a wnaeth, myned* 'what he did was to go,' historical present; in a series of consecutive actions verb-nouns may be used instead of verbs; the word order may be changed from the normal VSO to SVO, OVS. Further inversion may occur in some passages, but these are not normally narrative, and what one is most conscious of is an aesthetic appreciation of the effect of balanced clauses or sentences which contrast with each other. Such smoothness of style is, however, not accidental as it appears to have developed over the years. The oldest of these tales, *Culhwch and Olwen*, reveals this polished narrative style in some sections, but its opening paragraphs are almost brutally cryptic as the simple sentences, often containing verb-nouns rather than verbs, lurch from one to another, echoing in their lack of progression the primitive ethos of the social fabric of this story. Part of the interest of *Culhwch and Olwen* is the variety of styles which it employs, ranging from the brief statements of the opening section to a number of examples of typically swiftly moving and smooth narrative, so that the story can be viewed by the critic almost as an archaeologist might examine the layers of his section.

The written stories are not markedly formulaic. Formulae are used for restricted functions, e.g. greetings, requests for news, oaths, but they play little or no part in the formation of style. Stories normally open with a phrase naming the hero and giving his status, kingdom, etc. That this is a stereotyped opening is suggested by the inverted ("abnormal") syntax of the sentence: within the narrative another phrase ("and one day . . .") denotes a chapter heading. There are set collocations of noun and adjective, descriptions of dress and appearance, conventional descriptions of combat and phrases denoting the passage of time (e.g. "and they spent the time in pleasant song . . .," "and when it was time to go to sleep, to sleep they went," "and however long they were on the journey, they came to . . ."), but within the context of a complete story such phrases do not draw attention to themselves by their frequency and they have a narrow functional role in composition.

The oral origins of "cyfarwydd style writing" account for the place given to dialogue and for the skill shown in the presentation of convincing conversations or exchanges. *Geraint and Enid* probably reflects the conventions of the oral storyteller most closely in that it contains a higher proportion of dialogue than any other story; much of it, however, is simply pleasantries and courtesies. Conversations tend to be reported fully, rather than reduced to what is significant for the story, whereas the other tales use dialogue meaningfully to reveal situations and to carry the narrative. The author of the *Four Branches* is the most assured of all the writers of the Middle Welsh *chwedlau*. Not only does he use dialogue as a narrative device, but he is able to give his characters recognizably individual forms of expression. He reveals oppositions, points to social distinctions, and paints delightfully naturalistic cameos in the conversations of his characters. Speeches of more than some four or five consecutive sentences are rare, for the author has the ability to see his story unfolding much as a dramatist sees his characters on a stage and situations are not allowed to develop in an unrealistic way. As an example of what I mean, we may turn to an episode in the first of the *Four Branches*. When a former suitor claims Rhiannon on her wedding feast, she draws up an elaborate plan to trick him when he is to return a year hence. All this must be whispered to her husband while the suitor stands before them awaiting a reply. The author, aware that Rhiannon could never have been allowed to defer her answer so long, makes the suitor interrupt harshly, "It is high time I have an answer," and thus makes use of his own narrative fault to strengthen the naturally dramatic quality of the scene. If it is correct to see in the confident handling of dialogue by the authors of the written *chwedlau* their debt to the oral storytellers, it is worth noting that *Cyfranc Lludd a Llefelys*, a tale which contains almost no dialogue or direct speech, did not achieve its written form as an independent literary story deriving directly from oral tradition, but that it has a learned Latin context since it first appears as an insert into Welsh versions of Geoffrey of Monmouth's *Historia Regum Britanniae*. The wit and bantering tone of some of the exchanges in the majority of the stories suggest that they were written in a sophisticated setting where wordplay and verbal fencing were agreeable diversions. Where the tales were written is not known, but their urbane tone suggests an aristocratic environment where good conversation and well-told narrative were appreciated. Though the stories do not show the same sophistication or attention to social mores as French romance, they reveal, if not courtly, certainly relaxed and civil attitudes.

Though much of the appeal of these stories lies in the flow of events objectively reported in as lively and logical a way as possible, the action is slowed or enlivened by descriptive passages, brief or extended. These are of two kinds, the one forming part of the narrative flow, the other a rhetorical embellishment. The former follows a familiar technique, that of the TV camera panning and finally centering on the significant object or person. The narrator brings his hero to a castle, a woodland glade, a beach, and progressing through a number of scenic features fixes the gaze upon whatever is central to the episode. The accumulation of details and the delaying of the significant feature is what gives the description force, for on the one hand the scene is presented from the audience's perspective and is shared with them, and on the other the central features or persons become more clearly marked. These features are presented with a judicious choice of significant characteristics which allow both protagonist and reader to become slowly aware of the meaning of what they see together. The result is that though such descriptions—especially in the hands of the author of the *Four Branches*—need not be obviously adjectival, the eye for detail, both external and in human behaviour, makes them highly realistic.

The other type of descriptive passage takes in a scene in its entirety. Their stereotyped qualities—hair, dress, jewelry, actions—and the fact that similar formalised scenes or descriptions may occur in more than one story, show these to be set-pieces. They arrest the narrative for a moment so that the audience can enjoy the warmth and colour (or the contrasting hideousness) which evoke awe and are appropriate to the marvellous and extravagant. In that sense, though not formalised in structure, these are rhetorical digressions, less consciously so than in French or Latin, but fulfilling a similar function. The device is more highly developed in *Culhwch and Olwen* which has two extended descriptions which are consciously rhetorical, and both of which fulfil a structural role. The description of Olwen's dress and torque is simple enough though colourful, but her person is described more fully than is usual in Welsh. Each sentence contains a conventional colour-comparison and there is a pattern of variation in the syntactical order of the comparisons. These comparisons conclude the description which is followed by a statement of the effect of the heroine's beauty, obviously intended as a formal closing sentence.

> She was sent for. And she came, with a robe of flame-red silk about her, and a torque of red gold around the maiden's neck with precious pearls thereon and rubies.
> Yellower was her head than the flower of the broom; whiter was her flesh than the foam of the wave; whiter were her palms and her fingers than the shoots of the marsh trefoil from amidst the fine gravel of a welling spring.

Neither the eye of the mewed hawk, nor the eye of the thrice-mewed
falcon, not an eye was there fairer than hers.
Than the breast of the white swan were whiter her breasts.
Redder were her cheeks than the reddest foxgloves.
Whoso beheld her would be filled with love of her. Four white trefoils
sprang up behind her wherever she went; and for that reason was she
called Olwen.[8]

The description of Culhwch has a similar purpose but is differently organized. It is a traditional portrait of the hero setting out on his adventure —
armed, lavishly equipped, mounted, his hounds eager but he himself motionless. Horse and equipment are named at the beginning of each sentence
but they are followed by extended descriptions which bring them vividly
before us. Here, however, words not only convey an impression of wealth
and colour but they are themselves used in a rhetorical pattern. Nouns have
two or more adjectives; *gorwydd* 'steed,' has four compound adjectives,
each with the same rhythm of a central stressed syllable flanked by un-
stressed syllables, *penllùchlwyt, pedwargàyaf, gauylgỳgwng, carngràgen*.
This oral stylistic device is used throughout the Middle Welsh narrative
tradition, not in extended paragraphs as in *Culhwch and Olwen*, but as
isolated descriptive phrases where a noun may be accompanied by two or
more compound adjectives (or a verb by like adverbs) made up of a
monosyllabic and a disyllabic (or even trisyllabic) word which has the same
rhythm as the Culhwch passage. Welsh forms compounds easily and some
compound adjectives are part of the normal lexicon, but these examples
have been especially created, a facility possibly learned in the bardic
schools as similar examples are found in more than one prose text and in
the poetry. The description of Culhwch is a well-designed paragraph and
its function both as a rhetorical digression and as a structural marker (for
which see below) is easily recognizable. Under what circumstances an
author may decide to use a flourish of adjectives with a single noun is not
so obvious, but they occur in *Peredur* and *Geraint* to denote energetic,
highly charged movement and emotion, especially therefore with reference to horses, knights, squires, in descriptions of combats, physical or
verbal. The *Dream of Rhonabwy* uses the technique of descriptive digression to a greater extent than any other tale. The author writes vivid but
traditional flowing prose, but the central part of his story describes two
groups of three messengers who are portrayed in a series of permutations
of colours and comparisons, with the result that the digression has
become an end in itself and effectively stops the narrative.

Whether or not this digression is seen as a "fault" depends on our
willingness to perceive it as one of several satirical and parodic elements

in this story which now appears to be more complex in intention than was formerly assumed. The incoherence and inconsequentiality of the central section are intended to reflect an unstructured dream-world, but the paradoxical elements and reversal of roles which appear here surely have satirical significance. The narrative structure of the tale may itself be a parody (as is suggested below), and as we shall see, the author has woven into his tale comments critical of contemporary society while the setting of the story in a particular and carefully specified locale may have had comic meanings for the first audience.

Culhwch and Olwen has another extended rhetorical passage, again in a conventional situation, — the porter's report of the hero at the gate. The porter lists the many and exotic regions of the world where he and Arthur have been, the fine men whom he has seen, but none can be compared to the young man at the gate. Some of the place-names have a geographical location, though here viewed conceptually, others are legendary, others simply euphonious, but in series and introduced by the repeated phrase "I have been . . ." they are used here to convey the inexpressibility of the hero's stature.

These narratives never include an address to the audience and the narrator does not interrupt his tale nor does he point to the significance of his story. There are, however, a few examples of authorial comment, though some may be scribal glosses. None is long enough to be termed a digression; they are more in the nature of asides which an oral storyteller will make to his audience and thus represent the narrator's comment rather than an author's intrusion. These may be remarks on characters (as in the catalogue in Culhwch and Olwen, or on Maxen in the Dream), references to inconsistencies within the text or to a variant tradition (e.g., that the hounds noted by the giant in Culhwch and Olwen were not the ones which took part in the hunt) or more frequently explanations of place-names, proverbs, or social customs and games. Both Geraint and Owain have comments on the office of porter to Arthur (the former in some detail). These stand outside the narrative and are directed at the audience though the reason for them may be that the role of Arthur's porter was the subject of conflicting traditions. We come closer to authorial intervention in the sententious comment at the opening of Peredur where it is said of the hero's father, "And as often is the case with those who follow arms, he and his six sons were killed," an overt criticism of knightly pursuits and tournaments. The narrator's comments in The Dream of Rhonabwy are of a different kind, for here, within the dream section, use is made of the technique of the omniscient guide who answers the hero's naïve questions about what and whom he sees around him. As this information is critical or satirical, these are in reality authorial comments on his own society and its failings which are part of the meaning of the story. In a word, the author is playing here the role of a narrator persona.

Though there is no direct address to the audience in these stories, the authors are always aware of their readers or listeners and write from their narrative perspective. In *The Dream of Maxen* both emperor and audience acquire knowledge of the dream-maiden's identity at the same time as the author delays revealing it as long as possible to heighten our expectations. Normally, however, though the audience will know where the hero is or under what guise he appears, he is portrayed within the bounds of the knowledge which the other characters have. Thus when Pwyll in the guise of Arawn fights with Hafgan in the first of the *Four Branches*, he is not named in the account of the combat, being identified simply, as "the man who was in Arawn's place." This is clearly an unsophisticated attempt to square the audience's knowledge with Hafgan's assumptions. A more controlled example of the description of the hidden identity of a character occurs in *Owain*. Arthur and his men search for the lost hero, who remains unnamed until, during his fight with Gwalchmai, the visor of his helmet is dislodged and his friend recognises him: "Owain!" he cries, as his knowledge and ours merge. The author of *Geraint* uses the watchman device to describe Edern's arrival at Arthur's court so that the unknown knight might be slowly recognised, but in both *Peredur* and *Owain* the motif of the all-conquering chivalric unknown is used more ironically.

There can be no doubt that the crisp, brisk style found in all these Middle Welsh tales is to be viewed as one element in the passage from an oral to a literary medium. Descriptive passages are suggestive rather than detailed, and in spite of some carefully controlled rhetorical sections there is in general a restrained tone to the writing, seen at its most economical in the *Four Branches*. The restraint never lapses into curtness and the Welsh "cyfarwydd style writing" is more obviously designed to bring pleasure to readers than for example, the more staccato style of the early Irish prose tales. The *Dream of Maxen* and *Owain* come closest to the norm, and, as the same style is found in fourteenth-and fifteenth-century prose translations and adaptations of Old French narratives, we can conclude that the literary tradition must have been as strong then as it had been a century earlier.

The "cyfarwydd style" was, however, a developing tradition, and within these stories there are a number of examples where individual authors have freed themselves from oral conventions. In both *Geraint* and the *Four Branches* the use of *uchod* 'above' to refer to a previous incident, where oral style would require a temporal reference, 'before,' is a sign of a written text. More instructive is to observe how the conventional opening formula has evolved in these written *chwedlau*. As has already been said, the formulaic tale opening had as its primary purpose the presenting of the hero's name and status ("X was king of/ruling at . . ."), and in most cases the story follows without any further introduction or explanation. *Owain* and *Peredur*, however, though making use of the formula, delay the narration of the story by including a leisurely description of the scene at court (*Owain*) or of events which preceded the circumstances in which the story is to happen (*Peredur*). The formula in these examples has obviously lost the function which it originally had, and the oral storyteller's need to open his tale directly and catch the attention of his audience immediately is not apparent. *Geraint* retains some of the formula, but the author recognises it has no role to play and attempts to use it simply as an opening statement which can be developed. His story opens, "Arthur used to keep court at Caerlion-upon-Usk . . ." but what follows is a description of the court and an account of its customs, none of which is strictly relevant to the story which is to be told. We have moved from what was an oral storytelling device to a literary convention. *Owain* shows the ultimate development, for although the story opens with the traditional formula, Cynon's tale-within-a-tale has a wholly nontraditional opening which dispenses with the conventions: "I was my mother and father's only son, and I was high-spirited and very arrogant."

The third of the *Four Branches of the Mabinogi* has another nontraditional opening which marks its written setting even more firmly: "After the seven men we spoke about above had buried Bendigeidfran's head facing France in the Gwynfryn in London, Manawydan looked upon the town of London and upon his companions and gave a great sigh. . . ." We may note also that *Lludd and Llefelys*, already observed as being somewhat removed from the oral tradition, lacks the formulaic opening phrase.

Owain has other examples of extending the bounds of conventional narrative devices. The author uses the passage of time formula not as an empty phrase, but as a means of conveying the hero's impatience as he awaits the next day's adventure. Taking the device of threefold repetition, a familiar method of increasing tension, (e.g., the three visits to the giant's court in *Culhwch and Olwen*, Peredur's infatuation for the empress, his three-day tournament with the earl's men, Pwyll's meeting with Rhiannon), the *Owain* author integrates it into the account of the Black

Knight's final hours—his death pains, the sacrament of extreme unction and his demise.[9]

The triple repetition of incidents may be integral to the structure of the narrative. It may be brought about unimaginatively as in *Lludd and Llefelys* where the three accounts of the defeat of the Coraniaid, though differently motivated, nevertheless reveal a monotonous similarity. The author of the *Dream of Maxen* shows greater skill in handling this device as the three journeys to Britain serve to move the story from a dream world through a geographical setting to an historical period, while the three accounts of the expedition to the fountain in *Owain* have subtle variations in tempo, detail, and purpose which help the development of the narrative.

All the Middle Welsh stories which we are discussing are carefully constructed. All have moved away from the chronological sequence and the single motivation of the folktale or from other simple patterns, as, for example, cumulative or frame stories, so that there can be no doubt as to their status as literary composed tales. *Culhwch and Olwen*, often claimed to be closest in style to the oral tales, superficially has the simple folklore structure of the hero's gathering up of helpers to fulfil the tasks with which the giant has burdened him; the tasks set become the motivation for a number of independent adventures. In fact, not only does this story have a variety of styles, but its structure is carefully organised into formally distinct parts. The stage is set and the quest theme is stated in the opening paragraphs of part one in the fractured style I described earlier. Part two begins with a rhetorical passage (the setting out of the hero), and the heroic ethos is sustained on his arrival at Arthur's court by the porter's speech. A ritualistic formula (*nod a nottych*, 'name what you will') reiterates the quest, and a catalogue of names with a formal closing sentence ends the section. The search for the heroine, related with some humour in normal narrative style, follows. Her discovery (opening part four) is marked by the second rhetorical passage and the quest theme re-appears, again ritualistically, *nod a nottych*, in a catalogue of tasks put into formulaic dialogue form which has a formal closing sentence. The location of the two catalogues at the end of sections two and four is significant as both of these sections open with extended rhetorical passages, and both mark major incidents in the narrative—Culhwch's request at Arthur's court following the introductory section one, and his request at the giant's court following the search for Olwen, section three. The fulfilment tales follow, the narration of which may be swift or leisurely, full or skeletal, single or repeated. Though related to the central theme by their link with the list of tasks imposed by the giant, these tales tend to have an independent existence, and the increasing pace of the story creates a sensation that the tale is disintegrating. The hunting of the boar Twrch Trwyth reimposes order and sets the narration on its feet again. This is a wholly self contained episode with its own introduction and development which follows an epic pattern of parleys and conditions. The minor characters are killed off in preliminary skirmishes, and only the two protagonists, Arthur and Twrch Trwyth, remain. The hunt rises to its climax and becomes exuberant, exultantly physical. An element of farce releases the tension of the closing stages and the cruel humour of the final episode with its new vocabulary of a lower social register changes the tone of the narrative, bringing it back to the normality of earthy existence. The vivacity of the narrative, the nature of its material, its inconsistencies and blind alleys, should not blind us to its formal structure and its logical ordering of elements, nor to the implications which these features have for a view of *Culhwch and Olwen*, in its present form, as an oral tale.

The other Middle Welsh stories are structured with similar care. They have an internal logic of episodes, and they have a similar tripartite pattern of two related sections joined by a bridging or interposed section. *Owain* has a^1, the journey and adventure at the fountain, which is brought to a conclusion in a^2, the account of the hero's rehabilitation; b, Arthur's search for Owain and the latter's seven-year sojourn at court, links the two main sections which carry the thematic development of the romance. a^1 is mirrored in a^2, and b is relevant to both. *Peredur*, however, has a^1, the hero's education and chivalric development, while a^2 continues and completes adventures begun in the earlier section: b contains independent tales about the hero which do not seem relevant to the thematic development of the romance. The same pattern is found in the *Dream of Maxen*. The story of the dream maiden (a^1) is the prologue to the historically significant role of the hero which appears in a^2, the account of the winning of Rome and the settlement of Brittany: between these two sections comes b which contains antiquarian material relevant to the historical theme. *Geraint* is bipartite as it lacks the bridging section. The story of the winning of Enid and the return to Cornwall are a prologue to the deeper theme of the estrangement and reconciliation of the hero and his wife. Arthur's court provides a degree of articulation, but there is no narrative link between the two parts which have different narrative patterns, the prologue showing interlace (as do parts of *Peredur*), the second section being more straightforwardly linear. The basically binary structure seen in all these tales is a well-known medieval method of ordering a narrative,[10] and its use in these Welsh stories suggest that their authors were aware of contemporary literary practices.

As has already been suggested, this is even more manifest in the *Dream of Rhonabwy*, which has been criticised for its lack of progression, its descriptive passages, and the inconsequentiality of its episodes. There now seems to be general agreement that these faults are intentional and that the story (an *ystoria* read from a book) is a pastiche of traditional episodes composed as a parody of interlacing and of the episodic style of a *roman d'aventure*. Episodes open, develop and are left, never to be returned to, narrative lines peter out, so that though there is much movement, nothing is ever concluded, and much remains unexplained.

However faithfully these stories may reflect their sources in traditional *cyfarwyddyd*, they reveal themselves to be the literary creations of individual authors who were indebted to the oral tradition for the basis of their style and material, but who drew on contemporary literary theory for their presentation. Careful structuring implies thematic development, and another sign of the literariness of these stories is that the narrative is given significance beyond the progression to a satisfying conclusion of a sequence of events. The significance may, of course, be traditional. The hero of the *Dream of Maxen* was an important figure in British traditional history, but the bringing together of the two themes of his marriage to a British queen and his establishment of Brittany underlines his role in that tradition. Even as fantastic a tale as *Cyfranc Lludd a Llefelys* appears first in Welsh versions of Geoffrey's *Historia*. But in the case of *Owain*, *Geraint*, and *Peredur* the *sens* reflects questions of chivalric modes of behaviour and knightly virtues, and it is the concern for correct standards in a courtly Arthurian society, expressed by means of a narrative of a knight's adventures, which justifies the use of the term "romance" to describe them. They are implicit and naturalistic rather than specific and chivalric in motivation, suggestive rather than rhetorical in their exploration of character, still revealing the objectivity of narrative rather than the personal voice of the author, but they represent in Welsh writing a major development which may be properly called "Welsh romance."

The *Four Branches of the Mabinogi* cannot be so easily labelled as this unified group of four stories has many features which set it apart from the other *chwedlau* which we have considered. The author is altogether more restrained and reserved than his fellows. He is specific in his location of events and is attentive to details. His precise use of words is a sign that language is important for him. In the second Branch the hero makes amends for the insult which his guest has received. The compensation is accepted with the wry comment that this cannot "uninsult" him (*diwaradwyddaw*). The word, attested in Middle Welsh only here, is an attempt to convey a concept central to the theme of the Branch. The author varies the rhythm and tempo of his sentences, isolating important words by changes in syntax: he delights in balanced antithesis and is a master of creating tension or atmosphere by the use of syntax rather than by description. His skill in writing dialogue not only sets up scenes of dramatic intensity but also creates the most convincing characters of medieval Welsh fiction, men and women who are, notwithstanding their typological or functional basis, imbued with personal characteristics revealed as much by the distinctive tone of their speech as by their actions.

The structures of individual Branches are interesting in that they tend to be more complex and less amenable to mechanistic patterning than the other stories which I have been discussing. This may be inherent in the nature of the material and its adaptation by the author, but it frequently suggests the ability to plan a narrative so that episodes, apparently introduced incidentally, are later revealed as being central to the plot. The cauldron of rebirth, which is Efnisien's means of expiation, first appears in an after-dinner conversation following the "uninsulting" referred to above, while the logic and motivation of the Fourth Branch defy an easy synopsis. The author uses juxtaposition of incidents, sometimes ironically; he experiments with non-linear (but not truly retrospective) narrative. It is, however, fairly easy to see how each branch relates to another and how incidents in one may have been motivated by those in another so that in spite of some inconsistencies a unity is apparent in the surface structure of the *Four Branches*. *Pwyll* (1) sets the stage historically and contains the germs of future episodes which will be developed in *Manawydan* (3) and *Math* (4). The gradual emergence of Manawydan, first as a mere name and then more substantially as a recognizable character in *Branwen* (2), prepares us for his major role in Branch 3, which is presented as a continuation of Branch 2. The only formal link which is lacking is that between branches 1 and 2. But these mechanical devices are not of the essence of the *Four Branches*, even assuming that the original material had already been organized as four sequential parts of a whole in the oral tradition.[11] The author needed an architectonic means which would unify the material at a deeper level than the plot. He seems to have found it in his use of keywords.

Branch 1 is a necessary preliminary to what will follow, but thereafter each Branch has its own theme and its own significant nouns which epitomize it: insult (*tremyg, gwaradwydd, sarhad*) in *Branwen*, friendship and fellowship (*cydymddeithas*) in *Manawydan*, shame (*cywilydd*) in *Math*.

All the main male characters in *Branwen* — Efnisien, Matholwch, Brân — believe they have suffered insults at the hands of others, and the theme of the Branch is the working out of the implications of these insults in the relationships of the characters. Insult, *sarhad*, is a legal term for injury which may also be physical, to one's honour or status, and which, as such, is open to redress in law. Brân's apology to Matholwch, his guest, is accompanied by full and complete legal compensation, so that the previous relationships of the parties should have been restored, as Brân assumed and as was symbolised by the use of the same seating arrangements at the second feast as at the first. But insult is not simply a legal matter. Matholwch cannot be "uninsulted" in personal terms and his injured feelings cannot be compensated. The injured Irish resolve to avenge the insult and the tragedy which the law was designed to prevent becomes unavoidable. It is impossible to read *Branwen* without being aware of humanity's violent and destructive propensities. Men's unwillingness to be reconciled leads to the devastation of "two good islands," but the terrible irony of life is that it is Branwen's attempt at reconciliation which is the occasion of the final slaughter. Human pride, described in the mythic episode of universal significance of the door which must not be opened (like the fruit which must not be eaten) lies at the root of humanity's woe.

Our author takes the seven survivors slowly from devastated Ireland to desolate Britain, but imperceptibly the atmosphere changes as life and light return. *Manawydan* is the brightest Branch of all, taking its tone from Pryderi's promise to his companion, "The best fellowship which I can offer will be yours if you desire it." The four characters delight in each other's company, so that they are sufficient unto themselves even when they find themselves a solitary group in the waste land. When Manawydan returns from a hunting trip without her son, Rhiannon's strongest stricture is "You have been a poor friend." It is, however, his sage understanding of events, motivated by his loyalty and chaste faithfulness, which restores the fellowship of the four and which brings life to desolate Dyfed.

Artistically, this was a necessary interlude after the gloom of *Branwen*, but the problem of suffering and the inadequacies of the law remain unresolved. The final Branch, *Math*, though superficially the one most full of magic and fantasy, is, in fact, the most human. Math, as do the other main characters, Pwyll, Brân, Manawydan, reflects life's just and moral forces. The magician Gwydion is amoral Man interested in ends not means, considering only methods of actions, not their rightness. Where *Branwen* is full of physical effort and *Manawydan* of cunning and sagacity, *Math* describes the easy short cuts of magic, or it does so until Gwydion's nephew is mortally wounded. For nothing shows the author's deep understanding of the pain of human existence more clearly than his refusal to allow the youth to be magically healed. The uncle-magician achieves humanity when he must nurse his nephew, suffering in himself the pain which is part of compassion. Magic within a fantasy world cannot touch life's suffering, because the real world has its own ordered law. When law is broken and men suffer insult, there is recompense. But the injury done to Math's standing in his own eyes, even more than to his status as king responsible for his servants, by the behaviour of his own kin, is beyond what the law can comprehend. His sense of outrage and shame remain. In *Branwen* the author described *sarhad*, legal insult; now he takes this a stage further and sees personal offence. The former can be paid for and justice can be satisfied. The latter has to do with injury to a personality, for the insult is not only wounding but shaming. The satisfying of the former leads to *tangnefedd*, the legal restoration of relationships, but the satisying of the other is *cerennydd*, friendship and reconciliation. When Math reflects to those who have insulted him, "My shame you cannot repay," he is acknowledging that what he feels is outside the scope of the law. Matholwch could not be "uninsulted" by legal compensation, but Math's reception of the two offenders after the completion of their punishment is an acceptance of the meaning of law, the flouting of which in *Branwen* had led to violence and war. To those who have shamed him, he says, "Legal rehabilitation (*tangnefedd*) you have received and you shall receive reconciliation (*cerennydd*)." Legal justice is necessary for the smooth working of society, but without the graces of forgetting and forgiving human pride will render the best systems unworkable.

In the *Four Branches of the Mabinogi* we are aware of a consistent attitude and a thematic unity. The material which these stories use is the most obviously native and traditional of all the *chwedlau*, and yet from it the medieval author has produced a work unparalleled in Middle Welsh literature. His moral view of life, tempered by his compassion for human frailty, has taken up the *cyfarwyddyd* which he found and has given it significance beyond that of his own time, not along the way of accepted contemporary literary conventions but along the road of personal conviction shaping a unique narrative form.

The antecedents of the eleven Middle Welsh stories which I have discussed in this essay lie in traditional tales recited by oral storytellers. We can never know the particular form of those lost versions but during the eleventh, twelfth, and thirteenth centuries, they were taken up by men of letters who, by subtly combining the virtues of the native oral tradition with the opportunities which literary composition granted, produced these new and personal retellings.

Brynley F. Roberts
University College of Swansea, Wales

Notes

1. For a discussion of the evidence and other references see Proinsias MacCana, *The Learned Tales of Medieval Ireland* (Dublin: Dublin Institute for Advanced Studies, 1980), pp. 132–41.

2. "The Poetry of Llywarch Hen," British Academy Sir John Rhŷs Lecture, 1932, republished in *The Beginnings of Welsh Poetry*, ed. Rachel Bromwich (Cardiff: Univer;sity of Wales Press, 1972), pp. 122–54; also *Lectures on Early Welsh Poetry* (Dublin: Dublin Institute for Advanced Studies, 1944). More recently the hypothesis has been refined and is currently the subject of much discussion.

3. See D. A. Binchy, "The Background of Early Irish Literature," *Studia Hibernica* 1 (1961), 7–18, esp. p. 11. Cf. my comments in "Geoffrey of Monmouth and Welsh historical tradition," *Nottingham Medieval Studies* 20 (1976), 29–40.

4. Perhaps a prosimetron form, or, as suggested by P. K. Ford in *Studia Celtica* 10/11 (1975–76), 152–62, a literary form wherein one person narrated an episode in which he played the parts of two or more persons.

5. See further "Ystoria," *Bulletin of the Board of Celtic Studies* 26 (1974), 13–20.

6. These are translated into English by Gwyn Jones and Thomas Jones, *The Mabinogion*, 2d ed., Everyman's Library, (London: Dent, 1974), Patrick K. Ford, *The Mabinogi and Other Medieval Welsh Tales*, (Berkeley: University of California Press, 1977), Jeffrey Gantz, *The Mabinogion*, (Harmonsworth: Penguin Books, 1976).

7. Robin F. Jones contrasts the collective effort of poet and public which produced oral epic poems, renewed and transmitted in each performance, with the writer who "by virtue of his *sens* and the process of writing, creates a less contingent, more highly personal individual work which in principle would be unthinkable and unknowable without him and which is fixed forever in manuscript." *The Nature of Medieval Narrative,* ed. M. Grunmann-Gaudet and Robin F. Jones (Lexington: French Forum, 1980), pp. 150–51.

8. Quoted, with a few adaptations, from the Gwyn Jones and Thomas Jones translation of *The Mabinogion*.

9. I have discussed stylistic and structural features of the Welsh *Owain* more fully in P. B. Grout et al., eds., *The Legend of Arthur in the Middle Ages* (Cambridge: D. S. Brewer, 1983), pp. 170–82.

10. See William W. Ryding, *Structures in Medieval Narrative* (The Hague: Mouton, 1971), p. 40.

11. The unity of the *Four Branches* has long been a matter of discussion dominated until recently by W. J. Gruffydd's view of them as being the heroic biography of Pryderi. For criticisms and other views, see Proinsias MacCana, *The Mabinogi* (Cardiff: University of Wales Press, 1977), J. K. Bollard, "The structure of the Four Branches of the Mabinogi," *Trans. Hon. Soc. of Cymmrodorion* (1975), 250–76, Jeffrey Gantz, "Thematic structure in the Four Branches of the Mabinogi," *Medium Aevum* 47 (1978), 247–54.

8. Sentence and Solas in the Old French Fabliaux

The anonymous author of *La Dame qui se venja du chevalier* describes the appropriate response to his literary efforts and to those of his fellow *fableors* as follows:

> Vos qui fableaus volez oïr,
> Peine metez à retenir;
> Volentiers les devez aprendre,
> Les plusors por essample prendre,
> Et les plusors por les risées
> Qui de meintes gens sont amées.[1]

This sounds straightforward enough, and nothing in the practice of other fabliau authors contravenes the idea that the statement employs its technical terms precisely. It implies that the generic term *fabliau* was perceived as encompassing two subspecies, *essample* and *risée*, whose distinction from one another is predicated on the comparative emphasis given to instruction or entertainment in the story, but whose essential identity as fabliaux embraces a spectrum of artistic intents ranging from the predominantly didactic to the predominantly risible.

The actual degree of humor discoverable in individual fabliaux is naturally impossible to quantify. However, in accordance with Bédier's generally accepted definition of works in this genre as "des contes à rire en vers,"[2] some humorous effect is clearly a constituent feature of all fabliaux, so that every *essample* is necessarily to some extent also a *risée*.[3] The exact nature and source of this humor cannot be postulated in terms applicable to every fabliau, but in the majority humorous effect can be seen controlling, in order to be realized through, the sequence of episodes comprising the plot. The humor in these fabliaux is uniform in nature, and derived from a single, ascertainable source. In order to make some correlations between the *solas* generated by this humor, and the *sentence* whose presence in certain fabliaux warrants their being classified

231

as *essamples*, a pragmatically useful if partial definition of *solas* can be posited which will differentiate narrative patterns somehow capable of producing an essentially similar humorous effect.

What I suggest accounts for the quality of *solas* in the fabliaux is the recognition of something quasi-magical, a kind of *mana*, attaching to the processes of cognition by which man attempts to know and understand the material world accessible to him through sense perceptions, and specifically to man's ability to interpret, or in a self-servingly creative way to manufacture, ambiguous signs. If conceived as existing externally to man, such *mana* may appear in two forms. One is the Babel demon who blights man's efforts to communicate effectively with his fellows; the other is a capriciously benign genie who can conjure from words sophistical solutions to all problems. An element of awe attaches to both figures. Anyone potentially may also possess *mana*, but women in the fabliaux seem especially gifted with this capacity as a birthright of their sex. "Fame est plaine de sanc agu; / Par lor engin ont deceü / Les sages des lo tans Abel," says one poet;[4] "Fame est féte por decevoir; / Mençonge fet devenir voir, / Et voir fet devenir mençonge," says another.[5] Both statements reflect the assumption that *mana* runs, as it were, in women's blood. Because it is likely to be cherished as one sees oneself possessing it, and feared as one sees it possessed by someone else, attitudes towards *mana* and towards those informed with *mana* may reflect some deep-seated ambivalencies. But I shall assume the effect of watching *mana* in action to be, unequivocally, *solas*, an effect compounded of intellectual fascination and the emotional pleasures of laughing at fellow victims and laughing with the expert practitioners of mystifying skills.[6]

If every *essample* is necessarily a *risée*, the reverse would not appear to be true. But the issue of the nature of *sentence* in the fabliaux is perhaps more complicated than that of *solas*. A statement by Bédier will make a useful point of departure for an investigation of the matter: "Il n'y a pas, en effet, de bourde ni de *trufe* si indifférente qu'on n'en puisse tirer quelque leçon. . . . Mais l'intention morale n'est jamais qu'accessoire. Elle ne vient que par surcroît" (p. 311).

It is certainly possible to agree with Bédier that any story whose narrative pattern generates, and decisively resolves, some conflict between individuals clearly differentiated from one another in their attitudes will necessarily imply a moral schema coincident with the system of rewards and punishments which pertains within its fictional world. A large number of fabliaux, specifically for our purposes those which exhibit the workings of personal *mana*, satisfy these conditions. The implied morality is normally not explicitly articulated, but on occasions it might be, as is the case with *Le Pliçon*, one of five extant fabliaux written by the four-teenth-century court poet Jean de Condé. It opens with some verses iden-tifying it as a *risée*: "Gens sont qui ont plus kier risées / Et mokeries desghisées / Oïr que ne face[nt] siermons" (*MR*, 6: 260). The story, which describes the trick whereby a wife engineers a lover's escape from her bedroom in the presence of her armed and irate husband, concludes with the following summary of its *sentence*:

> Li tours fu biaus et grascieus,
> Plain[s] d'engien et maliscieus;
> Si fu à grant pourfit tournés,
> Car grans maus en fu destournés.
>
> [*MR*, 6: 263]

By keeping a cool head in circumstances dangerous enough to induce panic, the wife defuses a potentially explosive situation charged with the possibility of bloodshed, and turns it into an occasion for merriment. She exploits personal *mana* not only to generate *solas*, but also, accord-ing to the author's own account of the morality implicit in his story, to effect the triumph of virtue.

Two further implications of Bédier's statement are open to serious ob-jection. Theoretically, nothing prohibits a fabliau from being conceived ex-clusively as entertainment.[7] In practice numerous fabliaux, specifically for our purposes those exhibiting the workings of impersonal *mana*, make no explicit claim to be informative or morally edifying, and do not satisfy the conditions necessary for drawing moral lessons from the fortunes of the protagonists. More importantly, Bédier fails to acknowledge that *sentence* in the fabliaux, unlike *solas*, is not uniform in nature and does not emanate from a single source. As a result, his remarks confusingly blur some necessary distinctions. When he discusses a moral intention which is ac-cessory and subordinate to the humorous effects aimed at in the story, he cannot possibly mean such morality as that articulated by Jean de Condé in the passage quoted from *Le Pliçon*. Since this morality is implied by the in-teraction of the characters and the contours of the plot, it derives from ex-actly the same source as the tale's *solas*, and under such circumstances *sentence* and *solas* are complementary and inseparable. Rather than the implicit moral lessons forming part of the audience's response to the story, he must mean the explicit claims for potentially edifying effects which, in the form of a conventional-looking *moralitas*, are appended to so many fabliaux as to constitute a standard feature of the genre.

Bédier, in conformity with his conception of the fabliaux as an escapist bourgeois literary genre—"un fabliau," he disparagingly asserts, "n'est qu'une amusette" (p. 309)—dismisses the moral element in the fabliaux from serious consideration once he supposes himself to have established its subordinate and inconsequential role. He at no point addresses directly the problems raised by the frequent appearance of passages making some pretence, at least, to interpret morally the tales of which they form a part. Per Nykrog did acknowledge the existence of such passages in a large number of fabliaux,[8] but being unable to assimilate them comfortably to his conception of the "courtois burlesque" nature of the genre, he proposed two tentative explanations of their presence: that the *moralitas* appears in accordance with the dictates of contemporary rhetorical theory, or that it is a vestige of the fable form from which it helps to confirm the fabliau's derivation. Both explanations, by assuming that the moral conclusion is not an integral part of the story, account very simply and comprehensively for the disjunction frequently discovered between some fabliaux and their *moralitas*.[9] But neither makes any distinctions between different kinds of fabliau-*sentence*, or considers how they might be related to a context of different kinds of narrative pattern, and both radically oversimplify what can be apprehended as a complex problem involving several significant variables.

I

Since fabliau-authors knew better than to spoil their jokes by attempting to explain them, *solas* in the fabliaux is always a matter of inference, while *sentence*, as noted, is frequently spelled out. As an initial methodological principle, the concept of *sentence* will be extended to include not only the terminal *moralitas* of the familiar type ("Par cest flabel poëz savoir . . ." "Par cest example vos deffant . . . " etc.), but also all occurrences of lines or passages in the text, before, after, or during the course of the action, when either the author, or one of the characters, or a group of characters speaking in unison makes some generalizing observation on the significance of the action, or interprets it in relation to an extra-textual frame of reference or system of belief. Occurrences of sentence so defined have been classified into five groups:

1. Authorial commentary on fabliau form.

There are a number of passages, normally presented as prologue, which explain and defend the genre. The following passage, from Nykrog's second version of *Le Chevalier qui fist les cons parler*, reflects the standard sentiments:

Aventures e enseignement
Fount solas molt sovent
E solas fet releggement,
Ce dit Gwaryn que ne ment.
E pur solas demostrer
Une trufle vueil comencer.
Quant um parle de trufle e rage,
Ne pense de autre fere damage.

[Rychner, 2: 39]

Most of these passages stress the value of humorous anecdotes to relieve
tension, dispel quarrelsomeness, ease sorrow, and lift depressed spirits,
making their case for the fabliau as an escapist and primarily entertaining literary form. As a result, the appearance of such introductory statements is helpful in identifying those works which the authors perceive as
belonging with literature written for the purpose of recreation. Use of the
word *trufle* to describe the work cited is significant in this respect.

2. Proverbs.

These are the briefest and simplest expressions of *sentence*. They appear with great frequency. Only proverbs which are in some respect
monitory have been recorded as important for the concern of this essay
(e.g., *Qui trop despent, il s'endete*); other proverbial phrases (e.g., *Tierce
fois est drois, Cui avient une n'avient seule*), and proverbial comparisons
(e.g., clichés such as *Pire de mal des denz*) have been ignored.[10]

3. Practical advice.

These passages, also of frequent occurrence, function in a fashion
analogous to that of monitory proverbs. They may be regarded simply as
expanded proverbs which lack the latter's epigrammatic quality and consequently do not have formally-fixed general currency. Both types of expression form part of a genuine but unsystematized and often internally
contradictory kind of wisdom. It serves to alert the agent to the existence
of options in behavioral responses to any situation (e.g., *Meauz vaut
bons atendres que folement enchaucier* [M: 1. 1248] vs. *L'en doit batre le
fer tandis cum il est chauz* [M: 1. 1449]) while leaving the choice of options to the agent's assessment of the particular circumstances in which
he is obliged to act. Neither proverbs nor passages of practical advice involve choices between right and wrong behavior as defined in accordance
with any absolute moral framework. The question addressed is rather
one of expediency, and the issue concerns not the moral right or wrong
but the rational validity or invalidity of actions undertaken in particular
circumstances. The nature of these passages, and the quality of internal

inconsistency in situations documented by fabliau narratives, are illustrated by two summary statements of this kind. The first, which reflects some Christian coloration derived from the doctrine associated with the schema of the seven acts of mercy, is from *Le Povre Clerc*:

> Cest fabliaus nos dit et raconte
> Q'an son respit, dit li vilains,
> *Que à celui doit l'an del pain*
> *Qu'on ne cuide jamais veoir;*
> Car l'an ne cuide pas savoir
> Tel chose qui vient mout sovant.
>
> [*MR*, 5: 200. Italics mine.]

The second, which shows its proverbial affiliations by incorporating a proverb in the final line, is from *Gombert et les deus clers*:

> Cis fabliaux moustre par example
> Que nus hom qui bele fame ait,
> Por nule proière ne lait
> Clerc gesir dedenz son ostel,
> Que il li feroit autretel;
> *Qui plus met en aus, plus i pert.*
>
> [*MR*, 1: 244. Italics mine.]

There are stylistic differences between the two passages. The first has an earnestness attributable to the author's sense of its conformity with orthodox Christian teaching. Jean Bodel, with his "qui bele fame ait" (clerks are lechers to the last man, but lechers of impeccable taste) shows a tongue-in-cheek awareness of his statement's pragmatic unconventionality. But there are occasions, as his story illustrates, when the advice would be valid and well taken, and the lightness of tone does not sanction denying its literal meaning on the grounds that it is ironic, or debar it from taking its place as necessary complement and counterbalance to the sentiments expressed at the end of *Le Povre Clerc*. Taken together as increments in the formulation of some theoretical fabliau-ethic, they suggest that life's experiences frequently present us a choice between two evils: in this instance either to refuse hospitality to itinerant clerks and be remiss in one's Christian duty to feed the hungry and provide shelter for the homeless, or to be hospitable and place the sexual security of the women of one's household in jeopardy. The sensible response to so pessimistic a view of the human condition is a cautious resolve to choose the lesser of two evils while taking care to avert or minimize the dangers thus courted, but there is no sure path to security, since the choice can be validated only by its consequences.

4.) Moral exhortation.

In common with passages of practical advice, passages of moral exhortation urge a particular course of action, but on the basis of its rightness by the standards of some ethical system, not because it is expedient in certain circumstances. A Christian ethical context of free will is assumed, and evil is seen as the result of a perverted will making wrong moral choices, so as to be potentially rectifiable by a direct appeal to guilty individuals to change their ways. Since these moral judgments do not depend, in the same way as those associated with proverbs or passages of practical advice, on the denouement of the plot for their validation by some contextual system of rewards and punishments, passages of moral exhortation may appear in initial as well as in final position. It is characteristic of fabliaux which function within a conventional ethical framework to begin and end with such moral exhortation, so as to emphasize the absolute nature of the moral issues raised and resolved in the course of the action. A typical instance is provided by *La Dame escoillée*, which begins with the following address to the audience:

> Seignor, qui les femes avez,
> Et qui sor vos trop les levez,
> Ques faites sor vos seignorir,
> Vos ne faites que vos honir.
>
> [*MR*, 6: 95]

The author's reformatory fervor in castigating what he perceives as a particularly opprobrious vice is attested by the tone of imperative advocacy evident throughout the passage, which continues for another eighteen lines and incorporates five uses of some form of the verb *devoir*.

Passages of moral exhortation frequently appear in conjunction with benedictions and curses, a tendency well illustrated by the concluding verses of *La Dame escoillée*, which complete the moral framework for this fabliau:

> Benoit soit il, et cil si soient,
> Qui lor males femes chastoient;
> Cil sont honi, et il si sont,
> Qui lor feme tel dangier ont.
> Les bones devez mout amer
> Et chier tenir et hennorer,   ?
> Et il otroit mal et contraire
> A ramposneuse deputaire.
> Teus est de cest flabel la some;
> Dahet feme qui despit home!
>
> [*MR*, 6: 115-16]

Curses may occasionally stand alone as summary moral commentary in
fabliaux which assume the same sort of conventionally absolute standards. The practice constitutes a mark of identity for Gautier le Leu,
who ends several of his fabliaux with a curse, but here is an example
from the anonymous *Le Provost a l'aumuche*:

> Cist fabliaux retret de cest cas,
> Que par emblers ont les avoirs.
> Mais Diex qui fu mis en la Crois
> Lor envoit tele povreté,
> Que povre gent tiengnent verté.

> [*MR*, 1: 112]

5) Complaint.[11]

In passages of complaint the author addresses the audience, and on
rare occasions one character addresses another, on a state of affairs
which both are assumed to find regrettable but to be incapable of changing. What inspires the complaint can usually be subsumed under the general concept of corruption, initially corruption of human nature in a
fallen world, but also by extension those social institutions over which
corrupt individuals exercise control, so that complaint may address
usurers, or judges who accept bribes, but also the economic or judicial
systems as a whole. The corruption is assumed to be so widespread (references to *le siècle* and *tot le mont* are commonplace), and of such long
standing, that no amelioration is to be looked for by an appeal to individuals to reform, corrupt human nature being regarded as intractable.
The tone is often nostalgic, cognizance of current evils coexisting with
belief in a prelapsarian state of innocence, or sense of some earlier
golden age in the history of social institutions when utopian standards
prevailed from which there has been a catastrophic and perhaps irreversi-
ble falling away. With regard to institutions, the abuses addressed are
those capable of being legislated out of existence, so that in some
measure an earlier, pristinely just and fair system might be restored. In
the meantime the author and his audience find themselves passively subject, as plaintiffs before a corrupt judge, or as customers exploited by
some entrepreneur's sharp practices, to whatever degree of malpractice
the present legal system tolerates. An example appears at the conclusion
of *Les trois Boçus*:

> Durans, qui son conte define,
> Dist c'onques Diex ne fist meschine
> C'on ne puist por deniers avoir;
> Ne Diex ne fist si chier avoir,
> Tant soit bons ne de grant chierté,

> Qui voudroit dire verité,
> Que por deniers ne soit eüs.
>
> . . . .
>
> Hoinz soit li hom, quels qu'il soit,
> Qui trop prise mauvés deniers,
> Et qui les fist fere premiers.[12]

By its nature complaint is closer to a lyric than to a narrative mode, and its most comfortable context is in non narrative or minimally narrative fabliaux such as *Le Pet au vilain* (MR, 3: 103–05), *Le Con qui fu fait a la besche*,[13] and *Le Roi d'Angleterre et le jongleur d'Ely* (MR, 2: 242–56).

Passages of complaint, insofar as they document situations regarded as in some sense vicious and potentially troublesome, take an unequivocally condemnatory stance towards the conditions complained against. But the spokesman assumes that these conditions constitute the regrettable but intractable background circumstances governing practical choices, rather than one term in a moral antinomy whose opposite term is promoted by authorial commentary and ultimately endorsed by the narrative contours. The important response to situations described in passages of complaint is not to condemn or condone them, but to know and understand them, because such knowledge and understanding will guide the protagonist in making expedient practical choices. It is not surprising, therefore, to find passages of complaint and practical advice appearing in conjunction in the fabliaux. The second version of *Les trois Dames qui troverent un vit* (MR, 5: 32–36) well illustrates this combination, a passage of complaint against corrupt judges being immediately followed by a passage of practical advice, sown with a heavy scattering of proverbs, on the most expedient course to pursue in the light of widespread judicial misconduct:

> Autresi font les jugeours:
> Covoiteus sont, jel sai de voir;
> Ja povres hons qui n'a avoir
> N'avra par eus droit en sa vie.
>
> . . . .
>
> Por ce, seignor, je vos chasti;
> Par essample vos mostre et preuve
> Que se nul de vos avoir treuve,
> S'il a compaing ne compaigne,
> N'atende pas que il s'en plaigne,
> Mès rende l'en toute sa part.
> Je di: *Cil se repent trop tart,*
> *Qui se repent quant a perdu;*
> Je di qu'il a trop atendu,
> Et si vous revoil fere entendre

Que *L'en pert bien par trop atendre*;
Mès en la fin fin [sic] di en apert:
Cil qui tot covoite, tout pert.

[Italics mine.]

All instances of isolable and bounded passages of sentence appearing in the fabliaux can be assigned to one or the other of these five categories.[14] They have been defined and illustrated at length in order that their significance as indicators for classifying fabliaux of which they form a part can be discussed with some measure of precision.

A minority of those known. II

Twenty-five fabliaux are without passages of *sentence* of any kind. It is not too bold a hypothesis to assume that among these may be found some tales in which total absence of any claim to value as vehicles for instruction may legitimately be interpreted to imply that the tales are *risées* whose main function was perceived as entertainment. This is a large enough group to offer some promise that a particular type, or particular types of story might be identified as especially associated with this category. To the evidence offered by the absence of *sentence* may be added that to be derived from passages of authorial commentary on fabliau form. When such passages appear in fabliaux otherwise bare of moralizing or interpretive commentary, they help identify these fabliaux as *amusettes*.

Both Jean de Condé's *Le Clerc qui fu repus derriere l'escrin* (MR, 4: 47–52), which the author labels a *truffe de verité*, and *Les deux Angloys et l'anel* (Reid, pp. 11–13) turn on some *quiproquo* which is not engineered by one character wishing to entrap another, but simply emerges out of the situation in which the characters find themselves. Because the clerk cannot see that the peasant is pointing at his food bin rather than the clerk hidden behind it when he says, "chieus là," and because the Englishman's version of French does not distinguish *anel* and *agnel*, the characters in both stories stumble into misunderstandings inherent in the linguistic-gesticulatory code. *Solas*, such as it is, depends on the audience being aware of some choice in articulating or interpreting a sign whose ambiguous nature is unknown to the protagonist. A distinguishing element in this group of tales is the absence of conflict stemming from some crucial misunderstanding deliberately created by one character in order to establish his superiority over another. No moral import can consequently be abstracted from such tales on the basis that success in the outcome of an intrigue implies endorsement of attitudes espoused by the trickster and condemnation of those espoused by the dupe. The character who suffers some misfortune

Any narrator could have turned such a tale into a moral one. The moral for *Le Clerc qui fu repris* could have easily been drawn as "don't apply to yourself before its necessary" *A gilous shal himself bigiled be.* Chaucer's Reeve makes his tale illustrate may thus be perceived as a victim of impersonal *mana.* If the audience feels superior to this victim in escaping the particular pitfall which constitutes the comic action, they nevertheless share his dependency on semiotic systems innately prone to generate confusions capable on other occasions of ensnaring them also.

If these two fabliaux are *risées*, so too must be *La Vielle qui oint la palme au chevalier.* This particular tale turns on an amphibology whereby the old woman of the title takes literally some advice intended metaphorically. Instead of offering a bribe to the knight whose provost has impounded her cows, she naively greases his hand with bacon fat. Although the story is introduced as "une fable por deliter," and despite the fact that the knight, once he has understood her simplicity, restores the old woman's cows without penalty, the author chooses to conclude with a passage of complaint against corrupt judges:

L'avanture de cest proverbe
Retrai por riches homes hautz
Qui plus sont desloiaus et faus;
Lor san et lor parole vandent,
A nul droiture n'entandent,
Chacuns à prandre s'abandone;
Povres n'a droit, se il ne done.

[*M,* 11: 1711–12; *MR,* 5: 157–59. Italics mine.]

[handwritten marginal notes:]
told on: the knight's provost is the one whose corruption (or overharsh...ness in interpreting the law) is exposed... right thro' his provost. Complaint against bailiffs... see Chaucer's Friar's tale.
But the "glose" and the "text" are often very tenuously related in the tales/homilies/anecdotes.

Clearly *La Vielle qui oint la palme au chevalier* is not primarily intended to make literal demonstration of judicial corruption, and the censure of dishonest and avaricious judges with which the author concludes is not morally justified by the behavior of the particular knight dispensing justice in this story. The author's concern is rather with *solas,* generated by the intervention of impersonal *mana* in its more mischievous form as it subverts the counsel given the old widow by her gossip.

A number of other fabliaux, the two versions of *La Male Honte* (Rychner, 2: 16–29), which contain passages of primarily political complaint, *Estula* (Johnston and Owen, pp. 6–9), *Le sot Chevalier,*[15] and three stories which utilize the same comic motif, *Les trois Boçus, Les quatre Prestres* (*MR,* 6: 42–45), and *Estormi,*[16] all belong to the same type. *Sentence* in *Les quatre Prestres* is confined to an appropriate proverb, *tieus ne peche qui encourt* (*M,* 1: 2034), which succinctly confirms the tale's association with other accounts of the manifestation of mischievous impersonal *mana. Les trois Boçus* contains only the passage of complaint quoted earlier. It may have been added in an effort to make morally more acceptable a story which casually portrays the death of a totally innocent victim. But the husband dies, in fact, not because he spent the profits from his usury to purchase a bride, but because his hump is so distinctive and unusual a feature that he is confused with the three hunchbacked minstrels accidentally killed at his house.

Stories which employ the motif of the operation of malign impersonal *mana* may be recognizable as *risées* on the basis that they appear without passages of explicit *sentence*. That *La Vielle qui oint la palme au chevalier* and *Les trois Boçus* contain passages of complaint does not, however, disqualify them as *risées* of this type. Passages of complaint in isolation from practical advice constitute a kind of lyric interlude which addresses concerns connected only tangentially with what has transpired within the narrative context. Such passages do not endorse the actions or attitudes of one character over those of a less favored fellow in a way which would permit abstracting any significant moral *sentence* from the opposition between them.

The author of *Estormi* loads the tale with a variety of different kinds of *sentence*, all but two passages ironic or misapplied. The tale's innate amorality is reflected in a comment by the husband, guilty of murdering three priests, on the unfortunate and demonically contrived death of the innocent fourth, "teus compere le forfet / Qui n'i a pas mort deservie" (ll. 586-87). The story ends with a passage of practical advice, to be tolerant of the slightly scandalous behavior of poorer family members who may in a moment of crisis turn out to be deliverers:

> Mes on ne doit pas, ce me samble,
> avoir por nule povreté,
> son petit parent en viuté,
> s'il n'est ou trahitres ou lerres;
> que, s'il est fols ou tremeleres,
> il s'en retret au chief de foiz.
>
> [620-25]

The single most important feature which protects this version of the story as entertainment, despite the desperate violence, is that the author, rather than attempting to make the fourth victim in some way responsible for his own death, trains attention instead on his unwitting assassin. This character is portrayed as an attractive rogue, much given to wine, women, and dicing. The practical advice is part of the process of rendering him as acceptable as possible. There are no morally significant oppositions to which the advice could be connected within the tale in such a way as to compromise its essentially recreational qualities.[17]

To the group of tales dependent on a pun or amphibology may be added, as further examples of stories intended primarily to amuse, those in which misunderstanding arises not from some ambiguity inherent in the semiotic code, but from the ineptness of those involved in its use. The confusion-mongers are either naive recipients of a message, children or animals, who fail to interpret the code correctly because inadequately versed in its use, or adults incapable of dealing effectively with a language not their own. Of this type are *Le Prestre et le mouton (MR, 6: 50), Le Prestre qui dist la passion (MR, 5: 80–81)*, two versions of *Celui qui bota la pierre* (Rychner, 2: 28–31), and two versions of *Le Prestre qui menga les meures* (Rychner, 2: 149–51). All conclude with passages of practical advice, addressed in some instances to the malefactors and apparently directed towards making them more proficient in their villainy. However, it is clear that the advice is not intended seriously, and it does not interfere with the generally good-natured fun at the wrongdoers' expense. *Le Prestre et le mouton* ends, "Il se fet bon de tot garder," while both versions of *Celui qui bota la pierre* urge that, "L'en se gart do petit oil." *Le Prestre qui fu mis au lardier (MR, 2: 24–30)* has the same advice, "Du petit ueil se fait bon guetier," and it belongs in spirit with this group, although it lacks the motif of a breakdown in communication. Both versions of *Le Prestre qui menga les meures* stress that, "Cil ne fait mie savoir / Qui tot son pensé dit et conte." *Le Prestre qui dist la passion* has a summary statement in which the banality of the sentiments expressed vies with the exaggerated insistence on their veracity:

> Par cest flabel vos vueil monstrer
> Que, par le foi que doi saint Pol,
> Ausinc bien chiet il à un fol
> De folie dire et d'outraige
> Con il feroit à un bien saige
> D'un grant sens, se il le disoit:
> Fous est qui de ce me mescroit.
>
> [MR, 5: 82]

Apparently the nature of the story, the motif of misapprehension on which the comic plot turns, identifies it unmistakably as a *risée* in a way understood and respected by fabliau-authors.

In all seven of these fabliaux, the character who misunderstands some signal, or is the ultimate victim of someone else's misunderstanding, is invariably a parish priest, but there is little apart from this fact to support the idea that these are all instances of anticlerical satire. Except for *Le Prestre et le mouton*, where the sheep kills the priest (his dead body turns up in *Le Segretaig* 4), he extricates himself comparatively lightly, even when taken in adultery; he pays a fine to the husband in *Le Prestre qui fu mis au lardier*, and escapes scot-free in *Celui qui bota la pierre*. There seems to be very little difference between the priests of *Le Prestre qui dist la passion* and *Le Prestre qui menga les meures*, who are guilty at worst of mild and momentary surrender to sloth or gluttony, and the priests in the other five fabliaux, who are guilty at best of committing adultery with their parishioners' wives. Sin and expiation are not the issue here, but rather a debilitating failure to function effectively in the difficult circumstances which beset their relatively debauched lives, so that they behave in a careless or clumsy fashion to their own undoing. One priest cannot keep his balance on the back of a horse; another's copulating on the kitchen floor mimics so approximately a ram's challenge to lock horns that he is butted to death. One priest is incapable of reading Latin to conduct divine service, while another inopportunely speaks Latin while being hauled away in a shoemaker's bacon bin. In order to facilitate sexual negotiations, the complacent priest of *Celui qui bota la pierre* coins a nonce phrase which, being taken literally by a carelessly ignored infant present at these proceedings, serves later to expose the priest's adultery.[18]

The simplest way to account for the role played by parish priests in these fabliaux would be to accept the misfortunes which befall them as punishment for dereliction of their pastoral duties, or hypocritical violation of the Christian principles which they preach and should be expected to practice. No doubt some of the animus directed at the *prestre*-figure in the fabliaux can validly be traced to this source. But such an explanation does not ring entirely true. One problem with it is that by these standards there are some startling disparities between the offense committed and the punishment suffered. If accepted, the explanation would consequently contribute to creating exactly the sense of fabliau morality as capricious and arbitrary which it is one purpose of this paper to combat. Despite the great divergency between the degree of their moral offense conventionally defined, all the priests exhibit a similar failure in *praxis*, a particularly pernicious failure by the standards of a literary genre in which opportunism is a major virtue, and practical advice the most common form of admonition. Priests in the fabliaux are the most numerous and most intrusive representatives of a doctrine of submission to the will of an anthropomorphically conceived supernatural power. This religious attitude is at odds with both an earlier belief in sympathetic magic and a later belief in science. Both the latter, because they promise control of the natural world, hold more attraction than religion for the doctrinaire pragmatist. Magic and the supernatural, as often noted, figure surprisingly little in the fabliaux. But science, particularly practical exploitation of the principles of epistemology, is all pervasive. There are very few admirable priests in the fabliaux. The rest may be condemned less on account of their shortcomings by conventional moral standards than for being what they are by virtue of their profession—representatives of religious attitudes which at a perhaps subconscious level the composers or purveyors of fabliaux found unsympathetic.

A second group, tentatively identifiable as *risées* because represented by more than one example among fabliaux with no passage of explicit *sentence*, is comprised of *Le Prestre qui ot mere a force* (Reid, pp. 14-18), and *Le Vilain Mire* (Johnston and Owen, pp. 56-66). To these may be added *Le povre Mercier* (Johnston and Owen, pp. 44-50), which has no *sentence* other than an authorial prologue testifying to the salutary effects of listening to entertaining stories:

> Elle doit bien estre escoutee,
> Car par biaus diz est oblïee
> Maintes foiz [i]re et cussançons
> Et abasies granz tançons,
> Car, quant aucuns dit les risees,
> Les fors tançons sont obliees.
>
> [5-10]

In all three of these works the characters whose *mana* puts them in control of events manage to confront their opponents with a quasi-choice, so loaded that the victim must opt for the alternative favoring the trickster. In *Le povre Mercier* a monk has to choose between recompensing a merchant for the loss of his horse or denying God. In *Le Prestre qui ot mere a force* a priest must acknowledge a stranger as his mother, and assume responsibility for her well-being, or face suspension. Trials, one civil and one ecclesiastic, figure as climactic scenes in both these stories, and are a feature of the type. *Le Vilain Mire* is considerably more episodic, and lacks the trial scene climax, but its place in the group is confirmed by the fact that it employs the "quasi-choice" motif twice, once in connection with the peasant himself, who is several times required to admit to an expertise in medicine which he does not possess or face a beating, and once when he offers the sick who have been committed to him for treatment the choice of acknowledging themselves cured or being burned alive.

The motif, complete with secular court scene, also appears in *La Vielle Truande*, which has already been noted as sharing an interest in the marginally criminal activities of low-life types. Here an aging prostitute engineers a young man into the situation where he must either have intercourse with her or acknowledge her as his mother and provide appropriately for her needs.

Throughout this group of tales characters suddenly and unexpectedly find themselves in situations from which no outcome totally free of adversity is possible. The implications of this view of the likely nature of experience are encapsulated in the summary statement of *La Vielle Truande*:

> Por çou vous di en la parfin:
> Teus cuide avoir le cuer mout fin
> Et mout repoint, n'est pas mençoigne,
> Qui set mout peu à le besoigne.
>
> [*MR*, 5: 178]

The trickster figures in these fabliaux exhibit that ability to force favorable solutions from crises which I have associated with possession of personal *mana*. With the exception of the mock-physician in *Le Vilain Mire*, however, whose abused wife is responsible for his initial dilemma, the dupes have not offended within the context of the tale. They are frequently total strangers to those who snatch the opportunity to coerce them into self-damaging decisions. Like the characters in the preceding group of tales, they may therefore see themselves as victimized by impersonal *mana*, for which the tricksters who momentarily and disconcertingly intervene in their lives act merely as material agents.

The motif appears in two other fabliaux which differ from the foregoing stories in that the person forced to choose between unpleasant alternatives *has* offended within the context of the tale, and the quasi-choice serves to absolve the character against whom the offense was committed from further persecution. Both fabliaux again conclude with a climactic court scene where the choice, in judgment-of-Solomon fashion, resolves the issue at trial in the defendant's favor. In *La Couille noire* (*MR*, 6: 90–94) a wife who has complained of her husband before an ecclesiastic court is tricked into making an overly emphatic denial of a counter charge he brings against her. In so doing she imprudently admits to some insanitary habits of personal hygiene, and her admission serves to exculpate her husband. Both charges promote some grotesque comedy stemming from blazoned vulgarity. In *Le Preudome qui rescolt son compere de noier* (Johnston and Owen, pp. 1–3), a man rescued from drowning brings suit against his rescuer because in the course of the rescue he lost an eye. The court, on the advice of a *fol*, offers him the chance of being returned to the sea, on the promise that, if he can save himself from drowning, he will be awarded compensation for his injury. He opts to abandon his plea.

In both these fabliaux the exercise of *mana* resolves an opposition between characters whom the narrative has already differentiated morally. The shift away from pure entertainment brought about by the creation of an implicit contextual moral scheme is registered by the nature of the explicit moral commentary. *Le Preudome qui rescolt son compere de noier* concludes with the following *moralitas*:

> Por ce vos di tot en apert
> Que son tens pert qui felon sert.
> Raembez de forches larron,
> Quant il a fait sa mesprison,
> Jamés jor ne vos amera.
>
> . . . .
> Ja mauvais hom ne savra gré
> A mauvais, si li fait bonté:
> Tot oublie, riens ne l'en est,
> Ençois seroit volentiers prest
> De faire li mal et anui,
> S'il venoit au desus de lui.
>
> [67-78]

Practical advice not to waste one's time on evildoers is vindicated by the passage of complaint which describes them as compulsive ingrates. This combination of complaint and practical advice is especially typical of fabliau *sentence*, moral censure in the form of complaint serving to provide the background information necessary to facilitate some purely expedient choice.

La Couille noire will serve to introduce a third group of fabliaux with which it has much in common, and which are also clearly identifiable as *risées*. They are either stories which exemplify Nykrog's idea of "franche et naive pornographie" (p. 216), or they are scatalogical. They aim to do biologically what such stories as *Boivin de Provins, Barat et Haimet,* and associated tales (see footnote 17) aimed to do socially— fascinate by describing outrageous behavior in a contrivedly amoral context. Stories of this type frequently exploit the unreal worlds of dream or supernatural grotesquery in some fantastical way. Among the twenty-five fabliaux entirely without any passages of *sentence*, this group is represented by *L'Anel qui faisoit les . . . grans et roides* (*MR*, 3: 51-53), *Le Sohait desvez* (*MR*, 5: 184-91), and one version of *Les trois Dames qui troverent un vit* (*MR*, 4: 128-32). With them belong both versions of *Le Chevalier qui fist les cons parler*, each of which begins with a statement on fabliaux as pure entertainment. That from Nykrog's version 2 has been quoted earlier. Version 1 begins as follows:

Neïs a ceus qui sunt pleins d'ire
Quant il sent bons fableaus lire,
Si lor feit il grant alejance
Et oublier duel et pesance
Et mavestie et pensement.

[Rychner, 2: 38]

La Crote (*MR*, 3: 46-48), which has as *sentence* only a brief statement on the advantages of brevity for an author intent on amusing his
audience, also belongs here. A peasant in this tale chews excrement to
win a bet, while another in *Le Vilain de Farbu* (*MR*, 4: 82-86) spits in his
soup to test its temperature. The bridegroom in *Gauteron et Marion*
(MR, 3: 49-50) believes his bride's vulgarly fanciful explanation for the
loss of her maidenhead, and voices a mock curse on the subject, the only
piece of pseudo-*sentence* in the story. *La Grue* and *Le Heron* (Rychner,
2: 9-14) are analogous stories combining humor associated with bizarre
sexual episodes (here the reification of the sex act, which can be paid and
repaid in barter) and humor associated with gluttony. *La Grue* has only a
concluding proverb commenting on the duenna's ineffectiveness as guardian of a young girl, *La male garde pest lo leu* (*M*, 1: 1207). *Le Heron* expresses more extensive *sentence* in two monologues (ll. 80-86 and
169-72) by the duenna character, who, by offering herself practical advice, sustains a running commentary on the action. Between these two
soliloquies she cites a proverb to the effect that, *Grant desturbir / Avint*
entre buche e cuilir (*M*, 689). This proverb surfaces again as the only explicit *sentence* in *L'Oue au chapelain* (*MR*, 6: 46-49), a tale which is also
meant as a *risée*. Its plot involves a fantasy featuring gluttony alone,
rather than sex or sex and gluttony together.

The final group of stories to be identified as *risées* on the basis of the
combined evidence that they appear without *sentence* or appear only
with an authorial statement about their value as entertainments I have
discussed elsewhere under the generic title of *jugements*.[19] In the first
category fall *Le Jugement des cons* (*MR*, 5: 109-14), *Jugement* [frag-
ment] (*MR*, 6: 154-55), and the second version of *Les trois Dames qui*
troverent l'anel (*MR*, 6: 1-7). The second category is represented by *Les*
trois Chanoinesses de Couloigne (*MR*, 3: 137-44) which has an opening
statement associating the work with literature for recreation and identifying it as a *truffe*:

Il n'a homme de si à Sens,
S'adès vouloit parler de sens,
C'on n'en prisast mains son savoir
Qu'on fait sotie et sens savoir.

Qui set aucunes truffes dire,
Ou parlé n'ait de duel ne d'ire,
Puis que de mesdit n'i a point,
Maintes foiz vient aussi à point
A l'oïr que fait uns sarmons.

[*MR*, 3: 137]

All depend for their humor on a climactically outrageous series of statements, jokes, or actions, all with a sexual bias, by the three women involved in each story. The author's attitude is clearly non-judgmental, in
that a standard feature is the concluding appeal to the audience to
decide, or to help the poet decide, which of the participants in what
amounts to a straightforward contest in bawdry should be awarded the
prize. The framework of competition suggests that these fabliaux as a
group are games, with no significance beyond provoking laughter.[20]

III

Of the remaining fabliaux with zero *sentence*, two groups clearly
break the rule that such fabliaux are necessarily *risées*. Their distinction
from other fabliaux without *sentence* is corroborated by the fact that
none are prefaced with statements extolling the entertainment value of
the genre.

The first of these groups is represented by *Le Vallet qui d'aise a
malaise se met* (*MR*, 2: 157-70) and *Les trois Dames de Paris* (*MR*, 3:
145-55). Both tales are remarkable for the extreme naturalism of their
style. Neither has a plot which sets characters in opposition to one
another so as to allow for the triumph of the more inventive, quick-witted,
and opportunistic, and both consequently lack the element of *solas*
associated with witnessing these qualities in action. They are essentially
tableaux de moeurs, or 'portraits,' whose affiliation with the Theophrastan
tradition could be indicted by such titles as "the poor but impetuous lover,"
or "drunken wives." Unlike the typical fabliau narrative, which turns on a
comic climax occupying only a few minutes of real time, the typical
tableau de moeurs develops in a steady, cumulative way over a comparatively extended period. There are no surprising reversals or
discoveries. On the contrary, the portrait character embarks enthusiasti-
cally on a course of action which the audience, and occasionally another
character in the story, perceive from the start as foolhardy and inevitably
self-defeating. The tale ends when the gap between the characters' resolutions or expectations and their actual conduct or experiences is revealed in

a climactic exhibition of folly, or grows so great as finally to make the protagonists themselves aware that their earlier attitudes were self-delusory.

The conduct of the portrait characters, conceived as exemplary of
attitudes or patterns of behavior which the author finds misguided or objectionable, is judged according to such conventionally bourgeois standards as financial responsibility or social decorum. If divergence from
these standards is shown inevitably to produce distressing consequences,
the *sentence* of these tales becomes perfectly clear, even when, as is the
case with the two tales under discussion, these standards are not evoked
explicitly in the stories themselves.[21]

Since a lack of self-knowledge is the issue in these fabliaux, conflict occurs primarily within the individual psyche, although when the
protagonists undergo some psychological growth the sensible attitudes
they are finally brought to embrace may have been articulated earlier by
wiser, more experienced characters in the story.

Philippe de Beaumanoir's *Fole Larguesce* (*MR*, 6: 53–67), which incorporates over a hundred lines of proverbs, practical advice, moral exhortation, and complaint[22] is cast essentially in this same mold. "The rashly
generous wife" would serve equally well as a title, and would register the
portrait qualities of the work. That we are engaged with moral values
defined independently of the tale which illustrates their significance is evident from the practice (observed earlier in illustrating moral exhortation as
a distinctive type of *sentence* from *La Dame escoillée*) of beginning as well
as ending a tale with a passage of moral exhortation:

> De fole larguesce casti
> Tous ciaus qui en sont aati;
> Car nus ne la puet maintenir
> Qui en puist à bon cief venir.
> Je ne blasme pas le donner
> Ne les bontés guerredoner;
> Mais il convient maniere et sens
> De soi tenir ou droit assens,
> Par coi on puist le gré avoir
> Des bons sans perdre son avoir.
>
> [*MR*, 6: 53]

When these same sentiments are reiterated in a concluding *moralitas*
they are combined with prayers and a benediction. As in the passages
quoted from *La Dame escoillée*, vice (prodigality, domineering self-
assertiveness) is defined by contrast with a corresponding virtue
(generosity, obedient self-effacement), and discussion of this virtue
forms part of the moralizing passage.

Also belonging with this group is Gautier le Leu's *La Veuve* (Livingston, pp. 159–83), a sensitively detailed portrait of a widow who drifts from the inertia of grief to a frenzied search for sexual fulfilment. There is no final moment of enlightenment for the widow, but only the long drawn-out demonstration of the erroneousness of her initial supposition that she could deny her nature by resigning herself to a life of chaste widowhood. Gautier le Leu's summary statement, the one passage of explicit and readily identifiable *sentence* in the work, is probably best understood as practical advice to husbands to be tolerant of their wives:

> Vos qui les dames despités
> Sovigne vos de ces pités
> Que vos sentés a icele eure
> Qu'ele est desos et vos deseure.
>
> . . . .
>
> Segnor qui estes auduïn
> Et gilleeur et herluïn,
> Ne soiés de rien en esmai:
> Li auduïn ont mellor mai
> Q'aient li felon conbatant,
> Qui les noisses vont esbatant.
> Gautiers li Leus dist en la fin
> Que cil n'a mie le cuer fin
> Qui sa mollier destraint ne cosse,
> Ne qui li demands autre cosse
> Que ses bones voisines font.

[563–89]

As in *Le Vallet qui d'aise a malaise se met* and *Les trois Dames de Paris*, there is no passage of explicit complaint in *La Veuve*. Its place in all three fabliaux is taken by the recital of a series of impetuous and imprudent actions whose self-deluding nature, apparent to the audience early in the story, is confirmed by the distressing circumstances to which they ultimately reduce the protagonists. The actions are clearly regarded as exemplary of class-related aberrations—youthful folly and feminine vanity, gluttony, or fickleness—which form the subject of passages of complaint in other contexts. But narrative diffusion of the materials of complaint ambiguates the author's stance in *La Veuve*. His account of the widow's behavior may be neutrally reportorial, or weighted to create a pejorative impression. The resultant ambiguity extends to the practical advice to husbands. Should they seek to control their wives' behavior or submit to tolerating it with as much grace as they can muster, and how is such a decision affected by the fact that individual women cannot be expected to behave differently from other members of their sex? The summary passage has as complex a relationship to the antifeminist tradition as the envoy to Geoffrey Chaucer's *Clerk's Tale*.[23]

None of the narratives in the four fabliaux so far identified as *tableaux de moeurs* exhibits the workings of *mana* in the operation of signs, and none of them consequently promotes the associated sense of *solas*. The pleasure derived from these tales does not stem from sudden and surprising reversals and discoveries, but rather from witnessing how a psychologically determined course of action brings the protagonist into conflict with a previously denied reality. The audience is equipped to anticipate the end result and derives gratification from seeing the aberrant behavior of the portrait character exposed by comparison with the conventionally sanctioned standards to which it may ultimately be forced to conform.

How the nature of *solas* in this group differs from that in the groups earlier identified as *risées* may be illustrated by a fabliau which shares some qualities with both groups, Jean Bodel's *Le Couvoiteus et l'Envieus* (Reid, pp. 5-7). The author begins by announcing that he plans to moralize his song, "Seignor, aprés le fabloier,/Me vueil a voir dire ap[l]oier" (ll. 1-2). The moral nature of the tale is evident from the title, which identifies the vices to be dealt with (cf., *Fole Larguesce*), and indicates that they will be treated as "portraits," so that a fully-developed personification allegory emerges. True to the moral nature of other portrait fabliaux, but in contrast to their predominantly naturalistic style, the vices exposed through the narrative are also the subject of an intercalated passage of complaint:

> Que covoitise si est tiex
> Qu'ele fait maint home honteus;
> covoitise preste a usures
> Et fait recouper les mesures
> Por covitié d'avoir plus aise.
> Envie si est plus malvaise,
> Qu'ele va tot le mont coitant.
>
> [19-25]

Exposure of the titular vices in *Le Couvoiteus et l'Envieus* is not accomplished through the development of a naturalistic action which gradually confronts illusion with the accumulated evidence of a contrary reality. Precipitation of a denouement which brings both characters to grief is controlled by Saint Martin's offer of a double benefit to the character refraining from making a wish. Such a stipulation prohibits the covetous man from wishing at all, and eventually prompts his envious companion into wishing for himself the loss of one eye, so that by the terms of the covenant his companion will lose both. The personifications of deadly sin suffer specifically because the vices which are all we know of their natures bind them to predictable responses to Saint Martin's offer. The poet therefore follows the same psychologically determined progression from optimistic illusion to cruel reality as occurs in the four fabliaux just discussed, and the story is as conventionally moral. But because Saint Martin's proposal is couched in precisely the terms necessary to transform a free gift into self-willed punishment, it exhibits that capacity to subvert an expected sequence of cause-and-effect relationships which has earlier been identified as a characteristic source of *solas* in the fabliaux. Thus in *Le Couvoiteus et l'Envieus* such *solas* perfectly complements a quite orthodox Christian moral *sentence*.

Conventional moral doctrine and *solas* are similarly interdependent and mutually supportive in the second group of fabliaux for which lack of explicit *sentence* is not proof that we are necessarily dealing with some form of *risée*. This group is represented by *L'Evesque qui beneï le con* (*MR*, 3: 178-85) and *Le Bouchier d'Abeville* (DuVal and Eichmann, pp. 13-28). Its distinctive feature is a form so precisely definitive of the moral values presupposed in its narrative development as to render authorial commentary and interpretation largely superfluous.[24]

L'Evesque qui beneï le con, as the title indicates, has much in common with those tales already discussed which exploit some kind of sexual grotesquery. But since the bishop is tricked into performing the bizarre ritual in order to expose his hypocrisy, the story is also brought into association with such other fabliaux as *La Nonette*, the second version of which[25] contains as *sentence* only the concluding couplet, "Pour ce, enfans, trop ne blamez / Ce dont, espoir, blamé, serez." Version 1, like *Le Lai d'Aristote* (another example of hypocrisy exposed), exhibits some concern with courtly love doctrine, and contains a passage of philosophic *sentence* on love articulated by a chorus of nuns, but it too concludes with an authorial statement stressing the roundedness of the form:

> Se cils ne ment qui fist che dit,
> On se doit mout bien aviser
> S'il a sour lui que deviser,
> ains que sour autrui on mesdie.

> [*MR*, 6: 269]

All three fabliaux deal with an affair, between a priest and his concubine or between young people in love, prohibited by an authoritative older figure whose effectiveness as a blocking character is destroyed when he or she is exposed as a *senex* or *matrona amans*. They are closely linked by content as well as form, and push towards a comedic resolution in the

happy reunion of temporarily parted lovers, or in the restoration free
from censure of an illicit and threatened ménage. Aristotle, in Henri
d'Andeli's fabliau, muddies the moral waters by suggesting, after he has
been revealed as a hypocrite, that the validity of his professed beliefs
might in fact be confirmed by his own failure to adhere to them. In
L'Evesque qui beneï le con and *La Nonette* exposure of hypocrisy serves
to define the offense, and so a very precise correlation is assumed to exist
between the tale's parts, the offense inviting and mandating the nature of
its own exposure and punishment.

  Le Bouchier d'Abeville belongs with an associated group of tales in
which typically the vicious character offends in such a way as to allow his
victim to turn the tables on him. Thus in *Le Bouchier d'Abeville* an ar-
rogantly self-assured and avaricious priest, who is living a debauched life
of luxury with his concubine, is cheated, robbed, and "cuckolded" by the
resourceful artisan he had the temerity to treat with contempt. The same
form appears again in *Le Prestre et le Chevalier*, which also lacks any
final authorial commentary on the tale's significance. However, the
values established by the form are articulated by the characters. The
priest's mistress observes, "Ne doit boire / Le vin malveis qui tel le brasse?
(*M*, 1: 1966), and earlier the priest himself, on discovering that his plan
to cheat the knight is going awry, makes a similar statement incorporating a related proverb:

> "Hélas!" fait il, "comme gaaingne
> Fait chix qui autrui veut dechoivre;
> *Tex cuide sour autruï boire*
> *Qui boit sour li, sour sa compaingne* [*M*, 2340]
> Et trueve bien après gaaingne
> Aussi com j'ai fait à le moie."
>
> [*MR*, 2: 74. Italics mine.]

The reversal whereby the knight turns the tables on the priest comes
about because he insists on a literal interpretation of one clause of an
agreement made between them after the priest has literally interpreted
another to his own advantage.

  In *Le Vilain au buffet* (*MR*, 3: 199–208) and *La Plantez* (*MR*, 3:
170–74), characters who are victimized by some sophistical play on
words or some cynical explanation for boorish behavior simply pursue
the same sophistry with surprisingly unfortunate consequences for those
who introduced it. A seneschal slaps the face of a peasant, invited to a
banquet and looking for somewhere to sit, with the remark that he
should squat on that *buffet*. The slap is later returned with interest by the
peasant, who makes it a rule always to repay what he has borrowed. An

innkeeper excuses his carelessness in spilling wine from a mug by maintaining that spilt wine presages good luck. After his offended customer
has pulled the stopper on his wine cask in the cellar, the hosteler is told
that he can hardly avoid having some stupendous stroke of good fortune
on the basis of his own earlier argument. In *Charlot le Juif qui chia en un
pel de lievre* (*MR*, 3: 222–26) the minstrel Charlot revenges himself on
the squire who paid for the minstrel's services with a hare's skin he sophistically claimed cost five pounds. The revenge takes the form of the
scatalogical trick described in the title, whereby the squire is enticed into
defiling himself. After an eleven-line introduction warning against playing
tricks on minstrels, who know how to defend themselves and are seldom
outdone in duplicity, the author concludes with another quip appropriate
to this type of literary form: "Rutebuez dit, bien m'en souvient: / Qui
barat quiert, baraz li vient."

The vicious characters in two of these tales, *Le Bouchier d'Abeville*
and *Le Prestre et le chevalier*, are parish priests. The stories in question
might readily be categorized therefore as belonging to the general body
of anticlerical satire. But even though designation of the malefactors as
priests clearly has some significance in this respect, its importance should
not be exaggerated. Nothing in the form of the stories requires this particular distribution of roles. In other stories in this group a seneschal (*Le
Vilain au buffet*), an innkeeper (*La Plantez*), and a squire (*Charlot le
Juif*) fill the priest's role without mandating any significant modifica-
tions of the form. That social status is in free variation in this schema is
apparent from the fabliau *Jouglet*, in which a minstrel suffers the same
scatalogical humiliation as the squire in *Charlot le Juif*. The minstrel is
on two occasions the subject of commentaries pointing out the appropriateness of his punishment in terms similar to those used in Rutebeuf's
fabliau, once by a character, "Qui merde brasse, merde boive," and once
by the author in a summary statement:

> Segnors, ce dist COLINS MALÈS
> *Teus cuide cunchier autrui,*
> *Qui tout avant cunchie lui.*
>
> [*MR*, 4: 127. Italics mine.]

Common to all these stories is the circumstance that they bring
together, as guest and host, two characters previously unknown to one
another. If the narrative action begins with a *tabula rasa*, it moves quickly
to establish a moral framework, since sojourn of one character at
another's establishment is governed by age-old and familiar customs.
The host must not abuse his authority as master of his house to exploit or

coerce his guest, and the guest must not abuse his host's hospitality. Whatever happens, the guest is expected to depart within a matter of hours, thus concluding all commerce with his host. A more neatly circumscribed action, or one more conducive to ludic manipulation of an arbitrarily segmented sequence of causally linked incidents, would be hard to imagine. The moral universe projected by this particular motif is strikingly simple.

In each instance, one of the two characters in the guest-host relationship (the host in all but *Jouglet*) seizes the initiative in attempting to defraud or humiliate the other, and this action suffices to identify him as the villain of the piece.[26] Since the ultimate victor in the quarrel which erupts between guest and host is responding to a prior offense by his opponent, the outcome accords with the requirements of conventional morality in satisfying a sense of justice. What is achieved must be acknowledged, however, as the rough justice of vengeance. In the course of the tales just discussed the sympathetic avenger-figures are responsible for rape, robbery, and numerous and varied acts of physical violence. In each instance, the putative victim is able to intervene in the causal sequence of events which appears logically certain, within the necessarily narrow temporal and spatial confines of the action, to bring him to misfortune, and to divert this sequence in such a way that the misfortune recoils on the malefactor. Although implicit fabliau morality is frequently at variance with conventional moral standards, and these standards are often ignored or violated in the intrigues which serve to generate *solas*, fabliaux do not by any means convey an impression of total moral chaos. Nowhere is the gratuitously aggressive exercise of *mana* for the sake of bullying an innocent victim or cheating him out of material goods allowed to succeed and to escape punishment.

The moral issues are more complex and enigmatic in a small group of fabliaux consisting of *Le Prestre crucefié*, Gautier le Leu's close analogue to this piece, *Le Prestre teint* (Livingston, pp. 255–69), and *L'Enfant qui fu remis au soleil* (MR, 1: 162–67). In *Le Prestre crucefié* a priest posing as a crucifix *corpus* to avoid detection and punishment for adultery is castrated by the wood-carver husband on the pretext of amending a flawed product of his craft. The priest in *Le Prestre teint* is threatened with and narrowly escapes a similar fate. An unfaithful wife in *L'Enfant qui fu remis au soleil* explains the presence of her illegitimate son by telling her husband that she conceived from swallowing a snowflake, and he later accounts for the boy's disappearance by claiming that he melted. Unfortunately for the reprobate wives, they find themselves dealing with

Snowchild Melting in the Sun
Janet Anderson

husbands whose ability to manipulate a signified reality in order to seize control of the present moment exceeds their own. Not only can these husbands accomplish their original purpose of avenging themselves on those who have profaned their marriage beds, but they do so while accommodating for the purpose of vengeance the very artifice by which those who have offended against them hoped to escape retribution. An apparently complex moral situation is suddenly and serendipitously resolved when the malefactors unwittingly create the ideal opportunity for their own punishment, by means which have no automatic moral sanction in real life terms, but which within the context of the tale are unchallengeable because logically consistent with their own fabrications to cover guilt.

In such tales as *Le Prestre crucefié* and *L'Enfant qui fu remis au soleil* there is a logical paradigm, based on the axiom that any false premise implies all other premises. Translated into narrative terms, this paradigm accounts for the pattern of crime and punishment constituting the tale's moral *sentence*, and the intervention in a contingent chain of events constituting the source of its *solas*. The association of the two parts, plot and counterplot, is so close that together they form an autonomous entity which effectively isolates itself from the flux of space-time experience. This independence is manifest in the absence of any moral exhortation, or any passages of complaint, since no constants need to be imported from the outside world of moral valuation or material circumstance to establish meaning. *Le Prestre crucefié* concludes with a passage of thinly veiled practical advice to husbands to deal with lecherous priests as the priest was dealt with in this tale:

> Cest example nous monstre bien
> Que nus prestres por nul rien
> Ne devroit autrui fame amer,
> N'entor li venir ne aler,
> Quiconques fust en calengage,
> Que il n'i lest ou coille ou gage.
>   [*MR*, 1: 197]

More typically, the moral significance of *L'Enfant qui fu remis au soleil* is allowed to speak for itself through the narrative, except for the final couplet incorporating a version of the proverb which has appeared in *Le Prestre et le chevalier* and *Jouglet*: "Bien l'en avint qu'avenir dut / Qu'ele brassa ce qu'ele but." It serves simply to emphasize the tale's "biter-bit" narrative structure.

The problem morally is that the wives who attempt ingeniously to explain away the apparently incontrovertible evidence of a prior infidelity, or to conceal from a husband the presence of a lover in the house (it is at the wife's suggestion that the priest in *Le Prestre crucefié* adopts his disguise) are exercising *mana* for purposes which in other fabliaux, *Le Pliçon* for example, are accorded the moral endorsement implied by their successful execution. Fabliau *mana*, by discovering the hidden possibility for alternative significance in apparently unequivocal signs, or the unexpected contrary instance to a generally observed rule, normally promotes a sense of freedom, particularly freedom from the exigencies of a rigorous moral system. To find *mana* used to enforce such a system through the punishment of those who have violated its dictates is consequently discomfiting. Admittedly, the wives are not the immediate victims of the husbands' vengeance. But because the wife initiated the sophistry which is assimilated into the husband's triumph, the castration of her lover or the selling into slavery of her son seems to be directed against her, and to resolve a fundamentally marital conflict. The wives who act to protect their sexual freedom are not such vicious figures, however, as the male rogues discussed earlier who cheat for the sake of material gain or to assert their own superiority. *Mana* itself is a morally neutral instrument of power and may as readily be invoked to enforce conformity with conventional moral standards as to evade them, but implicit fabliau morality generally favors the exercise of *mana* by wives for the latter purpose. A presentation which runs counter to such practice creates the impression that in these fabliaux the very perfection of the form is distorting a generally more balanced fabliau morality, and moving it in the direction of the rigorously enforced male dominance exemplified by the satirically antifeminist fabliaux discussed next. I shall return to the issue of antifeminism, marital conflict, and fabliau morality in the following and final segment.

IV

The immediately preceding tales, which generally balance *sentence* and *solas* in a structure creating the conditions for their mutual complementarity, may be contrasted with certain fabliaux in which *sentence* takes sufficient precedence over any concern with the kind of *solas* I have been discussing as to inform them with the quality of anticlerical or antifeminist satires.

Anticlerical moral sentiment of this sort may be found in Gautier le Leu's *Connebert* (Livingston, pp. 219–32), which ends, typically, with a curse:

Car fussent or si atorné
Tuit li prestre de mere ne
Qui sacremant de mariage
Tornent a honte et a putage!

[303–06]

By comparison with the husbands in *Le Prestre crucefié* or *L'Enfant qui fu remis au soleil*, whose only decision concerning the exacting of vengeance is not to neglect the opportunity presented to them, the husband in this story is shown agonizing over the dilemma of how to avenge his honor without endangering himself for assaulting a member of the priesthood. He solves the problem by surprising the priest with his wife, dragging him off, and nailing him by the scrotum to the anvil block in his forge, which he then puts to the torch. To save his life the priest is obliged to mutilate himself with a razor the smith has left available for that purpose.

The outcome, castration of a lecherous priest by the husband of one of his amorous conquests, is the same in *Connebert* as in *Le Prestre crucefié*, but there is a considerable difference in the spirit of the two works. The clerical status of the lover in *Le Prestre crucefié* is incidental in the sense that any seducer trapped as the priest was trapped could plausibly have adopted the same disguise, and neither the moral significance of the story nor its appeal as a neatly fashioned construct would have been affected by the change to a nonclerical protagonist. In *Connebert*, by contrast, it is not the priest who inadvertently suggests the nature of his own punishment, but the vengeful smith who cunningly machinates to have the priest mutilate himself, so as to be sophistically guiltless of a dangerous offense. Rather than a general condemnation of adultery illustrated in the person of an errant parish priest, *Connebert* aims its satiric barbs specifically at those not simply guilty of adultery, but guilty of blatantly exploiting the assumed protection of their privileged clerical status. It is the calculated abuse of power, social rather than sexual vice, which prompts the bitter animus evident in this story, and only the clerical status of the victim logically accounts for the precise form of the vengeance exacted. While the concatenation of incidents in *Le Prestre crucefié* diffuses conventional moral concern with the fitting of punishment to crime by structurally transcending the issue, *Connebert* makes a focal point of justifying the aspiringly "heroic" secular morality of the betrayed and vengeful husband.[27]

What is true of anticlerical satire in the fabliaux holds good for antifeminist satire also. A case in point is provided by *La Dame escoillée*, whose opening and closing passages of moral exhortation have already been quoted. In the course of the action the son-in-law and mutilator of the wife guilty of lording it over her husband articulates sentiments clearly echoing those of his author-creator: "Molt a qui bone feme prent, / Qui male prent, ne prent nient," and "Feme ne fait vilté greignor / Que de vill tenir son seignor." Although, with the exception of the opening and closing passages of authorial commentary, *La Dame escoillée* makes no departures from the narrative mode, the author twice refers to the work as an *essanple*, and exceptionally the structure of this fabliau reflects its exemplary function, in that it progresses through a series of episodes which show the son-in-law killing two greyhounds for failing to catch a hare, killing his horse for stumbling, mutilating his cook for disobeying instructions on seasoning a meal, and beating his wife senseless for countermanding his orders to this unfortunate servant, before reaching the climactic "castration" of the willful older woman.

There is an elaborate feigning in this scene that a preconcealed pair of bull's testicles have been removed from the mother-in-law's body, thereby purging her of the "mannishness" which corrupted her being. A typical fabliau plot features an initial interference with reality by some malefactor which provides an opportunity for retaliation by the injured party such as to appear to absolve his action from judgment by conventional moral standards. By that criterion, this mock castration offers us a pseudo-fabliau episode, since contingent linking of crime and punishment emanates only from the minds of the woman's persecutors, who posit for what they conceive as objectionable behavior a physical cause appropriate to excuse their mock-surgical cure.

The maniacal cruelty of this sadistic hoax is for the purpose of dissuading a married daughter from following in the footsteps of her mother, whose role as a model for rebellion against patriarchal authority it finally destroys. The satiric norm recommended, absolute and unquestioning obedience to masculine authority, is certainly articulated with great clarity. What makes the satire so devastatingly strident is that the fake castration episode attempts to confect some witty correspondence, imbued with a sense of rightness and inevitability, between transgression and punishment. This works only if the male protagonists, the author, and the audience he supposes himself to be addressing share the view that a woman who asserts her independece to the point of acting in a manner contrary to her husband's wishes has usurped his role and transformed herself into a hybrid monster guilty of an offense of the same order of criminality as adultery or rape by a male felon.

Whatever semblance of poetic justice the story achieves is imposed by the machinations of a passionate moralist who assumes to himself the roles of accuser, judge, and executioner. Rather than an exemplary story of crime and punishment wherein the wish for a utopian state of social justice finds itself momentarily and mysteriously fulfilled, *La Dame escoillée* confronts us with the manifesto of a moral crusade. Gestures in the direction of fabliau wit create a less than adequate façade to conceal the tale's unabashed support for the imposition of male dominance by the use of superior physical force.[28]

The single issue of contention in *La Dame escoillée* and associated texts is dominance in marriage, the authors unanimously endorsing the idea of absolute and overt male supremacy. For this position they have, of course, the support of the Church, for which male dominance served to confirm divine order, as female usurpation of that prerogative offered further evidence of the social and moral chaos occasioned by the fall. But in the fabliaux there is litle if any Christian doctrinal bolstering of the male position. The matter is dealt with exclusively in secular terms. The key moral concepts, as in *Connebert* and associated anticlerical texts, are *honte* and *deshenor*, and masculine pride is defended as passionately and single-mindedly as in a typical *chanson de geste*.[29] The behavior of the women who reject masculine authority is depicted as criminal rather than sinful, and the response is punitive rather than salvatory, the husband acting almost in the manner of a feudal lord suppressing rebellion in the fiefdom of his domicile.

In the anticlerical and antifeminist satires represented by *Connebert* and *La Dame escoillée* implicit *sentence* extrapolated from the plots accords exactly both with the passages of moral exhortation explicitly stating the morality of the tale and with conventional social and religious moral standards. In these tales *sentence* is clear and unequivocal. But *mana* is somewhat too curiously elicited from the circumstances of the plot to manifest that phenomenon's usual degree of spontaneity and is furthermore enlisted in the service of a dogmatically repressive, male-dominated social order, so that the recreational quality of *solas* is noticeably weakened. The sentiments inspiring this kind of anticlerical or antifeminist satire occur only sporadically in the fabliaux, however, and the passages of moral exhortation in which such sentiments find expression are as atypical of *sentence* throughout the fabliau corpus generally as is the particular type of narrative structure they purport to interpret morally.

V

The largest single group of fabliaux is comprised of those which, like *Le Pliçon* and *L'Enfant qui fu remis au soleil*, feature a conflict between husband and wife clearly enough focused so that some moral principles are implied by their narrative development. Unlike *La Dame escoillée*, however, they contain no passages of moral exhortation identifying them as satires. A return to the issue of the relation of *sentence* and *solas* in these tales may be made by way of a fabliau in which the morality implied by the narrative is partially at odds with that inferred by the author. This conflict helps focus the potentially different nature of implicit and explicit morality in the fabliaux.

As the title suggests, the wife in *Le Chevalier qui fist sa fame confesse* mistakenly supposes herself ill to the point of imminent death, summons her father confessor, but then unwittingly makes confession to her husband, who has returned disguised as a priest in hopes of verifying the reality of her reputation for spotless virtue. In response to his invitation that she unburden her soul, the unsuspecting wife embarks on a damning account of the needs of her sex:

> A paine porroit l'en choisir
> Fame qui se puisse tenir
> A son seignor tant seulement.
> Jà tant ne l'aura bel et gent;
> Quar la nature tele en ont,
> Qu'els requierent, ce sachiez vous,
> Et li mari si sont vilain
> Et de grant felonie plain,
> Si ne nous oson descouvrir
> Vers aus, ne noz besoins gehir,
> Quar por putains il nous tendroient,
> Se noz besoins par nous savoient;
> Si ne puet estre en nule guise
> Que n'aions d'autrui le servise.
>
> [MR, 1: 183]

Her personal transgressions, which include casual sexual encounters with numerous servants, and an affair of five-years' standing with her nephew, are sufficiently monstrous to mortify her mock-cleric husband, and certainly substantiate her account of the general immorality of her sex.

The fictional circumstances under which the lady supposes herself to be making this confession would seem to guarantee its authenticity, and make it a most damaging indictment. On first analysis, it is tempting to suppose that an author intent on articulating antifeminist sentiments has hit upon a particularly effective device whereby the deviousness and depravity of women are attested by one of their own number in a context which defies any challenge to the factual veracity and emotional sincerity of her statement. Had the story been different, and had the lady in fact died, that is how it must have been interpreted. But unexpectedly she recovers, and conscious of his unaccustomed coldness towards her realizes that it was to her husband in disguise that she made her confession. Only momentarily nonplussed, she confronts him with the truth, which he admits. Did he think her so dull, she asks, as not to have recognized him right away? For the insulting suspicion which led him to test his loving wife's well-merited reputation for virtue, he deserved to be punished, and so she invented a series of outrageous escapades specifically intended to wound his pride and shock his sensibilities.

Because, in order to obtain her confession, the knight had resorted to trickery, and because this compromised his position in a way his wife is quick to exploit, he has no means of countering her argument, or refuting her claim that she had not been fooled. He cannot consequently recapture for himself the grounds of certitude necessary to sustain his scandalized condemnation of her character. What is true for the knight, however, is not necessarily true for the audience, which knows, because privy to authorial omniscience, that in fact the wife did not recognize her husband, and that her subsequent claim to have done so is a lie. Does the literary ploy of the confession work then as an effective vehicle for the expression of antifeminist satire despite the wife's ability within the tale to evade demonstrable proof of her guilt? One can confidently assert that it does not, for the very good reason that the audience's response is not equivalent to that of a better-informed member of the cast of characters, subject to a fictional truth-value system analogous to that pertaining in real life. For the audience the wife's confession is neither true nor false in these terms, but the invention of an author who has attributed to her such experiences, thoughts, and feelings as he chose. The important corollary to the recognition of this fact is that to the extent the author assigned the wife a confession which can be repudiated within the fictional world, the content of that confession has no absolute validity and no relevance to social issues in isolation from that world. What the author proposes, the author also disposes, and by so doing confirms the autonomy of his creation. It is, one can see, the very enormity of the wife's sexual transgressions which makes her later claim—that they were invented to shock—plausible.

Before I appear to be implying more praise than the anonymous author of *Le Chevalier qui fist sa fame confesse* merits, I would like to consider another, later segment of the wife's confession:

Ne jà ostel n'ert à honor
Dont la dame se fet seignor;
Et fames ceste coustume ont,
Et volentiers toz jors le font,
Qu'elles aient la seignorie
Sor lor seignors; por c'est honie
Mainte méson qu'est sanz mesure,
Et dame avoire par nature.

[*MR*, 1: 185]

Certainly it does no violence to the verisimilitude of the story that a wife guilty of asserting mastery would confess this fault as a sin to her confessor. Nor is it inconceivable that manipulation of her husband occurred in the context of a psychological relationship sufficiently subtle as to leave him unaware of her dominance and his submissiveness. But by comparison with the segment on sexual offenses quoted earlier, the wife's admission that she has been guilty of aspiring after dominance of her husband is artistically inept. Adultery is necessarily clandestine. If it has not been detected, then plausibly no evidence remains that it took place, and once admitted it can be as readily denied. Only the confession itself needs to be accounted for. By contrast, admitting a previously unrecognized dominance in marriage would be neither believed nor understood unless there were some long-standing pattern of behavior which could be retrospectively interpreted so as to confirm the assertion, and that evidence would remain even if the assertion were subsequently denied. Unlike the confession of adultery, confession of dominance is not retractable, and that is what makes it incongruous in the context of this tale. That the wife's claim about going along with the mockery of a confession as a means of punishing him for his suspicion and duplicity is not challenged by the husband on the grounds that certain statements she made are clearly incompatible with any such purpose undermines the logical rigor and weakens the narrative coherence of the story.

What is wrong ultimately with the wife's admission of culpability in regard to seeking marital dominance is that it makes us all too aware that we are listening to the unmediated voice of the author. Apparently tempted by the opportunity which the wife's confession offers for a particularly damning indictment of women's follies and vices, he uses it to express some knee-jerk antifeminist sentiment on what *La Dame escoillée* and associated texts bear witness to be an especially sensitive issue, oblivious of, or despite, the disruption this inevitably causes to the overall integrity of his literary artefact.

The author of the version of the story which has survived to us apparently did not invent the plot but reworked material which came to him with its essential sequence of episodes already formulated. The potential of the story as he received it was something different from what he understood, and somewhat better than he had the artistic ability to realize, although he is sufficiently faithful to his source not to have marred beyond recognition what that potential might be. He seems to have perceived it as an antifeminist satire, and probably thought that by extending the range of vices admitted in the wife's confession he was simply adding cumulatively to the tale's *sentence*. In fact he is distorting it. As long as the wife's confession encompasses only those transgressions from which her later repudiation will exculpate her, the question of whether she did or did not recognize her husband before making her confession, and whether consequently that confession is true or false, is rendered irrelevant. Certainly our estimate of her in conventional moral terms would be different if we as audience knew she was a virtuous woman who lied to shock her husband rather than a depraved woman who lied to save her skin, but either way, once the husband has yielded to the temptation to test his wife through trickery, he hears what he deserves to hear. The need to pursue some absolutist obsession to know certain truth has precipitated him into a torturing paradox of uncertainty from which there is no escape. According to the ethical system which can be extrapolated from the essential features of the plot, it is the husband who transgresses and suffers. He has dared to disturb the universe with his hubristic supposition that he can know naked truth, and he is punished by discovering that for the particular issue on which he wanted reassurance the truth is unknowable.

By disguising himself as a cleric in order to trick his wife into an unwitting confession, the husband in *Le Chevalier qui fist sa fame confesse* is ambiguating a sign in the manner associated with the exercise of *mana*. But from the frustration of his endeavors in the further development of the plot, which reveals the wife's superior ability to summon *mana* to her aid in escaping any evil consequences of her earlier gullibility, it is clear that by the moral system implicit in this fabliau the husband's action exemplifies the same kind of gratuitous aggression as comes to grief in *Le Prestre et le chevalier* and associated works. A number of other fabliaux, *La Saineresse* (DuVal and Eichmann, pp. 105-09), *Les deux Changeors* (*MR*, 1: 245-54), and *La Borgoise d'Orliens* and its analogues (Rychner, 2: 80-99) follow closely the pattern of *Le Chevalier qui fist sa fame confesse*. All present the wife's trickery as a response to some offense on the part of her husband, who has boasted that he can control his wife's behavior so as to guarantee her fidelity, or has attempted to achieve such control by clandestine surveillance or the recruitment of spies and informers.[30]

Other fabliaux, in which the husband has not offended within the context of the tale except by his very existence as *le jaloux*, resolve the conflict between a husband and wife in similar fashion. The women are successful practitioners of *mana* in manipulating control of their husbands, and the narrative pattern, by dissolving the logical consequences of anterior misdeeds into confusion and uncertainty, evolves towards freedom from the trammels of institutionally approved socio-moral standards of behavior. *Sentence* in this group of fabliaux is so uniform as to be almost monotonous in its consistency.

Several of these fabliaux contain as *sentence* only a passage of antifeminist complaint, of the kind already quoted from *La Fame qui fist batre son mari* and *Les Perdriz* in support of the assertion that women are by nature of their sex credited with possession of *mana*. Similar sentiments are expressed by Marie de France at the conclusion of *Le Vilain qui od sa feme vit aler son dru*:

> Pur ceo dit hum en repruvier
> que femmes sevent engignier:
> les veziëes nunverables
> unt un art plus que li diables.[31]

Alternatively, these particular fabliaux offer passages of practical advice to husbands, either, as in *Le Vilain de Bailluel*, not to believe their wives: "Mes li fabliaus dit en la fin/C'on doit por fol tenir celui/Qui mieus croit sa fame que lui" (*MR*, 4: 216), or, in harmony with a system of expedient choices such that opposite courses of action are not mutually exclusive, to believe their wives rather than the evidence of their own senses.[32] Most commonly, antifeminist complaint and practical advice occur in conjunction, in a manner which reflects their interdependence. Such is the case, for example, with the summary passage in *La Sorisete des Estopes*:

> Enseignier voil por ceste fable
> Que fame set plus que deiable,
> Et certeinemant lo sachiez.
> Les iauz enbedeus li sachiez
> Se n'é à esciant dit voir.
> Qant el viaut ome decevoir,
> Plus l'an deçoit et plus l'afole
> Tot solemant par sa parole
> Que om ne feroit par angin.

De ma fable faz tel defin
Que chascun se gart de la soe
Qu'ele ne li face la coe.[33]

The tales which the foregoing discussion associates with one another have quite unjustifiably provided the source for much of the evidence usually cited in illustration of antifeminist sentiment in the fabliaux. Most of them certainly contain passages of complaint accusing wives of being particularly skillful at what are several times referred to as the "devilish" arts of deception, but this is to accuse them expressly of practicing with consummate craft that *mana* which accounts for the *solas* in stories demonstrating its operation. It cannot be regarded as an unequivocally negative quality, and it is nowhere in these fabliaux inveighed against in passages of moral exhortation. With the exception of the few tales associated earlier with *La Dame escoillée* (see footnote 28), where such passages do occur, fabliaux do not depict women in the monastic tradition of antifeminist satire as morally inferior creatures who are to be shunned as a precaution against falling into deadly sin, or kept so rigorously subservient to their husbands' authority that their penchant for debauchery has no opportunity to manifest itself. There is consequently no defensible reason for regarding the portrayal of women in the genre generally as a rancorously satiric reflection of "un dogme bien défini, profondément enraciné, que voici: les femmes sont des êtres inférieurs et malfaisants."[34]

Comparison of *Le Prestre crucefié* and associated texts on the one hand, with *Le Chevalier qui fist sa fame confesse* and associated texts on the other, indicates that the opposed positions giving rise to marital conflict are the same in both sets of works. Husbands champion the cause of male dominance, which rests on a foundation of patriarchal social and religious authoritarianism, and normally entails jealous sexual guardianship of potentially promiscuous wives. Wives champion the cause of sexual vitality, which assumes freedom from the strictures of institutionalized male authority, and normally entails some conspiracy to escape from a husband's surveillance and control into the pleasures of an illicit sexual escapade.

As long as the opposition is conceived in these totally incompatible terms, the only outcome possible is that one party to the dispute will completely vanquish the other. Both resolutions are adequately represented by fabliaux which generate, from similar sources in the exercise of *mana*, an authentically fabliau sense of *solas*. The resolutions are therefore achieved at the expense of denying in one group of fabliaux the validity of attitudes which in the other group are endorsed by the success ultimately attributed to them. In such tales as *Le Prestre crucefié*, implicit *sentence* accords well with the conventional morality of a heroic, patriarchal society. The narrative evolves towards complete assimilation of *ethos* into *logos*, so that at the conclusion the husband's superior ability in the manipulation of words gives him the virtual power of life and death over the other protagonists in what he successfully transforms, with their unwitting assistance, into a totally conceptualized world. The problem with this resolution is that the exercise of *mana* in the service of sexual vitality exactly parallels similar practices in such works as *Le Pliçon*, where it successfully achieves its ends. Defeat of a female endeavor of this kind therefore carries with it the suggestion of a different outcome and creates in the denouement of such stories a somewhat sterile and gloomy sense of repressiveness.

In such tales as *Le Chevalier qui fist sa fame confesse*, where wives engineer opportunities for extramarital sexual adventures, divert suspicion about the existence of such liaisons, or escape the consequences of their discovery, the narrative pattern moves away from a conceptually structured world and towards the ideal of existentially pure "being," effectively free from any schema of moral valuation. Implicit sentence in these fabliaux is opposed to conventional morality as reflected by the passages of explicit *sentence*, which combine antifeminist complaint and practical advice to men and are a standard feature in tales of this type. Complaint, as already noted, acknowledges women's skill in the exercise of *mana*, and the sexual vitality which utilizes *mana* as the means for achieving its free expression. Passages of practical advice suggest that men are deficient in just those qualities which their wives are shown to possess. They are urged either to accept gracefully the role of *wihos suffrans* to which such deficiency necessarily condemns them, or to work at acquiring those same skills, so as to be capable of outmatching women in what the latter's habitual success implies is their own special area of expertise. The narrative development suggested, if husbands were able to comply with the behavior patterns which fabliau-authors recommend for them, would parallel that in the contrasting works represented by *Le Prestre crucefié*. The *moralitas* to a number of these tales also suggests, therefore, a different resolution, more conformable in this instance to conventional moral expectations.

Since conflict involving adultery cannot end in success for the husband without mandating defeat for the wife, and vice-versa, no individual fabliau treating this theme can explore the possibility of reconciling the attitudes espoused by the respective parties to the dispute, even though the varying fortunes of such attitudes in the fabliau corpus as a whole intimates that some positive value may be attached to each. Setting, in absolute opposition on the level of dramatic conflict, attitudes not necessarily so antithetical as to defy all possibility of their being reconciled, reflects a weakness inherent in the form of fabliaux dealing with adultery and reflects also a limitation imposed on the genre by the exaggerated popularity of this theme.

A reconciliation of these attitudes is achieved in *La Dame qui aveine demandoit pour Morel sa provende avoir* and *Le Pescheor de pont seur Saine*. Both portray the fortunes of initially ideal marriages. The relationship in the former tale is described in these romantic terms: "Tristans, tant com fu en cest monde, / N'amna autant Ysoue la blonde / Cum si .II. amans s'entr'emmerent / Et foy et honnor se porterent" (*MR*, 1: 319). The same combination of circumstances, that the wives are sexually vigorous but also hypocritically unwilling to acknowledge the intensity of their desires, places the future happiness of the lovers and the stability of their marriages in jeopardy, because sex threatens to become embroiled in a partisan struggle to assert supremacy.

The hypocrisy of women as exemplified by the wife in *La Dame qui aveine demandoit* is the topic of a brief passage of antifeminist complaint by the author: "Fame, selonc sa nature, / La riens, que miex ara en cure / Et tout ce que miex li plaira, / Dou contraire samblant fera" (*MR*, 1: 332). The husband in this story tries to moderate his wife's demands by shifting responsibility for initiating sex to her, insisting, on the pretext that he does not want to offend by making unwelcome overtures, that she utilize the formula of the title—"black beauty wants her oats"—to signal her feelings, and promising that a request so couched will never be refused. Once the wife has overcome her initial outrage at this affront to the delicacy of her feelings, she boldly employs the formula with unrelenting frequency, so that the husband, now doubly trapped by his own rash promise, becomes increasingly debilitated, and begins to despair of his very survival. He finally extricates himself from his dilemma by defecating in the marriage bed in response to the last, unanswerable request from his wife, telling her that the supply of oats being totally depleted, black beauty must now content herself with bran.

The gesture, despite its stupefying obscenity, is recognizably an instance of the exercise of personal *mana*. Its capacity to effect the primary purpose of denying the wife sex, while accommodating the husband's promise never to refuse a request for oats, logically parallels the capacity of the husband's action in *La Prestre crucefié* to effect punishment of the priest while accommodating this lecher's pretence to be a carved wooden image of Christ crucified. The audience is left to assume that the outcome for the married couple is a reconciliation, and a future relationship based on the sort of moderation the author in a final passage of practical advice recommends to husands generally among his audience:

> A vous di, qu'iestes mariez;
> Par cest conte vous chastiez;
> Faites à mesure et à point,
> Quant verrez lieu et tens et point.
>
> [*MR*, 1: 329]

The marriage portrayed in this fabliau suffers some degradation in passing from romantic illusion to sordid reality, but there is clearly some compensatory gain in razing so unstable a structure in order to build again from its foundation.[35] The fabliau concludes with a positive sense of balance and harmony from which the possibility of both husband and wife progressing towards an equal and equally fulfilling partnership is by no means excluded.

What is true in this respect for *La Dame qui aveine demandoit* is true also for *Le Pescheor de pont seur Saine*, a somewhat more light hearted tale because the wife's hypocrisy about an unproblematic level of sexual desire is the source of conflict, rather than a level of sexual activity so elevated as to be beyond the husband's capacity to sustain. The functions of the characters, in that it is the husband who displays personal *mana* in exposing the wife's charade of at best merely tolerating the physical aspects of their marriage, are the same in *Le Pescheor de pont seur Saine* as in its companion piece. So too are the contours of the narrative, which take the relationship from mutual satisfaction through a period of strain to restored happiness and increased honesty and stability.

The fisherman-husband in this story, irked with his wife's insistence that sex is not only not important to her happiness, but a barely supportable annoyance, takes advantage of his discovery of the floating body of a dead priest, whose amorous escapades have proven fatal for him, to cut off and pocket the priest's penis, which he then produces before his wife with the explanation that he was accosted by three knights determined to deprive him of his choice of some member, and that he chose as he did because her avowed distaste for sex made this the most dispensable. After his wife has berated him, and begun preparations to sever their relationship, so that the hypocrisy of her earlier claims has been fully exposed, the husband reveals the truth to her, and they are happily reconciled. The fabliau concludes with the now familiar combination of antifeminist complaint and practical advice to men:

Seignor, fols est qui fame croit
Fors tant comme il l'ot et la voit.
Je di en la fin de mon conte
Que, s'une fame avoit un Conte
Le plus bel et le plus adroit
Et le plus alosé qui soit,
Et fust chevaliers de sa main
Meillor c'onques ne fu Gavain,
Por tant que il fust escoillié,
Tost le voudroit avoir changié
Au pior de tout son ostel,
Por tant qu'ele le trovast tel
Qu'il la foutist tost et sovent.
Se dames dient que je ment,
Soufrir le vueil, atant m'en tais,
De m'aventure n'i a mais

[MR, 3: 75]

The slightly fantastical description of the intensity of women's sexual desire, and of the extremes to which they may go to achieve its satisfaction, recalls the similar statements in *Le Chevalier qui fist sa fame confesse*, and acquires extra sophistication from being clearly intended for presentation to a mixed audience.

Invention of an encounter with three knights, and reference in the *moralitas* to the figure of Gawain, like the reference to Tristan and Isolde in *La Dame qui aveine demandoit*, may be intended to suggest both points of contact with and distance from the concerns of courtly romance. But the ethos of *Le Pescheor de pont seur Saine* is equally remote from what might be assumed as the similar fabliau world conjured up by the episode of the hapless priest who has been killed in pursuit of another man's wife. The two fabliaux with which we are dealing examine, in a significant way which neither the exquisite refinement of courtly romance nor the crude scurrility of the bawdier fabliaux can quite duplicate, the topic of physical love and its relationship to marriage, without recourse to the dauntingly unromantic "marriage debt" concept as understood by such commentators as the husband in *Le Menagier de Paris* and his peers.

Whatever is positive and promising in the marital relationship at the conclusion of these two fabliaux stems from resolution of a conflict between female sensuality on the one hand and male ability to manipulate *mana* on the other. But because sensuality and ingenuity are in significant respects similar phenomena, inexhaustible sexual vitality and fertility of imagination both serving some concept of plenitude, the outcome does not require obliteration of one quality by the other. What finally emerges in both tales is the possibility of a marriage based on tolerance and cooperation. The touchstone of such an ideal reveals the excess of other domestic strife fabliaux, both the duplicitous insurrection of the wife in *Le Chevalier qui fist sa fame confesse* and the tyrannical dominace of the husband in *Le Prestre crucefié*. *La Dame qui aveine demandoit* and *Le Pescheor de pont seur Saine* employ familiar fabliau devices to orchestrate intrigues which produce a very typical sense of *solas*, and seem in addition close to some center of gravity of moral concerns in the fabliaux. The centrality is reflected not only in the balance which results from the mediation, through the pattern of episodes, of conflicting desires on the part of the protagonists, but also from the unusual range of emotional attitudes which the tales assimilate into an effective unity.

Passages of *sentence*, specifically antifeminist complaint and practical advice to husbands, which in other fabliaux seem partially at odds with the narrative development in that they attribute to wives characteristics not particularly manifest in their behavior, or offer to husbands advice not put into practice within the confines of the story, are here perfectly integrated with the details of the plot. Instead of a narrative pattern predominantly concerned with a conflict between individuals which moves towards or away from punishment of one partner in a marriage for some offense committed against the other, conflict in these fabliaux involves such issues as the deleterious effect of hypocrisy on a married couple's need to establish and maintain honest dialogue, and aims to amend some defect in the nature of their relationship, so that the narrative moves from illusion to reality in a pattern which ultimately proves salutary for both partners.

In such fabliaux as *La Dame qui aveine demandoit* and *Le Pescheor de pont seur Saine* the threat to a happy resolution of conflict comes predominantly from hypocritical deceit and willful misunderstanding. Therefore passages of complaint aimed at dispelling confusion about unpalatable but true facts, and practical advice aimed at articulating the alternatives for action in light of the facts thus registered, precisely serve the ends of the moral *sentence* implied by the narrative pattern.

Fabliau ethic is not concerned with salvatory morality, but with the strategies and tactics of survival in a space-and-time-bound world whose physically closed nature makes survival itself difficult, and limits the possibility of individual progress towards a materially affluent and emotionally gratifying life. The absolutism of conventional Christian asceticism is alien to the dialectic spirit of the ethical system which pertains generally in all fabliaux except those identified by the presence of passages of moral exhortation at satires, or *tableaux de moeurs* which paint characters with the palette of a conventional moralist. The fabliau system of morality may tolerate duplicity and positively endorses opportunism and expediency. The purely aesthetic reconciliation, with regard to degrees of significance and subtlety, between the moral significance of the story and the author's interpretive comments will vary according to the artistic skill and perspicacity of the individual *fableor*. But in general there is little persuasive evidence for regarding the authors of fabliaux as literary hacks who stumble unconsciously into incongruities, or as such slaves to literary convention that they struggle unsuccessfully to accommodate generic or rhetorical devices alien to the form of their compositions. They appear rather to be competent craftsmen in their chosen medium, whose statements as to the moral implications of their works are in principle to be taken seriously.

These statements usually harmonize with the moral precepts which can be abstracted from their respective narratives, as long as the nature of the morality involved is properly understood. Admittedly, even when the necessary distinctions in the type of fabliau, whether *example* or *risée*, and in the type of *sentence*, whether proverb, practical advice, complaint, or moral exhortation have been made, there remain a scattering of fabliaux in which moral commentary seems inexplicably irrelevant or perverse. But these are by no means sufficiently numerous to justify the view that as a general rule passages of commentary are "determinedly cudgelled" from works deliberately immoral in conception,[36] or that these passages can be dismissed as "merely a perfunctory conventional appendage" to works with which they have no organic relationship.[37] The argument dependent on these assumptions, that passages of moral commentary provide evidence for the generic derivation of the fabliau from the Aesopic fable,[38] is also mooted if the perception of their extraneousness is illusory, since the argument for derivation rather than merely parallel development depends expressly on conceiving such moralizing passages as redundant and poorly assimilated vestiges of an ancestral form. Moral commentary in the fabliaux, although frequently at odds with Christian ethical principles, expresses an internally consistent system which harmonizes with the moral implications of fabliau narratives. It should therefore be recognized as integral and significant, rather than tangential and trivial, in any valid effort to understand and assess the place of this body of popular narrative materials in the literary art of the later Middle Ages.

Roy J. Pearcy
University of Oklahoma

Notes

1. Text in *Recueil général et complet des fabliaux des XIIIe et XIVe siècles*, ed. Anatole de Montaiglon and Gaston Raynaud (Paris, 1872–90), 6: 24–33. Unless otherwise noted, all fabliaux are cited and quoted from this edition. Quotations are followed immediately by the identification *MR*, with volume and page number (there are no line numbers).

This paper was written during tenure of a fellowship at La Fondation Camargo in Cassis, France, and I would like to take this opportunity to thank the Foundation for providing support to pursue this project in such idyllic surroundings.

2. Joseph Bédier, *Les Fabliaux: études de littérature populaire et d'histoire littéraire du moyen âge*, 1st ed. 1895, 6th ed. (Paris: Champion, 1969), p. 30. Subsequent quotations of Bédier are from this edition. Page references are given in parentheses following the quote in the text of the paper.

3. Such an assumption is implicit in the articles anthologized in *The Humor of the Fabliaux: A Collection of Critical Essays*, ed. Thomas D. Cooke and Benjamin L. Honeycutt (Columbia: University of Missouri Press, 1974).

4. *La Dame qui fist batre son mari*, ll. 87–89. Text in Jean Rychner, *Contribution à l'étude des fabliaux*, 2: Textes (Geneva: Droz, 1960), 87, hereafter identified following quotations in the text as Rychner 2.

5. *Les Perdriz* (*MR*, 1, 193).

6. It is beyond the scope and purpose of this essay to delve into the relationship between fabliau *solas* and general theories of comedy, but some interesting speculation on this relationship may be found in Willem Noomen, "Structures narratives et force comique: Les Fabliaux," *Neophilologus* 62 (1978), 361–73.

7. The case for the independence from conventional moral strictures of works conceived for the purpose of entertainment, with careful and extensive documentation of this theoretical position from medieval sources, may be found in Glending Olson, *Literature as Recreation in the Later Middle Ages* (Ithaca: Cornell University Press, 1982).

8. Per Nykrog, *Les Fabliaux: étude d'histoire littéraire et de stylistique médiévale*, nouvelle éd. (Geneva: Droz, 1973), pp. 100–03.

9. See, for example, discussion of this issue in Thomas D. Cooke, *The Old French and Chaucerian Fabliaux: A Study of Their Comic Climax* (Columbia: University of Missouri Press, 1978), pp. 86–96.

10. For proverbs appearing in the fabliaux, see particularly J. Morawski, *Proverbes français antérieurs au XVe siècle*, Classiques Français du moyen âge 47 (Paris: Champion, 1925) and S. Singer, *Sprichwörter des Mittelalters*, 3 vols. (Berne, 1944–47). Hereafter proverbs recorded by Morawski are identified by their numerical listing, (*M*: 1) etc. There is an interesting article on the various ways in which proverbs may be integrated into fabliaux by Elisabeth Schulze-Busacker, "Proverbes et expressions proverbiales dans les fabliaux," *Marche Romane* 28 (1978), 163–74. The author concludes that the didactic or pseudo-didactic

tendencies in the fabliaux may transform what would otherwise be a purely decorative stylistic feature into a constitutive element.

11. For the convenience of the terminology, I am making a distinction between complaint and moral exhortation analogous to the distinction between complaint and satire drawn by John Peter, *Complaint and Satire in Early English Literature* (Oxford: Clarendon Press, 1956). Peter defines complaint differently from the way it is used here, however (see particularly pp. 9–10).

12. Text in *Cuckolds, Clerics, and Countrymen: Medieval French Fabliaux*, trans. John DuVal, ed. Raymond Eichmann (Fayetteville: University of Arkansas Press, 1982), p. 42.

13. *Fabliaux et Contes des poëtes françois des XI, XII, XIII, XIV, et XVe siècles*, ed. M. Méon and E. Barbazon (Paris, 1808), 4: 194–96.

14. The classification is not absolutely exhaustive, but neglects nothing of major importance. There are, throughout the fabliau corpus, a scattering of philosophic or Christian-religious *sententiae* (and sometimes, in conjunction with the latter, of prayers), but they are usually no more than brief relative clauses attached to the grand abstractions when these crop up during the course of a story. Typical are the following: "li Mors, qui roi, duc, ne conte / N'espargne" (*Le Vescie a Prestre, MR*, 3: 106); "Amors, qui les siens justise" (*Auberée*; text in *Twelve Fabliaux*, ed. T. B. W. Reid [Manchester: Manchester University Press, 1958], p. 55, l. 51). Such expressions often appear to be little more than tags introduced for the sake of rhyme. They rather confirm than deny Bédier's contention (p. 317) that *l'esprit gaulois* of the fabliaux "manque de metaphysique." There are, in the fabliaux, no passages of complaint against Fortune, a lacuna which sets them apart not only from the courtly romances with which they are conventionally contrasted, but also from such works as *Le Roman de la Rose* and *Le Roman de Renart* with which they are generally assumed to have the most in common. Lengthy encomia to *Amors* and *Larguesce* appear in *Le Lai d'Aristote* (Reid, pp. 70–82), and *sententiae* of the kind we are dealing with here appear also in a small group of fabliaux, to include *Auberée* and *Un Chivalier et sa dame et un clerk* (*MR*, 2: 215–34), which share the interest of Henri d'Andeli's story in courtly love themes. Philosophic *sententiae* are found also in the group comprised of *Le Prestre qu'on porte* (*MR*, 4: 1–40) and the various versions of *Le Sacristain*. Most of the tales mentioned are unusually long and episodic, show a greater-than-average concern with psychological action, and lack the focal exercise of *mana* by some character who thereby sets in motion an intrigue capable of generating the particular form of *solas* described as characteristic of fabliaux generally.

15. Text in Charles H. Livingston, *Le Jongleur Gautier le Leu*, Harvard Studies in Romance Languages 24 (Cambridge: Harvard University Press, 1951), 185–97.

16. Text in *Fabliaux français du Moyen Age*, ed. Philippe Ménard (Geneva: Droz, 1979), p. 46.

17. Developing the figure of the street-wise underworld character, whose exploits hold a fascination relatively free of moral censure for the more respectable reader, is a feature of a number of other fabliaux which contain no particularly serious passages of *sentence*. *Boivin de Provins* (Ménard, pp. 47–57) has only the proverb *bon larron est qui autre emble* (*M*, 1313), replaced in *Barat et Haimet* (*MR*, 4: 93–111) with the addition of the practical advice that "Male est compaignie a larron." The world of prostitutes described in the former appears again in *La vielle Truande* (*MR*, 5: 171–78), discussed more fully with the next group of tales. *Le Prestre et les deux ribaus* acknowledges the story-teller's duty to relate *biaus mos*, and concludes with advice emphatically more practical than moral:

"Et por ce fet il bon aprendre / Guile et barat, ce est la somme, / Quar mestier ont eü maint homme" (*MR*, 3: 67). The world of the gigolo, and the techniques of one of the attractively brash exponents of this trade, are the subject matter of *Le Foteor* (*MR*, 1: 304-17), which concludes with the proverb *Qui va, il lesche, / Et qui toz jors se siet, il sèche* (*M*: 2144). It is distinctively a hustler's motto.

18. With this group belong two fabliaux in which the misreading of signs is engineered, but in a congenial and innocuous spirit. One of these, *Les trois Aveugles de Compiegne* (Ménard, pp. 109-18), begins with a statement of the value of fabliaux as entertainment: "Fablel sont bon escouter: / maint duel, maint mal font mesconter / et maint anui et maint mesfet (ll. 7-9). *Le Meunier d'Arleux* (*MR*, 2: 31-45) ends with a general celebration. Both conclude typically with passages of practical advice, blandly benign in these instances. *Les trois Aveugles* summarizes its moral concerns thus: "On fet a tort maint homme honte." *Le Meunier d'Arleux* requires four lines to express the same tautology: "Et vous anonce bien et dist / C'onques ne vous prenge talens / De faire honte à bones gens. / Qui s'en garde, il fait que sages."

19. Roy J. Pearcy, "The Genre of William Dunbar's *Tretis of the tua mariit wemen and the wedo*," *Speculum* 55 (1980), 58-74.

20. Two other fabliaux without any passages of explicit *sentence* may be included in this category. *Les trois Meschines* (*MR*, 3: 76-80) has no competition, but does end with an appeal to the audience to decide which of three girls should bear the cost of some wasted makeup they had jointly purchased. The story, like others in this group, is blatantly vulgar, and shares some features with the pornographic and scatalogical tales discussed as an independent group earlier. It is emphatically a *risée. Une seule Fame qui a son con servoit .c. chevaliers* (*MR*, 1: 294-300) is of the climactically outrageous type, whereby after the death of one of two women responsible for satisfying the sexual needs of fifty knights each, the surviving prostitute who conspired to have her coworker murdered saves her skin by agreeing to assume her victim's duties in addition to her own. The connection with the *jugement* type is clearer in the analogue to this fabliau which appears in the story told by Sir Baldwin in the Middle English verse romance *The Avowynge of King Arthur, Sir Gawan, Sir Kaye, and Sir Bawdewyn of Bretan*, where three women are involved, and assumption of the duties of two successively murdered women by the surviving member of the trio has the conventional triadic climactic effect. See *Middle English Metrical Romances*, ed. Walter Hoyt French and Charles Brockway Hale (1930; rpt. New York: Russell & Russell, 1964), 2: 605-46.

21. I have attempted to articulate these standards for *Les trois Dames de Paris* in "Realism and Religious Parody in the Fabliaux: Watriquet de Couvin's *Les trois Dames de Paris*," *Revue belge de philologie et d'histoire* 50 (1972), 744-54.

22. To these types of *sentence* may be added dramatic monologue, whereby the wife in this story registers the possibility for significant psychological change (*MR*, 6: 62). Similar passages occur in *La Vieille et la lisette* (text in A. Hilka and W. Söderhjelm, eds., *Petri Alphonsi Disciplina Clericalis: III Französische Versbearbeitungen*, Acta Societatis Scientiarum Fennicae, 49 [Helsinki, 1922], pp. 30-32), and in some of the works, particularly *Le Lai d'Aristote*, listed in footnote 14, with which *Fole Larguesce* and other *tableaux de moeurs* have affinity.

23. Similarities between Gautier le Leu's portrait of the widow and Geoffrey Chaucer's portrait of the Wife of Bath have been examined by Charles Muscatine, "The Wife of Bath and Gautier's *La Veuve*," in *Romance Studies in Memory of Edward Billings Ham*, ed. U. T. Holmes (Hayward: California State College, 1967), pp. 109-14.

24. Of the twenty-five fabliaux asserted to be without passages of *sentence* of any kind, I have classified sixteen into groups. Of the nine remaining fabliaux, *Le Femme qui charma son mari* from the *Disciplina Clericalis* belongs with the fabliaux discussed later in this essay which typically incorporate passages of antifeminist complaint combined with practical advice to husbands. In the *Disciplina Clericalis* such sentiments are assimilated into the frame discussion between father and son (see, for example, the exchange following *La Piere au puis* in this collection of tales). *La Feme qui cunqui son baron* (Bédier, pp. 344–46), and *Le Cuvier* (*MR*, 1: 126–31) similarly describe successful ruses by women to smuggle lovers out of their houses after the unexpected return of their husbands, and belong in this same category of supposedly cautionary tales. Analogues to *Le fol Vilain* (Livingston, pp. 148–58), and *La Damoiselle qui ne pooit oït parler de foutre* (Rychner, 2: 120–34) also contain passages of antifeminist complaint and practical advice which determine the place of these fabliaux in the proposed taxonomy. There finally remain unclassified *La Gageure* (*MR*, 2: 193–96), *Le Prestre et le Leu* (*MR*, 6: 51–52), *Saint Pierre et le jongleur* (Johnston and Owen, pp. 67–77), and *Le Segretain I* (*MR*, 5: 115–31).

25. For the text of this fabliau see Gaston Raynaud, "Une nouvelle version du fabliau de *La Nonnette*," *Romania* 34 (1905), 278–83.

26. To assert that the distribution of roles is arbitrary in terms of the *solas* to be derived from the contours of a particular plot structure is not to deny that the pleasure might be intensified if this distribution was in conformity with, and helped to confirm, the expected prejudices of the author and his assumed audience. Given the fact that itinerants, whether secular minstrels or *clerici vagantes*, are firmly associated with the composition and dissemination of fabliaux, it is not surprising that virtue is found almost exclusively in those who have to petition for food and lodging, not in those who exploit their positions as expectedly charitable dispensers of alms or as entrepreneurs offering a public service. That the fabliaux make little distinction between the two is apparent from a passage of complaint against innkeepers in Gautier le Leu's *Le Prestre teint*: "A l'entrer lor fet bele chiere, / A l'essir est d'autre maniere. / Bien set conter quant quant qu'il i met, / Neïs le sel qu'el pot remet; / Les auz, le verjus, et la leigne, / Ne let rien qu'a conter remaigne" (Livingston, p. 256). The ruse is precisely that practiced by the priest in *Le Prestre et le chevalier*.

27. Criticism of the abuse of clerical privilege, tacitly implied by the nature of the intrigue in *Connebert*, is explicit in other fabliaux. See, in this regard, Gautier le Leu's own *Le Prestre teint*, and particularly *Constant du Hamel*, where the tyranny of petty officialdom is articulated in a passage of perverted *sentence*, addressed by a parish priest to his fellow conspirators, a provost and a forester, on how a peasant's wife is to be treated to make her more acquiescent to sexual overtures: "Qui de li se veuille entremetre, / De son chastel l'estuet jus metre, / Tant que besoing, poverte et fain / La face venir a reclain. / Ainsi doit on servir vilaine; / Fol est qui autrement s'en paine" (*MR*, 4: 171–72). The preoccupation with adultery in *Connebert, Le Prestre teint*, and *Constant du Hamel* may in part be attributable to the pervasiveness of this motif throughout the fabliau corpus, but what gives these tales a distinctive satiric bite is passionate concern with the issue of social injustice.

28. Other fabliaux which assume the propriety of husbands subjecting their supposedly errant wives to cruel abuse fall into the same category. *L'Home qui avoit feme tencheresse* from the *Fables* of Marie de France describes how a husband conspires to let his contentious wife drown by directing would-be rescuers to look for her upstream, arguing that it is the right place to look for a woman who never acted otherwise than contrarily. See no. 95, *Se uxore mala et marito eius,* in *Die Fabeln*, ed. Karl Warnke, Bibliotheca

Normannica, 6 (Halle: Niemeyer, 1898), 307-10. As with *La Dame escoillée*, the dominant male figure is here responsible for formulating the sophistical analogy on which depends whatever degree of wit the story exhibits. Three versions of *Le Pré tonduz*—the fabliau with this title (*MR*, 4: 154-57), *Dame Joenne* (text in A. Lângfors, "*Le Dit de Dame Jouenne*: Version inédite du fabliau de *Pré tondu*," *Romania* 45 [1918-19], 99-107), and another fabliau by Marie de France, *La Contrarieuse* (no. 94, *De homine et uxore litigiosa*, in Warnke, pp. 304-06)—all depict the beating of argumentative wives. *Dame Joenne* and *Le Pré tonduz* itself show their affiliation with *La Dame escoillée* by their construction as a series of exemplary episodes, and both are deficient in narrative interest, tending towards becoming purely *tableaux de moeurs*. Both conclude with the statement that the husband cursed his wife, "A deiables la commanda," which parallels the ending of *La Dame escoillée*. That these several fabliaux recommend physical chastisement as a means of controlling unruly wives is perhaps the most salient single factor identifying them as a unified group, but they share other characteristics. Most are either themselves early, or they have affinities with other works which antedate the full flowering of the fabliau phenomenon in the thirteenth century. This is evidently the case with the fabliaux from the *Fables* of Marie de France, and both the early circulation and the *exemplum* qualities of *Le Pré tonduz* tale-type are attested by its appearance among the *exempla* of Jacques de Vitry. The closest analogue I know to *La Dame escoillée*, which tells of a husband who bleeds his wife almost to death as a means of quelling her overly bold spirit, appears uniquely in *Li Romans des sept sages*, ed. H. A. Keller (Tübingen, 1836), ll. 2470-807.

29. *Le Pèlerinage de Charlemagne*, for example, begins with just the kind of domestic squabble which occurs in the fabliaux. See Roy J. Pearcy, "Chansons de Geste and Fabliaux: *La Gageure* and *Berenger au long cul*," *Neuphilologische Mitteilungen*, 79 (1978), 76-83. Nykrog (pp. 88-89) notes the possible parody of the process of trial by combat in *Sire Haine et Dame Anieuse*, another instance of a husband physically beating a factious wife.

30. A number of fabliaux have jealous guardianship of wife or daughter as a central motif, and explicitly condemn surveillance as often productive of the specific evils it is designed to prevent. Of this kind are *L'Espervier* (*MR*, 5: 43-51); *L'Esquiriel* (*MR*, 5: 101-08); and *La Dame qui se venja du chevalier* (*MR*, 6: 24-33).

31. No. 45, *Iterum de muliere et proco eius*, in Warnke, p. 152. Similar statements are made by the author of *La Borgoise d'Orliens* (Johnston and Owen, p. 23): "Fame a trestout passé Argu;/Par lor engin sont deceü/Li sage des le tens Abel."

32. See, for example, the passage of *sentence* spoken by the husband in Marie de France's *Le Vilain qui vit un autre home od sa feme* (no. 44, *De muliere et proco eius*, in Warnke, p. 147): "Chescuns deit mielz creire e saveir/ceo que sa femme dit pur veir/que ceo que si malvais ueil veient,/ki par veüe le foleient." Similar sentiments are expressed in the *moralitas* of *Le Chevalier a la robe vermeille* (*MR*, 3: 43).

33. *MR*, 4: 165. Identical sentiments are expressed in Rutebeuf's *La Dame qui fist trois tors entor le moustier* (*MR*, 3: 152), and briefer, but essentially similar statements are to be found in *La Dame qui fist entendant son mari qu'il sonjoit* (Rychner, 2: 147); *La Saineresse* (DuVal and Eichmann, pp. 108-09); and *Les deux Changeors* (*MR*, 1: 254). The latter is brief enough to be quoted as exemplary of the rest, and illustrates clearly the close relationship with the passage quoted from *La Sorisete des Estopes*: "Par cest fablel prover vous vueil/Que cil fet folie et orgueil/Qui fame engingnier s'entremet;/Quar qui fet à fame .I. mal tret,/Ele en fet .x. ou .xv. ou .xx./Ainsi ceste aventure avint."

34. Bédier, p. 321 His views are disputed by Richard Spencer, "The Treatment of Women in the *Roman de la Rose*, the *fabliaux*, and the *Quinze joyes de mariage*," *Marche Romane*, 28 (1978), 207–14. Spencer reviews several of the fabliaux I have discussed in this paper, and reaches similar conclusions on portrayal of women and the matter of antifeminist satire in the fabliaux. See also Raymond Eichmann's introduction to *Cuckolds, Clerics, and Countrymen*, pp. 6–10.

35. I have commented briefly on *La Dame qui aveine demandoit pour Morel sa provende avoir* as an illustration of the movement from illusion to reality in the fabliaux, in "Modes of Signification and the Humor of Obscene Diction in the Fabliaux," in *The Humor of the Fabliaux: A Collection of Critical Essays*, ed. Thomas D. Cooke and Benjamin L. Honeycutt (Columbia: University of Missouri Press, 1974), pp. 163–96.

36. Johnston and Owen, p. xv.

37. Reid, p. x.

38. The idea that the fabliau and fable are closely related forms, and that common features, particularly the concluding *moralitas*, are to be explained as derived from fable practices, was apparently arrived at independently in the period 1957–58 by Nykrog (pp. 248–54), Johnston and Owen (pp. xv–xviii), and Reid (pp. x–xi).

9. Jacques de Vitry, the Tale of Calogrenant, La Chastelaine de Vergi, and the Genres of Medieval Narrative Fiction

"Tria sunt item, quae praestare
debeat orator ut doceat, moveat,
delectat." Quintilian, *Institutionis
Oratoriae*, 3. 5. 2.

In the third book of his *Institutio Oratoria*, Quintilian turns to the duties of the orator and to the kinds of questions an orator is likely to treat.[1] The purpose of an oration, he says, is to instruct, to move the emotions, or to delight the audience. This tripartite division of rhetorical purpose, Quintilian thinks, is better than the usual division of oratory into (1) that which relates to things, by which I assume he means objective facts, and (2) that which concerns the emotions, "because both 'things' and emotions will not always be present in the subjects the orator has to treat."[2] While this is true enough since some orations certainly will be factual and instructive, while others will produce strong emotions, it is also true that still other speeches will both instruct and "move" the emotions at the same time and that all speeches are capable of charming or delighting the listener.

When we try to classify the generic shapes of specific works we want to choose categories that overlap with each other as little as possible in order that we may distinguish one literary kind from another. Although Quintilian's three duties of the orator are clearly capable of overlapping in any oration, I hope to show that they nevertheless provide invaluable principles for the classification of medieval narrative fictions when viewed and defined in a way that is more modern and precise than Quintilian's way of looking at them.

281

Quintilian's duties of the orator were passed down to the Middle Ages as part of the course in rhetoric. Rhetoric and grammar were eventually taught as accessories to dialectic which dominated the thinking of the thirteenth century. Even the narrative poetry of the period began to take its structural organization from the dialectically organized university disputation.[3] The result was a blurring of the distinctions between the *prodesse* or 'useful' function of poetry and the *justa persuadere* or 'persuasive' function of rhetoric.[4] We should not be surprised to find then that the duties of the orator were assumed by the medieval narrative poet whose recited stories were fashioned with the intention of instructing, moving, or delighting a listening audience.[5]

Since Quintilian's concern in the passage cited above is with what is expected of an orator, he does not speak of *genera* or kinds of orations in connection with these three oratorical purposes. In fact, ancient and medieval theoreticians never thought to classify kinds of narrative according to authorial intention. To infer a writer's intentions on the basis of the text he produces is a subtle process, requiring the tools of modern critical analysis, for unless what the critic says can be backed up by the text, it is bound to be subjective. Moreover, authors usually do not state their intentions clearly or even honestly in some cases. However, we can know what effect an author hoped his narrative would have upon his audience if we study the way in which his devices function together in the narrative as a whole. I will have much more to say about devices throughout the course of this paper. But, for the moment, let me return to Roman and medieval theoreticians who believed that poems could be distinguished from one another according to the style — humble, middle, or sublime — in which they were written.

Narratives whose aim was to instruct were supposed to be in the humble genre, with a simple, clear style that appealed to the reason. Narratives that delighted were expected to be in the middle genre, written in an adorned, charming style. These narratives would appeal to the hearer's sensibility. Finally, the kind of narrative that moved an audience was supposed to represent the sublime genre, written expressively and forcefully. It would affect the listener's will and move him to tears.[6] As will soon become apparent, narratives that move us in Quintilian's sense of the word can make us laugh, cry, or snicker — they can even make us very angry — and so, for that matter, can narratives that teach us things. In short, the medieval genres, humble, middle, and sublime, simply don't describe medieval works in a way that enables us to distinguish them from one another. Nevertheless, as I said a little earlier, ancient and medieval rhetorical theory does offer a means for classifying narratives in a more meaningful way than even modern genre critics have done to date.

Among modern theoreticians, the emphasis has been upon the value of isolating organizing principles—that is, central principles which govern all the functions of the various parts of the work—in order to classify different kinds of stories.[7] Mary Doyle Springer, for example, is a holistic critic who, following in the footsteps of the late Sheldon Sacks of the Chicago School, discerns "mutually exclusive principles of wholeness" amongst the contemporary stories she attempts to classify in her *Forms of the Modern Novella.*[8] Although there are some things in Professor Springer's book with which I strongly disagree, her main point—that all of the devices in a story function together in the service of the organizing principle—has proven, for me at least, extremely useful. Taking the narrative aims which medieval writers inherited from Quintilian—*docere, movere,* or *delectare*—as my set of organizing principles, I found that the medieval narratives I looked at—and incidentally modern ones as well—fell into three mutually exclusive categories.

Having suggested that Quintilian's *docere, movere,* and *delectare* were by no means mutually exclusive, that in fact they were likely to overlap in any given work, let me now show why they become mutually exclusive when viewed in a more enlightened perspective than Quintilian's

If the *chief purpose* of a narrative were to be instructive, then, in the jargon of holistic critics, all of its devices would theoretically function together at the service of this narrative aim. Thus while we might be emotionally moved or delighted by such a work, or both moved and delighted by it, that which moved or delighted us would be subordinate to the narrative purpose which was to instruct. As an example, most of us love a good story. The better the story, the more delighted we are. But let us suppose that the aim of that story were to point out a kind of behavior to which we were susceptible and which the author considered foolish or reprehensible. Rather than tell us directly to avoid such behavior, a skilled writer might create a character who behaved in just the way he wanted us to avoid behaving, and rather than be heavy-handed or serious about it, he might try to "move" us to laughter. Clearly, the more we laughed at the character, the more delighted or entertained we would be by the story, and the less willing we would be to behave in the foolish way the character was behaving. Thus in moving us to laughter and by entertaining us in order to reach his chief narrative goal, which was to instruct us, the author would have transformed the other two possible narrative goals

—Quintilian's "movere," and "delectare"—into devices which functioned together with all the other devices in the work at the service of the propadeuctic aim of the work.

The kind of narrative that instructs is clearly ethically oriented, by which I mean that it is concerned with the morality or wisdom of human actions or behavior. I decided to name the kind of tale which fulfilled the orator's duty to instruct (Quintilian's "docere") "apologue" because Sheldon Sacks had already used the term to designate a form that subordinates all of its fictional devices to the making of a statement.[9] The kinds of tales that would be included in this category are stories we call fables, exempla, parables, and apologues.

It is easy to see that there could also be non-ethically oriented narratives which were not in the least concerned with instruction.[10] These kinds of stories would seek to entertain or delight an audience, and, not containing any lesson, would be quite distinct from apologues. The only tales that come to mind at the moment are jokes like *La Male honte* and *Du chevalier qui fit*. . . . Such narratives are non-ethically oriented because their sole purpose is to get a laugh. It is also possible, in theory at least, to have a non-ethically oriented anecdote that is primarily a mood piece, almost a lyric poem in prose. Marie's "Chievrefoil" comes close to being just that, but because "Honeysuckle" is a picture of perfect earthly love, it falls into the *docere* category—we learn a lot about how to love from this very short story.

It is clear that a story whose narrative aim was Quintilian's "delectare" would very likely seek to "move" us emotionally in order to achieve its special ends. But, as in apologue, the author's attempt to elicit an emotional response from us would be a device which, like all the other devices in the work, was subordinate to the chief narrative purpose. This second kind of story had no name in traditional criticism that I could find. In fact, I was hard pressed to discover good examples of the type, perhaps because, as John Gardner argued in *On Moral Fiction*, narratives that are not moral tend to be trivial. They are usually not great works of art.[11] In search of a neologism for the kind of narrative that merely seeks to delight or charm, i.e., to elicit a purely emotional response from us, I decided I needed a word with a Greek root and the suffix "logue" to complement the term "apologue." My friend, Thomas Bergin, forthwith produced the wonderfully apropos "rhapsologue."[12] Henceforth all those narratives whose principal aim was to inspire pity, fear, ridicule, laughter, or any other emotion rather than to teach a lesson or agitate the listener with an unresolved problem—my third kind of narrative fiction—would be "rhapsologues" in my mind.

Now it is clear that all fictions must reach us emotionally in some way in order to achieve their particular narrative goals. This being the case, then Quintilian's third oratorical aim would seem meaningless in the scheme of things I have been outlining. However, the Latin "movere" has a number of meanings which help us to discern a third mutually exclusive category of narrative fiction. The kind of story I have in mind is written by the sort of author who likes to act as a gadfly. He wants to move his audience in the sense that Latin "movere" has of 'stirring up trouble,' 'tormenting,' or 'upsetting' them. "Movere" has yet another meaning which very precisely describes the kind of tale I am talking about: that of 'causing' the hearer 'to turn what has been said over and over in his mind,' to 'ponder' the values being set forth at various levels of the narrative.[13] As we might expect, such stories can be instructive as well as upsetting, but their didactic function is subordinate to the quizzical function, as in the case of the *Yvain* where what we learn about the proper uses of chivalry is overpowered by our feelings of uneasiness about what Chrestien tells us were the "good old days" when people knew how to love. Similarly, in the *Chastelaine de Vergi* (= *ChV*), although the narrator persona's lesson about discretion is useful as far as it goes, the rigidity with which he presents that lesson becomes a device, the function of which is to underscore the fact that the lesson is inappropriate to the circumstances detailed in the tale proper.

The author of my third kind of story is an agitator; he does not tell his listener what he means by his tale. On the contrary, he often lies to him, telling him anything that furthers his desire to reach his audience through indirection. But once the listener has "heard the tale with his heart" as Chrestien de Troyes' Calogrenant would say, he knows there is something wrong with the arguments that have been put before him. In a satirical story like Chrestien's tale of Calogrenant the hearer / reader may laugh heartily at the foolishness of the narrator, but once he stops laughing, he is left with a very uneasy feeling. What did it all mean? In a tragic tale like *ChV*, it is the sense of the narrator persona's inequity that leaves the hearer / reader feeling agitated, perhaps even enraged, if he becomes really involved in the story. The medieval listener knew the narrator persona in *ChV*, who was performing the tale before him, had said things that were unfair and wrongheaded. Far from being an open and shut case — an "exemplum," or subtype of apologue, as the narrator persona calls his story at l. 951, the tale as a whole is open-ended.[14] While the narrator argues that the tragic incidents of the poem are the fault of the knight who failed to keep his love affair secret, the events of the

exemplum that is supposed to prove this hypothesis very plainly show
that the poor knight was a victim of tragic circumstances beyond his control. It was clear to me that if this tale was an exemplum, it had been
deliberately turned on its ear. I wondered if the poet had inverted the
genre of his principal source, Marie de France's "Lanval," an elegant
apologue, the way he had so many of its structures.[15] As it turned out,
this is exactly what he had done. Although space did not permit me to
analyze both *ChV* and "Lanval" here, it was possible to do a detailed
comparison between *ChV* and one of Jacques de Vitry's sermon exempla.
The exercise proved extremely fruitful because, in comparing and contrasting these opposing tale types, I was able to discern a watershed for
the directions taken by ethically oriented narrative fiction. On the one
hand was the traditional exemplary tale that teaches a lesson: the
apologue; on the other hand, the quizzical story that questions its own
norms and perhaps disconcerts a too complacent audience. To my surprise and delight, the medieval tales I had chosen to examine stood shimmering on the threshold of the modern novel. The gap between these
stories and later representatives of the same kinds of tales suddenly
closed for me because I had begun to see them all in a new perspective:
from a viewpoint that was able to take in and then move beyond the
idiosyncracies of individual devices and narrative surfaces.

My third kind of narrative was the most difficult to name. For a
very long time I felt that it ought to be designated by some form of the
word "novel" because Henry James, whose theory of the novel has traditionally set the trends in modern criticism of that form, was apparently
aware of the principle I had discovered.[16] Unfortunately, the term
"novel," as it is used by modern critics, is applied indiscriminately to all
three of my genres of narrative fiction so that it seemed psychologically
unwise to attempt to redefine it. Once again Professor Bergin came to my
rescue, this time fashioning the splendid "aenigmalogue" for me: indeed,
a tale that "troubles" its audience by causing them to "turn it over and
over in their minds" long after the poet's voice is still — a profoundly disturbing, puzzling, enigma of a tale.

In the pages that follow, I will be concentrating upon the kinds of
tales that either instruct or agitate the audience because I am only interested, for the moment, in ethically oriented fiction. It was Martianus
Capella who said that in the larger sense, the result of all discourse is to
raise doubts and to cause the hearer to assent to a proposition.[17] I will
take issue with Martianus only for not having gone far enough, because
what I have found is that the chief result of all ethically oriented discourse

is to raise doubts and to cause the hearer to assent to a proposition, or to raise doubts in order to undermine a proposition. In the latter case, the audience is sometimes left dangling, the problem is left unsolved, the tale remains open-ended. And it is not just the satirist who wishes to puncture myths. Literature has many moods, and artists have different temperaments. Since medieval literature in particular is a kind of game the rules of which are embedded in the text, the author is capable of donning many disguises and playing many tricks.[18] He may tell us the truth if he plays the preacher, but he can choose to play any part he wishes because he is the master of the game. One thing we as readers can do is to study the way in which his devices function within the text as a whole. Is he being ironic? Or can he be being serious? If ironic, why? to what purpose? How does this instance of irony affect our view of his characters? of his narrator? the way we view the text as a whole? What is he trying to say to us, and why can't he just say it and be done with it?

Fortunatus said the rhetor veiled his thought on account of modesty or fear or both.[19] Medieval writers believed that veiled thought was superior to plain speech when the lesson to be learned was precious. They spoke enigmatically in order that the unworthy might not besmirch the bright truth that lay hidden beneath the veil of fiction.[20] But sometimes, as in the case of Chrestien's tale of Calogrenant, the truth might be so painful for the audience to hear that they would not hear it unless it were veiled. This is usually the reason for an author's choice of indirection. Human defensiveness does not allow us to see our own faults unless we can forgive ourselves for them. An author lets us forgive ourselves by showing us a character who behaves like us. We laugh at the character because we see ourselves in him, but, at the same time, we stand back and deny that we ever behaved like that. That we fault the fictional character for the vices that lie within ourselves is healthy and good because it allows us space to grow and change.

Satire, tragedy, comedy, irony, and allegory have variously been called genres and modes throughout the ages. Without wishing to quarrel with these terms, I do know that I have found in my enquiry into the kinds of stories that either instruct or agitate an audience that satire, tragedy, comedy, irony, and allegory have all turned out to be devices that function at the service of the narrative purpose. For this reason, I would like to call them "moods." In Volume 2, *Chaucer and the Craft of Fiction*, I will be focusing upon Chaucer's *Merchant's Tale* which is a very sophisticated apologue that proceeds, as aenigmalogues usually do, through indirection. An example of remarkable sustained irony, and thus of indirection, this tale communicates its statement through a complex allegorical system that nevertheless spoke very clearly to Chaucer's audiences. After analyzing this tale, it becomes clear that although the mood of the story is satiric, Chaucer's aim is not merely to ridicule his Merchant narrator. Rather, he is concerned with the proper uses of marriage as these relate to the attainment of the supreme Good, which is God. As Professor Springer was at pains to demonstrate in her book, "satires" usually have a moral standard built into them, and the good in these works is not only visible, but conspicuous.[21] The purpose of satiric narrative then is to instruct or to question through the devices of irony and ridicule and the use of a moral standard against which to measure the ridiculed object. The same is true in narratives we call tragedies and comedies. Unless the tragic or comic narrative is non-ethically oriented, i.e., purely for entertainment and nothing else, then the pity, fear, laughter, and tears we are made to experience are all a means to an end. We either learn something from the experience of such narratives, or else we are left to puzzle out a meaning the author never tells us.

Before turning to Jacques de Vitry's preaching exemplum, it is perhaps expedient to address the objections of the many critics who believe that genres are in a constant state of flux and that literary kinds may be distinguished from one another on the basis of their content. What I am arguing here is that there are only three kinds of narrative fiction and that these appear to remain constant throughout literary history.

First a word about content as a basis for generic classification. If we accept the concept that a genre is a form, it is illogical to classify a literary kind according to what the story is about. As far as I am concerned, genres are shapes, formal constructs or "moulds," to use Henry James' word for it,[22] into which the author pours his thoughts, if I may be permitted the metaphor. Because unconscious human thought tends to be fragmentary, the writer needs these forms in order to limit and direct his artistic choices. Thus while it is perfectly true that devices and the anecdotal content or the superficial trappings of narratives come and go with the ebb and flow of cultures, the generic categories I have been describing here do not vary, being fundamental to the way in which the human mind deals with complex verbal constructs. Once I had selected the moral thrust of the work as my organizing principle, the resulting paradigm revealed itself to be extremely flexible. The author could use any devices he chose, as long as these devices functioned together in the service of the narrative purpose. In both kinds of ethically oriented tales I had chosen to focus upon — apologue and aenigmalogue — the behavior of the characters could have tragic, comic, or ridiculous consequences, and, in both kinds of tales, the attitude of the author or narrator towards his characters might be caring or detached. In other words, both the apologue and the aenigmalogue could be composed in any mood the author liked without his having to alter the generic paradigm within which he had chosen to work. It seemed that I had discovered a fundamental pattern for the process of literary creation. The pattern I was observing appeared to reflect the way in which the mind of the literary artist organizes formless thought and disparate narrative materials into mutually exclusive communicable wholes. It was so simple that the reader had no difficulty in correctly apprehending the narrative and yet so complex that the author could create within his chosen paradigm to his heart's content.

Critics will argue that stories with special names and distinctive surfaces, like lays and fabliaux, form generic categories of their own. Nevertheless, when we think about it, this isn't true. Most of Marie de France's lays, for example, are really elegant apologues. As with "Chievrefoil," we learn a great deal from the experience of these stories whose protagonists serve as exempla of the kinds of behavior to emulate or avoid in love and marriage. As for the fabliau, 'little fable,' the name of this type of tale may be ironic because some fabliaux, far from being moralistic are ribald stories. But, whether or not the tale is naughty, it is the form of the story, not its content, that determines its generic shape. Thus if a given fabliau turns out to be a purely delightful ribald tale, then it is non-ethically oriented—a rhapsologue. If it instructs us in some way—and Roy Pearcy's paper shows that the sentence of a number of fabliaux involves a lesson in expediency or practical wisdom—it is an apologue.[23] Finally, if it is open-ended or enigmatic, designed like *ChV* to agitate its public, it is an aenigmalogue.

To illustrate the importance of logical classification in genre studies, let me quote Hans Robert Jauss' opinion of Jean de Meun's portion of the *Roman de la Rose*: the book is, he tells us, "du genre de l'encyclopédie laïque" . . . "où se croisent—réunies dans le cadre traditionnel de l'allégorie amoureuse—des formes de la satire et de la parodie, de l'allégorie morale et de la mystique (à la suite de l'école de Chartres) du traité philosophique et des scènes de comédie. . . ."[24] In the first place, the encyclopedia is not a fictional genre, and Jean de Meun's book is eminently fictional. Further, I have explained why, from my point of view, allegory and satire are moods, or bundles of devices which are subordinate to the moral thrust of the work, and not genres. Parody, of course, is a device, and mysticism and philosophy are matters of content, not form. This lumping together of moods, devices and subject matter results in Jauss' viewing great literary masterpieces as generic salads, and this kind of thinking impedes our understanding and appreciation of the artistry of medieval narrative. For it is certain that Jean de Meun had a definite purpose in mind to which all the other materials in his book are subordinate. Charles Muscatine, for example, has called Jean's *Roman* an overt and serious disputation."[25] As I have already suggested, it was the medieval university disputation that served as the exemplar for much medieval moral fiction, open-ended tales being the most faithful to the spirit of their non-fictional model because they stimulate inquiry into the truth, while propadeuctic tales are presentations or representations of moral truths.[26] Surely it is in the Boethian construction — the juxtaposed dramatic monologues of the various characters, Reason, Friend, False Seeming, Nature, Genius, the Duenna, which form a dialectic on the proper uses of love and generation — that the unifying principle of the *Roman* is to be found and hence the generic category of the work.

While I agree with Jauss that "Entre les formes et les genres du Moyen Age et la littérature actuelle, il n'existe pas de continuité historique *visible* ou réperable,"[27] (italics mine), I hope to show that there is indeed an invisible continuity; that the forms of medieval narrative fiction are very much those of modern fiction. What differs is the content, the thematic preoccupations of the age, and some of the devices, though not all.

If my explanation of the genres of medieval narrative fiction has appeared somewhat simple, the business of classifying actual stories is extremely complex, requiring an intimate knowledge of the author's devices and the way in which these function together within the work as a whole. One thing, however, makes the task easier: although the apologist and the "aenigmologist" may employ the same devices — a formal *quaestio* or disputation topic posed within the tale proper, a dialectical gross structure, unreliable narrators, allusiveness to create that telescopic kind of narrative economy so typical of the best medieval tales, bits of lyric poetry enchased within the story, rhetorical constructs such as exempla, enthymemes, epicheiremes, and figures of thought and diction — these function in entirely opposite ways, depending upon whether the narrative is an apologue or an aenigmalogue. Thus, while the appearance of an unreliable narrator in a tale does not ensure that the narrative is an aenigmalogue, the function of that unreliable narrator within the generic paradigm helps to classify the work. For example, the *ChV* narrator persona adopts a patently untenable stance against the male protagonist.

Because, as we shall see, all the other devices in the story function together to undercut the narrator persona's condemnation of the knight, his "lesson" or "exemplum" as he calls it is rendered irrelevant. The tale is an aenigmalogue because the public is left to ponder an insoluble issue. Chaucer's Merchant narrator is also unreliable, for while claiming that women are responsible for the woe that is in marriage, the tale he tells clearly demonstrates that lecherous men are the cause of their own marital misery.[28] The reason Chaucer's narrative is not an aenigmalogue is that all the devices in the tale, including the unreliable narrator, are made to function at the service of a complex moral statement which is clearly communicated through the intricately wrought allegorical system of the work.

In short, because the same device functions differently within different generic paradigms, the way it functions may be considered a clear generic signal.[29] This being the case, I would like to focus upon just a few of these signals to show how they work in two opposing tale types, Jacques de Vitry's exemplum about Aristotle being ridden by one of Alexander's concubines, and *ChV*. Among the devices I have singled out are the relation of the frame or prologue-epilogue arrangement to the tale, the degree to which the reader is made to sympathize with or "care" about the characters,[30] the reliability of the narrator, the organization of fundamental concepts and of the diction deployed to evoke those concepts, and the use of allusion and lyric. Ideally we would expect to find an identity between the frame and the tale it encloses, that the narrator is thoroughly trustworthy, that we are kept at a fair distance from the characters — if their behavior is reprehensible — that allusions to other texts and lyric bits lend authority to the "lesson," or moral, and that the organization of important concepts and the key words used to accent these concepts — the verbal structure or "conjointure"[31] — drive home the main point in propadeuctic narrative. By contrast, one would expect that in open-ended narrative the frame would jar with the tale, as it does in *ChV*, allusions and lyric would undermine the narrator, as they do in *ChV*, that we would be made to care very much for the wronged characters, as we are for the *ChV* knight, and that the verbal *conjointure* would underline the fact that the central problem has no solution, thus keeping the audience in a state of anxiety, which once again turns out to be the case in *ChV*.

However, the fact of the matter is that *ChV* is an ideal specimen, which is why I have chosen to analyze it. In the hands of an extremely skilled apologist like Geoffrey Chaucer, the aenigmologist's devices may be made to serve the moral to the apologue. Thus we get not only unreliable narrators teaching us a moral lesson in spite of themselves, but the whole bag of aenigmologist's tricks to undercut that narrator — allusions he doesn't understand, lyric he debases because he is too crass to appreciate it, the use of outlandish language or dramatic impropriety, and the mock moral.

It was probably because Saint Augustine was disposed to accept rhetoric among other worldly devices as a viable method for communicating the word of God that the exemplum became something of an institution during the Middle Ages. Indeed, it would be difficult to imagine a medieval treatise or literary piece of any seriousness that did not employ examples to illustrate the argument or theme of the work. The subject matter of these anecdotes was rich and varied, being drawn from the nearly inexhaustible wealth of story materials that flooded Western Europe: eastern apologue, biblical narrative, classical myths and fables, histories and religious tales of all kinds were all pressed into service by writers and moralists alike.[32] But whatever the content of the exemplum, its structure was rhetorical in origin, ultimately stemming from Greek oratory.

In Book I of his treatise, the *"Art" of Rhetoric*, Aristotle defined the exemplum as one of two viable modes of rhetorical demonstration: "Now all orators produce belief by employing as proofs either examples or enthymemes i.e., rhetorical syllogisms and nothing else. . . ."[33] In recording how central the exemplum was to rhetorical argumentation as practiced in his day, Aristotle was to ensure its role at the very core of literature, because all narrative fiction tends to be "exemplary," being fundamentally an anecdotal art of persuasion.[34] As I said earlier, even enigmatic fictions set examples for us, although this kind of story is distinguished by the fact that, despite its exemplary qualities, some basic issue is left unresolved or is resolved in such a way that nothing in the narrative tells us what the right solution might have been. Thus, for example, Yvain learns the proper uses of chivalry, but his relationship with Laudine, which is one of the focal points of the narrative — indeed the prologue is about love during the golden age of chivalry — left a great deal for a courtly public to wonder and argue about.[35]

The classical exemplum, it must be remembered, was often precisely an "example," that is, a very brief evocation of real or fictional authorities, places, or events to illustrate an abstract point. Such an example could be as short as a proper name or a proverb and as long as a fable. While it never achieved the status of a literary genre, the exemplum in the hands of medieval apologists became an extended dramatized narrative with surprisingly developed literary qualities.[36]

With this necessarily brief account of the exemplum, let me turn to Jacques de Vitry's retelling of the tale of Aristotle being ridden by Alexander's wife. The piece is found in the *Sermones Feriales et Communes* (ca. 1229-40) and is based upon Henri d'Andeli's *Lai d'Aristote* (before 1225).[37] Exhibiting marked literary qualities, among which, its rhetorical balance, the use of lively, believable bits of dialogue, and the freshness of its very brief descriptive material, de Vitry's exemplum is typical of the kind of highly developed little narratives found in other medieval collections such as *Le cento novelle antiche o Libro di novelle e di bel parlare gentile detto anche Novellino*, whose diminutive tales are remarkable for their compression.[38] The exempla of the "Novellino" are viewed by Italian critics as precursors of the Boccaccesque tale, and, as I hope to show, the narrative technique of the French preaching exemplum is very much related to that of the early French apologue and aenigmalogue. But let us eavesdrop on the sermonist as he endeavors to wake up his congregation:

De Aristotile et uxore Alexandri

. . . in Ecclesiastico: "Qui se iungit fornicariis, erit nequam" et Apostolus Ia ad Corinthios: "Modicum fermentum totam massam corrumpit." Quod certo experimento, ut dicitur, probavit Aristotiles. Qui instruens Alexandrum adhuc adolescentem inter alia dixit ei, ut non multum frequentaret uxorem suam quam nimis diligebat, eo quod pulcerrima erat. Cumque se a frequentibus eius amplexibus subtraheret, illa valde cepit dolere et studiose inquirere, unde proveniret in viro suo tanta et tan subita mutacio. Cumque pro certo didicisset quod magister eius Aristotiles istud procurasset, post multas cogitaciones et cordis anxietates viam et modum repperit, quibus se de Aristotile vindicaret. Et cepit ipsum frequenter intueri deambulans in orto; et respiciens per fenestram camere in qua studebat homo ille, et oculis ridentibus et verbis lascivie cepit robur eius emollire; et aliquando discalciata et vestes elevans atque tibias denudans coram ipso ambulabat. Et ita in amorem et concupiscenciam suam mentem eius enervatam voluntati. Cui illa respondit: "Credo quod temptare me vis et decipere. Nullo enim modo credere possem quod homo tanta sapientia preditus talia vellet attemptare." Cumque ille perseveraret pulsans, dixit illa: "In hoc sciam quod ex corde me diligis, si ea que tibi dixere pro amore meo facere non recusaveris. Cras hora matutina domino meo adhuc dormiente ad me in ortum istum exibis et super pedes et manus ambulando, ut te quitare possim, incurvaberis." Cum autem miser carnali *concupiscencia* captivatus, *illectus et abstractus* consensisset, illa voti compos effecta accessit ad Alexandrum et ait illi: "Cras mane parati estote, et videbitis, utrum magistro vestro qui a vobis alienare me volebat, credere debeatis!" Cum igitur

Aristotle Being Ridden by Alexander's Wife
Janet Anderson

mane facto regina Aristotilem equitaret, rege superveniente et ei improperante ac mortem comminante, post multam erubescenciam et confusionem ad se tendem reversus magister respondit: "Nunc pro certo perpendere debes, quod fideliter adolescencie tue consului. Si enim versucia mulieris et malicia tantum prevaluit, quod senem et prudentissimum inter omnes mortales decepit et captivum duxit, et qui multis et magnis conclusi magistris michi conclusit: quanto magis te decipere, allicere et circumvenire prevaleret, nisi exemplo meo tibi caveres." Quo audito rex ira sedata magistro suo prudenter respondenti pepercit.

According to Eccles. 19: 3, "And he that joineth himself to harlots will be worthless, and the Apostle Paul in 1 Cor. 5:6, "[Know you not that] a little leaven is enough to leaven the whole batch!" In fact Aristotle demonstrated it by certain proof, so the story goes. Instructing Alexander, when he was still a young man, he said to him, among other things, that he should not frequent one of his wives so much whom he loved excessively because she was very beautiful. And when [Alexander] drew away from her frequent embrace, she began to grieve exceedingly and to enquire anxiously how such a great and sudden change had come over her husband. But when she found out for certain that [it was] his tutor Aristotle who had brought it about, after much thought and anxiety she discovered a way to get even with Aristotle. And strolling in the garden, she began to gaze upon the master him[self]. Frequently looking through the window of the room in which the man studied she began to weaken his will with smiling eyes and lascivious words. And she would walk barefoot from time to time, lifting her dress and revealing her legs in front of him. And she even led his weakened mind into such a state of love and desire for her that he began asking [her] to comply with his wishes. [Then] she replied to him, "I think you wish to tempt and deceive me. For in no way could I possibly believe that a man endowed with so much wisdom should wish to seduce someone like me." As he persisted, she said, "In this I shall know that you love me sincerely, if you do not refuse to do what I shall ask [of] you for Love's sake. Tomorrow at matins, while my lord is still sleeping, you will come to me to this garden, [and you will] bend [over] so that I may ride you like a horse." However, when the unhappy man, seized by carnal desire [led astray and witless] consented, having gratified her wish, she went to Alexander and said to him, "Tomorrow morning be ready and you will see whether you ought to believe your tutor who wanted to alienate me from you!" Thus, when it was morning, the queen rode on Aristotle's back with the king arriving unexpectedly and abusing him, threatening death to him. Returning at last to his senses after much blushing and confusion, the master answered, "Now surely you must consider how faithfully I was watching out for your youth. If indeed the malice and cunning of the woman so prevailed that she deceived and held an old man captive, the most prudent of all mortals, and who has argued with many great masters, it demonstrated to me how much more

power she might have over you [whom she could so much more easily]
deceive, allure, and defraud, unless you guard against her [through]
my example." When he heard this, the king's anger was assuaged, and
he spared his tutor who was replying so prudently.[39]

Unlike modern narrative where the prologue-epilogue arrangement
has been subsumed by the story, medieval narratives very frequently were
framed by thematic materials. This device of conditioning the public to
respond to the tale in certain ways is significant for determining the generic category of the tale depending upon the way in which it functions. In
the case of the sermon exemplum, the public is given a theme to con-
template, and that theme is then illustrated by the tale. In the aenigmalogue, the frame may be made to jar visibly with the tale, as in *ChV*,
where the so-called *exemplum* seriously undermines the lesson being
taught in the prologue and epilogue.

The frame of de Vitry's preaching exemplum is made up of those
general remarks, proverbs and maxims surrounding the anecdote enchased within the larger sermon. In this particular exemplum, since the
editor was interested primarily in the stories themselves, we have the
preacher's opening commentary, but not the moralizing remarks which
perhaps followed the relation of Aristotle's misadventure. As stated in
the text, the purpose of the tale about to unfold will be to illustrate two
biblical aphorisms: (1) that lust, or "the joining of oneself to harlots,"
renders all men worthless (Eccles. 19:3) and (2), that "a little leaven is
enough to leaven the whole batch" (1 Cor. 5:6) by which Saint Paul
meant that a fornicator must be excommunicated from among the Corin-
thians lest he contaminate all of them. At the very outset of the exemplum proper, then, the pagan Aristotle is made to assume a Jeromian
stance when he warns Alexander not to be a too ardent lover of his wife.[40]
Since the formidable seductive powers of Alexander's queen are able to
confound the reason of Aristotle himself, the most rational of men,
"prudentissimum inter omnes mortales," the exemplum illustrates very well
how a little leaven can make the whole batch rise and that women are
potentially dangerous to a man's soul. So treacherous is this woman that
she even succeeds in causing a momentary rift between her powerful husband and his famous tutor. Alexander's queen is obviously the leaven
"fermentum" in the tale. Because we are made to see how carnal desire
confuses both Aristotle's and Alexander's judgment, the story certainly
demonstrates how great a danger woman, as sex object, is to all men, if
even the most prominent representatives of clerisy and chivalry from one
of the greatest civilizations in human history, become weak and worthless

in her power. In short there is an absolute identity between what the preacher/narrator *tells* us in the frame and what his exemplum *shows* us.[41] As in other medieval exempla, the anecdote serves as a paradigm for future human conduct. The listener learns what to expect from the fair descendants of Eve and how to guard against the wiles of women by avoiding their frequent perilous embrace.

The exemplum proper begins with an admonition by Aristotle to his pupil, Alexander, to avoid the woman, and it ends with a second admonition, this time offering reasons demonstrated by Aristotle's fall, for avoiding the woman: "quanto magis te decipere, allicere et circumvenire prevaleret, nisi exemplo meo tibi caveres." In a word, the gross structure of this exemplum forms three concentric circles: the biblical maxims of the frame, introducing the tale, and which probably found an echo in the continuation of the sermon, surround Aristotle's warnings against the woman, which, in turn, enclose Aristotle's own experience as irrefutable proof: "Quod certo experimento . . . probavit Aristotiles" and "nisi exemplo meo tibi caveres." It is not unusual to find this kind of structure in short narrative. We will see it again in *ChV* for example. But when we come to study that aenigmalogue, it will become apparent that while the frame structure will still describe a circle, the "lesson" to be gleaned from the inscribed "exemplum" will be at odds with that of the frame. In other words, although the frame and the tale have the same gross structural configuration in both the exemplum and the aenigmalogue, this device functions in opposite ways in the two kinds of narrative.

The second most significant device I would like to examine here is that of making the reader care for certain characters, or, alternately, keeping him at a fair emotional distance from them. The characters in the Aristotle exemplum are much more vivid than was usual in the classical rhetorical exemplum, but, for all that, they are still extremely flat.[42] We are never allowed to develop any sympathy for them. Rather we are expected to accept unquestioningly the authority of the preacher/narrator and to identify with either Alexander or Aristotle. If anything, we are supposed to be terrorized by what the woman represents. As the Wyf of Bath's fifth husband, the good clerk Jankyn, knew, lechery, even with a wife, imperils the soul. "Never give thy soul into a woman's power, and let her command the fortress of it, to thy shame" (Eccles. 9:2)!

If we are kept at a fair emotional distance from the "harlot" in the story, her wicked power is nevertheless colorfully described in a lively gesture portrait. As in the fictional gospels of the Apocryphal New Testament, the preacher lingers over the description of the temptation.

This is because he wishes to dramatize, as graphically as possible, how dangerous the woman is. She must be made to seem so delightful that even the congregation is tempted by her. As the late Salvatore Battaglia explained in his *Giovanni Boccaccio* . . . ,[43] medieval man did not shrink from the Enemy (i.e., the Devil) rather he believed it was necessary to confront evil in order to be truly good. Except for the narrator's explanation that Alexander loved her because she was so beautiful, the portrait of the queen is all gesture: "deambulans in orto," "respiciens per fenestram," "oculis ridentibus et verbis lascivie," "discalciata et vestes elevans atque tibias denudans." This dramatization of her seductive power through the crystallization of her gestures is preceded by an inside view of her maliciousness, a technique the *ChV* poet uses in his handling of the duchess, another of Eve's literary sisters: "post multas cogitaciones et cordis anxietates viam et modum repperit, quibus se de Aristotile vindicaret" (cf. *ChV* ll. 551–64, where the duchess plots how to get the secret out of the duke by using the wiles of her sex).[44] This inside view of Alexander's queen and the gesture portrait are capped with a sample of her deceitful words to Aristotle: "Credo quod temptare me vis et decipere" (!) (Again, compare her taunt, "In hoc sciam quod ex corde me diligis, si ea que tibi dixere pro amore meo facere non recusaveris" with the *ChV* duchess's temptation of the duke, ll. 577 ff.). Of course, ironically, it is the woman who seeks to tempt and deceive, not poor old Aristotle. Finally, having dealt with the master, we witness her manipulation of the pupil. We hear her prick Alexander to come see for himself whether or not Aristotle is to be trusted. Thus we have *seen* and *heard* how this "harlot" degrades men, makes wise men behave foolishly and turns them against one another through her treachery. We are now fully prepared for Aristotle's condemnation of her: "Si enim versucia mulieris et malicia tantum prevaluit . . . quanto magis te decipere etc. . . . ." The preacher / narrator has carefully calculated his audience's response to the woman: she corrupts and must therefore be avoided, no matter how beautiful, regardless of how tempting.

It must be clear from all I have been saying that the reliability of the preacher / narrator is unimpeachable. Every word that drips from his lips is THE TRUTH. Even so, the narration of this exemplum is a bit more complex than at first appears. Ostensibly, the tale is told by de Vitry, whose vision is omniscient (he sees into the minds and hearts of his characters and he knows how *all* men and women behave). However, the experience he relates is Aristotle's, and it is his example from which we must profit. Thus, to resort to Jamesian terminology, when Aristotle's discovery in the garden by his young, irate pupil, Alexander, embarrasses him into recovering his senses, he becomes a "reflector" for the preacher. Our extended inside view of his temptation establishes him as a second narrator. In fact, his personal experience, as dramatized for us in the story, coupled with his renown as *the wisest man*, makes Aristotle a more reliable witness than de Vitry himself: "Quod certo experimento . . . probavit Aristotiles." Coming from Aristotle, then, the condemnation of the woman carries enormous authority: "If she deceived me, who am the wisest of men, then how dangerous she must be to simple men!"

A number of critics have remarked that the novella seems to have a polarized structure which revolves about a central symbol.[45] Nevertheless, as I hope will become apparent by the end of this paper, while this kind of structure may be typical of a number of short narratives, it is not generically significant in and of itself. However, the way in which the tension between the narrative poles is maintained or resolved may signal generic differences. In the exemplum we are examining, Alexander represents the chivalric pole while the significantly more loquacious Aristotle stands for the clerical pole of the tale. Critics who look for central symbols in short fictions would perhaps find that this story revolves about the woman, or Eve figure at its center as she casts her malicious spell over both knight and cleric alike. Certainly it is significant that although there is a certain amount of tension between the two men because of the woman, this conflict is resolved when Aristotle manages to demonstrate through his own foolishness the truth of the lesson he had attempted to teach his pupil at the beginning of the story. It is because the initial polarization or dialectic is resolved that we cannot apprehend this tale as anything but exemplary. If the author pitted the world's greatest philosopher against the world's greatest knight, it was because the knight and the cleric represented the highest professional goals that medieval society had to offer. If these two great pagan authorities could arrive at the same conclusion as the narrator/preacher, namely that woman (i.e., lechery) is to be avoided, then what must the common man think except that this is the absolute truth?

The polarization between clerisy and chivalry forms part of the rhetorical balance one finds in many well-wrought tales throughout the early history of western narrative. Major concepts, sometimes embodied by characters, tend to be juxtaposed to one another. Naturally, such antitheses are reflected in the diction that is used to express these concepts. Thus in the Aristotle exemplum, *adolescens* and *rex* are set in opposition to *magister*, *senex*, and *prudentissimus*:

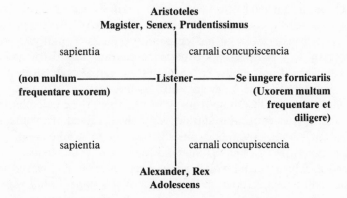

Aristoteles
Magister, Senex, Prudentissimus

sapientia   carnali concupiscencia

(non multum————————**Listener**————**Se iungere fornicariis**
frequentare uxorem)   **(Uxorem multum**
                                              frequentare et
                                              diligere)

sapientia   carnali concupiscencia

Alexander, Rex
Adolescens

Although, as I said before, the tale might be said to revolve about the woman, my diagram of the verbal structure depicts the medieval listener at the very heart of the tale. The reason for this is that the preacher has deliberately involved his listener as deeply as possible in the narrative by claiming that apprehension of the meaning will determine the destiny of his mortal soul. By employing characters with whom this implied listener would have identified, the narrator ensures the involvement he seeks from his audience. The fact that the usually prudent Aristotle and the more sensuous Alexander find themselves in the same dilemma, and that that dilemma is one which the medieval Christian listener was certain to have experienced himself, shows that no matter how disciplined or what the estate of the man in question, he is still capable of losing his soul through the sin of fornication.

A little thought quickly reveals that whereas the polarization of concepts in the de Vitry exemplum is intentional, the antithetical treatment of diction is sporadic and unsystematic, indicating that it was probably unconscious. By contrast, the rhetorical patterning of the diction in *ChV* is both intricate and deliberate, as we will see presently.

In addition to antitheses as both figures of thought and figures of speech, the little sermon exemplum we have been examining utilizes the kind of convoluted repetition typical of rhetorical argumentation and which was to become a major device in narrative fiction.[46] Through the figures of thought known as *commoratio*, or dwelling on the point, and *expolitio*, refining or polishing an idea through varied repetition, the main theme of the exemplum, the treacherousness of the woman, is reworked again and again, but in such varied ways that we do not notice how the point is being driven home. The theme is introduced in a general way via the two biblical maxims of the frame. Our first glimpse of the queen's feminine wiles comes very early on when, through the narrator, we enter her mind as she realizes Alexander suddenly shrinks from her embrace. Through the preacher, we see the lustful strumpet's tearful efforts to discover the reason for his behavior, and we become a party to her vengeful nature. Such an inside view would immediately have evoked in the medieval listener's mind a certain type of woman. We have already seen how through a gesture portrait and two snatches of her conversations with Aristotle and Alexander we are made to *see* and *hear* how dangerous she is. All these instances are examples of varied repetition or *expolitio*, and, of course, of dwelling on the point. Further, by dramatizing her corruption of the two men, the point is made yet again. After so many repetitions in such varied guises, Aristotle's warning has the force of truth. In short, the public has been artfully manipulated and persuaded. Alexander's queen, upon whom this narrative centers, becomes an emblem for all the mischief of which womankind is capable.

Naturally, a good deal of the persuasive force of the piece is lost on us moderns because most of us, at least, no longer harbor superstitious fears of women. Moreover, in this egocentric age we live in, it is difficult for us to visualize human beings as pure types in the manner of a theocentric culture like that of medieval Europe. Neither do we fancy being visibly manipulated by an intrusive author / narrator. Nevertheless, if we are to enter into the medieval imagination, it is necessary to understand and to accept as viable literary devices, these fundamental, albeit dated, features of the psychology and style of the age.

By now I hope it is clear that in spite of its sermonizing tone, the exemplum we have been examining is a piece of literature. Its dramatic qualities, at least partly attributable to the connection between pulpit and stage, the economical description of gestures, rudimentary dialogue, and inside views of the characters' minds are all "novelistic" techniques, that is, devices characteristic of those fully developed fictional narratives I call apologues and aenigmalogues. The polarization of concepts and of the words which express these concepts, around a central character or emblem, is a structure derivable from classical forensic rhetoric or legal narrative, where the lawyer had to argue round and round the point adjudicate.[17] It is this distinctive rhetorical patterning which was to become typical of much short narrative fiction. However, the verbal system of correspondences, usually a network of synonyms and antonyms, has a very special function in an aenigmalogue like *ChV*. Whereas the apologist may use convoluted repetition to get his statement across, the function of *expolitio* in the aenigmalogue is to dwell upon both sides of a question, as in a medieval disputation, so that the central problem is never resolved.

La Chastelaine de Vergi is an anonymous short verse narrative of the thirteenth century (ca. 1250–78). A minor work, *ChV* has nevertheless captured the imagination of a number of well-known critics because it is a beautifully made tale. One of its most intriguing and appealing features is that it transforms into narrative fiction the ideals and concerns of thirteenth-century noble society as celebrated in the Provençal love lyric. What is even more interesting is that the vehicle via which this transformation takes place is a dialectical or scholastic structure which is very like that of the *geu-parti*, a lyric debate between rival poets about some rule of love.

In the prologue a general rule, that to tell the secret inevitably leads to woe, is confronted with a specific case, that of a knight who tells the secret of his love for the lady of Vergi, and whose love affair ends in tragedy. While the tale does successfully demonstrate that no one, not even the duke of Burgundy, is to be trusted with the secret, the narrator persona's claim that the tragedy came about *because* the knight told the secret is untrue. Rather, the lovers lose their lives because the knight finds himself in a situation whose only possible outcome is his death. In a word, whether or not the knight tells the secret, given the chain of circumstances which lead to the telling, is irrelevant because as soon as the duke threatens to hang or banish him, woe and death are certain to follow. The *only* way for the knight to prove his innocence, the duke tells him, is to reveal the identity of his mistress. Had the poet really been attempting to teach his audience the value of discretion, as the narrator persona says he is, he would not have chosen an extreme case that so sorely tests the rule, throwing the system that produced the rule, with all the behaviors that the rule implies, into doubt. In short, while a superficial reading might convince us that this tale is an apologue, a careful study of its devices shows that it is an aenigmalogue, the author's chief purpose having been to agitate, or "move" his public. As I said in the introduction to this paper, a tale that moves us can also be instructive, but if its principal aim is to make an audience question the materials it has put forward, then it is an aenigmalogue.

In the pages that follow, I will be relying to some degree upon that element of audience reception that can be known on the basis of the text. While we cannot know how an audience in fact received a text, we can determine what the author expected from his audience by his use of certain devices and by his allusions to other texts. For example, Jacques de

Vitry expected the men in his audience to know who Aristotle and Alexander were so that they could identify with them. Otherwise the force of his exemplum would have been lost. He also expected them to have certain attitudes about marriage and sex; otherwise the Jeromian stance he takes would have met with surprise or opposition. Extracting these facts from the text helps us to construct an implied audience and, of course, to determine the narrative purpose. In *ChV*, the audience would have to have been courtly and elegant. They would have to have been familiar with the *joc partit, oarystis, alba, planh*, and *canso* in order to fully enjoy the peformance. They must have appreciated the dialectical and rhetorical devices which abound in this narrative because the scholastic ring of the tale is very important to its meaning. It is also clear from the text that the author expected them to be familiar with the Tristan material and the biblical tale of Potiphar's Wife from Genesis 39.

When the story of the Lady of Vergi begins, the lady's lover, through his chivalric virtues, has so risen in the favor of his powerful liege lord, the reigning duke of Burgundy, that he has become his favorite. The knight's political position occasions numerous visits to the court until, at last, he is unlucky enough to catch the lustful eye of the duchess. This wanton, but influential, woman pursues the love-distracted knight until, at last, he is forced to reject her, albeit as gently as possible in the circumstances. Alone in bed with the duke, an enraged duchess accuses her husband's vassal of having tried to woo her. The poor duke spends a night of terrible anguish torn between his love for his wife and his friendship for his favorite courtier. The next day the duke confronts the knight, demanding that he divulge the name of his mistress as proof of his innocence, the rationale behind his demand being that a true lover cannot love two persons at the same time. Although he has sworn never to reveal the chastelaine's identity on pain of losing her love, the knight has also rashly promised the duke under oath to answer any question he may put to him. Thus when the question turns out to involve the name of his mistress, the knight finds himself in a terrible dilemma or *geu-parti*. If he refuses to oblige the duke, then he will be banished as a perjurer, in which case he stands to lose both his lady and his honor. On the other hand, if he betrays the chastelaine, and she discovers it, the knight will lose her as surely as if he had been banished. In other words, he is torn between a deep emotional need to remain in the same country as his mistress since, in Frederick Goldin's terms, she is his mirror and thus inextricably linked with his identity,[48] and the equally pressing socio-economic need to be reconciled with his liege lord. Just as the lady represented the

courtly ideal, the crown of the knight's career as a courtly man, his liege
lord also held his life in the balance. To foresake his home would have
meant a life of wandering and perhaps starvation unless the knight could
find another protector. And even when he did find another lord, he
would surely have to prove himself all over again. It could not have been
given to everyone to save a foreign kingdom for a foreign lord as the
romances would have us believe. The Eliducs were surely the exception to
the rule. In reality, to be a knight errant meant to risk being killed or
maimed, and many were those who perished. Knight errantry also meant
being poor unless prowess, political finesse, and luck won the favor of a
rich and powerful lord who, like the duke of Burgundy, had fiefs to
grant. More likely than not, service to a foreign lord would go unre-
warded, as it does in Marie de France's *Lanval*.

Torn between the oath of secrecy he has sworn to his mistress and
the oath of loyalty he has sworn to his lord, the knight is certain that
whatever he decides will lead to his death:

> Cil ne set nul conseil de soi,
> que le geu a parti si fort
> que l'un et l'autre tient a mort.
> [268]
> The knight could find no counsel
> in his ruinous dilemma;
> he considered that whatever choice he made would lead to death.

Since he cannot live without his lady, and because either solution
would result in her loss, the knight's dilemma is an irrevocable death
sentence. Thus when the duke promises to keep his love affair a secret,
the knight decides to trust him. Upon hearing that the knight loves the
chastelaine, who is his niece, the duke begins to believe that his vassal
cannot have asked his wife for her love. Naturally he requires more
tangible proof than an oath, and so he accompanies him to the chastelaine's manor where he sees and hears the lovers' amorous greeting and
farewell. Clearly the duke's presence at their tryst is the most treasonous
violation of the lovers' covenant possible and yet, what other choice did
the knight have? Tristan, we remember, chose banishment from Iseut to
preserve their honor, and they both eventually died for it. The knight has
chosen the opposite path, but, alas, he has only put off the inevitable for
a little while because the wicked duchess wheedles all the details of his
secret out of her husband. At Whitsuntide, when the duke's subjects are
gathered together at his court, the duchess viciously confronts the chastelaine by alluding to a little lap dog which has long served as a private
signal between the lovers. The chastelaine dies of a broken heart, believing

her lover has betrayed her secret because he has been carrying on an affair with both her and the duchess at the same time. Thus her concern is with the very tangible matter of her love's fidelity rather than with his defilement of some ineffable courtly ideal. Coming upon the expired chastelaine and hearing a little serving girl's account of her last moments, the knight perceives that he is the cause of her death and kills himself. The narrator persona prattles on in the epilogue, as he had in the prologue, that the whole mess was the knight's fault because he had failed to keep his pact with the chastelaine.

In the *ChV* narrative the lady of lyric is brought to life with consummate art. Once animated, however, this ideal woman simply cannot exist in the real world because no man can measure up to her impractical expectations, and she herself is bound to be flawed. As Frederick Goldin wrote of Provençal love service:

> To place all our hopes in an idealized human being: to turn our life into service to another person whom we have nominated to justify us; to seek in her for the image of our future perfection—such a personal submission is full of peril, because it is based on a lie, projecting onto the lady an ideality that her flesh and blood must betray . . .[49]

During the passage from song to narrative the lyric situation—adoring man striving to win and keep the love of a lady who embodies the ideals of courtly society and who thus mirrors the man's progress in that society—undergoes some modification.[50] In *ChV*, where, unlike lyric, the love has been consummated, the lady idealizes the man, perhaps even more than he does her, looking to him to supply her with an identity. As in the "mirror lyrics" described by Goldin, the moment when the love object is recognized as a mere reflection of the lover's self is perilous. In the narrative, where the lyric situation is developed to its logical conclusion, the outcome is tragic. As in the myth of Narcissus, which Goldin believes underlies the *canso*, once the idealized image falters, showing itself to be unworthy of the lover's adoration, the lover must die or learn to love another rather than himself. Like Narcissus, the chastelaine cannot live unless the image she idolizes returns her love perfectly. His apparent infidelity shatters her identity, and she perishes.

Critics before me have already classified this story as a "novella."[51] However, because, as I explained earlier, the word "novella" originally signified "any tale" I feel that the term has no value for the description of literary kinds. In fact, our tolerance of imprecise generic terminology—regardless of how traditional the term—only perpetuates misconceptions about the works we are trying to classify. For example, to call *ChV* a "precursor of the novella" as Söderhjelm and Dubuis have done is to assume that novellas have a particular structure in which *ChV* does not fully participate.[52] Although I do not deny that this little masterpiece of early narrative fiction does have some imperfections, it in no way falls short of being a perfect aenigmalogue.

One of the most visible devices for creating an aenigmalogue is the use of an unreliable narrator, or a narrator with limited vision. The narrator persona in *ChV* makes a logical, cogent argument for the law of secrecy in love,[53] which is wise and good as far as it goes. But in the exemplum, which is supposed to prove that the knight brought the tragedy upon himself by revealing his mistress' identity, the knight finds himself ensnared by the duke in a *geu-parti*, or insuperable dilemma about whether or not to tell the secret. The dilemma is posed in such a way that it makes no difference whether the knight reveals or conceals his mistress' name because whichever choice he makes will lead to death. The poet's use of the *geu-parti* in this way renders the whole question of secrecy irrelevant because the tragedy hinges upon the knight's predicament, not upon the telling of the secret. Thus what we eventually learn from this narrative is not discretion, but a mistrust of the system of love service that depends upon adherence to the letter of its laws. In the process, we also learn to be suspicious of the judgment of a narrator whose literal mindedness blinds him to the inequities brought about by a code he himself never questions. In short the narrative voice in *ChV* is one of the earliest examples in the French short story of what Henry James would later call a "flawed center of consciousness," and this, of course, makes it a very exciting moment in the history of narrative fiction.[54] As far as I know, the earliest examples of unreliable narrators in French literature occur in the "romances" of Chrestien de Troyes.

A number of medievalists will object to the comparison of medieval "text enunciators" with Jamesian narrators and reflectors. As Peter Haidu puts it, "Late nineteenth- and early twentieth-century 'point of view' implies and depends upon contemporary views of the uniqueness of subjects, the relativization of 'perspectives,' and a potential solipsism that it would be difficult to sustain as operative in the twelfth century" (p. 24).

Let me say right away that I agree with Professor Haidu. Like all fictional characters, medieval narrators are the embodiments of ideas, but unlike modern characters who are life-like becuase of the psychological stuff of which they are made, medieval characters are fashioned from traditional materials. Nevertheless, even a character like Chaucer's

Merchant narrator, stitched together from scraps of iconography, takes on the appearance of a "real person" in the tale he tells. Like many a modern narrator, he lies to his audience, deliberately misleading them lest they discover his selfish sinfulness. His motivation, however, is not psychological, but iconographical. He is a figure for the devil, and as such, he must act out the sins he embodies in a way that is verisimilar. By representing himself as a victim of women's wiles, the Merchant attempts to obfuscate the fact that lecherous men are responsible for much of the woe that is in marriage. The medieval listener was expected to play an active role in Chaucer's narrative by "separating the chaff from the grain," or discarding the sinful surface of the tale—which he nevertheless was supposed to enjoy because it is hilarously funny—in favor of the moral philosophical lesson which is promulgated through the complex allegorical system of the text.

Non-Chaucerians usually counter that Chaucer is a special case. Notwithstanding, Chaucer learned to write by reading the French poets. All of his devices can be found in earlier literature; what makes him "different" is that he was a genius at pushing those devices to the limits of their capabilities. What I am saying then is that although medieval characters are not psychologically rounded or "real" in our modern sense of the word, they are still used as devices, the narrative function of which is the same as that of their modern counterparts.

When medieval characters are made to speak, they usually do so in one of several ways: (1) they tell us the entire truth like the Preacher/narrator of the Aristotle exemplum, (2) they tell us as much of the truth as they know, as in Marie de France's lays, (3) they tell us the truth as they see it, which is what the narrator persona in *ChV* does, or (4) they deliberately mislead us or lie to us, as do Chaucer's Merchant and Chrestien's Calogrenant. As far as I am concerned, a narrator, be he medieval or modern, who is less than omniscient, is a "flawed center of consciousness," or "unreliable," in the restricted sense I have outlined for these terms here.

If I may be forgiven a further excursus on this important and controversial matter, I would like to analyze Chrestien's Calogrenant because he is a fine example of a medieval narrator whom we learn to mistrust very early on in the story. Like Chaucer's Merchant, Calogrenant has a double function: He tells an entertaining story—in this case badly—which misrepresents his role somewhat because he would like to minimize the shamefulness of his defeat in battle. Thus, while he is not an evil character like the Merchant, he is also not completely truthful. Like

Chaucer, who undermines his Merchant in the General Prologue to the *Canterbury Tales*, Chrestien subtly lets his audience know that this narrator is not to be trusted. He gives Calogrenant a prologue to deliver that is totally out of character for a knight. The inappropriate scholastic tone of this speech makes it a signaling device, the purpose of which is to alert the audience as to the role they are expected to play in listening to the tale. The device is not unlike Chaucer's when he has his evil Merchant begin his tale "Wepying and wayling" like Boethius, i.e., a moral philosopher![55]

It seems fairly certain that most medieval listeners would have perceived Calogrenant as representing the foppish concerns of the arrogant, and perhaps young, noblemen whom the poet very clearly wishes to reach in this romance.[56] Chrestien's provocative intent lies behind Calogrenant's long-winded speech about hearing with the heart:

> . . . or escotez!
> Cuers et oroilles m'aportez,
> car parole est tote perdue
> s'ele n'est de cuer entandue.
> De cez i a qui la chose oent
> qu'il n'entandent, et si la loent;
> et cil n'en ont ne mes l'oïe,
> des que li cuers n'i entant mie;
> as oroilles vient la parole,
> ausi come li vanz qui vole,
> mes n'i areste ne demore,
> einz s'an part en molt petit d'ore,
> se li cuers n'est si esveilliez
> qu'au prendre soit apareilliez;
> car, s'il le puet an son oïr
> prendre, et anclorre, et retenir,
> les oroilles sont voie et doiz
> par ou s'an vient au cuer la voiz;
> et li cuers prant dedanz le vantre
> la voiz, qui par l'oroille i antre.
> Et qui or me voldra entandre,
> cuer et oroilles me doit randre,
> car ne vuel pas parler de songe,
> ne de fable, ne de mançonge.
>
> [149]
>
> Now listen! . . .
> Lend me your hearts and ears
> because words are lost
> when they are not understood.
> Some people hear what is said,
> and, not understanding what they hear, they praise it,
> but they have heard nothing more than the sounds
> when they have not understood with their hearts.

The words come to the ears
just like the wind which flies,
but they neither stop nor tarry,
rather they quickly depart
if the heart is asleep
and not disposed to grasp what is being said.
Now if a person can take the words into his ears,
shut them in and retain them,
the ears are the passage
through which the voice reaches the heart.
Then the heart takes into the chest the voice
which has entered through the ear.
Whoever would understand me now
must lend me both his heart and his ears
because I speak not of dreams,
fables or lies.

It is Chrestien, not Calogrenant, whose words we are supposed to take into our hearts. In fact, this long, clerkish preamble in the mouth of a knight is startling to say the least.

Calogrenant's comparison of his own voice to the wind is not without irony on the part of the author. The knight's protest must also strike us as slightly inappropriate considering that everyone is already listening to him with rapt attention and that the queen has commanded him to continue his tale. (l. 136) Our first impression of this story then is that the teller is affected and silly. Although we are not disposed to trust the sarcastic seneschal, Keu, we cannot help but remember his characterization of this man as having little sense (l. 76). It must also have struck the medieval audience that, unlike most medieval storytellers, this fellow has no lofty moral purpose to emphasize. Rather, in contrast to Chrestien's own proud prologues, Calogrenant's tale redounds not to his honor but to his shame (l. 60). If he means his story as an example of what not to do, he never says so. Rather he greatly emphasizes its value as an adventure. Since the adventure turns out to have been a mishap, even he becomes depressed at the close of his tale, which proves as vain and empty as his prolgoue. As his windy preamble suggests, he and his kind are full of vanity. The prologue is followed by another outlandish statement:

Il m'avint plus a de set anz
que je, seus come *païsanz,*
aloe querant aventures,
armez de totes armeüres
si come *chevaliers* doit estre . . .

[173. Italics mine.]

Seven years ago
when I, all alone like a *peasant,*

> set forth in search of adventures
> fully armed
> as befits a *knight* . . .

Why does Calogrenant compare himself to a peasant?[57] Surely there
were all sorts of people who traveled alone — minstrels, knights errant,
mendicant friars, for example. The term is all the more incongruous
because peasants did not set out in search of knightly adventures, and, as
Calogrenant himself is quick to point out, he was armed the way a knight
is supposed to be. It would seem that just as this eager courtier was the
first to leap to his feet at the sight of the queen, whom he further attempts to impress with a pretentious prologue to his tale, he is trying to
get attention again by shocking his noble listeners as they surely never expected him to compare himself to a peasant. His solicitude and silliness
are indeed annoying, and we begin to sympathize just a little with
grouchy Keu.[58] It is clear, when we think about it, that Calogrenant's
overblown prologue and his bizarre comparison of knights errant to
peasants are Chrestien's devices the function of which is to undercut
Calogrenant's authority as a narrator. How can we take him seriously?
If there is a lesson to be learned from his tale, we must conclude that it
lies outside of his perception.

As the story progresses, Calogrenant eloquently proves that he is not
the "bravest or the best man" that Keu ever insulted (l. 112). He is not
only afraid of the wild bulls, bears, and leopards — should we believe him
about the bears and leopards? Only the bulls are mentioned by the narrator when Yvain repeats Calogrenant's adventure (l. 792) — but also of
the herdsman he encounters, whom he describes in exaggerated terms
that remind us of his prologue:

> Uns *vileins* qui resanbloit Mor,
> leiz et hideus a desmesure,
> einsi tres leide criature
> qu'an ne porroit dire de boche,
> assis s'estoit sor une çoche,
> une grant maçue en sa main.
> Je m'aprochai vers le *vilain*,
> si vi qu'il ot grosse la teste
> plus que roncins ne autre beste,
> chevox mechiez et front pelé,
> s'ot pres de deus espanz de lé,
> oroilles mossues et granz
> autiex com a uns olifanz,
> les sorcix granz et le vis plat,
> ialz de çuete, et nes de chat,
> bouche fandue come lous,

danz de sengler aguz et rous,
barbe noire, grenons tortiz,
et le manton aers au piz,
longue exchine torte et boçue; . . .

[286. Italics mine.]

There was a *peasant* who resembled a Moore
who was incredibly ugly and hideous;
such an ugly creature was he
that it is impossible to describe him in words.
He was sitting on a tree stump
with a huge club in his hand.
When I approached the *peasant*
I saw that his head was thicker
than a nag's.
His hair was matted and his forehead hairy,
and more than two hands wide.
He had huge hairy ears
like an elephant,
his eyebrows were bushy and his face flat,
he had eyes like an owl and a nose like a cat,
his mouth was cleaved like a wolf's,
his teeth were sharp and yellow like a boar's,
his beard black, his moustache twisted,
and his chin was attached to his chest,
he had a long spine, crooked and hunched;[59]

Our narrator has no trouble whatever identifying this hideous monster as a "peasant." This peasant, he says, is like a "Moore." We might readily believe that the man was ugly, but that he had ears like an elephant, eyes like an owl, a nose like a cat, and a mouth like a wolf is too much. Our experience of Calogrenant has taught us that he is full of such nonsense. Chrestien's courtly audience must have howled with laughter when, after this second windy preamble to an adventure that never seems to get off the ground, the monster who is expected to charge at any minute, stands stock still:

An piez sailli li *vilains*, lués
qu'il me vit vers lui aprochier;
ne sai s'il me voloit tochier,
ne ne sai qu'il voloit enprendre,
mes je me garni de desfandre,
tant que je vi que il estut
en piez toz coiz, . . .

[312. Italics mine.]

The *peasant* rose quickly to his feet
when he saw me approaching him;
I don't know if he wanted to harm me,
I have no idea what he wanted to do,

> but I readied myself to fight
> until I saw that he was standing
> very quietly . . .

It is very clear that Calogrenant's perception is not to be trusted. He goes to a lot of trouble to get us to "hear with our hearts" a tale that has no moral, he compares himself to a peasant because he travels alone, fully armed, like any knight errant, he is terrified of a meadow full of grazing cattle, and readies himself to do ferocious combat with a quiet peasant who turns out to be far more reasonable than he:

> et je cuidai qu'il ne seüst
> parler, ne reison point n'eüst.
> Tote voie tant m'anhardi
> que je li dis: "Va, car me di
> se tu es boene chose ou non."
> Et il me dist qu'il ert uns hom.
> "Quiex hom ies tu — Tex con tu voiz;
> si ne sui autres nule foiz.
>   [323]
> and, thought I to myself, that he didn't know how
> to speak, that he was incapable of reason.
> Nevertheless, taking courage
> I spoke to him: "Tell me now
> what manner of creature are you — good or evil?"
> And he replied that he was a man.
> "What kind of man?"
> "Such as you see;
> I have never been otherwise."

We would expect a peasant to be fearful, or at least impressed, and to display the basest ignorance in the presence of a nobleman. It wouldn't surprise us to see a rough-hewn, uneducated man perceive a knight errant as a creature from another world as does the fearless, young Perceval when he mistakes five Arthurian knights for angels. Perceval falls to the ground and piously says his prayers. In the *Yvain*, it is Calogrenant who cowers in awe of the peasant, he weapons readied for dire combat because he mistakes the peasant for an evil giant.[60] In fact, the world of Calogrenant's tale is all upside-down when compared to that of the opening scenes of the *Perceval*. In the latter romance, the ignorant country boy is "nices," 'silly,' the knights, cool and rational, although they become irritated at the boy's foolish questions. By contrast the scene from the *Yvain* features an unflappable peasant and a knight who asks irritatingly simple-minded questions. Worse still, the peasant talks of his bravery in handling his herd (l. 342), while the knight yearns wistfully for an adventure in order to prove himself! (l. 359) The peasant doesn't know anything about adventures, but he directs Calogrenant to a place where he can prove his bravery (l. 366–405). The passage closes significantly with the "chevalier-vilain" opposition typical of this tale:

> que, se tu t'an puez departir
> sanz grant enui et sanz pesance,
> tu seras de meillor cheance
> que *chevaliers* qui i fust onques."
> Del *vilain* me parti adonques
> qui bien m'ot la voie mostree.
>
> [402. Italics mine.]
>
> And if you can get out of there
> without great harm
> you will have had better luck
> than any *knight* that ever lived."
> Then I took leave of the *peasant*
> who had shown me the way.

When Calogrenant finally arrives at the adventure for which we have all been waiting, he is utterly shamed. By pouring water on a marble stone at a fountain, he creates a terrible storm which fells the trees in Esclados li Ros' woods (l. 499). This huge, red-headed knight appears in a fury, summarily knocks Calogrenant to the ground with his lance, and leads his horse away. Afraid to pursue his attacker, Calogrenant sits dejectedly by the fountain (l. 546). Forced to abandon his heavy arms, he returns on foot, in shame, truly like a peasant (l. 556) Unlike the knights who had challenged Esclados before him, Calogrenant is neither killed nor taken prisoner. For one thing, he must live to tell the tale, but we also suspect that Esclados had such contempt for him that he just let him go:

> Ensi alai, ensi reving;
> au revenir por fol me ting.
> Si vos ai conté come fos
> ce c'onques mes conter ne vos.
>
> [575]
>
> Thus I went, thus returned;
> When I came back I thought myself a fool,
> And like a fool I've told you
> What I never wanted to tell anyone.

I think we can see now that Calogrenant's vision is far from clear; his point of view seriously flawed. He realizes dimly that he is a fool, but the verbal and situational confusion in his tale between knighthood and peasantry surely escapes his notice. If his story shows anything at all it is that . . . *molt valt mialz . . . un cortois morz c'uns vilains vis*! 'a dead courtier is better than a live peasant!' (l. 32). The proverb, as Tony Hunt points out (p. 85), is a reversal of Eccles. 9: 4, "a live dog is better than a dead lion," by which is meant that it is better to be a live sinner than a dead man, because there is always hope for the living. Chrestien seems to have meant that it is better to be dead than to exist in a base condition. But there is possibly an echo of another proverb in the Calogrenant sequence: *vera rustice potius quam falsa diserte*. 'It is better to tell the truth like a peasant than to lie eloquently.'[61] Calogrenant has lied to us loquaciously. The fact that Calogrenant's tale is so outlandishly told also reminds us of the Horatian principle:

> Interdum speciosa locis, morataque recte fabula, nullius veneris, sine pondere et arte faldius oblectat populum, meliusque moratur quam versus inopes rerum nugaeque canone.[62]
> It is better to have a fable with natural characters and justly described customs in a style without grace or art than a harmonious but insignificant poem without substance.

The yarn Calogrenant spins is both unnatural and insignificant. In comparison with Chrestien, he comes off as a pretty bad storyteller! There were those in Chrestien's audience who would remember either the text of Jerome or that of Horace, or both. These listeners would have laughed even harder than the others when they heard Calogrenant's nonsensical tall tale.

As far as our putting our trust in him as a narrator is concerned, even he knows that his veracity is suspect:

> Par mi le voir, ce sachiez bien,
> m'an vois por ma honte covrir.
>
> [524]
>
> I'm going to tell you the strictest truth
> in order to hide my shame.

What he in fact does is to exaggerate the dangers he encounters to hide his shame.[63] What does it all mean? If Arthur and his court are the source of "modern" courtesy, which has fallen into disrepair as Chrestien's narrator persona claims, then what is Chrestien saying to his contemporaries about themselves when Arthur and his court all turn out to behave like peasants?[64] Keu, as we have seen, is rude, Calogrenant, silly, and as for Arthur himself, he shocks everyone by toddling off in the midst of a feast for what we have every reason to suspect is a little afternoon delight with the queen, followed by a nap (l. 42).[65] One wonders how many of the Calogrenants in Chrestien's audience realized that he had insulted them. Certainly, his tale of Calogrenant is an aenigmalogue—a story that presented such an aenigmatic surface to its audience that even if they guessed the author's meaning, they could never be absolutely certain of it. After the laughter at Calogrenant had died down, some of them — the ones hit hardest by the satire — must have felt disturbed by it. Chrestien had played the gadfly well, like a true aenigmologist.

In short, unreliable narrators existed long before Henry James.[66] How else could James have been able to theorize about them so glibly? He didn't invent them; they were always there, but he did develop them and endow them with psychological attributes and functions which medieval narrators did not have. The problem in *ChV*, however, is that there is no formal distinction made between the author and his narrator persona. Like most narrators charged with telling the story, he has neither a face nor a name. This does not mean, however, that he *is* the poet; rather, he is one of the poet's masks, and like all the other characters in a book, the mask is only a projection of the writer who wears it. The *ChV* audience could not have felt at ease with a tale that creates enormous sympathy for its male protagonist, while blaming him for a chain of tragic events that are very clearly out of his hands. Like the *geux-partis*, or lyric debates about controversial questions in love, this poem must have stimulated a great deal of discussion among its public after its performance.

Lest anyone insist that it is unheard of for a medieval author to disguise himself behind the mask of a flawed center of consciousness, let me remind my reader of the naive Chaucer persona in the *Canterbury Tales* who is a terrible storyteller, and who goes about praising his vicious fellow pilgrims. As his friends knew very well, Chaucer was an illusionist, hiding behind a series of masks, one of which was his narrator persona. His public understood how quick-witted the real Chaucer was, and they must also have guessed that he saw right through his corrupt fellow travelers. Similarly, Chrestien dons a mask at the beginning of the *Yvain* where, as we have already seen, he tells us that Arthur and his world represent the golden age of courtesy. But we have also seen that this turns out to be a lie because Arthur and his knights are boors — live peasants! The point is that to an even greater extent than modern literature, medieval literature is an elaborate game.[67] if we wish to play the game well, then we must study the text to discover the rules by which we are to play. And the very first thing that must be suspect is the narrating voice, which more often then not is likely to be a disguise.

The thematic filiation between *ChV* and medieval lyric poetry, specifically, medieval song, was first explored by Paul Zumthor in his "*La Chastelaine de Vergi*: de la chanson au récit," the subtitle of which may be roughly translated as 'the passage from song to narrative.'[68] It is difficult not to agree with Professor Zumthor that *ChV* shows a great deal of influence from the lyric upon both its content and its form. Since the *geu-parti* is so central to both the construction and the meaning of this narrative, I would like to explore the relationship between this lyric form and *ChV* in some depth.

The *geu-parti* was a spirited dispute between two poets in six ten-line stanzas which were dialectically arranged. Each of the stanzas had a metrical pattern that was typically 7-7-3-7-7-3-7-7-7-7 and a rhyme scheme of the type a-b-a-b-b-a-a-c-c. Like the medieval disputation, after which it was patterned, the *geu-parti* was "acted out" before a chamber of noble men and ladies in the same way the formal classroom dialogues between medieval master and student took place while the rest of the class looked on.[69] Perhaps the *geu-parti* is best described as a parlor game, the staging of which was not unlike that of a dramatic skit. After each poet had argued on opposite sides of the topic, the final decision as to which one of them was right, was left up to a judge, elected from among the noble men and ladies in the courtly audience. Unfortunately none of these "opinions" has come down to us, but works like Marguerite de Navarre's *Heptaméron* — sixteenth century — give us a very good idea of the kind of lively discussions which followed the telling of controversial tales and undoubtedly the heated metrical arguments of the *geus-partis*.[70] We have all experienced rudimentary forms of the theater that are similarly bare-boned. It seems to me that the passage from the *geu-parti* to a narrative like *ChV* is made possible by the fact that not only the drama, but poetry of all kinds were performed during the Middle Ages. Like the songs and plays of the period, medieval tales were recited for live audiences, with the poet himself or a *jongleur* miming the various characters, perhaps to the accompaniment of musical instruments. No wonder the structure of the *geu-parti* — which had such potential for dramatization — derived from the medieval disputation, resembles that of *ChV*, a form of performed narrative fiction also derived from the medieval disputation![71]

The *disputatio* was a school exercise which was dialectically organized. The master or teacher presented the question to the student, giving him a choice between two propositions. The student then argued for his chosen proposition while the master or another student upheld the opposing argument. At the end of the exercise, the master "determined" or gave the right answer to the argument.[72] The theatrical potential of the *disputatio* is evident. But it was the alternance between opposing propositions — i.e., dialectic — that made it an ideal exemplar for early episodic narrative, which, like the romanesque churches of the eleventh and twelfth centuries, was constructed in massive parallel or antithetical blocks.[73] The following is an outline of the gross structure of the *disputatio* where "a" designates the proposition chosen by the student and "b," the teacher's or another student's objections to proposition "a":

1. Question (a or b?)
2. Proposition in answer (a)
3. Objections to propositions (b)
4. Determination by master (a or b)
5. Answers to objections (optional) (a)[74]

Given the importance of the disputation in the medieval educational process, we should not be surprised to discover that the extremely popular *geu-parti* has a gross structure which is identical to the dialectical patterning of the disputation. In fact the *geu-parti* is fundamentally the application of this school exercise, the purpose of which was to sharpen the intellect, to problems of love rather than to problems in theology or logic as in the schools. If the *geu-parti* was well loved by the noble ladies and gentlemen who gathered together to form the first literary salons of France, it was because that generation enjoyed the intellectual challenge such literature could offer to the reader or listener.[75]

Typically, the *geu-parti* had six stanzas. The purpose of the first stanza was for one of the two rival poets to state both sides of the question to be discussed. Thus, in the example below J. Bretel asks J. de Grievéler which course of action is preferable to the true lover: to renounce the favors of his lady for fear of compromising her (a), or to enjoy his lady at the risk of jeopardizing her reputation (b). It will be noted that this is precisely the choice with which the *ChV* knight is faced when his liege lord demands to know the name of his mistress. In the following passage from the Långfors collection of *geus-partis*, I have marked the alternate propositions with the letters (a) and (b):

> Grieviler, dites moi voir:
> Le quel cuidiez vous sans faille
>   Qui miex vaille
> Pour ami faire valoir
> Et vivre a mains de bataille:
>   Ou qu'il faille
> A sa joie recevoir,
> Pour paour de percevoir,
> Ou qu'il goe en percevance,
> Dont sa dame ait mesestance?
> Grieviler, tell me truly:
> Which do you think best enables
> the true lover to be worthy

and to live with the least amount of strife?
Either that he renounce his joy   (a)
Out of fear of being discovered,
Or that he enjoy his lady openly (b)
Thereby causing her grief.[76]

Grieviler, the one to whom Bretel directs his question opts for proposition (a) and so in the second stanza we get his proposition in answer to the question:

—Sire, quant de ce savoir
M'avez enquis, ja frapaille
        Ne merdaille
Ne saront de mon voloir
Riens fors par adevinaille.
        Ne vous chaille
Aussi d'eus metre en espoir,
Dont cele se puist doloir
Que vous amez d'amour franche;
L'amour c'est droite vaillance.
Sir, since you have asked me,   (a)
The riff-raff and scoundrels
Will never know my heart
Unless they take a guess.
Don't you worry
About giving that lot any hope
For which she might grieve
Whom you love with a true love.
Love is a very prize.

To which Bretel responds by developing proposition (b):

—Grieviler, qui puet avoir
Ce pour quoi il se travaille,
        Prendre l'aille.
Qui le grain voit aparoir
Et dont n'en prent fors la paille,
        sa vitaille
Pert par son povre savoir.
On puet au jour d'ui veoir
Qu'avoir mal aquis avance
Plus que ne fait astinance.
"Grieviler, he who can obtain   (b)
the thing after which he strives,
let him seize it.
He who sees the grain appear,
but who satisfies himself with the chaff,
Loses his nourishment through his ignorance.
Nowadays anyone can see
that it is better to have stirred up gossip
than to abstain from pleasure."

The positions having been clearly stated in capsulized form by each poet in the first three stanzas, the argument heats up now as Grieviler calls Bretel false and a rogue, for it is villainous to take pleasure of one's lady without first giving thought to the consequences:

> Mès il n'est nulz de grant vaille
> > Qui assaille
> Sa dame en liu ou paroir
> Puist. . . .
> But there is no lover of any worth
> Who assails
> His lady in a place where they can be seen . . .

This of course is a variation of proposition (a), and, as we might have expected, Bretel counters with an enlargement upon proposition (b) in the fifth stanza:

> Qui le met en nonchaloir
> Pour poour, il fait enfance,
> Quar bon fait prendre pitance
> He who forsakes his suit
> through fear, behaves childishly,
> because it is best to take one's portion [due].

The encounter ends with a return to proposition (a) in the sixth stanza which closes with a sentence, presumably the equivalent of the *determinatio* in the disputation:

> Amours pert bien sa semaille
> > Et l'entraille
> Dont le cuer veult decevoir.
> On devroit celui ardoir
> Qui met a deshonnorance
> Ce qu'il aime par samblance
> Love loses his seed
> on a heart that seeks to deceive.
> He who dishonors the lady he loves
> by making a show of his affections
> ought to be burned at the stake.

In short, the dialectical organization of the *geu-parti* is identical to that of the medieval disputation, following the pattern a–b, a, b, a, b, a. However, as I said earlier, the official "opinions," which were purportedly handed down by a distinguished authority figure chosen from the audience, are lost. If such judgments really were a part of the game,[77] then the sixth stanza in the extant *geu-parti* merely represents a third objection to the proposition in answer to the question, while the lost judgements must be considered the equivalent of the *determinatio* in the disputation.

Now the gross structure of *ChV*, by which I mean the syntax of its three largest divisions — its prologue, exemplum, and epilogue — when viewed in relation to the proposition set forth by the narrator in the prologue, is a variation of the very pattern we have been examining in the disputation and *geu-parti*. The principal difference between *ChV* and its sources is that the narrative poem omits the question stage, beginning instead with a proposition. Thus in the prologue we are told that it is foolish to reveal the secret of one's love affair to even the most trustworthy of friends since one never knows who will betray one. One's secret is almost certain to be broadcast to EVERYONE with the result that the love affair must end in woe and shame for the lovers. Clearly, then, this is the narrator persona's proposition (a) which his narrative is designed to prove. However, the exemplum he chooses is an ambivalent one for, while it proves that when a love affair is revealed the result is certainly shame and woe for the lovers, it also shows that it is not always possible to keep the affair a secret and, at the same time, to preserve it. As a result of what happens to the poor knight in the tale proper, the whole question of secrecy and the kind of relationship that exists between courtly lovers is thrown open for discussion. Thus the exemplum offers some very strong objections (b) to the narrator persona's proposition (a). Since the exemplum does demonstrate the dire consequences of the knight's decision to reveal his mistress's name, this part of the poem also offers answers to the objections (a). Finally, in the epilogue, the narrator returns to his original argument, that it is always better to keep one's secret no matter what the circumstances. This last section of the narrative poem corresponds to the *determinato* (a) in the disputation or the final stanza of the *geu-parti*. In short, the patterning of the prologue-exemplum-epilogue sequence is a, b–a, a.

Using Aquinas' *Summa Theologica* († 1274) as an example, James J. Murphy has shown one of the ways in which the disputational structure was appropriated by written narrative. In the following diagramatic representation, I have altered Murphy's wording slightly in order to demonstrate that the dialectical patterning of the *quaestiones* in the *Summa Theologica* is identical to the structuring of the episodes in *ChV*:

Proposition	(a)
Objection 1	(b)
Objection 2	(b)
Objection 3	(b)
Transition	(a or b)
Reply to Objection 1	(a)
Reply to Objection 2	(a)
Reply to Objection 3	(a)[78]

Now if we look at the eight sections which constitute the episodic structure of *ChV* we find that the prologue (1) corresponds to the proposition (a) — that a man should never divulge the secret of his love.[79] Following the prologue is a Potiphar's Wife sequence. Like Potiphar's lustful wife in Genesis 39, the duchess unsuccessfully tempts the young hero and then, angry at his rejection of her love, falsely accuses him to her husband (2). The sequence ends with the longest *scène à deux* in the poem (ll. 144-272) which focuses upon the duke's unjust accusation of his vassal (3). We may equate sections (2) and (3) with the objections to the proposition (b, b) since these are the scenes which demonstrate that the knight had very little control over the events which led to his "betrayal" of his mistress's secret. Section 4, the lovers' tryst, is a highly ambivalent scene because, on the one hand, it shows the "profanation" of the love affair by the presence of the spying duke (a) but, on the other hand, the same scene eloquently demonstrates just how great a loss it would have been for the poor knight had he chosen banishment instead of confiding in the duke (b). Thus if we let the prologue, or proposition section, equal (a) and the objection scenes equal (b) we get the following pattern for the first half of the poem: a, b, b, a-b, with the fourth section serving as a transition between the objections and the replies to the objections. In sections 5, 6, and 7, the love affair is indeed progressively revealed to EVERYONE, just as the narrator had predicted in the prologue. The pattern for these three scenes is a, a, a. Finally, as I have said, the epilogue is equivalent to the *determinatio* in the disputation so that the episodic structure of the entire poem is very similar to the patterning of the individual parts in the *Summa Theologica*: a, b, b, a-b, a, a, a, a. Thus while the *ChV* poet was probably influenced by the form and subject matter of the *geu-parti*, the shape of his narrative indicates that he owes as much to the disputation and the written narratives derived from it as he does to the *geu-parti* itself.

The genesis of the dialectical structure of *ChV* can be diagrammed in the following way:

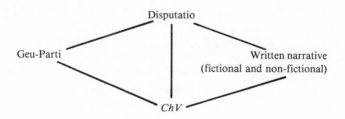

Given the educational system of the day, it is likely that the *ChV* poet had been taught the proper way to dispute as a boy.[80] It is therefore also likely that he learned to apply the dialectical method to composition as part of his education. Certainly his teachers would have encouraged him to imitate the *auctores*, and, by extension, admired contemporaries in whose works he may have observed the application of the disputational pattern to writing. The fact that his entire narrative centers about the *geu-parti*, or 'dilemma' which is posed at l. 269 — whether or not, given the special circumstances of the situation in which he finds himself, the knight should tell the duke the name of his mistress — proves that the dramatic verse form was at least a contributing factor to the dialectical organization of *ChV*. But whatever we make of the data, it is evident that the fictional narrative, like its lyric and pedagogical sources, is dialectically structured, and that this method of constructing narratives was the logical product of a medieval education.[81]

Although the gross structure of the poem is designed to demonstrate the narrator persona's proposition, that to tell the secret leads to woe, there are a number of devices in the work that ensure its reception as a narrationalized *geu-parti* rather than as a disputation, or scholastic enquiry into and proof of the truth of a proposition. The most visible of these is the poet's allusion to the *geu-parti* at l. 269, which has the function of reminding the audience that matters such as the rule of secrecy were debatable issues. The author gives not a hint as to what alternative solutions the knight might have found to his horrible plight, leaving such considerations up to his audience to puzzle out for themselves. The allusion also underscores the fact that the author is engaging in a literary game that is not unlike the game played by lyric poets when they argue about questions of love. The fact that this particular *geu-parti* is described as being . . . *si fort / que l'un et l'autre tient a mort* 'so tough that the knight considers either solution will lead to his death,' is the poet's way of telling his listener that this particular game / dilemma (*geu*), unlike those the listeners had probably seen performed at court, is so extreme, that the only possible determination is the knight's death. Because of this dilemma, they certainly could not have concluded, as the narrator persona does, that the whole mess came about because the knight told the secret. Rather, the poet had presented the knight in such sympathetic terms, that his circumstances can only have been viewed by the *ChV* public as unfair. They must have regretted that he and his mistress lacked the ability to communicate about the threats being posed to their love by the duchess's lust and the duke's insistence upon learning the identity of the knight's mistress in order to assure himself that the duchess's charge against the knight was false. Was such inability of lovers to communicate about practical matters a flaw in the system of love service? Was it because the partners had to maintain an idealized view of each other that such tragedies could come about? Certainly if, as I have been arguing here, the poem is the transformation of lyric concerns into narrative, then the lovers were simply mirrors of each other, each seeing in the other, an idealized projection of himself. Given the adoring posture of the courtly man in courtly lyric, it is easy to see that the mistress was unapproachable except on her terms. He dared not trouble her with political or practical problems. Rather she stood above and apart from the petty concerns of society, utterly isolated in the man's mind like the chastelaine in her garden. And, as the chastelaine herself says, both she and he assumed their hearts were one (l. 798), which is to say, that whatever the one did, the other was sure to understand without its having to be spoken of. Unhappily, as things work out, the knight's plight and the actions he takes are both issues that ought to have been discussed, just as the chastelaine's feelings after she suspects the knight of having betrayed her, are something that ought to have been discussed between the lovers. It is clear that what is wrong with the world of this poem is the lovers' decision to live in a fantasy-world. The moment they are touched by reality— like Narcissus at the fountain—they are destroyed.

The *ChV* poet's allusion to the *geu-parti* at l. 269 is not the only occasion upon which he uses material from the lyric as a device to create sympathy for the knight. In the same scene he incorporates an entire stanza from one of the chastelain de Couci's crusade songs into his tale. Because the song conditions the reader's response to the knight, let us examine it carefully.

As is frequently the case when bits of lyric appear in the midst of a medieval story, the function of the stanza is to serve as a signaling device and as an ethical yardstick by which the poet meant his public to measure both the narrator persona and the characters in his poem. As a result of the contrast in style between the inserted lyric stanza and its surrounding context our attention is drawn to the fact that there are certain similarities between the lyric poet de Couci, and the *ChV* knight which cause us to sympathize with or "care" very deeply about the knight and thus to mistrust the case the narrator persona is making against him. The hero's transgression against the law of secrecy, we suddenly realize, is being unfairly condemned by the voice telling the tale. Even if we imagine that the poet read his own poem to the courtly audience for whom it was written, his purpose, as I have been suggesting, was to make them angry with the rigid viewpoint of his narrator persona or his "disguise." If this seems difficult to visualize, let us remember that Chrestien de Troyes and Chaucer did not hesitate to "put" their audiences "on" in this way.

For the modern reader, the differences in line length, meter, and rhyme between the intercalated lyric stanza and the narrative context in which it is embedded are eye-catching. But the medieval listener very likely had a tremendous advantage over us because it is probable that either the reader who "performed" or recited the poem, or a musician who shared the "stage" with the reader, sang the stanza to the accompaniment of a musical instrument. As a result the medieval public would have enjoyed the full emotional impact of both the plaintive lyrics and the haunting melody which accompanied it.[82]

Certainly ll. 293–94 of the narrative would have served as a striking cue if indeed there was a musician involved in the production:

> Si est en tel point autressi
> com li chastelains de Couci,
> qui au cuer n'avoit s'amor non,
> dist en un vers d'une chançon:
> [The knight] was as miserable
> as the Castellan of Couci
> who, his heart full of love,
> said in a stanza of one of his songs:

As it turns out, de Couci, who was considered a model lover in his day, was guilty of the very same trangression as the knight, for, like him, de Couci too revealed the identity of his mistress to their enemies, the *losengier*, or 'vicious gossips' who jealously meddle in the affairs of lovers. How then can we agree with the *ChV* narrator persona who claims the knight got what he deserved? Any listener with a heart could see that what happens to the poor knight for telling his secret was no fault of his own because the same thing would also have happened to him for not having told it. As the text very clearly says, "either choice would lead to death" (l. 270). One choice, of course, was to tell the secret; the other was banishment. The narrator persona conveniently ignores the fact that this second choice very likely would have produced the same result as the first. The chastelaine probably would never have consented to share the knight's exile because life beyond the settlements was truly brutal. This is why heroines like Iseut and Nicolete are depicted in such heroic and sympathetic terms. Moreover, our chastelaine is supposed to be the niece of the duke of Burgundy, which means that she would have been extremely reluctant to forsake her social position, her manor house, and her noble friends for a harsh life in the forests among wild animals and brigands. Keeping in mind the romantic terms of the fiction, and considering the lady's devotion to the knight and his to her, she would surely have died of a broken heart had he left her. And he, because he could not live without her, would have killed himself, just as he does at the end of the story, or at best, he could have lived the kind of miserable existence Tristan does at the side of Iseut aus Blances Mains. Certainly the various solutions the knight might have chosen were explored in the discussions that followed upon the recitation of this controversial narrative. In any case, if the poet had wanted his audience to believe the knight could have invented an ingenious solution, he would never have assured them that there was no solution. It is clear that he chose an extreme case in order to throw the system that supported the law of secrecy into doubt. If then the knight had no choice, then the narrator persona must be unfair in blaming him for the catastrophe, and if the narrator persona is unfair, then what indeed are we to make of the tale? It may be tragic, but it is no less a "put on" than Chrestien's *Yvain* or Chaucer's *Canterbury Tales*.

When the *ChV* public heard de Couci's song being sung, they no doubt recalled his story and his poetry. Seeing that the knight was in a *geu-parti*, they may well have remembered that de Couci poses a dilemma about the very same problem — breaking the law of secrecy — in one of his other songs.

We do not know just how de Couci transgressed against the law of secrecy, but we are told that just as he was about to receive one of the various rewards the lady could parcel out to her suitor, the whole affair was broadcast by some evil spies or gossips, i.e., the *losengier*.

> Si coiement est ma doleurs celee
> Qu'a mon samblant ne la recounoist on;
> Se ne fussent la gent maleüree,
> N'eüsse pas soupiré en pardon:
> Amours m'eüst doné son guerredon.
> Maiz en cel point que dui avoir mon don
> Lor fu l'amour descouverte et moustree;
> Ja n'aient il pardon.[83]
> My sorrow is so secretly hidden
> That no one could discover it from the way I look;
> Were it not for the evil folk,
> I would never have had to sigh for pardon:
> But just as I was to have my reward
> The love affair was revealed and laid bare
> May they [the losengier] never be forgiven.

That this mishap came about because of some lack of discretion on the part of the poet becomes clear in the very next song in the Lerond edition, which begins:

> Merci clamans de mon fol errement,
> Ferai la fin de mes chançons oïr,
> Quar trahi m'a et mort a escïent
> Mes jolis cuers que je doi tant haïr;[84]
> Begging forgiveness for my folly,
> I will make an end to my songs,
> Because my tender heart has deliberately betrayed
> and slain me for which I must hate it;

The chastelain de Couci so captured the imagination of his contemporaries that an entire "romance" was written about him and his lady shortly after the composition of *ChV*.[85] Certainly, even if the *ChV* poet's audience did not remember the words of de Couci's songs, they were aware that the story which emerges from these lyrics involved some breach of the law of secrecy by the poet, his subsequent estrangement from his mistress and, finally, his sorrowful departure for the Holy Land where he was soon to meet his death. By the time *ChV* was written the lyric poet had grown to legendary stature and was admired for his constancy in love.[86] In the very poem where he laments his folly (Lerond's Chanson VI), de Couci poses a little *geu-parti*, just as the *ChV* poet would later do in his narrative, about the problem of secrecy in the love affair:

> As fins amans proi qu'il dient le voir:
> Li queuz doit mieuz par droit d'amours joïr,
> Cil qui aime de cuer sanz decevoir,   (a)
> Si ne s'en set mie tres bien couvrir,
> Ou qui prie sanz cuer pour decevoir   (b)
> Et bien s'en set guarder par son savoir?
> Dites amant, qui vaut mieuz par raison:
> Loiauz folie u sage trahison?
> I pray true lovers to be my judges:
> Which man has a better right to love's reward,
> He who loves truly without deception,   (a)
> although he does not know how to be as
>   discreet as he might be
> or the false lover who woos a lady in   (b)
>   order to deceive her
> but has learned through experience how to be discreet?
> Tell us, all you who love, which qualities
>   make a man more worthy:
> Loyal folly or wise treason?

Indeed, unlike the *geu-parti* in *ChV*, the song gives so few real details of the case that it would be very difficult to measure de Couci's guilt.

Surely the function of the *geu-parti* theme in the song is to invoke pity for the speaker, or to minimize his fault so that his lady and the audience may look upon him with more favor. This is also true in *ChV*, where it is the audience's sympathy that is sought. The point is, however, that if even the most courtly of lovers can be caught in an indiscretion by the *losengier*, then how can we blame the knight for not having been able to accomplish the impossible — keeping the affair a secret from those who pry into other people's love affairs? Further, the lyric poet's "crime" was really just as serious, if not more so than the *ChV* knight's, because in de Couci's case, there was no crisis, no conflict of allegiances to motivate his indiscretion. And yet, de Couci was never blamed by any of his contemporaries. Rather he seems to have been an object of admiration for all those who loved. Froissart lists him among Love's martyrs.[87] If they thought de Couci's transgression against Love's law was pardonable, then how sorry the courtly audiences must have felt for the poor knight who finds himself in such a terrible bind! In fact, those contemporaries who summarized the poem have nothing but sympathy for the knight. It is significant that not one of them finds fault with him for revealing his mistress' name. One of them, Perrot de Neele, even admires the knight's cleverness in choosing the solution he does, calling him "gentle, valiant, clever, and ingenious."[88]

At this point it might be useful to recall that in Marie de France's "Lanval," which is an analogue of *ChV*, the hero is not only fully pardoned by his mistress, but also allowed to continue enjoying her favors indefinitely. Lanval's crime, in fact, is very grave indeed, because he compromises his lady's honor in a fit of rage. It is true that, like the *ChV* knight, Lanval's own honor is at stake because his lord's wife, whom he has just brutally rejected, accuses him of homosexuality. Nevertheless, his reaction is both thoughtless and gratuitous because he is not faced with a life-threatening dilemma. However, despite Lanval's lack of courtesy, he receives all a lover can desire, while the elegant and sensitive *ChV* knight is sentenced to death. Was it fair that the knight should be condemned by the *ChV* narrator persona for committing a fault so similar to that of Lanval or de Couci and in such extenuating circumstances? The narrator persona meanly insists that the poor knight got just what he deserved when he lost both the chastelaine and his life. It was because he could count upon the sympathy of his medieval public for his hero that the *ChV* poet caused his narrator persona to be monstrously unjust. The fellow's rigid treatment of the knight is of the essence of the tragic mode because a true tragic action involves the isolation of an undeserving victim from society. The knight is the pathetic hero, "isolated by a weakness which appeals to our sympathy because it is on our own level of experience," the "our," of course, referring to the courtiers of the *ChV* poet's noble public who could identify with the knight. If Northrop Frye's definition of the low mimetic mode is accurate, it would make *ChV* the first "domestic" tragic narrative in French, even though it is a tale about noble men and women.[89] In a word, the author deliberately set up an insufferably biased narrator persona whose blindness to the equity in the situation was sure to provoke his audience. The device was singularly well-suited to the author's purpose, which was to excite their anxiety about the impracticality of the courtly code.

To sum up then, the *ChV* poet uses allusions to the lyric to signal his audience that there is more to his story than meets the eye and to create sympathy for the knight. This is part of the way he opens his tale up in spite of the dogmatic stance of his narrator persona. Because of the way in which the allusion to the *geu-parti* and the quotation of de Couci's song function within the work as a whole, serving the poet's principle purpose, "movere," these devices become generic signals. There are, of course, a number of other constructs in *ChV* which also reveal the generic category of the work to us when we study their function within the poem as a whole. Among these is a cluster of rhetorical devices which work together to sap the narrator persona's point of view and thus to transform his "exemplum" into an aenigmalogue. Let us turn first to the poet's use of certain figures of thought, as they were called by the popular pseudo-Cicero: enthymeme, exemplum, and epicheireme.[90] The figures of diction, synonomy, and antithesis, will be treated in conjunction with the figure of thought known as *expolitio*, or 'refining.' It is through the continual refining or subtle redefinition of the antinomous pairs of synonyms originally set up in the prologue that the poet undermines his narrator persona's rigid verbal polarities and thus his inflexible linguistic definition of the problem of secrecy.

The *ChV* narrator persona is a maddeningly logical fellow. Not only is the tale he tells dialectically constructed, in the manner of a medieval treatise, but his persuasive rhetorical style shows him to be a skilled disputant, who has a strong sense of balance in both his arguments and his diction. This together with the conspicuous lack of ornamental rhetoric in this poem indicates that we are indeed dealing with an imitation of disputational literature and the scholastic method. The only difficulty with this impeccably logical construct is that the narrator persona is totally insensitive to the realities of the problem he thinks he has resolved. For what he does, in essence, is to argue for the letter rather than the spirit of the law of secrecy, and, as a general rule, literal-minded narrators are misguided. His cold-blooded logic jars horribly with the pathos of the knight's situation.

Aristotle described the enthymeme and exemplum in his *"Art" of Rhetoric* as being the only two viable forms of rhetorical argumentation. In the *Poetics* he spelled out the importance of rhetoric in developing *dianoia* or 'thought' in fiction, referring his reader back to his rhetorical treatise for the details.[91] Although most medieval writers did not read Greek, there was no need for them to do so in order to have access to Aristotelian rhetorical theory since the relationship between rhetoric and poetry that Aristotle had adumbrated in his treatises had been dealt with in Latin by the curriculum authors, particularly by Priscian and Cassiodorus.[92] Further, these principles were put into practice in the various exercises boys were made to do as part of their education. And so an author like the *ChV* poet would have become skilled at the use of enthymemes and exempla in literary contexts during his youth. We should not then be surprised to find him exploiting both these rhetorical devices novelistically. I say "novelistically" because, while the narrator intends his enthymemes and exempla as a "logical demonstration of his proposition"—that Love's secret must be kept regardless of the circumstances— the rigidity of his logical schemes only creates more sympathy for the poor knight, and this sympathy is what ultimately convinces us that the narrator has blinders on. In other words, what began as logical schemes are turned into literary devices.

The enthymeme is a rhetorical syllogism, consisting of a thesis and antithesis for premises, and a synthesis as its conclusions—that is, an argument from opposites. Its premises are general statements, or *sententiae*, as opposed to the logical propositions of the dialectical syllogism. The enthymeme was marvellously well-suited to literary fiction because it reached probable rather than certain conclusions.[93] Further it was not necessary to state all the premises of the enthymeme as in the syllogism. Following upon the conclusion of the enthymeme, the *exempla* or 'examples' served as its epilogues. Thus a full-blown rhetorical oration, as for instance, an ancient law case, would begin with a proem—the literary prologue—argue through a series of enthymemes or epicheiremes—arguments from consequents rather than from opposites—and exempla, and end in a peroration or recapitulation of the principal arguments (i.e., the equivalent of the epilogue in literature).[94] This is very similar to the structure of *ChV*, except that in place of a series of exempla, there is only one extended exemplum. Hence the narrator persona's phrase at l. 951: "et par cest example. . . ." He seems to have meant that his tale was supposed to have been a logical demonstration of the arguments in his prologue. By choosing an exemplum which shows that it was impossible for the knight to have protected his love affair from those who pry into other people's business, the *ChV* poet created a narrative which is the exact reverse of an exemplum, that is, an aenigmalogue. For, as we remember, the exemplum is a subtype of apologue, or a narrative whose chief purpose is to instruct, while the aenigmalogue is a narrative that agitates or moves its public, raising doubts and more questions than it answers. That he should have produced an enigmatic tale by turning an exemplum on its ear is wholly in keeping with medieval compositional habits. For, as I have shown elsewhere, medieval writers were in the habit of amplifying what was brief and abbreviating what was long in their source materials, which is to say that they often turned their models upside-down to get a new narrative.[95]

The first twenty lines of *ChV* consist of two maxims or sentences, a conclusion drawn from their opposition and an exemplum to illustrate the conclusion. With the reader's indulgence, the following is a somewhat liberal paraphrase of ll. 1–4: "Whenever a certain kind of person protests that he knows how to guard secrets [*conseil* 'secret,' is a metonym for the love affair] he appears so loyal that the lover naturally puts his trust in him." This is the first maxim or premise to the opening enthymeme. The second premise, ll. 5–8: "But if one does trust these people who appear discreet by telling them all about one's secret, and if they gossip about it. . . ." The conclusion begins at l. 9: "then he who has revealed his secret loses the joy of love," and is elaborated on through l. 18, where the exemplum is finally introduced: "just as it happened in Burgundy, to a valiant knight and his lady of Vergi. . . ." If I have had to supply the logical linguistic connectives "whenever;" "if," and "then" in my paraphrases, we must remember we are dealing with poetry rather than an oration destined for the forum or the declamation halls. The function of the remainder of the prologue is to describe the lovers' covenant and their long state of uninterrupted bliss, so that the reader may truly regret the destruction of such a perfect love affair. From the narrator persona's point of view then, the purpose of this prologue is to establish the importance of keeping one's love affair a secret from everyone, and to fill in the background for the extended example which is presumably going to illustrate this general rule.

As in the classical oration, the epilogue (ll. 944–57) recapitulates the thesis, adding whatever arguments may be drawn from the "ocular demonstration," to use the ancient rhetorical definition of the exemplum:

I   Ha, Dieus! Trestout cest encombrier
       et cest meschief por ce avint

	qu'au chevalier tant mesavint	EXEMPLUM
	qu'il dist ce que celer devoit	
	et que desfendu li avoit	
	s'amie qu'il ne le deïst	
	tant com s'amor avoir vousist.	
II	Et par cest example doit l'en	SENTENCE
	s'amor celer par si grant sen	
	c'on ait toz jors en remembrance	
	que li descouvrirs riens n'avance	
	et li celers en toz poins vaut.	
III	Qui si le fet, ne crient assaut	CONCLUSION
	des faus felons enquereors	
	qui enquierent autrui amors.	

God! To think that all this woe resulted	
because the unfortunate knight	EXEMPLUM
told what he should have hidden	
and what his lady had forbidden him to tell	
as long as he wished to have her love.	
And from this exemplum we should learn	
to hide our love affairs.	SENTENCE
Let it be remembered	
that in matters of the heart,	
nothing's gained by candor	
while secrecy is always well-advised.	
He who lives by this	CONCLUSION
need never fear	
the evil curiosity of those	
who pry into other people's love affairs.	

Clearly, ll. 944–57 are an enthymeme whose exemplum is its first premise—the exact reverse of the prologue—so that the superficial structure of the poem, like that of the Aristotle exemplum we studied earlier, describes a circle. But unlike the Aristotle exemplum, the *ChV* narrator persona's tale jars with its frame, as we have seen. Like the master in a disputation, our narrator shows us both sides of the question, and although he determines the dispute for us, as it was right for the master to do, he has shown us too much of the other side for us to accept his conclusions. It just isn't true that "He who lives by this need never fear the evil curiosity of those who pry into other people's love affairs." For we have seen that just as de Couci fell prey to the *losengier* the knight could not escape sorrow at their hands no matter what he did. The narrator persona is so taken up with his own rhetoric that he even has the duchess argue logically, using epicheiremes, or arguments from consequents. The following passage is taken from the second scene in the poem, where the duchess successfully convinces her husband that his favorite knight has asked her for her love:

	—Certes," dist ele, "j'ai duel grant	
PREMISE I	*de ce que* ne set nus hauz hom	MAXIM
	qui foi li porte ne qui non;	
PREMISE II	*mes* plus de bien et d'onor font	MAXIM
	a ceus qui lor trahitor sont,	
	et si ne s'en aperçoit nus."	CONCLUSION

[114. Italics mine.]

	—I am certainly grieved said she	
I	when I see that powerful lords	MAXIM
	cannot distinguish between their loyal	
	servants and the traitors at their courts	
II	Rather they favor and even reward	MAXIM
	the traitors in their service.	
	Thus they never perceive that	CONCLUSION
	they are being betrayed by false friends.	

I have underlined the logical conjunctions *de ce que, mes*, and *si* to show how the author himself marked the three stages of the duchess's epicheireme. It should be clear that Proposition II, "Great lords honor and reward the traitors among their servants" is simply a more precise phrasing, through *expolitio*, of Proposition I, "Great lords cannot distinguish between traitors and loyal servants." The conclusion to this chain of thought, "Thus they do not perceive it when they are betrayed" is a third reworking (*expolitio*) of the first premise. If this were the only instance of the duchess's use of formal rhetorical schemes one might pass it off as an accident. But the fact of the matter is that every time she speaks, the duchess formulates an epicheireme. Admittedly, her logic is often flawed, but her speech has a scholastic cast to it. Thus, just to cite one more example, her temptation of the knight (scene 1) is couched in a series of epicheiremes, beginning with the following:

	—Sire, vous estes biaus et preus,
PREMISE I	
PREMISE II	ce dïent tuit, la Dieu merci!
CONCLUSION	Si avriiez bien deservi
	d'avoir amie en si haut leu
	qu'en eüssiez honor et preu,
EPILOGUE	que bien vous serroit tele amie."

[60]

	Sire, you are both handsome and brave
PREMISE I	
PREMISE II	so say all, may God bless me.
CONCLUSION	Thus you have earned the right
	to have a lady friend of high degree
	who might bring you honor and profit.
EPILOGUE	Think about it. That kind of friend could be
	useful to you.

The purpose of the first two premises is to establish that the knight is worthy of a highborn mistress because this household knight was certainly of a considerably lower social station than the duchess. Premise I states that the duchess finds the knight well-qualified, while the second premise corroborates her personal findings by alleging that everyone shares her opinion of him. The argument, which is clearly marred by fallacies, is based on what Aristotle called *Tekmeria*, or 'signs.'[96] The conclusion which inevitably follows from the duchess's "demonstration" of the knight's courtliness is that he should choose a mistress from among the highest ranks of society, someone—and it is not difficult at this point to guess who that someone might be—who could help him to advance in his career. Tacked onto the conclusion in the form of an epilogue which naturally arises from the conclusion through *expolitio* is the rather seedy proposition that such an alliance could be useful to the knight. I could go on and on with examples of the duchess's use of false logic to seduce the duke. But the point I want to make here is that because the villain is made to use rhetorical schemes for the purpose of misleading others, we learn to mistrust the narrator persona's rhetoric as well. Why indeed should we believe him when the evil duchess misuses the art of persuasion just as learnedly as he? Although this rather technical-looking device is very difficult for the modern reader to appreciate, we must remember that the educated members of the *ChV* poet's audience were very much aware of such matters since, like the author, many of them also knew how to dispute, or had at least been exposed to the art of disputation at university or at court. I am not saying that the medieval listeners would have stopped to analyze the rhetorical figures the poet was using as I have been doing here, but I am saying that they would have been accutely aware of the scholastic tone of the tale, and, I submit, they probably found it amusing that the duchess, a woman, could so pervert the art of rhetoric to serve her own mendacious purposes. What we have in the duchess is a literary relative of those loquacious female apologists, Jean de Meun's Nature and Chaucer's Wyf of Bath.

Just as the narrator persona's dialectical demonstration, which incorporates rhetorical chains of reasoning, is undercut by the exemplum he is made to choose and by the scholastic ring of his character, the duchess's speeches, so the logical order of this narrator persona's diction becomes blurred in ways he certainly never intended. While his inflexible view is expressed in stark antitheses in the prologue, this rigid patterning breaks down in the exemplum where the antonyms become synonyms for each other. The key words in *ChV* are made to revolve about a central symbol, the secret or "conseil."[97] In other words the verbal structure

of this narrative is a convoluted relative of the kind we encountered in
the Aristotle exemplum. Because the word "conseil" is a metonym for the
love affair, *qui le conseil a descouvert* "who has revealed his secret," i.e.,
love affair, a number of words and expressions which also signify either
the lovers' pact of secrecy or the love affair itself are drawn into the
semantic sphere of the term "conseil." Thus synonyms the narrator uses
for "conseil" (ll. 3 and 10) in his prologue and epilogue are *covenant*
'pact' (l. 23), *amor* 'love' (ll. 6, 11, 13, 17, 950, 952, and 958), *uevre* 'affair' (l. 6) and "joie" 'joy,' which is also a metonym for the love affair.
Now as far as the narrator is concerned *joie* is always safeguarded when
the lover conceals his secret "celer le conseil" whereas to tell the secret to
anyone at all, "descouvrir le conseil" is to risk the loss of "joie": "cil joie
en pert" and thus to incur sadness, "dolor" and shame, "vergoigne":

> Et quant vient que on s'i descuevre
> tant qu'il sevent l'amor et l'uevre
> si l'espandent par le païs
> et en font lor gas et lor ris.
> Si avient que cil joie en pert
> qui le conseil a descouvert,
> quar, tant com l'amor est plus grant,
> sont plus mari li fin amant
> quant li uns d'aus de l'autre croit
> qu'il ait dit ce que celer doit.
> Et sovent tel meschief en vient
> que l'amor faillir en covient
> a grant dolor et a vergoingne
>
> [5. Italics mine.]

> And when it happens that the lover
> trustingly reveals his love affair
> to them the losengiers
> they tell everyone,
> making light of precious secrets.
> Thus he who reveals his secret
> Loses his joy
> because the greater the love
> the more sorrowful true lovers
> when one of them believes
> the other to have spoken what
> he should have kept concealed.
> And often such woe befalls them
> that love must come to an end
> with great sadness and shame.

The verbal pattern of the prologue may be diagrammed in the following
way. I have placed the lover at the center because he is to be focal

point of the narrator's exemplum, the character who serves as a model of good or bad behavior for the reader/listener to follow.

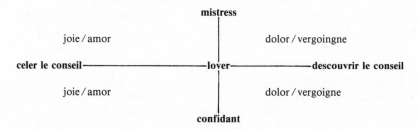

However, as we have seen, the knight stands to lose his "joy" whether or not he tells the secret:

> Quar s'il *dit* la *verité pure*,
> qu'il dira s'il ne se parjure,
> a mort se tient, s'il *mesfet* tant
> qu'il *trespasse le couvenant*
> qu'a sa dame et a s'amie a,
> qu'il est seürs qu'il la perdra
> s'ele s'en puet apercevoir.
> Et s'il ne *dit* au duc *le voir*,
> parjurés est et foimentie,
> et pert le païs et s'amie.
>
> [271 Italics mine.]
>
> Because if he told the truth [i.e., the secret]
> which he must do to avoid perjuring himself
> he was as good as dead
> for having breached
> his lady's covenant.
> He was certain to lose her
> if she ever found him out.
> And if he lied to the duke,
> he would lose both his lady and his home.

In the passage just cited I have italicized the key words and expressions which are being used as synonyms for those in the prologue. Since *la verité pure* 'the truth' the knight is being asked to tell is the name of his mistress, it is clear that *dire la verité* 'to tell the truth' is being used synonymously here with *descouvrir le conseil* 'to reveal the secret.' *Trespasser le couvenant* 'to breach the covenant, and *mesfere* 'to do a misdeed' are also near synonyms for "descouvrir le conseil" in this passage. As we might have expected, the result of such treason is the loss of the lady, "la perdra" and death, "a mort se tient." But instead of finding, as we do in the prologue, that to hide the secret ensures security, *ne pas dire le voir* 'not to tell the truth'—i.e., a synonym for *celer le conseil*—will inevitably result in not only the loss of the lady but also the loss of the lady but also the loss of the knight's home and his honor. To refuse to answer the duke's question, is to perjure himself since the knight is sworn to tell the truth: "parjurés est et foimenti." In short, it makes little difference whether the knight chooses to hide or to reveal his mistress' name because either way he loses. If we now try to diagram the verbal structure of the entire poem, we find that in lieu of the narrator persona's neat polarities, what we get is a graphic picture of the pretty verbal pickle the narrator persona has inadvertently gotten himself into.[98]

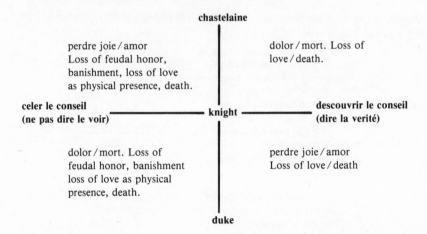

It is clear that the verbal patterning of this aenigmalogue is quite a bit more complex than that of the preaching exemplum we examined earlier. But what is significant is that it mirrors very faithfully the dialectical construction of the larger blocks of the tale. For like the prologue-exemplum-epilogue sequence, where the exemplum belies the arguments of the frame with which it is dovetailed, the verbal polarities also lose the crisp definition they had in the prologue, only to comingle inextricably. Apparently, this narrative is open-ended or enigmatic from its largest structural units all the way down to the smallest details of its microstructure.

This brief glimpse of the rhetorical patterning of concepts and diction in *ChV* will give the reader an idea of the vast web of antinomous pairs of synonyms which characterizes the poem's deep structure and which is essential to the poet's way of manipulating our reaction to its surface structures. The highly complex verbal patterning constitutes one of the more brilliant examples of *conjointure* in medieval French literature.

I have greatly simplified my discussion of the verbal patterning in *ChV* for the sake of clarity. However, running alongside the central theme of secrecy is a secondary theme, with its own special cluster of key or theme words, which is extremely important to our understanding of the meaning of this narrative. The theme I have in mind has to be one of the great topics of the Middle Ages: the problem of distinguishing between appearance and reality. Very briefly, the characters in the poem are all victims of false appearances. The duchess fails to perceive that the courteous knight is love distracted and so foolishly chases after him. The knight is taken in by the duke's apparent strength of character and protestations of trustworthiness. Not realizing the irony in his parallel situation with the duchess, the duke, in his turn, allows himself to be fooled by his wife's claims of loyalty. As for the chastelaine, she all too readily believes that the duchess has become her lover's new mistress. And so, like the knight and duke, she accepts lies as truths. This state of affairs is reflected in the verbal structure through the cluster *croire-cuidier / mescroire* 'to believe-trust / misbelieve-mistrust,' — *estre loial-dire la verité-le voir dire / estre trahitres-trahir-decevoir-moustrer-paroir-fere samblant par faintise-dire mençonge* to be loyal-to tell the truth / to be a traitor-to betray-to deceive-to pretend or feign-to lie.' Since to tell the truth means to tell the secret, as we saw earlier, the whole problem of secrecy comes under the influence of the theme of appearance and reality. Thus, while it would appear that to tell the secret and to lie to one's feudal lord are both morally wrong, the knight finds himself in a situation where in order to avoid perjuring himself to the duke, he must tell the truth. Unhappily, the truth he has innocently promised to tell turns out to be the secret of his love affair. Would it have been morally better had the knight perjured himself in this case? Would it have been wiser? These are questions the author leaves up to us to debate.

A second, equally important aspect of the theme of appearance and reality in this poem is the constant play between literature and life. Each of the characters entertains his own private literary fantasies. The duke wants to believe his wife truly loves him (see ll. 635 ff., 647 ff.) His courtly language shows he wishes to maintain a romantic relationship with the duchess, based upon literary models of the day. The knight, as we have seen, is identified with the tragic figure of the chastelain de Couci. He further finds himself torn between literature and life in that he must choose between the chastelaine's idealized form of love service and his feudal allegiance to his lord. And the chastelaine wants to live a literary romance: *je cuidoie que plus loiaus / me fussiez, se Dieus me conseut, / que ne fu Tristans a Yseut* 'I thought you more loyal to me, so help me

God, than Tristan to Iseut,' she wails, thereby revealing that she expected the knight to behave as though he were a character in a book rather than a real person (l. 758). All three are led into the final catastrophe through their unrealistic fantasies and resulting misapprehension of reality. What we have in the final analysis is two juxtaposed pairs of lovers, three of whom are disappointed in love because they have modeled their real life relationships upon literature. The fourth, the duchess, is not a lover with fine sentiments, but an evil lecher whose sinfulness and cruelty eventually crush the delicate sensibilities of the other three characters.

Thus far we have examined a number of devices which function "aenigmalogistically" in *ChV*. Lyric, as we remember, was used as a signal and a means to make us care about the hero. Similarly, the courtly themes of the *losengier* and the *geu-parti* were used as devices to make us sympathize with the knight. As for the narrator persona, the fact that his exemplum jars with its frame shows quite clearly that there is something very wrong with this character's perception of the problem. Further, his use of dialectic and rhetoric backfires because the villain's scholastic turn of mind makes us lose confidence in these constructs as vehicles for truth. Finally, the verbal patterning of the poem is such that the narrator persona's hopelessly rigid perspective becomes seriously blurred. All of these devices ultimately function together to make the narrator persona appear extremely unfair and thus to cause us to sympathize with the knight.

If I had to name a device upon which this aenigmalogue depends more than any other for its peculiar generic shape, I would have to say that it was the poet's expert manipulation of caring and distancing. Our trust in the narrator persona definitely diminishes in direct proportion to the amount of sympathy we feel for the knight. In fact the more unjustly the knight is treated by the narrator persona, the duchess, the duke, and even the chastelaine, the more upset we become about what is happening to him and the less willing we are to blame him for the misfortune that befalls him. An important part of this process through which the author manipulates our reaction to his tale is the way in which we are kept at a distance from all the other characters. This is especially true of the duchess with whom we can feel no sympathy whatever, despite the fact that another author might well have made us feel for her by telling the story from her point of view. *Phaedra* is a good example of what I mean. Since the devices of caring and distancing are so important to the way this tale works, I would like to focus upon the characterization of the lovers in the remaining pages of this article. I shall be particularly concerned with the problem of verisimilitude or the believability of the characters because if we cannot believe in them, then we cannot be persuaded to care about what happens to them. If we feel that a story is illogical, we cannot get emotionally involved in it. Unfortunately, the seven hundred years that have elapsed since the composition of this particular tale have effaced much of the cultural background we need to have before we can confront it with a "willing suspension of disbelief."

Anyone who has read E. M. Forster will recall that fictional characters tend to be either "psychologically rounded" or "flat,"; that is, types having little or no psychological depth.[99] Since everything a "flat" does is predictable, such characters can be summed up by a formula. Thus we say that the duchess is the "Potiphar's Wife figure" in the tale because she behaves very much like the lustful wife who desired Joseph in the thirty-ninth chapter of Genesis. By contrast, a rounded character, like a human being, is capable of surprising us by his behavior. It is generally assumed that the characters in early fiction are flat, which is not an altogether unfair assumption since Freud and Jung were far in the future, and medieval writers were more interested in representing humanity typologically than individually. This is because the medieval writer was motivated by the impulse to exemplify right and wrong kinds of behavior rather than to explore the infinite diversity in human nature. However, these writers were, like the authors of all eras, fascinated with human behavior. Thus, although their thinking was platonic, or ideational, we frequently get characters which are believable, if not exactly psychologically rounded. In Chrestien's *Perceval*, for example, the portrait of the hero as an awestruck boy before the five knights he meets in the forest, or the charming quarrel between Little Small Sleeves and her sister were obviously written by a man who knew and loved children.

Of all the characters in *ChV* none could be flatter than the chastelaine, whose formula might be "she loved the knight discretely." But, alas, she did not love him perfectly. Is it not an imperfection, albeit a very human one, to wish one's lover were the incarnation of a magnificent literary hero, a warrior of superior wit and steadfastness? And isn't it very human to wish to be adored by such a flawless man? So even though the chastelaine's character is hardly what E. M. Forster would have called "rounded," it is complex considering how little space is devoted to developing it in the poem. We have only the chastelaine's long lament — an extended inside view, which takes up approximately one ninth of the entire poem, ll. 733–834 — to tell us what she is really like. The fact that the chastelaine wastes so little time in concluding that the knight has been physically unfaithful to her (ll. 737–44) gives us an idea of how close she really comes to loving perfectly. If she cannot imagine any other excuses for her lover's betrayal, doesn't this indicate a deep underlying mistrust of him? That we are supposed to interpret in this way is shown by the linguistic parallels drawn between her accusations of her absent lover and the duchess's very similar accusations of her husband in an earlier scene (cf. ll. 744 and 588 and 791-2 and 583-84). Whereas in the scene between the ducal couple, the duchess's accusations are a deliberate deception, the same words in the chastelaine's monologue show that the chastelaine is deceiving herself. The difference between the two women is that the duchess uses appearances to distort reality while the chastelaine lives in a world of appearances, untouched by reality.

Throughout her monologue, the chastelaine returns again and again (*expolitio*), as if reciting a litany, to her own true love and loyalty as contrasted with the knight's betrayal. This concentrated use of *expolitio* has the mimetic effect of fragmenting the flow of her speech. This is how the poet represents her anxiety through rhetorical devices. The passage also abounds in hyperboles: she loved him more than herself (l. 763), more than heaven (l. 776). She complains that she did all his bidding (ll. 787-88) but of course we know from the prologue that the knight had to wait humbly in a remote corner of her garden until he was fetched by a little dog (ll. 33-39) Yet the narrator never details the sacrifices the chastelaine made for her lover, and, by the same token, the knight never complains, as his mistress does, about the sacrifices he has had to make. This is because, according to the courtly code, it was the man who had to undergo an endless series of tests and humiliations to prove his love. How ironic is the chastelaine's notion that their hearts were one: *Qu'a lui amer estoit si buen / qu'a mon cuer prenoie le suen* 'because it was so good to love him I took his heart for mine.' While she was measuring him against an idealized Tristan, he was plainly styled after the more human chastelain de Couci. Of course the greatest irony of all is that Tristan's fidelity wavered when he married Iseut aus Blanches Mains, whereas the *ChV* knight's heart is perfectly true even until death. So, like the knight and duke, the chastelaine is meant to be a noble character with human flaws. She reminds me of the lover in the "mirror lyrics" who is crushed by the discovery of his lady's imperfections. Like the two men, she rises above her human frailty when she pardons her lover (ll. 826-27). The knight's finest moment is when he kills himself and the duke's is when he metes out justice by murdering his beloved wife. Certainly, because we are allowed inside her mind for an extended sympathetic view, we come to care quite a bit about the chastelaine, whose death must touch us with its poignancy. If we do not see very much of her before her monologue it is because her imperfections and frailties could scarcely have been presented with such delicacy were we to have been granted a better view of her. Further, by keeping her at a great distance throughout the poem and saving her condemnation of the knight until the very last, the poet makes sure we know she is being a bit unfair to the knight.

Many modern readers of this tale scoff at the fact that the chastelaine dies of a broken heart. The scene is hopelessly romantic and unrealistic, they complain. Since I am concerned here with the verisimilitude of the characters in this poem, I think it is important to clear up this misconception about the heroine. Surprisingly, there is absolutely nothing unrealistic in the chastelaine's extreme reaction to her lover's betrayal because, as her monologue reveals, she has become fixated on him. Thus upon discovering that the object of her obsession may no longer share her desire for an exclusive relationship, in which she has complete control over him, the chastelaine no longer has any reason to go on living. Like the lover in the lyrics she has come face to face with the realization that what she has loved in her beloved is the idealized projection of herself. Physiologically speaking, when a person becomes extremely overwrought, the frontal cortex of the brain is capable of sending the heart muscles into fatal fibrillation.[100] It is this physiological phenomenon which the *ChV* poet records so faithfully at ll. 835-9;

> A cest mot de ses braz s'estraint,
> li cuers li faut, li vis li taint;
> angoisseusement s'est pasmee,
> et gist pale et descoloree
> en mi le lit, morte sanz vie.
> With that she clutched her breast,
> her heart failed, her face grew pale,
> she fainted with horrible anguish,
> and lay drained of color,
> pale and lifeless on the bed.

The occurrence of death by a "broken heart" is not so uncommon as we might think. In an article entitled "Emotional Stress and Sudden Death" in *Psychology Today*, George Engel writes:

> One common denominator emerges from the medical literature and the 275 press reports on sudden death. For the most part, the victims are confronted with events that are impossible to ignore, either because of their abrupt, unexpected, or dramatic quality or because of their intensity, irreversibility, or persistence. The individual experiences or is threatened with overwhelming excitation. Implicit, also, is the idea that he no longer has mastery or control over the situation or

> himself, or fears that he may lose what control he has. This may be in-
> ferred from the frantic, disorganized activity displayed by some of
> these people before collapse, and from the paralysis or inactivity ex-
> hibited by others etc."[101]

The event which triggers the chastelaine's collapse is the duchess's revelation that she knows the lovers' secret. With that the chastelaine's very
reason for being is taken away since, as she says in her monologue, she
lived only for the knight. (ll. 801–06) Isn't the real issue behind the
chastelaine's complaint that she has lost control over the knight to the
duchess? And what could be more frantic or disorganized than her last
moments which are represented by a pitifully fragmented syntax:

> Et quant j'ai avant perdu lui,
> ne puis aprés itel anui
> (que sanz lui por qui je me dueil
> ne puis) vivre ne je ne vueil.
>   [815][102]
> And when I have first lost him,
> I cannot, after such a shock
> I mean, without him for whom I grieve
> I cannot live nor do I wish to live.

It seems to me that our medieval poet has very accurately represented a
psychological event which we are only now beginning to understand. I
see absolutely nothing "romantic" or inconsistent in the chastelaine's
behavior. Rather, the poet has portrayed his heroine with brilliant insight.

The chastelaine's role in the garden scene (ll. 374–489) is highly
poeticized. In fact, what the poet has done in this episode is to narra-
tionalize the lyric *oaristys* or union of lovers and the *alba* or poem about
the separation of the lovers at dawn.[103] Through the eyes of the duke, we
see the chastelaine's silhouette (ll. 423–24) as she races eagerly from her
chamber to greet the knight, throwing her arms about his neck and kissing him a hundred times (ll. 400–403). The fact that the word "saillir" (l.
400) is also applied to the young serving girl who overhears the lovers'
death monologues (l. 903) suggests the author may have conceived of the
chastelaine as a young woman.

Scholars have argued about whether or not our heroine was married, because the poet never tells us. Raynaud, Lorenz, Frappier, and
Dubuis assumed there must have been a husband if the love affair had to
be kept a secret, while Reed and Foulet think she may have been a young
widow because, they reason, if there had been a husband he would never
have allowed the lovers to be buried in the same sarcophagus at the end
of the story.[104] Iseut aus Blances Mains, we recall, refused to permit her

husband Tristan and his sweetheart to share a grave.[105] But then Tristan's envious wife had the power to dispose of the lovers' bodies as she wished, whereas it is clear that the chastelaine's husband would have been at the mercy of his powerful liege lord, the duke of Burgundy. Let us not forget that the French lord had absolute power over marriages.[106] Thus, having found a husband for his niece, the duke could just as easily take her and the land away again:

> The heads of such houses set out to find the best possible match for the heiresses that were theirs to bestow and did not hesitate to break a first marriage if the expectations of the young woman had increased.[107]

It is also important to consider that a castelanie was a military fief, the chief function of which was the protection of a castle felt by the lord to be of stategic importance. Chrestien's *Yvain* attests to the difficulty in the Middle Ages for a woman to hold a fief for any length of time, without a husband to defend it for her. It is probable that if a castelane's wife were widowed, her lord would have "married her off to the highest bidder" in order to ensure the continued safety of his castle.[108] Thus, Carl Stevenson concludes that:

> . . . by a series of legal devices, it was arranged that a fief should pass from one mature man to another for the holder was normally required to perform military service.[109]

In short, it is likely that our heroine had a live husband. Since the duke shows no concern about the marital status of his niece, this suggests that he was satisfied that her husband was carrying out his obligation in the matter of protecting his castle at Vergi.

Nor should we forget that the medieval marriage was generally one of convenience, which had nothing whatever to do with love. If the wife was a gift from the lord upon whom the husband depended for his very survival, then surely the lord could dispense with her dead body as he saw fit. It was precisely because of these loveless matches that the fantasy of adulterous love between married women and single men became so popular. Thus, in *ChV*, which, as we have seen, is a "courtly" narrative, we are doubtlessly meant to assume that the husband is somewhere in the background, but that, as in courtly lyric, he is simply unimportant to the poem. Finally, although Reed and Foulet interpret the chastelaine's remark about her "sire" ("mon seignor") at l. 714, as a reference to the duke rather than to her husband, I think the context and simple logic demand that it be the husband who comes to his wife's mind when she is publically accused of adultery:

—Je ne sai quel acointement
vous penssez, ma dame, por voir,
que talent n'ai d'ami avoir,
qui ne soit del tout a l'onor
et de moi et de mon seignor."

[710]

I do not know what "friend"
you have in mind, my lady, truly.
For I desire no "friendship"
if it honor not
both myself and my lord [i.e., my husband].

In any event, I do not share the opinion that one of the more important reasons for the secret in this tale is that the chastelaine has a husband lurking about in the background. Rather I feel that the gratuitousness of the lovers' pact is essential to the meaning of the story because the whole point of the covenant is that it represents the kind of demand for absolute, unquestioning obedience required of a Lanval or a Lancelot by their intractable mistresses.[110] The knight's crime is not that he thoughtlessly endangers the chastelaine's marriage or her reputation, but rather that his indiscretion is a form of disobedience, which, as in the *Lanval* or the *Charrete*, is a grave threat to the mistress's desire to have complete control over her lover. The fantasy is understandable in an era when women were mere chattels among the possessions of their husbands and when men were violent and brutish. However, regardless of the motivation for the pact of secrecy, the chastelaine's reference to her sire at l. 714, coupled with the fact that she simply could not have remained a widow without much pressure from her powerful uncle to marry while she had charge of one of the most strategically important strongholds in all of medieval Burgundy, convinces me that we are meant to assume that we are dealing with the traditional love triangle of courtly lyric from which the husband is usually conspicuously absent.

Now I suppose there will be some who will object to the fact that the chastelaine manages to receive her lover so easily at home. Where is the husband then, they may ask? The answer is that, for the medieval listener, the text provided more than enough information to explain this difficulty. For if we read very carefully, we notice that, rather than greet her lover at the castelanie, that is, at the fortified building of which her husband had charge, the chastelaine has her knight come to her manor house. Whereas the medieval listener would have realized this right away from the few descriptive details in the text, we have to ponder over the problem for some time before we can visualize it. To begin with, although there were living quarters on the upper floors of the feudal castle, these were rough accomodations the purpose of which was to house personnel for the defense of the lord's property. Great barons like the duke of Burgundy, his counts, and his more powerful castelanes had manor houses where they stayed when they were not engaged in military duties and which were situated upon great estates which brought them revenue in the form of poultry, pork, and produce.[111] It would appear from the description of the chastelaine's house that it is a manor rather than a rough castle since castles did not have walled gardens (see *angle*, 'the corner made by the coming together of two walls,' at l. 33, *jardin*, 'garden' at l. 378 and *vergier*, 'garden,' or 'orchard,' at l. 381), courtyards (see "prael," at l. 396) and chambers suitable for a courtly tryst on the ground floor (see *D'iluec vit en la chambre entrer / le chevalier. . . .*) 'From there behind a huge tree the duke saw the knight enter the chamber presumably the bedchamber,' at l. 392). In short, if the husband was off guarding his lord's castle, as he was supposed to do, it would have been an easy matter for the chastelaine to entertain her lover at their country estate.

If I have gone into a great deal of detail in explaining this rather sketchy character, it is because the reader has to believe in the chastelaine if he is ever going to sympathize with the knight. Our bewilderment with a culture that is not only foreign but also remote in time from our own easily causes us annoyance when the author provides so few details about the society being represented by the characters in his poem. We hastily conclude that he was a bad writer, never realizing that, on the contrary, we are poorly informed readers. What is worse, our irritation and frustration destroy the illusion of the fiction for us. As a result, we cease to care about any of the characters and so easily miss the point the author was trying to make. Spoiled by the photographically descriptive techniques of modern fiction, we grow impatient with the ancient poet's suggestive art. We are simply not used to being asked to draw our own mental pictures from a simple linesketch. All we learn of the chastelaine's physical appearance is that she has beautiful arms and eyes (ll. 401 and 476).[112] It is up to us to imagine the rest. What a clever way for an author to make his heroine represent every man's ideal woman! Had the *ChV* poet described her in detail, he would have given us an individual lady rather than the type of the beautiful courtly lady, and, as I explained earlier, medieval poets deliberately strove to create types rather than individuals. Thus it should not surprise us that, as in the sermon exemplum, our impression of the chastelaine comes from a gesture portrait and representative snatches of her thoughts through her eager greeting of the knight in the garden, her reluctant farewell at the end of their tryst, and her bitter, lonely lament (*planh*) on the following Pentecost. Nevertheless, some important things

are implied about the moral side of our heroine's character from the way
the knight thinks and talks about her with the duke.

If the chastelaine, whose name is also the title of the poem, is conspicuously absent throughout most of the narrative, the knight is constantly present. This is because he is a victimized hero, whose happiness
and destruction are both brought about by the chastelaine's bookish notions about love. It is she who demands absolute secrecy and contrives
elaborate means to implement the love covenant by training her little dog
to fetch her lover. Like the chastelaine, the knight is undeniably a "flat."
But this probably would not have stopped the medieval audience from
coming to care about him deeply, as witnessed by references to the knight
in contemporary literature (see my notes 86 through 88), because, in their
eyes, he typified the perfect courtly lover. From the very beginning, the
knight is depicted by the narrator as *preu et hardi* 'brave and valiant' (l.
19), *biaus et cointes* 'comely and refined' (l. 43) and *biaus et preu* 'brave
and handsome' (l. 60) by the duchess. He is apparently valorous enough
because it is through his feats at arms, presumably in tournaments and
local skirmishes (l. 45), that he becomes a favorite of the powerful duke
of Burgundy. Since, in addition to being favored by the duke, the knight
is beloved by both the chastelaine and duchess, he is obviously courtly,
or, as we might say, a gentleman, courtliness being the medieval measure
of lovableness.

The very first time we see the knight tested is at ll. 45–59 where he is
so preoccupied by his love for the chastelaine that he fails to notice the
duchesses' outrageous flirting. The second test is dramatized as a
dialogue between the duchess and knight. Remaining extremely humble
and courteous, the knight successfully guards his own, his lord's, and his
lady's honor, while trying to save face for the duchess by pretending not
to fully understand her proposition (ll. 73–80). And again, when she
comes dangerously close to revealing her love for him (l. 84) he replies
very carefuly with all the finesse of the perfect courtier:

> Ma dame, je ne le sai pas;
> mes je voudroie vostre amor
> avoir par bien et par honor, etc.
>
> [88 ff.]
>
> My Lady, I do not know [if I have won your love],
> but I would like to have your friendship honorably. . . .

Handsome, diplomatic, courteous, humble, loyal, distinguished at arms, in
short, the perfect medieval lover, such is our early impression of the knight.
We cannot help but share the anxiety and rage of such an admirable and

sympathetic character at having been so falsely accused by his friend and liege lord:

> —Certes," dist il, "ce est granz deus
> quant proësce avez et beauté,
> et il n'a en vous lëauté.
> Si m'en avez mout deceü . . ."
>
> [156-9]
>
> "It is a very great pity," said he, [the duke]
> "to see how valiant and fair of form you are
> but so lacking in loyalty!
> I am very disappointed in you . . ."

How appalling this is, following upon the knight's brave defense of his lord's honor before his lord's lascivious wife (ll. 94-6). And just to make us all the more upset on behalf of the knight, the duke is made to rage on about his disappointment in him for twenty lines (through l. 176). By this time, we fairly ache for the knight to tell the duke what an evil creature his wife is. How can we not share his righteous indignation? (ll. 178-80): *D'ire et de mautalent esprent / si que tuit li tramblent si membre. . . .* 'When the knight heard this his very limbs trembled with indignation. . . .' But what is uppermost in the knight's mind, as befits the lover of lyric poetry, is not the loss of his own honor, but the possible physical separation from his lady, which would result from his banishment:

> dont il set qu'il ne puet joïr
> se n'est par aler et venir
> et par reperier ou païs
> dont li dus veut qu'il soit eschis.
>
> [181-4]
>
> and he was quite wretched
> when he thought of his mistress
> in whom he could no longer delight
> were he to be banished.

Were he to be deprived of her presence, his identity as a courtly man would be lost, just as her identity as the courtly lady is lost when she believes he has betrayed her.

His second thought is for his honor (ll. 185-7). Once again, as in the scene with the duchess, the political animal in him emerges and, without accusing the duchess directly, he nevertheless defends himself at her expense (ll. 195 and 204). Depressed by his lord's continuing distrust, the knight lets slip a fateful oath: *si n'est riens que je n'en feïsse / par si que j'en fusse creü* . . . 'There is nothing I wouldn't do in order that I might be believed.' (l. 208.) It is this very moment which is the turning point in his life. As in a fairytale, where the hero's almost inaudible wish is instantaneously granted, the knight has unwittingly unleashed the powers of darkness[113] Thus when the duke claims to have found a test of his innocence, the knight eagerly agrees to it before hearing what he will be asked to say or do (ll. 225–37). He further seals his fate by swearing to answer whatever question the duke may ask (ll. 238–39). Upon discovering that he has promised to reveal his mistress's name on pain of banishment, the knight is discomfitted. It is only fitting that a man who thinks like the chastelain de Couci (ll. 291–92), and thus one who has styled himself after literary models, should find himself in a predicament which is so like a *geu-parti* (l. 269). In this reference to contemporary lyric poetry, as I have already explained, the author gives us the key to his narrative aim — he wants us to know that he is arguing *in utramque partem* 'on both sides of the question,' and that we are to react to his poem as we would to a *geu-parti*, that is, by weighing all the evidence before passing judgment upon his hero.[114] The knight's dilemma is very real, because, as we have seen, it is not at all certain that there is a "right choice." In fact, since telling the secret turns out to be a way of clearing not only his own honor, but the duke's as well, it may actually be viewed as a very good thing to do in this situation. But what if the duke should tell the chastelaine? The knight would surely lose her then, and he could not live without her. Utterly baffled, he is like the chastelain de Couci, feeling that "his heart should break / and yet, it goes on beating to his shame." (ll. 301–02) So torn is the knight that he begins to cry (ll. 308–11).

Let me hasten to point out, lest the reader form the erroneous impression that the knight is being portrayed as a weakling, that tears were not considered unmanly in the Middle Ages. On the contrary, epic grief scenes and lyric poetry were filled with manly weeping. (See, for example, the Roland and the poems of de Couci.) When the duke sees the knight's distress, he immediately attempts to pry the knight's secret from him, claiming to be trustworthy all the while: "You don't trust me as you ought. Do you think that I would tell anyone your secret? Why, I'd rather have my teeth pulled one by one." (ll. 316–22) His behavior recalls the narrator's warning in the prologue: "Beware of friends / who boast their loyalty . . . for they too easily inspire trust." The knight's response is very interesting because it raises the question as to why he did not ask leave to consult with the chastelaine before revealing her identity to the duke:

> . . . je voudroie mieus morir
> que perdre ce que je perdroie,

se le voir dit vous en avoie,
et s'il estoit de li seü
que l'eüsse reconneü . . .

[326. Italics mine]

I would rather die than lose
what I would lose
were I to tell the truth to you
and were she to learn that I
had published her name for any reason.

The point is not that this perfect, loyal and courtly knight is a sneak, but that the chastelaine's covenant, like that of the Lanval fay or Queen Guenevere's demand for unequivocal obedience from her lover in the *Charrete*, was so arbitrary it would not allow for any extenuating circumstances. To tell her that he even considered revealing her identity to anyone under any circumstances would incur her irrevocable wrath. Thus, by that very pact of secrecy, whose purpose was to perpetuate their love, the chastelaine had undermined the communication so necessary to lovers.

The knight is modeled upon literary heroes like Lanval and Tristan, but, unlike these Breton heroes of yore, he is supposed to represent a "real" person, a contemporary of the audience. Thus he is depicted as a young Burgundian nobleman in love with the wife of a Burgundian castelane. Moreover, he is identified with another young nobleman, also from the north of France, the castelane of Coucy, who was in fact a real, rather than a fictional person. It is very significant that the story takes place in contemporary France rather than in the Brittany of the dark ages, because this mimesis shows us that the author was deliberately juxtaposing literature and life. What happens to the fictional knight is what might happen to any real person who was expected to emulate literary heroes. The point is that the literary rules won't work in real life. The chastelaine is too unyielding and it is her stubborn clinging to her illusions which ulitmately causes the destruction of the couple. Even at his death, the knight's adherence to the literary ideal is beyond reproach (ll. 885-900). Ironically blaming himself for his mistress's death, he runs himself through with a sword: *Mes je ferai de moi justise / por la trahison que j'ai fete.* 'I will do justice to myself for the act of treason I have committed.' (ll. 894-95) We are reminded of the pathetic suicide of Pyramus, who coming upon Thisbe's bloodied veil, blames himself for arriving too late at their rendezvous to save her from the lion.[115] No medieval listener would ever have held poor Pyramus responsible for Thisbe's death. Similarly, as we have seen, it is the chastelaine's mistrust of the knight that kills her, his betrayal being merely a symptom that something is terribly wrong with their relationship. Thus when like Pyramus the knight accuses himself of having killed the chastelaine, the audience would only have admired the delicacy of his sensibilities and pitied him all the more. In the end, the knight loses the very thing for which he made such an unwise compromise, the chastelaine's physical presence; the chastelaine dies believing her knight was not the equal of her romantic idol, when, as irony would have it, he was really more loyal than Tristan, and the duke's illusions of a courtly or romantic relationship in his marriage are shattered along with his very life (ll. 939-40). He foresakes women and marriage, not only as a penance for his role in the catastrophe, but also because he is thoroughly disillusioned with earthly delights. Rejected by the knight, the duchess cannot even manage to manipulate her husband as much as she would like to think she can because the one promise he keeps is to execute her for her betrayal. By juxtaposition to the lovers, the ducal couple forms a subplot. By showing these two sets of thwarted romantic expectations side by side — marriage and illicit love — the author planted the seeds of doubt in the minds of his audience as to the advisability of urging real lovers to model their relationships upon literature. It is clear from the events of the tale that the consequences of attempting to impose such standards in real life are disastrous. As we have seen, the demand for absolute secrecy about the love affair, i.e., unwaivering obedience, was the most unreasonable standard of all.

If this play between literature and life seems artificial, we should keep in mind that (1) artificiality of plot or language is a common device in narrative for calling attention to the fact that we are not supposed to take the story at face value and (2) the medieval audience delighted in pondering the hypothetical problems of lovers, as witnessed by the popularity of the *geu-parti* during the thirteenth century. Moreover, if at first the author's anguish seems silly, we must remember that, in those days, young people's role models were literary heroes rather than film or rock stars. The false standards imposed by television and cinema have ruined just as many modern-day love relationships as did courtly literature in those days. Thus it takes surprisingly little "archeology" on our part to demonstrate the universality of a poem, which, at first glance, may have appeared quite antiquated.

If we are made to sympathize with the knight and chastelaine, we are kept at a very great distance from the wicked duchess whose portrayal is handled in much the same way as that of Alexander's queen in the sermon exemplum. We are made to fear and to dislike her through inside views of her evil machinations and overheard dialogues with other characters. Because she was so obviously modeled on Potiphar's Wife from Genesis 39, the *ChV* poet's audience easily would have apprehended her as the type of the evil seductress. Thus a wealth of unpleasant associations immediately would have come to bear upon the duchess whom they could not help but despise. It is because he relied so heavily upon a rich tradition that the medieval author could elicit strong emotion from his audience for a character who is just a "flat."

By contrast with all the other characters in this tale, the duke appears to be an early experiment in round characterization, which means that, unlike a "flat," the duke surprises us. Now I am not claiming that this experiment represents a conscious effort on the part of the poet to break with the traditions of his time, but merely that the needs of his narrative led him to stray away from the traditional techniques of his contemporaries. The problem the author faced with the duke was that this character had to play several different roles. He was first of all to be the powerful duke of Burgundy, the largest duchy in France. To be sure, there was a wealth of material at the author's disposal for fleshing in the type of the ruler. However, at the same time, the duke had to be a husband deeply in love with his wife. He must treat her with extreme courtesy and be taken in by her without becoming the foolish husband of the *fabliau*. He is also the fond and indulgent uncle of the chastelaine, and, finally, the friend and patron of his "nourri" 'ward,' the knight. It is clear that the character of the duke presented a tremendous challenge to an author who, to judge from the other characters in the story, was used to working only with types. Many another medieval writer simply would have destroyed his poem by clumsily combining the several types required. Now while I will not go so far as to say that the *ChV* poet was completely successful by modern standards, what he did do with the duke is admirable when measured against the standards of the day.

What strikes one about the character of the duke is the range of emotions he is allowed to have and still be believable. At ll. 144-53, we see the husband/ruler tossing and turning all night because he is upset to learn that his favorite vassal has insulted his wife. His fury during his interview with the knight and his joy following the tryst are equally powerful and yet psychologically true emotions. In fact, there are many "realistic" qualities in the portrayal of the duke, among which, his tenderness and patience with his wife (especially at ll. 519-28, 613-18 and 631-34), whom he addresses as "bele dame" (l. 635), "ma bele suer" (l. 613), and "ma douce amie" (l. 541). One is also struck by the duke's sincerely perplexed attitude during his wife's long speeches (ll. 122, *Je ne sai por qoi vous le dites* 'Why are you saying this to me?' 587, *a qoi*? 'But how can this be?' and 593, *. . . de qoi . . . por Dé*? " 'By God, I do not understand!' cried he." Finally, throughout the entire poem, we never forget that he is a powerful man, striving to mete out justice with great pain to both himself and to those who depend upon him. In short, the duke was a very complex and difficult character for a medieval poet to represent with his traditional, typal art.

We may wonder why the duke trusts his wife after learning she is a liar (ll. 425-26). The most consistent explanation I have seen is that which emerges from Emilie P. Kostoroski's reading of the tale.[116] It is because he is so anxious to maintain a courtly relationship in his marriage that the duke overlooks his wife's duplicity: "Because he loves her he believes her," (l. 647). This is why, when he returns from the lovers' tryst, where the knight has exculpated himself, he does not call the duchess a liar, but merely proclaims his vassal's innocence, adding "so let's just forget about it." (ll. 541-49) What is fairly clear from the author's treatment of the duke is that he is not meant to be a *fabliau* type. As Kostoroski remarks, had the duke not wished to treat the duchess as his courtly mistress, rather than as a wife, he simply could have "asserted his rights as her husband and lord."[117] It is therefore illogical to assume that he gives in to her on account of his sexual desire as R. Dubuis implies.[118] It would be a mistake to read the scene in question as if it were a *fabliau* with noble characters because, unlike the *fabliau* husband, the duke is no fool. Rather, he is a man fully cognizant of his power over his wife, who feels pity for the poor tormented creature: *Et li dus tel pitié en ot / qu'il li a dit: 'Ma bele suer . . .'* "The duke pitied her so, he said: 'My lovely sister . . .'" (l. 612) If the duke compromises his feudal principles it is in order to preserve a romantic relationship with his wife:

> And so he said to her: "My lovely lady,
> I know not what to do,
> since I so trust in you
> I should not hide a single thing."
>
> [ll. 635-39]

He is therefore understandably enraged ("dervé," l. 910) when he discovers that not only has she betrayed him, but that she has caused him to betray the lovers. His anger is heightened by the fact that as a feudal ruler he must have prided himself on being fair and just. The open-mindedness of this powerful feudal lord with the knight is exemplary, considering what charges the duchess has brought against his vassal. The duke shows the same open-mindedness to his wife, with the result that when she takes advantage of his liberality, he unhesitatingly carries out the punishment he promised her when he confided in her (ll. 641 ff.). It is clear then that the text itself provides a logical reason for the duke's misplaced trust in his evil wife, but the poet's handling of the narrative in this instance is sufficiently ambiguous to have misled several excellent critics. Nevertheless, even though the psychological richness of the duke caused the author a great deal of difficulty, he did succeed, I feel, in creating one of the earliest rounded characters in French literature. Responding, I think, to the complexity of the duke's character, Pál Lakits exclaimed that he was "le vrai héros tragique . . ." of the poem.[119] However, as was the case with the chastelaine, who might very well have been another author's tragic heroine, the *Ch V* poet deliberately keeps us at far too great an emotional distance from the duke for us to be able to sympathize with him. The reason for this, of course, is that the focal point of this tale is the tragic dilemma of the knight.

The foregoing pages have been devoted largely to the problem of verisimilitude. This is because the credibility of a character is essential to the degree to which the reader may be made to sympathize with him and thus to enter readily into the author's imagination. A single conspicuous tear in the veil of illusion is enough to dispel all the fiction writer's magic.

I have tried to show that *Ch V* is an interesting experiment in characterization which, despite some difficulties, is successful for the period. Certainly the author handled devices of caring and distancing adroitly since even the most naive reader will express sympathy for the knight and chastelaine, and dislike of the duchess. Further, most readers will also grasp the fact that the chastelaine is a very unreliable narrator when the time comes for her to speak at last. It would be difficult to miss the point that her mistrust of the knight is unfair. Finally, the duke is such an interesting character that a number of critics have tried to explain his behavior.[120] Of these critics, very few have failed to react to the unusual "human" qualities of this character which are atypical for the period, and which are certainly never found in the husband of the *fabliau*.

Because this particular aenigmalogue is dominated by the voice telling the tale, the unreliability of the narrator becomes one of the most important generic signals in the poem. The fact that the poet never differentiates himself from his narrator persona might make us think that his opinions were the same as those of the teller of the tale, but if we did think that, it seems fairly clear to me that we would be wrong. How then, can we be sure that the narrator persona is a mask, or disguise, behind which the poet hides both his face and his true feelings? For one thing, in spite of all his logical constructs, the narrator persona's exemplum shows up his blindness because instead of demonstrating how true his "lesson" is, it makes us doubt his word about the knight's guilt very seriously. This comes about because, very simply, the events of the exemplum make us feel so sorry for the knight that we cannot believe the narrator persona when he says the catastrophe was the knight's fault. Further, the narrator's repetition and amplification of his 'lesson'—which as we have seen is simply inappropriate to the exemplum—in the epilogue is maddening. It has even deeply annoyed a number of modern critics, who apparently did not know what to make of it.[123] In a work so impeccably styled as *ChV*, if a device irritates us very much, we ought first to ask ourselves if that isn't precisely what it was designed to do. The epilogue in *ChV* makes us want to jump up and shout at the narrator persona, or the poet—as I suggested earlier, the author himself may have recited his work—for being so blind to the knight's unwarranted agony. And that reaction carries with it a desire to go back over the exemplum in order to show the fellow what a fool he is. This is probably exactly what the medieval audiences did. They liked the poem, as evidenced by its twenty extant medieval copies, because it was provocative and they could argue about it for hours, if not for days, afterwards. Moreover, there are a number of other devices in the exemplum which tell us how the poet wanted us to read his poem if we are alert. As I explained, the *geu-parti* to which the poet refers at l. 269, was a kind of cue for the medieval audience. Once they had heard that the knight's dilemma was a *geu-parti*, they could hardly have failed to realize that there could be no solution to the central problem posed in this narrative. Moreover, they would certainly have remembered some of the *geus-partis* they had seen performed about the very problem which lies at the center of this work, the law of secrecy. In a word, their experience with the "courts of love," as the noble companies of knights and ladies convened to witness the *geus-partis* were called, predisposed them to pass judgment upon the poet's tale, rather than to accept the narrator's lesson passively. The author's brief allusion to the poetic debates of his day merely served as a catalyst to ensure the desired reaction.

Again, the poet's use of lyric, and perhaps even of the music that accompanied the intercalated song, must have created a lot of sympathy for the knight, which works against the narrator. Further, his utilization of the *chanson* (ll. 295-302), and his narratonalization of the *oaristys* (ll. 392–449), *alba* (ll. 450–76) and *planh* 'complaint' (ll. 732–834), all lyric forms of the day, are a visible demonstration that he was juxtaposing a literary ideal to "real life." His listeners probably had no difficulty in apprehending his meaning, whereas we so easily miss the point. I doubt the medieval audience could have sat calmly by, after hearing the narrative, without questioning those ideals at least within themselves. We must remember that medieval courtesy was a code governing intercourse between men and women, and, as we all know, no subject is of greater interest or more likely to produce strong emotional responses in any age.

I hope it is clear that all the devices in this tale function together to create in us a sense of irritation, anxiety, and injustice at the fate of the knight. For, as in de Vitry's sermon exemplum, we are being manipulated by the author's dialectico-rhetorical organization of the various constructs which make up his narrative. However, unlike de Vitry's moralistic little anecdote, but like all the others of its kind, the narrative aim of this story is to make us question its norms rather than to accept them blindly. And this, of course, is what makes *ChV* an aenigmalogue, or the opposite of an apologue.

Leigh A. Arrathoon
Solaris Press

𝕹otes

1. ed. H. E. Butler, 1 (Cambridge: Harvard University Press, 1965), 399–401. The questions an orator may treat are either legal or rational. These questions in turn are divided into indefinite questions (which the Greeks call "theses" and the Romans call propositions, general or philosophical questions) and definite questions (for which the Greek word is "hypotheses," and the Roman word, "causes"). An indefinite question, or thesis, is non-specific as in "Should a man marry?" A definite question, or hypothesis, is specific as in "Should Cato marry?" For a more detailed discussion of oratorical theses and hypotheses, see Wesley Trimpi, *Muses of One Mind: The Literary Analysis of Experience and Its Continuity* (Princeton: Princeton University Press, 1983), pp. 3–79. I wish to thank Professor Trimpi for his useful comments on the rough draft of this paper. I am also grateful to Peter Haidu whose comments and suggestions proved very helpful indeed.

2. Quintilian, p. 397.

3. See Tony Hunt, "The Dialectic of *Yvain*," *Modern Language Review* 72 (1977), 285–99 and "Aristotle, Dialectic, and Courtly Literature," *Viator* 10 (1979), 95–129.

4. Edgar De Bruyne, *Etudes d'esthétique médiévale: De Boèce à Jean Scot Erigène*, 1 (Bruges: "De Tempel," 1946), 46.

5. ibid., 1:60.

6. ibid., 1:235.

7. On organizing principles, see Sheldon Sacks, *Fiction and the Shape of Belief* (Berkeley: The University of California Press, 1964), John F. Reichert, "Organizing Principles

and Genre Theory," *Genre* 1 (1968), 1-12, Judith Leibowitz, *Narrative Purpose in the Novella* (The Hague: Mouton, 1974), E. San Juan, Jr., "Notes Toward a Clarification of Organizing Principles and Genre Theory," *Genre* 1 (1968), 257-68, Mary Doyle Springer, *Forms of the Modern Novella* (Chicago: University of Chicago Press, 1975).

8. op. cit., n. 7, p. 22.

9. Springer, p. 22.

10. Glending Olson, *Literature as Recreation in the Later Middle Ages* (Ithaca: Cornell University Press, 1982). See also Roy J. Pearcy, "*Sentence* and *Solas* in the Old French Fabliaux," *The Craft of Fiction: Essays in Medieval Poetics,* pp. 231-80.

11. (New York: Basic Books, 1978), pp. 5-6.

12. Private conversation in February 1984.

13. My definitions of *movere* are taken from John C. Traupman, *The New College Latin and English Dictionary* (New York: Amsco School Publications, 1966).

14. See Emilie P. Kostoroski, "Quest and Query and the *Chastelaine de Vergi*," *Medievalia et Humanistica,* n.s., 3 (1972), 179-97.

15. See Arrathoon, "The Elegant Apologues of Mary of France," to be published.

16. Henry James also seems to have been aware of the *docere-movere* dichotomy because, in the critical prefaces he distinguishes between "obvious apologues" like "Flicker-bridge" and "The Story In It," which he describes as a "deep and straight . . . dive into the deep sea of a certain general truth . . ." (*Theory of Fiction: Henry James*, ed. James E. Miller, Jr. [Lincoln: University of Nebraska Press, 1972], pp. 284-5) and *Daisy Miller*, which I would consider an aenigmalogue and which James calls a "shapely nouvelle." In fact, in his preface to this tale, James wrote of his heroine that she was ". . . a figure of which the only fault is touchingly to have transmitted so sorry a type to have, by a poetic artifice, not only led our judgment of it astray, but made *any* judgment quite impossible." (p. 269) Finally, James' constant concern for the story shows his awareness of the third medieval narrative purpose, entertainment (*delectare*).

While finding the kind of obviously manipulative rhetoric used by medieval writers distasteful — the "goody" moralizing as he called it — James was certain that morality is essential to the success of the work. A writer needs a natural sense of morality — a moral imagination, he thought:

> Be the morality false or true, the writer's deference to it greets us as a kind of essential perfume. We find such a perfume in Shakespeare; we find it, in spite of his so-called cynicism, in Thackeray; we find it, potently, in George Eliot, in George Sand, in Turgenieff. They care for moral questions; they are haunted by a moral ideal . . . Charles de Bernard's talent is great — very great, greater than the impression it leaves; and the reason why this clever man remains so persistently second-rate is, to our sense, because he had no morality. By this we of course do not mean that he did not choose to write didactic tales, winding up with a goody lecture and a distribution of prizes and punishments. We mean that he had no moral emotion, no preferences, no instincts — no moral imagination, in a word. (ibid., pp. 302-3.)

17. De Bruyne, 1: 98.

18. Per Nykrog, "Playing Games with Fiction: *Les Quinze Joyes de Mariage, Il Corbaccio*, and *El Arcipreste de Talavera*," *The Craft of Fiction: Essays in Medieval Poetics*, pp. 423-52 and John Gardner, *On Moral Fiction*, passim.

19. De Bruyne, 1: 47.

20. ibid., 1:97. Cf. Charles G. Osgood, *Boccaccio on Poetry, Being the Preface and the Fourteenth and Fifteenth Books of Boccaccio's Genealogia Deorum Gentilum, an English Version with Introductory Essay and Commentary* (Princeton: Princeton University Press, 1930), pp. 42, 61, and 79.

21. Springer, p. 97. Unlike me, Springer and Sacks consider satire a genre. Cf. Robert Scholes, "Les modes de la fiction," *Poetique* 32 (1977), 507-14.

22. James, p. 107.

23. Pearcy, "*Sentence* and *Solas* in the Old French Fabliaux."

24. Hans-Robert Jauss, "Littérature médiévale et théorie des genres," trans. Eliana Kaufholz, *Poétique* 1 (1970), 83.

25. *Chaucer and the French Tradition* (Berkeley: University of California Press, 1969), p. 74.

26. Hunt, "Aristotle, Dialectic, and Courtly Literature," p. 106. For the ancient and medieval traditions of declamation, see Trimpi, esp. pp. 46, 235, 253, 306, 307, 309-13, 321-23, 328-29, 334-35. Although we disagree as to the organizing principles and genres of narrative fiction (see his pp. 211-12, 255-56, and 358), like me, Professor Trimpi sees rhetorical *quaestiones* as providing the basis for the "novella," or what I would call narrative fiction (both long and short). See his pp. 306, 340-43. Unlike Professor Trimpi, I do not think that just because a tradition exists, it must be "right." The traditional terms for literary kinds are, for the most part, useless and confusing, which is why I am attempting to erect an entirely new system here.

27. p. 98.

28. See Malcolm Pittock, "The Merchant's Tale," *Essays in Criticism* 17 (1967), 26-40, Emerson Brown, Jr., "Biblical Women in the *Merchant's Tale*: Feminism, Antifeminism, and Beyond," *Viator* 5 (1974), 387-412, and Arrathoon, "The Two Saras of Chaucer's *Merchant's Tale*," *Ball State University Forum* (1984), in press.

29. Springer discusses signals, pp. 24, 40, 126.

30. Springer, citing Sacks, p. 104. Cf. Peter Haidu, *Aesthetic Distance in Chrétien de Troyes: Irony and Comedy in Cligés and Perceval* (Geneva: Droz, 1968).

31. See F. Douglas Kelly, "The Source and Meaning of *Conjointure* in Chrétien's Erec 14," *Viator* 1 (1970), 179-200, *Sens and Conjointure in the Chevalier de la Charrette* (The Hague: Mouton, 1966). See also Arrathoon, "Antinomic Cluster Analysis and the Boethian Verbal Structure of Chaucer's *Merchant's Tale*," *Language and Style* (1984), in press, Arrathoon, *The Lady of Vergi, Edited and Translated with an Introduction, Variants, Notes, and a Glossary* (Merrick, N.Y.: Cross-Cultural Communications Press, 1984), Paul Zumthor, "Recherches sur les topiques dans la poésie lyrique des XIIᵉ et XIIIᵉ siècles," *Cahiers de civilisation médiévale* 2 (1959), 409-27, and Springer, pp. 28, 120, 122, 123. In this paper I shall be dealing with theme words rather than isotopies. See Peter Haidu, "Text and History: the Semiosis of Twelfth-Century Lyric as Sociohistorical Phenomenon (Chrétien de Troyes: 'D'Amors qui m'a tolu,')" *Semiotica* (1980) for the semiotic approach to the verbal structures of medieval literature. Another interesting approach is J. D. Burnley's in his "The Morality of the *Merchant's Tale*," *Yearbook of English Studies* 6 (1976), 16-25 and "Chaucer's *Termes*," *Yearbook of English Studies* 7 (1977), 53-67.

32. Robert J. Clements and Joseph Gibaldi, *Anatomy of the Novella: The European Tale Collection from Boccaccio and Chaucer to Cervantes* (New York: New York University Press, 1977), and Janet Levarie Smarr's introduction to her *Italian Renaissance Tales* (Rochester, MI: Solaris Press, 1983).

33. Aristotle, *The "Art" of Rhetoric*, trans. J. H. Freese (Cambridge: Harvard University Press, 1967), p. 19.

34. See Wayne C. Booth, *The Rhetoric of Fiction* (Chicago: University of Chicago Press, 1974), Salvatore Battaglia, *Giovanni Boccaccio e la riforma della narrativa* (Naples: Liguori, 1969), p. 11, n. 1: "La esemplarità, insomma, e appannaggio inalienabile della narrativa in quanto tale," Gardner, whose principal thesis is that art instructs (see, for example, his pp. 30 and 108–09), and Trimpi, who treats the rise of literary fiction, and, in particular, the drama and "novella," from the fusion of ancient philosophical and rhetorical discourse, especially forensic rhetoric. See pp. 68–71 of his "The Quality of Fiction: The Rhetorical Transmission of Literary Theory," *Traditio* 30 (1974), and *Muses of One Mind*, pp. 371–81 on the exemplum. Pp. 382–90 of the same book deal with the morality of medieval fiction. Perhaps it is useful to say here that I began to work on the passage from *controversia* to medieval narrative fiction in 1970 when I was still in graduate school, but not having the fine classical background that Professor Trimpi has, I abandoned the project until I discovered his two *Traditio* articles in 1975, which gave me the confidence to pursue my original course. The first of these articles, "The Ancient Hypothesis of Fiction: An Essay on the Origins of Literary Theory," *Traditio* 30: 1–118, appeared in 1971.

35. Tony Hunt, "Beginnings, Middles, and Ends: Some Interpretative Problems in Chrétien's *Yvain* and Its Medieval Adaptations," *The Craft of Fiction: Essays in Medieval Poetics*, pp. 83–117, shows that the problems raised in the *Yvain* are far from being resolved by the conclusion to the romance which fails to reconcile love and chivalry. In fact, the reason Hunt gives for Chrestien's having utilized Calogrenant's tale in place of a conventional prologue is that he wanted to "alert his audience to the complexities in this most sophisticated and problematic romance." Cf. Peter Haidu, "Romance: Idealistic Genre or Historical Text?" *The Craft of Fiction: Essays in Medieval Poetics*, pp. 1–46. The *Charette* can also be viewed as problematic, if we accept the very tempting interpretation of A. H. Diverres, in his "Some Thoughts on the *Sens* of *Le Chevalier de la Charrette*," *Forum for Modern Language Studies* 6 (1970), 24–36. Finally, the hypocrisy of Fenice in the *Cligés* must certainly tell us that Chrestien was at odds with his female patrons. Surely the men in the audience held their sides with laughter when the nude Fenice was rudely awakened by a pear falling from the tree above her because they certainly would have viewed the pear in this context as a phallic symbol. On pear symbolism, see Karl Wentersdorf, "Imagery, Structure, and Theme in Chaucer's *Merchant's Tale*," *Chaucer and the Craft of Fiction* (Rochester, MI: Solaris Press, 1985) and Bruce A. Rosenberg, "The 'Cherry-Tree Carol' and the *Merchant's Tale*," *Chaucer Review* 5 (1971), 266–76. Further, how could they have taken the scene as anything but a burlesque of courtly love when an intruder's leg is hacked off by the lover / hero and made to fall into the *locus amoenus*? I should think the women in Chrestien's public would have been amused or infuriated or both, and I can easily see a heated battle of the sexes following the recitation of the author's quizzical tale.

36. On the exemplum, see Salvatore Battaglia's "Premesse per una Valutazione del 'Novellino,'" *Filologia Romanza* 2, no. 6 (1955), 259–86, *Giovanni Boccaccio*, "L'esempio medievale, l'esempio nella retorica antica," *Filologia Romanza* 6 (1959), 45–82, Trimpi,

Muses of One Mind, pp. 345, 378–81, and Roger Dubuis, *Les Cent Nouvelles nouvelles et la tradition de la nouvelle en France au moyen âge* (Grenoble: Presses Universitaires de Grenoble, 1973), p. 488: "L'exemplum connaît une évolution logique et inéluctable: cessant d'être considéré comme un moyen de démonstration il trouve en lui-même sa propre raison d'être. Sa valeur 'exemplaire' n'est pas, pour autant, necéssairement abolie, mais le plus souvent, elle passe au second plan."

37. *Die Exempla aus den Sermones feriales et communes des Jakob von Vitry*, hg. von Joseph Greven, *Sammlung mittellateinischer Texte*, hg. von Alfons Hilka, 9 (Heidelberg: Carl Winter, 1914), 15, also cited by Maurice Delbouille, *Le Lai d'Aristote de Henri D'Andeli* (Paris: Société d'Edition "Les Belles Lettres," 1951), p. 39. Delbouille is rather harsh in his criticism of de Vitry's exemplum (see his pp. 50–53), when he compares it to d'Andeli's *Lai*, objecting to the fact that the exemplarist makes Alexander's concubine into a legitimate wife.

38. See Smarr.

39. I would like to thank Professor H. C. Kim of the Department of Foreign Languages and Literatures at Washington State University for correcting my English translation of the Latin. Let me hasten to assume responsibility for any liberties taken with the original.

40. Jerome, *Adversus Jovinianum*, trans. Philip Schaff and Henry Wace, *A Select Library of Nicene and Post-Nicene Fathers of the Christian Church*, Ser. 2, 6 (Grand Rapids, MI.: Wm. B. Eerdmans Publishing Co.), 281. See also John T. Noonan, Jr., *Contraception. A History of Its Treatment by the Catholic Theologians and Canonists* (New York: Mentor-Omega, 1965), for the classical influences on the doctrine.

41. See Booth, chap. 1, "Telling and Showing."

42. E. M. Forster, *Aspects of the Novel* (New York: Harcourt, Brace, and World, 1927), esp. pp. 67–69.

43. p. 5.

44. The line numbers cited in the text refer to my edition of the poem as it appears in the *Lady of Vergi*.

45. It should now be clear that those critics who look for the "falcon" or central symbol in "novellas" because they believe Boccaccio's ninth tale on the fifth day, which revolves about a falcon, is a model novella, are merely pointing to a rhetorical scheme that is typical of much short narrative fiction. In fact, Boccaccio's famous falcon tale is really a fable or species of apologue. The "falcon" theory is Paul Heyse's, see E. K. Bennett, *A History of the German Novelle*, (London: Cambridge University Press, 1934, rpt. 1949, 2nd ed. revised and continued by H. M. Waidson, 1961, rpt. 1965, 1970, 1974), pp. 13–16.

46. See Springer, pp. 45, 64, 122–23.

47. See Eren Branch, "Rhetorical Structures and Strategies in Boccaccio's *Teseida*," *The Craft of Fiction: Essays in Medieval Poetics*, pp. 143–60 and Trimpi, chap. 12.

48. *The Mirror of Narcissus in the Courtly Love Lyric* (Ithaca: Cornell University Press, 1967), passim.

49. ibid., p. 87.

50. ibid., p. 99.

51. See, for example, Pál Lakits, *La Châtelaine de Vergi et l'évolution de la nouvelle courtoise* (Debrecen: Kossuth Lajos Todományegyetem, 1966), esp. p. 51, where the term "nouvelle" is finally defined in a footnote. See also "La Chastelaine de Vergi, Marguerite de Navarre et Bandello," *Mélanges*, 1945, 1. *Etudes littéraires*, Publications de la faculté des

Lettres (1946), 89 and Paul Zumthor, *Essai de poétique médiévale* (Paris: Seuil, 1972), chap. 8, "Du Roman à la nouvelle." By contrast, Jean-Charles Payen, "Structure et sens de 'La Châtelaine de Vergi,'" *Moyen Age* 2 (1973), 229, reads the poem as a misbegotten exemplum, finally concluding that it is a romance. I wish I had the space here to show that some "romances" are aenigmalogues while others are apologues because Payen's generic demonstration misses the mark. Nevertheless, I do agree with him that the purpose of *ChV* is "démontrer le caractère chimérique de l'idéal courtois . . ." (p. 228). But I do not see the prologue and epilogue as "une double concession aux lois implicites du genre et au besoin d'une justification morale inventée après coup . . ." (p. 214) Rather, as we shall see, the opposition between the frame and the tale, or "example," as the narrator persona calls it, constitutes a viable literary device, the function of which is to signal the reader that something is amiss with the narrator's point of view. Thus, like all the other devices in this aenigmalogue, the prologue-epilogue arrangement is necessary to our correct apprehension of the genre and meaning of the poem.

52. Werner Söderhjelm, *La Nouvelle française au XVe siècle* (Paris: 1910, rpt. Geneva: Slatkine, 1973), p. 6 and Dubuis, p. 525.

53. Andreas Capellanus, *The Art of Courtly Love*, trans. John Jay Parry (New York: W. W. Norton, 1969), pp. 184-5. Andreas states the law of secrecy in the following way: "When made public love rarely endures" (p. 185). Jean Frappier described one reason for this rule of love: "Le secret est une règle essentielle de la fin'amor, non seulement en raison d'une prudence banale [by which Frappier meant the need to protect the lady from vicious enemies like the duchess of Burgundy in *ChV*] mais aussi parce qu'il convient de comprendre l'amour comme une chose sainte, qu'on ne saurait profaner." From "Vues sur les conceptions courtoises dans les littératures d'oc et d'oil au XIIe siècle," *Cahiers de civilisation médiévale* 2 (1959), 140. It is significant that the chastelaine utters not one syllable about her lover's "profanation" of their love while she is very concerned with the practical issue of his fidelity to her.

54. The Calogrenant episode which I am about to analyze has been studied in some depth by Paul R. Lonigan, "Calogrenant's Journey and the Mood of the 'Yvain,'" *Studi Francesi* 58 (1976), 1-20. See also P. S. Noble, "Irony in *Le Chevalier au Lion*," 196-208, Peter Haidu, *Lion-Queue-Coupée: l'écart symbolique chez Chrétien de Troyes* (Geneva: Droz, 1972), Roger S. Loomis, "Calogrenanz and Crestien's Originality," *Modern Language Notes* 43 (1928), 215-22, who sees Calogrenant (< *Cais li Grenanz*, 'Kex the Grumbler') as a double for Keu in his role as foil for the Arthurian heroes. The text I will be citing is *Yvain, ou le chevalier au lion*, ed. Jan Nelson, Carleton W. Carroll, and Douglas Kelly (New York: Appleton-Century-Crofts, 1968). The line numbers will be cited in the text proper. The translations are mine.

55. See Arrathoon, "Antinomic Cluster Analysis."

56. Lonigan's impression of Calogrenant and mine are similar: "Calogrenant," Lonigan writes, "is a pompous, pretentious individual who delights in being the center of attention; and he intends to hold it as long as he can by means of his story telling ability." (p. 10. Cf. pp. 3-4.)

57. In *Lion-Queue-Coupee*, p. 20, Peter Haidu gives one possible explanation:

> . . . Erec et Enide partiront "en aventure" mais ils auront abandonné
> tout ce qui n'est pas symbole personnel. Entre le moment où ils s'habil-
> lent et celui où ils quittent la cour interviennent les prières du père et
> des compagnons d'Erec: s'il veut partir, qu'il le fasse dans les formes,
> en emmenant des compagnons et d'argent, *car ne doit seus aler filz de*

> *roi. . . .* Car se mettre en route sans ces apanages de la noblesse peut être le signe d'une dégradation sociale. Ainsi du moins pensera Calogrenant, qui dira avoir quitté la cour d'Arthur *seus come paizans.*

While agreeing with Professor Haidu, it does strike me that Calogrenant is no king's son. Can it be that Chrestien is making of him for being pretentious? But see the same author's "Romance: Idealistic Genre or Historical Text?", *The Craft of Fiction: Essays in Medieval Poetics*, pp. 1–46.

58. I am much indebted to Robert Miller's forthcoming analysis of Chaucer's Squire in his "Chaucer's Rhetorical Rendition of Mind: The *Squire's Tale*," *Chaucer and the Craft of Fiction*, as the Squire and Calogrenant seem to have certain similarities of character and storytelling ability. John L. Grisby sees Calogrenant's "chatty nervousness" as giving him away as an "inexperienced storyteller," p. 272 of "Narrative Voices in Chrétien de Troyes: A Prolegomenon to Dissection," *Romance Philology* 32 (1979).

59. This ugly portrait is discussed by Alice Colby, *The Portrait in Twelfth-Century French Literature* (Geneva: Droz, 1965), pp. 170–73. Cf. Lonigan, p. 13.

60. Lonigan, p. 13. On the "reversal of roles between the knight and the peasant," see Haidu, "Romance: Idealistic Genre or Historical Text?"

61. De Bruyne, 1: 94.

62. ibid., 1: 228.

63. Lonigan, pp. 11, 17.

64. ibid., pp. 35, 36.

65. Haidu, *Lion-Queue-Coupée*, p. 36. Pp. 37–40 discuss Calogrenant's cupidity when he stays with the vavassor. As Peter Haidu's analysis shows, even this amorous adventure ends in failure when it is interrupted by a call to the evening meal. Cf. Longian, p. 10.

66. On the distinction between the narrator-persona mask and the implied author, see Booth, p. 73, Leo Spitzer, "Note on the Poetic and the Empirical 'I' in Medieval Authors," *Traditio*, 4 (1946), 414–22, Nykrog, and Goldin, p. 69: "The lady and the audience are to be constructed not as actual persons with dates, but as presences in the lyric, implied and to a great extent invented by the poet, who should be similarly regarded: the historic poet invents the "I" who speaks." The same is true of narrative.

67. Nykrog. Charles A. Owen, *Pilgrimage and Storytelling in the Canterbury Tales: The Dialectic of "Ernest" and "Game"* (Norman, OK.: University of Oklahoma Press, 1977).

68. Paul Zumthor, "De la chanson au récit: La Chastelaine de Vergi," *Vox Romanica* 27 (1968), amplified and reprinted in *Langue, texte, énigme* (Paris: Seuil, 1975), 217–36, 77–95, was the first to link this narrative with medieval song. See also Haidu, "Text and History," Eugene Vance, "Le combat érotique chez Chrétien de Troyes: De la figure à la forme," *Poétique* 12 (1972), 544–71.

69. On the disputation and the dialectical structure of the *partimen* or *joc partit*, see Glynnis M. Cropp, "The Partimen between Folquet de Marseille and Tostemps," *The Interpretation of Medieval Lyric Poetry*, ed. W. T. H. Jackson (New York: Columbia University Press, 1980), pp. 91–112. The debate Crop analyzes is between a married Genoese merchant and a poor married gentleman, Raimon de Miraval. (pp. 92–93.) The same article contains a useful short bibliography on the *partimen* genre, n. 12.

70. See Marguerite de Navarre, "Heptaméron," *Conteurs français du XVIᵉ siècle*, ed. Pierre Jourda (Bruges: Pléïade, 1965), pp. 1106–08, for example. It is interesting that the chastelaine's jealousy is an important point in the discussion which follows Marguerite's reworking of the Old French original.

71. See Crop, pp. 94–95 and 109. Perhaps the Ancients were right to classify some eclogues—poetic dialogues between shepherds—as a form of drama. See De Bruyne, 1: 157, 210. It seems to me that the *geu-parti*, like the eclogue, might also be more appropriately dealt with as a form of drama rather than as lyric.

72. Urban Tigner Holmes, Jr., *Daily Living in the Twelfth Century, Based on the Observations of Alexander Neckam in London and Paris* (Madison: University of Wisconsin Press, 1952), pp. 122–3, describes the disputations.

73. For studies on the parallel or dialectical construction of medieval narratives, see Haidu, *Aesthetic Distance*, Hunt, and James J. Murphy, *Rhetoric in the Middle Ages: A History of Rhetorical Theory from St. Augustine to the Renaissance* (Berkeley: University of California Press, 1974).

74. Murphy, p. 103.

75. Edmund Reiss, "Chaucer and His Audience," *Chaucer Review* 14 (1980), 390–402 and De Bruyne, 1: 103.

76. *Recueil Général des Jeux-Partis*, ed. Arthur Långfors (Paris: Champion, 1926), 1:111, no. 30. All further references will be cited in the text proper. The translations are mine. For other *geus-partis* about the law of secrecy, see 1: 355, and 2: 15.

77. On the *partimen* as "game" see Charles Camproux, "On the Subject of an Argument between Elias and his Cousin," *The Interpretation of Medieval Lyric*, ed. W. T. H. Jackson (New York: Columbia University Press, 1980), 77–78.

78. Murphy, p. 103.

79. *La Chastelaine de Vergi*, ed. F. Whitehead, 2nd ed. (Manchester: Manchester University Press, 1951, rpt. 1961), p. xxxi. Whitehead was the first to divide the *ChV* narrative into seven "scènes à deux" between (1) the duchess and knight, (2) duchess and duke, (3) duke and knight, (4) knight and chastelaine, (5) duchess and duke, (6) duchess and duke, (7) duchess and chastelaine. Although I accept Whitehead's division, I do consider the complementary lovers' monologues at the end of the poem as an eighth "scène à deux."

80. According to John Gardner, in his chapter on Chaucer's education, *The Life and Times of Chaucer* (New York: Knopf, 1977), Chaucer went to school as a boy, but many members of noble families were educated at home by the clergy.

81. Medieval school boys and university students learned to compose from several different sources. In the first place there were the very difficult rhetorical exercises known as the *Progymnasmata* which drilled students in narrative technique. Donald L. Clark has given a precise idea of these in his "The Rise and Fall of the Progymnasmata in Sixteenth and Seventeenth Century Grammar Schools," *Speech Monographs* 19 (1952), 260:

> The first two were narrative exercises in retelling FABLES and TALES from poetry and history. Next came the expository exercises of CHREIA and PROVERB, which taught the boys to develop a topic by iteration, enthymeme, contrast, illustration, example and the testimony of authority. REFUTATION and CONFIRMATION were argumentative exercises in analyzing such myths as that of Apollo and Daphne to show that the story was or was not obscure, incredible, impossible, inconsistent, unfitting, or inexpedient. The exercise of COMMONPLACE gave practice in enlarging on praise of virtue and dispraise of vice. The next exercises of ENCOMIUM and VITUPERATION taught how to praise a person or thing for being virtuous and to dispraise a person or thing for being vicious. The exercise of COMPARISON made but a slight step forward, showing which of two is better or worse. The exercise of IMPERSONATION or PROSOPOPOEIA, required

the pupil to compose an imaginary monolog which might appropriately be spoken or written by an historical, legendary, or fictitious person under given circumstances. The exercise in DESCRIPTION, in Greek ECPHRASIS, was designed to train the boys in vivid presentation of details of sight or sound. The THESIS was an exercise in deliberative oratory, arguing for or against a general question such as Should a man marry or seek office. The final elementary exercise, LEGISLATION, gave the boys practice in speaking for or against a law, usually one from ancient history.

See Ray Nadeau's English rendering of the actual exercises in his "The Progymnasmata of Aphthonius in Translation," *Speech Monographs* 19 (1952), 264-85. See also Trimpi, *Muses of One Mind*, 321-8.

Of course it may be argued that Priscian's translation of Hermogenes' *Progymnasmata* in his *Preexercitamenta*, presumably the only source of the text for the Middle Ages, left no traces in medieval library catalogues beyond the eleventh century. However, as Murphy has pointed out, p. 131, "The devices of Hermogenes . . . are not inconsistent with ordinary grammatical training in composition and might well have been incorporated into medieval literary instruction without much explicit acknowledgment of source."

The second model for composition, and particularly for the aenigmalogue, may have been Seneca the Elder's *controversiae* and *suasoriae* (See Sénèque le Rhéteur, *Controverses et suasoires*, ed. Henri Bornecque, [Paris: Garnier, 1932], for the text). Trimpi also sees the Roman declamation as the source of the modern "novella" in his "The Quality of Fiction," and *Muses of One Mind*. Cf. Branch. Further, Murphy asserts that the controversies did not "serve as models for discourse, but rather as sources of tales or exempla." (p. 131.)

The Senecan declamations are a collection of political and legal orations delivered by various declaimers in the Roman schools of declamation during the period when public oratory was forbidden. The *suasoria* was a fictitious political speech whose purpose was to pursuade some mythological or historical figure to follow a given course of action. Similarly fictitious was the *controversia* or law case. Bornecque describes the structure of these exercises in his introduction to his edition of them in French, op. cit., p. ix:

> Une fois le sujet posé, ceux qui le traitent commencent par exposer les arguments qui, étant donné les textes de lois invoqués, prouvent la culpabilité ou l'innocence de l'accusé; ils les présentent isolément, sans qu'on leur demande de se préoccuper de les enchaîner; ce sont les avis, les *sententiae*. Puis on s'efforce de grouper, en un plan simple et logique, les arguments précédemment fournis: c'est la *divisio*. Généralement elle se compose de deux parties, qui ont rapport, l'une au droit, l'autre à l'équité: l'accusé pouvait-il, devait-il agir de cette façon? Après les *sententiae* et la *divisio*, l'on trouve les couleurs (*colores*): ce sont les motifs, indépendants de la loi, allégués pour expliquer, pour excuser, pour colorer, en quelque sorte, les paroles ou les actes qui sont à la charge de l'inculpé.

Indeed, medieval narratives frequently begin with *sententiae* (i.e., maxims, the literary equivalent of the laws in the *controversiae*) which are then illustrated or refuted through the fiction which follows the prologue (i.e., the *divisio*). Moreover, it is apt to be the discrepancy between the letter of the law and questions of equity, i.e., the moral ramifications of the hero's acts, which forms the basis of aenigmalogues, because the aenigmologist's purpose is often to make us question some belief we thought was truth. The aenigmologist who cultivated the "courtly romance" wanted to make his readers think about problems in love and marriage. See Trimpi for a thorough discussion of the role of equity in the development of fictional narrative. Finally, the *colores* or rhetorical figures used to plead, explain, or excuse the acts of the hero are what form the complex verbal patterning of some courtly narratives.

A third and final exercise, the dialectically structured university disputation, had perhaps the greatest influence of all upon literary discourse. Murphy defines it as "a formal discussion of a subject by two or more people who take opposite or differing sides." (p. 102.) One cannot help but notice the similarity of the disputation with the Provençal *joc partit* or *geu-parti* in Northern French. The disputation was used in the classroom "for the interpretation of texts, the testing of hypotheses and examination." (p. 103.) Murphy adds that "It had the great advantage of focusing attention upon a proposition and upon the 'proofs' for that proposition, while allowing maximum flexibility for the consideration of differing opinions . . . Outside the classroom the methodology was translated directly into a pattern for writing." (ibid.) The dialectical oppositions in the disputations could be resolved through the negation of one of the propositions or through *coincidentia oppositorum*. (Hunt, "Aristotle, Dialectics, and Courtly Literature," p. 108.) Thus the disputational paradigm could serve as a pattern for both open-ended and propadeuctic narrative.

82. See *Les Chansons du Châtelain de Coucy*, ed. Francisque Michel, suivies de l'ancienne musique, ed. M. Peine (Paris: Crapelet, 1830), p. 190.

83. *Chansons attribuées au Chastelain de Couci (fin du XIIe-début du XIIIe siècle)*, ed. Alain Lerond (Paris: Presses Universitaires de Frances, 1964), Chanson 5, p. 78. rev. Félix Lecoy, *Romania* 86 (1965), 409–13.

84. ibid., p. 82.

85. Jakemés, *Le Roman du Castelain de Couci et de la Dame de la Fayel*, ed. Maurice Delbouille (Paris: Société des anciens textes français, 1936), (after 1285).

86. See *Chansons attribuées au Chastelain de Couci . . .* , ed. Lerond, p. 19, where the editor quotes Delbouille as follows: "dès le XIIIe siècle, le châtelain était cité au nombre des amants parfaits et semblait prêt à entrer dans la légende. Dès la première moitié du siècle, Eustache le Peintre le place à côté de Tristan et de l'illustre Blondel de Nesle [dans la chanson R. no. 2116] . . . Au XIIIe s. encore, un auteur inconnu écrit sur le modèle de la pièce célèbre du châtelain *A vous amant, ains qu'a nulle autre gent* . . . une chanson qui commence ainsi:

> Li chastelains de Couci ama tant
> Qu'ainc por amors nus n'en ot dolor graindre;
> Por ce ferai ma complainte en son chant.
>> [chanson R. no. 358.]"

87. *Oeuvres de Froissart, Poésies*, ed. A. Scheler, 1 (n.p.: 1870), 217.

88. Judging from contemporary summaries of *ChV*, the medieval readers of the poem viewed what happens to the knight as a cruel stroke of fortune. For example, Christine de Pisan wrote of *ChV* in her *Débat des deux amans:*

> Et du Vergy la tresbelle assouvie
> Chastellaine, qui de riens n'ot envie
> Fors de cellui a qui voit plevie Amour loyale;
> Mais elle et lui orent souldee male
> Par trop amer, car mort en jeurent pale:
> Si ont fait main et en chambre et en sale
> A grant doulour . . .

According to the poetess, the chastelaine and knight loved each other too much. Could this be a gloss on ll. 775 f. where the chastelaine confesses that she loved the knight more than anything in the world, even more than God's paradise which she would have foresaken for the knight's love?

As for Martin Le Franc, he lays the blame upon the envious ones who cannot bear to see lovers happy. It is significant that in his opinion no matter how hard lovers try to keep their affair a secret, the envious ones can always find a way to discover it. I quote from Le Franc's *Champion des dames*:

> Que diray je du chevallier
> Qui tant amoit covertement
> la chastelaine du Vergier?
> Fait on riens tant secretement
> Que fausse Envye appertement
> Ne congnoisse, die et descelle?
> Je l'ay apris, Dieu scet comment,
> Entre envyeux rien ne se celle.
>
> Seulement par le chiennet duit
> Le temps et l'eure congnissoit,
> Et n'avoit aultre saufconduit
> Quant il y entroit ou yssoit.
> Envie qui contrepensoit
> Neantmains tout le fait accusa,
> Et congnut on que vray estoit
> Quant une mort les encusa.

The above cited quotations are both taken from Gaston Raynaud, "La Chastelaine de Vergi, *Romania* 21 (1982), 157. A more contemporary commentator, Perrot de Neele (ca. 1288), lays the blame entirely upon the duke and duchess. In other words, like Martin Le Franc, he blames the *losengier* for the tragedy rather than the knight.

> . . . Si ores coment la ducoise
> Onques de priier ne s acoise
> Au duc: de par amor li die,
> Si li cevaliers a amie,
> Car bien percut, que li dus sot
> L'amor, que li chevaliers ot.
> Tant le blangi et tangona,
> Que li dus si s'abandonna
> Que la verite l'en descueure,
> De co il fist moult vilaine oueure . . .

> [456]

(Quoted from p. 751 of Leo Jordan's transcription in his "Peros von Neele's gereimte In-haltsangabe zu einem Sammelcodex. Mit Einleitung und Glossar zum ersten Male herausgegeben," *Romanische Forschungen* 16 [1904]). The section of Perrot's summary concerning *ChV* has been edited by R. E. V. Stuip in his edition of the text as it is found in MS *A* (B.N. ms fr. 375) (The Hague: Mouton, 1970), pp. 20–22. Nowhere in his ninety-two line summary of *ChV* does Perrot find fault with the knight. Rather, he seems to have perceived him as a brave and intelligent character who is to be admired for the ingenious-ness of the solution he finds to his horrible dilemma. Although Perrot does not say so, these are precisely the qualities for which Tristan was famous: "Coment li cevaliers gentieus, no-ble, valiant / Qui tant ert sages [clever] e soutieus [ingenious], / Ne vit s amie a la carole:"

(ibid., l. 59) In short; not one of the three medieval poets who summarized *ChV* blamed the knight for the catastrophe, as the *ChV* narrator persona does. Rather, the knight is seen as the perfect courtly lover whom a senseless tragedy has befallen. If contemporary readers did not even give the narrator persona's point of view a tumble, why should we take it so seriously?

89. *Anatomy of Criticism: Four Essays* (Princeton: Princeton University Press, 1959), p. 38.

90. See Cicero, *Ad C. Herennium: De Ratione Dicendi (Rhetorica ad Herennium)*, trans. Harry Caplan (Cambridge: Harvard University Press, 1968).

91. Aristotle, *The Poetics*, p. 73: "All that concerns thought may be left to the treatise on rhetoric, for the subject is more proper to that inquiry . . . . Under the head of thought come all the effects to be produced by the language. Some of these are proof and refutation, the arousing of feelings like pity, fear, anger, and so on, and again exaggeration and depreciation."

92. See *Readings in Medieval Rhetoric*, ed. Joseph M. Miller, Michael H. Prosser, Thomas W. Benson (Bloomington: Indiana University Press, 1973).

93. Trimpi, pp. 20–21.

94. See Trimpi, *Muses of One Mind*, p. 253 (Cf. Trimpi, "The Quality of Fiction," p. 64) for the structure of the Roman *controversia*.

95. See Arrathoon, "La Châtelaine de Vergi: A Structural Study of an Old French Artistic Short Narrative," *Language and Style* 7 (1974), 151–80, for a detailed account of the inversion of "Lanval" by the *ChV* poet. This article was first written as a seminar paper in 1970 at Princeton during the time when Claude Lévi-Strauss's structural anthropology was so much in vogue. See also my review of L. G. Donovan, *Recherches sur le Roman de Thèbes* (Paris: Société d'édition d'enseignement supérieur, 1975), *Romanic Review* 71 (1980), 88–89 and Vance, p. 569.

96. See *The "Art" of Rhetoric* for the fallacies of signs.

97. Wolf-Dieter Lange, "Höfische Tradition und Individuelles Leben in der 'Chastelaine de Vergi': Ein Beitrag zum Stil des altfranzösischen Versnovelle," *Zeitschrift für Französische Sprache und Literatur* 75 (1966), 20, was the first to remark upon the *conseil celer / conseil descouvrir* polarity in *ChV*. See also Zumthor's important study on verbal clusters in twelfth-and thirteenth-century lyric poetry, and the way in which these clusters tend to adhere to a particular motif or theme: "Recherches sur les topiques dans la poésie lyrique des XIIe et XIIIe siècles." It was in this article that Professor Zumthor made his well-known remarks about the craftsmanship of medieval poetry: "Le caractère fondamental de l'art littéraire est sans doute sa technicité" (p. 409), and "La littérature et les arts plastiques ont alors en commun un caractère artisanal, un rythme d'atelier . . . ils travaillent sur des exempla, sur des schémas techniquement cohérents" (p. 427). Cf. Frappier's brief remarks on the *Canso* in his "Vues sur les conceptions courtoises . . ." p. 138 and R. Guiette, "D'une poésie formelle en France au moyen âge," *Revue des sciences humaines* (1949), 61-68. Finally, see Arrathoon, "Antinomic Cluster Analysis. . . ."

98. See the glossary in Arrathoon, *The Lady of Vergi*, for a complete list of synonyms, near synonyms, antonyms, and key words in the poem.

99. Forster, pp. 67–82.

100. *Psychology Today*, July 1980, p. 124.

101. ibid., November 1977, pp. 153-4.

102. See the note on these lines in the Arrathoon edition of the poem.

103. See Alfred Jeanroy, *Les Origines de la Poésie lyrique en France au moyen âge. Etudes de littérature française et comparée* (Paris: 1889), pp. 14-15 for a description of the *oaristys*, Paul Zumthor, "De La Chanson au récit . . . ," and J. Saville, *The Medieval Erotic Alba, Structure As Meaning* (New York: Columbia University Press, 1972).

104. Raynaud, p. 150; Emil Lorenz, *Die Kastellanin von Vergi in der Literatur Frankreichs, Italiens, der Niederlande, Englands und Deutschlands mit einer Deutschen Übersetzung der Altfranzösischen Versnovelle und einem Anhange: Die Kastellan Legende* (Halle: 1909), pp. 108 ff.; Frappier, "La Chastelaine de Vergi, Marguerite de Navarre et Bandello," p. 101; Dubuis, p. 522, n. 33; Joselyne Reed, "La Chastelaine de Vergi: Was the Heroine Married?" *Romance Notes* 16, (1974), 197-204, and Alfred Foulet, private conversations at Princeton, 1970-73.

105. Thomas, *Le Roman de Tristan*, ed. Joseph Bédier, 1 (Paris: Firmin Didot, 1902), 416, n. to l. 3124.

106. Marc Bloch, *Feudal Society*, trans. L. A. Manyon (Chicago: University of Chicago Press, 1961, 1971), 1: 222.

107. Carl Stephenson, *Mediaeval Feudalism* (Ithaca: Cornell University Press, 16th printing, 1975), p. 27.

108. ibid. It is a matter of history that the Castelanie of Vergi was passed down from father to son during the years preceding the composition of *ChV*. See Ernest Petit, *Histoire des ducs de Bourgogne de la race capétienne* (Dijon: La Marche, 1889).

109. ibid. This, of course, is why all the landed ladies in Chrestien's *Yvain* are so eager to marry the hero. It was not for Yvain's *beaux yeux*, but because these women desperately needed a big, strong husband to secure their fiefs for them.

110. Most critics give two reasons for the law of secrecy: (1) the danger that envious gossips or a jealous husband will ruin the relationship and (2) the fear of profaning the love affair and of offending the delicate sensibilities of the lady. (See Lakits, pp. 33-34 and Frappier, "La Chastelaine de Vergi, Marguerite de Navarre et Bandello," p. 101). However, in the "Lanval," which is the most immediate source of *ChV*, the whole point of the fairy mistress's injunction of secrecy seems to be to instill obedience in the hero. As I have been saying in this article, it is the chastelaine's belief that she has lost control over the knight, which causes her heart to "break." In fact, it is because the chastelaine is not a fay that she falls victim to the villainous duchess. Had she been omniscient like the lady of the tent or Guenevere, who knows of Lancelot's momentary hesitation before the cart, she would have known the exact extent of the knight's crime. But because the chastelaine is only human, i.e., a rationalized fairy mistress, she learns of the knight's transgression much later and completely misunderstands his motives.

In reply to Lakits's charge that it is an insult to tell a *fin amant* he must keep the affair a secret (p. 34), the spate of debates about this very point during the thirteenth century shows that if the lady wanted absolute secrecy she would have had to make that clear.

111. Stevenson, pp. 72-73; Bloch, 1: 241-45, and Brian Tierney, *The Middle Ages*. 1, *Sources of Medieval History*, 3rd ed., (New York: Knopf, 1978), p. 287 f.

112. See Whitehead, p. xxxi, for a discussion of the "technique of exclusion" in this poem.

113. See my "La Châtelaine de Vergi: A Structural Study of an Old French Artistic Short Narrative," for a comparison of *ChV* with the fairy tale. It is important to keep in mind while reading this text the residual magic it retains from its long forgotten Celtic origins, as filtered through "Lanval."

114. Trimpi, *Muses of One Mind*, pp. 309 and 334.

115. *Piramus et Tisbé, Poème du XIIe siècle*, ed. C. de Boer (Paris: *Classiques français du moyen âge*, 1921), ll. 766 ff.

116. op. cit., n. 14, pp. 192-4, 196, n. 7, and 197, n. 18. In fact, my reading of the poem is very much in agreement with Kostoroski's whose main thesis is that *ChV* is a "quest for perfect love and a query about the system within which the   love could exist" (p. 180). Her view is echoed by Payen, p. 217.

117. p. 193. See also Lakits, p. 73.

118. p. 521

119. p. 73.

120. See, for example, Frappier, "La Chastelaine de Vergi, Marguérite de Navarre et Bandello," Lakits, Dubuis, Kostoroski, and Payen.

121. A. Pauphilet, for example, simply removed the epilogue when he reprinted the Raynaud/Foulet text, with some modernized spellings, in his *Poètes et Romanciers du Moyen Age* (Bruges: Pléïade, 1963), 351-74: "Nous supprimons ici quelques vers ou le poète tire la morale assez platement évidente, de ce beau récit" (p. 374). Pauphilet's crippling emendation is one of the more obvious examples of what can and does happen when the editor has misapprehended the genre of the work. See also Dubuis, p. 521.

10. Le "Jeu de saint Nicolas" de Jean Bodel

Prologues

L'intérêt qu'un grand nombre de médiévistes ont porté au *Jeu de saint Nicolas* de Jean Bodel ne tient pas seulement à la beauté de l'œuvre, mais au fait que le genre dramatique de cette pièce semble se soustraire à toute formulation univoque.

Dans une optique historico-sociologique, on accepte difficilement qu'un écrivain s'écarte d'une tradition formelle établie pour faire œuvre nouvelle, raison pour laquelle la critique savante n'a pas manqué de déceler dans cette œuvre des faiblesses de composition. Ainsi chaque étude en suscite une autre pour confirmer, nuancer ou invalider telle ou telle interprétation.

Il faut bien reconnaître que les études sur le *Jeu de saint Nicolas*[1] offrent le spectacle d'un ensemble de travaux dont le caractère disparate — mais faut-il s'en étonner? — fournit une fois de plus la preuve qu'il n'y a en fin de compte d'interprétation que dans et par le travail de "l'imaginative compréhension." Celle-ci relève d'une pratique de lecture des textes qui exige une sorte de mémoire, toujours en retrait, mais prête à intervenir pour faire résonner la langue et presque à l'insu du sujet qui l'aurait comme apprise "par cœur."

Toute proportion gardée, il en va de même pour l'expérience analytique dont la nature fondamentalement esthétique fait dire à Wittgenstein qu'elle consiste à voir quelque chose "comme quelque chose" mais qu'à ne pas l'éprouver du dedans comme telle," cette cécité aspectuelle sera *apparentée* au manque d'oreille musicale."[2]

Le lecteur, confronté au texte, s'engage dans une aventure imprévisible dont le jeu est chaque fois à ré-inventer, car il ne s'agit pas de redire ce que le texte transmet dans sa langue spécifique, ni encore moins de refaire le travail du philologue, qui reconstruit selon certaines règles conventionnelles l'archéologie du texte, mais d'ajouter, par le travail de la glose, ce que Marie de France appelle, dans le Prologue des *Lais, un surplus de sen.*[3]

Située dans l'entente de l'œuvre-modèle, la glose, livrée à plusieurs programmes de vérité,[4] devient l'imagination allégorique au travail et dont l'écriture oscille entre le commentaire et le récit, fécondés en plusieurs directions par la force d'incitation du texte. La lecture n'enregistre donc pas purement et simplement le texte comme un document daté, figé dans des sens constitués et dont il s'agit de tirer des effets de savoir objectif, mais correspond à un travail de transformation d'où résulte que le lecteur ré-invente à son insu ce qui lui revient aujourd'hui d'un passé toujours encore à venir à travers la parole retentissante de l'oeuvre. C'est dire qu'une telle actualité ne serait pas grand'chose si elle ne se donnait pas comme actualisation des réserves temporelles d'une langue dont l'historicité est à situer dans l'épaisseur même de l'oeuvre: langue mémoriale, intertextuelle, volume, dont la glose sauvegarde dans la parole son libre espace de jeu en sa plus grande extension.

Telle est aussi la structure du *Jeu de saint Nicolas* car, retorse, déroutante, se prêtant à plusieurs ententes, elle a pu solliciter chez les critiques les interprétations les plus divergentes. S'agit-il d'une représentation liturgique ou semi-liturgique où le souffle épique, en résonance avec le fait historique des Croisades, côtoie le fabliau? Faut-il voir au contraire dans ce *Jeu* une pièce entièrement profane, gouvernée par le comique qui atteint toutes les scènes? D'autres vous diront qu'il faut nuancer: la pièce de Jean Bodel présente un mélange de gravité et d'humour dont les registres variés manifestent la subtilité d'un art savamment calculé.

Dire que Jean Bodel a tiré de la "légende dorée" d'un des saints les plus populaires en Europe la matière d'une représentation c'est d'abord reconnaître un processus d'invention tout à fait courant au moyen âge. Ce qu'il faut en revanche souligner c'est la manière subtile dont le poète, opérant sur cette tradition rhétorique (le merveilleux hagiographique), en produit un spectacle sans précédent.

L'action de la représentation se joue sur deux scènes: l'une prend toutes les apparences d'un spectacle édifiant, fondé sur des croyances traditionnelles bien connues par les auditeurs (les miracles de saint Nicolas); l'autre scène, dissimulée sous le jeu ambigu de l'art, représente un Saint qui protège, de son "image," et récupère les biens, les richesses, le trésor de ceux qui acceptent de croire en lui:

> Riens qui en se garde soit mise
> N'iert ja perdue ne maumise,
> Tant ne sera abandonnee,
> Non, se chis palais ert plain d'or,
> Et il geüst seur le tresor:
> Tel grasse li a Dieus donnee

[526-31]

(Rien qui soit mis sous sa garde ne sera perdu ni détérioré, si longtemps soit-il laissé à l'abandon, non, même si ce palais était plein d'or,
pourvu que saint Nicolas fût couché sur les richesses. Voilà la vertu
que Dieu lui a donnée.)

On prévoit aisément que ce pouvoir du Saint ou de sa statue ne manquera pas d'efficacité dans la mise en oeuvre des miracles et de la conversion, opérée par l'un de ses dévots, le "preudome" miraculeusement
échappé au massacre des Chrétiens par les Sarrasins. On se souviendra
que, surpris en prière devant la statue, le preudome emprisonné obtiendra
la grâce du roi à condition que l'effigie de saint Nicolas protège le trésor
royal exposé à la foule sans autre gardien que l'image du Saint. Si d'a-
bord il y a un raté dans l'opération du miracle, du fait que les voleurs de
la taverne s'emparent du trésor, l'apparition de saint Nicolas dans le rêve
des truands les oblige par la suite à restituer ces richesses et à remettre l'image en son lieu.

Ainsi le preudome, qui sauve sa peau, obtient de plus la conversion
du roi et de ses alliés à l'exception d'un des quatre émirs, celui d' "outre
l'Arbre sec," qui feint de se convertir, mais garde sa fidélité à Mahomet.

On devine la fonction que la figure du Saint va pouvoir assumer dans
l'imagination du poète et dans son art, dont l'autre scène se dérobe sous
le semblant hagiographique de l'action. Nous y reviendrons.[5]

Ce qu'il faut d'abord souligner c'est la manière dont le théâtre de
Jean Bodel se déploie d'un bout à l'autre dans un espace mouvant où
toutes les oppositions entre la fable épique d'un Orient lointain et la
proximité d'une taverne de style arrageois (mais en pays sarrasin), entre
les dieux et le Dieu chrétien, perdent leur sens réel et leur différence. D'où
résulte que le prétendu "réalisme" d'observation qui caractérise les
truands de la taverne arrageoise, par exemple, fait partie du même
monde fantastique que les "turqueries" qui animent la fable épique orientale. Dans le *Jeu de saint Nicolas*, actions et personnages sont livrés au
vertige des ressemblances d'un monde double où Païens et Chrétiens
reflètent mutuellement leur image inversée: monde divisé, aliéné, qui fait
coexister dans l'homme le païen et le chrétien, l'impénitent et le croyant,
le transgresseur et le fidèle. De même le poète porte en lui deux âmes,
sollicitées en sens contraire: l'une dissimule le culte idolâtre de l'image, le
dieu caché du désir "sarrasin" de l'art, sous les couleurs d'une rhétorique
de l'orthodoxie l'autre reste soumise à l'institution chrétienne.

Ainsi le trait fondamental, qui marque le champ d'action du *Jeu de
saint Nicolas*, c'est l'instauration d'un espace structurant soustrait, dans

l'ensemble, à toute vraisemblance chronologique mais strictement opéra-
toire du fait que, en faisant résonner les scènes les unes par les autres,
Jean Bodel intègre le temps de la succession à la vision d'un présent simul-
tané où les actions des personnages, toujours à deux faces et réversibles
selon l'angle de vision, sont entièrement soumises à l'attraction du songe.

Comme nous le disions, c'est l'ambiguïté miroitante qui fait structure dans le *Jeu de saint Nicolas* où triomphe, à tous les niveaux, l'extraordinaire fascination des doubles, mais dont l'humour de Jean Bodel
s'amuse simultanément à rompre les charmes sans jamais porter atteinte
pour autant à la puissance d'enchantement de l'oeuvre.

A bien lire le prologue, on s'aperçoit du reste que tous ces glissements,
ces oscillations, ces fuites dans l'équivocité, ce clair-obscur, sont délibérément voulus par le poète. Il pourra sembler singulier que le "prêcheur" du
Jeu articule dans le prologue un long discours, qui, référé à la tradition,
relate sous la forme d'un récit (ravivé par l'insertion d'un dialogue v. 30 sq.)
les principales étapes de l'action de la pièce. N'est-ce pas que l'auteur se
coupe à l'avance de tout effet de mystère ou d'imprévu? En réalité, il n'en est
rien si l'on considère que l'auteur introduit dans le drame des éléments
nouveaux: le messager Aubéron qui annonce l'invasion des chrétiens, les
alliés du roi, l'apparition de l'Ange, les crieurs du royaume et de la cité, le
tavernier, les voleurs, autant de personnages qui, absents du résumé, sont
de nature à donner au miracle une tout autre tournure.

Il faut noter par ailleurs que, si le prologue dans son ensemble est
d'une clarté exemplaire, en revanche il tourne un peu à l'obscurité au moment où le "prêcheur" conclut son discours en ces termes:

> Pour che n'aiés pas grant merveille
> Se vous veés aucun affaire;
> Car canques vous *nous* verrés faire
> Sera essamples sans douter
> Del miracle representer
> Ensi com *je* devisé l'ai.
> Del miracle saint Nicolai
> Est chis jeus fais et estorés.
>
>   [106-113. C'est moi qui souligne.]

(Ne vous étonnez donc pas, si vous assistez à quelque malencontre; car
tout ce que vous nous verrez faire sera, n'en doutez pas, un essai fidèle
de représenter le miracle comme je l'ai raconté. Ce miracle de saint
Nicolas est la matière dont notre *jeu* est fait et composé).

Il ne fait pas de doute que Jean Bodel tient à prévenir ses auditeurs
de ce qu'il pourrait y avoir d'étonnant, pour eux dans le spectacle des

choses surprenantes, insolites ou qui pourraient choquer. Mais en insérant le *je* dans le *nous* (v. 108 et 111), le "prêcheur" du prologue tient à marquer sa différence avec les forces plurielles d'une mise en œuvre qui conduit le poète au-delà de ses propres intentions. Du même coup, par l'écart entre la tradition du miracle telle qu'elle est racontée en raccourci dans le prologue (*comme je devisé l'ai*, v. 111) et la représentation (v. 110), désignée par le mot *essamples* (v. 109), Jean Bodel revendique sa part d'invention, car si *essample* signifie "modèle," "figure,"[5] ce mot, par son contexte relève ici de la libre invention "tropologique" d'une matière liturgique ou hagiographique traditionnelle.

La question est alors de savoir ce que cette œuvre présente d'effectivement surprenant.

Un critique a pu relever certaines divergences entre le prologue et le texte et, à partir d'arguments—à notre avis, précaires—, s'étonner par exemple qu'il existe en territoire sarrasin une "chapelle" alors que ce même critique ne s'étonne pas du tout de trouver une taverne arrageoise en pays sarrasin.[6] Nous n'entrerons pas dans ce débat tout simplement parce qu'il suffirait de peu pour accorder le prologue et le récit car le premier dit bien que chrétiens et païens "étaient voisins" (v. 10) et que "chaque jour il y avait entre eux la guerre" (v. 11). On peut donc fort bien admettre que les guérillas quotidiennes, les avancées et les retraites répétées ne manquaient pas de laisser des traces païennes ou chrétiennes dans les zones-frontière.

Quant à la situation géographique qui caractérise les lieux de la pièce, il est tout à fait clair que leur indétermination est voulue, comme le montrent d'ailleurs à l'évidence les toponymes qui projettent dans un au-delà fabuleux les territoires d'origine des alliés du roi d'Afrique: "outre Pré Noiron, la terre où poussent les ourtons" (v. 355-56); "outre Grise Wallengue où les chiens foirent de l'or" (v. 362-3); "outre mer . . . terre chaude et ardente . . . pleine de rubis et d'émeraudes" (v. 368-72); "outre l'Arbre sec, où il n'y a d'autre monnaie que des pierres de moulin" (v. 374-77).

Le problème ne se laisse donc pas aborder par des arguments de vraisemblance mais par une logique imaginative, génératrice de l'indétermination et des doubles, qui gouverne toute la représentation.

Par ailleurs, le fait même que l'auteur de la pièce prévienne le lecteur laisse supposer que les surprises auxquelles celui-ci doit s'attendre sont en quelque sorte prévues par la stratégie du poète qui intègre le "problématique" dans la vision globale de l'oeuvre.

L'analyse que nous proposons, n'étant pas en mesure de rendre compte de toutes les surprises que nous réserve la mise en oeuvre poétique du miracle, s'articule sur deux points fondamentaux: la figure de saint Nicolas et la scène de la taverne. Au sujet de celle-ci, notons-le, les commentateurs ont relevé, entre autres choses, la disproportion produite par l'excessive longueur donnée au traitement de cette scène qui occupe environ la moitié de la pièce.

Le jeu et le "fust" de saint Nicolas[7]

Saint Nicolas n'échappe pas à cette loi de structure qui vise l'indétermination et d'abord parce qu'il apparaît sur la scène en personnage dédoublé, jouant non seulement de son "image," dont il surveille les effets d'efficacité, mais comme apparition fantomatique surgie dans le rêve des voleurs. De plus les appellatifs qui désignent la statue vont jouer un rôle important dans ce processus de déstabilisation du principe d'identité.

Appelée *sanlanche*, au sens de "simulacre," "image" par le preudome (v. 32), *fust* c'est-à-dire "morceau de bois" par le roi (v. 31), la statue est considérée par l'émir d'Orquenie et par d'autres comme un *Mahommet cornu* (v. 458 et 513), alors que les voleurs y voient un *cornu menestrel* (v. 999) au sens de "canaille" certes, mais aussi de "*ménestrel*."

Faut-il voir là un trait d'humour du poète, vu le risque de paganisation "mahométane" de la statue, dans les formes verbales *maumet* (v. 1261) *maumise* (v. 527) du verbe *maumetre*[8] ("péricliter," "détériorer"), employées par le preudome pour désigner les personnes ou les choses mises sous la protection du saint ou de sa statue? On ne sait.

Ainsi l'objet saint revêt peu à peu un aspect *abject*, mais n'en obéit pas moins à la logique de la pièce qui provoque un mouvement dont l'oscillation constante empêche le lecteur de fixer l'identité de l'image.

Il en va de même pour la matière dont est faite la statue, car si l'appellatif *fust* laisse supposer qu'elle est de bois, Rasoir, le cerveau de la bande des voleurs, semble en douter:

> Ains gist uns mahommés deseure,
> Ne sai ou de fust ou de pierre;
> Ja par lui n'en ora espiere
> Li rois, s'on li taut tout ou emble

[779-82]

(Au contraire, on a couché par-dessus un fétiche, en bois ou en pierre, je ne sais: ce n'est sûrement pas par lui que le roi apprendra quoi que ce soit, si on lui rafle tout.)

Ce processus de dégradation est encore plus complexe du fait que la statue de saint Nicolas et son double païen s'insèrent dans une symétrie.

Comparée au "Mahomet chrétien" la statue de Tervagan, vénérée par les Sarrasins, présente des ressemblances troublantes. Si l'image de saint Nicolas recouvre de son aspect fruste le trésor du roi, celle de Tervagan, laide en-dessous, mais recouverte d'or, présente les signes inversés du dehors et du dedans de la statue chrétienne:

> A! fieus a putain, Tervagan
> Avés vous dont souffert tel oeuvre?
> Con je plaing l'or dont je vous cuevre
> Che lait visage et che lait cors!
> [134-7]

> (Ah! fils de putain, Tervagan, avez-vous donc permis pareille oeuvre?
> Comme je regrette l'or dont je vous couvre ce laid visage et ce laid corps!)

Et c'est encore trop peu dire, car Tervagan revêt une couverture d'or qui ne fait que s'accroître chaque fois que le roi veut obtenir des oracles propitiateurs:

> Et si prometés Tervagan,
> Dis mars d'or a croistre ses joes
> [162-3]

> (Et promettez donc aussi à Tervagan dix marcs d'or qui iront grossir ses joues.)

Mais c'est aussi vrai pour le *fust* minable de saint Nicolas qui redouble le volume du trésor païen:

> —Che m'est avis qu'il est doublés—
> Et li sains Nicolais gist sus!
> [1394-5)

> (—à mon avis, il est doublé—et le saint Nicolas est étendu par-dessus.)

Quant à savoir de quelle matière est fait le dessous de la statue de Tervagan, que le roi couvre d'injures, on ne peut que le supposer à partir des menaces du roi en fureur qui projette d'*ardoir et de fondre* l'idole (v. 140): le premier verbe se rapportant vraisemblablement à un dessous ligneux et le deuxième à sa surface dorée.

Vues dans cette perspective les deux statues, dont l'une se couvre de l'or royal du roi et l'autre le recouvre, suggèrent des ressemblances diaboliques fort peu conformes à l'image chrétienne dont le support devrait coïncider avec le Saint qui habite le ciel. Mais ce Saint est-il identiquement celui qui visite le rêve des voleurs et les oblige à rendre le trésor volé? On pourrait en douter ne fût-ce qu'en raison de la vulgarité du langage de cette apparition qui ressemble étonnamment au parler des truands de la taverne (v. 995) non moins qu'à la manière dont le roi traite Tervagan de *fius a putain* (v. 134). Saint Nicolas ne s'exprime pas autrement à l'égard des voleurs:

Fil a putain, tout estes mort!

[1281]

L'intervention de saint Nicolas est-elle l'effet d'un miracle authentique ou bien l'effet d'un rêve surgi de l'ivresse des voleurs travaillés par l'angoisse de leur forfait? Les voleurs ont-ils fait un mauvais rêve qui se prolonge sous forme d'hallucination ou bien ce rêve est-il un signe authentique de l'irruption du surnaturel? Un doute demeure. Jean Bodel jouant de l'indécidable fait balancer le lecteur entre le miracle et le cauchemar, à moins que ce ne soit un mélange des deux.

Certes, selon la logique du semblant surnaturel, Jean Bodel feint d'introduire un rapport de cause à effet entre la prière du preudome et l'apparition de saint Nicolas, dont l'image, en un premier moment, n'a pas tenu ses promesses. Soit, mais demandons-nous comment Jean Bodel représente cette apparition? D'où vient-elle? Il faut reconnaître qu' ici encore, Jean Bodel manœuvre de façon à produire dans l'enchaînement de l'action un effet de clair-obscur qui rend absolument impossible l'interprétation univoque de ce visiteur nocturne. Parallèlement l'image sainte est toujours sur le point de tourner au fétiche ou de ressembler à la statue de Tervagan.

L'équivoque maintenue par Jean Bodel n'épargne pas non plus le preudome, dont la dévotion à saint Nicolas et la croyance en ses miracles apparaissent parfois branlantes. Si le sage chrétien surpris en prière devant son *Mahommet cornu* ne parvient pas à convaincre par sa foi le lecteur c'est aussi en raison des conseils de l'ange. Celui-ci en effet a cru bon de rappeler au preudome, lors de l'invasion sarrasine, l'ordre des préséances qui exige que Dieu soit invoqué avant ses saints. Et tout se passe comme si la dévotion du preudome risquait de basculer dans un culte trop zélé qui fait oublier Dieu pour son serviteur et le modèle pour son image. Si bien que la foi et l'idolatrie, que sépare un abîme, n'en offraient pas moins le péril de la ressemblance, la seconde suppléant à la carence de la première par le culte de l'idole:

En Damedieu soies bien chiers,
Et en saint Nicolai après,
Car tu aras sen haut confort,
S'en foy te voit seür et fort.

[492-5]

(Mets toute ta confiance en Dieu, et en saint Nicolas *après lui*: tu auras son souverain réconfort, s'il voit ta foi sûre et inébranlable.)

Pour peu que le lecteur garde ses distances à l'égard du piège de l'imaginaire hagiographique, une question se pose: que signifie le fait de cette grâce accordée au preudome, unique rescapé du massacre, lors même qu'elle l'exclut de la jouissance immédiate du paradis[9] promis à ceux que l'Ange encourage à sacrifier leur vie?

> Metés hardiement vos cors
> Pour Dieu, car chou est chi li mors
> Dont tout li pules morir doit
> Qui Dieu aime de cuer et croit
>
> [420-3]

> Exposez hardiment votre vie pour Dieu, car vous allez trouver ici la mort dont doivent mourir tous ceux qui aiment Dieu sincèrement et ont foi en lui.)

Privilège accordé au preudome ou punition pour ce fléchissement de la foi authentique (v. 423) qui le fait pencher vers le fétichisme et lui fera ainsi mériter la prison et les peines qu'il endure?

Aux yeux de certains interprètes, la scène a pu sembler sublime, pour nous c'est autre chose: l'Ange, stéréotype obligé, depuis longtemps, du merveilleux épique, a tout l'air de réciter de très haut, comme une sorte de revenant distrait, son rôle ennuyeux, dont le signe reste nettement en dehors de l'horizon du *Jeu*. Autrement dit, en faisant mimer par l'Ange son propre stéréotype codé, Jean Bodel fait basculer le merveilleux épique, et avec lui toute la scène, dans le champ des doubles parodiques, substituant ainsi à la gravité de l'épisode son effet de ressassement. Qu'on admette ou non cette interprétation, il n'en résulte pas moins des paroles de l'Ange que, à les appliquer au sort réservé au preudome, celui-ci, pâle et piteux, décidément ne semble pas appartenir à la race privilégiée des chevaliers du Christ.

Non moins problématiques sont les scènes relatives à la conversion produite par le miracle. N'oublions pas que c'est dans le retour du trésor volé que le roi a vu le signe du miracle:

> Preudom, il a bien commenchié,
> Car mes tresor est revenus;
> Assés sont li miracle apert,
> Puisqu'il fait avoir che c'on pert.
> Mais je n'en creïsse nului!
>
> [1430-4]

> (Sage chrétien, il a très bien commencé car mon trésor est revenu, Les miracles sont tout à fait évidents puisqu'il fait retrouver ce qu'on perd. Mais j'avoue que je n'aurais là-dessus cru personne!)

Se convertir aux biens éternels, comme fait le roi, sans rien perdre des jouissances terrestres, et ceci grâce à l'image du Saint, bien sûr, n'y a-t-il pas là de quoi rendre suffisamment suspecte la foi nouvelle du monarque païen? D'autre part, vue sous l'angle du trésorier du ciel, cette conversion, monnayée en quelque sorte par une opération de change (la vie du preudome contre le trésor du roi), reste une spéculation particulièrement efficace. D'où résulte que Jean Bodel, sans jamais trop appuyer sur les extrêmes, produit un flottement qui rend le preudome et le personnage de saint Nicolas les plus équivoques de tous, les plus étrangement suspect et finalement sans identité propre.

A la fois complice et protecteur de la convoitise du roi, le Saint, partagé entre son image et son modèle, exerce sur les voleurs une autorité dont l'action de justice rendue semble couvrir une main mise céleste sur les richesses de la terre, sans que la chrétienté doive y perdre la face.

S'il est vrai, comme disent certains folkloristes que les dieux ont survécu dans les Saints de la "légende dorée" du moyen âge, —entendons bien les Saints créés par la littérature, grande pourvoyeuse de miracles— c'est Jean Bodel, fort de son art et de son humour, qui porte à la scène l'extraordinaire puissance de fascination que la fiction est capable d'exercer sur l'imagination des croyants.

Fruit de la clairvoyance humoristique et du pouvoir d'enchantement de la langue, le *Jeu de saint Nicolas* découvre ses engins pour mieux les couvrir à la manière d'un mouvement de marées soumises à l'attraction céleste. Ainsi le vol du trésor et sa restitution obéissent à une stratégie qui utilise le raté du miracle pour mieux asseoir la fonction de l'image protectrice, dont nous aurons encore à parler.

Pour ce qui concerne le preudome on pourrait encore relever un autre effet de brouillage. N'est-ce pas qu'il fait figure de menteur, lors de la non-intervention du Saint, qui rend inefficace sa statue? En revanche l'oracle païen de Tervagan a tout l'air, quel que soit le sort que le roi lui réserve, de dire la vérité. Bref, on est en droit de se demander si le *Jeu* auquel se prête saint Nicolas est encore celui d'un personnage céleste ou la machination du plus rusé des dieux sarrasins parmi les élus du ciel chrétien.

C'est dans cette perspective, toujours double, qu'il faut situer la scène finale de la conversion du roi. N'était-ce la rébellion du quatrième allié, l'émir" d'outre l'Arbre sec," cette scène ressemblerait à une victoire chrétienne absolue. Malheureusement tout se brouille, car le geste de refus, par où Jean Bodel déplace l'authenticité de la foi du côté du païen rebelle, vient porter au spectacle une brèche qui empêche la pièce édifiante de se refermer sur elle-même. Car si la possession du trésor, travestie en miracle, provoque la conversion du roi et des trois émirs, celle-ci engendre à son tour la violence du roi qui force l'émir "d'outre l'Arbre sec" à s'agenouiller devant la statue de saint Nicolas.

Toute la scène s'éclaire, dès lors, d'une lumière douteuse car les néo-
phytes chrétiens, qui ont renié leur Mahomet pour un *Mahommet cornu*,
disons "équivoque," se voient traités d'infidèles par la bouche d'un païen
dont le discours est digne de la ferveur d'un martyr chrétien:

> A! rois, pour Mahommet, merchi!
> Ne me fai pas mes dieus renoier!
> Fai me anchois le teste soier
> Ou mon cors a cheval detraire
>
> [1501-04]

(Ah! roi par Mahomet, merci; Ne me fais pas renier mes dieux! Fais-moi plutôt couper
la tête ou écarteler par les chevaux.)

L'émir rebelle n'imitera pas le roi, mais s'adressant à saint Nicolas
par un souci d'authenticité à outrance, remet pour ainsi dire les choses
en place:

> Sains Nicolais, c'est maugré mien
> Que je vous aoure, et par forche.
> De mou n'arés vous fors l'escorche:
> Par parole devieng vostre hom,
> Mais li creanche est en Mahom.
>
> [1507-11]

> (Saint Nicolas, c'est bien malgré moi que je vous adore, je succombe à
> la violence. De moi vous n'aurez que l'écorce: en paroles je deviens
> votre homme, mais la foi véritable reste en Mahomet.)

Libre à nous d'entendre dans l'écartèlement souhaité par l'émir, qui
voudrait se faire couper *le teste*, la voix détournée d'une allusion au dé-
chirement du "texte" lui-même: l'histoire, parfaitement *devisee* (racontée)
dans le prologue, est pour ainsi dire "divisée," dans la représentation, en
deux langages opposés dont la parole de foi, comme celle exhibée par
l'émir, reste finalement une parole de surface, une "écorce."

Par ailleurs, la singularité de ce rebelle, resté exceptionnellement fidèle
à Mahomet sous le masque du converti, invite à le rapprocher du personnage non moins unique du preudome, seul rescapé du massacre, mais dont
l'idolatrie semble par moment masquer sa foi en Dieu. Égalité dans la
différence certes, mais tout semble indiquer que l'émir prend la relève de ce
ferment païen qui couve sous le vêtement chrétien du preudome non moins
que sous l'œuvre d'un jeu dont l'édification est la règle imposée.

Nous voici reconduit du même coup à ce qui constitue, selon nous,
la stratégie fondamentale de la pièce: la couverture en ceci qu'elle permet
de faire coexister, entre le dedans et le dehors, deux âmes contradictoires,
dont nous verrons mieux, au cours de l'analyse de la taverne, la raison de
cette cohabitation.

Il ne fait donc pas de doute que la loi d'indétermination, qui structure le jeu des doubles dans l'oeuvre de Jean Bodel, déstabilise non seulement les effets de signifiance mais rend délibérément équivoques les frontières entre les lieux et leur au-delà chrétien ou païen démultipliés en des pays de l' "outre," entre les messagers du ciel, Ange ou saint Nicolas, et Aubéron, le messager du roi, dont les pas rapides annulent les distances et le temps.

Il en va de même pour tous les personnages: de loin ils diffèrent, de près ils se ressemblent, ils habitent la même contrée du rêve et parlent la même langue: arrageoise ou sarrasine qu'importe si le nom d'*Arras* semble avoir déteint sur celui du *Sarras*in.

La taverne

La taverne est un motif fréquemment utilisé dans la littérature médiévale. On le trouvera dans *Courtois d'Arras*, dans le *Jeu de la Feuillée* d'Adam de la Halle, dans le *Roman de la Rose*, chez Rutebeuf et même dans la chanson courtoise. Il s'agit là d'un lieu commun qui peut revêtir des fonctions et des significations diverses, mais qui n'en reste pas moins un signifiant littéraire.

Pour l'auteur du *Roman de la Rose*, par exemple, le monde ressemble à une taverne de buveurs où *Fortune*, la tavernière de Jupiter, tire de ses deux tonneaux, l'un rempli d'une liqueur douce, l'autre d'une liqueur amère, un breuvage dont le mélange fait "soupes" (v. 6794). *Johans Chopinel* (c'est sous ce nom que figure [v. 10535] dans le texte le futur auteur du *Roman*: Jean de Meun), comme tout le monde, sera abreuvé des tonneaux de Jupiter "dont l'un est clair et l'autre trouble" (v. 10602), à cette différence près que la vocation poétique de ce personnage est liée à ce breuvage divin. Car si boire la *chopine*[10] (selon le vers 6798 du *Roman*), c'est avaler le doux et l'amer de l'existence, la résonance de ce substantif dans le nom de *Chopinel* destine ce poète, dès sa naissance, à composer les mélanges des doubles contraires dont le *Roman de la Rose* sera à la fois la pharmacopée et la "soupes."

Ainsi *Johans Chopinel*, assigné par son nom même à la lignée des "buveurs de lettres," fait partie des grands soiffards de la littérature qui, depuis les Goliards au moins, nous conduiront à Villon-Cotart[11] et à combien d'autres, Mais on sait qu' il appartiendra à Rabelais d'ouvrir tout le champ de signifiance de cette fable *gigantale* selon laquelle, depuis toujours, on n'écrit qu'en buvant.

Du reste, ce rapport entre la taverne et l'art[12] figure en un prodigieux raccourci, dans une chanson du troubadour Arnaut Daniel (12e s.). Pour célébrer la toute puissance de la Muse, traitée d'usurière, le poète déclare, et pour cause, que sa dame est devenue la patronne de l'atelier et de la taverne:

> Tant a de ver fait renou
> C'obrador n'a e taverna[13]

> (Et en vérité elle a tellement fait l'usurière qu'elle est devenue la pa- tronne de l'atelier et de la taverne.

> *Autre traduction*: De mes vers elle a tellement abusé qu'elle est deve- nue la patronne de l'atelier et de la taverne.)

N'excluons cependant pas, et pour une autre entente du vers 27 l'anagramme inséré au début: *tant a de ver* qui se recompose dans le mot *taverne*, ou presque, donnant à entendre en un *surplus de sen* que l'*obrador* ou le travail abusif de la dame sur les vers a fini par créer le lieu, soit la taverne, par la lettre.

Arnaut Daniel, comme le note Toja, reprend ici un lieu commun de la rhétorique médiévale[14] qu'on rencontre aussi chez Guillaume IX, dans une chanson où le mot *obrador* désigne la fabrique, l'étude, la boutique d'art.[15] L'*obrador* c'est identiquement l'*ergasterium* que Dante utilise dans le *De vulgari Eloquentia* au sens de lieu du travail poétique.[16]

Dans le texte d'Arnaut Daniel, l'"atelier" est posé en synonyme de "taverne," à moins que celle-ci ne soit le complément indispensable du premier,[17] à savoir cette taverne du diable où l'on boit et l'on joue pour de l'argent, comme l'écrit le *Ménagier*: "si est le moustier au déable, ou ses disciples vont pour le servir."[18]

Ce côté diabolique de la taverne est manifeste dans la parole de Pincedé, l'un des voleurs du trésor protégé par la statue. Chassé de la taverne, le truand renonce à ce marché du diable:

> Segneur, or est pis que devant:
> Anemis nous va enchantant
> Qui nous cuide faire honnir.
> Avoirs puet aler et venir;
> Mais s'on nous escille et deffait,
> Nous ne serons jamais refait.
> Honnis soit ore tés marchiés!
>
> [1334-40]

(Messieurs, cette fois, ça va plus mal qu'avant. Le diable est en train de nous ensorceler et il compte bien nous faire mettre à mal. La richesse peut aller et venir; mais si l'on nous met en pièces et qu'on nous extermine, jamais nous ne serons remis sur pied. Alors, au diable un marché pareil!)

Si Arras est devenu dans la tradition littéraire un espace fabuleux de la poésie et des arts c'est aussi parce que la taverne en était le complément indispensable, l'espace clos réservé aux assoiffés de vin, d'évasion et de jeux. Lieu privilégié de la création poétique, Arras l'est à tel point que Dieu lui-même, devenu malade, y recouvra la santé.[19]

De la taverne du *Jeu de saint Nicolas*, on a trop parlé en termes, il est vrai, de "réalisme," alors que, colorée de tous les traits du quotidien, cette taverne, intégrée à la grande structure onirique du *Jeu*, n'en participe pas moins du rêve dont elle concentre les potentialités. Dans l'œuvre de Jean Bodel, la taverne prend valeur paradigmatique d'autant plus que, comme nous le verrons, la mise en jeu du trésor royal dans cette taverne ressemble singulièrement à l'aventure que met en "jeu" le travail du poète opérant, dans l'atelier de ses rêves, sur la matière précieuse du trésor public de la langue.

Voilà qui explique du même coup pourquoi, dans cette œuvre, la taverne occupe une place centrale et prépondérante. Et si Jean Bodel déclare dans le prologue que tout est *essamples*, voire symbole dans son œuvre, la taverne, antre ou creusent des songes et des jeux, dissimule sous des semblants réalistes sa dimension de métaphore spéculaire du *Jeu*. Tout concourt à cette lecture à voir comment s'agence parfaitement l'homologie des forces antagonistes.

La scène de la criée, devant la taverne, fait dès le début le trait d'union entre le dehors et le dedans. Quant aux mots *tresor* et *restor* conjoints à la rime (v. 1217-8), la relation entre ces deux termes, dont le premier est l'anagramme du second (dérivé de "restaurer") fait, signe en direction d'une réinstauration de la langue poétique, véritable centre de gravitation de tout le *Jeu de saint Nicolas*.

Comme le dit fort justement Guillaume le Clerc, dans son *Bestiaire rimé*, le trésor est ce fond de tradition ancienne où l'écrivain va puiser la matière d'une invention nouvelle:

> Issi ert le sage escrivein (. . .)
> . . . Qui de son tresor met avant
> Les velz choses e les noveles
> qui ensemble sont bones et beles.[20]

(C'est le sage écrivain [. . .] qui de son trésor promeut [. . .] les vieilles choses et les nouvelles qui mises ensemble, sont bonnes et belles.)

Il suffit du reste de parcourir les traités de rhétorique latine de l'Antiquité et du Moyen âge pour s'apercevoir que le mot *thesaurus* désigne toutes les richesses culturelles que la mémoire a déposées dans les lieux communs du langage et de ses fables.

Les quelques aspects que nous allons examiner de ce qui a trait aux activités des personnages de la taverne, devraient nous permettre de mieux saisir le subtil enjeu de ce *Jeu* où l'image posée sur le trésor en un premier moment, écartée ensuite, puis remise en place à la fin, assume une fonction fondamentale, voire décisive dans l'ensemble de la pièce.

L'*outrevin* et le pays de l'*outre*

Il s'agit tout d'abord de comprendre le sens et la portée de cette dispute qui surgit brusquement entre les deux crieurs au seuil de la taverne: Raoulet, le crieur de vin, et Connart, chargé par le roi d'annoncer que son trésor et ses richesses seront désormais accessibles à tout le monde sans la moindre surveillance. Le seul gardien est un *fétiche cornu*; il est mort, puisqu'il ne bouge pas (v. 585-6). Le miracle, s'il se produit n'en sera donc que plus manifeste.

Les gens sont fatigués de boire, raison pour laquelle Raoulet est requis par le tavernier de vanter son vin. Prenons garde cependant que, sous l'image populaire de cette criée, c'est tout l'inverse qu'il faut lire: non pas le langage du vin, mais le vin du langage, ce "jus" qui n'est pas exactement le *Jus de saint Nicholai*, mais le savoir qui le met en jeu, selon le dire d'un autre poète:

> Jus, qui me fait scavant? C'est le vin
> ou ce bon jus de pomme.[21]

(Quel jus me rend savant? c'est le vin ou ce bon jus de pomme).

L'ivresse des mots, leur saveur ne se laisseront donc connaître qu'à les faire demeurer sur la langue, comme le dit Raoulet, dont le boniment est digne d'un poème:

> Cler con larme de pecheour,
> Croupant seur langue a lecheour:
> Autre gent n'en doivent gouster!
>
> [648-50]

(Limpide comme larme de pécheur, s'attardant sur la langue des gourmets: les autres ne doivent pas y toucher.)

Si le mot *lecheour* a ici de toute évidence le sens de "gourmets," n'oublions pas que ce même terme est fréquemment appliqué aux *losangiers* les poètes tricheurs, séducteurs, mais connaisseurs tout aussi expérimentés dans la langue que les poètes authentiques.[22]

Raoulet d'ailleurs n'a pas manqué de charger de cette nuance les "paroles" de son rival:

> Oiiés quel *lecherie* a dite
> Qui me roeve crier notorne!
>
> [615-6]
>
> (Ecoutez donc quelle insolence il me dit, celui-là qui exige que je sonne
> la retraite!)

Ceci se passe au moment où la dispute éclate entre les deux crieurs.
A noter tout d'abord qu'elle tourne principalement autour d'une question
de voix, dont Jean Bodel ne manquera pas d'exploiter à son compte les
effets de "langue" chez les deux crieurs.

Connart, le crieur du trésor royal, possède une voix forte comparée
à celle de Raoulet qui se voit reprocher de crier trop faiblement par *gille*
(ruse) et donc suspecté en sous-œuvre de truquer et son boniment et le
vin. Or, si Connart reproche à Raoulet d'avoir une voix trop basse, ses
invectives ne revêtent toute leur portée, dans la langue de Jean Bodel,
qu'à condition de les reconduire à leur dimension poétique:

> Fui, ribaus, lai ester te gille,
> Car tu cries trop a bas ton!
> Met jus le pot et le baston,
> Car je ne te pris un festu. (607-610)
>
> (Fuis crétin, renonce à ton imposture, car tu cries bien trop faiblement!
> Mets bas le pot et la baguette! Vraiment, je ne t'estime pas un fiferlin.)

La *gille*, comme ruse ou tricherie est encore un mot familier au monde de
la littérature. D'autre part si le mot *baston* pouvait avoir le sens de
"mesure du vers" ou "vers" tout court[23] on se rendra compte que ce n'est
pas par hasard que Jean Bodel fait rimer *bas ton* et *baston* en une parfaite homophonie et qu'il utilise ici un genre d'altercation dont on
retrouve des échos dans les jeux-partis et les fréquentes attaques des
poètes courtois contre les *losangiers*.

La trouvaille de Jean Bodel, c'est de produire pour l'oreille et
l'écriture un effet d'équivalence entre la voix basse et comme en retrait du
crieur de vin et celle du vers en contraste avec la voix bruyante et domi-
nante du crieur de la trésorerie royale ou du *thesaurus* de la langue au
sens le plus officiel de ce terme. Ainsi la dispute des deux crieurs, sous
des apparences très réalistes, ajuste les forces rivales de deux langages,
celui de la loi et celui de la poésie. Car si Raoulet, pour faire goûter son
vin utilise le cri scandé par la frappe régulière de la baguette sur le
gobelet, Jean Bodel de son côté reste le vrai crieur qui tourne la scène du
boniment en événement poétique. Ne perdons jamais de vue que le poète
reste l'unique chanteur de la scène, le secret buveur de mots. N'est-ce pas
aussi et surtout que Jean Bodel veut sous-entendre ici que c'est le battement

du vers qui compense la faiblesse du crieur de vin et l'obscurité de ce *trobar clus* opposé à un *trobar leu* décidément trop clair?

En somme, ce duel de mots joue sur une autre scène l'affrontement de deux voix que Jean Bodel, tout comme le tavernier pacificateur qui accorde les discordes des crieurs (v. 628 sq.) et les rixes des buveurs (v. 1163 sq.) va tenter d'harmoniser dans son œuvre. Deux voix se trouvent donc ici en concordante discordance, entendons bien celle de la loi bruyante et impérieuse des *connarts* — car c'est ainsi que le poète fait sonner le nom du crieur royal (v. 619) — et celle du petit crieur de vin, voix secrète de la poésie qui chante l'ivresse à l'écart de la loi.

Cela revient à dire que le poète exploite la langue instituée pour y faire circuler ses rythmes mystérieux. Encore faut-il ajouter que si le poète triche avec la langue du roi ce sera, n'en doutons pas, pour mettre une sourdine au signifié toujours trop bruyant ou faire du réalisme un trompe-l'oeil qui demande qu'on regarde tout de même un peu au-delà de ce qui est représenté.

Disons donc en résumé que l'altercation, dans l'ouverture de la scène de la taverne, met en place les deux registres antithétiques de l'action, autour desquels s'organisent les métaphores de la langue en vue d'un accord possible mais qui restera toujours aussi problématique.

Ainsi le vin, source des richesses du tavernier et de l'ivresse des buveurs s'oppose au trésor du roi menacé non seulement par la soif des ribauds de la taverne, mais encore, et peut-être davantage, par la force protectrice, inhérente à la couverture chrétienne du *fust*, qui fait en quelque sorte main mise sur les richesses du roi et sur son pouvoir.

Ce danger qui menace la puissance royale, séduite par l'image protectrice ou par la conversion, renvoie à tout un processus d'allégorisation mis en branle par la chrétienté. Rien de plus remarquable que cette stratégie "poétique" de la catholicité médiévale couvrant de sa cape les richesses du paganisme antique ou sarrasin — autrefois destinées à grossir les joues de Tervagan — pour mettre cet or au service non pas de l'oracle, mais de l'orthodoxie chrétiennne qui sauvegarde, à la faveur de l'allégorie, la beauté des œuvres païennes, en redouble le trésor et la jouissance, laquelle serait interdite sans l'image chrétienne.

Insouciants du pouvoir, qu'il s'agisse de l'Eglise ou du Roi, les voleurs, vus sous cet angle, prennent tour à tour les attitudes ambiguës d'alliés du roi contre l'imposition de l'image chrétienne, qu'ils écartent, et de complices de saint Nicolas au moment où celui-ci exige non seulement la réinstauration du trésor mais de son image. C'est là du moins ce qui ressort du texte et de l'insistance que marque, sur ce point précis, la voix menaçante du saint homme:

Gardés tost qu'ele i soit remise

[1295]

et encore

Et metés l'ymage deseure

[1298]

L'humour noir du paradoxe c'est que les mécréants arrageois, insensibles à la grâce, qui fait ici échec—mais non à la violence de cette voix—deviennent à leur insu l'instrument diabolique de l'imposture du miracle, mais dont le roi et son sénéchal, également à leur insu, entre sommeil et veille, accueillent les effets d'authenticité et de preuve avec d'autant plus de conviction que le fétiche s'est révélé particulièrement efficace pour la sauvegarde du trésor volé et restitué. N'est-ce pas pour le roi une raison suffisante de se convertir à la foi chrétienne?

Il ne saurait être question ici de reprendre tout ce que les commentateurs ont écrit, et très pertinemment, de cette scène de la taverne où déjà le déchiffrage du langage des voleurs est un travail en soi, très finement conduit par A. Henry. Notre but sera plutôt de montrer l'enjeu de toute cette "turquerie" et le truquage d'une conversion dont le tour qu'elle prend dans le parler du roi ressemble à une sorte de retour du refoulé plus ou moins caché dans la métathèse *truquier* du verbe *turquier*, "tourner," "convertir":

Preudom, il muert de duel et d'ire
De che c'a Dieu me sui turkiés.

[1517-18]

(Sage chrétien, il [Tervagan] crève de douleur et de rage, parce que je me suis donné à Dieu.)

Il s'agira surtout de creuser le sens de l'abandon, après tout sans heurts, de ce "marché du diable" entrepris par les voleurs. Pourquoi cette acceptation facile? Pourquoi cette folie de Tervagan? Pourquoi enfin l'émir refuse-t-il de se se convertir?

Certes les jeux de dés (par où l'on sollicite le hasard), la tricherie, les mélanges de vin, les tensions, les éclats, l'ivresse, le rêve, sont autant de phénomènes qui se laissent aisément transférer de la taverne à l'atelier du poète, de même que le côté oraculaire, dionysiaque souligne le caractère païen de la poésie tout en suggérant une symétrie entre le rôle du Tavernier vis à vis des joueurs et celui du roi à l'égard de Tervagan. La similitude des lettres entre les noms de *Tavernier* et de *Tervagan* pourrait servir d'indice, voulu peut-être par l'*obrador* Jean Bodel.

Bien qu'en marge de la loi, le Tavernier n'en impose pas moins ses règles aux clients de la taverne, surveille les comptes par l'intermédiaire de son valet, Caignet, attentif surtout à Cliquet, le plus démuni de tous.

N'est-ce pas qu'il a déjà mis en gage la cape qui recouvrait sa misère corporelle? Si la richesse du Tavernier n'égale pas le trésor du roi, l'oeil du maître veille à ce que les buveurs, qui jouent toujours à crédit, n'empochent pas les besants du sac. Et tout se passe en fin de compte comme si le sac d'or avait joué un mauvais tour aux voleurs, *fait une wide* (v. 1345) comme dit Cliquet, Bodel, jouant sur l'entente du mot *wide* au sens de "vide" et de "ruse" ou mot d'esprit (*witz*).

Décidément les besants resteront imprenables, d'où s'impose la conclusion qu'il n'est permis de jouer avec de pauvres avoirs ou avec des richesses qu'à condition d'observer la règle qui interdit de se les approprier. N'était-ce la présence du tavernier, la bacchanale des joueurs finirait toujours dans le désordre des rixes où, faute de cape, on paierait de sa vie. N'oublions pas surtout que l'espoir du trésor à conquérir augmente les paris, le trésor étant désigné par Rasoir comme une prise à crédit sur le *hart* ("gibet," v. 1058) aussi bien que sur l'art, selon l'à-peu-près homonymique qu'on rencontre dans le *Roman de Renart*.[24]

Rien de ces folles dépenses ne sera jamais payé car tout, dans l'intérêt de l'œuvre, doit concourir à maintenir cette béance liée au fantasme de la mort. Comment pourrait-on douter que le trésor de la cour n'aurait été dissipé, en tant que valeur boursière, livrée aux jeux insensés des buveurs?

Toute proportion gardée, la taverne fait donc pendant au palais royal où Tervagan meurt "de douleur et de rage" quand il perd le soutien du roi, autrement dit, quand le cadre païen de sa crédibilité s'effondre, mais cette fois au profit de l'image chrétienne.

C'est dans cette perspective qu'il s'agit de comprendre, du moins en un premier moment, le péril qui menace le jeu continu avec les richesses de la langue, ses ensorcellements qui risquent la folie, l'écartèlement, la "mise en pièce" de la raison et du corps qui paie de son "besant" d'or, si l'on peut dire. Seule, par conséquent, la restitution de l'image gardienne de ce trésor redoutable est ce qui permet de conjurer les périls du *Jeu*. Car ce qui fait miracle dans l'image c'est que, dans l'économie du drame, elle sert de garde-fou au poète. S'il ne veut pas perdre la tête ou être mis en pièce comme le craint l'émir d' "outre l'Arbre sec," ou Pincedé,[25] le poète, déchiré par la brisure du rythme dionysiaque, sera contraint de feindre d'adorer le fétiche chrétien pour sauver l'œuvre.

Le nom évocateur de l'émir rebelle, de même que sa stature enveloppant le germe d'un futur toujours problématique qui sauvegarde l'ouverture (païenne) de l'œuvre, révèlent la dimension signifiante de l'au-delà poétique. Le lieu de la langue restera toujours ce pays sans nom, ce pays de l' *outre* dont seuls les bords, protégés par l'image, empruntent des noms variés: *outre Pré Noiron, outre Wallengue, outre mer, outre l'Arbre sec.*

Or, cette langue de l'*outre*, dont le fonds fait toujours grimoire défiant toute traduction, figure à la fin de l'œuvre dans le baragouin de Tervagan. Renié par le roi, Tervagan s'abandonne à sa propre folie:

> Palas aron ozinomas
> Baske bano tudan donas
> Geheamel cla orlaÿ
> Berec. he. pantaras taÿ.
> [1512-15]

La statue de Tervagan se trouve donc dans l'impossibilité de se garantir de l'or du roi qui lui servait de couverture. Que cette statue ait été détruite ou non importe moins que son langage sibyllin faisant écho aux dernières paroles de l'émir d' "outre l'Arbre sec" qui feint de se convertir en se couvrant de cette "écorce."[26] Quant au fond, païen sans doute, il se situe entre la folie de Tervagan et l'ivresse incontrôlée des joueurs de la taverne. Mais pour ce qui concerne l'émir, ce fond recouvert par l'écorce ne causera aucune inquiétude au roi, pas plus que celui-ci ne se soucie de déchiffrer le grimoire de Tervagan:

> Mais n'ai mais soing de son prologe
> [1519]
> (Mais maintenant je me moque de son sermon)

Tout est rentré dans l'ordre, ou pour le moins les apparences sont sauvées. Voilà pourquoi il fallait montrer le jeu des alternances, car à se débarrasser radicalement de l'image, il ne resterait que le grimoire de Tervagan dont les sonorités ne donnent plus rien d'autre à entendre que le reste irréductible d'une langue devenue illisible.

Ce qui, dans le "Jeu" de Jean Bodel rassemble l'écriture et sa fable, ce n'est pas le souci de l'édification, bien qu'il fasse partie des effets de l'œuvre, mais la sauvegarde du miracle de l'art, le travail du symbolique, bref tout ce qui fait de l'œuvre un rêve éveillé, dont la langue possède la clarté du vin qui "mange sa mousse." Rien d'autre, à bien entendre cette métaphore, que le grand art de rendre volatile la matière langagière, mousse légère où pétille l'esprit de l'œuvre, si bien que, à garder ce vin sur la langue, on sentira l'*outrevin*, non moins que le vin de l'*outre* du *Jus de saint Nicholai*[27] comme le laissait entendre déjà Raoulet dans sa criée:

> Vois con il a mangüe s'escume
> Et saut et estinchele et frit!
> Tien le seur le langue un petit
> Si sentiras ja outrevin.
> [655-58]

(Vois comme il mange sa mousse et sautille et brasille et pétille! Garde-
le sur la langue quelque peu et tu sentiras, je t'assure, un supervin.)

Un lecteur moderne pourra difficilement s'empêcher d'entendre des
résonances homonymiques entre la préposition et le substantif *outre*.
Or, comme le substantif, semble-t-il, n'est pas encore employé au 13e
siècle,[28] reste la lecture comme effet d'après coup, par contingence, comme si le temps, qui ne cesse de réécrire les œuvres à sa manière en les do-
tant d'une vie nouvelle, au hasard de rencontres fortuites ou non, mais
parfois merveilleuses, s'était chargé de réaliser dans l'écriture homonymique des deux *outre* ce rapport virtuel que l'œuvre donne à imaginer entre le
fust-statue et le fût de vin en tant qu' enveloppes des trésors de la langue.

Il est important de relever que comparé à, d'autres poètes — Gautier
de Coinci, par exemple, chez qui on trouve une véritable inflation du jeu
de la lettre — Jean Bodel n'abuse jamais de ce procédé. N'oublions pas
qu'il s'agit d'une représentation dramatique, c'est-à-dire d'une action
dont le mouvement est mis en spectacle et donc destiné à faire *voir* ce qui
est donné à entendre.

Si Jean Bodel définit comme *essample* son œuvre, c'est parce que
l'ordre symbolique du jeu prend ici la relève de ce que d'autres poètes in-
vestissent dans les jeux de mots. Il est clair que c'est par le jeu du symbolique qu'une relation s'instaure entre le palais royal et la taverne, entre
l' "image" rigide et sèche comme la pierre ou le bois, et l'image hallu-
cinante du rêve.

Jean Bodel ne spécule jamais sur le *fust* de la statue et le "fût" de vin,
ni sur le *Jus* (cas sujet de "Jeu") et le "jus," liqueur ou vin, il faut même
souligner que les homonymes de ces deux termes ne figurent jamais dans
le texte alors qu'il sont couramment utilisés au moyen âge. En revanche,
Jean Bodel force pour ainsi dire le lecteur-spectateur, et ceci en raison
même de la fonction de l'*essample*, à s'interroger sur cette mise en scène
de la couverture et à se demander pourquoi la statue n'a pas fonctionné
avant le vol. Dès lors, le lecteur est porté à produire lui-même ce rapport
"inouï" en dépassant le signifié, un peu à la manière dont le poète dépasse
le miracle de la légende, non pas selon l'Ecriture, mais "selon son
écriture" (v. 61):

> Mais pour abregier le miracle,
> M'en passe outre, selonc l'escrit
>
> [60–61]

et fait goûter son *outrevin*:

> Si sentira ja outrevin

Ainsi l'*outrevin*, en sa subtile liaison, fait signe vers ce vin de l'esprit et du mot d'esprit où le "jus" et le "jeu" se confondent dans le rêve des buveurs ivres.

La nécessité s'imposait donc au poète de rendre le fétiche à sa fonction de crédibilité et de couverture. Il fallait d'une part jouer ce péril sous la fable orgiastique de la taverne, risquer la perte du trésor public en comptant sur la chance afin que, livré aux jeux du hasard et du calcul, cet or revienne transmuté dans le rêve qui restitue à l'image sa puissance de miracle. Il fallait montrer d'autre part que l'œuvre a besoin du fétiche pour se préserver du désastre de la folie: stratégie de protection certes, mais qui n'en est pas moins commandée par l'inaccessibilité de l'Autre ou de l'outre.

Ainsi le "Jeu" s'ordonne, se recompose au rythme du "comptoir," celui du Tavernier en l'occurrence, voire se conclut selon toutes les règles, mais à distance du vertige qui ne cesse de menacer le théâtre de la Poésie.

Roger Dragonetti
University of Geneva

Notes

1. Nous mentionnerons ici, une fois pour toutes, les principales études auxquelles nous sommes redevables d'informations précieuses et de suggestions dont la force stimulante n'a pas consisté à reprendre le même point de vue, mais à suivre au contraire une voie différente dans l'interprétation que nous proposons du *Jeu de saint Nicolas*, dont voici le titre original: *C'est li Jus de saint Nicholai.*

L'édition utilisée est celle d'Albert Henry, *Le jeu de saint Nicolas de Jean Bodel.* Bruxelles: Presses Universitaires de Bruxelles, 1962.

Voici d'autres travaux sur le sujet: Charles Foulon, *L'œuvre de Jehan Bodel.* Paris, 1952; Ida Del Valle de Paz, *La leggenda di S. Nicola nella tradizione poetica medievale in Francia* (Florence: 1921); A. Henry, voir l'introduction dans l'édition précitée, p. 7-44 et les notes, ainsi que les articles suivants du même auteur: "L'Ancien français 'escat,'" *Etudes de lexicologie française et gallo-romane*, (Paris: 1960, p. 110-120); "La Partie de hasard dans le Jeu de saint Nicolas," *Romania* 81 (1960), 241-43. Cfr. aussi A. Adler, "Le Jeu de saint Nicolas, édifiant, mais dans quel sens?" *Romania* 81 (1960), 112-121.

Pour les publications les plus récentes, voir H. Rey-Flaud, *Pour une dramaturgie du moyen âge* (Paris: Presses universitaires de France, 1980); J. Dufournet, "*Du Jeu de saint Nicolas au Jeu de la Feuillée,*" chap. 3, p. 71-93 de l'ouvrage intitulé: *Sur le Jeu de la Feuillée, études complémentaires* (Paris: SEDES), 1977. J.-Cl. Aubailly, *Le théâtre médiéval profane et comique* (Paris: Larousse, 1975), p. 17-26. M. Zink, "Le Jeu de saint Nicolas de Jean Bodel, Drame spirituel," *Romania* 99 (1978), 31-46.

2. *Philosophische Untersuchungen (Philosophical Investigations)* (Oxford: B. Blackwell, 1953), p. 208. Texte cité par J. Bouveresse, dans son étude, "Une illusion de grand avenir, la psychanalyse selon Popper," *Critique*, no. 346 (Mars 1976), p. 304.

3. *Les Lais de Marie de France*, ed. Jean Rychner (Paris: Champion, 1968), v. 15–16.

4. Nous reprenons cette expression à Paul Veyne, *Les Grecs ont-ils cru à leurs mythes; Essai sur l'imagination constituante* (Paris: Seuil, 1983). Voir aussi du même auteur, "L'histoire conceptualisante," *Faire de l'histoire* (Paris: Gallimard, 1974), 1: 62–92.

5. Cf. Tobler-Lommatzsch, au mot *essanple*: modèle, étalon de poids et de mesure, symbole, parabole et comparaison.

6. Cf. A. Henry, éd., *Jeu de saint Nicolas*, note au vers 458, p. 195. Il s'agit bien évidemment de l'hypothèse émise par l'éditeur du texte.

7. Le mot *fust* signifie en ancien français: "morceau de bois," en l'occurrence, comme ici, "statue." Le même mot peut avoir le sens de "fût," récipient en bois d'un liquide, tonneau.

8. Voir *supra*, le texte cité à la p. 2 et les vers 1260–1:

> Je me sui mis en vostre garde
> ou nule chose ne maumet
> Je (le preudome) me suis mis
> sous votre protection, et là
> rien ne périclite.

9. Cf. v. 401–07.

10. Cf. voir aussi le verbe *chopiner*. dans Godefroy, 9.

11. Cf. l'édition de Rychner-Henry: *Le Testament Villon* (Genève, Droz, 1974), v. 1238–65.

12. Parmi les tavernes de la littérature on pourrait citer le bordel de la Grosse Margot, *ibid.*, v. 1591–1626. Cf. aussi la *Ballade de bonne doctrine, ibid.,* 1692–1719.

13. Voir l'édition Toja (Sansoni: 1961), chanson 10, v. 26–27.

14. Ibid., p. 280 note au vers 27–28.

15. Edition Pasero (Modène: 1973), chanson 6, v. 1–3.

16. Mengaldo, *De Vulgari Eloquentia*, 2. 4. 1, n. 5, p. 160, in *Opere minori* (Milano: Ricciardi, 1979).

17. Le mot *taberna* dans l'Antiquité revêt deux sens: 1) boutique, magasin, librairie; 2) mauvais lieu, taverne, Cfr. Ernout-Meillet, *Dictionnaire Etymologique*.

18. Cité par Littré au mot *taverne*.

19. Voir à ce sujet la remarque d'Alfred Adler dans son étude, *Sens et composition du Jeu de la Feuillée* (Ann Arbor: University of Michigan Press, 1956), p. 33.

20. Edition Reinsch, v. 815–820.

21. Cf. Godefroy au mot *jus*.

22. Voir notre ouvrage, *Le gai savoir dans la rhétorique courtoise* (Paris: Seuil, 1982), p. 62–67.

23. Dans la *Bible de Macé de la charité,* (fin du XIIIe siècle), éd. J. R. Smeets (Leiden: 1967), p. 72. l'*escorce des baston* (v. 2061) désigne le sens obvie des vers (*bastons*) en opposition au sens caché:

> quer en l'escorce des bastons
> soulement la letre notons.

24. Voir notre article "Renart est mort, Renart est vif, Renart règne," *Critique*, nos. 375–6, (Septembre 1978), 783–98.

25. Cf. *supra*, texte cité p. 33, vv. 1334–40.

26. Cf. *supra*, texte cité p. 17, vv. 1507–77.

27. Cf. *supra*, n. 1.

28. Cf. Godefroy, tome X, au mot *outre* substantif, attesté à partir du XVe s. Le Tobler-Lommatzsch ne mentionne pas ce terme qui devient courant au XVIe siècle, selon le Dictionnaire de Huguet.

11. Truth, Half-Truth, Untruth Beroul's Telling of the Tristan Story

> "Por honte oster et mal covrir
> Doit on un poi par bel mentir." [2353-4]

Thus does the hermit Ogrin, with more policy than principle, counsel Tristran and Iseut — not that they greatly require such encouragement. To efface shame and conceal evil through the skillful lie, so that they may continue to enjoy their illicit *amours*, is a perennial concern of the lovers; the variety of the stratagems they employ, and with what success, rivets the attention of the reader.

The element of deceit is particularly marked in the versions of this story set down in writing in the twelfth century. These comprise the originally full-length (but now fragmentary) verse romances of Béroul and Thomas, and three short episodic poems: the *Lai du chevrefeuille* of Marie de France and the two *Folies Tristan*, those of Berne and Oxford.[1] In these poems, with far greater singleness and intensity than in the thirteenth-century prose renderings, we encounter a situation that by its very nature makes for both faith and unfaith, truth and falsehood. Nothing so banal as a mere tale of adultery, with two lovers indifferent to all around them and especially the wronged spouse, greets us here. On the contrary, we are faced with divided loyalties, conflicting obligations, and shifting emotions, as the main characters perceive and deceive each other. It is this psychological and moral component, more than the social circumstances and far more than the dangers involved, that creates the extraordinary tension in this tale, perhaps the best-known secular story in medieval Western Europe.

This essay will focus on the 4,495 lines (partial and complete) that we have the good fortune still to possess of the single surviving manuscript of Béroul.[2] Whether or not this is the most ancient treatment of the

story to have been preserved is still in dispute;[3] indeed, the whole traditional opposition of *version commune* and *version courtoise* has been
called into question.[4] Perhaps it is not too rash to propose, however, that
Béroul's text seems here and there to evoke a less-developed stage of
society than does, for example, the narration of Béroul's more-or-less
contemporary Thomas, and it clearly appeals to some rather primitive
emotions. The feelings involved are basically strong and simple ones:
love, hate, fear, jealousy, and vindictiveness. Their expression here,
though, and the actions they inspire, are very complex indeed, owing
largely to the personal and social forces at play. An adulterous triangle
is, of course, by nature unstable, whether the individuals who compose
it are equal, independent entities or whether they are differentiated in
rank, rights, social custom, and religious sanction. A triangular relationship in a work of literature having medieval society (with its norms and
taboos) as its backdrop is particularly asymmetrical, for it posits a large
inequality among the interested parties. Husband and wife are far from
possessing equal rights; and as for the wife's lover, he has no rights at
all — except such as are, if only as a literary convention, granted him by
author and hearer or reader. For the adherents of this other, rival, and
subversive code, personal happiness takes precedence over the claims of
Church and feudal society; love conquers all, and so it should. This, at
least provisionally, appears to be the judgment of those legions of medieval writers who celebrated love outside and often in defiance of marriage.[5] Béroul's sympathies are clearly with the lovers; yet he is far from
relegating the husband to the background. Marc in fact is very much
present and active in as much of Béroul's narrative as has been preserved.
Some of the longest and most dramatic scenes are those in which all three
of the principals confront each other or at least are within earshot of
each other. Even when they are separated each is aware of the other — or
others — and indeed to the point of obsession.

  A further complication in what might seem a sufficiently complex
and dangerous situation is the fact that Marc and Tristran are not
strangers to each other, nor are they merely connected politically as king
and subject. Tristran is Marc's near relation; in fact, they are nephew and
uncle, and each is the other's closest kin.[6] On top of this, Tristran has in
the past preserved Marc's crown, and saved his people, by fighting and
killing the formidable Morholt; by so doing, he willingly became Marc's
man, his liegeman as well as kinsman, with the privilege of entrée into the
royal bedchamber. Furthermore, it is through his efforts that Iseut has
become Marc's consort and queen. Marc is deeply in his debt for all these
services; and on the other hand Tristran as vassal is dependent on his

lord's generosity; at one point he has been reduced to pawning his *hernois* (military equipment), as he tells Iseut in Marc's hearing, and this implies that he has no fief and, in fact, nothing at all that does not come from the hand of his uncle and suzerain. He and Marc are consequently linked by two of the strongest bonds known to medieval secular society: kinship, and the relationship of suzerain and vassal. Both of these are to be stressed, if one is to grasp the drama of the tale. Of blood relationships among male literary characters, a particularly significant and frequent one is that of uncle and nephew,[7] especially if the nephew is a sister's son. Among familiar examples are Charlemagne and Roland, Arthur and Gauvain, William of Orange and Bertran. The older man is *in loco parentis*, the younger *in loco filii*; the real father or son (whether dead or absent) is often simply passed over in silence. Yet in the *Tristran* romances of Béroul and others, uncle and nephew become rivals and bitter enemies; and this constitutes a paradoxical and indeed scandalous state of affairs. Scandalous, too, is the violation of the feudal relationship, for the link between lord and vassal (forged of service owed to the lord, protection owed to the vassal, and fidelity owed to each by each) was one of the strongest forces holding medieval society together.[8] Fidelity included keeping a respectful, if gallant distance from one's lord's wife; and adultery was a form of treason.[9] To make matters worse, Marc is not only Tristran's uncle and suzerain but also his king; and for a subject to become the paramour of his sovereign's wife was tantamount to not ordinary but high treason.

This, then, is the dynamic of Béroul's *Tristran*: there is a king who claims authority over a young nobleman by virtue of being his uncle, his feudal lord, and his sovereign, and over his wife in his multiple capacity as her husband, lord, and king. There is a queen who enjoys royal honor but whose authority is all derivative, contingent upon the king's good pleasure and her ability to please him; as a foreigner far removed from home and kinsmen, she has no allies of her own except for Brengain, her compatriot and confidant—and for Tristran. And then there is Tristran, the national savior, Marc's right arm, unmistakably and unchangeably Marc's inferior in the social and political order, whereas in another sphere, the republic of lovers, he occupies a different rank, on a par with the queen and independent of all obligations (whether feudal or familial) to the king. Marc, as Iseut's lawful husband, possesses her body and assumes to possess her heart, as would be normal and proper. Improperly and abnormally, and perforce surreptitiously, Tristran has Iseut's heart—and her body as well, whenever the opportunity presents itself. Iseut shares herself with both men, giving the reality of her passion

to Tristran while treating her husband to an artful counterfeit of affection and respect. The narrative structure is the *raison d' être* for the basic
mode of expression of this tension-filled romance; and in its turn the
mode of expression, as used by the three main characters, perpetuates the
shaky balance of psychological forces among them. This mode is ambiguity; it permeates the text.

Ambiguously, the lovers communicate, both by language and by signs
intended to convey their true thoughts and feelings to each other while
concealing them from Marc and his supporters. Tristran and Iseut are
conscious of no moral constraints. This is no Abelard-and-Heloise situation, with the lovers warring against a shared and deeply-held sense that
fornication is sin, and that to yield to fleshly temptations is to fall from
grace.[10] No such scruples assail these literary lovers. They are untroubled
by them during the three years of the potion's efficacy, and they are every
whit as undisturbed by them when, the spell broken (but their love continuing; see their leave-taking, ll. 2653–2814), they separate, Iseut then
resuming her married life. The problem as they envisage it is not a moral
but a practical one: how to enjoy their illicit passion without being
caught. Their prudence, their furtiveness, spring from no sense of guilt,
only from a knowledge of danger and a determination to carry on their
liaison in spite of it. That they succeed in this is due in large part to divine
favor,[11] still more to their own quickness of wit, their ability to improvise
colorable explanations for extremely dubious behavior. Lying seems to be
for both second nature. Each is capable of putting on a virtuoso performance with no advance warning, no time to prepare or rehearse, no opportunity even to agree beforehand as to who will say what.[12]

The Tryst

Owing to the accidents that have befallen Béroul's text, it is as play-
actors that the lovers first appear before us. The fragment begins during
a highly dramatic scene: Tristan has summoned Iseut to a nocturnal
rendezvous. Once there, they realize severally that they are not alone.
Marc, informed by his dwarf-astrologer that this meeting is imminent,
has preceded them into the palace garden and there climbed a tree,
whence he spies on his wife and nephew. His cleverness, though, is no
match for that of the lovers; each of them, unbeknownst to the other,
promptly detects the king's presence by noticing his reflection in the
water of the fountain.[13] Iseut and Tristran now face a formidable task:
to warn each other that they are being observed, to account for their being alone together in a highly compromising situation and obviously by

prior agreement,[14] to show by their distance and coolness that there is nothing culpable between them, and to allay Marc's suspicions to the point where he will again trust them and ignore their detractors at court. Iseut speaks first, and her words are a tissue of lies, half-truths, and equivocations, with an artful admixture of fact to make them plausible. Her first speech, ostensibly to Tristran, in reality to both men, deserves to be quoted in full.

> "Sire Tristran, por Deu le roi,
> Si grant pechié avez de moi,
> Qui me mandez a itel ore!"
> Or fait senblant con s'ele plore.   8
> . . . . mie
> . . . . mes en vie
> . . . . ceste asenblee
> . . . . s'espee   12
> . . . .
> I . . . .
> Conme . . . .
> Par Deu, qui l'air fist et la mer,   16
> Ne me mandez nule foiz mais;
> Je vos di bien, Tristran, a fais,
> Certes, je n'i vendroie mie.
> Li rois pense que par folie,   20
> Sir Tristran, vos aie amé;
> Mais Dex plevis ma loiauté,
> Qui sor mon cors mete flaele,
> S'onques fors cil qui m'ot pucele   24
> Out m'amistié encor nul jor!
> Se li felon de cest' enor,
> Por qui jadis vos conbatistes
> O le Morhout, quant l'oceïstes,   28
> Li font acroire, ce me senble,
> Que nos amors jostent ensenble,
> Sire, vos n'en avez talent;
> Ne je, par Deu omnipotent,   32
> N'ai corage de drüerie
> Qui tort a nule vilanie.
> Mex voudroie que je fuse arse,
> Aval le vent la poudre esparse,   36
> Jor que je vive que amor
> Aie o home qu'o mon seignor.
> Et, Dex! si ne m'en croit il pas;
> Je puis dire: de haut si bas!   40
> Sire, molt dist voir Salemon:
> Qui de forches traient larron,

Ja pus nes amera nul jor.
44   Se li felon de cest' enor
        . . . .
        . . . .
        . . . .
48   . . . .
        . amor deüsent il celer.
        Molt vos estut mal endurer
        De la plaie que vos preïstes
52   En la batalle que feïstes
        O mon oncle. Je vos gari;
        Se vos m'en erïez ami,
        N'ert pas mervelle, par ma foi!
56   Et il ont fait entendre au roi
        Que vos m'amez d'amor vilaine.
        Si voient il Deu et son reigne!
        Ja nul verroient en la face.
60   Tristran, gardez en nule place
        Ne me mandez por nule chose;
        Je ne seroie pas tant ose
        Que je i osase venir.
64   Trop demor ci, n'en quier mentir;
        S'or en savoit li rois un mot,
        Mon cors seret desmenbré tot,
        Et si seroit a molt grant tort;
68   Bien sai qu'il me dorroit la mort.
        Tristran, certes, li rois ne set
        Que por lui par vos aie ameit;
        Por ce qu'eres du parenté
72   Vos avoie je en cherté.
        Je quidai jadis que ma mere
        Amast molt les parenz mon pere,
        Et disoit ce que la mollier
76   Nen avroit ja [son] seignor chier
        Qui les parenz n'en amereit;
        Certes, bien sai que voir diset.
        Sire, molt t'ai por lui amé,
80   Et j'en ai tot perdu son gré."[15]

All here is calculated to allay the suspicions of the eavesdropper: indignation (you ought not to have sent for me), rigor (I shall never grant such
an interview again), anxiety (the king is mistrustful; if he knew of this
meeting he would kill me [implying that no such meeting has taken place
hitherto]), and a protestation of innocence (the king is quite mistaken,
and misled, in doubting my fidelity). This last assertion is shored up by
what sounds like the strongest and most solemn kind of oath;[16] in fact it is
a cryptic affirmation of her unchanged passion for Tristran, with, as an

added touch, an allusion to their first union. There follows a plain false-hood (you have no desire to be my lover),[17] a half-truth (I wish for no love-affair that would bring disgrace), and another lie (I would rather be burned to ashes than love anyone other than my husband).[18] Then comes a justification for Tristran's friendly attitude toward her (she healed his wound) and hers toward him (he is her husband's kinsman): in short, all that links them is an innocent affection unfortunately misrepresented by ungrateful and envious men. Interspersed in this remarkable speech are allusions to facts, facts well known to Marc and to all his court: that Tristran fought and killed the Morholt, Iseut's uncle (all for the common weal), that among the beneficiaries of his bravery are those very *félons* who are now his accusers, that he was gravely wounded during the com-bat, and that it was Iseut who restored him to health. Throughout, Marc is treated with grave respect.

I have singled out this passage because it is representative of the thick tangle of truth and falsehood, appearance and reality, of which Béroul's romance is very largely composed. It is representative at least in quality, though perhaps not throughout in quantity, for Iseut's speech carries devi-ousness to the point of enfolding a lie within a lie. Her assertion of loving no one "fors cil qui m'ot pucele" leads us back to a part of the tale not in-cluded in the Béroul fragment. Other versions, though,[19] tell of a decep-tion, non-verbal but nevertheless most effective, practiced on Marc during his wedding night: since by then Iseut was no longer a virgin, her faithful maid-of-honor Brengain was persuaded to act as substitute for the bride. Hence Marc, in assuming that he had possessed Iseut as a virgin, was deceived; and he remains deceived (as Iseut well knows, and presumably Tristran as well), when he overhears this fascinating speech.[20]

The scene continues in much the same vein. When Tristran begins to speak he takes up the theme already sounded by Iseut: Marc's men have made him believe lies about us. This should suffice (although Béroul does not say so specifically) to make Iseut realize that Tristran has grasped the situation and that between them there is a good chance of carrying it off. As for what is going through Tristran's mind, Béroul per-mits no doubt:

> Qant out oï parler sa drue,
> Sout que s'estoit aperceüe;
> Deu en rent graces et merci,
> Or set que bien istront de ci.

> [97–100][21]

He now has but to find a pretext for their meeting. He begs her to inter-cede for him with the king, so that in departing from the court he will be able to retrieve his military equipment, which he in his poverty has had to pawn; and with Iseut's firm negative the improvised charade is safely concluded. There is, though, one last, magisterial touch: Tristran's monologue for Marc's benefit after Iseut has returned to the palace. Weeping, leaning on the stone that edges the fountain, he laments his misfortune: he must not only depart, but go away destitute: no arms, no horse, no companion but Governal. Without equipment, even the livelihood of a mercenary knight will be closed to him; and all this misery results from the lies people have told his dear uncle. Small wonder if that dear uncle, perched in his tree, is moved to real tears by the pathetic scene and at its conclusion is entirely convinced of now being in possession of the truth. His wife and nephew were and are clearly innocent; therefore those who have denounced them have not (by a curious mental operation) been honestly mistaken but have deliberately misrepresented the state of affairs. Lying is going on (this, of course, is true), and Marc thinks he can identify the liars: they must be the dwarf and the three *félons*. He thus judges the dwarf:

> "Las!" fait li rois, "or ai veü
> Que li nains m'a trop deceü:
> En cest arbre me fist monter,
> Il ne me pout plus ahonter;
> De mon nevo me fist entendre
> Mençonge, porqoi ferai pendre . . ."
>
> [265-70][22]

As for the three barons, his advisers,

> En son cuer dit or croit sa feme
> Et mescroit les barons du reigne,
> Que li faisoient chose acroire
> Que il set bien que n'est pas voire
> Et qu'il a prové a mençonge.
>
> [287-91][23]

He is not yet, however, sure of the facts to the point of dropping his investigation. Promptly, just after Tristran and Iseut have severally had the chance to relate the night's adventure to their respective confidants, Marc puts the queen to the test: will she tell the truth about the nocturnal tryst? Without preamble he opens with a formidable charge:

> "Roïne, ainz vien a vos parler
> Et une chose demander;
> Si ne me celez pas le voir,
> Qar la verté en vuel savoir."
>
> [391-4][24]

Marc's subsequent question ("Have you seen my nephew?") is an implicit falsehood, i.e. it implies an ignorance that he does not in fact possess. Once again, as we by now expect, he is no match for his wife. With a show of fear and trembling, and protesting that Marc will not believe her although her account of the tryst will be factual, she proceeds to recapitulate all that she knows Marc has overheard earlier that night. Naturally she passes this *viva voce* examination with flying colors: "Li rois sout bien qu'el ot voir dit." (l. 459)[25] Marc is seduced by this demonstration of veracity into completely letting down his guard, promising never to suspect them again and revealing that he had witnessed the rendezvous beneath the pine tree. Iseut, far from letting her own guard down, is all feigned amazement: "Sire, estïez vos donc el pin?" (l. 475)[26] Marc goes so far as to confide how he had been persuaded to take that undignified vantage point, and even adds what he had felt while listening to the two of them: pity for Tristran's great battle (with the Morholt), compunction for his poverty, pity again at observing their innocent and distant behavior; he even mentions his slight laugh (or smile)[27] that accompanied his decision to take no further action. This constitutes unconditional surrender; he is by now completely in Iseut's hands. Drawing both on his old authority and on his new-found security and reassurance, he affirms to Iseut and, shortly thereafter, to her and Tristran together, his total confidence in them. Thus through clever play-acting on the one side, and complacent delusion on the other, the threatened equilibrium of forces is reestablished.

The Trap

Reestablished, soon to be shattered again. As Béroul remarks,

> Ha! Dex, qui puet amor tenir
> Un an ou deux sanz descovrir?

$$(573-4)^{28}$$

Not, seemingly, Tristran and Iseut. For lovers who, as we have seen, can be exceedingly clever and circumspect, they can also be amazingly indiscreet. Three barons are (or pretend to be) scandalized by their behavior:

> Qar, en un gardin, soz une ente,
> Virent l'autrier Iseut la gente
> Ovoc Tristran en tel endroit
> Que nus hon consentir ne doit;
> Et plusors foiz les ont veüz
> El lit roi Marc gesir toz nus.
> Quar, quant li rois en vet el bois,

Et Tristran dit: "Sire, g'en vois",
Puis se remaint, entre en la chanbre,
Iluec grant piece sont ensenble.

[589-98][29]

They go to Marc, not with the above report but with the bare assertion
that his queen and nephew are lovers; and this suffices to reawaken Marc's
suspicions and persuade him to set a trap. This takes the form of an
urgent but fictitious mission that will take Tristran from the court before
dawn, doubled with the stratagem of flour sprinkled on the floor of the
bedchamber that the royal couple share with Tristran. The trap looks as
though it will be a failure (or perhaps more accurately, one should put it
that the hearer or reader expects it to be a failure, given Tristran's usual
prudence, ingenuity, and superiority over others). In fact, Tristran does
in the night detect the dwarf in the act of strewing the flour, does remark
on the abnormality of such behavior, does surmise that its purpose is to
detect movement from one bed to the other, and does conclude that it
would be folly to cross the intervening space (at least on foot):

"Qui iroit or, que fous feroit;
Bien verra mais se or i vois."

[714-5][30]

Walking being ruled out, Tristran resorts to leaping to the royal couch as
soon as the coast seems clear, returning in the same way when he hears
Marc and the dwarf coming back. For once, though, his own cleverness
has betrayed him; in place of footprints he has left blood on the floor,
and for good measure in Iseut's bed. When Marc and his barons,
bursting in, see that Tristran's wound is bleeding afresh, the evidence
seems conclusive.[31] Here again, though, we are in the realm of ambiguity,
not verbal this time but evidential. There is strong presumption of guilt,
enough at least to convince Marc:

"Trop par a ci veraie enseigne;
Provez estes," ce dist li rois.

[776-9][32]

Yet the lovers have not actually been caught *in flagrante delicto*, that is
to say that no one—*not even the reader*—can be certain beyond a shadow
of a doubt that on this particular occasion Tristran and Iseut committed
adultery. Béroul's language, just like the drops of blood, is inconclusive:

La plaie saigne; ne la sent,
Qar trop a son delit entent.

[733-4][33]

As to the nature and duration of the *delit*, Béroul is silent. *Felix silentium* (if not *felix culpa*), for the lack of real eyewitness testimony creates a legal loophole through which all the main characters, once the immediate furor has died down, will to their common relief be able to slip.[34] The faint possibility of their not having had intercourse *that* time perhaps accounts for Marc's readiness, much later in the romance, to be publicly reconciled with his wife.

A further explanation of the king's remarkable inclination to forgive and forget on that occasion is provided (although Béroul makes no overt connection) by an intervening passage occurring during the lovers' long stay in the Morrois Forest. To it they have fled to escape execution for the crime of adultery. Marc there pays them a furtive daytime visit as they lie sleeping. To this episode, one of the most famous of the entire Tristran corpus, we now turn.

The Morrois

The fugitives, rather than leaving Cornwall for foreign parts, opt to remain in the great, dense forest not far from Marc's court. There they subsist on what Tristran kills, and his *mestre* Governal cooks. Hunters, they are also hunted: Marc's followers are on their trail. Tristran and Iseut know great hardship; but while the potion grips them they do not repine. One day, while sleeping, they are surprised by a forester, who recognizes them, hastens to the court, and returns guiding the enraged king. Marc has every intention of killing them both. Seeing them in an apparently innocent posture he relents, blocks with his gloves a sunbeam that is falling on Iseut's face, exchanges rings with her and swords with Tristran, and returns home; there he refuses to tell anyone where he has been or what he has done. The lovers, at last awakening, realize that Marc has been there. Panic-stricken, they quit the Morrois and flee in the direction of Wales.

The reader who has followed the story thus far will have noticed the importance of signs, and the accurate or inaccurate reading thereof, in Béroul's romance.[35] The tableau of the sleeping lovers comprises a complex of phenomena: the makeshift shelter, the tattered clothing, the emaciated flesh, the unconscious, vulnerable bodies, their spatial relationship. The chief sign is the drawn sword between them. This is reinforced by other details: Iseut is clad in her *chemise*, Tristran in his *braies*; and although they have their arms around each other there is still some distance between them and their lips are not touching.[36] Here again, as in the garden tryst, Marc is cast in the role of an observer fervidly attempting to decipher and interpret the evidence of his senses, and prepared to act according to his conclusions. In the tryst scene it was with ambiguous words that he had to grapple; here it is with ambiguous signs. These add up to a whole that is not so much compromising to the couple as confusing to the spectator. Another and important difference from the tryst scene is that this time no deception is deliberately being perpetrated by the lovers. They did not expect visitors; they are unaware until afterwards of having had any. If, this time, Marc is not only suspicious but murderous, the fact is not astonishing; for the accusation made with much *éclat* in the royal bedchamber has never convincingly been denied; and in addition to this the putative lovers have been living together in the woods for some considerable time, with excellent opportunity for further lapses. Strangely, though, the logical processes and false conclusions of the tryst scene are recapitulated here, and this time all in Marc's head. His is an if/then type of reasoning: If Tristran and Iseut are lovers, they will show it in speech, action, or posture. The absence of amorous words, acts, or attitudes is for him a proof of innocence.[37] This reasoning process receives sufficient prominence to make the reader pause.

To go back to the tryst scene, we remember that during it the already suspicious husband spied on his wife and nephew to see whether they would betray themselves. By the time they had finished their conversation and gone their several ways he had observed their meeting from first to last and heard all their words (ll. 258–60). He concluded that he had been the victim of a lying deception—not on the part of the people observed but on that of the dwarf who had denounced them, since their words and deeds as he has witnessed them had not corresponded to his preconception. What this was, he himself articulated:

> "Or puis je bien enfin savoir;
> Se feüst voir, ceste asenblee
> Ne feüst pas issi finee;
> S'il s'amasent de fol' amor,
> Ci avoient asez leisor,
> Bien les veïse entrebaisier;
> Ges ai oï si gramoier.
> Or sai je bien n'en ont corage."
>
> [298–304][38]

After he confidingly told Iseut of his presence during the scene, adding his feelings of pity and relief and his resulting decision to take no action, Iseut cunningly reinforced the conclusion he had drawn, even using (necessarily without knowing it), some expressions of his soliloquy:

"Or savez bien certainement,
Molt avion bele loisor;
Se il m'amast de fole amor,
Asez en veïsiez senblant.
Ainz, par ma foi, ne tant ne quant
Ne veïstes qu'il m'aprismast
Ne mespreïst ne me baisast.
Bien senble ce chose certaine,
Ne m'amot pas d'amor vilaine.

And then the finishing touch:

Sire, s'or ne nos veïsiez,
Certes ne nos en creïssiez."

[494-504][39]

By the time this episode has come to an end, several notions seem firmly fixed in Marc's rather simple mind: seeing is believing; people who are amorously inclined toward each other will necessarily speak and behave in an amorous manner if they think themselves unobserved; a lack of such words and acts on any occasion is a clear proof of innocence; he and Iseut have had an entirely frank discussion. The fact that reality, even the reality of passionate lovers, is complicated eludes him. That it continues to elude him is amply demonstrated in the forest scene. To this we may again address ourselves.

Marc, finding his wife and nephew asleep, takes the complex of signs as a demonstration of their innocence. We readers, however, well know that Tristran and Iseut are still in the grip of their passion, the three years of the potion's effect not yet being past. It is only when the spell is ended that Iseut can say to the hermit Ogrin that she and Tristran are friends, good friends, nothing more:

"De la comune de mon cors
Et je du suen somes tuit fors."

[2329-30][40]

Why, then, on that particular day, when Marc comes to their hut, are they (still potion-held) lying in such an innocent posture? There is abundant explanation for this in the text itself (to which one might add some facts taken from psychological and historical reality).

The lovers are sleeping in broad daylight because Tristran has returned weary from following a stag he had been hunting: he must hunt, after all, to survive. This is not the first time we are told of his napping with Iseut in the daytime; it had happened before (1673 ff.). Why on this occasion do they sleep so soundly that, in spite of the utter stillness ("Vent ne cort ne fuelle ne trenble," l. 1826), they are unconscious of being twice discovered? First comes the *forestier*, tracking them like beasts by their successive sleeping-places and approaching close enough to recognize them. Then, led by him, appears someone more formidable, King Marc, who goes right into their leafy shelter, brandishing his sword. Rapidly assessing the situation, he checks the fall of his raised weapon, busies himself with gentler acts, leaves the shelter, and rides away. He manages to accomplish all this without disturbing the sleepers. By now readers may find their credulity strained to the breaking point; Béroul, though, has prepared us for all this, at least in part, through the earlier scene. There, too, the lovers lay sleeping in their bower, without sentinel either animal or human; there, too, someone approached them closely without waking them. On that occasion, fortunately, it was Governal, coming to attach to the bower itself the severed head of one of Tristran's enemies and thereby arranging a pleasant surprise for his master. On both occasions the weather is warm, Governal and the horse are away, the dog is not mentioned; in short, all is conducive to deep mid-day slumber. Are we inclined to accept as not totally improbable the first of these scenes? If so we are at least partially prepared to accept the second, even to the extent of believing that two people—granted that they are weary with exertion, weakened by privation, and oppressed by breathless stillness and heat—could sleep through such an event-filled afternoon.[41] The capital event, of course, is Marc's reading of the signs; and if ever there was an instance of overreading, this is it. It is true that Béroul gives no explanation of the separating sword, nor of the other signs; it is also true that the *argumentum ex silentio* is fraught with perils. One ought not to be intimidated by these considerations to the point of not looking hard, once again, at this fascinating tableau.

Béroul accounts for none of the arrangements made by Tristran and Iseut as they compose themselves for their siesta. The very lack of authorial comment here might suggest that a number of things are being taken for granted, and were not challenged during the telling of earlier drafts of the tale or readings of the written version, before it was committed to parchment in the version we possess. What does the text relate? That a pair of outlaws lie down to sleep in broad daylight, unattended, in a makeshift shelter, within two leagues of their mortal enemies; that they keep their clothes on, and that the man has his only weapon handy; that he has previously and very recently (ll. 1673–1745) slept so deeply, in similar weather, as to be insensible of the approach of Governal; and that this time when at last he awakens, upon hearing his lover cry out, his first, instinctive act is jump up and seize his sword:

Tristran, du cri qu'il ot, s'esvelle,
Tote la face avoit vermelle;
Esfreez s'est, saut sus ses piez,
L'espee prent com home iriez.

[2077-80]⁴²

This sword is no chastity symbol, and Marc is totally mistaken in reading
it as a proof of chastity. Not that Tristran is incapable of arranging ambiguous or deliberately misleading signs; we have seen that deception is
his second nature. But this time he was not expecting an audience.⁴³
What he did anticipate was the possibility of being surprised by an enemy
or enemies; this, after all, is the consideration that makes the lovers and
their faithful companion fearful and nervous and keeps them daily on
the move, like tracked animals in the forest. Tristran knows, because the
hermit Ogrin has informed him (ll. 1370-6), that a reward of a hundred
marks has been offered for him, and that every *baron* in the kingdom has
pledged to bring him in, dead or alive; he also knows on lying down with
Iseut that they are alone, Governal having gone off with the horse. (In
fact, the Morrois forest was generally shunned [ll. 1661-7, 1719-28]; but
Tristran is unaware of this.) What could be more natural than to keep his
weapon close to hand? A savage, lying down to sleep in the open, would
place club or spear beside him; a modern soldier would do the same with
pistol or rifle. Tristran is a knight, and his weapon is a sword. He puts it
where he can get at it; lying on his side, he naturally places it not behind
him but in front of him — which incidentally means that it is between him
and Iseut. One is reluctant to belabor the obvious; but what was obvious
to Béroul and his audience is not necessarily so to modern readers.⁴⁴
Béroul wrote from the cultural experiences of his own time; he did not
dwell upon, nor spell out, what could then be taken for granted.⁴⁵ There
is no indication in Béroul's narration that a separating sword is
automatically, in the world of his sub-creation,⁴⁶ understood as a sign of
chastity.⁴⁷ In support of this we may observe that Marc is alone in so
understanding it; and even he does not subsequently bring it up again,
even in justification of his astonishing decision to take Iseut to himself
once again as his queen. If this sword, in combination with other signs, is
conclusive evidence of the good behavior of an unjustly-accused wife,
and if the unjustly-accusing husband subsequently has a change of mind
or heart, why in the world does he not adduce what he has seen in order
to avert or diminish his own public embarrassment? If we reread the rest
of Béroul's text with this question in mind, the silence of the point
is astounding.

As for Tristran and Iseut, ignorant of Marc's visit until it is over, their reaction on realizing it is sudden, violent, and unpremediated. Tristran, leaping to his feet, grips the substituted sword, and only then scrutinizes it:

> Regarde el brant, l'osche ne voit;
> Vit le pont d'or qui sus estoit,
> Connut que c'est l'espee au roi.   (2081-83)[48]

As for Iseut, she too immediately detects a substitution:

> La roïne vit en son doi
> L'anel que li avoit doné,
> Le suen revit du dei osté.
> Ele cria; "Sire, merci!
> Li rois nos a trovez ici."
>
> [2084-88][49]

With the greatest rapidity they assess the situation and conclude that it is dangerous:

> Il li respont: "Dame c'est voirs.
> Or nos covient gerpir Morrois,
> Qar molt li par somes mesfait.
> M'espee a, la soue me lait;
> Bien nos peüst avoir ocis."
> "Sire, voire, ce m'est avis."
>
> [2089-94][50]

It is worthwhile to pause here and note how far Béroul's lovers diverge in their reaction from those of Thomas (as preserved in Gottfried's version). The latter, also realizing that they have been visited and that their visitor was Marc, feel considerable relief as they awake, take stock, and become aware of how they must have looked: they have slept, and been surprised, in a quite noncompromising attitude.[51] In contrast, Béroul's lovers, who are quite prepared to make capital of anything that may serve their ends, make no capital of this, and indeed never refer to it again. This fact, I think, is significant; and the lack of critical attention it has aroused is not easy to account for. Let us put the matter in the simplest terms.

(1)   The separating sword does not function in Béroul as a *guardian* of chastity.

(2)   Nor is it designed by the lovers as a *symbol* of chastity, for a deliberately contrived symbol implies an audience, or at least an expected or potential audience, to see and correctly understand it. That audience is not Marc, nor is it any other character in the story. Far from arranging a charade for the benefit

of the king or his vassals, or subjects, or servants (and this exhausts all the possibilities in their particular situation), Tristran and Iseut are in perpetual flight from them.

(3) The lovers, learning that they have been surprised, do not speculate on, or indeed take the slightest notice of how their sleeping arrangements must have appeared to their visitor.

(4) Nor do they attempt retroactively to convert what they well know Marc has observed into a proof of innocence, even when they initiate the negotiations that they hope will return Iseut to her husband's good graces.

Nevertheless, the sword *functions* as a symbol of chastity. It so functions because Marc reads it as such. We have here what is perhaps the most complex and subtle of all the many untruths in Béroul's *Tristran*: a false impression unintentionally created by two characters who in other circumstances have consciously and repeatedly deceived, by words and signs, without the slightest compunction. Furthermore, the victim of this unplanned and indeed unwitting deception is the same person who earlier had been victimized, deliberately and successfully, by the pair, during the tryst scene. We recall that they had then (by keeping a decorous distance from each other, as well as by establishing a verbal formality), carried off their joint effort to convince Marc of their innocence of carnal passion. In the Morrois episode, by contrast, there are no words spoken, nor is there any conscious attempt to deceive. Yet deception occurs. This time it is Marc who without any prompting interprets the complex of signs and makes of them a guarantee of innocent behavior: the space between the sleeping bodies, the clothes they are wearing, the interposed weapon. It is Marc who converts a functional sword into a symbolic sword, and brings it into alignment with his reading of the scene as a totality. Once he has made this assessment, the king generalizes it: not only, he concludes, have these two not had carnal relations just prior to his arrival, but they have not had them at all during their lengthy forest sojourn:

> "Dex!" dist li rois, "ce que puet estre?
> Or ai veü tant de lor estre,
> Dex! je ne sai que doie faire,
> Ou de l'ocire ou du retraire.
> Ci so[n]t el bois, bien a lonc tens;
> Bien puis croire, se je ai sens,
> Se il s'amasent folement,
> Ja n'i eüsent vestement,
> Entrë eus deus n'eüst espee,

Autrement fust cest' asenblee."

[2001–10][52]

Whereupon he takes pity on them, and spares their lives.

Here, for once, an untruth is created by a plain failure of comprehension on the part of the victim, rather than by a deliberate deception. The error is induced to some degree by Marc's perennial readiness not to believe the worst of persons who once were, and who remain, dear to him.[53] At the same time one may legitimately connect it with the experience related in the earlier episode.[54] We may also be permitted to see in this forest scene an explanation of Marc's ready assent to the proposal of a reconcilation with his queen, and his later acceptance without demur of Tristran's protestations of his and Iseut's innocence when the dramatic meeting actually takes place:

> "Rois, ge te rent Iseut la gente;
> Hon ne fist mais p[lu]s riche rente.
> Ci voi les homes de ta terre
> Et, oiant eus, te vuel requerre
> Que me sueffres a esligier
> Et en ta cort moi deraisnier
> C'onques o lié n'oi drüerie
> Ne ele o moi, jor de ma vie.
> Acroire t'a l'en fait mençonge. . . ."

[2851–9][55]

This is a bare-faced lie, and no less so that there is no formal oath involved. We note too that for once the denial of *drüerie* is unaccompanied by any modifying phrase that might at a pinch render it formally true.[56] Tristran's affirmation is enough for Marc; he takes his wife back without further ado and is on the point of readmitting Tristran as well to his household when he is dissuaded by the three troublemaking barons. Tristran will be sent away for a year, to avoid scandal and permit the king to verify the queen's faithfulness. Tristran, who had already promised the hermit Ogrin to depart for Brittany (l. 2610), or his native Loenois,[59] if his uncle would not retain him and, tutored by Ogrin, had sent to Marc a written offer to go and serve another king in Scotland,[58] renews to Marc personally, during the reconciliation scene, his intention to go to Loenois if he may not remain at court. Informed that in fact he must leave, he states inconsistently that he will go to a king who is at war.[59] Nevertheless he carries out none of this announced program. Marc and his barons escort Tristran part of the way toward the sea; but when they leave him Tristran, far from going into foreign parts, promptly takes a side road that leads him to the home of Orri the forester, who had many a time provided him and Iseut with a bed. In so doing he carries out not his pledge of absenting himself, which he had made to Marc on his own initiative (following Ogrin's recommendation), but Iseut's request just before they both returned to court:

> "Por Deu vos pri, beaus douz amis,
> Que ne partez de cest païs
> Tant qos saciez conment li rois
> Sera vers moi, iriez ou lois.
> Gel prié, qui sui ta chiere drue,
> Quant li rois m'avra retenue,
> Que chiés Orri le forestier
> T'alles la nuit la herbergier. . . ."
>
> [2811-18][60]

There he is to await Iseut's messages, and there he does wait, hidden underground, the better part of a month (l. 3031), until once again the three barons raise the question of Iseut's past conduct. There Perinis finds him, sent in secret by Iseut with the news of the date and place of her formal disclaimer, her *escondit*. This, once the issue of her chastity has again been raised, is the only way in which it can be settled once and for all, given the supposed absence of Tristran and therefore the impossibility of having him defend by combat the point at issue. Since Tristran is in fact not absent but merely in hiding nearby, and regularly kept abreast of developments, it is because of yet another premeditated deception on the part of the lovers that the last and most spectacular of all the untruths in Béroul's romance is played out.

The Oath

This last complete episode in Béroul's truncated narrative is, from start to finish, stage-managed by Iseut.[61] She proposes the proof, she sets the date, she requests King Arthur and his followers as impartial witnesses (and subsequent defenders if the matter is ever raised again), she chooses the place and requests that the totality of Marc's subjects be there. (In so doing, she has the opportunity to communicate with Tristran, secretly ordering her messenger to visit him on his way to Arthur's court.) Curiously enough, although her instructions to Tristran are most specific with regard to the day, the place, and the disguise he is to assume, she does not reveal even to him what she intends to do nor what his rôle is to be. Nevertheless on the day before the *escondit* these two seasoned actors play their parts to perfection. Tristran, in his character as begging leper, asks alms of all who approach his station at the edge

Iseut Being Carried across a Stream on the Back of her Lover,
Tristran, who is Disguised as a Leper
Janet Anderson

of the swampy Mal Pas barring the way to the Blanche Lande, and with false directions sends them into the deepest parts of the marshy stream. Iseut does not arrive until almost everyone has crossed over; she sends her small escort across and then, with all eyes upon her, arranges the trappings of her palfrey to keep them from the mud and drives the animal to the other bank with a blow of her whip. Now, standing alone in her magnificent robes and perfect beauty, with the two kings and their retinues observing her anxiously,[62] she turns to the only person remaining on her side of the Mal Pas, the "leper," and unceremoniously commands him to take her on his back and carry her over the muddy foot-bridge. Safely over, she rudely dismisses him. Tristran's feigned self-abasement and reluctance and Iseut's feigned hauteur are a show put on for the benefit of the spectators; in reality they are united in heart and (however briefly) joined in close physical contact as well.

The latter circumstance, since it is observed by everyone present, is crucial in Iseut's subsequent *escondit*, for it permits a substitution of oaths. This is Arthur's formulation of the charge to her:

> "Entendez moi, Iseut la bele,
> Oiez de qoi on vos apele:
> Que Tristran n'ot vers vos amor
> De puteé ne de folor
> Fors cele que devoit porter
> Envers son oncle et vers sa per."
>
> [4191-6][63]

Stepping nimbly around this proposed formula, to which she could not swear without perjuring herself, she proposes another, seemingly more comprehensive, in fact far narrower in scope. (She is quite within her rights, having previously [l. 3232-4] declared to Marc that she would take no oath except one of her own devising.)

> "Seignors," fait el, "por Deu merci,
> Saintes reliques voi ici.
> Or escoutez que je ci jure,
> De quoi le roi ci aseüre:
> Si m'aït Dex et saint Ylaire,
> Ces reliques, cest saintuaire,
> Totes celes qui ci ne sont
> Et tuit icil de par le mont,
> Q'entre mes cuises n'entra home,
> Fors le ladre qui fist soi some,
> Qui me porta outre les guez,
> Et li rois Marc mes esposez;
> Ces deus ost de mon soirement."
>
> [4197-4208][64]

This, of course, is technically true, a fact that presumably accounts for her coolness and self-confidence when taking this most solemn oath. Yet her intention is to hoodwink her audience (and manipulate God, for good measure). That her success is complete is attested by the assembled multitude, who repeat her words in chorus (ll. 4219-30). The next speaker is King Arthur; in the hearing of all the barons of both courts he pledges henceforth to support Iseut against her detractors. Marc in his turn invites Arthur to blame him if he should ever believe a *félon* concerning his wife. As to God, the remaining witness of Iseut's mendacious oath, nothing is said.[65]

Thus concludes the last complete episode of Béroul's romance. A delicate balance of psychological and social factors has once again been restored, based on a continuing deception and illusion. Marc is convinced of his wife's past faithfulness and of no present or future danger from Tristran since the latter is presumably far away; whereas Tristran, still lurking in the neighborhood, resumes his furtive visits to the queen when her husband is absent.[66] In spite of the lapse of time and much intervening incident, nothing has changed in any real sense since the tryst scene. Tristran and Iseut are still lovers; Marc remains the doting husband; all three are, in their several ways, content.

Béroul's telling of their story is, as we have seen, largely made up of a complex interplay of truth and untruth. The main characters, and some of their associates as well, repeatedly find themselves in situations where they lie or are lied to, spy or are spied upon, doubt the sincerity of speeches and acts, attempt to verify the suspicion, search for the inner thoughts of others while concealing their own, even tell the truth secure in the conviction that it will be misunderstood. Marc, Tristran, and Iseut are much akin in their willingness to mask their feelings, hide or disguise their persons, play on verbal and physical ambiguities, indulge in outright lying in word and deed. Tristran and Iseut have considerably more skill in this game than does Marc; in each crisis they emerge the *de facto* winners. Their triumph is enhanced by their victim's delusion that he has succeeded in grasping the truth, that he knows whom he may and may not trust; this in turn creates the opportunity for a new episode in which he can be practised upon once again. The characters and their relationships remain static. Hence the tension obtaining in the opening lines is unabated when Béroul's romance breaks off; it ends, as it began, with dissimulation.

Barbara Nelson Sargent-Baur
University of Pittsburgh

Notes

1. A recent and most useful bibliography of the Tristran literature in Old-French verse is by David J. Shirt, *The Old French Tristan Poems, A Bibliographical Guide*, Research Bibliographies and Checklists, 28 (London: Grant and Cutler, 1980).

2. For a description, see *The Romance of Tristran* by Béroul, ed. A. Ewert (Oxford: Blackwell, 1939, 1970), 1: ix-xii. All quotations of the text will be taken from this admirable edition. The name Berox appears twice in the text and presumably identifies the author, who is otherwise unknown.

3. Dating hangs on several clues, but largely on the expression *mal dagres* (l. 3849), interpreted by many as *mal d'Acre*, which (if indeed it is the *mal d'Acre*, i.e. an illness first identified and publicized during the Third Crusade), puts Béroul's poem as we have it after the siege of Acre (1190-1). It should be noted that even if the reading *mal d'Acre* is correct, the expression may be a later interpolation in the text. The question of dating has been warmly disputed. See Ewert edition, 2: 34-36, and Shirt, *Old French Tristan Poems*, pp. 50-51. For that matter, single vs. double authorship is very much a live issue; see Shirt, *Old French Tristan Poems*, p. 50 ff.

4. The opposition of *version commune* (Béroul, Eilhart von Oberg, Berne *Folie*) and *version courtoise* (Thomas, Gottfried von Strassburg, Oxford *Folie*) has been vigorously challenged by Pierre Jonin in *Les Personnages féminins dans les romans français de Tristan au XIIe siècle, étude des influences contemporaines* (Gap: Ophrys, 1958), especially Pt. III, chaps. 2 and 3.

5. This is not the place to go into the vast literature on the subject of "courtly love." For an introduction to the bibliography, see Douglas Kelly, *Chrétien de Troyes: An Analytic Bibliography*, Research Bibliographies and Checklists, 17 (London: Grant and Cutler, 1976), p. 123 ff.

6. Marc's parents are not mentioned; his father must necessarily be dead; his sister (Tristran's mother) in the full-length accounts died in childbirth and in any case does not appear in the fragmentary text. Tristran's father is not mentioned in Béroul, nor is any sibling or other relative.

7. See W. O. Farnsworth, *Uncle and Nephew in the Old French Chanson de Geste: A Study of the Survival of Matriarchy* (New York: Columbia University Press, 1913).

8. For a recent discussion of this, see Georges Duby, *La Société chevaleresque*, tr. as *The Chivalrous Society* (Berkeley: University of California Press, 1977), and also A. Dessau, "L'Idée de la trahison au moyen âge et son rôle dans la motivation de quelques chansons de geste," *Cahiers de Civilisation médiévale* 3 (1960), 23-6.

9. See John Benton, "Clio and Venus: An Historical View of Courtly Love," in *The Meaning of Courtly Love*, ed. F. X. Newman (Albany: S.U.N.Y. Press, 1968), pp. 26-27 and n. 26.

10. For a discussion of a moral view stressing intentions rather than acts, and possibly deriving from Abelard, see Jean-Charles Payen's review of A. Vàrvaro, *Il "Roman de Tristran" di Béroul,"* in *Le Moyen Age* 71 (1963), 604-6, and the much longer treatment of the subject by Tony Hunt in "Abelardian Ethics and Béroul's *Tristran*," *Romania* 98 (1977), 501-40.

11. Such authorial comments as "Bele merci Dex li [= Tristran] a fait" (l. 960) and "Oez, seignors, de Damledé / Conment il est plains de pité; / Ne vieat pas mort de pecheor: / Receü out le cri, le plor / Que faisoient la povre gent / Por ceus [= Tristran et Iseut] qui eirent a torment" (ll. 909–14) make it clear where Béroul thinks God's sympathies lie. See the remarks of Jean Frappier in "Structure et sens du *Tristan*: version commune, version courtoise," *Cahiers de Civilisation médiévale* 6 (1968), 447–9.

12. In "Le *Tristan de Béroul, un monde de l'illusion?*" *(Bulletin bibliographique de la Société Internationale Arthurienne* 31 [1979] 230), Jacques Ribard suggests persuasively that "le *Tristan* de Béroul se présente comme un univers du mensonge." His subsequent observation, that "Tout le monde y ment, peu on prou" is not strictly accurate, for the three barons, at least, do not lie, nor does the dwarf Frocin.

13. This is another detail not included in the fragment we possess; but Iseut mentions it shortly after this scene, in the account of it that she had given to Brengain (l. 345 ff.).

14. The Oxford *Folie* provides information on this score. Tristran would whittle chips of wood and toss them into the stream that flowed toward (near? alongside? through? — the line is defective) Iseut's chamber; this was a prearranged signal, used whenever Tristran wished to speak alone to Iseut. Se *La Folie Tristran d'Oxford*, ed. Ernest Hoepffner, Publications de la Faculté des Lettres de l'Université de Strasbourg, Textes d'Etudes, 8 (Paris: Belles Lettres, 1943; rpt. 1963), l. 777 ff.

15. "'Sir Tristran, in the name of God the King, you do me so great a wrong to send for me at such an hour.'" Now she pretends to weep . . . . "'In the name of God, who made the air and the sea, do not send for me another time. I tell you, Tristran, once and for all, that I should certainly not come. The king thinks, Sir Tristran, that I have loved you unlawfully; but to God I swear my faithfulness — may He smite me if any man ever had my love except for him who had me as a virgin! Even if the traitors of this realm, for whom long ago you fought the Morholt, when you killed him, make him believe (it seems to me) that we are lovers — Sir, you have no such desire. Nor, by almighty God, do I have any inclination toward a love-affair that would dishonor me. I would rather be burned and my ashes cast to the wind any day, than have love with any man but my lord. And yet, God! he does not believe me. I can say: what a downfall! Sir, Solomon spoke truly: He who saves a thief from the gallows will never be loved by him. If the traitors of this realm . . . . They ought to conceal love. You had to endure much pain from the wound you received in the battle that you fought with my uncle. I healed you. If you were friendly toward me because of that it was no wonder, by my faith! And they have given the king to understand that you love me with a forbidden love. May they see God and His kingdom! Never would they look Him in the face. Tristran, take care not to send for me, in any place, for any reason; I should not be so rash as to dare to come. I stay too long, I do not wish to lie; if the king knew a word of this, I should be torn limb from limb (yet that would be most unjust); I know that he would put me to death.'

'Tristran, indeed, the king does not know that for his sake I have loved you. Because you were related to him I have held you dear. I believed, long ago, that my mother loved my father's kin dearly; and she used to say that the women who wouldn't love her husband's kin wouldn't cherish her husband. Indeed, I know that she spoke the truth. Sir, for his sake I have loved you well; and on that account I have lost all his favor.'" J. C. Payen's translation of l. 24, "celui qui m'épousa vierge" misses the point. (*Les Tristan en vers* [Paris: Garnier, 1974], p. 3.)

16. For a discussion of this ambiguous oath (and others), see Brian Blakey, "Truth and Falsehood in the *Tristran* of Béroul," in *History and Structure of French: Essays in the Honour*

of Professor T. B. W. Reid, ed. F. J. Barnett, A. D. Crow, C. A. Robson, W. Rothwell, and S. Ullmann (Oxford: Blackwell, 1972), pp. 25-27. The later note by Francis Bar, "Le Premier Serment ambigu d'Iseut dans le poème de Béroul," *Bulletin bibliographique de la Société Internationale Arthurienne* 29 [1977], 181-4, neither cites' this essay nor goes beyond it. In "Du style de Béroul," *Romania*, 85 (1964), 522, Guy Raynaud de Lage takes up the oaths employed in this first surviving episode: "Dans ces 572 premiers vers, le nom de Dieu apparaît trente-deux fois, sauf erreur, *et en raison inverse de la sincérité des personnages*: car Iseut le prononce quatorze fois; Tristan, dix fois; Brengain, quatre fois; Marc, deux fois; Governal, une fois; le narrateur, une fois; il est vrai que Tristan et Iseut parlent plus longuement que les autres personnages, et il faut en tenir compte." This enumeration is cited by Jean Subrenat, who adds to it similar matter in other passages from Béroul's text and then draws an odd conclusion: "Il est impossible de ne pas considérer toutes ces invocations, tous ces appels à Dieu comme sincères" ("Sur le climat social, moral, religieux du Tristan de Béroul," *Le Moyen Age* 82 [1976], 249. Italics mine.)

17. B. Blakey ("Truth and Falsehood," pp. 26-7) takes *talent* (v. 31) to mean "will" and specifically the will to commit adultery, and considers that they did not intend this, the potion having annihilated their volition. Since what is under discussion in Iseut's speech is not, formally, adultery but carnal love, and since *talent* normally means "desire" rather than "will," I take Iseut's statement to be a deliberate lie.

18. Pierre Jonin takes this as another equivocation, "seigneur" (l. 37) being applicable to both men, Tristran being "celui qu'elle reconnaît pour son seigneur." One should note, however, that in Old French this word, used by or of a woman, normally means "husband." See P. Jonin, "L'Esprit celtique dans le roman de Béroul," in *Mélanges de langue et de littérature médiévales offerts à Pierre Le Gentil* (Paris: Société d'Edition de l'Enseiquement Supérieur et Centre de Documentation Universitaire Réunis, 1973). p. 410.

19. E.g. Eilhart's, l. 2726 ff.

20. Since the episode of the wedding-night substitution does not occur in Béroul's fragment, we are obviously dealing with conjecture here; but the first part of Béroul's extant text agrees so closely with Eilhart's that the conjecture is by no means unreasonable.

21. "When Tristran had heard his mistress speak, he knew that she had noticed [Marc's presence]. He thanks God for it; now he knows that they will extricate themselves from this."

22. "'Alas!' says the king. 'Now I have seen that the dwarf has greatly deceived me. He made me climb this tree; he could not humiliate me more. He gave me to believe a lie about my nephew; I'll make him hang for it.'"

23. "He says in his heart that he now believes his wife and disbelieves the barons of the realm, for they gave him to believe something that he well knows not to be true and that he has found, by testing, to be a lie." Curiously, Marc assumes that only two categories are possible in communication: truth and falsehood. The possibility of an honest mistake seems not to occur to him.

24. "'Queen, I come rather to speak to you and to ask something. Do not hide the truth from me, for I want to know the truth.'"

25. "The king knew well that she had spoken the truth."

26. "'Sir, you were in the pine tree, then?'"

27. "Souef m'en ris" (l. 492). *Rire* may mean either "to laugh" or "to smile" and signify an assortment of states of mind; see my article "Medieval *ris, risus*: A Laughing Matter?", *Medium Aevum* 43 (1974), 87-96.

28. "Ah, God! Who can carry on a love affair for a year or two without revealing it?"

29. "For, in a garden, under a grafted tree, they saw noble Iseut the other day with Tristran, in a situation such as no one ought to accept. And several times they have seen them lying naked in King Marc's bed. For, when the king goes to the forest and Tristran says 'Sir, I'm coming,' he stays behind and enters the bedchamber. There they are together for a long time."

30. "'If anyone went [there] now, he would act foolishly. He [the dwarf] will see it very well, if I go there.'"

31. It seems so not only to Marc and his supporters but also to some modern critics, e.g. Pierre Le Gentil, "La Légende de Tristan vue par Béroul et Thomas: Essai d'interprétation," *Romance Philology* 7 (1953–54), 114, and Pierre Jonin in his otherwise very useful examination of legal matters in *Les Personnages féminins dans les romans français de Tristan au XIIe siècle, étude des influences contemporaines*, pp. 61–73. In her review article of Jonin's book, Rita Lejeune draws our attention to the fact that the evidence is only circumstantial; see *Le Moyen Age* 66 (1960), 147. A probing analysis of the evidence and what can legitimately be made of it is found in Stephen G. Nichols, Jr., "Ethical Criticism and Medieval Literature: *Le Roman de Tristan*," in *Medieval Secular Literature: Four Essays*, ed. William Matthews (U. C. L. A. Center for Medieval and Renaissance Studies Contributions: 1) (Berkeley: University of California Press, 1965), pp. 74–76.

32. "'There is a very clear sign here; you are proven [guilty],' says the king."

33. "The wound bleeds; he does not feel it, for he is too intent on his pleasure."

34. The fact remains that the lovers do fulfill the original prediction of Frocin, who had said that Tristran, if he loved the queen *folement*, would go and speak to her before his departure (ll. 655–62); and Frocin is justified in the eyes of the audience, if not in Marc's.

35. A fascinating examination of some of the signs in Béroul's text (but excluding the sword and the other details of Marc's visit to the lovers in the Morrois) is contained in John Grisby's "L'Empire des signes chez Béroul et Thomas: 'Le sigle est tut neir'," in *Mélanges de langue et littérature du moyen âge et de la renaissance offerts à Charles Foulon*, 2 (*Marche Romane* 30 [1980], 115–25).

36. There is nothing in the text to suggest that Tristran and Iseut make love before falling asleep, as F. Xavier Baron asserts in "Visual Presentation in Béroul's *Tristan*," *Modern Language Quarterly* 33 (1972), 108.

37. T. Hunt makes Marc out to be irresponsible and changeable ("Abelardian Ethics and Béroul's *Tristan*," p. 520); yet Marc abandons his plan of killing the lovers only when he decides, on weighing the visual evidence, that they are *not* lovers: "De fole amor corage n'ont" (l. 2013). There are some judicious observations on Marc's preoccupation with the search for truth (as a pre-condition of administering justice) in Colette-Anne Van Coolput, "Le Roi Marc dans le Tristan de Béroul," *Le Moyen Age* 84 (1978), 35–51.

38. "'Now at last I can be sure; if it [= the accusation] were true, this meeting would not have ended thus. If they loved with a guilty love—they had ample opportunity here—I should have seen them kiss each other. I heard them lament so much! Now I know well that *that* is not in their minds.'"

39. "'Now you know, for a certainty. We had a fine opportunity. If he loved me with a guilty love you would have seen ample sign of it. But, by my faith, you did not see him approach me in the slightest, nor misbehave nor kiss me. It appears quite certain that he did not love me with a disgraceful love. Sir, if you did not see us just now, surely you would not believe us.'" (My translation of the first two verses is postulated on a punctuation different from that in the Ewert edition.)

40. "'We are quite free, he of the possession of my body, I of his.'"

41.   One notes with some astonishment that they are asleep when the forester arrives, and go on sleeping all during the time he hastens to court (two leagues away), has an interview with Marc, waits while the latter arranges to slip away and join him, and subsequently guides him back to the spot—a round trip of about eight miles, some of it through thick woods. Clearly this implies a considerable lapse of time. On the other hand, the sunbeam that touched Iseut's face when they first lay down is still on it when Marc arrives, a circumstance suggesting that a strictly literalistic calculation in this area is not really appropriate.

42.   "Tristran awakens at the cry he hears; he was quite scarlet in the face. He took fright, he jumps to his feet, he takes the sword like an angry man." This, by the way, is a recapitulation of his reaction in the preceding scene, when upon awakening he perceived the (severed) head of one of his enemies: "Tristran s'esvelle, vit la teste, / Saut esfreez, sor piez s'areste" (ll. 1739-40) ["Tristran awakens, saw the head, jumps up frightened, pauses when he is on his feet."] The single differentiating element is the sword; in the first scene it is not near at hand, whereas in the second it is, and Tristran seizes it.

43.   Moshé Lazar is mistaken in stating in *Amour courtois et fin'amors dans la littérature du XIIe siècle* (Paris: Klincksieck, 1964), pp. 153-4, that the sword was placed between them "pour faire croire à Marc qu'ils ont vécu chastement dans la forêt," and that Béroul says that "le roi chassait dans la forêt." According to the text, no one, or almost no one (the place where one of Tristran's enemies was killed by Governal is not really specified), hunts in the Morois; certainly Marc does not. Why, then, should the lovers arrange "toute une mise en scène spectaculaire" on that day of all days? Anthime Fourrier hits the nail squarely on the head: "Pour l'amant traqué de la version commune, il ne s'agit pas d'une préméditation, mais d'une élémentaire précaution: quoi de plus facile, pour un agresseur, que de passer la main sous la feuillée et de subtiliser une épée qu'un dormeur imprévoyant aurait laissée près du pourtout de la hutte? La seule place où Tristan puisse la mettre, et dégaînée, c'est entre Iseut et lui." (*Le Courant réaliste dans le roman courtois en France au moyen-âge*, I [Paris: Nizet, 1960], p. 87).

44.   For Bernard Heller, e.g., it was "une précaution qu'ils ont prise," neglecting to specify what it might have been a precaution against; see "L'Epée symbole et gardienne de chasteté," *Romania*, 35 (1907), 40. Gertrude Schoepperle Loomis called the separating sword "incomprehensible" (and this in regard to the Tristran story in general, not merely Béroul's telling of it); she could only account for it as being "perhaps a fossil of Celtic traditions" (*Tristran and Isolt, a Study of the Sources of the Romance* [Frankfurt and London, 1913; 2nd ed. 1959; rev. ed., New York: Franklin, 1970], 2: 431). Pierre Jonin attributes the presence of the separating sword to "un hasard providentiel" (*Les Personnages féminins*, p. 27); while in *Il "Roman de Tristran" di Béroul* (Turin: Erasmo, 1963, p. 164; English translation, *Béroul's "Romance of Tristran"* [Manchester: Manchester University Press, 1972], p. 115), Alberto Vàrvaro can only term it fortuitous: "la sua posizione appar casuale e involontaria, cosa assai strana se si considera che i due amanti sono abbracciati . . . . " Scholars are happy in being, on the whole, sheltered from the harsher realities of life; this on occasion has its drawbacks, in that it encourages them to seek literary or mythological or philosophical explanations for details that may well be rooted in the conditions of daily life and the universal instinct for survival in a dangerous environment.

45.   Eilhart von Oberg, working presumably from the same (oral or written) version of this material, makes this placement of the sword between the lovers a normal thing from the start of the forest life, whenever they lie down to sleep. He does not distinguish between day and night arrangements, between times when Kurneval is there and times when they are alone together. Eilhart's text has Kurneval unaccountably absent when the lovers are discovered by the forester, although it is early morning. He comments that Tristant's

custom of laying his sword between himself and Ysald is "strange" ("ain fremder manne sinn," "ein vromder manne sinn," l. 4592), a remark suggesting an imperfect grasp of the circumstances; but by making this sleeping arrangement a regular procedure he takes away from the discovery of the lovers in that particular posture any element of abnormality (as well as removing from the sword any symbolic value for the readers). We note, too, that Eilhart's Marke at this time draws no conclusions of any sort from the separating sword. (Later, l. 4865 f., he tells his courtiers how Tristrant and Ysald were lying and swears that Tristrant had not made her his "wife"; see Eilhart von Oberg, *Tristrant*, ed. Danielle Buschinger [Göppingen: Kümmerle, 1976], p. 360 f.) The Berne *Folie* shows Tristan, playing the fool before Marc, referring without comment to the separating sword (l. 196 f.); in the Oxford *Folie* Tristran reminds the queen of their being discovered in the forest, "Mais Deus aveit uvré pur vus, / Quant trovat l'espee entre nus; / E nus rejeümes de loins" (ll. 881-83 — providentially, the sword was between them *and* there was some considerable distance between them. (See *Les Deux Poèmes de la Folie Tristan*, ed. Joseph Bédier [Paris: Firmin-Didot, 1907].) Gottfried von Strassburg (presumably following in this a vanished portion of Thomas's text) gives a significantly varying account: the fugitives hear all day long the sounds of a hunt in the forest and half-expect that Marke will come upon them if they fall asleep; consequently, *on that particular day*, they take care to lie apart and with the sword between them; see for an English translation of Gottfried's *Tristan*, that of A. T. Hatto (Harmondsworth: Penguin, 1960, rpt. 1969), pp. 269-73.

46. "Sub-creation" is borrowed from J. R. R. Tolkien, who uses it in his essay "On Fairy-Stories" (in *Essays Presented to Charles Williams* [Oxford University Press, 1947; rpt. in *Tree and Leaf* [London: Unwin, 1964]).

47. For the motif of the separating sword in European fiction in the eleventh and twelfth centuries, consistently used as an intentional device to ensure chastity, one may consult Helaine Newstead's "Isolt of the White Hands and Tristan's Marriage," *Romance Philology* 19 (1965-6). She notes, of Tristran and Iseut, that "the usual purpose of the separating sword, to perserve chastity, is incompatible with their situation," (p. 158) and terms this element in the Tristran story a "conspicuous if unexplained feature"(p. 159).

48. "He looks at the blade, he does not see the notch; he saw the golden pommel that was at the top; he recognized it as the king's sword."

49. "The queen saw on her finger the ring she had given him; she saw [that] her own ring [had been] taken from her finger. She cried, 'Mercy, sir! The King has found us here.'"

50. "He answers her: 'Madam, it's true. Now we must leave the Morrois, for, to him, we are very guilty. He has my sword; he leaves me his own; he might well have killed us.' 'Indeed, sir, it seems so to me.'"

51. Thomas, *Le Roman de Tristan*, ed. Joseph Bédier (Paris: Firmin-Didot, 1902, 1905), I: 243.

52. "'God!' says the king, 'What may this be? Now that I have seen so much of their way of life, God! I don't know what I should do: kill, or withdraw. Here they have been in the woods for a very long time; I may well believe, if I have any sense, that if they were lovers they wouldn't have any clothes on and there wouldn't be a sword between them. This neighboring would be different.'"

53. One of the most touching expressions of this occurs when Tristran delivers to his uncle's window a letter soliciting a reconciliation. Tristran awakens Marc and in haste identifies himself; as he flees into the night, he is pursued by Marc's voice repeatedly calling him to stay for him, his uncle: "'Por Deu, biaus niés, ton oncle atent!'" (l. 2473) One could also cite the passage, situated before Marc's forest visit, in which Marc gives the outlawed Tristran unstinting praise as a knight (ll. 1469-72).

54. P. Le Gentil's perceptive remarks on the episodic rather than global nature of Béroul's narrative deserve attention ("La Légende de Tristan," p. 111). Nevertheless it is not unreasonable to suppose *some* connection from scene to scene; for in his depiction of his characters, and his attitude toward them, Béroul is highly consistent.

55. "'King, I restore to you the noble Iseut. Never did anyone make so rich a restitution. I see here the men of your land; in their hearing I wish to ask your permission to clear myself and to defend myself in your court [by swearing] that never in all my life have I been in love with her or she with me. They have made you believe a lie. . . .'" One should note that the word *drüerie* normally refers to the kind of love-affair that includes carnal relations.

56. This sets it apart from such equivocations as appear in 32-34 and 57 (quoted above), 407-8, and 2574.

57. This is most likely Lothian; see Ewert, ed., 2, note on l. 2868.

58. ll. 2408-9; 2610. *Frise* probably denotes Dumfries, or Scotland in general. Tristran had already mentioned this to Iseut in l. 2246. For the identification see Ewert, ed., 2, note on l. 2246.

59. The MS is suspect here. As we have them, 2925-26 read "A qant que puis vois a grant joie, / Au roi riche que l'en gerroie." The author's own text may have read "A qant que puis vois en Gavoie," and so corresponded with the barons' earlier recommendation about Tristran, in ll. 2631-32: "Au riche roi aut, en Gavoie, / A qui li rois [escoz] gerroie." Presumably *Gavoie* is Galloway. See Reid, *Commentary*, note on ll. 2925-26.

60. "'I pray you, for God's sake, my dearest friend, that you do not leave this country until you know how the king will be toward me—angry or undecided. I, who am your dear love, beg that when the king has taken me back you will go and take shelter for the night at the home of the forester Orri . . . .'"

61. The episode receives a brilliant analysis in Vàrvaro, *Il Roman de Tristran*, chap. 4, pts. 1 and 2.

62. "Li roi prisié s'en esbahirent, / Et tuit li autre qui le virent" (ll. 3901-2).

63. "'Listen to me, fair Iseut; hear the declaration expected of you: that Tristran has never had for you a vile or dishonorable love, none but that which he was duty-bound to have for his uncle and his uncle's wife.'"

64. "'Lords,' says she, 'Thanks be to God, here I see holy relics. Now hearken to what I swear and what I affirm to the king here present: so help me God and Saint Hilary and these relics and this shrine, and all those that are not here, and all those throughout the world, that never did a man come between my thighs except for the leper who made of himself a beast of burden and carried me over the ford, and my husband King Marc. These two I except from my oath.'" For l. 4203, see Reid, *Commentary*.

65. Not by Béroul; Gottfried's comment runs "Thus it was made manifest and confirmed to all the world that Christ in His great virtue is pliant as a wind-blown sleeve. He falls into place and clings, whichever way you try Him, closely and smoothly, as He is bound to do. He is at the beck of every heart for honest deed or fraud. Be it deadly earnest or a game, He is just as you would have Him" (Hatto translation, p. 248).

66. Vàrvaro, *Il Roman de Tristran*, English translation, "Postscript, 1971," p. 203.

12. Playing Games with Fiction Les Quinze Joyes de Mariage, Il Corbaccio, El Arcipreste de Talabera

Fiction is, semantically speaking, a variant of the lie — *enuntiatio falsa cum voluntate fallendi*, as St. Augustine defines it:[1]

> In that part of the western division of this kingdom which is commonly called Somersetshire there lately lived (and perhaps still lives) a gentleman whose name is Allworthy . . .

No, there never was such a gentleman, nor could this nonexistent gentleman, whose existence is so neatly located in space and in time by this text, develop any interest in the likewise nonexistent Tom Jones, whose coming into existence is "enunciated" a little later, and whose subsequent doings and sayings are described in vivid detail over the following 900 pages or so. Yet Fielding is not a simple liar, for obvious reasons: between him and the reader of his mendacious text there is a tacit understanding, a sort of "social contract" stipulating that he, the storyteller, can tell us events that have not occurred, as if they had, without incurring our blame, for *we* know that *he* knows that *we* know that what he tells us is *fiction*. The understanding is that we will even take pleasure in his enunciation of untruth *cum voluntate fallendi*: between the writer of fiction and his reader there is an elaborate collusion, the reader ardently desiring to be taken in, and the storyteller doing his best to satisfy that desire. This establishes literary fiction as a variant of the *joke*, or as a *game*, according to Thomas Aquinas' elaborations on the basic teachings of St. Augustine.[2]

Fiction is in itself a game, played between the writer and the reader, a game which presupposes that a certain balance is maintained between these two conflicting rules: the reader is to be persuaded to believe in what is being told, and at the same time to be kept aware of the fact that what he is being induced to believe in is not the truth. In the above lines quoted from Fielding, the localization in space and in time contributes to the persuasion side—the name of the worthy gentleman, on the contrary, is a clear signal indicating that the narration is a fabrication, the figment of a mind, *fiction.*

Actually, Fielding's "realistic" opening lines follow a time-honored and apparently ubiquitous pattern. It was used (to mention some random examples) by the Kashmiri Brahmin Somadeva (12th century A.D.) in his Sanskrit *Brhatkathasaritsagara* ("Ocean of the Rivers of the Great Romance"):

> On the banks of the river Godavari lies the kingdom of Pratisthana; and in that kingdom long ago there was a famous king named Trivikramasema, the son of Vikramansena, and Indra's equal in might . . . [3]

And it was used, off the shores of the other end of the Eurasian continent, by Somadeva's contemporary Marie de France, when she wrote her lay about the Nightingale (*Aüstic*) in French:

> En Seint Mallo en la cuntree
> Ot une vile renumee.
> Deus chevalers ilec maneient
> E deus forz maisuns i aveient.

It seems, indeed, that in all the various cultures across the globe, when fictional storytelling emerges from the oral tradition and becomes preserved in writing, the standard practice is to authenticate the trustworthiness of the narration—partly, one might think, as a vestige from the primordial ancestor of playful fiction (seriously truthful narration of events that had actually occurred), and partly because the very situation in which the storytelling takes place is in itself so loaded on the side of disbelief that a hefty antidote is considered necessary at the outset. Nobody is taken in, of course: the ritual words "Once upon a time . . . " have in themselves become a signal indicating that we are going to be taken for a ride. And we go along, willingly. Such is the rule of the game.

The straight game of fiction is played between these two poles: acceptance and nonacceptance, belief and disbelief. The storyteller proves his craftsmanship by maintaining both in a certain equilibrium by the skill with which he navigates between Scylla and Charybdis: if disbelief becomes too strong, the reader may refuse to go along, tossing the book aside unread, with mockery or disgust; if belief becomes too strong, the entire situation changes: fiction is perceived as truth (or as something presented as truth), the text is perceived as a historical document, and the storyteller is no longer appreciated as such. He is seen as a mirror, an inert instrument, a reporter, a historian — or a simpleton.

But within these boundaries of the basic and well-established game, there is the additional possibility of playing games with the game. One of these games-within-the-game — so prestigious in European tradition that it is not perceived as a game at all[4] — consists in heightening the level of verisimilitude in the tale, by telling events that appear convincingly probable in themselves, and by suppressing the signals that could remind the reader that he is in a world of fiction, the cruder ones, such as Fielding's, Stendhal's, or Balzac's chatty side remarks from narrator to reader, or even the more subtle ones that merely might remind the perceptive reader that there *is* a narrator between him and the events. The opposite game consists in making the task of persuasion harder, in stacking the cards against the storyteller by telling tales so improbable ("fantastic") that the reader would want to refuse them, and then of showing the craftsmanship it takes to compel the reader to go along anyway and accept the unacceptable.

Fielding was, technically, a middle-of-the-roader. He had, in his day, on one side the technicians of radical make-believe, who used the potentially very persuasive "novel by letters" or fictional memoirs,[5] and, on the other side people like Swift, who lured their readers into accepting the unacceptable (albeit by means of this particular form of *imitatio* called allegory). Later in the same century Diderot played all kinds of games with fiction: one of his *contes* has as its title *Ceci n'est pas un conte*; his novel *La Religieuse* was not at first *bona fide* fiction, since it was initially a hoax, intended, created, and used as an outright lie, a practical joke victimizing a particular individual (the poor man went out of his way to help the lady in distress, though not as far as Diderot and his mischievous friends had wanted him to); in *Jacques le Fataliste* he alternates teasingly and aggressively between the construction and the de(con)struction of fictional illusion, switching back and forth between passages where he deceives the reader, and passages where he pushes his fictional reader around and mocks him for his credulity.

In the nineteenth century, the literary scene was dominated by a game called "realism," and though not many have believed that Rastignac, Emma Bovary, or Raskolnikov ever existed in flesh and blood, the institution of fiction, as a valid alternative manifestation of reality before the mind, became so strongly established that the terms *mimesis* or *imitatio* were considered inadequate: the realistic novel was more true than those terms could express. (In the process, the word *fiction*, when used about literature, lost its original, derogatory ring, at least in English; it became a neutral technical term, no longer emphasizing, as before, the element of untruth.) This is why avant-garde writers in the mid-twentieth century felt the need to set out on an iconoclastic crusade to undercut, sap, blow up, and demolish the reader's supposedly unsuspecting belief in fiction as an accepted alternative form of reality (*faire concurrence à l'Etat Civil*, as Balzac liked to say). In *Le Nouveau roman*, Jean Ricardou presents a nice graph, showing *la trajectoire folle de tout élément fictif* as pulled between two mutually contradictory dimensions, *l'illusion référentielle* leading into the regions labelled *euphorie du récit* (my "belief"), and *l'illusion littérale* leading into the regions labelled *contestation du récit*: the reader's realization that what he experiences are just words on a page, cannot coexist with his euphoria at living the narrative as if it were live reality, and the hero a person he has really met.[6]

But writers had not waited for Diderot or Borges before they began playing games with the game of fiction. Medieval writers played them too, a rich variety of them. One might suppose that it was much easier for them, as they had not been brought up with the peculiar idea that fiction is *better* if it is presented in earnest as reality. Up until the mid-17th century (and beyond), fiction was enjoyed as fiction, as a lie, as untruth, as an elegant or surprising use of words to create an artificial, enthralling universe. This difference between the attitudes of post-nineteenth-century readers, and the presupposed readers of earlier ages, has led to much misunderstanding of medieval fictional writing, and to many an unjust evaluation of medieval storytellers.

The following pages will consider two sets of texts representing two different types of games played with fiction by medieval writers; one set, consisting of one book, representing the kind of game in which the writer stacks the cards against himself, against the "narrative euphoria"; the other set consisting of two texts which have, in fact, been taken by modern readers to be more or less raw truth, personal confession, simplistic straightforwardness.

II

Les Quinze Joyes de mariage[7] deserves an honorable place in the Hall of Fame for successful literary freaks, together with other more famous notables such as *Aucassin et Nicolete, Gargantua, Jacques le Fataliste*, Michel Butor's *La Modification* and others.[8] What these works have in common is only this, that they are so extraordinary in their form and technique that none of them can be taken as a direct model by other writers who want to practice literary craftsmanship: any later text which shows the same technical characteristics will immediately be denounced as imitation or plagiarism. There are tricks that can be used only once.

But is the *Quinze Joyes* a work of fiction in the modern sense of the word? If we are to believe the signals given by the text itself, it is not. Nevertheless Nicolas de Troyes turned "Joys" 1 and 5 into a *nouvelle* (no 52) in his *Grand Parangon de nouvelles nouvelles* (1535), and Werner Söderhjelm treated the entire collection as a major work in his study of *La Nouvelle française au XVe siècle* (1910), an attitude that has been followed by several other, more recent readers.[9] And the late medieval *nouvelle*, for all its protestations of authenticity, is unquestionably a classical case of the basic game of fiction. Other critics, however, have taken a different stance, the most noteworthy representative of this school of thought being Jean Rychner: in the introduction to his critical edition of the text, far from classifying the "joys" as *nouvelles*, he even declares himself reluctant to accept them as narrative (p. xxiii).

A closer look at the text will explain how these differences of opinion could arise, by showing how this text functions as such. Surely the author would smile in his grave if he could follow the learned debate: it proves that he has been very successful indeed with the particular game he was playing.

The title of the book should have served as an early warning: "The (Seven) Joys of Mary" was a well-established sub-genre of sublimely exalted devotional poetry; "marriage," on the other hand, for all the practical usefulness of the institution, is anything but exalting—in medieval literature it is traditionally seen as grotesque or ridiculous, a standard joke. So the title conveys meaning on two levels: it says what it says at face value, but it says it in a double-faced way which makes us foresee a tongue-in-cheek text, a literary amphibian belonging simultaneously to two incompatible realms.

A long-winded prologue (148 lines) obliterates this fleeting impression of subtlety: the author is obviously a well-meaning bore, scholarly and pedantic, definitely not very intelligent, heavy-handed as a writer. He lets himself get carried away into elaborate and irrelevant digressions (lines 19–54): he repeats himself (*la chartre*, lines 8–17; *la fosse*, lines 60–6; *la nasse*, lines 69–79), and his transitions, when he has gotten too far off his track, are brutally inelegant (lines 55–7[10], line 79, and especially the long key phrase explaining the title, lines 102–23). By the time we reach his final philosophizing about whether or not the sufferings endured in marriage will ease the husband's access to Paradise, considering

that the sufferers seem to like it, we have become convinced that this man
cannot be very bright. His concluding remarks on the uselessness of his
writing would push us over the brink of impatience, were it not for the
final sentence, which makes us prick up our ears, for it is as two-faced as
the title, though in a different way:

> . . . et pour ce en icelles joies demourront tousjours et fineront
> miserablement leurs jours.

This is too good to be true, and in fact we soon discover that the
final sentence had more to it than met the eye immediately. It establishes
a ritual: each of the following fifteen texts is in fact sandwiched between
a ritual beginning: *La (n^e) joie de mariage si est quant* . . . and a no less
ritual conclusion . . . *tousjours et finera miserablement ses jours*. The
stage is set.

La première joie de mariage si est quant . . . The prologue had
spoken of *ceulx qui sont en mariage*; the main texts use the singular *il,
elle*, but that does not mean that they refer to individuals: *le jeune
homme, le pouvre homs,* etc. in the first paragraphs refer to a *type*, to a
paradigmatic young man, not to a particular person. This is clearly sig-
naled in several ways: expressions such as *selon l'estat dont il est* (l. 7), *a
l'aventure* (l. 8), and *souvent* (l. 21) indicate that we are dealing with a
type that has numerous variants. What we are told remains "typical." So
Rychner was right: this is not a narrative, let alone a *nouvelle*. We are
definitely not in the realm of fiction; this claims to be a sociological study.
Consequently it is kept in the present tense, the timeless present used
about general truth: proverbs, laws of nature, and the like.

The next paragraph begins with an *Or* . . . , but that does not
change anything: our writer has merely moved on to the description of a
subsequent phase. It is as though he were lecturing and had projected
another slide on the screen: here the young man is married. But then
something happens:

> Sa femme convient mectre en estat ainxin qu'il appartient et a l'aven-
> ture el avra le cuer bon et goy et avisa l'autre jour a une feste ou el fut
> les autres damoiselles, bourgeoises ou aultres femmes de son estat qui
> estoient abillées a la nouvelle fasson; si appartient bien a elle que elle
> soit abillée comme les aultres.

[30–36]

Six lines, and we are in a different textual universe; seven more lines,
and we will be even further removed from anything we have met so far in
this book. The turning point is, in retrospect, the future tense (*el avra*);
apparently it corresponds with *a l'aventure* (cp. "as likely as not"), but it

is much stronger: "let us assume that." It zooms in on an individual case, and the following *passé simple* (*avisa*), strengthened by the indication of time (*l'autre jour*; not "some days before") conjures up before the reader's mental eye a specific, though nameless woman. The paradigmatic list of possible guests (*ou aultres femmes de son estat*) is not a signal strong enough to neutralize this perception, and the following sentence (in *style indirect libre*) confirms the experience of specificity by taking us into the intimacy of what must be an individual mind.

The focus on an individualized specimen of the class "young wives" naturally leads to an individualization of *le compaignon dont j'ay parlé* (l. 42), almost retroactively (at this point the category of spouses is referred to in the plural, ll. 38-41), and before we know it the text has embarked on a one hundred line long stretch of pure dialogue (ll. 44-142), lively, personal and "mimetic," convincingly "real" to the reader, whose attention is caught and who is now definitely enjoying himself. The professorial narrator has vanished; the timeless present tense, which at first took on the character of a "historical present" (l. 42), becomes the present as used in stage directions: *dist il, fait elle*. We find ourselves carried away in an irresistibly "euphoric" flow of realistic *fiction*.

Not totally, though. The characters have become so vivid that they steal the show, and the narrator (whom two pages earlier we took for a clod) has faded discreetly away, but he is still very much there, not only with his *dist il* and *fait elle:* he keeps watch over his text, and every time one of the spouses mentions a name, he censors it, replacing it with a *tel* (as in *la dame de tel lieu et la femme de tel*, l. 84), which was most definitely not what the characters spoke originally. Thereby he gives a clear and unequivocal signal that we are still in the paradigmatic mode, but we hardly notice it: it is as if the narrator who has set all this going (not as a sorcerer's apprentice; as a master sorcerer himself) is almost ironically demonstrating how powerless even sharp signals become if they go against the overriding "narrative euphoria."

The transition to a second act of the nightly conversations in bed — contrasting the coldly manipulative behavior of the wife (lines 151-6) to the nervously affectionate response of the husband (lines 157-60) — is kept in the future tense. The reference point in time is last night's dialogue, told in the present tense, but we remain in the realm of the inevitable: here, a present tense would have taken on the character of a conventional "historical present," i.e. a perception emphasizing the individual case; in order to maintain the fiction of non-fiction, the aura of universal principle that is to be given to this most specific "scene from private life" (as Balzac would have said) a tense connoting relentless regularity is needed, and the future serves that purpose very adequately.

But as soon as the second dialogue (lines 162–80) has come to an end (and the wife has successfully made her "sting"), the narrative shifts back into an emphatically "paradigmatic" language: there are several examples of the characteristic *a l'aventure* and the like (*aucuneffois*, l. 191), and a very curious sentence which leads on to a subsequent stage of events:

> [the husband] a l'aventure vient prendre le drap et la penne et s'en oblige aux marchans ou emprunte ou engaige dix ou .xx. livres de rente ou porte vendre le vieil joyau d'or ou d'argent qui estoit du temps de son bisaieul, que son pere luy avoit gardé. Et fait tant qu'il vient en sa meson garny de toutes les chouses que la dame lui demandoit . . .

The narration literally fans out over a wide variety of individual possibilities, aligned by means of the conjunction *ou*, — one of them (or rather two) developed into a glimpse of affectionate detail (*le joyau d'or ou d'argent qui . . .*): any decent family will have such an heirloom, treasured as unique and personal, and to which the family will refer using the definite article. But this broadening of the perspective lasts only for a short moment: the story continues on a single track. Yet the effect of the "fanning out" lingers on in the reader's mind: we have been conditioned to experience this single track as running through the lives of an infinite number of families at several social (financial) levels, in the past, in the present, and in the future.

Actually, "the husband" in our "story" did not sell valuables; he borrowed, and the dramatic conclusion of the text, the financial ruin of the family (detailed in the form of a monologue for the wife, ll. 225–35), springs from that fact. When the chain of events has been brought to this point, the narrator takes over completely, reasoning about the situation hereafter in general terms, with address to the reader (*Ne demandés point . . .* , l. 224). But he does not, for that, move back to general terms: at the moment when he might have been expected to talk about married couples in general, in the plural, expounding the universal "moral" of his half-fable, he pointedly continues to say "he" and "she," thereby confirming our impression of having witnessed a single experience, perhaps exemplary but nevertheless individual — i.e., fictional.

It is easy to see why this double-faced text has puzzled twentieth-century readers and prompted them to take very different views of its status as a text. W. Söderhjelm and others after him focused on the fact that a story has been told, a sequence of events involving characterized protagonists and displaying lively, convincing "realism" in the detail (the dialogues). Jean Rychner gives overriding weight to the passages of "paradigmatic" fanning out (*a l'aventure* = "maybe," "as likely as not," and the alternative *ou* passages), and he finds that these ways of writing are incompatible with narrative in general:

> Les événements d'un récit sont nécessairement singuliers et imposent en quelque sorte leur singularité au narrateur, qui n'a plus le choix. Sous l'apparent réalisme et la prétendue soumission à l'objet des *QJ* se cache tout au contraire une très puissante appropriation du réel, que l'auteur plie à sa vérité.
>
> [p. xxiii]

These observations by Rychner are of course perfectly judicious and justified; only he may, so far as I can see, have missed the point. The writer (as distinct from the narrator, the "I" in the text) is definitely not of those who would let the events "impress their singularity upon him"; he is very much in charge, shaping his text as he wants. His characters were not there *before* the text; they are created *in* and *with* the text, and that text has certain characteristics that seem to be very much willed, chosen, crafted. This writer is definitely not a simple-minded automaton; the *narrator* may be, the *writer* is not; he is a joker, and a subtle one, too. His game consists of oscillating back and forth over the borderline between universal truth and specific individual event, alternatively sending signals indicating one and the other of these in such a way that the reader is kept constantly (and delightfully) in doubt as to whether the narrative is of one type or of the other. The result is stylistically extraordinary, a unique performance in the history of fiction, presenting the specific (i.e., fictional) "singularity" of a *novella* with all the general (i.e., non-fictional) trappings of universality.

In one respect, however, I thoroughly agree with Jean Rychner: this is definitely not a *novella*. As a story it may be a "scene from private life" in the sense of Balzac or of Maupassant, a "slice of life" in the naturalistic manner, contemplating the goings-on in human society from the detached vantage point of a biologist who describes human behavior as he would look at the behavior of some strange animal species. (The narrator, and perhaps the writer, actually presents himself, in the Prologue, as a person who has no share in this kind of game — that is, he is "objective," an outsider who has no personal involvement in the phenomena he describes.) But if the story told (for a story has been told, after all) satisfies the nineteenth-century criteria for a short story, it certainly does not meet the prerequisites for a medieval *novella*, which are that the plot has to be something singular, remarkable, striking — "news." Or rather (we are hopelessly entangled in the games played by this mischievous writer), the narrative *is* striking — but linguistically, stylistically, narratively, it is presented as if it were not, as if it were the rule, a law of nature. A non-*novella*, or even an anti-*novella*: a *novella* cannot, by definition, be told in the present tense of universal principle. And *that* is, to the best of my judgment, the point of it: what we are told is a scandal, an outrage, a personal tragedy for the man—excellent material for a *novella*. But it is told in a way which transforms the event into a non-event, which forces us to perceive it as the very texture of normal, ordinary, current, even universal, daily life, the run of the mill. *This* is the game that is being played here, a very subtle game indeed—devilishly subtle.

The following fourteen "Joys" all make use of the same stylistic-technical devices, routinely but in varying proportions. The role of the narrator, telling what happens or reasoning about it, tends to become more predominant in the later texts ("Joys" 8, 10, 12, 13, 14), with the result that they are almost skeleton plots. Perhaps an indication that the writer was getting tired or low on inspiration. In a couple of median "Joys" he pushes his sociological didacticism to the point of formulating general laws, somewhat outrageous "laws":

> Et est toute condition de femme de sa nature telle: quelque mary que el ait, jasoit que el soit bien aise et ne lui fault riens, elle met tourjours son entente a metre son mari en aucun songe ou pencee.
>
> ["Sixièsme Joye," lines 11-15]

> . . . sachez: de quelque condicion qu'elle soit, proude femme ou aultre, il y a une reigle generalle en mariage, que chacune croit et tient que son mary est le plus meschant et le moins puissant au regard de la matere secrete que touz les autres du monde.
>
> ["Septiesme Joye," lines 6-11]

> Et sachés que les hommes font le contraire de ce que dit est, car quelques femmes qu'ilz aient, ilz croient generallement qu'elles soient meilleures que toutes les aultres. Aucuneffois la reigle faut, mes c'est entre aucuns ribaux desesperez et sans raison qui n'ont aucun entendement.
>
> [Ibid., lines 87-92]

The other "deconstructional" traits— the alternatives (*ou . . . ou*) and the recurring *a l'aventure*—appear throughout, but they are by no means evenly distributed over the text: characteristically, they appear either in transitional explanations preparing a lively "scene" (as in the first "Joy"), or in a glimpse in the course of a "scene," as an aside remark or in a minor detail (the narrator cannot be bothered), for instance in the second "Joy" when a cousin or a friend of the wife comes to talk to the husband: *Lors la cousine ou la commere dira: Par Dieu, mon compere ou mon cousin. . . .*

The technique of letting a plot grow out, as it were, of a thicket of alternative possibilities is practiced with particular complexity in the exceptionally long fifth "Joy." The only basic trait needed at the outset is some kind of inequality (rank, age) between the spouses (a digression on how that could have come about, lines 27-42, prefigures the full orchestration of the same theme in the eleventh "Joy"): all other specifics are irrelevant. When the "story" begins, the wife has a lover, and we are invited to witness three independent, separate "scenes" between the spouses in bed: one (lines 67-149) in which she refuses her favors to the husband (she is expecting her lover next day, perhaps for a short but intense visit, perhaps for long, more relaxed enjoyment); a second scene (lines 150-96) describing an intercourse during which the wife is unwilling and grumpy; and a third, similar episode (lines 198-264) in which she is very lively and eagerly participating — because she wants her husband to buy her new clothes (cp. first "Joy"). Then comes the transition to what is going to be the real story: the husband may buy the clothes (and she will use her finery to attract more lovers), or then again, he may not. If he does not, she will "ditch" her lover (who is, *a l'aventure*, young and impecunious) and engage in a long and elaborate comedy in several acts (lines 271-488!) in order to attract a potentially more generous admirer into her bed. In this story (which emerged out of one possible outcome of one out of three parallel scenes in bed), the lead role is played by the chambermaid Jouhanne (the only two characters in the entire book who have names are this girl and her namesake, perhaps her alter ego, in the fifteenth "Joy"), and the intrigue is presented almost entirely in the form of pure dialogue between these two scheming women. Not until a number of frocks have been acquired in this questionable way does the husband reappear in the text: he gets suspicious in line 502, he quarrels bitterly with the wife in line 510, and in line 523 he ends his life in utter misery. . . .

These unusual devices, playfully sabotaging *l'euphorie du récit* at the level of the sentence or the paragraph inside the "Joys" (but promptly swept aside by potent waves of "narrative euphoria"), have their counterpart at the level of the macrostructure of the book: the sequence of "Joys" and the thematic relations between them. The unspecific anonymity of the main protagonists, husband and wife, and the fact that the dialogues between them are written by the same author, more or less in the same style, establishes a sort of identity between *dramatis personae* from one "Joy" to another. But only in the way well-known and easily recognizable comedians can appear in different shows: the "Joys" are not sequels to one another, nor are they independent stories; they are alternative routes starting out from the same typical, joyous homeymoon (with one exception), branching off at different points, but all eventually leading to the same, ritually repeated conclusion: the husband spending the rest of his life in torment and misery. . . .

The first four "Joys" demonstrate this principle clearly. In "Joy" 1 the husband is ruined by the excessive expense in buying finery for the wife; in "Joy" 2 he is not ruined, but the finery turns the head of the woman, who goes to parties and gets seduced; in "Joy" 3 all this is irrelevant (it may have taken place and it may not); the crucial point is that she gets pregnant (charming descriptions of the sollicitous husband caring for her)—what corrupts her here are the mature women who gather around the childbed. "Joys" 4, 6, and to some extent 5 branch off at different points ("Joy" 4 is specific: after six or seven, nine or ten years of marriage; in "Joy" 6 it is stated that the marriage may have gone through all of the above "joys," or some of them, or none): the main topic of these is the woman's humiliating refusal to fullfill her wifely duties, specifically to provide food at unusual hours under special circumstances (pleasant descriptions of the man trying to fix something himself).

A couple of later "Joys" bypass all these phases entirely. In the tragic "Joy" 9, the man has managed to be a respected master of his own house for twenty or thirty years (then he falls ill, and the wife, working together with the oldest son, has him declared of unsound mind and locks him up in isolation); in the equally tragic "Joy" 13 the man is a noble figure who goes on a crusade for lofty motives (when he returns after years of captivity, he finds that his loving wife has remarried); in "Joy" 14 the marriage remains happy and unclouded (but the wife dies and the man makes the mistake of taking a second wife). Some other "Joys" are located on isolated circuits of a different nature; in 12, war comes to the region, and the man has to do military service while at the same time evacuating his family; in 11, the focus is on what precedes the marriage (a girl has become pregnant, and an innocent and naïve, but eligible bystander is trapped by the in-laws into a precipitous and ill-advised marriage). "Joy" 8 is a borderline case: after two, three, or four childbirths (or more or less, line 11) another child is born with such difficulty that the wife vows a pilgrimage (to Notre-Dame du Puy in Auvergne, or to Rocamadour, or to several other places); the non-plot of this non-story merely describes the husband's backbreaking toil as a travel organizer. (They actually do go to Le Puy.)

The remainder of the stories (if, indeed, they are stories: some are, others are not) present more or less conventional tales of adultery, some poorly developed (7, 10), others fully orchestrated. "Joy" 6 looks like a variant of 4 (the wife's refusal to cook), with a variant of the endings of 2, 5, or 7 (the cuckold's jealous rage) grafted onto it. The masterpiece in this somewhat weak group is "Joy" 15 (a relatively early text, placed at the end of the book for the effect?), which starts out at the point where the husband realizes that he is being cuckolded (a situation which can come up in many different ways), and moves into a very long (lines 46–318), very detailed and very specific, exceptionally *fabliau*- or *novella*-like description (in vivid dramatic form) of how the wife, her maid, her mother, her lady-friends, and her confessor in coalition manage to crush the poor man's revolt completely, and reduce him to utter misery.

The implicit claim that stories as specific and individual as the complex maneuvers in "Joys" 11 (the entrapment of the unsuspecting youngster) or 15 are specimens of universal truth is of course outrageous. The same observation applies to the specific dialogues reported, for example in the first "Joy." It is inconceivable that the author should not be aware of this fact, and yet he drones on, keeping up the unacceptable claim that white is black and black is white, by his stylistic techniques at the level of the sentence or the paragraph as well as by his narrative techniques in general and by his overall framework at the level of the macrostructure of the book. We are forced to conclude that he must have known what he was doing: he was playing games with us, the readers, as well as with the literary genres. What he has produced is technically unique, one of the most extraordinarily sophisticated texts in French literature. He is having fun, and so are we.[11]

But even this reassuring conclusion is not allowed to stand unchallenged by this strange writer. In an Epilogue, more well-intentioned, apparently, than stylistically elegant or even understandable, he (assuming that the epilogue and the book are by the same man),[12] states that his intentions have been, at least partly, to write in honor and praise of women! And what is more, he seems to be serious here, not ironical. The problem is that husbands let themselves be cowed (*abestis*, the word had come up several times in the "Joys") and stultified, and the writer (somehow I feel, paradoxically, that it is the writer who speaks here, and not a narrator-mask) has come to the conclusion that this is brought about by *la nature du jeu*. He feels that there may be a remedy for this, but he refuses to put it in writing (some ladies might take offense): ask him personally, and he will explain. It is tempting to assume that he has a "male chauvinist" solution in mind, of the type known as "The Taming of the Shrew," but that would probably be wrong again: in the final lines of the epilogue (lines 48-61, only in three manuscripts) he volunteers the surprising information that he has written his book at the request of *certaines demoiselles*; if they want another book by him, taking a different view, he will be delighted to write on an even better topic: the injustice, grief, and oppression that men, in general, inflict, *par leurs forses et sans raison,* on women, weak, defenseless, and obedient, "without whom they would be unable to live."

III

The author of *Les Quinze Joyes* openly plays the game of telling fiction while emphatically denying that it is fiction, and while undermining in various ways the "belief," or the "euphoria" which narrative fiction normally tries to build up in the reader. The two works that are now to be examined seem — at least to me — to be playing the opposite game, that of creating a fiction that has been made so convincing that it is normally taken to be non-fiction by modern readers to whom the relationship between the writer and his work is not known from extraneous channels of information. In fact, both these works are currently taken by twentieth-century scholars to be outright projections of the writer's self; both are literary works, not historical documents, and so the problem I will raise can be condensed into one simple question: Does the "I" which appears in these texts as the speaking (writing) subject, actually coincide with the "I" of the writer? Or is it a mask, a narrator "I" which is markedly distinct from the "I" of the writer — a fictional character? I will try to argue in favor of the second possibility.

Boccaccio's "opusculum" *Corbaccio*[13] is not one of the author's major achievements, and relatively scant attention has been paid to it by critics, or so it might seem. A suspicious reader of Boccaccio biographies may, in fact, realize that the dark colors most biographers lavish on the picture of the writer's later years have not merely been prescribed by the disappointments he is known to have suffered; the alleged bitterness has a hidden function, which is to explain — i.e., excuse — the foul deed he committed by writing the *Corbaccio*: the man who wrote that awful text is not "our" Boccaccio, the gentle lover of Fiammetta, the brilliant creator of the *Decameron*, the distinguished scholar who was Petrarch's close friend. Something must have changed him.[14]

The text opens, on a solemn note, with the tritest of medieval exordia: he who has something to say should not remain silent; "I," having been favored with a merciful and healing intercession by the Virgin, less than anyone (469: 3). Deeply dejected over a love affair, B (my symbol for the narrator "I") contemplated suicide, but after reasoning with himself (470-73: 4-6) he decided to live, and to spend the evening with his friends. The party turned out to be enjoyable, and the following night B had a remarkable dream. He was walking through a pleasant landscape which, however, gradually turned forbidding and frightening. As he anxiously tried to find his way out, a vaguely familiar human figure, clad in luminous red, approached him (476: 8) and blamed him for being there. At that point, B realizes that it is a ghost, but a friendly one. When B questions him, the ghost explains that the place is called "the Labyrinth of Love," "the enchanted Valley," "the Valley of Sighs and Misery," or more crudely, "Venus' Pigsty." (479: 10). He further explains that he has been sent from Purgatory (his red garment is fire) on a mission inspired by the Virgin in order to save B. After a speech by the ghost against love in general, B is asked to tell his sad story (485: 14). A friend had praised a certain widow, and B fell in love with her; he managed to catch sight of her as she was sitting in a church, and sent her a polite declaration of love. She replied, in neutral but highfaluting terms. He sent a second letter, but before a second reply could arrive, he overheard the lady talk mockingly about him to a certain man, her lover, known as "the second Absalom" because of his vulgar pretention to male beauty. That was the end of that love affair (491: 18).

The ghost points out that a man of B's age (mid-forties) should have known better (492: 19), especially an intellectual, a man of letters (494: 20). Then he goes over the traditional catalogue of women's vices, at length and with vehemence (495-508: 22-30), extolling the nobleness of the male sex as compared to the wretched females (508-11: 30-32). From these general considerations he moves on to specifics, giving an atrocious moral portrait of his wife's vanity, her gluttony, her desperate (but effective) makeup practices, her greed, her lecherousness, etc. (511-30: 32-44), followed by an even more abominable description of her in the nude (face, breasts, belly, intimate parts) when she wakes up in the morning (531-36: 44-47) — a textbook exercise in the description of outrageous, monumental hideousness. Being married to this monster had finally killed him, and the "portrait" goes on to outline her objectionable behavior in widowhood (536-41: 47-50). One final touch: while haunting the house as an unseen ghost, the ex-husband had witnessed a scene where the woman, in bed with her lover, had discussed B and his timid advances in harshly derogatory terms (543: 51). In a long exordium (544-52: 52-58), the ghost exhorts B to realize that there are better things he can do with his life than waste it on an infatuation with "a rattling, withered, unwholesome old woman who is fodder for the dogs rather than for men."

B expresses gratitude for the guidance (552: 58) and accepts the penitence prescribed; he will have masses said for the ex-husband's soul, and he will write against that woman. The sun rises, tracing a luminous path before B's feet, and the ghost disappears. B is lifted out of the valley (559: 62). The next day he discusses the dream with his friends; they interpret it for him and encourage him to write his little work of castigation, waiting for God to strike that awful creature with the ultimate punishment (561: 63).

To many twentieth-century readers of Boccaccio, this is a pamphlet of personal mudslinging, written by a man so incensed that he has lost all decency and all sound judgment. The tale about the infatuation with the widow is taken to be strictly autobiographical,[15] and so the role of the critic is to excuse the author of the *Decameron* for having been so stupid, so thin-skinned, and so gross in his later years. That may well be, yet I am unable, personally, to bend myself to such a view: the gentle, intelligent Boccaccio could not possibly be capable of such behavior. But this question should not be debated on the basis of mere subjective sentiment.

Apart from the author's use of a first-person narrator, two substantial traits can be given as proof for the biographical reading: B had spurned business and had pursued literature instead, "with greater enthusiasm than loftiness of mind" (495: 20), a possible allusion to the *Decameron*; and the lovers, overheard by the ghost, had reason to suggest that B "go back to weeding onions," a possible allusion to Certaldo, Boccaccio's hometown, famous for its onions. The rest of the argumentation for the biographical reading is pure conjecture; based on the emotionality of the text, and perhaps on the singularity of the association between the widow and her "second Absalom." Against the biographical reading can be cited the silliness of the "love story," the inconsistent picture of the widow (she is little known, even to her neighbors, at the beginning of the text, but known to everyone for her sinful ways in the end), the outrageous exaggerations in the "portrait," and the style of the entire text, complicated and pedantic, old-fashioned, different from Boccaccio's usual ways of writing. More specifically, B is said always to have had a particularly fervent devotion for the Virgin—this is why she sends the ghost to his rescue (482: 12)—a significant trait which does not apply to Boccaccio as a person. N. R. Cartier, a firm advocate of the autobiographical reading, nearly admits that there is no proof either way, but feels that he has to "give the author the benefit of the doubt" and to consider that Boccaccio is actually writing about himself.[16] The argument is double-edged: to my judgment, the "benefit of the doubt" would weigh in favor of the hypothesis that Boccaccio was *not* writing about himself.

The reading I am going to suggest is based on the assumption that I have managed to identify that mysteriously attractive old hag, the *corbaccio*, by making use of a clue given in Boccaccio's text. The ghost explains, at the outset (481: 11), that he is in Purgatory expiating the sins of greed for money, and excessive passivity in tolerating the behavior of his wife. That is to say that he is placed somewhere between the fourth and the fifth circles according to Dante's topography, between the end of Canto 18 of the *Purgatorio* (passivity) and the body of Canto 19 (greed). At that precise point Dante (the narrator) has a dream: he sees a hideously ugly woman, whose song nevertheless attracts him irresistibly—the Siren.[17] A sacred female figure (the Virgin ? or merely her deputy?) appears, and to break the spell cast on the dreamer she tears the clothes off the alluring corruptress, thereby revealing her stinking belly. Dante wakes up, horrified. Virgil knows what it was he had seen in his "dream": the age-old witch—*l'antica strega*—who has caused the sins atoned for in the circles into which they are proceeding (greed, profligacy, gluttony, voluptuousness). At the beginning of Canto 18 Virgil had explained what is good, true love; at the beginning of the following canto, the vision of the ambiguous siren, unmasked by divine intercession (the Virgin's?), marks the beginning of the presentations of "bad love" (cp. the *antica lupa* who is cursed by Dante in the beginning of Canto 20).

Boccaccio's entire text is obviously modeled after Dante's, regardless of how one chooses to understand it: the allegorical landscape, the bewildered "I," the insightful but personally doomed predecessor sent as a guide by divine mercy, the solemnly didactic and religious tone. But seen in that perspective, Boccaccio's text can only be a humoristic, lowly counterpart to Dante's sublimity (the solemn tone does not contradict this perception)—the only possible alternative would be to see the *Corbaccio* as painfully inept: if Boccaccio was imitating Dante *seriously*, he would be a literary dunce as well as a morally despicable character. So let us give him "the benefit of the doubt"—he deserves it—and let us assume that his *picciola operetta* is not an act of revenge directed against a particular woman, not even a serious treatise against women in general, but a joke, a parody—not of Dante: of sinister and embittered misogyny.

The first advantage gained by this approach is that our dear Boccaccio is restored to us as we know him, playful, witty, intelligent, and mischievous. The second advantage is that the *Corbaccio* finds its place in what is almost a well-established literary sub-genre, often misjudged in modern times: the humoristic, parodic, allegedly misogynistic *Remedium amoris*, not infrequently cultivated by the very same writers who, elsewhere, write in love of Love. Andreas Capellanus is the classical example of this tradition: the third book of his *De Amore* does not by any means prove that the classical legislator of courtly love had turned into a woman-hater in his old age.[18]

Let us suppose, then, that Boccaccio had a fancy to write a *Reprobatio amoris*, medieval style (i.e., pretending to free the reader from Love in general, not merely from the love of a particular woman, as was the scope in Ovid's *Remedium*), crystallized around the thematic nucleus of the Siren, the *antica strega* who in Dante stands for the negative aspects of love, and that he decided to do it in his own characteristic way, giving it a "realistic" fictional setting, while maintaining the Dantesque touch. He imagines a deeply unhappy (but ridiculously inept) lover who has thrown himself headlong into the folly of an "affair" which resembles *fin amor* (falling in love after having heard about the lady—*la princesse lointaine*), but which is nevertheless a very down-to-earth enterprise— "bourgeois," if you wish. And he constructs a bizarre female figure having the basic contradictory characteristics of Dante's Siren (old and ugly, yet sexy and alluring), but which is also a relatively plausible character within the framework of contemporary Italian city life. He calls her *corbaccio*, "old crow," a peculiar nickname for a real woman, but significant because it retains the element of the Siren's birdshaped nature while reviling her song. . . . Like Dante (the narrator!), the would-be lover finds himself lost in a hostile, allegorical landscape, where he is accosted by a supernatural guide, the counterpart of Virgil, but also of the sacred woman who unmasks the Siren in the dream. And who, indeed, would be better suited for the task of (literally) unmasking an old earthly "siren" than her disenchanted husband? The fiction is in strict accordance with the established stereotypes in the medieval lore of Love.

If one looks at the text in this way, the allegorical-supernatural staging of the *Corbaccio* really becomes very funny. Actually we *have to* look at in it this way: in the text, we never meet that abominable woman; we merely get a description of her as seen by two pairs of male eyes. Nor are the atrociously misogynistic discourses proffered by B; they are put in the mouth of an embittered, defeated husband—a figure which is traditionally ridiculous by essence. Of course it is Boccaccio who has written all this, but when reading him we should not forget that technically he has inserted two masks between himself—the writer of the text—and what is seen and said: the ghost, who is the actual, outspoken, militant hater, and stupid B, who is the narrator reporting the discourses of the ghost. Both are characters in the story, and both have their motives for speaking and writing as they do, motives that are not necessarily those of the actual writer.

What Boccaccio's own motives for writing this story may have been is a matter of conjecture.[19] The autobiographical reading contends that his motive was to pour out the bitterness that is expressed in the ghost's discourses, that he *is* B. My suggestion is that his motive may have been to play a literary game, which ultimately consists of creating the two fictional characters, B and the ghost, oldish and embittered, each telling his story and listening to each other in a fictional setting which ingeniously combines two incompatibles: Dante-like solemnity, and *fabliau*-like, willed platitude. The conception is bizarre and bewildering, to us at least, for it is derived from a form of humor that is unfamiliar to us. But it was common in the Middle Ages: we have just seen something similar at work in *Les Quinze Joyes* (especially in the prologue).

The outcome of it, the text as it stands, is not without a certain resemblance to the *Decameron*; the *Corbaccio* could, in a way, be read as a sort of mini-anti-Decameron: by its "*cornice*," the *Decameron* is the radiant book of good love, of youth; the *Corbaccio* is the sombre book of bad love, of grumpy old age. Yet even B has to laugh at the ghost's caricatural descriptions (516: 35), and even the ghost knows very well what it takes to be an ardent, triumphant, youthful lover (493: 20): all he says is that this is not a game for old people, that B is making a fool of himself.

But does writing about grumpy and ridiculous old men indicate that the writer himself has become a grumpy and ridiculous old man? *Non sequitur.*

IV

From around the year 1500, the title *Il Corbaccio* — meaningful though somewhat obscure in Italian — was Hispanicized into *El Corbacho*[20] — a configuration of letters devoid of meaning in medieval Spanish — and applied to a beloved book from the beginning of the 15th century, a book which has absolutely nothing in common with Boccaccio's *picciola operetta*, technically. The only significance that can be attributed to the apocryphal title "*El Corbacho*" is that it is a reference to *Il Corbaccio*, indicating that this is somehow the counterpart of that, and the only apparent element the two books have in common is the shrill and absolute hostility to lovemaking and to women expressed in both.

As far as form goes, the Spanish *"Corbacho"*[21] is a treatise in three or four parts. Part 1 (38 chapters, 98 pages) describes the havoc love wreaks in people's lives and in the world at large; Part 2 (14 chapters, 78 pages) pictures the abominable immorality of women; Part 3 (10 chapters, 34 pages) presents the four temperaments in general, and especially in their relationship to lovemaking. A Part 4, of a very different nature (4 chapters, 89 pages), is directed against the "common talk of fays, fortune, signs, and planets," that is, against various popular beliefs that incite people to shrug off their personal responsibility for their actions, and lull them into the illusion that they are not masters of their own destiny. The following discussion will almost exclusively refer to the first two parts, the most characteristic and those that have made the book famous.

Famous and influential, at least in the sixteenth century: my brief and objective summary of the contents does not reveal where the power of this book resides. Among modern historians of Spanish literature it is considered an established fact that *"El Corbacho"* is a seminal pioneer work which has introduced popular street language, colorful, vivid, and graphic, into the tradition for writing: *La Celestina* is clearly marked by its influence, and a more remote echo is heard when Sancho and his likes are speaking in *El Quijote*, just to mention two major and often quoted monumental works. *"El Corbacho"* may not be, in itself, a major masterpiece of Spanish literature, but it is respected as an extraordinary stylistic achievement, and beloved by those who find their way to it, because of its festive popular vitality.

Like the *Quinze Joyes*, and like the *Corbaccio*, this Spanish treatise begins with a very solemn prologue, marked by the accents of the most severe Christian faith, inviting the reader to love only God, and to turn his back on all the miseries of the sinful, carnal world. The tone is that of a preacher, and more specifically, as the preacher moves into the substance of his subject, "a pulpit-thumping, roaring, sneering, malicious, lusty, and, with it all, a sincere and immensely energetic denouncer of sin" (Simpson, p. 1).

The voice that rises from these pages is obviously full of its subject, bubbling over with indignation. At first in rhetorical outbursts addressed to the reader (or the listener), then, gradually more and more (especially in Part 2), making use of vivid dialogued scenes to illustrate the reprehensible conduct that mars lives caught in the grip of carnal sins. These dialogues between husbands and wives, or between lovers, bear a remarkable resemblance to those we have heard in *Les Quinze Joyes*. . . .

But as the reader is letting himself be carried—with considerable amusement—on the irrepressible flow of this truculent moralizing, he may be visited by a nagging doubt: is this really to be taken seriously or is it a joke? Is the writer really being himself, using his colorful language to captivate the reader so that a seriously meant message can come across, or is the whole thing a stylistical-rhetorical exercise *meant to* provoke the reaction it unquestionably produces in the modern reader—merriment and laughter? Here again, does the writer stand behind his text personally, expressing his own sincere convictions? Or is the voice heard in the text that of a "narrator," a mask, a fictional character to whom this emotional discourse is subtly attributed? In other words, is *"El Corbacho"* a work of fiction?

The consensus among modern critics is that it is not; even L. B. Simpson, presenting his translation as a humoristic book, considers the author to be "sincere"—unwittingly funny. The question cannot be discussed on the basis of conjecture about human nature; reality constantly defies imagination, and improbable as it may seem, rambling fanatics like this have certainly existed (and still exist).

Yet only a look at the table of contents in *"El Corbacho"* may strengthen the suspicion that this text should not be taken at face value. The first eighteen chapters of Part I are devastating enough: Love is displeasing to God; it causes death, violence and wars; it brings out hatred for parents, kin and friends; it drives people mad; it leads to crime; etc. But then (chapters 19–29) our moralist sets out to prove that love leads to the transgression of the Ten Commandments, one by one, and furthermore (chapters 30–36) that it leads straight to the Seven Deadly Sins, one by one. This is simply too much. But again; how are we to know to what excess—terrifying or ridiculous—a man can be led by ardent fanaticism? Are there other clear signs in the text that could tell us how it should be understood?

There are.

In all the printed editions (but not in the manuscript) the book has an epilogue in the form of an open letter in which the writing subject—"I"—admits to having indulged in *diversas e muchas imaginaciones*. He suggests that anyone who wants to enjoy the love of ladies should burn this book immediately, and then proceeds to recount a dream he has had: thousands of ladies gathered around him, blaming him for having written the book, and punishing him angrily. He wakes up, unhappy, in bed, exclaiming "Woe to him who sleeps alone!"—The final "date" given to the "letter" is couched in astrological terms (Jupiter in the sign of Venus!)—i.e., contradicting Part 4.

Some critics, such as von Richthoven consider this Epilogue to be genuine, written by the author of the book himself, without fully realizing how badly this undercuts the main body of the text.[22] Others, such as Martín de Riquer, consider it to be apocryphal, since the thought and the style are so totally different from what we find in the other parts: it must have been added by the printers in order to soften the objectionable harshness of the main text. But this merely displaces the problem without solving it, for whoever wrote the epilogue clearly assumed that the person who would buy the book might feel offended by its strident anti-feminism: one may ask then who the prospective buyers were, and why they would buy the book at all if its contents shocked them so badly. Mario Penna omits the Epilogue in his edition, but discusses it in his introduction, pp. xlvii-l,, leaning towards it authenticity: what he suggests is to consider it as a joke. A strange kind of joke from the pen of a merciless fanatic!

For my part, I would go the other way around, not only taking the Epilogue to be authentic, but even considering the possibility that it is here, and here alone, that the writer comes close to revealing his true self (as was the case in *Les Quinze Joyes*?). This idea might appear outrageous, were it not for one or two other signs that point in the same direction.

As already mentioned, the nickname of the book, *"El Corbacho,"* is clearly apocryphal: its authentic name is indicated with great care and precision on the first page:

> Libro compuesto por Alfonso Martines de Toledo, Arcipreste de Talavera, en hedat suya de quarenta años. Acabado a quinze de março, año des nascimiento de Nuestro Salvador Jesuchristo de mill e quatrocientos e treynta e ocho años. Syn bautismo, sea por nonbre llamada Arcipreste de Talavera dondequier que fuere levado.[23]

In the following Prologue, Alfonso Martínez de Toledo presents himself as Bachelor of Canon Law, Archpriest of Talavera, and Chaplain of the King of Castile—to which can be added that he was Treasurer of the Cathedral of Toledo, fourth dignitary in rank after the Archbishop himself. So this was no vulgar or unsophisticated fanatic; to the extent that his career can be reconstructed, his ascent through the ecclesiastical ranks to the top was rapid and brilliant. What is strange and remarkable about the title page is that the author (who was Archpriest of Talavera) literally (and almost blasphemously) christens his *book* "The Archpriest of Talavera." The *book* carries the author's own title, but only one of his titles, and (although he was proud of it) not the most prestigious one. The meaning of the title page can only be that the book is play-acting, that in this book the high-ranking church dignitary Martínez de Toledo appears *in the role of* Archpriest of Talavera.

Before we follow this track further, a digression will be helpful. Like other "misogynists" before him (the anonymous author of the *Quinze Joyes*, Boccaccio . . .), Martínez de Toledo draws heavily on the literary tradition. In particular, his dependence on Andreas Capellanus' bk. 3 — *De reprobatione amoris* — is extremely significant. Mario Penna reproduces Andreas' text *in extenso* (pp. 229-39), indicating in the margin where Martínez de Toledo has borrowed from it. The conclusion is obvious: up to the point where he starts out on the Ten Commandments and the Seven Sins, he must have written with Andreas' book under his eyes; on every or every other page there is a borrowing, and these hidden quotations appear in the same order as they appeared in *De reprobatione*! The borrowings from Andreas reappear in Part 3 about female vices,[24] somewhat more scattered (but not much). Again, this impulsive and festive writer is definitely no ordinary, simple-minded, ascetic hothead spontaneously spilling over with his heart's indignation.

So *El Arcipreste de Talavera*, to use its correct name, a book against bad love, is modeled after Andreas Capellanus' *De reprobatione amoris*. If we look around, with this insight in mind, our mental eye will immediately and necessarily fall upon *El Libro de Buen Amor*, written about one hundred years earlier, around 1340, by Juan Ruiz. But as was the case with *"El Corbacho,"* the title *Libro de Buen Amor* is apocryphal, in this case modern, coined by Menéndez Pidal in 1898: in Martínez de Toledo's day it was known as *El Libro del Arcipreste*, or *El Arcipreste de Hita*.

El Arcipreste de Hita is one of the loveliest and most lovable books in European literature, deeply different in spirit, tone, and outlook from what has come to be considered as characteristically Spanish after the times of *los Reyes Catolicos*.[25] It is a capricious, poetic, and multifarious hymn to life, a gentle and playful declaration of love to Love, ranging from bodily love-making, high and low, to the love of God and the love of the Virgin (it contains several poems of the "Joys of Mary" variety).

The identity of the author has long been shrouded in mystery, but recently the veils may have begun to fall. Juan Ruys (or Rodriguez) de Cisneros was no ordinary small-town priest, not any more than Martínez de Toledo was. He was of prestigious nobility, though born out of wedlock (like his five brothers), to a Spanish aristocrat who spent twenty-five years as a prisoner in Muslim Andalucia.[26] Back in Christian Spain, Juan Ruiz enjoyed the personal favor of Popes, Archbishops, and Bishops (several were his next of kin), and, from a relatively early age, held several prestigious positions in the Church: Archdean of Medina del Campo, Canon in Palencia, in Sigüenza, in Burgos, etc. (Interestingly, it has not yet been proved that he was Archpriest of Hita . . .).

A hypothesis begins to take shape: what Alfonso Martínez de Toledo wrote (with Andreas Capellanus' book lying open before him) was originally intended to be a playful and unserious, or downright parodic *Reprobatio amoris*, by "the Archpriest of Talavera," to match the Book of Love, by "the Archpriest of Hita." It can only be a hypothesis, a suggestion, but at least one final fact can be alleged in support of it.[27]

El Libro del Arcipreste, or *El Libro de Buen Amor*, ends on a comically sad note: the Archbishop Gil transmits a decree from the Pope, severely prohibiting any cleric or married man from having a mistress, married or single. The penalty for transgressing the decree will be excommunication. In a long epilogue (twenty strophes of *cuaderna vía*), the Papal pronouncement is brought to the clerics of *Talavera* by their *archpriest*, and the news brings distress to the entire clergy. They all gather in the chapel, under the presidency of the dean, to voice their protest against this unreasonable piece of legislation. They decide to appeal it, as did the minor orders. And that is the end of the book.

So, if there is nothing precise in *El Arcipreste de Talavera* to link it explicitly to *El Arcipreste de Hita*, there is a solid anchoring place in *El Libro de Buen Amor* to which a *Reprobatio amoris*, a subsequent *"Corbacho,"* could be logically attached: listen now, this is what that sinister Archpriest of Talavera must have been like, who came to spoil the pleasures of his flock on that sadly memorable occasion. Together, the two books form a structure comparable to Andreas Capellanus' *De amore libri tres*: two on how to embrace love; one on how to be scared away from love.

V

A few concluding remarks at the end of this meandering itinerary.

The parallel though different analyses of the *Corbaccio* and the *Arcipreste de Talavera* mutually confirm each other. If I am right in my analyses, the two texts have more in common than the strident "antifeminism" they seem to express: they both belong to a same technical type of writing within a similar literary sub-genre. The fact that the contemporary Spanish readers (printers) gave the name of Boccaccio's text to Martínez' text is in itself a strong indication that they perceived the two texts as related in this way — and not as independent outpourings of two men who had in common only a somewhat disgusting bitterness against women.

This consideration can be further generalized. For example, an analysis of the *Lamentationes Matheoli*,[28] a major source for *Les Quinze Joyes*, could very well arrive at a conclusion closely similar to what is proposed here for the Italian and for the Spanish texts. In a general way, it is probably always wise to approach medieval "anti-feminist" writings, of whatever nature they may be, with the idea that, harsh as they may seem, these texts could well be facetious and humoristic, written to provoke laughter. The modern reader will find this tactless and in bad taste (much as he may laugh himself as soon as he hears the word "mother-in-law"), but the modern reader should not refuse to accept what seems to be historical facts: deplorable as it may appear to many (as in fact it did to Christine de Pisan), the very topic of women's nastier sides was apparently a standard joke in the Middle Ages, a joke enjoyed by many women, too, and — what is more — not infrequently indulged in by men who were really fond of women.

My final consideration reaches back to what was discussed in my prologue. The mental heritage (or conditioning) we have all received from nineteenth-century realism, with its respect for authenticity, for sincerity, for "personal inspiration" — and its corollary, the low opinion in which we tend to hold purely formal exercises — leads us astray when we are dealing with medieval texts, and indeed with most texts written before 1800. The medieval writer had no need of mid-twentieth-century experimental writing to teach him that writing merely consists of aligning words on a page, that it is not the sincere confessions of a heart. He did not, normally, see it as his task to be a personal witness about Truth; he understood himself above all as a rhetorician, a conjurer with words, a craftsman.

Per Nykrog
Harvard University

Notes

1. *De Mendacio*, chap. 4: "Nemo autem dubitat mentiri eum qui volens falsum enuntiat causa fallendi: quapropter enuntiationem falsam cum voluntate ad fallendum prolatam manifestum esse mendacium." Cp. chap. 5:" . . . falsum aliquid enutiare cum voluntate fallendi . . ." Similar expressions in *Contra Mendacium*, chap. 12.

2. *Summa Theologiae*, 2a 2ae, Quaest. 110, art. 2: ". . . mendacium jocosum est quod fit causa ludi . . ." and: ". . . mendacium jocosum quod fit placendi cupiditate. . . ." 'It is sinful, but the sin is venial' (art. 4).

3. Somadeva, "Brhatkathasaritsagara," *Tales from Ancient India*, translated from the Sanskrit by J. A. B. van Buitenen (Chicago: University of Chicago Press, 1959, 1973), p. 11.

4. It is on purpose (and partly as a game) that I have quoted Augustine and Thomas Aquinas for their moralistic analysis of the lie, and not the mainstream literary theories stemming from Aristotle. According to those, fiction is justified as *mimesis*, or *imitatio naturae*, for epistemological and didactic purposes (an imaginary model demonstrating how life functions and destinies are shaped). The Aristotelian approach focuses on the relation story / reality; what I want to focus upon is the relationship between storyteller and reader.

5. The *Lettres portugaises* (1669, model for the "novel by letters") are a fiction created by their presumed translator, Guilleragues, but they were taken to be authentic throughout the 18th century. The *Memoirs* of Madame de la Guette (1681) are authentic, but were long considered to be fictional (the author claims to be a close friend of Madame de Sévigné, but there seemed to be no mention of her in the *Letters*; modern critical editions, however, justify the claim: the earlier printed editions had simply cut out all mention of this unimportant lady; see F. R. Freudmann: *The Memoirs of Madame de la Guette, A Study* [Genève: Droz, 1957].)

6. Jean Ricardou: *Le nouveau roman* (Paris: Seuil, 1973), p. 30.

7. *Les .XV. joies de mariage*, ed. Jean Rychner (Genève: Droz, 1963) hereinafter referred to as *"Joies."* On the reception of the text, see Rychner's Introduction, pp. lvii–lix (*Le Succès*). There are four 15th-century manuscripts, one 15th-century printed edition, two 16th-century printed editions, reprinted several times in the 16th and the 17th century, at least two editions from the 18th century, numerous reprints and new editions from the 19th and 20th centuries. An Elizabethan English translation (*The Batchelars Banquet*, 1603), was reprinted, F. P. Wilson ed., (Oxford: Clarendon Press, 1929). The Catalogue of the Bibliothèque Nationale lists the work under *La Salle, Antoine*, who was long assumed to be its author.

Balzac lists *"les Seize Joyes du mariage"* at the origins of the ancestry to his *Physiologie du Mariage* in the preface to the 1830 edition (*Contes drôlatiques précédés de La Comédie humaine*, ed. R. Pierrot, [Paris: Bibliothèque de la Pléiade, 1959], 11: 158). His own work is, of course, much more ambitious and much more complex, but by one of its facets — the ironically harsh tone — the family relationship is undeniable. Balzac's fascination with 15th-and 16th-century storytelling is well known, and he must have enjoyed this specimen; to what extent it actually inspired him to write his *Physiologie* in the way he did is, however, a matter of conjecture.

8. *Aucassin et Nicolete*, this utterly marginal text, looms large in the modern consciousness of 13th-century literature, and justly so: it seems to have been written somewhere around 1220, and *nobody else* at that time (or, indeed, for a long time afterwards) was able to write French prose as this unknown writer did. See also the intriguing article by D. D. R. Owen, *"Aucassin et Nicolette and the Genesis of Candide," Studies on Voltaire and the 18th Century*, 41 (1966), 203-17. *Jacques le Fataliste* should be placed next to *Tristram Shandy*, which set Diderot going on his strange conception — *La Modification* is, and will possibly always remain, the only novel written as "stream of consciousness" referring to the subject as *vous*.

9. E.g. R. Bossuat, who places the text in the chapter on *La Nouvelle* in his *Manuel bibliographique de la littérature française du Moyen Age* (Melun: Libraire d'Argences, 1951). Jens Rasmussen in *La Prose narrative française du XVe siècle* (Copenhagen: Munksgaard, 1958), p. 61 is more cautious in his assessment; what is important to him is the distinction narrative / non-narrative, not the distinction fiction / non-fiction, but he does include the text as a major specimen of narrative prose in his analyses.

10. See Jean Rychner's discussion of this obscure passage, *Joies*, p. 142. In spite of my best efforts, I cannot make sense out of the reading preferred by Rychner; the equally possible reading that he rejects seems preferable to me.

11. As can be seen in Jean Rychner's *Notes* to his edition (*Joies*, pp. 141-69), Jean de Meun's *Roman de la Rose* has been used extensively as a source for ideas in the *Quinze Joyes*. In particular the "story" told by *la vieille*, in hypothetical construction and various verb forms indicating the future, comes quite close to the technique discussed here (ed. E. Langlois [Paris: Firmin-Didot, 1914-24], and ed. D. Poirion. [Paris: Garnier-Flammarion, 1974], ll. 14203-14380).

12. The textual tradition for the epilogue is remarkably complicated, see Jean Rychner's edition, *Joies*, p. 139.

13. Quoted here after Giovanni Boccaccio, *Opere in versi - Corbaccio - Trattatello in Laude di Dante* (etc.), ed. Pier Giorgio Ricci (Milan: R. Ricciardi, 1965), translated as *Boccaccio's Revenge - A Literary Transposition of the Corbaccio (The Old Crow)* by Normand R. Cartier (The Hague: Nijhoff, 1977). Page references in the following are to the Italian edition, followed by the page number in the English version, separated by a semicolon.

14. The autobiographical reading seems to originate in Henri Hauvette 'Il Corbaccio': Une confession de Boccace, *Bulletin italien* 1 (1901), 3-21, rpr. in H. Hauvette, *Etudes sur Boccace (1894-1916)*, ed. C. Pellegrini (Turin: Boltega d'Erasmo, 1968). It was taken up with full force by E. Hutton, *Giovanni Boccaccio, A Biographical Study* (London: J. Lane, 1910), p. 181 ff. and, more recently, by Th. C. Chubb, (*The Life of Giovanni Boccaccio* [New York: Boni, 1930], pp. 184-91 and by N. R. Cartier in his translation quoted above (note 12). P. G. Ricci writes, in his introduction to the volume containing the text, about *una grande crisi psicologica* and of *acerbissime esperienze* (pp. ix-x).

15. Chubb uses the very words of B in the *Corbaccio* to tell the sad story in his *Life of Boccaccio*.

16. Cartier, *Boccaccio's Revenge*, p. ix. On the same page the translator refers to the "deliberately didactic style," and to the "complicated, pedantic style" of the text.

17. Dante Alighieri, *The Divine Comedy*, trans., Ch. Singleton, *Purgatorio* 1. Italian Text and Translation, pp. 200-205 – 2. Commentary, pp. 450-54 (Princeton: Princeton University Press, 1973).

18. Andreas Capellanus: *De Amore libri tres*, ed. E. Trojel, (Copenhagen: 1892), also ed. G. Ruffini (Milan: Guanda, 1980). French translation by Cl. Buridant; *Traité de l'amour courtois*, (Paris: Klinksieck, 1974); English translation by J. J. Parry, *The Art of Courtly Love* (New York: Columbia University Press, 1941, rpr. 1959).

19. As could be expected, Vittore Branca does not accept the crudely autobiographical reading, though he does feel baffled by the text. He sees it as a composite literary work, not directly personal, but marked by a "trace of disappointment, grievously painful for the man of fifty who, despite his religious and spiritual convictions, was not yet able to detach himself from the world and its pleasures." (*Boccaccio: The Man and his Works*, trans. R. Monges [New York: New York University Press, 1976], p. 142. This reading understands Boccaccio's motive in creating the narrator (B) as a kind of satire directed against himself. . . .

20. Modern Spanish *corbacho*, "whip" (cp. French *cravache*) seems to be a more recent word in the language (after 1600); its ultimate origin is Turkish. See J. Corominas and J. A. Pascual: *Diccionario crítico etimológico castellano e hispánico* (Madrid: Gredos, 1980), in which any connection between the medieval book title and the more recent word is emphatically denied.

21. Alfonso Martínez de Toledo, *Arcipreste de Talavera - Corvacho, o Reprobación del amor mundano*, ed. Martín de Riquer (Barcelona: Seleccìones bibliófilas, 1949), or: *Arçipreste de Talavera*, ed. Mario Penna (Turin: Rosenberg and Sellies, 1955 ?). English translation (pts. 1-3) by Lesley B. Simpson, *Little Sermons on Sin - The Archpriest of Talavera* (Berkeley: University of California Press, 1959). The basic scholarly work on sources, background, etc. is Erich von Richthoven, *"Alfonso Martínez de Toledo und sein Arcipreste de Talauera, ein kastilisches Prosawerk des 15. Jahrhunderts," Zeitschrift für Romanishe Philologie* 61 (1941), 417–537. There is one manuscript of the text (dated 1466), four incunabula, and four printed editions from the first half of the 16th century. The title *"El Corbacho"* appears in the second 15th-century printing (1498) and in most of the 16th-century editions as a sort of aside remark in the colophon: . . . *o segund algunos llamado coruacho*. Boccaccio's text had been introduced on the Hispanic peninsula by a Catalan translation (Martín de Riquer, ed., p. 11)—Narcís Franch: *El "Corbatxo" de Giovanni Boccaccio*, ed. F. de B. Moll (Mallorca: Ed. de l'Obra del Diccionarí, 1935).

22. Von Richthoven hypothesizes that the author, having suffered blame from charming ladies, added the postscript at a later date, at a time when his style had become more fluent and elegant than the learned, dry, familiar, and unpolished prose he had written earlier (p. 464, note 1). But if these ladies had taken him seriously, there would hardly have been any basis for a reconciliation (nor would he have wished to reach one, had he been writing in earnest). It is also more than questionable that he should have written the way he did out of mere clumsiness; familiar style in writing is what comes last in a personal development, not first.

23. "This book was composed by Alfonso Martínez de Toledo, Archpriest of Talavera, at the age of forty years. It was completed on the fifteenth day of March, in the year of Our Savior Jesus Christ, 1438. Without the benefit of baptism let it be called, whithersoever it may be borne, "The Archpriest of Talavera." (trans. L. B. Simpson).

24. The parts on the Ten Commandments and on the Seven Sins are, according to von Richthoven (p. 454, note 3), based on the *Compendium theologiae veritatis* (by Albertus Magnus ?). But only for the presentation in chapters and a few quotations: the idea of bringing in love in this connection, and specifically the examples told, are entirely Martínez' own. And a very significant idea it is, too.

25. Juan Ruiz, *Libro de Buen Amor*, edited, with an Introduction and English Paraphrase, by Raymond S. Willis (Princeton: Princeton University Press, 1972). See also the important chapter on this text in Américo Castro, *La Realidad de España* (Mexico: Editorial Porrúa, 1954), *Réalité de l'Espagne, histoire et valeurs* (Paris: Klincksieck 1963).

26. Em. Sáez y J. Trenchs, "Juan Ruiz de Cisneros (1295/96-1351/52 autor del *Buen Amor*," *El Arcipreste de Hita*, Actas del Primer Congreso internacional sobre el Arcipreste de Hita, ed. M. Criado del Val (Barcelona, S.E.R.E.S.A., 1973), pp. 365–68. A strong influence from Islamic culture on the book had been noticed by several scholars, e. g. Américo Castro, *La Realidad de España*. I am indebted to my colleague, Professor Francisco Márquez Villanueva, for orientation in these developments in Juan Ruiz scholarship.

27. The archpriest was a stock character in medieval Spanish humoristic narrative; he is expected to be crude and selfish, harsh on other people's peccadillos and very attentive to his own pleasures. See E. J. Webber: "La Figura autonoma del arcipreste," *El Arcipreste de Hita*, op. cit., note 25, pp. 337-42.

The colophons to the early editions of Martínez de Toledo's book actually state: "Here ends the Book of the Archpriest of Talavera, which deals with vices and virtues and Reprobation of crazy love (*loco amor*), in men as well as in women, according to some called "Corbacho."

28. *Les Lamentations de Matheolus et Le Livre de Leesce de Jean Le Fèvre de Resson*, 2 vols, ed. A. G. van Hamel (Paris: E. Bouillon, 1892–1905). It is a Latin original from the late 13th century, freely adapted into French in the 14th century. On the heavy borrowings from this work in the *Quinze Joyes*, see Jean Rychner's edition, pp. xiii–xiv, especially the notes, pp. 141–69.

The narrator in the *Lamentations* is a priest who had been present at the Synod where a strict prohibition against clergymen's cohabitation with mistresses was decreed. He had nevertheless continued his life with his Peronelle, and it had cost him his status in the clergy. Now he addresses to his former colleagues in the diocesis of Thérouanne (Pas-de-Calais) a long description of his miseries: his poverty, his insufferable wife, women in general, etc. His poem shows obvious and striking borrowings from Ovid. In the conclusion he recants and expresses the wish that he may be allowed to spend eternity together with his dear old Peronelle. The last part of the poem is a series of long, amicable characterizations of a dozen clergymen, all connected with Therouanne. There definitely seems to be a good possibility of reading the Latin original (not the later translation) as a friendly joke written by a Thérouanne priest, "showing off" his scholarship for the amusement of his colleagues and friends. The Latin original does not appear to have reached beyond a close, local circle.

13. The Mediterranean's Three Spiritual Shores: Images of the Self between Christianity and Islam in the Later Middle Ages

When Jean Cocteau was invited to contribute an essay to the German miscellany on autobiography *Formen der Selbstdarstellung*, he replied that everything he wrote was autobiographical. And Salvador Dali, among many, if asked for another self-portrait, could doubtless have asserted that all his painting was as autobiographical as a self-portrait.

Indeed, when we try to understand the nature of autobiography we invariably end up with an elusive genre and a ubiquitous theme, hard to define precisely in literary terms and analyzable in human terms only with the most abstract, even if at times penetrating, generalities.

And yet we are witnessing a fully justified, lively interest in autobiography in recent years, which some specialists date from the first landmark study by a French historian of philosophy, Georges Gusdorf, in that very miscellany *Formen der Selbstdarstellung* I have just cited (1956), and then evolves through other landmark studies such as, first and foremost, Roy Pascal's *Design and Truth in Autobiography* (1960).

Some recent research has rightfully chosen a rather broad context, namely the discovery of the self or self-consciousness — an epistemological, psychological, and anthropological approach that transcends the literary genre without precluding the possibility of fastening on literary and artistic qualities.

We then end up with two distinct yet convergent phenomena: the literary genre of autobiography and the literary emergence of an analysis of the self or of the inner psyche as both a human and a literary event. This twofold purpose is now my subject since, in the course of my studies of this question, I have concluded that the two cannot really be separated.

Traditionally, autobiography has tended to be defined as a subgenre of biography, the notable distinction within the genre being that the subject-object is the self. But we have increasingly come to realize that the identification of autobiography with self-biography is inadequate. For not only have poems, novels, even plays begun to be analyzed autobio-graphically (i.e., for what they have in common with formal autobi-ography), but even in formal autobiography the definition of the self has received a wider connotation than as a historical, objective revelation of a detached "factual" object. Hence the distinction between fact and fic-tion, history and literature, "truth" and "poetry" has somehow broken down, and we have begun to look upon the literariness of the autobi-ographic narrative as though it should be granted the same leeway of "design" (i.e., structure imposed retroactively) as all fictional literature.

This is now the challenge before us: to delimit, define, and distinguish the degree, quality, and peculiarity of this fictional element in auto-biography as distinct from the rest of literature. But this "liberalization" of the autobiographic form, as it were, also works in reverse, by reflecting itself on all literature. If it is true that a work does not have to fit the classic, traditional mold to deserve classification as autobiographical, it is equally true that we are entitled to look even at the most conventional, "imitative," "literary" works of literature for the elements of personal, individual, direct experience they contain—elements which perhaps represent their inner *raison d'être*, the catalyst that made the author write those works and no others. To sum up by looking at it in another way, we can say that there is as high a degree of "fiction" in autobiography as there is autobiography in the most "detached" fiction.

For who would deny that Yeats, Joyce, and Proust—to take three modern authors whose poetic narrative moves on the highest qualitative level—are autobiographical? But if we think of "design" as the a posteri-ori imposition of a pattern on past events (like Augustine and Dante tell-ing us, in the *Confessions* and the *Vita nuova*, how they reached truth through ignorance when they reviewed, from the vantage point of ac-quired truth, their past accomplished progress through ignorance), is this essentially different from the fictional narrator's representation of a sym-bolic action in which the characters acquire meaning because the writer tells their actions while knowing more than they know, since he sees where they are going (where *he* makes them go)?

Insofar as it relates to historiography, (auto)biography is subject to the famous Aristotelian distinction (in the *Poetics*) between the par-ticularity of history and the universality of literature. But not only is the successful autobiographer's self typically invested with an emblematic, programmatic, exemplary value (something he shares with the object of some perceptive biographers); he also shares this feature with the sort of poet who, by an irrepressible "lyrical" disposition, never actually speaks but of himself—take Dante and, even more clearly, Petrarch. Furthermore, such poets are symbolically autobiographical even while they are never "particular," never historically accurate. When a writer describes himself, he almost inevitably draws upon a conventional body of transmitted images, forms, and perceptions. Hence his individual 'I' tends, by the nature of the medium, to become to some degree impersonal, collective, and symbolic, so that we can speak, as has been done, of a "rhetoric of the self-portrait" just as we have a rhetoric of any other literary genre.[1]

Dante and Petrarch professedly speak of themselves within the framework of literary schemata. In the case of Dante, these are the universalistic, theological, and ethical notions drawn by him from as disparate but, in his mind, convergent traditions as those of Virgil, Augustine, the Provençal poets, and Guinizelli (specifically, this latter, for the *donna angelo*). Likewise and yet differently, Petrarch tests his perceptions of the self against classical authorities before expressing them in prose or verse because, as he tells us, of the infinite chain of personal experiences only those that "check out" against recognized *auctores* are worthy of publication (in his own new, "personal" form).

Boccaccio presents a notorious case of the inextricability of fiction and autobiography. Ever since Vincenzo Crescini made the mistake of trying to extract a consistent, continuous autobiographical web from the allusions in Boccaccio's fictional narratives, with especially heavy reliance on the two "novels," the *Filocolo* and the *Fiammetta*, critics have had a field day exploding the myth the author himself had created. For he was a genuine narrator who would look upon himself — or at least his name — as essentially one more character for his stories, so that his birth in Paris from a royal lady, his falling in love with the noble Fiammetta of the Counts of Aquino, his being jilted by her and revenging himself through the *Fiammetta* and the *Corbaccio*, where he would reverse the practical and the sentimental roles — all this was nothing but "fiction," another of his fascinating stories. It is the other way around with his contemporary Petrarch, who was constantly exposing his inner self, though always through the intermediary of "authorized" literary conventions in form and topic, even when dealing with, writing "to" or "about," historical characters (for instance in his *Lives of Illustrious Men*, in his historical anecdotes of the *De Remediis*, in the creation of the character and role of Augustine in the *Secretum*, who is, at the same time, both the historical personage and one side of Petrarch's personality).

Some specialists have stressed this "fictional" and exquisitely literary ingredient in the autobiography. William L. Howarth, "Some Principles of Autobiography" (1974), asserts:

> Autobiography is thus hardly "factual," "unimaginative," or even
> "non-fictional," for it welcomes all the devices of skilled narration and
> observes few of the restrictions — accuracy, impartiality, inclusive-
> ness — imposed upon other forms of historical literature.
>
> [p. 365].

Both Georges Gusdorf and Roy Pascal had noted before that "design" is an essential aspect of autobiography — design meaning the process of interpretation and attribution of "meaning" to external facts. Cf. Gusdorf, "Conditions," in James Olney, ed., *Autobiography*, p. 37:

> This lived unity of attitude and act is not received from the outside;
> certainly events influence us, they sometimes determine us, and they
> always limit us. But the essential themes, the structural designs that
> impose themselves on the complex material of exterior facts are the
> constituent elements of the personality.

Indeed Pascal seized on this term, "design," and displayed it as first principle to be investigated in his authoritative book. Again Gusdorf, in "Conditions," p. 42:

> Moreover, the illusion begins from the moment that the narrative
> CONFERS A MEANING ON THE EVENT.
>
> [Emphasis mine.]

But we must start with some clear and broadly accepted definitions (the most expedient of them probably to be found in Roy Pascal), which will implicitly serve to separate the genre of autobiography from the broader theme of self-discovery. First, autobiography must have a plot, tell a story — the story of a life in the world, hence be dramatic and relate an individual personality, seen from within, to its social outside world. It must then be both social and "private . . . secret . . . intimate" (Pascal, p. 1). And the story must be made up of "concrete experienced reality" of the spiritual identity of the individual (Misch). If the narrative is not self-centered but rather other-centered, it makes not an autobiography but a memoir, and most political autobiographies (and the good ones are rare) belong more to this other group, except when the self, the individual politician, has acted out of a powerful spiritual source or motivation. Such exceptional status marks out, for instance, Gandhi's autobiography (Pascal, p. 7). Look at his titles: *The Story of my Experiments with Truth* and *Satyagraha* (= Soul Force) *in South Africa*.

Since we are dealing with the story of a life, time becomes an essential ingredient. We are then confronted with the relationship between past and present. This distinguishes autobiography from another allied genre or sub-genre of it, namely the diary or personal chronicle. In this respect autobiography is a review of a life from a particular moment in time, with a coherent, retrospective, ex post facto design, and also, although not coextensive with the former, an inner truth or rather sincerity to it — which can be plainly contradictory to outer, objective truth. This covers several possible genres, yet it also excludes several, and especially the diary or journal, which moves through a prolonged chain of moments in time. This latter's message as to the meaning of life cannot, therefore, be planned coherently and intentionally beforehand, as in the autobiography.

"Autobiography is," conclusively, "the shaping of the past. It imposes a pattern on a life, constructs out of it a coherent story." The center is the self, but the world must be present — otherwise we cannot have real communicable experiences along with the unfolding of a dramatic story. This excludes and partly disqualifies true mystical experiences. Yet the world is present, typically, only as the setting against which the personality arises and which forms and determines it. "The coherence of the story," on the other hand, "implies that the writer takes a particular standpoint, the standpoint of the moment at which he reviews his life, and interprets his life from it" (Pascal, p. 9).

Because of the particular manner in which past and present interface in the autobiography, a sort of circularity obtains whereby, as it were, "the beginning is in the end . . . the end in the beginning" (Pascal, p. 12); we get a "subtle penetration of the past by the present" (Pascal, p. 13). We could say that Aristotle's definition of the plot, as something having a beginning, a middle, and an end, acquires a special retrospective dimension, since the progress from beginning to end is still chronologically there, but psychologically it becomes reversed, or at least subjected to an inherent to-and-fro movement that distinguishes the genre.

At the same time, an autobiography "is an artistic failure if . . . its end is assumed from the beginning," for instance if the story of a disabused communist makes us feel the coming disillusionment from the beginning, as in Arthur Koestler's autobiography (Pascal, p. 17).

At this point one can take one further step that virtually bridges the gap between autobiography and all the broader literature of self-consciousness, which encompasses a great deal of lyric poetry and almost any possible form, including the novel. For we must hold firm that an autobiography must decisively include "the meaning an event acquires when viewed in the perspective of a whole life" (Pascal, p. 17), since it lies in the very nature of autobiography that it gives meaning, ex post facto, to the chaotic and potentially absurd sequence of an individual's lifetime sensations and apprehensions of the infinitely unpredictable environmental setting, and every event as selected and narrated by the autobiographer is given a meaning only within his or her whole life story, whose general design is superimposed on the past at the moment of composition—the present. It is easy to see how, aside from this particular, global dimension, the essence of autobiography becomes the finding of *Selbstbesinnung*, consciousness of the self, which can also, and in a sense always is, a fictional, imagined, objectified, and distanced self, like another character created by a narrator, or a lyrical detached self by a poet.

Lest we misunderstand the above insistence on coherence, unity, and design in the self-portrait, we must never forget that the self, and typically the self of a (good) autobiography, is "Protean," like Rembrandt's sixty-two self-portraits, or Dürer's self-representations in different symbolic roles, not like the "shocking" "biographer's" portraits we find appended to autobiographies by the editors (Pascal, p. 18). For those portraits are fixed, timeless, and static, which the autobiographer's self-portrait cannot and must not be.

And to return to Aristotle, once again for his distinction between poetry and history, the autobiographer's history is not particular, but universal, not objective, but imaginary, not realistic, but symbolic. It represents the past not as it was, but as he thinks it was, that is, as it might or should have been from his point of view. For autobiography is memory, hence not reconstruction but interpretation (Pascal, p. 19).

If we now turn back to the first stage or pivot of our definition, the need for privacy or secret intimacy, we see how it clearly spills over into the broader area of self-consciousness beyond the genre, because the way the self emerges in autobiography depends on psychological evolution and discoveries that are not limited to that genre. Montaigne's essays are not, by our definition, an autobiography, since they lack a narrative plot, yet autobiographical they undoubtedly are, and the portraiture of the individual in the novel or in biography—a subgenre of historiography, quite remote from *auto*biography—clearly evolves in a way that reflects the growing and changing consciousness of the intimate, secret self.

We now reach a decisive borderline that determines our characterization of the genre and its broader implications. At this point the question arises: Is autobiography as we know it eternal and universal? The answer has usually been a firm "no." With some qualifications, most specialists seem to agree that autobiography is a western European genre that started with St. Augustine's *Confessions*, hence was tied to the introduction of Christianity. Even though Georg Misch, the most detailed surveyor of the genre, wrote two large volumes on pre-Christian ancient autobiography, he and all others have tended to conclude that true autobiography is a result of the Christian revolution, with its unprecedented focusing on the individual inner man, the soul, as the only value beside God, hence on the need and institutionalized practice of absolute intro-spection, self-examination, and confession. As St. Bonaventure in the thirteenth century was to put it with his memorable formula: *in te ipsum redi; transcende et te ipsum*, the Christian's turning to the self away from the world—*itinerarium in seipsum*—is the first stage of the movement to God—*itinerarium mentis ad Deum*.

If this is so, we are bound to wonder: is there really no true auto-biography outside Christian Europe? Has not the source of Christianity, Judaism, produced autobiography? Perhaps the Book of Job? And does the introspection of the Christian not extend to that immediate offshoot of Christianity, Islam? Would there be anything equivalent to European autobiography in Oriental literature, perhaps through Christian in-fluence, literary, or broadly spiritual, or psychological? If we grant, for example, that Buddhistic or Taoistic total concentration on the pure con-sciousness of the inner self does not qualify for the genre because it also rejects an essential Christian ingredient, the sense of dramatic conversion through experience of evil in the space and time *of the world* (since Chris-tian virtue is not pure, but a continuous dialectic struggle with *the other*, Satan and sin), we may then exclude this vast geographic area from autobiography as a strictly defined genre, but surely we remain with the clear availability of private, intimate self-analysis and psychological analysis at least outside the genre. And some specialists insist that Japan offers very early examples of fine autobiography even before the in-troduction of Buddhism.

But we cannot proceed any further without entering a basic distinc-tion, which descends from a segment of the definition given above. When I said that political autobiography is rare because it tends to fall into reminiscence or memoir, which is other-centered instead of self-centered, I could have added that most ancient, pre-Christian, and later non-Christian autobiography tends to fall precisely into that variety, which is not true autobiography. That is to say, we witness here a sort of paradox. The absolute, God-sanctioned dignity of the Christian soul, slave or master, made it possible to view the story of any Christian conversion as worth telling, which is akin to that modern, western phenomenon of extreme individualism that has produced all forms of virtual or overt narcissism—never before as evident as in our contemporary culture. One the opposite side of the spectrum, while the basic collectivism of pre-Christian and non-Christian civilization made it presumptuous and indis-creet to put the individual ego to the fore, it also gave the leaders that special status of authority whereby they could see themselves as different

and godly, hence deserving to boast of their individual achievements because they enjoyed the exalted status of public concerns.

Most ancient as well as modern non-Christian autobiographies are of
this "political," public kind, more, as we said, like memoirs. But, just as
Georg Misch, without invalidating his basic definition, did not hesitate to
give so much space to them, the self-descriptions of this kind do have a
place in the history of the genre, if one keeps the distinction in mind.

Since it is so clearly part and parcel of autobiography, the question
of individualism is an important one. Aristotle (*Politics*) had observed
that European tribes outside Greece were incapable of organization into
states because the strong individualism of their members could not be
properly and nationally harnessed. On the other hand, oriental populations reduced all their cultural life to that of the state, with no room left
for the free expression of individuality. Only the Greeks were capable of
combining both, the organized life of the state alongside the free expression of individual values—although they refused to form units larger
than was necessary in order to make an examined political life possible.[2]
This evaluation is confirmed, as far as our subject is concerned, by
Georges Gusdorf in the 1956 article where he attributed the rise of autobiography to the change from the collectivism of archaic societies to the
modern sense of individualism. We could say that Aristotle's summary
perception can be applied, *mutatis mutandis*, to the contrast between the
self in autobiographic form of the three shores of the Mediterranean, the
European Christian on the one side, and the African and Asian Islamic
on the other.

This comparison should be instructive for specialists of autobiography, in light of the fact that they have tended to restrict their surveys to
Europe alone, with only a few samplings from other areas—mostly twentieth-century ones, like Gandhi's. Indeed, it is difficult to draw up a list of
accepted texts. Roy Pascal, for instance, in his final bibliography of important autobiographies lists neither Dante's *Vita nuova* nor Vico,
Dostoevsky, Proust, and Karl Gustav Jung, and of non-Europeans lists
only Ssu-Ma-Ch'ien (Se-Ma-Ts'ien), not discussed in the text.

To anticipate my conclusion, let me say that despite the reservations
of most students of the question, I hope to contribute to the demonstration of the cosmopolitan nature of autobiography. Pascal, for example,
has remarked that of all literary genres the autobiography is the least national or regional. My contribution should lie not in this general statement, but rather in showing how it might be applied specifically to a major
non-European area—this being something that is very seldom done. The
only broad attempts I know of are those of James Olney with reference

to third-world literature, mainly black African. Of course one must include North America in western, European literature in this context.

In undertaking the following experiment I am aware of the strong inclination in some quarters toward denying validity to the extension of autobiography not only geographically beyond Europe, but also, and more typically, chronologically toward the remote past. This restrictive attitude is particularly strong in recent French critical speculation on the subject, and has been given a particularly trenchant voice by Philippe Lejeune (strongly opposed by Gusdorf), who denied the possibility of speaking of autobiography before the mid-eighteenth century because individualism, a modern western psychological phenomenon, did not exist before that date. Eloquent as it may sound at first, Lejeune's approach remains unconvincing in its peremptoriness, and historically shallow.[3]

The meaning and value of non-western autobiographies can be realized more fully when we compare and contrast them with parallel western samples. Accordingly, I plan to engage in a sort of Plutarchian exercise in "parallel lives" (*si parva licet*). I shall use four outstanding models from the Islamic world: Avicenna's, al-Ghazāli's, Tamerlane's, and Ibn Khaldûn's autobiographies, which are not mentioned at all in any existing treatment of the subject.[4]

Avicenna or Abu 'Alī al-Husain Ibn-Sīnā (980–1037), found his place in history as the greatest of Arabic physicians, equally renowned as a mathematician and philosopher, whose works continued to be used for centuries even in European universities. A child prodigy who before he was twenty was already regarded as a master teacher, and who spent a vigorous life of adventure and intrigue at various courts, admired, flattered, and feared, he left a brief autobiographic account of his accomplishments that makes us think immediately of the later Abelard's letter on his troubles, the famous *Historia calamitatum*, as well as Petrarch's letter to posterity.

The most personal brush-strokes in his autobiography remind us of Petrarch's own self-portrait as a man who, wholly consumed by a passion for literature, methodically arranged his whole days and much of the nights around his literary activities, but not without a constant and deep concern for the fate of the soul. Similarly, Avicenna tells us, "everytime I was perplexed in a question . . . I went to the Mosque and beseeched the author of everything to unveil to me the difficult and closed meaning. At night I came back home; I lit the lamp in front of me, and I began to read and write. When I was overcome by sleep, I was accustomed to drink a glass of wine which gave me strength. After that I began again to read. Then at the end I fell asleep, and I dreamed about those same questions . . . and thus it happened that for several of them I discovered the solution in sleeping." A wonderful passage indeed, providing a link in the intriguing chain of authorities that lead, without necessary mutual quotation or even influence, through Petrarch down to Machiavelli's celebrated letter to Vettori, where he described his intimate communing with the Roman classics, who courteously and humanely conversed with him through their writings and obligingly answered all his queries when he addressed them in the privacy of his study.

Avicenna then boasts of having mastered "the cycle of the sciences" at the age of eighteen and that he then "possessed it by heart. Now it has ripened in me, but it is always the same science, I have not renewed it since." With this proud consciousness of his unparalleled achievement, he feels alone and lonely, as Abelard and Petrarch also did, especially when the latter spoke of himself as being *velut in confinio duorum populorum*, between two generations of ignorance, both before and ahead of him. Indeed, Avicenna concludes that his autobiographic account describes "what was at that time the forlorn and miserable situation of science." This loneliness of sage and scientific genius was expressed in a poem he quotes, where he had written: "I am not big, but there is no city which contains me; my price is not high, but I am wanting a buyer."[5]

Our second author, al-Ghazāli (1059–1111), was considered Mohammed's greatest disciple, as a teacher and a saint. As with Avicenna, Persian was his native language though they both used mainly Arabic in their writings and lived in various Eastern Mediterranean Arab countries. al-Ghazāli is perhaps best known in the West for his attack on all philosophical systems, a vast work whose title, *The Incoherence of the Philosophers*, occasioned Averroes' famous later counterattack, under the genial title *The Incoherence of Incoherence*. His spiritual autobiography bore the title *The Deliverer from Error*. In it he recounts his spiritual itinerary from the crisis that made him lose his faith in orthodox Islam, then look for answers in the examination of *Kalām*, the orthodox Muslim scholasticism, then move on to *Falsafa*, the Greek-based metaphysical systems, and finally to the peace of mind that he found in *T'lim* or Sufism, the mystical doctrine of those who accept, without criticism, the teaching of an infallible Imâm or divinely inspired sage.

In al-Ghazāli as well as in our next examples one sees how our definitional parameters apply outside the European tradition, even though, especially in the case of al-Ghazāli, the general strictures hold true whereby the mystics are to be regarded as borderline cases insofar as the description of the intuitive union with God tends to transcend the dramatic narrative of personal worldly experiences. This would apply, however, only to the last phase of al-Ghazāli's book, and even then the above objection would be no more disqualifying than in the cases of a Suso (Seuse) or Teresa de Ávila, who nevertheless enter any survey of autobiography better than just marginally. The remainder of al-Ghazāli's book, the bulk of it as it happens, falls into the same class as, say, in this respect, Augustine's retracing of his successive intellectual experiences, from pagan to Christian schools, from heresies to orthodoxy.

The successive phases of the intellectual experience are strikingly similar, both singly and in their order, to the Bonaventuran *itinerarium mentis ad Deum* a medieval European sage could have gone through. We start with an almost Cartesian rationalism *avant la lettre*: "I recognized that certitude is the clear and complete knowledge of things, such knowledge as leaves no room for doubt nor possibility of error and conjecture . . ." (*ULA* 2: 9). No faith will be given to the maker of miracles and a formal stand of antifideism will be taken (10). Next came the realization that nothing enjoys that degree of certitude but sense perceptions and necessary principles (10), and this led to an implicit state of thoroughgoing scepticism which lasted about two months (12). The deliverance came not from "a concatenation of proofs and arguments," but from "the light which God caused to penetrate into my heart" (12). This "light which illuminates all knowledge," what the Christians called Grace, was explained by the Prophet on the verse of the Scriptures: "God opens to Islam the heart of him whom he chooses to direct" (12)—a revelation, as it were, of Augustinian, Lutheran, and Calvinistic predestination.[6]

After examining one by one all the systems of medieval scholastic theology (Mohammedan), and then those of Greek metaphysics, al-Ghazāli turns, finally, to Sufism, where he has the conclusive revelation that the Sufis do hold the answers, through God's election and consequent possession of intuition and truth by means of mystical ecstasy (13, 26). In his own way al-Gazāli shows the relative unity of the Mediterranean area at least through the Judeo-Christian-Islamic traditions.

The third example I have chosen is the amazing autobiography of Tamerlane, or Timur-Lenk, Timur-the-Lame, Marlowe's Tamburlane (1336-1405). The ill-famed Tartar chieftain who, after conquering all western Asia and India overthrew the Turkish Sultan Bajazet in 1402 and threatened Europe as heir to the Turkish empire on eastern European lands, yet spared that continent to turn his fury toward China, like his alleged ancestors Genghis Khan and Kublai Khan, is said to have dictated to his scribes a story of his adventurous life as latter-day Attila or Genghis Khan at the end, or fifth book, of his *Institutes*, an exposition of his policies and methods of conquest and government for the benefit of his heirs.

The story of Timur's original biographies and the parallel question of his autobiography are complex, contradictory, and in part controversial. Some of the texts are in Arabic, others in Persian, like the *Memoirs* or fifth book of the *Institutes*, and some of them are not available in complete printed form except in Arabic, like another text, by Ibn Khaldūn, will be my last example.

The records ordered and left by Timur were first redacted by Nizām al-Dīn Shāmī, a court writer, in the 1404 *Zafar Nāma* 'Book of Victory' in Persian, a sober text, supposedly responding to Timur's own stylistic injunctions. It was then reworked after Timur's death, in 1424, by Sharef-ud-Din (Sharaf al-Dīn 'Alī Yazdī), in a rather florid expanded style under the same title. Two other biographies are extant, but the most interesting is still one more text, an Arabic counterpart of those "official" versions. It was completed in 1435 by Ahmed Ibn 'Arab shāh, an important Arab historian born in Damascus and a deported prisoner of Timur's who reflected the hostile viewpoint of the conquered.

The extensive text of the *Institutes* is a puzzling case because this Persian text was put forward only in the early seventeenth century in India by a certain Abū Tālib al-Husaynī, who presented it as written in Timur's own hand. Arguments to support its authenticity are advanced by some specialists (e.g., Harold Lamb, pp. 311 f.), even though it is rather generally regarded as apocryphal. Even while Timur, though a violent autocrat, was no barbarian, he is unlikely to have left any record in his hand, since he probably did not write (he was severely injured from his youth in his right hand, right elbow, and right leg above the knee). The language, Persian, was one of the three languages he was known to master, along with Mongolic and Turkish (he could not understand Arabic).

The text is, however, interesting and revealing enough to deserve attention and to warrant our taking limited risks with it. At the very least, it deserves a place within our subject as a very clever and well-informed *fictitious* autobiography. The "design" legitimately imposed by the autobiographer on his own subjective self will have been replaced here by an alien interpreter who may have managed to create a willful image that was probably quite close to the one the hero himself might have wanted to project in an authentic autobiography. Be that as it may, the divergences with the versions of the *Zafar Nāma* are notable. Where the *Institutes* present Timur as a merciful and generous minister and ruler, the *Zafar Nāma* does not hesitate to boast of the massacres that struck the horrified imagination of most foreign observers. By contrast, one of his most memorable acts of inhumanity, the massacre of 100,000 Hindus before the battle of Delhi, is not even mentioned, for instance, by 'Arab-shâh, who had an interest in picking up the most unflattering events.

The cruel monster who could have claimed "to set the murderous Machiavel to school" as preposterously and effectively as Shakespeare's Richard III (*Henry VI*, pt. 3),[7] indeed does seem to enact a Machiavellian program in those memoirs by setting down his official record in a deceptive garb of pious, respectable upholder of the true religion of Islam, as a fated instrument of an all-merciful and humane Allah, he who, instead, had been all lion and all fox in the real ways of his violent and destructive conquests.

A western reader might have dismissed it as simply a sort of *Mein Kampf avant la lettre*, a mere act of self-whitewashing and rhetorical propaganda, with the difference that Tamerlane's *Institutes* do not even contain the blunt, brutal statement of true methods, purposes, and goals to be pursued, that dramatize Hitler's disarming "sincerity." But the oriental reader might very well have received that record as an honest, nay Allah-inspired statement of a true warrior of the faith, who did not and should not regard violence against infidels as a form of inhumanity.

In this formal sense Tamerlane's apparent autobiography is some-what like Gandhi's, *mutatis mutandis*. Even if we rejected his religious motivation as an ex post facto design or afterthought, we might assume that he saw his career and achievements, and wanted them remembered, "sincerely," in that light. In this sense it also matches, once again, and again somewhat paradoxically, St. Augustine's. Their lives are the incomparable work of destiny, fate, or God. The difference with Gandhi lies in the difference of their Gods, Gandhi's being a non-personal one: hence God was not working through him, but he was working for a superior truth that was his God.

Some literary genres are ancient, hence grounded in classical theory (the epic, tragedy, comedy), others are modern (take the novel, the novella, and bourgeois drama). The latter are much more elusive and subject to drastic transformations in time and space. Autobiography, for one, is a most unstable genre, that will look different if we start with Augustine, Petrarch, Cellini, Montaigne, or Rousseau; if we do want to take in all these richly disparate models, we will have to envision a drastically changing chain of historical and cultural perspectives.

If some structural features of Tamerlane's "autobiography" show analogy with those of Augustine or al-Ghazāli, others remind us of a Cellini. It is this latter case at the very start, where he recalls some clear portents surrounding his birth and infancy which were taken as signs of future greatness by the family and the sages who were consulted. This allows him to inscribe his story in the book of fate, thus giving his future achievements the sanction of Allah. We read Cellini's similar early feats as an echo of the myths that were learned in school, such as those of Hercules, but their function remains the same.

This divine sanction comes back one final and conclusive time at the end of Tamerlane's book, thus closing the full circle of a God-directed career. Just as St. Augustine conceives his *Confessions* as a hymn to God, who has deigned to perform the stupendous miracle of turning such a wretched, humble pagan creature to Himself and making him His instrument, so does Tamerlane remind his successors, conclusively, that his royal title has been, from the first, Ameer Sahiba Kurraun, meaning Lord of the Conjunction, that is of the planets at his birth, and in the end he wants to be remembered as the Restorer of the Religion of Mohammed. It can indeed be said that he used fully, as Machiavelli would have wanted, the power of religion to prop up his rule, not as a useful occasional aid, but, sincerely, as the very center of a legitimate ruler's calling. He did so without having become a full orthodox convert. Aside from the fact that orthodox Islamic milieus, especially the Egyptian caliphs, always regarded Timur as a heretic and half-pagan, he never doffed the garb of a true Muslim, starting with the turban, and fought as many Muslims as infidels. He also did not hesitate to seek alliances with infidels and even Christians in Europe—something the orthodox Turkish rulers never conceived of at the time. On the other hand in his famous mausoleum in Samarkand, still extant, he wanted to be buried, embalmed (an unMuslim practice), next to but on a lower level than Sayyid-Baraké, the sage he treated as his protector for the coming Last Judgment Day.

To attain his goal he had to sacrifice his private life and tranquillity, choosing a career of toil and sweat for the sake of a godly commonweal. "I shut my eyes to the soft repose which is found in the bed of ease," he says (p. 201), "and to the health which follows tranquillity. From the twelfth year of my age I suffered distresses, combated difficulties, formed enterprises, and vanquished armies." He was, it would appear, an activist through and through, a despiser of peace, a warrior and a conqueror. The self-portrait of the heroic leader is thus achieved.

Is this a medieval crusader or a Renaissance individualistic hero? If we listen to the minutely described stratagems by which he successfully manipulated the rivalry of chieftains and overlords to his own advantage, always appearing as the loyal servant even while he prepared for the ultimate usurpation, we might see the shadow of Cesar Borgia behind the Tartar warlord. But there is no easy way to classify such overwhelming, charismatic personalities in their unscrupulous struggles toward personal success. We can only understand them in the historical contexts of their own cultures, even while the patterns fall under abstract categories. The success of a Tamerlane is more like the story of an Ayatollah than that of a Renaissance prince or a feudal warlord.

We must fall back on that oriental need for, and acceptance of a collectivistic way of life that was defined by Aristotle, which we will call an ethical state, namely a state that, perhaps in the name of a God, is felt as the necessary creator of moral values, a state that is more than the sum of its parts and of its citizens, a state that turns the natural instincts of citizens from potential vices to actual virtues for the benefit of a community. A state, in short, that Machiavelli, though a republican at heart, could understand.

The proud self-praise of a Tamerlane cannot be situated outside the middle-eastern tradition of autocratic rulers who placed themselves, by virtue of the very social system that produced them, on a monumental, super-human pedestal which sanctioned their god-like superiority for all posterity. Autobiographic writings could serve the same purpose as mummification, Egyptian pyramids, Assyrian bas-reliefs, and all kinds of inscriptions or effigies in stone under eastern or Roman rule. Conversely, the official self-praise of an exalted ruler cannot be assimilated to the individualistic self-consciousness of an excellent craftsman, such as a Cellini. The only individual worthy of attention in a collectivistic, autocratic society such as that of medieval Islam could be nothing short of a sultan, an Imâm, a recognized sage, or a prophet, hence even a full-fledged self-portrait as that of Tamerlane does not belong in the same class as that of a Cellini — self-portrait of a humble subject cherished by kings and pontiffs, but always at some distance and with no guarantee on the social plane.

The medieval and Renaissance western autobiography borrows from the epic (ancient and chivalric) and from the medieval hagiographic legend the exemplary image of the hero and the saint, so that the writer strives, only half-consciously, to produce an image of himself wherein his person becomes a paradigmatic *legenda*. The circumstances of Hercules' birth and growth, his achievements or "labors," are combined with the superior moral features of the Christian saint, his isolation and his inner power, and a new personal hero will emerge in a secular, mundane key. This has been discovered in Cellini, for instance, and is akin to the "image" that is "fictionally" attached to Tamerlane's person, with the added translation of the Christian saint into the Muslim sage and leader. But a version of the same ingredients was equally present in Avicenna and al-Ghazāli, in a more spiritual context.

These inherited epic and hagiographic features were part of the craft of fiction in the respective medieval genres, since the "legends," secular or religious in turn yet never exclusively one or the other, did draw on some kind of real events, but only after they had been gradually and somewhat imperceptibly turned into standardized forms to fit the individual character at hand. The outcome is that the mimetic process of representation of reality has become literary "fiction" by merging both outside physical and historical reality and literary models into patterns to be adapted and reproduced in strings of particular texts.

In Islam as well as in ancient or medieval Europe one could have powerful individualities, even an Abelard or a St. Bernard, but Etienne Gilson was wrong in offering them as an argument to deny the Burckhardtian thesis of Renaissance individualism.[8] For individualities, even powerful ones, are everywhere, but individualism is another matter: it is a widespread phenomenon that potentially invests all members of a society, regardless of their status or professional success. Indeed, Cellini's story is not the record of a triumphantly successful artist, but, quite the contrary, the apologia of an individualistic personality who, toward the end of his life, and after having achieved his greatest works, realizes that he has failed to persuade his society of his true greatness, starting with the Medici duke, and wonders, to himself and to his readers, why things have gone wrong.

Nor has Tamerlane's book anything in common with the western autobiographic accounts of the confessional type—a genuine Christian phenomenon impossible in other cultures. St. Augustine institutionalized into a new literary genre the Christian sacrament of confession, and no one but a Christian could do that, even if the Latin word *confessiones* also contained the additional, and even prior meaning of "witnessing"— in praise of God's glory.

Incidentally, it has been said (cf. Georges May, *L'autobiographie*, p. 25) that the Christian element of confession is not necessary to explain western autobiography, because the purely secular confessions à la Rousseau do not address themselves to God but to generations of men. Yet this tends to overlook the pressure of the traditional heritage by focusing on autobiography in the modern, romantic and post-romantic sense.

For one last word on Tamerlane's stunning work (whether his own or not), it does confirm one essential feature of Roy Pascal's definition as seen above. It conspicuously contains an ex post facto "design," clearly superimposed on the chain of prior events. This design is partly, and more than is normally acceptable, a big lie, since that scourge of the earth overlooked the bloodiness and sheer destructiveness of his empire-building. More than that, it repeatedly asserted a basic policy as a secret of his success—a policy that is apparently denied by the record, namely that of being always merciful and clement toward the enemy and of never turning into enemies those who could be friends and allies. Precious little of this is part of the record. As the text puts it, that policy was the Sixth Maxim of his Twelve-Point Program, namely: "Sixth: By justice and equity I gained the affections of mankind; my clemency extended to the guilty as well as to the innocent . . . by benevolence I gained a place in the hearts of men . . . I delivered the oppressed from the hand of the oppressor . . . those who had done me injuries, who had attacked my person, and had counteracted my schemes . . . when they threw themselves on my mercy, I received them with kindness, conferred on them additional honors, drew the pen of oblivion over their actions. . . ." And again under Maxim Eight: ". . . cruelty and oppression, which are the destroyers of posterity, and the parents of famine and of plagues, I cautiously shunned" (201–203). One can safely speculate that, had Hitler won his war, his dutiful successors would have presented such an image of him through their propaganda machine.

The truth of the matter is that by his own account Tamerlane never felt any loyalty to anyone but himself, and all his life schemed and intrigued in order to advance his own chances to get to the top by taking advantage of the weakness of his superiors. The most involved situation and his decisive chance occurred in the year of Hegyra 758, when he was twenty-two. Faced with the alternative of siding with his trusting Sultan, Amyr Kurgen, or with the league of chieftains in revolt against the Amyr, he chose the former course, not out of loyalty or righteousness, but, as he says candidly, "having reflected that it would be much easier at some future time to dispossess one person, than to have to contend with ten rivals" (p. 194). All this and much more he relates not in order to show what a clever Machiavellian knave he really was, but that he was the only man in the realm who deserved first place by implicit inherent right.

The fourth and last Islamic text I wish to discuss is connected, in part, with that of Tamerlane. I mean Ibn Khaldūn's autobiography, whose first chapters appeared as the last chapters of his monumental *Kitâb al-'Ibar*, a history of the Islamic world, and was later continued and completed in what can be a separate autobiographic work, published after World War II both in Arabic and by Walter Fischel in an English translation.[9]

Ibn Khaldūn (Tunis 1332 – Cairo 1406) is celebrated as the greatest African Muslim historian, and his autobiography also relates, as one of the salient events in his later life, his journey from Cairo to Damascus in 1401, to accompany the Mamlūk Sultan al-Nāsir on a campaign against Tamerlane, who was laying siege to the Syrian capital and within a few months would manage to capture it and sack it. Under circumstances that are left unclear Ibn Khaldūn left besieged Damascus for a meeting with Tamerlane in his royal tent. The conversations are described in great detail, even though in probably incomplete form. The two hit it off so well that such visits to the royal tent went on over a period of perhaps a month and a half on as many as perhaps 35 different occasions (Fischel, p. 113), after which, Damascus having fallen in the meantime, Ibn Khaldūn took his leave from the Mongol lord still on very friendly terms, and returned to Cairo.

The most striking and historically valuable aspect of this account is a confirmation of what is recorded in other sources, namely Tamerlane's high respect for intellectuals, sages, and saintly personages, which contrasts with his scorn for the popular masses. In the repeated massacres of his military career he was reputed to have ordered the separation of such scholarly types from the populace, this latter being destined to mass slaughter, soldiers first. This respect for the intelligentsia seems surprising, odd, and contradictory to some historians of Timur, but they don't seem to take into account that it was a Mongolic tradition. Genghis Khan is known to have displayed the same kind of respect, preserving the intelligentsia of the vanquished and decimated populations. Rather than a degree of intellectualism, it may be all-embracing superstitiousness. Concomitantly, Ibn Khaldūn's account reveals the famous scholar's pride and trust in his ability and right to deal with the powerful, even the most violent and untrustworthy, if not on an equal footing as a Michelangelo or a Cellini would have expected, at least on friendly terms of mutual respect, interest, and admiration.

I should now like to conclude by drawing some general inferences with regard to autobiographic performances as a whole not only on the literary, aesthetic, or artistic plane, but on the anthropological one as well. For Gusdorf ("Conditions") the last critical phase in our analysis of autobiography ought to be, precisely, a consideration of its anthropological significance. Beyond the positivistic fallacy of searching for factual accuracy, and the literary-minded reader's search for artistic coherence, we find in a true autobiography a symbol of an externalized consciousness, the creation of the self by the self. Thus, for example, as I should like to interpret it, Cellini does not produce the individualistic artist of the Renaissance, he searches for one, and produces the picture of a failure in crime. The way he looks at himself as in a mirror toward the end of his life is a questioning pose: Why, he wonders, is a true artist in an artists' age not recognized by his society and its leaders when he has produced his highest and most enduring accomplishments? God must be on his side, but what mistakes has he made as a man if not as an artist? Perhaps the world will listen to his story and find him, in the end, a good man, forgive him for his faults, recognize him and accept him at long last. But the question, in the end, leaves him a saddened observer of his own portrait.[10]

Somewhat analogously, I submit, the propagandistic self-portrait offered by Tamerlane (perhaps through the mediation of his immediate successors or ministers) is an act of externalized consciousness, a creation of the self by the self at the moment of his life when he was, at long last, ready to look back on his career and eager to make a coherent, meaningful story of it, out of a hectic, chaotic succession of sound and fury that meant perhaps nothing but strong stuff in a power play. Without that autobiography and the parallel biographies Tamerlane would not have been a real person, either for us, or perhaps even for his own people, since the record of his deeds and the results of his conquests were largely lost in an almost complete disintegration of an empire built on nothing, apparently, but force, violence, cruelty, and short-term personal charisma. The verdict of history — political, social, and institutional history — is that of an accomplishment as barren as the deserts he treaded on. But the portrait of the autobiography presents us with a person, a human being we can understand, analyze, and evaluate, the being he probably wanted to see in himself and wanted others to see in him. This, and it is no small matter, may be the durable "anthropological" meaning and value of that "autobiography," as that of many another.

Supposing we have no reason to believe that any of the facts reported in the *Mulfuzat Timury* is false, we might still raise the question as to whether the book is not, historically speaking, a lie, since the image of the protagonist may be, in the end, a fabrication (whether or not of Timur's own will). And this question can be repeated for any autobiography. This means that a story has been made by selecting certain facts, arranging them according to a given end, with the addition of particular interpretations — which is the "story" of any autobiographic "fiction."

Aldo Scaglione
University of North Carolina

𝔑𝔬𝔱𝔢𝔰

1. Cf. Michel Beaujour, *Miroirs d'encre: Rhétorique de l'autoportrait*, passim.

2. Cf. Henry Paolucci, *A Brief History of Political Thought and Statecraft* (Whitestone, N.Y.: Griffon House Publications, 1979), pp. 10–15. See Aristotle, *Politics*, trans. T. A. Sinclair (Baltimore, Md: Penquin Books, 1962), bk. 7, chap. 7, p. 269.

3. See Lejeune, "Autobiographie et histoire littéraire," in *Le Pacte autobiographique*, pp. 311–41 and in *Revue d'histoire littéraire de la France* (1975), with approving reference,

p. 315, to Paul Zumthor, *Essai de poétique médiévale* (Paris: Seuil, 1972), pp. 68–69 and 172–74, "Autobiographie au Moyen Age?", *Langue, Texte, Enigme* (Paris: Seuil, 1974). But see G. Gusdorf's strong demurrers in the debate following Lejeune's paper, pp. 931–36, with Lejeune's self-defense. For Gusdorf, "l'autobiographie c'est la littérature de la première personne," and it will not do to deny the existence of autobiography in the Middle Ages on the ground that there was "no individuality" in that age. At least for Gusdorf (and many others), there was.

4. The texts of Avicenna, al-Ghazāli, and Tamerlane are conveniently available in vol. 2 of the *University Library of Autobiography*, hereafter referred to as *ULA*. My quotations of these texts are from this anthology. Tamerlane's text in *ULA* is from Stewart's translation of the *Mulfuzat Timury*.

One of the most authoritative Arabists, Gustav von Grünebaum, deals with lyric, autobiography, and biography in chap. 8, "Self-Expression: Literature and History" of his *Medieval Islam: A Study in Cultural Orientation* (Chicago: University of Chicago Press, 1962), which mentions neither Avicenna nor Tamerlane, and al-Ghazāli only briefly together with Ibn al-Haitham (d. ca. 1039). He also mentions the Egyptian physician 'Alī b. Ridwān (d. 1061), Ibn al-Muqaffa' (d. 757) as translator of the autobiography of the Sassanian physician Burzōē, and Nāsir-i Khusraw (d. 1088), besides al-Muhasībī. Ridwān professes to represent the true follower of Hippocrates: his work may be assimilated to the tradition of Galen's (d. ca. 200) letter on his life and correct sequence of listed works. Khusraw tells the story of his reform and conversion. Al-Haitham and al-Ghazāli seem to be in the line of Augustine, although the former does not find his mental peace in religion but in Aristotelianism and Galenic science. Al-Muhāsibī, Ibn al-Haitham, al-Ghazāli, and similar intellectual, mystical, or ascetic autobiographers differ from their European counterparts in that they concentrate more on the self and exclude all characterization of their contemporaries. Their works are more like confessional monologues.

If one goes further chronologically one can reach the interesting case of 'Abd al-Wahhāb al-Sha'rānī (d. 1565), whose autobiography *Lata'ifu 'l-Minan* "is a record of the singular spiritual gifts and virtues with which he was endowed, and would rank as a masterpiece of shameless self-laudation, did not the author repeatedly assure us that all his extraordinary qualities are divine blessings and are gratefully set forth by their recipient *ad majorem Dei gloriam*." Cf. Reynold A. Nicholson, *A Literary History of the Arabs* (Cambridge: Cambridge University Press, 1956 [1907¹]), p. 465. One might want to think, once again *mutatis mutandis*, of Augustine's predicament.

5. On Avicenna, see F. Rosenthal, "Die arabische Autobiographie," 24 f. For text of quotations, cf. *ULA* 2: 3–5.

6. The comparison with Augustine has been made by Arabists: cf. F. Rosenthal, "Die arabische Autobiographie," pp. 12–15 on al-Ghazāli, esp. fn. 15, with reference to H. Frick, *Ghazâlis Selbstbiographie*. The conclusion is that the differences remain more meaningful than the similarities, especially on the level of the revelations of the inner personality. Also citing G. Misch, 1. 2: 410 ff., 456 ff.

For a translation of al-Ghazāli's basic theology in the text of the "Jerusalem Credo" see R. Gramlich, "Muhammad al-Gazzâlîs [. . .] Fundamentaldogmatik," *Saeculum* (1980), and for a recent analysis of some of his theology, M. S. Stern, "Notes on the Theology [. . .]," *Islamic Quarterly* (1979).

7. Act III, sc. ii, where Richard is speaking as Gloucester. See *The Complete Works of W. Shakespeare*, ed. W.J. Craig (Oxford: Oxford University Press, 1943), p. 581.

8. See my discussion of Gilson's position on this question in my *Nature and Love in the Late Middle Ages* (Berkeley: University of California Press, 1963; Westport, Conn.: Greenwood Press, 1976), pp. 23–32.

9. Part of it in W. J. Fischel, *Ibn Khaldûn and Tamerlane*. An intriguing text in the tradition of the Mongol rulers can be read in the *Bābur-nāma* (Memoirs of Babur), transl. Annette Susannah Beveridge. More memoirs than autobiography of the famous ruler of Transoxiana and Hindustan, extraordinarily detailed in reporting on battles, movements, adventures, family ties, and all sorts of personal acquaintances, it is the record of a highly literate and artistically-minded statesman.

10. On the "mirror," see Jacques Lacan, "Les stades du miroir comme formateur de la fonction du Je," *Revue française de psychanalyse* 4 (1949), elaborating on the role of the mirror for the child's gradual process of evolving self-consciousness. Gusdorf referred to Lacan and noted the fact that autobiography would have predated the mirror (but the mirror is really more ancient than the sophisticated devices especially studied by Lacan).

References

Bābur-nāma (Memoirs of Babur), translated from the original Turki Text of Zahiru'd-dîn Muhammad Bābur Pādshāh Ghāzî by Annette Susannah Beveridge. 2 vols. New Delhi: Oriental Books Reprint Corp., 1970 (reprt. of 1922 ed.).

Barbier de Meynard, Charles Adrien Casimir. Transl. of al-Ghazāli, *Munkid min ad-dalâl*. *Journal Asiatique*, 7e Série, 9 (1877): 3–93.

Beaujour, Michel. *Miroirs d'encre: Rhétorique de l'autoportrait*. Paris: Seuil, 1980.

Bruss, Elizabeth. "L'autobiographie considérée comme acte littéraire." *Poétique* 17 (1974), 14–26.

Butler, Lord. *The Difficult Art of Autobiography*. Oxford: Clarendon Press, 1968.

Fischel, Walter J. *Ibn Khaldūn and Tamerlane*. Berkeley: University of California Press, 1952.

Fragner, Bert G. *Persische Memoirenliteratur als Quelle zur neueren Geschichte Irans*. Wiesbaden: Steiner, 1979. See Einleitung.

Frick, Heinrich. *Ghazalis Selbstbiographie. Ein Vergleich mit Augustins Confessionen*. Veröffentlichungen des Forschungsinstituts f. vergl. Religionsgeschichte an d. Universität Leipzig, 3. Leipzig: J. C. Hinrichs, 1919.

Goldberg, Jonathan. "Cellini's *Vita* and the Conventions of Early Autobiography." *Modern Language Notes* 89 (1974), 71–83.

Gramlich, Richard. "Muhammad al-Ghazzalis kleine islamische Fundamentaldogmatik." *Saeculum* 31 (1980), 380–98.

Grünebaum, Gustav E. von. *Medieval Islam: A Study in Cultural Orientation*. Chicago: University of Chicago Press, 1946, 1953, 1961; Phoenix ed., 1962. See chap. 8: "Self-Expression."

Gusdorf, Georges. "De l'autobiographie initiatique à l'autobiographie genre littéraire." *Revue d'histoire littéraire* 75 (1975), 957–94.

Gusdorf, Georges. "Conditions and Limits of Autobiography." Trans. James Olney. In *Autobiography: Essays Theoretical and Critical*. Ed. James Olney. Princeton: Princeton University Press, 1980. Pp. 28–48.

Howarth, William. "Some Principles of Autobiography." *New Literary History* 5 (1974), 363–81.

Ibn 'Arabshah, Ahmad ibn Muhammad. *Tamerlane, or Timur, the Great Amir*, trans. J. H. Sanders from the Arabic Life by Ahmed ibn 'Arabshah. London: Luzac, 1936.

Lamb, Harold. *Tamerlane*. Garden City, N.Y.: Garden City Publ. Co., 1928.

Lejeune, Philippe. "Autobiographie et histoire littéraire." In *Le Pacte autobiographique*.

Paris: Seuil, 1975, pp. 311-41, and in *Revue d'histoire littéraire de la France* 75 (1975), 903-930.

Mandel, Barrett J. "The Autobiographer's Art." *Journal of Aesthetics and Art Criticism* 27 (1968), 215-26.

May, Georges C. *L'Autobiographie*. Paris: Presses Universitaires de France, 1979.

Misch, Georg. *Geschichte der Autobiographie*. vol. 3, pt. 2, 2nd half. Bern: Francke, 1949. Pp. 905-1076.

Muhammad Abul Quasem. "Al-Ghazali's Theory of Devotional Acts." *Islamic Quarterly* 18, 3/4 (1974), 48-61.

Nicholson, Reynold A. *A Literary History of the Arabs*. Cambridge: Cambridge University Press, 1956 [1907¹].

Nizam al-Din Shami. [. . .] *Histoire des conquêtes de Tamerlan, intitulée Zafarnama*. Ed. Felix Trauer. Monografie Archivu Orientalniho, 3. Prague: 1937.

Olney, James. "Autobiography and the Cultural Moment: A Thematic, Historical, and Bibliographical Introduction." In *Autobiography: Essays Theoretical and Critical*. Ed. James Olney. Princeton: Princeton University Press, 1980. Pp. 3-27.

Olney, James. *Metaphors of Self: The Meaning of Autobiography*. Princeton: Princeton University Press, 1972.

Pascal, Roy. *Design and Truth in Autobiography*. Cambridge: Harvard University Press, 1960.

Reichenkron, Günter and Erich Haase. *Formen der Selbstdarstellung. Analekten zu einer Geschichte des literarischen Selbstportriats. Festgabe f. Fritz Neubert*. Berlin: Duncker & Hunblot, 1956.

Renza, Louis A. "The Veto of the Imagination: A Theory of Autobiography." In *Autobiography* etc., ed. J. Olney, pp. 268-95.

Rosenthal, Franz. "Die arabische Autobiographie." In F. Rosenthal, G. von Grünebaum, and W. J. Fischel, eds., *Studia Arabica* 1. Rome: Pontificium Institutum Biblicum, 1937. Pp. 1-40.

Rosenthal, Franz. *A History of Muslim Historiography*. Leiden: Brill, 1952. Pp. 151 ff.

Scholes, Robert, and Robert Kellogg. *The Nature of Narrative*. Oxford: Oxford University Press, 1966.

Sellheim, Rudolf. "Gedanken zur Autobiographie im islamischen Mittelalter." (19. Deutsche Orientalistentag in Freiburg.) *Zeitschrift der deutschen morgenländischen Gesellschaft*, Supplement 3, 1 (975), 607-612.

Shapiro, Stephen A." The Dark Continent of Literature: Autobiography." *Comparative Literature Studies* 5 (1968): 421-54.

Sharaf al-Din 'Ali Yazdi. Trans. F. Petis de la Croix, *Histoire de Timur-Bec*. Trans. F. Petis de la Croix. 4 vols. Paris: R. M. d'Espilly, 1722. Eng. ed. *The History of Timur-Bec* . . . Trans J. D. Darby. London: for J. Darby, 1723, 2 vols.

Spengemann, William C. *The Forms of Autobiography: Episodes in the History of a Literary Genre*. New Haven: Yale University Press, 1980.

Stern, M. S. "Notes on the Theology of al-Ghazzali's Concept of Repentance." *Islamic Quarterly* 23 (1979): 82-98.

Timur, *The Mulfuzat Timury, or Autobiographical Memoirs of the Moghul Emperor Timur*. Trans. Charles Stewart. London: J. Murray, 1830.

Unversity Library of Autobiography (The) [15 vols.]; 2: *The Middle Ages and Their Autobiographers*, with an Introduction by Charles J. Bushnell. [n.p.] National Alumni, 1927.

14. The Character of Character in the Chansons de Geste

The relationship between character and plot confronts the literary critic with a chicken and egg problem of ostrich proportions. How far can we dissociate what a literary character is from what he does, and supposing such dissociation to be operable, which is the proper, primary level of description in any text? Should we say, for instance, that Othello is a character liable to violent jealousy, and so can be set up to kill his ever-loving wife, or do we say that the killing of an unjustly suspected wife leads us to perceive her murderous husband as violently jealous? Do texts differ in this regard? As with Shakespeare plays, some *chansons de geste* are assigned titles featuring a principal character (*Chanson de Roland, Aiol, Gaydon, Chanson de Willame*), others an aspect of the action (*Charroi de Nîmes, Prise d'Orange, Siège de Barbastre, Aliscans*). The prologues of some, like the *Couronnement de Louis*, announce the matter that is to follow as centered primarily on character:

> De Looÿs ne lerai ne vos chant
> Et de Guillelme au cort nes le vaillant,
> Qui tant soffri sor Sarrazine gent;
> De meillor home ne quit que nus vos chant.
>
> [7-10]¹

Others, of which *Girart de Roussillon* is an example, summarize part of the plot:

> Ceste muet de Folcon e de Folchui,
> Et de Girart le conte la vos revui,
> Quant prestrent guere a Charle el e li sui,
> Per quant sunt espandut de sanc mil mui.
>
> [12-15]

Critics of medieval literature writing in a traditional idiom have explored the *chansons de geste* both with an assumption of the primacy of plot, and from the point of view of character; their choice reflects their generation. Among the more senior, this judgement on the *Roland* by

475

Edmond Faral has been much (if incorrectly) cited: "Les idées [. . .] constituent le principe vital de [la *Chanson*], [. . .] mais ce que ces idées ont, à l'application, de force poétique et de beauté morale, c'est dans l'âme des personnages qu'il faut le chercher."[2] This passage is quoted with approval by Le Gentil in 1955 and 1967,[3] and by Misrahi and Hendrickson in 1980.[4] Le Gentil continues, "Rien de plus exact: dans notre poème, les caractères commandent l'action et les problèmes posés le sont dans et par des 'études d'âmes'" (p. 123). Tony Hunt is representative of the younger school when he asserts, of the same poem, "[the poet] is not interested in motivation but in repercussion [. . .] [His] technique is entirely the result of his interest in tragedy as the product of *action*, not *character*"; and, later in the same article, "Too much emphasis has been placed on the *Roland* as a psychological drama."[5]

There are good reasons why we should not simply turn our backs on this issue.[6] The gross categories of "actor" and "plot" are those to which the reader reacts first, and beyond which the naïve reader rarely progresses. Through them interest, sympathy, and excitement are elicited in the reader, and ethical and especially political themes conveyed.[7] They are universals of narrative; to quote the words of Barthes, "the characters [. . .] constitute a necessary plane of the description, outside of which the commonplace 'actions' that are reported cease to be intelligible, so that it may safely be assumed that there is not a single narrative in the world without 'characters' or at least without 'agents'."[8] They are not far from being universals of criticism, too, to judge by the frequency with which titles on "The hero" continue to appear in bibliographies.[9] Finally, the relationship between *dramatis persona* and plot in a fiction will relate to (though not necessarily correspond with) contemporary prejudice about the relation between character and action in the real world. This should certainly qualify it as a legitimate concern of literary history; the more so in a genre such as the *chanson de geste* which belongs to a para-historical or even historical mode of discourse.[10]

Important though this area of investigation seems to me, it is clear that most literary theorists have their sights trained towards other horizons. Receptional aesthetics with its revalorisation of literary history and concern to explicate reader reaction was an obvious place to look; and indeed an article on "Levels of identification of hero and audience" by Hans Robert Jauss[11] testifies to the recognition accorded to the notion of hero in this critical school. His aim in this article is to revise Northrop Frye's famous modes (mythic, marvellous, high and low mimetic, and ironic)[12] from a receptional standpoint, suggesting modes of reader identification with character ranging from the admiring to the ironic. Comparing the two studies, however, it seemed to me that Jauss was even less interested than Frye to examine how the hero is constituted (through "characterization," authorial intervention, emplotment, or whatever), and while he suggests ways in which the reader can react to character, he says nothing about how he or she perceives it in the first place.

Hard-core structuralist theory also proved a disappointing hunting ground. In *La Sémantique structurale*, Greimas formulates admirably the question which preoccupies me when he acknowledges the possibility of opting between a character-based and a plot-based description of a given corpus of mythological material.[13] The researcher could either (1) identify a series of plots in which the god is active, and so attribute a set of functions to him ("description fonctionnelle"), or else (2) identify a range of descriptions of him ("description qualificative"). The results of these approaches would be, he says, ("dans certaines conditions") complementary and "comme convertibles de l'un à l'autre modèle: le dieu pouvait agir conformément à sa propre morale; ses comportements itératifs, jugés typiques, pouvaient lui être intégrés comme autant de qualités" (pp. 172-3). Sadly the discussion goes no further. Greimas offers no argument for his decision in favour of a functional analysis (one presumes he is merely bowing to the force of the formalist tradition transmitted by Propp),[14] nor does he investigate under what conditions the two descriptive models might cease to be equivalent.

Greimas' approach, then, assumes the primacy of plot and the subordination to it of "character." "Actantial categories" (the term is Greimas'), which are the primary unit of analysis, do not correspond directly with individual surface structure characters but with the roles that underly them. They are held to be reducible to six: Subject (the agent), Object, Adjuvant (the role of any person or element assisting), Obstruant (any element that hinders the activity of the agent), Destinataire (the indirect object of beneficiary) and Distinateur (the role under whose auspices, or with regard to which, the Subject is activated). These actantial categories are identified by reducing successive stages of the plot to minimal narrative units of "deep structure" (that is, to sentences summarizing the surface text), and by reading off the grammatical functions within those sentences as the corresponding category, i.e. grammatical subject = Subject, grammatical Object = object, etc. But as Greimas' conception of deep structure—like that of another discipline one can think of—has got deeper with the years, it is not always easy to determine how the actantial categories are realised by the actual characters in a particular text.[15] Application of his theory to the *chansons de geste* has produced some startling results. According to one self-confessedly experimental reading of the *Roland*, for example, it appears that God, who is not a "character" at all, is Destinateur and Destinataire, and at times also Adjuvant, namely three out of the total of six categories, whereas Roland is Subject under the modality of will (*vouloir*) only (though with some *savoir*)[16], and as such inferior to Charlemagne who combines *vouloir, pouvoir, faire, savoir,* and *devoir.* Such an analysis, one might pardonably observe, if it lacks an excessive regard for character, is not over-preoccupied with plot either.[17]

More *nouvelle vague* criticism (one is tempted to call it *nouveau vague*), with its diligent glossing of arbitrarily chosen fragments of surface structure text (referred to, since Barthes, as "lexies" or "reading units"), has no interest in crude mimetic categories such as actor and plot which are simply so much noise on its semiotic codes. In an ingenious analysis of a fragment of Chrétien's *Perceval* by Jean-Michel Adam,[17] for instance, the action — Perceval's meeting with the first knights he has ever seen — and his character of naïve persistence, simply disappear down the cracks between the semiotic building-bricks that realise the *"isotopies"* of nature and religion versus chivalry.

This paper — mercifully — does not set out to offer a broad theory of how character and plot should best be defined and integrated into literary criticism. More modestly I investigate some of the ways in which they interact in a body of literature whose exciting narrative stance has always attracted both theoretical and practical criticism — the *chansons de geste* of the twelfth and thirteenth centuries — with particular reference to the text among them best known to me, that of *Raoul de Cambrai.*

It is manifest that one way an author can present his actors as primary, the action as flowing from them, is by serving up slabs of circumstancial and atemporal description of a character, and then offering morsels of incident as being merely illustrative of his or her nature. The example of Balzac leaps to mind. It was to defer consideration of this style of authorial "characterization" that I began with a reference to Othello rather than a narrative hero, since in this respect the *chansons de geste* have always been compared with the theatre. This commonplace of epic criticism is clearly formulated by Misrahi and Hendrickson: "We learn to know and judge epic figures as we do those of medieval theatre, by what we see them do" (p. 360).

The element of portraiture, which is in any case slight, is so traditional in content that its aim can only be to categorize, not individualize.

I have pointed out elsewhere that the descriptions of hero and villain in the *Roland* are substantially alike.[18] Attempting a character sketch of Raoul in *Raoul de Cambrai* based on observations *ex persona poetae* and by other characters, I found that nothing was said about Raoul that was not also said of at least one other character. If he is handsome, so are Bernier and Gautier.[20] Did he inherit his clear face from his mother, and his fierceness from Guerri?[21] But then fierceness is found among the Vermandois too.[22] Other people can be wise on occasion, and then carried away on a tide of uncontrollable emotion.[23] Raoul may be a marvellous knight, but so are Bernier, Rocoul, and others;[24] as for the qualities of nobility, valour, rank, and breeding, they are two a penny.[25] He is not alone in his bad qualities either. His tendency to perfidy and immoderateness is shared by the king and even by virtuous Bernier.[26] The poet, in short, makes no attempt to particularize his central character through description. Indeed, a recent series of articles by Moroldo has shown that the descriptive elements which make up the portraits in the *Chanson de Roland* are taken from a common stock which does not differ materially through six other *chansons de geste* of varied tone and date.[27]

This is not to say that epic characters necessarily lack "psychological depth" (though some do), but that perceiving it involves a moral and imaginative effort on the part of the reader/hearer (with perhaps an actor's contribution from the jongleur).[28] While literary characters should not be confused with real people, the fact remains that epic heroes are knowable in a way similar to that in which we know other people in real life; whereas the heroes of a novel whose author is constantly imparting insights about them are known to us more as we know ourselves.[28] This gives epic characters a directness and an otherness which challenge the reader/hearer's imagination along lines which are suggested and guided chiefly by the plot. The descriptive element in the *chansons de geste* is therefore not such as would lead to a distinction between characterization and emplotment; rather one would see them as indissolubly bound up together.

Another feature of the composition of these poems that militates against a dissociation of character from action is repetition. The emplotment of *chansons de geste* is intensive rather than extensive; character and plot are at once reduced in scope, though often with a corresponding gain in intensity: the hero is of such a type that he unrelenting repeats the same action; the plot is so organized that certain aspects of the hero are insistently brought into play.

In the Loheren cycle, the families of Lorraine and Bordeaux do battle unstintingly through thousands of lines of siege and countersiege, sortie, ambush, and the occasional pitched battle (this clearly perceived as more glamorous). Not surprisingly, then, the character of the Loheren heroes emerges as grim and embattled, as austerely resolute as their unvarying text.[30] The *Couronnement de Louis* reveals a comparable sobriety of invention. William starts by protecting young King Louis at home; then he frees Rome from agressors; then he protects Louis at home; then he frees Rome from aggressors (incidentally protecting Louis); and finally he protects Louis at home. In the simplest imaginable way the plot analyses the character of its hero into two principal facets which it then proceeds to dramatize, viz. feudal competence at home and abroad.[31]

The *Chanson de Guillaume* repeats a single though more extended cycle: feasting, resting, setting out to fight, fighting, returning, feasting, resting, setting out to fight, etc.[32] Only one character, William himself, survives this punishing routine repeatedly; his true grit marks him as the hero. Other characters achieve only part of it. Thiebaut and Esturmi feast and rest to perfection, but when it comes to setting out to fight they turn tail and run away: clearly they have no grit at all. Vivien sets out to fight and fights, but does not return: he is a figure of doomed youth, inspiring but unsuccessful. Girart possesses more of the strength of his uncle, for he sets out to fight, fights, returns, feasts, rests, sets out to fight, and fights, but then fails to return. His score is midway between Vivien and William. Rainouart, finally, completes the cycle successfully but only once, and so lacks the solidity of William's achievements which, in any case, he burlesques. The Frankish warriors are thus all carved of one material. William is the complete man whose nephews are partial copies of himself, and in comparison with whom the cowards are shown to be totally inadequate.

In *Raoul de Cambrai* there are four types of scene in which the hero appears: court scenes (with the king), family scenes (in which I include his meeting with Bernier's mother), council scenes (with his vassals, including Bernier), and fighting scenes. We should not, however, be misled by this apparent diversity. Nearly all the characters whom Raoul meets are subsumed to the role of enemies, and he behaves throughout in a spirit of violent antagonism, threatening the king, insulting his uncle and his own and Bernier's mother, and hitting his vassal with a stick.

This belligerence is invested with ambiguity. As heroic bravery, it is endorsed in Raoul's encounter with the forbidding Vermandois knight, John of Ponthieu, who is almost a giant. Raoul is on the verge of panic when he remembers his father's courage before him and gains the victory through sheer force of character and pride of lineage (ll. 2744–8). In a macabre dissection scene following the death of both knights (l. 3239 ff.),

Raoul's heart is found to be as big as that of an ox, while John's is the size of a child's. These scenes present Raoul's warlike temperament *in bono*. For the most part, however, his violence is perceived as excessive and misdirected, an effect largely achieved through the patterning of scenes. Starting at ca. l. 900 the order of events is as follows: (1) Raoul decides to go to war to claim the Vermandois, (2) quarrels with his mother, (3) sets off on the campaign threatening destruction, (4) quarrels with Bernier's mother, (5) destroys Origny, (6) quarrels with Bernier, and finally (7) fights the Vermandois army. This interleaving of scenes connected with actual fighting (1, 3, 5, 7) and scenes of domestic or feudal conflict (2, 4, 6) shows Raoul's aggressivity spilling out into relationships which should be peaceable and supportive.

For much of the text, Bernier is presented as the exact opposite of Raoul. He also appears in the same types of scene but manifests an aversion to violence. He avoids quarrelling with Raoul's mother and his own; he makes only a peaceful protest to the king; he is reluctant to fight; and he endures extraordinary ill-treatment from his overlord before obtaining his release — which he does by proposing himself as victim to Raoul's assault.[33] For both characters, emplotment and characterization are handled with radical simplicity and are in practice impossible to dissociate.

The concatenation of similar scenes is the most obvious compositional principle in the *chansons de geste*, most of which are structurally open-ended: one could devise additional scenes at little cost to the imagination, or else abridge them with no sense of irreparable loss. The episode is their basic unit of composition, just as the *laisse* is of the episode. It is probable that the episode was also the commonest unit of performance: one can imagine an audience clamouring for "the bit where . . . " and certainly the *jongleurs*' catalogue in the romance of *Flamenca* lists many items which are in fact episodes from larger works.[34]

This fragmentation in practical performance no doubt partly accounts for the tendency to invest individual scenes with drama at the expense of overall coherence, which is well attested in the *chansons de geste*. Consistency in the presentation of individual characters may well be sacrificed to heighten the clash between them. When Ganelon is brought before Marsilie in the *Roland*, for instance, he infuriates the Saracen king by demands purported to come from Charlemagne but which formed no part of the Frankish deliberations as reported in the preceding scene, and therefore seem to be Ganelon's own invention. Only a few lines before, Ganelon had seemed fearful even to undertake the embassy, but now he is emboldened to the point of greatly increasing the dangers inherent in it. The payoff of an exciting scene, with Ganelon and Marsilie almost coming to blows, quite eclipses the incoherence of characterization that produced it;[35] as T. Hunt observes, the *Roland* poet is more interested in *interaction* than in *identity*.[36]

In her monumental study of *Huon de Bordeaux*, M. Rossi traces a similar lack of consistency in the central character. Initially Huon demonstrates a lucidity and good sense unusual in an epic hero. Once he is under the magical protection of Auberon, however, the plot risks stagnating: excitement and danger can only be revived when Auberon's friendship is withdrawn, and this has to be engineered by Huon's provoking him with hitherto uncharacteristic *folie*.[37] By adopting a laxer standard of consistency, the poet achieves the double drama of conflict with Auberon and physical risk to his hero. Concern with action as primary has made characterization take second place.

A third example of a text where the personality of a major character is bent to meet the author's conception of the story-line is the *Charroi de Nîmes*.[38] The essentially reduplicative structure whereby in the first half William argues with King Louis and in the second has a battle of wits with the Saracen kings Otran and Harpin sustains the hero in a dramatic conflict of personalities without, however, masking the fact that his own personality undergoes a considerable shift in the process. In the first scene he is all righteous anger as he defends the ideal of an enlightened feudalism that would reward the meritorious while protecting the weak; in the second he emerges as a wily play-actor, a knight disguised as a merchant pretending to be a thief, sardonic manipulator rather than innocent victim, his high-mindedness replaced by bravado and deceit.[39]

In the *laisses similaires* of the better epics, an act is presented from different standpoints which, taken together, are less contradictory than complementary. In the same way, differences in the presentation of a character from one episode to another may be reducible in a creative reading to a coherent presentation of a moral or political theme. In such a case, character is subordinated to a plot conceived not just as a series of acts but as the articulation of an ethical point of view. In the *Charroi de Nîmes*, for instance, the inconsistencies of William's behaviour may be partly neutralised by subsuming them to an apologia for the petite *chevalerie*.

In *Raoul de Cambrai*, the pacific Bernier occasionally rises to Raoul's implacable belligerence, while Raoul declines into moderation and goodwill. After their rupture and Bernier's return to his family with news of the invasion, his prudent father and uncles adopt a policy of appeasement. An ambassador is sent to Raoul's camp who behaves with exemplary decorum (not in the least like an Irishman, l. 2154) and pledges the Vermandois to assist in the reconquest of the Cambrésis from Giboïn. Even Guerri is struck by the generosity of their offer (ll. 2170–73), but Raoul is unbending and accuses him of cowardice. In a second embassy scene, however, the roles are reversed. Bernier is insulting and provocative, calling down a curse on Raoul and enumerating his grievances against him. At first incensed, Raoul is moved by Bernier's message of peace. From *fix a putain* (l. 2252) he switches to addressing him as *ami* (l. 2287), promises to accept the terms and looks forward to renewed friendship (ll. 2286–90, 2296–7). It is because of Guerri's obstinacy and wounded pride that the offer is rejected. Learning this, Bernier is filled with vindictive delight: he thanks God for the war, defies Raoul and at once rushes to attack him, thereby killing an unarmed man who had run to Raoul's defence.

A second diptych, composed of duels, demonstrates a similar changeover of roles between Bernier and Raoul's successor and nephew, Gautier, who is a watered-down version of his uncle. First Gautier, with uncharacteristic moderation, challenges Bernier to single combat in order to avoid further bloodshed. He prepares for the fight by scrupulous attendance at religious services (ll. 4290–5); courteous in word and deed, he ministers at Aliaume's death bed and then actually saves Bernier's life (l. 4715 ff., 4745 ff.). Bernier's pride or folly in insisting that their two seconds, Guerri and Aliaume, should fight as well, is condemned by both of them (ll. 4710, 4731–5). In the events surrounding the second duel, however, Gautier with ruthless intransigence rejects repeated appeals for peace from the king (l. 5139), Bernier (ll. 5181 ff. and 5267 ff.), the abbé of St. Germain (l. 5295 ff.) and the whole Vermandois family (l. 5346 ff.). His piety shows a marked decline, for he is reluctant to yield to the abbé's offer of absolution, and does so only with a bad grace: "con je le fas dolent" (l. 5360). Bernier, by contrast, has been conciliatory from the start, excusing Gautier to the king on the grounds of his youth (l. 5163), offering him his sword (l. 5256 f.), and prostrating himself on the ground (l. 5365, etc.).

In such scenes the author's conception of character is manifestly subordinate to his desire to expose the psychology of vendetta and reprobate the incessant renewal of strife. This principle of applauding the doves and blackening the hawks — unless, of course, they are engaged in a worthwhile warlike crusade—is constant in the so-called epic of revolt, and applies without regard to the integrity of individual characters. Sub-renat comments on the *dénouement* of *Gaydon* that the hero

> "maintient ses exigences certes et, en cela, ne change pas, mais il se rend compte aussi, de lui-même cette fois-ci, que la solution du conflit n'est pas dans les armes. [. . .]
> "Et curieusement, à ce moment-là, c'est Riol le sage qui devient plus violent. Ce renversement d'attitude entre les deux personnages souligne le caractère plus conciliant de Gaydon."[40]

In *Girart de Roussillon* the judgments passed on the hero by both author and characters reflect his swings of mood between conciliatoriness and bitter antagonism towards Charles Martel, and it is no coincidence that the extraordinarily long and laudatory description of Foulques occurs shortly after he has condemned Girart's implacability (l. 4832 ff.) and immediately before this line: "E sapçaz d'esta gera mout li desplaz" (l. 5010).[41]

Bertrand de Bar-sur-Aube retained something of this spirit in his often fatuous recasting of the same legendary material in the *chanson de geste Girart de Vienne*. Burlesque though the grounds of Girart's resentment against his sovereign are (he has been tricked into kissing the queen's toe instead of Charlemagne's, and the emperor has refused to punish his wife for this shameful outrage!), he persists in belligerent opposition until he successfully takes Charlemagne's godson, Lambert, prisoner. At once he changes character: hoping to win back Charles's friendship, he offers to waive a ransom demand; and now it is Charlemagne's turn to appear in a bad light. When Oliver, Girart's nephew, comes to his court to sue for peace, the emperor is intent on revenge (ll. 4020-1). He wants to humiliate his opponent, even though legally he himself is in the wrong (ll. 4046-8). Even when accused of treachery by Roland, there is no longer any question of rancour on Girart's part: his moral stock has risen as ineluctably as Charlemagne's has declined.[42]

One means whereby an author can spell out the moral thrust of his tale so that even the dullest wit shall perceive it is by writing in a divine intervention. Since this device deprives the human actors at least temporarily of that agency which is the principal form of expression of character, it again tends to diminish the status of the actors *vis-à-vis* the plot. This is the more true when, as sometimes happens, God is transparently an alias for the author's undistinguished moral prejudices, and the characters dangle puppet-like from unsubtle strings.

An example of such a scene occurs in *Girart de Vienne*. Roland, Charles's champion, and Oliver, Girart's champion, are to fight a duel to determine whether or not Girart has been guilty of irregularity in his feudal obligations. This episode, the most protracted of the text and apparently perceived by the author as its high point, lasts for some thousand lines (from the arming of the heroes, l. 4880 ff., to a conclusion ca. l. 5957), during which the poet spares us nothing of how they vie with each other in prowess and gentility. So many blows, or such nice manners, should, one feels, bring a conclusion to the point at issue: but not a bit of it. God literally brings the curtains down on their efforts by envelopping both combatants in a dense cloud (l. 5891 ff.) while an angel announces that they would be better employed fighting side by side against the Saracens in Spain (ll. 5908–5920).[43] The heroes at once fall in with this way of thinking. The duel is abandoned, and Charlemagne and Girart reach a reconciliation by quite another means. While this divine intervention does facilitate a realisation of the many promptings of mutual affection and esteem between the two young knights, it also deprives their great show of courage and endurance, their eager championship of their respective uncles, and their bitter political arguments of much of their point. The characters, in other words, are sacrificed to the author's concern to express his somewhat banal view of the proper purpose of chivalry (and also, incidentally, to bring them into line for the *Chanson de Roland*, to which his text is a retrospective introduction).

The two redactions of the *Moniage Guillaume* exemplify different approaches to the use of angelic intervention. The shorter first redaction, which proceeds at a *fabliau*-like pace, dispenses with a "psychological" consideration of William's sanctity by assigning an angel to summon him first to the monastery of Genevois-sur-mer (ll. 58–60), then to his hermitage at St. Guillaume le Désert (ll. 820–37), leaving William to a relatively uninhibited exercise of his former, worldly characteristics of pugilism and voracity, with splendid comic effect. The second redaction takes William's holiness much more earnestly. The angel vanishes, to be replaced by much explicit comparison between monasticism and knighthood, and rather too much pious meditation. The result is a far more serious view of character which is not without interest, despite its dampening effect on the cartoon-strip style of comedy of redaction 1.

Even when God is not a direct participant, the ambiance of the Old French epic tends to the religious and moral. In so far as they are "structured" at all, the stories display patterns of reward or punishment measured according to the preoccupations of the author, rather than of success or failure in terms of the desires or intentions of the characters. Heroes and traitors are alike exemplary, and a chief requirement of "realism" is to confer sufficient density on a character for the audience to engage with the type (not an individual) and thereby concur with the author's judgment on it. How characters act will show what they are made of, and elicit audience response; the ultimate test, however, is not what they do, but what happens to them. Thus E. B. Vitz writes of the *Roland* that "religious causation (God's will, revealed or unrevealed) undermines human agency as a narrative force in plot structure," and "men are responsible for their actions, but their actions are not responsible for what occurs."[44] She uses her observations of this and other texts to argue against the validity of a Greimasian notion of "Subject" for medieval literature; certainly I think they confirm that a sense of divine purpose is one way in which characters can be said to be subordinated to plot.

The classic reward for good conduct is a fief and a wife, always beautiful and preferably rich. W. C. Calin has argued that in *Aymeri de Narbonne*, the themes of the conquest of a city and the winning of a bride, which together make up most of the action, are interrelated: with land comes power and position, and with marriage a lineage to maintain it.[45] Aymeri's career in this *chanson de geste* is merely an amplification of that of nearly all his relatives, for his grandfather won the fief of Monglane and the lovely Mabille (*Garin de Monglane*), his son William wins Orange and "la belle Orable" (*Prise d'Orange*), and his grandson becomes king of Andrenas and marries Gaiete (*Guibert d'Andrenas*). Those whose careers involve more danger or excess are rewarded with martyrdom (Renaut de Montauban, Roland (?)), or sainthood (Garin Le Loheren, Girart de Roussillon), or at least with glory. Whoever wrote the second death scene of Vivien in the *Chanson de Guillaume* clearly felt it was less incongruous for the hero to appear to die twice over in very different circumstances than for his efforts to go unacknowledged, and hence rewarded him (l. 1988 ff.) with a touching end, in an odour of sanctity, attended with the last rites by his dear uncle, and in a Christian-symbolic setting of fountain and olive tree, even though he had been cut to pieces in a desert landscape some ten to fourteen days before.[46] Conversely punishment usually takes the form of death without honour. Characters like Raoul in *Raoul de Cambrai* and Isembard in *Gormont et Isembard* are "des maudits qui ne sont pas tout à fait des damnés, puisqu'ils se repentent et que Dieu leur laisse une chance de le fléchir, mais des maudits qui n'ont pas droit à un autre sort que la calamité de la mort subite."[47] Outright traitors are condemned in court (Ganelon in the *Chanson de Roland*), summarily executed (Acelin in the *Couronnement de Louis*, l. 1884 ff., or Makaire in *Aiol*, l. 10900 ff.), or insouciantly killed with a blow from William's tremendous fist (as Aymon le viel in the *Charroi de Nîmes*, l. 678 ff.),[48] all lending their weight to the conviction expressed in *Fierabras* that "Tous jours vont traïtours à male destinée; U en pres un en loing, jà n'i aront durée."[49]

Happily the hand of Providence is sometimes more discreetly gloved. In the events leading up to the hero's death in *Raoul de Cambrai* there is a conviction of fatality combined with confusion as to its operation. Cursed by his mother, sacrilegious and blasphemous, Raoul seems an obvious target for divine retribution, and yet his actual death is presented in almost wholly secular terms.[50] Is Bernier an agent of the Almighty? The poet spares us this conviction; but then he excels in conveying a sense of the tangibility of moral questions together with the elusiveness of moral answers. A scene which shows a similar, masterly reluctance to dilute the complexity of human problems with an infusion of divine justice is the death scene of Garin in *Garin le Loheren* (ll. 16511–93). It is a martyrdom of a sort: Garin is murdered by the treacherous Bordelais as he kneels at an altar in penitence for the sins of a violent life. Yet before he is dead, a follower with commercial flair and a quick eye to a future saint piously hacks his right arm off for use as a relic: which assault Garin pardons before he dies. Sanctity or burlesque? An air of ambiguity pervades the episode, proof against the easy answer or pat judgment. Two final, and more obvious examples of a sense of the numinous adding to the significance of a human drama without detracting from the alterity and integrity of the characters are the deaths of Roland and Vivien.

I will conclude this paper by considering two features of the composition of the *chansons de geste* which seem to me positively to privilege character *vis-à-vis* the individual events of the plot, and to confer on certain heroes an almost mythic status.

In these poems the distinction between "subject" and "fable" drawn by the Russian formalists and taken over by more recent critics with the terms "*récit*" and "*histoire*"[41] is more than a theoretical construct, it is a vital part of the mechanics of composition and reception. Whereas in modern fiction there tends to be a systematic blurring of the two, the Old French epic poets are quite clear that their narrative (or "*récit*") is only one possible rendering of a tale ("*histoire*") from which it is conceptually distinct. Without wanting to go into the subtleties of this distinction here, the devices by which it is most straightforwardly indicated include allusions to sources or other, rival versions; summaries of the *histoire* in prologues and elsewhere; recapitulations and prospections or prophecies which temporarily suspend the flow of the *récit* to reveal at least a partial overview of the *histoire*; and tense usage which opposes an unfolding, present tense *récit* against a complete and known past tense *histoire*.

The "normal" situation is for author and audience to share in this knowledge of the existence of the *histoire* while the characters slog along the line of the *récit*, experiencing and acting as though it were the ultimate reality. At times, however, the characters are received into the complicity of author and audience; they gain insight into the totality of the story in which they figure; and though they continue to enact the roles apportioned to them and to feel the emotions that are their lot, they do so with a curiously enhanced stature which can border on myth.

The commonest device whereby a character learns more about the plot of his text is the prophetic dream. From the structured diversity of dream-lore inherited from Classical Antiquity the authors of *chansons de geste* fixed on one form only: the dream which comes true.[51] It usually forewarns of trouble, conflict, death, or some other disaster. The dreamer is temporarily removed from the flow of the *récit* to perceive some part of the underlying story.[52] In *Raoul de Cambrai*, for instance, Aalais learns of Raoul's death (ll. 3511-20), Beatrice of her husband's (ll. 8467-76). In the *Chevalerie Ogier*, the hero dreams that Charlemagne's army will pursue him (ll. 8213-21). On waking he learns that he has just been betrayed in Castel Fort and that the enemy are upon him. This stock device is amusingly parodied in the *Roman de Renart*, Branche II, ll. 131-60.

Although belonging to a recognizably rhetorical convention, as the *Renart* version shows, these dreams do not utterly conflict with mimetic realism, and do, indeed, reflect contemporary folk belief. More uncanny is when the characters intuit the plot without the need for such mediation. In the *Chanson de Roland*, for instance, Charlemagne receives veiled premonitions of future strife from his angel, but Roland himself appears to have a hotline to foreknowledge.[54] In the opening council scene he is the only one of Charlemagne's barons to discern Marsilie's treachery behind his lavish offers of peace (l. 196 ff.). He seems to divine Ganelon's guilt at the time of his appointment to the rearguard, when he breaks out in violent recrimination of his stepfather and alludes to the earlier scene of Ganelon's being chosen for the embassy — that scene being, of course, the reason for Ganelon's betrayal (ll. 763-65). He expresses no surprise at Oliver's announcement that the Saracens will attack, and quashes his denunciation of Ganelon (ll. 1008, 1026-7), only admitting his guilt later (l. 1457). This admission is accompanied by a prediction of Charlemagne's vengeance (l. 1459). His forecasts of the battle are proved true, though not exactly as he anticipated: fierce blows are struck, great honour won, the Saracens are vanqished or slain, Charles hears the horn and returns. Only as the battle draws towards its close does Roland reckon the full cost of these achievements to himself and his men in the so-called lament:

> Barons franceis, pur mei vos vei murir,
> Jo ne vos pois tenser ne guarantir.
> Aït vos Deus ki unkes ne mentit!
> Oliver frere, vos ne dei jo faillir,
> De doel murra[i], se altre ne m'i ocit.
>
> [1863-68]

Embracing martyrdom, Roland anticipates Charles' arrival on the field to honour their remains (ll. 1922-31), and also his grief at the irreparable loss to his imperial army (ll. 1985-7). The death scene with the mediating angel sets the seal on Roland's participation in a mythic or quasi-divine level of awareness. As a character, he enjoys an exalted status mysteriously situated above the blow-by-blow unfolding of the action as expounded by the *récit*, a status aligned within the text with God and the angels, and outside it with the foreknowledge granted to author and audience.

Vivien in the *Chanson de Guillaume* presents an interesting mixture of true and false prediction of his future. On the eve of the battle his sober realism is contrasted with the Dutch courage of the inebriates Thibaut and Esturmi: they imagine they can win without reinforcements, but Vivien advises sending for William because "Od poi conpaignie ne veintrun pas Arabiz." (l. 71) The next morning he amplifies this advice: Thibaut should assess the enemy's strength, and then either engage battle or conceal his troops until William can be sent for: with God's help, the victory will be theirs (ll. 171-82). In the course of reconnoitring, Thibaut rashly exposes himself to enemy view and Vivien, feeling the Franks will be dishonoured if they do not at once attack, embarks on a policy of desperation. Though he assures Thibaut they will win, he does so quoting the drunken arrogance of Esturmi (cf. ll. 68 ff. and 207 ff.). A more realistic appraisal of the prospective encounter in ll. 245-51 contains predictions of the deaths of cowards, lesser men, and youngsters, and recognition that only God's power can overcome the heathen. As the battle takes its tragic toll, Vivien is divided between desperate hope that William or Louis will come to bring them victory and realisation that his followers are going to receive a martyr's death (ll. 485-6, 561-2, 573; 502, 538, 545-7). For a moment of terrible misapprehension, he takes Girart's cry of *Monjoie* for the arrival of William or Louis (ll. 453-54); this lack of true perception culminates in two despairing and false predictions, that he himself alone will win the fight, even though all his companions flee (l. 589 "Jo les veinterai ben solunc la merci Deu"), and that William and Louis will arrive in time, on that very day (ll. 751-2). As his last knights are cut down around him, however, Vivien returns to his former lucidity which now, with tragic prescience, encompasses his defeat and death:

> Forz sui jo mult, e hardi sui assez,
> De vasselage puis ben estre sun per; [ie. William's]
> Mais de plus loinz ad sun pris aquité,
> Car s'il fust en l'Archamp sur mer,
> Vencu eust la bataille champel.
> Allas, peccable, n'en puis home gent
> Lunsdi al vespre.
>
> [830-6]

Through this mixture of erroneous belief and terrible lucidity, the author of the *Chanson de Guillaume* gives his hero a stature comparable with Roland's while stressing his greater humanity.

The device of authorial prophecy is used with particular insistence in *Raoul de Cambrai*, making it the more remarkable when certain of the characters suddenly join with the author in announcing what will happen next.[55] From the outset, the audience has been alerted to grief that will follow from Louis's gift of a fief to Raoul (cf. vv. 516-17, 536-37, 639-40, 697-98, 745-46, 778-780, etc.). Quarrelling with her son about his intended campaign, Aalais too predicts that the longed for investiture will in fact bring death to its recipient:

> Qui te donna Peronne et Origni,
> Et S. Quentin, Neele et Falevis,
> [Et] Ham et Roie et la tor de Clari,
> De mort novele, biax fix, te ravesti.
>
> [987-90; cf. -1004-06]

Asking how he expects to win such a war, she taunts him with an inquiry after Bernier: what will become of him (l. 1077)? Raoul's reply is perhaps unwittingly prophetic: Bernier will help his family if the need arises (l. 1085; contrast the rather different declaration of intent by Bernier in ll. 944-5).[56] In a flash of clairvoyance, Aalais puts her finger on the nub of the whole plot:

> Bien le savoie, a celer nel vos qier,
> Ce est li hom dont avras destorbier,
> C'il en a aise, de la teste trenchier.
>
> [1089-90]

Again this prophecy echoes, but how much more strikingly, predictions already made by the author (see ll. 6-11, 391, and 741). Raoul therefore proceeds to the war against the Vermandois as the plot and his own logic require, but he does so both as a character enmeshed in the *récit*, and as a participant in a dialogue regarding the *histoire* which exactly parallels a similar dialogue engaged between author and audience. This is a highly effective device for privileging the heroic characters over the action.

My last point concerns discrepancies between *histoire* and *récit* which operate to undermine the credibility of the presentation of events and focus instead on the intensity of character reaction as the only reliable reality. In his highly influential study of *L'art épique des jongleurs*,[57] Jean Rychner established a terminology for classifying the various ways in which *laisses* could be grouped together. *Laisses parallèles* were those in which similar events were presented in similar terms, so that what might be conceived as successive parcels of narrative are in fact presented as "juxtaposed": "à moments similaires successifs correspond une expression similaire répétée" (p. 88). It is relatively easy to find examples of such *laisses*; a typical instance would be the series in *Raoul de Cambrai* where the supporters of the Vermandois arrive one after the other and pledge themselves to kill Raoul (*laisses* 97 [end], 98, 99 + 100, 101, 102, 103) (and cf. Rychner, pp. 83-93). The term *laisses similaires* is initially used to apply to certain groups of laisses in the *Roland* where this lyric "juxtaposition" is particularly marked: *laisses* 40-42 (Ganelon treats with Marsilie), 83-85 (the first horn scene), 133-8 (Roland sounds the horn), etc. Being principally concerned with formal elaboration (though there is no clear formal distinction drawn between *laisses parallèles* and *laisses similaires*) Rychner prefers to avoid determining the narrative reference of such sequences. Commenting on *laisses* 40-42, for instance, in which Marsilie asks Ganelon when Charlemagne will desist from war and is told, never so long as Roland is alive, he writes:

> Faut-il dire, d'ailleurs, la ou les questions de Marsile? Sous cet ensemble statique, les réponses de Ganelon marquent à chaque fois quelque progrès; ce n'est pas, à vrai dire, un progrès narratif, mais un progrès psychologique et dramatique, dévoilant peu à peu ses pensées secrètes, suggérant, insinuant la trahison. [. . .] Il ne faut donc pas chercher à savoir, sur le plan de l'événement, si Marsile a réellement posé trois fois la même question, car les laisses similaires retiennent le récit dans une halte bien plus lyrique que narrative. (pp. 94-5)

In most of the examples which Rychner goes on to discuss, however, it is clear that the distinguishing feature of *laisses similaires* is the fact that they offer multiple reports of the same event. In *laisses* 174-6 of the *Roland*, for instance, it would not be reasonable to suppose that Roland delivered his glove to a descending angel any more than once; likewise in *laisses* 206-7, we cannot imagine that Charlemagne found Roland's body twice. The examples adduced from other texts (pp. 100-107) confirm that whatever his formal definition, in practice for Rychner *laisses parallèles* are those where different events are described in similar terms and *laisses similaires* are those where the same event is presented more than once in slightly different ways.

This leaves a very considerable number of instances outstanding of which, as in the case of the Marsilie—Ganelon scene, it is impossible to assert whether it is the event or merely the description that is repeated. The narrative becomes unreliable on a quite simple and fundamental issue of plot but supplies instead a very insistent image of a character in the grip of an intense experience or emotion. Since the *laisse* patterns of the *Roland* have attracted so much critical attention, I will illustrate this from *Raoul*.

Nearly all the "lyric" patterns of *laisses* in this text occur in the purportedly older core (up to ca. l. 3740), and focus on the character of the hero. The scene confronting Raoul and his mother, *laisses* 48–54, contains a repeated pattern of maternal admonishment followed by a display of anger from Raoul. In *laisses* 48 and 49 Aalais's warning that the gift of the Vermandois means death is reiterated; in *laisses* 50 and 51 Raoul issues dire threats against the men of Arrouaise if they refuse their support; and in *laisses* 52 and 53 Aalais expatiates on his vassals' faults. Are they both so furious that they keep repeating what they have just said? or is their anger and sense of mutual injury being dwelt on repeatedly by the poet as a technique of amplification (*expolitio*)?

Laisses 77 and 78 create a similar ambiguity around the growing conflict between Raoul and Bernier. In *laisse* 77 Raoul threatens to drive the Vermandois brothers across the sea and seize every penny they own; Bernier replies that this would be outrageous treatment for such worthy knights. In *laisse* 78 Raoul's threats are repeated in more emphatic terms; the penny's worth of land, for instance, becomes:

> . . . le montant d'un denier
> De toute honnor ne de terre a baillier,
> Ou vif remaigne[n]t, ou mort puise[nt] couchier.
>
> [1633-5]

and "Tant que il soient outre la mer fui" (l. 1621) becomes "Outre la mer les en ferai naigier" (l. 1636). Bernier's reply is likewise amplified. To the defense of Herbert's sons as fine knights is added criticism of Raoul (l. 1639), warning that even if his campaign is successful he will not find it easy to hang on to the Vermandois (l. 1643), and the wish to be revenged on Raoul for his many crimes against him (ll. 1645-51). The descriptions contained in these two *laisses* are different but not incompatible, and so it is impossible to assert whether they record two exchanges, or one. What is, however, unmistakable is the escalation in both provocation and remonstrance, and the consequently sharpened focus on the conflict between the two knights. One cannot be sure exactly what they said on any precise occasion, but one forms a very strong impression of their capacity for emotional antagonism: an impression, that is, of character at the expense of a precisely informed grasp of plot.

The ensuing quarrel between Raoul and Bernier contains further patterns of repetition which create uncertainty about the narrative flow precisely as they emphasize the emotions of the participants.[58] The final phase of this episode is Raoul's offer of reparation for the blow which he has struck Bernier. In the middle of *laisse* 85 he promises a public act of atonement ("Droit t'en ferai voiant maint chevalier," l. 1745), which Bernier angrily rejects: not till the blood flowing down from his head returns there of its own accord, and not till he can obtain revenge (?), will he consider such an offer (ll. 1746-55).[59] In *laisse* 86 Raoul's offer is amplified to occupy nineteen lines (1759-77) and is followed by a murmur of approval among the Franks: "Ceste amendise est bele! Qi ce refuse vos amis ne vieut estre" (1778-9). *Laisse* 87 then combines elements from both these preceding accounts. Raoul urges Bernier to accept reparation; Bernier refuses in almost identical terms to those which he had used before; and Guerri amplifies the reaction of the Franks, condemning Bernier for his obduracy in the face of so splendid an offer (1792-5). Once again details of who says what when are effaced before Raoul's urgent desire to placate, and Bernier's furious implacability.[60]

This study quite explicitly forestalls any temptation to regard it as definitive by the logic-defying concern for symmetry with which it marshalls two arguments in favour of the inseparability of character and plot, and two each for the primacy of the one over the other. Perhaps the whole investigation should be reoriented away from formal relations towards an examination of reference: after all, the fact that in the *chansons de geste* the issues of honour and dishonour, loyalty and treachery, wealth and destitution, life and death are all superimposed and mutually reinforcing is what makes these narratives impressive, their heroes moving even today and clearly far more so to contemporary audiences in a community still strife-torn and in many ways primitive. One framework of reference for this type of study which has already yielded promising results is medieval law; further theoretical approaches are suggested by medieval personality theories and the philosophy of action. My main concern here has been to challenge the easy assumption that either character or plot has a simple, unanalysable priority of status in the economy of a literary text.

Sarah Kay
Cambridge University

Notes

1. Editions cited are as follows:
   Aiol: chanson de geste, ed. J. Normand and G. Raynaud (Paris: Didot, Societé des anciens textes français, hereinafter referred to as S. A. T. F., 1877).
   Le charroi de Nîmes (. . .), ed. Duncan McMillan (Paris: Klincksieck, 1972).
   La chevalerie Ogier de Danemarche, ed. Mario Eusebi (Milan: Istituto Editoriale Cisalpino, 1963).
   Les rédactions en vers du "Couronnement de Louis," ed. Yvan G. Lepage (Geneva: Droz, Textes li Héraires français, 1978). The text cited is the *AB* version.
   Garin le Loheren (. . .) ed. Josephine E. Vallerie (Ann Arbor: Edwards Bros. Inc., 1947).
   Girart de Roussillon, ed. W. Mary Hackett (Paris: Picard, S. A. T. F., 1953-55).
   "Girard de Vienne" de Bertrand de Bar-sur-Aube, ed. Wolfgang van Emden (Paris: Picard, S.A.T.F., 1977).
   La chanson de Guillaume, ed. Duncan McMillan (Paris: Picard, S. A. T. F., 1949-50).
   Les deux rédactions en vers du "Moniage Guillaume," ed. Wilhelm Cloetta (Paris: Didot, S.A.T.F., 1906, 1911).
   Raoul de Cambrai, ed. P. Meyer and A. Longnon (Paris: Didot, S.A.T.F., 1882).
   Le roman de Renart, ed. Jean Dufournet (Paris: Garnier-Flammarion, 1970).
   La chanson de Roland, ed. Frederick Whitehead, 2nd ed. (Oxford: Blackwell, 1946).
   I would like to take this opportunity to thank my colleagues Dr. G. S. Burgess and Dr. O. A. C. Waite for their helpful and learned advice with this paper.

2. Edmond Faral, *La Chanson de Roland, étude et analyse* (Paris: Mellottée, Collection Chefs d'oeuvre de la littérature expliqués, 1933), p. 261.

3. Pierre Le Gentil, *La Chanson de Roland,* first printed 1955; 2nd ed. rev. (Paris: Hatier, Collection Connaissance des Lettres, 1967), p. 123.

4. Jean Misrahi and William Lee Hendrickson, "Roland and Oliver: Prowess and Wisdom, the Ideal of the Epic Hero," *Romance Philology* 33 (1979-80), 357-72, p. 359.

5. Tony Hunt, "Character and Causality in the Oxford Roland," *Medioevo Romanzo* 5 (1978), 3-33, pp. 12-13. See also his article "The Tragedy of Roland: an Aristotelian View," *Modern Language Review,* 74 (1979), 791-805; Sarah Kay, "Ethics and Heroics in the Song of Roland," *Neophilologus,* 62 (1978), 480-91; and François Suard, "Le personnage épique," in *Proceedings of the 5th Conference of the Société Rencesvals, Oxford 1970* (Salford: University of Salford Press, 1977), 167-76.

6. Cf. the defence of character study by Marguerite Rossi, *Huon de Bordeaux,* (Paris: Champion, Collection Nouvelle Bibliothèque du Moyen Age, 1975), 463-67.

7. See for example John Bayley, "Character and Consciousness," *New Literary History* 5 (1973-4), 225-35.

8. Roland Barthes, "An Introduction to the Structural Analysis of Narrative," *New*

Literary History 6 (1974-5), 237-72, pp. 256-57 (translation, with additional material, of an essay originally published in *Communications* 8 [1966]).

9. E.g. Norman T. Burns and Christopher J. Reagan, eds., *Concepts of the Hero in the Middle Ages and the Renaissance* (Albany: State University of New York Press, 1975); Micheline de Combarieu du Grès, *L'idéal humain et l'expérience morale chez les héros des chansons de geste, des origines à 1250* (Aix-en-Provence: Publications de l'Université de Provence, 1979).

10. See D. J. A. Ross, "Old French," in A. T. Hatto, ed., *Traditions of Heroic and Epic Poetry*, i, *The Traditions* (London: Modern Humanities Research Association, 1980), 79-113, pp. 90-91: "In the Middle Ages the *chansons de geste* seem generally to have been accepted as having a basis of valid historical fact."

11. Hans Robert Jauss, "Levels of Identification of Hero and Audience," *New Literary History* 5 (1973-4), 283-317.

12. Northrop Frye, *Anatomy of Criticism: Four Essays* (Princeton: Princeton University Press, first published 1957, p.b. 1966), pp. 33-4 (1966 edition).

13. A. J. Greimas, *Sémantique structurale: recherche de méthode*, (Paris: Seuil, 1966). It has been pointed out to me that by trying to integrate a theory of narrative within a theory of poetry, Greimas risked losing sight of the specificity of either.

14. "Dans l'étude du conte, la question de savoir *ce que* font les personnages est seule importance; *qui* fait quelque chose [est une] question qui ne se pose qu'accessoirement," V. Propp, *Morphologie du conte* (Paris: Seuil, 1970), p. 29, cited by Michel Mathieu, "Les acteurs du récit," *Poétique* 5 (1974), 357-67, p. 357, who endorses this bias.

15. A. J. Greimas, "Les actants, les acteurs et les figures," ed. Claude Chabrol *et al.*, *Sémiotique narrative et textuelle* (Paris: Larousse, Collection Université, 1973), 161-76.

16. A further refinement to the theory is the introduction of modality permitting the nature of the Subject's agency to be analysed according to whether its "deep structure" action implies the presence of a modal verb.

17. Larry S. Crist, "Roland, héros du vouloir: contribution à l'analyse structurale de la *Chanson de Roland*," in *Mélanges de Philologie et de Littératures Romanes offerts à Jeanne Wathelet-Willem, Marche Romane* No. spécial (1978), 77-101. See also Patricia Harris Stablein, "The Structure of the Hero in the Chanson de Roland: Being and Becoming," *Olifant* 5 (2) (Dec. 1977), 105-19, which suggests that the role of hero is divided between Roland, Oliver, and Charles. Recent studies of other medieval genres influenced by a functionalist approach include Pierre Gallais, "L'hexagone logique et le roman médiéval," *Cahiers de Civilisation Médiévale* 18 (1975), 1-14, 133-48; Donald M. Maddox, *Structure and Sacring: The Systematic Kingdom in Chrétien's "Erec and Enide,"* French Forum Monographs 8 (Lexington: French Forum, 1978); and several studies by Evelyn Birge Vitz including "Narrative Analysis of Medieval Texts: *La fille du comte de Pontieu*," *Modern Language Notes* 92 (1977), 645-75. Vitz is critical of Greimas' concept of the Subject which, however, she seeks always to equate with a single surface structure character.

18. Jean-Michel Adam et Jean-Pierre Goldenstein, *Linguistique et discours littéraire: Théorie et pratique des textes* (Paris: Larousse, Collection Université, 1976), pp. 108-120.

19. Sarah Kay, "The Nature of Rhetoric in the Chanson de Geste," *Zeitschrift für Romanische Philologie* 94 (1978), 305-20, p. 316.

20. Cf. *Raoul de Cambrai*, ll. 347, 515, 625, 1549, 1555 (Raoul) with ll. 395, 591, 5596 (Bernier) and 3824, 4326, (Gautier).

21. Cf. ll. 392, 399, 831, etc. (*Raoul . . . o le vis cler* and variants) with ll. 30, 364, 1217, etc. (*Aalais . . . o le vis cler*, and variants); ll. 506 (Raoul's *fier contenant*) with l. 3579 (Guerri's *fiere contenance*). Guerri has a *fier vis* and *fiere veüe* in ll. 2534, 1208; Raoul's *coraige* is *fier* in ll. 1629, 1728, etc.

22. Cf. ll. 1365 (Marsent), 2024 (Wedon), 4501 (Bernier) and 5385 (Ybert).

23. Raoul is *saige*, l. 781, as also Guerri, ll. 1045, 2012, and Gautier, l. 3998, but of all three is it repeatedly said that *le sens quide / quida changier* (e.g. ll. 3081, 3402, 4505).

24. Cf. l. 2819 (Raoul) with l. 2906 (Rocoul), and also, though the formula is a slightly different one, with ll. 146 (Giboïn), 790 (the hostage Wedon de Borbone), and 1316 (Bernier).

25. Raoul is frequently *ber* (e.g. l. 836), as are Giboïn (e.g. l. 116), Guerri (e.g. l. 295), Louis (e.g. l. 844), and Gautier (e.g. l. 4946); the term *gentis*, used of Raoul (e.g. l. 372), is also used of Wedon (e.g. l. 1980), Bernier (e.g. l. 4264), and the abbé (l. 5310); Raoul is *preu* in ll. 534, 5170, as are Gautier (e.g. l. 4794), Guerri (e.g. l. 3221), Bernier (e.g. l. 3436). The qualificatives *au coraige vaillant* and *cortois* are likewise shared: cf. ll. 338, 2408, 2658, 4916, 4917, and 372, 5386, 5514, 5553.

26. Cf. ll. 2010, 881, 5169 and 2883, 778. This consistency of characterisation in the poem is commented on by Italo Siciliano, *Les chansons de geste et l'épopée. Mythes — Histoires — Poèmes*, Biblioteca di Studi Francesi 3 (Turin: Società Editrice Internazionale, 1968), 399: "Tout divers qu'ils soient, les preux et les sages du *Raoul* ont sensiblement la même taille, tous sont coupés dans la coulée d'une larve ardente et mouvante. Exception faite pour la triste Marsent, ils s'assemblent et se ressemblent. Toute porportion gardée, Aalais, Raoul, Guerri le Sor, Bernier, Garnier [Siciliano means Gautier], Aliaume sont de la même race et de la même force. Ici c'est le choeur qui chante la chanson et qui en fait l'unité, et c'est un choeur inquiet et inquiétant qui s'agite, court d'un bout à l'autre de la pièce, tourne en rond, s'épuise en interminables disputes, vit et périt de sa violence."

27. Arnaldo Moroldo, "Le portrait dans la chanson de geste," *Le Moyen Age* 86 (1980), 387-419 and 87 (1981), 5-44.

28. Cf. Barthes' assertion, in "The Structural Analysis of Narrative," p. 263, that the creation of "psychology" in a fiction presupposes mobility of stance from 3rd to 1st person and back again, which is transparently based on post-medieval narrative.

29. Cf. Jean Frappier, *Les chansons de geste du cycle de Guillaume d'Orange*, 1 (Paris: Société d'édition de l'enseignement supérieur, 1955), pp. 173-4: "les personnages existent de l'intérieur, ils ne révèlent pourtant leur nature morale que de l'extérieur, par leurs gestes, leurs paroles et leurs actes [. . .] Sans chercher à rendre nos héros plus complexes qu'ils ne sont, sachons goûter une simplicité expressive et franche qui parvient à montrer ou à suggérer la qualité des âmes."

30. The treacherous Bordelais, with whom for the most part the initiative lies, are more obviously imbued with "personality." In a sensitive study aimed at differentiating Garin from his brother Begon, Anne Iker Gittleman notes that often it is the absence of a descriptive element or motif that characterises Garin, to whom she attributes "une grandeur dépouillée": see *Le style épique dans "Garin le Loheren,"* (Geneva: Droz, 1967), p. 215.

31. Cf. W. W. Ryding, *The Structure of Medieval Narrative* (The Hague: Mouton, 1971), pp. 45-6.

32. Cf. Beate Schmolke-Hasselmann, *Boire et mengier: essai d'une analyse structurale de la "Chanson de Guillaume,"* paper read at the 17th International Congress on Medieval Studies, Kalamazoo, May 1982. I would like to thank Dr. Schmolke-Hasselmann for kindly sending me a copy of this as yet unpublished paper.

33. See Pauline Matarasso, *Recherches historiques et littéraires sur "Raoul de Cambrai"* (Paris: Nizet, 1962), p. 146.

34. *Le Roman de Flamenca*, ed. Ulrich Gschwind (Berne: Francke, 1976), vol. 1, 621 ff., and vol. 2, notes to ll. 630-1, 641-2, 677-8.

35. Cf. Suard, "Le personnage épique" (cited in fn. 5), p. 168, for another example of possible inconsistency in Ganelon.

36. Hunt, "Character and Causality in the Oxford Roland" (cited in fn. 5), p. 11.

37. Rossi, *Huon de Bordeaux,* p. 484.

38. *Pace* D. D. R. Owen, "Structural Artistry in the Charroi de Nîmes," *Forum for Modern Language Studies* 14 (1978), 47-60.

39. In a fascinating article "Type et individu dans l'autobiographie' médiévale," *Poétique,* 6 (1975), 426-45, Evelyn Birge Vitz attempts a study of the medieval concept of personality based on Abelard's *Historia Calamitatum.* A part of her exposition deals with the question of consistency: concerned to present his experiences more from the point of view of their intensity (and of his own superiority, or extreme sensibility) than of their fundamental unity, Abelard allowed various parts of his career to appear completely compartmentalised one from another.

40. Jean Subrenat, *Etude sur "Gaydon", chanson de geste du XIIIe siècle,* Etudes Littéraires. (Aix-en-Provence: Editions de l'Université de Provence, 1974), pp. 210-11.

41. For a study of the pacific ethos of *Girart de Roussillon,* see René Louis, *De l'histoire à la légende: 2, Girart, comte de Vienne, dans les chansons de geste* (Auxerre: Imprimerie Moderne, 1947), 1: 405-16. Cf. also the remarks under the heading *Condamnation de l'attitude belliqueuse* in vol. I of Micheline de Combarieu's *L'idéal humain,* p. 147 ff.

42. For further inconsequences in *Girart de Vienne,* see Ryding, *Structure of medieval narrative,* pp. 51-2.

43. There is a similar scene in *La Chevalerie d'Ogier de Danemarche,* ll. 10454-70. A more successful analogue is the supernatural fire which consumes the standards of Girart and Charles Martel in *Girart de Roussillon,* thus forcing an end to their battle at *Vaubeton* (l. 2874 ff.), since it operates as an effective metaphor of the violence and irascibility of the two antagonists, as also of the cauterising process of self-examination in the two camps following this disturbing experience. Charles Martel is pronounced to be accursed of God (ll. 2906-26); despite a rehearsal of his grievances, Girart is condemned by his uncle for not seeking peace (ll. 3018-30). God's intervention is in harmony with, but does not cause, the signal act of personal abnegation which actually finalises the peace negotiations, namely Tierri's voluntary exile (ll. 3122-35, especially ll. 3123-4: "Ne place a Damlideu, au manne rei, Que ja mais per mon cors nus on gerrei!"). In this case, the credibility and integrity of the characters seem to me to have been maintained alongside the expression of God's will.

44. Evelyn Birge Vitz, "Desire and Causality in Medieval Narrative," *Romanic Review,* 71 (1980), 213-43, pp. 223-24.

45. W. C. Calin, *The Epic Quest: Studies in Four Old French Chansons de Geste* (Baltimore: John Hopkins University Press, 1966), especially pp. 5-31. Calin stresses the hero's representative character, p. 23: "All of society participates in Aymeri's quest."

46. See Minette Grunman, "Temporal Patterns in the *Chanson de Guillaume,*" *Olifant,* 4 (1) (Oct. 1976), 49-62, p. 56.

47. Jean-Charles Payen, *Le motif du repentir dans la littérature française médiévale (des origines à 1230)* (Geneva: Droz, 1967), p. 180.

48. For remarks on William's celebrated rabbit punch, consult Frappier, *Guillaume d'Orange,* 1: 94-96. On the *post mortem* prospects of traitors, see Payen, *Le motif du repentir,* p. 158 and notes.

49. Quoted by William Wistar Comfort, "The Character Types in the Old French *Chansons de Geste,*" *Publications of the Modern Language Society of America* 21 (1906), 279-461, p. 356. Cf. also *Garin le Loheren,* l. 6357, "Hom desloiax ne puet longues garir," cited by Micheline de Combarieu, *L'idéal humain,* 1:98.

50. See my article *La composition de "Raoul de Cambrai,"* forthcoming in the *Revue Belge de Philogie et d'Histoire.*

51. See Sarah Kay, "The Contrasting Use of Time in the Romances of *Jaufre* and *Flamenca*," *Medioevo Romanzo* 6 (1979), 37–62, especially pp. 39–40 and notes.

52. See Herman Braet, *Le songe dans la chanson de geste au XIIe siècle, Romanica Gardensia*, 15 (Gent: Romanica Gandensia, 1975), 198.

53. On the integration of the dream to other forms of *annonce*, see Braet, *Le songe,* p. 103 ff.

54. Thus E. Vance writes in "Roland et la poétique de la mémoire," *Cahiers d'Etudes Médiévales* 1 (1975), 103–115, p. 106: "Les héros du *Roland* non seulement parlent-ils dans les mêmes formules métriques que le poète, mais ils ont recours aux mêmes épithètes, aux mêmes listes, voire à la même pré-science que le poète." This article has appeared in English as "Roland and the Poetics of Memory," in *Textual Strategies: Perspectives in Post-Structural Criticism,* ed. Josué Harari (Ithaca: Cornell University Press, 1979), 374-403.

55. For some other, less convincing examples of the characters of *Raoul* predicting their own future, see Carlo Pica, "*Raoul de Cambrai*: crisi di un sistema," *Cultura Neolatina* 40 (1980), 67–77, pp. 71–72.

56. The Brussels fragment of *Raoul de Cambrai* adds after the passage corresponding to ll. 944-945 "Mais tant vous di que ie lor aiderai; Se pooir ai, sachiez ie vous nuirai," which would, of course, deprive Raoul's words of their prophetic force. See A. Bayot, "*Raoul de Cambrai* (Brüsseler Fragmente," *Revue des Bibliothèques et Archives de Belgique,* 4 (1906), 412-29.

57. Jean Rychner, *La chanson de geste: essai sur l'art épique des jongleurs* (Geneva: Droz, and Lille: Giard, 1955).

58. *Laisses* 82-83 repeat in very similar terms Bernier's account of his mother's forcible abduction by Ybert; the mention of his mother's nobility in the very short *laisse* 80 is amplified in *laisse* 81.

59. The text is not very clear; Meyer suggests the possibility of a lacuna between ll. 1754 and 1755. I would punctuate and translate as follows:

> Ja enver vos ne me verres paier
> Jusqe li sans qe ci voi rougoier
> Puist de son gre en mon chief repairier.
> Qant gel verai, lor porrai esclairier
> La grant vengance qe vers ton cors reqier —
> Je nel laroie por l'or de Monpeslier.
>
> [1750-55]

"You will not see me reconciled with you until the blood that I see running red returns to my head of its own accord. When I see that, then I shall give vent to the terrible vengeance I desire against you—not for all the gold of Montpellier would I forego it!"

60. A further example of ambiguity is presented by *laisses* 143, 144, 147, and 151 describing Ernaut's flight from Raoul on the battlefield.

List of Contributors

Leigh A. Arrathoon is the Editor-in-Chief of Solaris Press. Dr. Arrathoon was born November 30, 1942. She received her A.B. from Hunter College in 1963, an M.A. in French and another in Spanish from Stanford University in 1966 and 1968, and her M.A. and Ph.D. in French from Princeton University in 1975. She has also studied at the Universities of Geneva, Lausanne, and Lille. Her dissertation research was carried out at Oxford University from 1972-3. She has published articles on Old French and Chaucer in *Language and Style, Romance Philology, Ball State University Forum*, and a translation of *La Chastelaine de Vergi* with *Cross-Cultural Communications Press*. She has also taught French and Spanish Language and French Literature at Stanford University as a teaching assistant, Princeton University, as a University Fellow, at the Convent of the Sacred Heart in Menlo Park, California, and Rider College in Trenton, New Jersey as an Assistant Professor.

Eren Branch was born September 8, 1944. She received her B.A. from Bryn Mawr College in 1966 (magna cum laude), her M.A. in English Literature in 1970, and her Ph.D. in English and Comparative Literature in 1975 from Stanford University. Dr. Branch spent her senior year at Yale University (1965-6) and studied Latin Literature and Palaeography at the University of Cincinnati from 1980-2. She has held an American Philosophical Research Grant (1982-3) and was a first alternate for an I Tatti fellowship from 1982-3. Dr. Branch has published in *Anglia*.

Roger Dragonetti is currently a full Professor of Medieval French Literature at the University of Geneva. He was born on November 9, 1915 in Gand, Belgium. He earned his Ph.D. in Romance Philology in 1943 and his University Teaching Doctorate in 1960, both from the University of Gand. Prior to that he was educated with the Jesuits at the Collège Sainte Barbe. In 1965, he was appointed to the Faculty of Philosophy and Letters at the University of Gand where he held the chair in French Literature. At Gand he taught French literary history, and the explication of medieval and modern French authors. On April 21, 1964, he was named an Officer in the Order of Leopold II by royal decree. He also received a first class civic medal by royal decree on April 21, 1967 for 25 years of good and

499

loyal services to his country. In 1975 Professor Dragonetti was elected to the Flemish Academy of Sciences and Belles-Lettres. He has written five books: *Aux Frontières du langage poétique, La Technique poétique des trouvères dans la chanson courtoise (Contribution à l'étude de la rhétorique médiévale), Dante Pèlerin de la Sainte Face (Etude sur la Divine Comédie), La Vie de la Lettre au Moyen Age (Le Conte du Graal),* and *Le Gai savoir dans la rhétorique courtoise (Flamenca et Jouffroi de Poitiers).* In addition he has given courses, seminars and lectures in the universities of Germany, France, Italy, Switzerland, and Belgium. Finally, he has published numerous articles in modern and medieval studies in *Studi Danteschi, Revue des études italiennes, Lingua e Stile, Yale French Studies, Modern Language Notes, La Revue des langues romanes,* and various *Festschriften.*

Peter Haidu was born in Paris on March 7, 1931. He received his B.A. from the University of Chicago in 1952, his M.A. and Ph.D. from Columbia University in 1961 and 1966. Since 1960 Professor Haidu has taught at Columbia University, Yale University, the University of Virginia, the University of Illinois, and U.C.L.A., where he has recently joined the French faculty. He has written two important books, *Aesthetic Distance in Chrétien de Troyes: Irony and Comedy in "Cligès" and "Perceval,"* and *Lion-queue-coupée: L'Ecart symbolique chez Chrétien de Troyes.* He is also the editor of *Approaches to Medieval Romance (Yale French Studies* No. 51: Summer 1975). Professor Haidu is at work on a fourth and fifth book, *The Semes of History: Structures of Contradiction in Medieval French Literature* and *Historical Semiotics: Essays Theoretical and Methodological.* Among his articles, the following are of special interest: "Text and History: The Semiosis of XIIth Century Lyric as Socio-Historical Phenomenon," "Semiotics and History," "The Hermit's Pottage: Deconstruction and History in *Yvain,*" "Towards a Problematics of Alterity: Making it (New) in the Middle Ages," "Narrativity and Language in Some Twelfth Century Romances," "Repetition: Modern Reflections on Medieval Aesthetics," and "The Episode as Semiotic Module in Twelfth Century Romance."

Tony Hunt is currently a Reader in French at the University of St. Andrews in Scotland. He was born in Bebington, England on March 21, 1944. Educated at Worcester College, Oxford from 1962–8, Dr. Hunt has published some 51 articles, among which "The Dialectic of *Yvain,*" "Aristotle, Dialectic and Courtly Literature," "Abelardian Ethics and Beroul's *Tristan*" "Chrestien and the *Comediae,*" "Prodesse et delectare: Metaphors of Pleasure and Instruction in Old French," and "La Parodie médiévale: le cas d'*Aucassin et Nicolette.*" He has been Treasurer of the Anglo-Norman Text Society since 1983, he is chief Bibliographer of the British Branch of the International Courtly Literature Society, a member of the Editorial Board of *Rhetorica,* and a trustee of the Eugene Vinaver Memorial Fund.

Sarah Kay is currently a Lecturer in the Department of French at the University of Liverpool. She was born in Birkenhead, England on November 12, 1948. She received her B.A. with honors in French from Somerville College, Oxford University in 1971, her M.A. in Linguistics from the University of Reading in 1972, and her Ph.D. from Oxford University in 1976. She has published articles on the *chansons de geste*, Northern French and Provençal romances, and the troubadours. She was awarded the Paget-Toynbee Prize for Old French Literature in 1973. Dr. Kay held the Kathleen Bourne Research Fellowship at St. Anne's College, Oxford from 1973-5. From April 1984 she has been appointed to a Lectureship at Cambridge and will be taking a Fellowship at Girton College from October 1984.

Douglas Kelly is currently a professor in the Department of French and Italian at the University of Wisconsin. He was born on July 17, 1934. He received his B.A. from the University of Southern California in 1956, his M.A. and Ph.D. from the University of Wisconsin in 1959 and 1962. He was an Assistant Editor for the *French Review* from 1964-8 and is currently an Assistant Editor for *Rhetorica*. From 1981-4 he was the International Vice President of the Société Arthurienne. He has written three books: *Sens and Conjointure in the Chevalier de la Charrette, Chrétien de Troyes: An Analytic Bibliography, Medieval Imagination: Rhetoric and the Poetry of Courtly Love,* and a fourth, *Invention and "Conjointure": the Art of Medieval Romance* is near completion. Of his twenty-four articles, "The Scope of the Treatment of Composition in the Twelfth- and Thirteenth-Century Arts of Poetry," "Theory of Composition in Medieval Narrative Poetry and Geoffrey of Vinsauf's Poetria Nova," and "The Source and Meaning of Conjointure in Chrétien's Erec 14," are especially noteworthy. Professor Kelly was a Romnes Fellow at the University of Wisconsin from 1974-9, held an ACLS fellowship from 1974-5 and an Institute for Research in Humanities fellowship at the University of Wisconsin from 1967-8.

Per Nykrog is currently a Professor at Harvard University. He was born in Copenhagen, Denmark on November 1, 1925. He earned his can. mag. at the University of Copenhagen in 1951 and his Ph.D. at the University of Aarhus, Denmark in 1957. Before coming to Harvard in 1970, he taught at the University of Aarhus. He was Dean of the Faculty of Humanities at Aarhus University from 1962-3. Professor Nykrog has written five books, including his well-known thesis on *Les Fabliaux* in 1957, and articles on the *Chanson de Roland,* Chrétien de Troyes, Gautier d'Arras, the *Jeu d'Adam,* the *Roman de la rose,* Antoine de la Salle, Rabelais, and various modern authors. He is a member of the Royal Danish Academy of Sciences. He also served as a correspondent for Denmark to the Société d'Histoire littéraire de la France, Paris 1965-79. In 1952 he won a gold medal from Copenhagen University, and he is a Knight of the Order of Dannebrog.

D. D. Roy Owen is currently a Professor in the French Department at the University of St. Andrews in Scotland where he has taught since 1951. He was born in Norton, Suffolk, England on November 17, 1922. He attended the University of Nottingham from 1942-3, St. Catharine's College, Cambridge from 1946-50, the Sorbonne and Collège de France from 1950-1. His M.A. and Ph.D. are from Cambridge University (1955). Professor Owen has published nine books, among which *The Evolution of the Grail Legend, The Vision of Hell, The Legend of Roland, Noble Lovers*, and *Arthurian Romance: Seven Essays*. He has published chapters on Arthurian Romance and Chrétien de Troyes in *European Writers: The Middle Ages and the Renaissance*, and articles and reviews in *French Studies, Modern Language Review, Medium Aevum, Forum for Modern Language Studies, Romania, Studi Francesi, Romance Philology, Speculum, Cahiers de Civilisation Médiévale, Zeitschrift für Romanische Philologie*, and the *Times Literary Supplement*. He is the founder and Editor of the *Forum for Modern Language Studies*. Professor Owen is preparing an elegant English translation of Guillaume Le Clerc's *Fergus* for Solaris Press.

Roy Pearcy He was born in Parkstone, Dorset, England on June 27, 1931. He was educated at Queen Mary College, University of London, graduating in 1959 with a first-class honors B.A. in English, and at Ohio State University, which awarded him his Ph.D. in 1963. Before joining the faculty at the University of Oklahoma, where he is currently a professor of English, he taught for five years at U.C.L.A., and he has also held half-year visiting professorships at the Universities of Kent at Canterbury, England, Sydney, and Queensland in Brisbane, Australia. Professor Pearcy's major research interests are in English and French popular narrative literature of the late Middle Ages. He has published articles on such figures as Chaucer and Dunbar and on the French fabliaux, in the *Chaucer Review, Neuphilologische Mitteilungen, Genre, Romania,* and *Speculum,* in critical anthologies, and in numerous other scholarly journals. He has articles forthcoming in *English Language Notes* and *Medium Aevum.* He is a member of the Medieval Academy of America and of the New Chaucer Society, for whom he edited the yearbook, *Studies in the Age of Chaucer,* from its inception in 1978 until 1982. On two occasions, in 1974 and in 1983, Professor Pearcy was awarded fellowships at La Fondation Camargo in Cassis, France, to pursue research in medieval French literature. Among his current projects are a translation of selected early branches of *Le Roman de Renart* for Garland, editions of the *Reeve's* and *Cook's Tales* for *A Variorum Edition of the Works of Geoffrey Chaucer,* and a volume of the Toronto annotated Chaucer Bibliographies covering scholarship on the *Reeve's, Cook's, Man of Law's,* and *Wife of Bath's Tales.*

Brynley Francis Roberts is currently a Professor and Head of the Department of Welsh at the University College at Swansea, Wales. He was born in Aberdare, Mid-Glamorgan, Wales, on February 3, 1931. He attended the University College of Wales in Aberystwyth from 1948-57. He earned his B.A. with first class honors in Welsh in 1951, his M.A. in 1954, and his Ph.D. in 1969. From 1954-6 he worked as a Russian translator in the Intelligence Corps. From 1952-78 he was Lecturer, then Reader, in Welsh at the University

College of Wales in Aberystwyth. In 1948 Professor Roberts held a J. D. Evans Scholarship at the University College of Wales at Aberystwyth. He also held a Cynddelw Scholarship from 1950–1. From 1952–4 he had a studentship at the University of Wales and was a University Fellow at the same university from 1956–7. From 1973–4 he held a Sir John Rhys Fellowship at Jesus College, Oxford. In 1962 he was awarded the Ellis Griffith Prize by the University of Wales. He is a member of the Druidic Order Gorsedd of Bards. He has published four books and two editions in Welsh and articles in the *Bulletin of the Board of Celtic Studies, Studies in Early Welsh Poetry,* and *Nottingham Medieval Studies.*

Barbara Nelson Sargent-Baur is currently a Professor and Director of the Medieval and Renaissance Studies Program at the University of Pittsburgh. She was born on January 8, 1928. She earned her B.Mus. from Lawrence College in 1951, her B.A. from the University of Wisconsin in 1954, her M.A. and her Ph.D. from Indiana University in 1957 and 1960. She was a Fulbright scholar from 1958–9 and held University of Pittsburgh summer stipends in 1972 and 1977. From 1968–72 Professor Sargent-Baur was Secretary-Treasurer and Bibliographer of the Société Rencesvals. Since 1981 she has been the Vice President of the International Arthurian Society, North American Branch. In 1971 she was Chairperson, French I, MLA. In 1978, she was Chairperson of the Division on Comparative Studies in Medieval Literature. She has been on the Editorial Board of *Olifant* since 1974, the Advisory Council of *Romance Philology* since 1980 and has served on the Advisory Board of *Speculum* from 1978–80. Professor Sargent-Baur has published four books: *Le Livre du Roy Rambaux de Frise, La France, son histoire, sa culture, François Villon: Le Testament et poésies choisies,* and *Aucassin et Nicolete: A Critical Bibliography* (co-author with Robert F. Cook). She has also published articles on Chrétien de Troyes, François Villon, *Aucassin et Nicolette,* and Andreas Capellanus in *L'Esprit Créateur, French Review, Romania, Medium Aevum, Romance Philology,* and *Le Moyen Age.*

Aldo Scaglione is currently W. R. Kenan Professor of Romance Languages and Comparative Literature at the University of North Carolina, Chapel Hill. He was born on January 10, 1925 in Torino, Italy and received a Doctorate in Modern Letters at the University of Torino in 1948. After having taught as a Lecturer at the University of Toulouse, France, he joined the faculty at the University of Chicago and, later, the University of California at Berkeley (1952–68.) He has also taught at Middlebury Summer School, Yale University, and at the Graduate Center at CUNY. He was a Herbert F. Johnson Research Professor at the Institute for Research in the Humanities in Madison, Wisconsin from 1981–2. From 1963–5, he was the Chairman of the Department of Italian at the University of California at Berkeley. Since 1975 he has been editor of the series *L'Interprete* and *Speculum Artium* (Longo). From 1971-5 he was the General Editor of *Romance Notes* and the "North Carolina Studies in the Romance Languages and Literatures." He is currently a member of the editorial boards for *Romance Philology, Studi Francesi, Studies in Philology,* "North Carolina Studies in Comparative Literature," and "Amsterdam Studies in the History of Linguistics." Professor Scaglione is the author of eight books, among which *The Classical Theory of Composition from Its Origins to the Present: A Historical Survey* and about a hundred articles on Italian Humanism, the Continental Renaissance, the history of rhetoric, and the history of language sciences. In 1951 he held a Fulbright Fellowship; from 1958-9, a J. S. Guggenheim Fellowship; from 1964-5, a Newberry Library Senior Resident Fellowship; a Senior Fellowship to the Southeastern Institute for Medieval and Renaissance Studies (Summer 1969); a Visiting Scholarship to Columbia University from 1971-2, and a Senior Fellowship of the Cini Foundation's 1973 Postdoctoral Program, Venice, Italy. Since 1972 he has been a Life Associate of the Renaissance Seminar at Columbia University. From 1980-1 he was President of the American Boccaccio Association. From 1981-4 he was Vice-President of the American Association of University Professors of Italian. He was Director of an NEH Summer Seminar on "Humanism, Latin, and Vernacular" at Chapel Hill in 1981. He received a certificate of merit from the International Association of Italian Language and Literature in 1973 and was knighted in the Order of Merit by the President of the Republic of Italy in April 1975.

Paul Joseph Zumthor is currently retired from the University of Montreal. He was born on March 3, 1915 in Geneva, Switzerland. He received his Baccalauréat ès Lettres, his Licence ès Lettres, and his Diplôme d'Etudes Supérieures from the University of Paris in 1933, 1935, and 1936. He earned his Doctorat ès Lettres in 1943 from the University of Geneva. From 1937-45, Professor Zumthor taught high school in Geneva and Bâle. From 1942-8 he tutored Medieval Literature at the University of Gröningen, and from 1952-71, at the University of Amsterdam. He taught at the University of Paris from 1970-1, and from 1972-80 he was a Professor of Comparative Literature at the University of Montreal. He has been an invited speaker at universities all over the world. Professor Zumthor has published seventeen books, the best known of which are *Langue et technique poétiques à l'époque romane (XI-XIIIe siécles), Guillaume le Conquérant et la civilisation de son temps, Essai de poétique médiévale, Langue, texte, énigme,* and over one hundred and twenty-two articles. Professor Zumthor is a Knight of the Legion of Honor and an Officer in the Italian Order of Merit.

Janet Anderson was born on March 13, 1949 in Royal Oak, Michigan. She is currently engaged in medieval book illustration and keylining for Solaris Press, as well as a number of private art projects, including building portraits, Christmas cards, note paper, murals, and occasional modern book illustration. Ms. Anderson is best known for her pen and ink drawings and watercolors of old and new Detroit scenes. Educated at Pratt Institute and the Center for Creative Studies, Ms. Anderson is completing a degree in printmaking with Dennis Galffy. She served as Art Director in 1981 in the U.S. Virgin Islands. One of the projects for which the artist is known is "Picture Detroit," a series of drawings and watercolors of Detroit and Michigan cityscapes, some of which were presented to Mayor Coleman Young. The collection was shown at the Bicentennial Celebration and is included in a permanent collection at the Detroit Historical Museum. Among the private collectors of Ms. Anderson's artwork are President Gerald Ford, Mayor Coleman Young, Governor Milliken, Carol Channing, Mrs. Edsel Ford, Henry Ford II, Judy Collins, and Governor Blanchard. Corporation Collectors include Burger King, Detroit Convention Bureau, E. F. Hutton, McDonald's, Michigan Congressional Offices, Wayne State University, and Wayne County Commissioners.

Index

507